"This is an excellent addition to the literature of communication surrounding corporate social responsibility in our digital age. It is an important pioneering work allowing authors with diverse disciplinary backgrounds to describe the state of the art (and science) in all its dimensions and what that state could and should look like in the future. Kudos are warranted for the editors and their contributors."
   —**Prof. Alex C. Michalos**, University of Northern British Columbia, Canada

"There is a continuous need to explore how organizations are communicating their socially responsible and sustainable behaviors to stakeholders. Therefore, this book provides a comprehensive guide to the extant theoretical underpinnings and empirical studies on corporate sustainability, social responsibility and ubiquitous digital media. I strongly recommend this book to academia and advanced undergraduate students in business and communications"
   —**Dr. Mark Anthony Camilleri**, University of Malta

"This timely book contains cutting-edge thinking at the confluence of two virtually seismic forces transforming global business today: corporate social responsibility and digital media. Together, the twenty-one contributions from scholars worldwide not only edify the reader on the nuts and bolts of effective CSR communication in today's hyper-connected media-saturated world but also challenge her to harness wisely the power of digital media in saving, literally, our planet and its people. In that, it is essential reading for every forward-looking business scholar and practitioner keen on optimizing business as a force for good."
   —**Professor Sankar Sen**, Zicklin School of Business, USA

T0321387

Communicating Corporate Social Responsibility in the Digital Era

Although literature on corporate social responsibility is vast, research into the use and effectiveness of various communications through digital platforms about such corporate social responsibility is scarce. This gap is surprising; communicating about corporate social responsibility initiatives is vital to organizations that increasingly highlight their corporate social responsibility initiatives to position their corporate brands for both consumers and other stakeholders. Yet these organizations still sometimes rely on traditional methods to communicate, or even decide against communicating at all, because they fear triggering stakeholders' skepticism or cynicism. A systematic, interdisciplinary examination of corporate social responsibility communication through digital platforms, therefore, is necessary, to establish an essential definition and up-to-date picture of the field.

This *research anthology* addresses the above objectives. Drawing on marketing, management, and communication disciplines, among others, this anthology examines how organizations construct, implement, and use digital platforms to communicate about their corporate social responsibility and thereby achieve their organizational goals. The 21 chapters in this anthology reflect six main topic sections:

- Challenges and opportunities for communicating corporate social responsibility through digital platforms.
- Moving toward symmetry and interactivity in digital corporate social responsibility communication.
- Fostering stakeholder engagement in and through digital corporate social responsibility communication.
- Leveraging effective digital corporate social responsibility communication.
- Digital activism and corporate social responsibility.
- Digital methodologies and corporate social responsibility.

Adam Lindgreen is Professor of Marketing at Copenhagen Business School where he heads the Department of Marketing. He also is a research associate with the University of Pretoria's Gordon Institute of Business Science. Dr. Lindgreen received his Ph.D. from Cranfield University. He has published in *California Management Review, Journal of Business Ethics, Journal of Product and Innovation Management, Journal of the Academy of Marketing Science*, and *Journal of World Business*, among others.

Joëlle Vanhamme is Professor of Marketing at the Edhec Business School. Dr. Vanhamme received her Ph.D. from the Catholic University of Louvain. She has been Assistant Professor of Marketing at Rotterdam School of Management, Associate Professor of Marketing at IESEG School of Management, and a Visiting Scholar with Delft University of Technology, Eindhoven University of Technology, Hull University's Business School, Lincoln University and the University of Auckland's Business School. Her research has appeared in journals including *Business Horizons, California Marketing Review, Industrial Marketing Management*, and *International Journal of Research in Marketing*.

François Maon received his Ph.D. in 2010 from Catholic University of Louvain (Louvain School of Management). After a visiting scholarship at the University of California, Berkeley, he now works as Associate Professor of Strategy and Corporate Social Responsibility at IESEG School of Management where he teaches strategy, business ethics, and corporate social responsibility. He is widely published in academic journals and books including *Journal of Business Ethics* and *A Stakeholder Approach to Corporate Social Responsibility*.

Rebecca Mardon is Assistant Professor of Marketing at the University of Cardiff's Business School. Dr. Mardon received her Ph.D. from the University of Southampton. Her research explores emerging consumer behaviours in digital contexts including the new ethical issues raised. Current projects include an exploration of digital materiality and work on tribal entrepreneurship within online spaces. Her research has appeared in *Journal of Consumer Culture, Journal of Marketing Management*, and *Journal of the Association for Consumer Research*, amongst others.

Communicating Corporate Social Responsibility in the Digital Era

Edited by
Adam Lindgreen, Joëlle Vanhamme,
François Maon and Rebecca Mardon

LONDON AND NEW YORK

First published in paperback 2024

First published 2018
by Routledge
4 Park Square, Milton Park, Abingdon, Oxon OX14 4RN

and by Routledge
605 Third Avenue, New York, NY 10158

Routledge is an imprint of the Taylor & Francis Group, an informa business

Publisher's Note
The publisher has gone to great lengths to ensure the quality of this reprint but points out that some imperfections in the original copies may be apparent.

British Library Cataloguing-in-Publication Data
A catalogue record for this book is available from the British Library

Library of Congress Cataloging-in-Publication Data
Names: Lindgreen, Adam, author. | Vanhamme, Joëlle, author. | Maon, François, author.
Title: Communicating corporate social responsibility in the digital era /
   Adam Lindgreen, Joëlle Vanhamme, François Maon and Rebecca Watkins.
Description: 1 Edition. | New York : Routledge, 2018. |
   Includes bibliographical references and index.
Identifiers: LCCN 2017036624 (print) | LCCN 2017037934 (ebook) |
   ISBN 9781315577234 (eBook) | ISBN 9781472484161 (hardback : alk. paper)
Subjects: LCSH: Social responsibility of business. | Business communication. |
   Social media.
Classification: LCC HD60 (ebook) | LCC HD60 .L556 2018 (print) |
   DDC 658.4/08—dc23
LC record available at https://lccn.loc.gov/2017036624

ISBN: 978-1-4724-8416-1 (hbk)
ISBN: 978-1-03-283729-1 (pbk)
ISBN: 978-1-315-57723-4 (ebk)

DOI: 10.4324/9781315577234

Typeset in Bembo
by Apex CoVantage, LLC

For Camilla, Emma, and Benjamin, with all my love – Adam

For my sweet, little girls Victoria and Zazou, with all my love – Joëlle

For Nicolas, Alexandre, and Filip, my favorite
half-brothers – François

For Nathan – Rebecca

Contents

Figures

Tables

About the editors

Adam Lindgreen

After studies in chemistry (Copenhagen University), engineering (the Engineering Academy of Denmark), and physics (Copenhagen University), Professor Adam Lindgreen completed an MSc in food science and technology at the Technical University of Denmark. He also finished an MBA at the University of Leicester. Professor Lindgreen received his Ph.D. in marketing from Cranfield University. He has been a Professor of Marketing at Hull University's Business School (2007–2010), the University of Birmingham's Business School (2010), where he also was the research director in the Department of Marketing, and the University of Cardiff's Business School (2011–2016). Under his headship of the Department of Marketing and Strategy at Cardiff Business School, the department was ranked first among all marketing departments in Australia, Canada, New Zealand, the UK, and the United States based upon hg indices of senior faculty. Since 2016, he has been Professor of Marketing at Copenhagen Business School, where he also heads the Department of Marketing. He also is a research associate with University of Pretoria's Gordon Institute of Business Science.

Professor Lindgreen has been a visiting professor with various institutions, including Georgia State University, Groupe HEC in France, and Melbourne University. His publications have appeared in *Business Horizons, California Management Review, Industrial Marketing Management, International Journal of Management Reviews, Journal of Advertising, Journal of Business Ethics, European Journal of Marketing, Journal of Business and Industrial Marketing, Journal of Marketing Management, Journal of the Academy of Marketing Science, Journal of Product Innovation Management, Journal of World Business, Psychology & Marketing*, and *Supply Chain Management: An International Journal*.

Professor Lindgreen's books include *A Stakeholder Approach to Corporate Social Responsibility* (with Kotler, Vanhamme, and Maon), *Managing Market Relationships, Memorable Customer Experiences* (with Vanhamme and Beverland), and *Sustainable Value Chain Management* (with Maon, Vanhamme, and Sen).

The recipient of the Outstanding Article 2005 award from *Industrial Marketing Management* and the runner-up for the same award in 2016, Professor Lindgreen serves on the board of several scientific journals; he is co-editor-in-chief of *Industrial Marketing Management* and previously was the joint editor of *Journal of Business Ethics* for the section on corporate responsibility. His research interests include business and industrial marketing management and corporate social responsibility. Professor Lindgreen has been awarded the Dean's Award for Excellence in Executive Teaching. He has examined dissertations, modules, and programs at numerous institutions including Australian National University, Unitec, University of Amsterdam, University of Bath's Management School, University of Lethbridge, and University of Mauritius.

Professor Lindgreen is a member of the International Scientific Advisory Panel of the New Zealand Food Safety Science and Research Centre, and he is a member of the Chartered Association of Business Schools' Academic Journal Guide (AJG) Scientific Committee in the field of marketing.

Professor Lindgreen has discovered and excavated settlements from the Stone Age in Denmark, including the only major kitchen midden – Sparregård – in the south-east of Denmark; because of its importance, the kitchen midden was later excavated by the National Museum and then protected as a historical monument for future generations. He is also an avid genealogist, having traced his family back to 1390 and published widely in scientific journals (*Personalhistorisk Tidsskrift*, *The Genealogist*, and *Slægt & Data*) related to methodological issues in genealogy, accounts of population development, and particular family lineages.

Joëlle Vanhamme

Dr. Joëlle Vanhamme is Professor of Marketing at the Edhec Business School. Dr. Vanhamme received her Ph.D. from the Catholic University of Louvain (Louvain School of Management). She has been Assistant Professor of Marketing at Rotterdam School of Management, Associate Professor of Marketing at IESEG School of Management, and a Visiting Scholar with Delft University of Technology, Eindhoven University of Technology, Hull University's Business School, Lincoln University and the University of Auckland's Business School. She is the joint editor of *Journal of Business Ethics* for the section on corporate responsibility. Dr. Vanhamme's research has appeared in journals including *Business Horizons, California Management Review, Industrial Marketing Management, International Journal of Research in Marketing, Journal of Advertising, Journal of Business Ethics, Journal of Consumer Satisfaction, Dissatisfaction and Complaining Behavior, Journal of Customer Behaviour, Journal of Economic Psychology, Journal of Marketing Management, Journal of Retailing, Marketing Letters, Psychology & Marketing, Recherche et Applications en Marketing*, and *Supply Chain Management: An International Journal*.

François Maon

Dr. François Maon received his Ph.D. in 2010 from Catholic University of Louvain (Louvain School of Management). After a visiting scholarship at the University of California, Berkeley, he now works as an Associate Professor of Strategy and Corporate Social Responsibility at IESEG School of Management where he teaches strategy, business ethics, and corporate social responsibility. In his research, Dr. Maon focuses mainly on topics linked to corporate social responsibility learning, implementation, and change-related processes, cross-sector social partnerships, and stakeholder influence strategies. He has published numerous articles in international journals such as *California Management Review, International Journal of Management Reviews, Journal of Business Ethics*, and *Supply Chain Management: An International Journal*. He has co-edited several special issues of academic journals and books including *A Stakeholder Approach to Corporate Social Responsibility* (with Kotler, Vanhamme, and Maon) and *Sustainable Value Chain Management* (with Maon, Vanhamme, and Sen). He serves on the editorial board of *M@n@gement* and is the founder and co-ordinator of the IESEG Center for Organizational Responsibility (ICOR).

Rebecca Mardon

Dr. Rebecca Mardon is Assistant Professor of Marketing at the University of Cardiff's Business School. Dr. Mardon received her Ph.D. from the University of Southampton. Her research explores emerging consumer behaviors in digital contexts including the new ethical issues raised. Current projects include an exploration of digital materiality and work on tribal entrepreneurship within online spaces. Her research has appeared in *Journal of Consumer Culture, Journal of Marketing Management*, and *Journal of the Association for Consumer Research*, amongst others.

About the contributors

Ana Adi

Professor Ana Adi is Professor of PR and Corporate Communication at Quadriga University of Applied Sciences in Berlin. Dr. Adi received her Ph.D. from the University of the West of Scotland. She has co-edited *Corporate Social Responsibility in the Digital Age* (2014). Her research interests include public relations measurement, storytelling and corporate social responsibility. She also blogs at www.anaadi.net and can be found on Twitter @ ana_adi.

Ezgi Akpinar

Dr. Ezgi Akpinar is an assistant professor of Marketing at Koç University. Dr. Akpinar received her Ph.D. from Erasmus University. She has published in *Journal of Marketing Research*, *Journal of Personality and Social Psychology*, and *Journal of Business Research*, among others. Her research interests include word-of-mouth marketing, social influence, and consumer behavior. She received the EMAC McKinsey Best Marketing Dissertation award. She has delivered presentations and moderated several sessions in leading conferences including Association of Consumer Research, Society for Consumer Psychology, and European Marketing Academy.

Mavis Amo-Mensah

Dr. Mavis Amo-Mensah is a Lecturer of Communications at the Department of Communication and Media Studies, University of Education, Winneba, Ghana. She is a Ph.D. student from Leeds Beckett University. Dr. Amo-Mensah is an alumna of the Chartered Institute of Public Relations (CIPR) and member of the Institute of Public Relations, Ghana. She serves as a member of the Integrated Reporting (IR) steering committee of the Center for Governance, Leadership and Global Responsibility (CGLGR) at Leeds Beckett University. Her research interests include strategic and corporate communication, corporate social responsibility, sustainability communication, and public relations.

Madhupa Bakshi

Professor Madhupa Bakshi is presently Professor in Media and Marketing Communication in the Department of Media Science at the Heritage Academy, Kolkata. She has published in *Journal of Business Ethics*, *Marketing Intelligence and Planning*, and *Journal of Media*

Business Studies. Her research interests include media branding, corporate social responsibility communication, and sustainability. She serves as a reviewer for many journals.

Mark Anthony Camilleri

Dr. Mark Anthony Camilleri is a resident academic lecturer in the Department of Corporate Communication at the University of Malta. Dr. Camilleri received his Ph.D. from the University of Edinburgh. He has published in *Tourism Planning and Development, Corporate Reputation Review, Sustainability Accounting Management and Policy Journal, Global Responsibility Journal*, and *Tourism and Hospitality Research*, among others. His books include *Creating Shared Value through Strategic CSR in Tourism* (2013), *Corporate Sustainability, Social Responsibility and Environment Management: An Introduction to Theory and Practice with Case Studies* (2017), and *CSR2.0: A New Era of Corporate Citizenship* (2017). His research interests include strategic management, corporate social responsibility, digital media, and tourism. He is a member on the editorial board of Springer's *International Journal of Corporate Social Responsibility* and he is also a member of the academic advisory committee in the Global Corporate Governance Institute (USA).

Suwichit Chaidaroon

Dr. Suwichit (Sean) Chaidaroon is Senior Lecturer of marketing communications at Westminster University's Business School. Dr. Chaidaroon received his Ph.D. from the University of Memphis and previously taught at Nanyang Technological University in Singapore, the University of Sydney, Australia, and California State University San Bernardino, US. He has published in *Asia-Pacific Public Relations Journal, Media Asia*, and *Journal of Public Relations and Advertising*, among others. His research interests include corporate and marketing communications, organizational communication and corporate social responsibility. He serves on the editorial board of *Journal of Public Relations and Advertising*.

Vidhi Chaudhri

Dr. Vidhi Chaudhri is Assistant Professor of Media and Communication at Erasmus School of History, Culture and Communication (ESHCC), Erasmus University Rotterdam. Dr. Chaudhri received her Ph.D. from Purdue University, USA. She has published in *Management Communication Quarterly, International Journal of Business Communication, Public Relations Review*, and *Journal of Corporate Citizenship*, among others. She is also (co-)author on several business cases and has contributed book chapters to *The Handbook of Crisis Communication, Corporate Reputation Decoded: Building, Managing and Strategising for Corporate Excellence*, and *The SAGE Encyclopedia of Corporate Reputation*. Her research interests include corporate social responsibility, crisis communication and corporate reputation, social media, and employee engagement.

Zhifeng Chen

Zhifeng Chen is a Ph.D. candidate at the University of Bath in England. Her main research areas are corporate social responsibility (CSR) and social and environmental reporting. Her Ph.D. focuses on stakeholders' responses to mixed messages about corporate social activities. She has presented her work at various conferences such as the *British Academy of Management annual conference* and the *IABS annual conference*.

Shuili Du

Dr. Shuili Du is Associate Professor of Marketing at the Peter Paul College of Business and Economics, University of New Hampshire. She received her Ph.D. in Marketing from the Questrom School of Business, Boston University. Dr. Du's research expertise lies at understanding various ways corporate social responsibility (CSR) and sustainability initiatives create social and business value. Her research has appeared in *Journal of Consumer Research, Management Science, Harvard Business Review, International Journal of Research in Marketing, Marketing Letters, Journal of Business Ethics, Journal of Product Innovation Management,* and *Journal of Business Research,* among others.

Francisca Farache

Dr. Francisca Farache is Senior Lecture and Course Leader of the MSc Marketing at Brighton Business School. Dr. Farache received her Ph.D. from Brighton Business School. She has published in *Journal of Business Ethics, Journal of Business Research, Corporate Communication: An international Journal,* and *Latin American Business Review,* among others. Her research interests include corporate communication, business ethics and corporate social responsibility.

Christian Fieseler

Professor Christian Fieseler received his Ph.D. in management and economics from the University of St. Gallen, Switzerland. His research is published in, among others, *Journal of Computer-Mediated Communication, Journal of Business Ethics,* and *New Media and Society.* Professor Fieseler's research interests center on organizational identity, corporate social responsibility, and computer-mediated-communication. His research is focused on the question of how individuals and organizations adapt to the shift brought by new, social media, and how to design participative and inclusive spaces in this new media regime.

Sarah Glozer

Dr. Sarah Glozer is Assistant Professor of Marketing at Royal Holloway, University of London and works within the Centre for Research into Sustainability (CRIS). Dr. Glozer received her Ph.D. from The University of Nottingham Business School and has published in journals including *Annals of Tourism Research* and *Journal of Management Studies.* Her research interests include corporate social responsibility (CSR), dialogue and communication studies, ethical markets/consumption, and social media marketing.

Urša Golob

Dr. Urša Golob is Associate Professor of Marketing Communications at University of Ljubljana. She has published in such journals as *European Journal of Marketing, Journal of Business Ethics, Public Policy & Marketing, Public Relations Review, Journal of Business Research, Journal of Marketing Communications,* and *Corporate Communications: An International Journal.* She has also authored or co-authored several book chapters on themes related to corporate social responsibility. Her research interests focus on corporate social responsibility, corporate communications and marketing. She is one of the co-founders of the International CSR Communication Conference.

Lina M. Gómez

Dr. Lina M. Gómez is Assistant Professor in the Digital Communication Program at the School of Social and Human Sciences at Universidad del Este (UNE), Puerto Rico. She has a Ph.D. in business with a concentration in corporate social responsibility and sustainability from Universitat Jaume I in Spain. Her expertise and research interests are in social media, public relations, and corporate social responsibility. Dr. Gómez currently leads the development of the Center for the Study and Research of New Media and Digital Technologies at UNE. In the last year, she has received both institutional and external grants from foundations to perform research projects regarding social media, university social, responsibility, and public health. Dr. Gómez also has published in journals such as *Public Relations Review* and *Developments in Corporate Governance and Responsibility*, and she has presented in many international conferences in public relations, corporate social responsibility, and social media.

Susan Grantham

Dr. Susan Grantham is Professor of Communications in the School of Communication at the University of Hartford. Dr. Grantham earned her Ph.D. from the University of Florida. Her research has been published in *Communication Research Report, Journal of Public Relations Research, Corporate Communications: An International Journal, Public Relations Journal*, and several other peer-reviewed journals. Her research interests include public relations roles, corporate social responsibility, and environmental and health communication.

Haiming Hang

Dr. Haiming Hang is a Senior Lecturer (Associate Professor) in Marketing at the University of Bath in England. His main research areas are consumers' judgement and decision-making, marketing ethics and advertising to children. His recent project focuses on children's response to new advertising techniques (e.g., product placement, advergames) that has been published in *Journal of Consumer Psychology, Journal of Advertising Research, Advances in Consumer Research*, and *International Journal of Advertising*. His research has been reported in different media such as BBC One Breakfast, Channel four News, BBC Radio 4; LBC Radio, *Observer, Independent*, and *Daily Telegraph*.

Robert L. Heath

Professor Emeritus Robert L. Heath, University of Houston, has written books, articles, chapters, encyclopedias, handbooks, and master series on public relations, issues management, rhetorical theory, CSR communication, strategic communication, risk communication, and crisis communication.

Claudia E. Henninger

Dr. Claudia E. Henninger is Lecturer in Fashion Marketing Management at the University of Manchester's School of Materials. Dr. Henninger received her Ph.D. from Sheffield

University. She has published in *the European Journal of Marketing, Journal of Fashion Marketing Management*, and *Journal of Cleaner Production*. Her book *Sustainability in Fashion: A cradle to upcycle approach* will be published by Palgrave MacMillan in 2017 (with Panayiota J. Alevizou, Daniella Ryding, and Helen Goworek). Dr. Henninger's research interests include corporate and social media marketing and sustainability.

Sally Hibbert

Professor Sally Hibbert is Professor of Consumer Behaviour at Nottingham University Business School. She has published in a wide range of international journals including the *Journal of Service Research, Journal of Business Research, Psychology & Marketing, Marketing Theory*, and the *European Journal of Marketing*. Her research interests centre upon health and wellbeing, altruism, and responsible consumption.

Christian Pieter Hoffmann

Professor Christian Pieter Hoffmann is Professor for Communication Management at the Institute of Communication and Media Studies, University of Leipzig, Germany. Professor Hoffmann received his Ph.D. from University of St. Gallen, Switzerland. He has published in *Journal of Management Information Systems, Corporate Communications: An International Journal, Journal of Public Affairs, Information, Communication & Society*, and *Corporate Reputation Review*, among others. His research portfolio is focused on strategic communication management, online communication, financial communication, and political communication.

Brian Jones

Dr. Brian Jones is Senior Lecturer in Marketing at Leeds Beckett University. Dr. Jones received his Ph.D. from the University of Bradford. He has published in *Journal of Marketing Management, Education and Training, Social Responsibility Journal, Journal of Research in Marketing and Entrepreneurship*, and *Journal of Enterprising Communities: People and Places in the Global Economy*, among others. His books include *Corporate Social Irresponsibility: A Challenging Concept* (with Tench and Sun), *Communicating Social Responsibility: Perspectives and Practice* (with Ralph and Sun), and others. His research interests include corporate social responsibility, enterprise education, entrepreneurial marketing, and social media. He serves on the board of three journals.

Asha Kaul

Dr. Asha Kaul is Professor of Communication at Indian Institute of Management, Ahmedabad, India. Dr. Kaul received her Ph.D. from Indian Institute of Technology, Kanpur, India. She has published *Effective Business Communication* (PHI, 2000), *The Effective Presentation: Talk Your Way to Success* (Sage, 2005), *Business Communication* (PHI, 2nd edition, 2009), co-author of the book, *Corporate Reputation Decoded* (Sage, 2014), and co-editor of two books: *Management Communication: Trends and Strategies* (Tata McGraw Hill, 2006) and *New Paradigms for Gender Inclusivity* (Sage, 2013). Her research interests include corporate reputation, social media, politeness and genderlect. Currently, she is working on Indian cases.

Jana Kollat

Jana Kollat is currently a doctoral candidate at the Institute of Corporate Development, Leuphana University of Lueneburg. Her research focuses on communication behavior in organizations and its underlying structures. With a background in media and communication studies, she is particularly interested in internal and external communication processes with regard to corporate social responsibility.

Jairo Lugo-Ocando

Dr. Jairo Lugo-Ocando is an associate professor of journalism studies and Deputy Head in the School of Media and Communication at the University of Leeds. He was a visiting fellow at the National University of Singapore, a visiting scholar in the international media, advocacy, and communications specialization in the School of International and Public Affairs at Columbia University, New York, a visiting professor of the doctoral program in media and communication at the Universidad de Malaga, and he has been invited as keynote speaker at several universities around the world. He has research and written about the relationship between public relations and CSR. Before becoming an academic, he worked as a political correspondent and news editor for several media outlets in Latin America and the United States.

Angela Mak

Dr. Angela Mak is an Associate Professor and Program Director of Public Relations at the School of Communication, Hong Kong Baptist University. She received her Ph.D. from the University of Oregon and previously taught at Monash University in Australia, Nanyang Technology University in Singapore and Iowa State University in the United States. Dr. Mak's research areas of expertise include social responsibility, community engagement, and cancer survivorship. She has published over 25 research articles in international peer-reviewed journals and book chapters including *Journal of Public Relations Research, Public Relations Review, Journal of Brand Management, Australian Journalism Review,* and *Journal of Nonprofit and Public Sector Marketing,* amongst others. Dr. Mak serves on the editorial boards of *Journal of Public Relations Research (2009–2015)* and *Asia-Pacific Public Relations Journal.*

Kateryna Maltseva

Kateryna Maltseva is a Ph.D. candidate in marketing at BI Norwegian Business School. She holds a BSc degree in sociology and a MSc degree in strategic marketing management. Ms. Maltseva is working in the field of consumer behavior and marketing communication. Her main interest is self-quantification and its implications. In her research, she focuses on how data obtained from self-tracking apps and devices affects individuals' well-being, performance, consumption habits, and satisfaction with products and service.

Prashant Mishra

Professor Prashant Mishra is presently Professor in Marketing at IIM Calcutta. He has published in *Journal of Business Ethics, Journal of Strategic Marketing, Marketing Intelligence and Planning,* and *Journal of Media Business Studies.* His research interests include consumer psychology, digital marketing, sustainability, and corporate social responsibility. He serves as a reviewer for many journals.

Majia Nadesan

Dr. Majia Nadesan is Professor of communication studies at Arizona State University. She has authored five books and numerous chapters and articles exploring biopolitics, economics, and risk. Her work on Fukushima appears in *Fukushima and the Privatization of Risk* (2013) and *Crisis Communication, Liberal Democracy, and Ecological Sustainability* (2016) explores captured crisis management that threaten liberal democratic futures.

Caroline J. Oates

Dr. Caroline J. Oates is Senior Lecturer in Marketing at Sheffield University's Management School. Dr. Oates received her Ph.D. from Sheffield University. She has published in *Psychology & Marketing, Journal of Marketing Management, Sociology, Journal of Marketing Communications, Journal of Consumer Policy*, and *International Journal of Advertising*, among others. Her books include *Advertising to Children on TV: Content, Impact and Regulation* (LEA Publishing, 2005; with Barrie Gunter and Mark Blades) and *Advertising to Children: New Directions, New Media* (Palgrave Macmillan, 2014; with Mark Blades, Fran Blumberg and Barrie Gunter). Her research interests include sustainability in marketing and marketing to children. She serves on the editorial board of the journal *Young Consumers*.

Augustine Pang

Dr. Augustine Pang is Professor of Corporate Communication (Practice) at the Lee Kong Chian School of Business, Singapore Management University. He received his Ph.D. from the University of Missouri, United States. Dr. Pang has published in *Corporate Communication: An International Journal, Journal of Public Relations Research, Public Relations Review, Journal of Business and Technical Communication, Asian Journal of Communication, Journal of Contingencies and Crisis Management, International Journal of Strategic Communication, Journal of Communication Management, SAGE Handbook of Public Relations* (2010), and *Handbook of Communication and Corporate Social Responsibility* (2011, Wiley-Blackwell), amongst others. His research interests include crisis management and communication; image management and repair; media management, and corporate communication management. He serves on the editorial boards of *International Journal of Business Communication* and *Asia-Pacific Public Relations Journal*.

Swaleha Peeroo

Dr. Swaleha Peeroo is Lecturer in Marketing at Université des Mascareignes, Maurtius. She received her Ph.D. from Leeds Beckett University. Dr. Peeroo has presented conference papers on social media at the Academy of Marketing Conference (2014), IEEE International Conference on Computing, Communication, and Security (2015), and IFIP Conference on e-Business, e-Services, and e-Society (2016). Her research interests cover social media, customer engagement, retail marketing, and corporate social responsibility.

Keith J. Perks

Dr. Keith J. Perks is a reader in marketing at Brighton Business School. Dr. Perks received his Ph.D. from Loughborough University and has an MBA from Manchester Business School. He has published in the *International Business Review, Journal of Business Research, Journal of Public Policy and Marketing, Corporate Communication: An International Journal*, and *Strategic Change*, among others. His research interests are in the areas of corporate and social responsibility, marketing systems, sustainability, business marketing and international marketing and entrepreneurship. He also serves on the editorial review board of *Industrial Marketing Management*.

Klement Podnar

Dr. Klement Podnar is Professor of Marketing Communications at University of Ljubljana. His work appears in journals such as *Journal of Business Research, European Journal of Marketing, Public Relations Review, Public Policy & Marketing, Journal of Marketing Communications, Corporate Reputation Review, Journal of Promotion Management*, and *Corporate Communications: An International Journal*. He has published a book titled *Corporate Communication: A Marketing Viewpoint* (Routledge, 2015). His research interests lie in corporate marketing and communication, corporate social responsibility and organisational identification. He serves on the boards of several journals and is the deputy editor of *Journal of Promotion Management*.

Mónica Recalde Viana

Dr. Mónica Recalde Viana holds a Ph.D. in Communication and is an Associate Professor at the Economics and Communication School, Universidad de Navarra (Spain). She regularly teaches undergraduate and postgraduate programs on human resources and advertising management. Dr. Recalde Viana has published on stakeholder management, corporate social responsibility and business communication. Her current research interests are focused on collaborative innovation and communication.

Isabel Ruiz-Mora

Dr. Isabel Ruiz-Mora is Lecturer in Advertising and Public Relations in the department of Audiovisual Communication and Advertising at the University of Malaga. She received her Ph.D. from University of Malaga. She was a visiting fellow at University of Stirling, University of Roskilde, and University of Sheffield. She has been a senior lecturer at Sheffield Hallam University. She has published in *Public Relations Review*; her book *Public Information and Communication for Public Participation in Spain* (Vernon Press) came out in 2016. Her research interests include CSR and the role of stakeholders and publics to create spaces for dialogue; also, she is interested in new methodologies of teaching in communication studies. She is co-editor-in-chief of the *International Journal of Public Relations* and vice chair of the Organisational and Strategic Communication Section of ECREA. Before becoming an academic, she worked as communication manager in several SME's in Spain.

Adam J. Saffer

Dr. Adam J. Saffer is an assistant professor at the University of North Carolina's School of Media and Journalism. He holds a Ph.D. from the University of Oklahoma. Dr. Saffer's research takes a network perspective to explore the areas of advocacy and activism, inter-organizational relationships, and new communication technologies in public relations.

Martin Samy

Dr. Martin Samy is a Visiting Professor at Kedge Business School, France. Formerly, he was Professor of Corporate Social Responsibility and Effectiveness Measurement at Leeds Beckett University. He received his Ph.D. from Monash University, Australia where he was a lecturer for seven years. Prior to being an academic, Dr. Samy had commercial experience as a financial manager of corporations in Singapore and Australia. He has been recognized in the Marquis Who's Who in the World in 2007 for his research in establishing a quality effectiveness instrument. His research interests are corporate social responsibility and financial performance research, where he has undertaken studies in Australia, UK, Indonesia, Bangladesh, and Nigeria. He has published in international journals such as the *Corporation Reputation Review, Journal of Global Responsibility, Sustainability Accounting, Management and Policy Journal*, and *Journal of Accounting & Organisational Change*. In 2013, he was awarded the prestigious "Innovation and Initiative Excellence Award" by Leeds Metropolitan University.

Wonsun Shin

Dr. Wonsun Shin is a senior lecturer in media and communications at the School of Culture and Communication, the University of Melbourne. Dr. Shin received her Ph.D. from the University of Minnesota. She has published in *New Media & Society, Communication Research, International Journal of Advertising, Computers in Human Behavior*, and *Journal of Health Communication*, among others. Her research interests include children and digital media, marketing communications, and consumer socialization. Dr. Shin serves on the editorial review board of the *Journal of Advertising*.

Ralph Tench

Dr. Ralph Tench is Professor of Communications and holds a Faculty of Business and Law management responsibility for 100 Ph.D. students as Director of Ph.D. programs, Leeds Business School, Leeds Beckett University. He has examined Ph.D. candidates in the UK, Europe, Africa, and Australia and is an external examiner for six UK universities. He has presented his research at academic and practitioner conferences around the world. Prior to returning to the university sector, Professor Tench was a national news and sports journalist and consultancy director. He is the president and past board director for EUPRERA (European Public Relations Research and Education Association) and is the former head of the Scientific Committee for the Association's annual congress. He sits on the editorial board for six academic journals. He is a member of the Institute for Leadership and the Chartered Institute of Public Relations as well as a Fellow of the Higher Education Academy.

Edward T. Vieira, Jr.

Dr. Edward T. Vieira, Jr. is Associate Professor of Marketing, Quantitative Methods, and Director of Research at the School of Management at Simmons College. Dr. Vieira received his MBA from Bryant University and his Ph.D. from the University of Connecticut. He has published in the *Journal of Business Ethics, Public Relations Review, Public Relations Journal, Corporate Communication: An International Journal, Applied Environmental Education & Communication, International Journal of Process Management and Benchmarking, Communication Research, Journal of Food Service, Journal of Media Psychology, Journal of Communication Studies, Journal of Applied Social Psychology, Journal of Children and Media, Educational Psychology, Reading Psychology, Journal of Hospitality & Tourism Research, Encyclopedia of Media Violence, Russian Journal of Communication, American Communication Journal, Journal of Family Violence*, and *Journal of the Academy of Nutrition and Dietetics*. His textbook *Introduction to Real World*

Statistics: With Step-by-Step SPSS Instructions will be published by Routledge in 2017. Dr. Vieira is on the editorial boards of several journals.

Damion Waymer

Professor Damion Waymer is Professor and Department Chair of Liberal Studies at North Carolina Agricultural and Technical State University. He holds a Ph.D. from Purdue University. His program of research centres on organizational discourse, particularly regarding PR, issues management, corporate social responsibility, branding, and strategic communication. His research projects address fundamental concerns about issues of power, race, class, and gender, specifically, how these social constructions shape and influence the ways that various stakeholders receive, react, and respond to certain messages.

Kun Yu

Dr. Kun Yu is Associate Professor of Accounting at the College of Management, University of Massachusetts at Boston. He received his Ph.D. in Accounting from the Questrom School of Business, Boston University. Dr. Yu's research interests include pension accounting, corporate governance, management compensation, corporate social responsibility, and sustainability accounting. He has published in the *Accounting Review, Accounting and Finance, Review of Quantitative Finance and Accounting*, and *Advances in Quantitative Analysis of Finance and Accounting*, among others.

Foreword and acknowledgements

Although literature on corporate social responsibility is vast, research into the use and effectiveness of various communications through digital platforms about such corporate responsibility is scarce. This gap is surprising; communicating about corporate social responsibility initiatives is vital to organizations that increasingly highlight their corporate social responsibility initiatives to position their corporate brands for both consumers and other stakeholders. Yet these organizations still sometimes rely on traditional methods to communicate, or even decide against communicating at all, because they fear triggering stakeholders' skepticism or cynicism.

A systematic, interdisciplinary examination of corporate social responsibility communication through digital platforms therefore is necessary, to establish an essential definition and up-to-date picture of the field. This examination ideally would

- Emphasize the role and use of corporate social responsibility communication through digital platforms;
- Outline key corporate social responsibility communications tactics, including social and environmental reporting, internationally recognized corporate social responsibility frameworks, and different means to involve stakeholders in two-way communication processes through digital platforms; and
- Examine the ultimate effectiveness of corporate social responsibility communication through digital platforms.

This *research anthology* addresses all of these objectives. Drawing on marketing, management, and communication disciplines, among others, this anthology examines how organizations construct, implement, and use digital platforms to communicate about their corporate social responsibility and thereby achieve their organizational goals.

The 21 chapters in this anthology reflect six main topic sections:

- Challenges and opportunities for communicating corporate social responsibility through digital platforms.
- Moving toward symmetry and interactivity in digital corporate social responsibility communication.
- Fostering stakeholder engagement in and through digital corporate social responsibility communication.
- Leveraging effective digital corporate social responsibility communication.
- Digital activism and corporate social responsibility.
- Digital methodologies and corporate social responsibility.

Challenges and opportunities for communicating corporate social responsibility through digital platforms

To start the first section, Sarah Glozer and Sally Hibbert contribute their chapter, "CSR engagement via social media: in theory and practice," in which they examine practitioners' views on and approaches to implementing corporate social responsibility communications through social media. Their primary focus is the extent to which corporate social responsibility communications can (and should) be integrated with marketing communications. To address these questions, they adopt an engagement lens that reveals three distinct perspectives on the integration of marketing with corporate social responsibility communications: avoidance, divergence, and convergence. Practitioners' reasoning about their implementation of corporate social responsibility communications relates strongly to differences in the orientation of their marketing and corporate social responsibility business functions, as well as contextual factors linked to the organization and broader environment. Noting the growing prominence of social media as a communications platform, these authors call for further research into the implementation of social media communications at the marketing–corporate social responsibility interface to produce practical implications for practitioners.

The second chapter, "Unlocking corporate social responsibility communication through digital media" by Mark Anthony Camilleri, also acknowledges that businesses increasingly embrace the dynamics of new digital technologies as means to communicate their policies and responsible initiatives through corporate websites, social media platforms, and other interactive channels. If Web 2.0 is considered a vehicle for marketing laudable practices, including non-financial reporting, then measures from technological innovation and corporate social responsibility might combine to explicate the rationale for using digital media to communicate about environmental, social, and governance issues. This quantitative study of 202 retail owner-managers reveals a positive, significant relationship between the perceived ease of use/perceived usefulness of online media for corporate social responsibility disclosures and stakeholder engagement. In addition, younger respondents engage even more in these ubiquitous technologies. Therefore, corporate social responsibility communication is more effective when it is readily available online, offering various opportunities for businesses to enhance their reputations and images as they engage with different stakeholders through digital media.

Prashant Mishra and Madhupa Bakshi next consider the "Strategic imperatives of communicating corporate social responsibility through digital media: an emerging market perspective." Based on interviews with senior corporate social responsibility and corporate communication executives in medium to large, public- and private-sector firms in the emerging market of India, these authors investigate the rationale for the use of digital media to communicate corporate social responsibility initiatives. It also explores the strategic imperative for digital outreach. The findings indicate that digital media for corporate social responsibility can mobilize stakeholders meaningfully. Strategically, such communication in the digital domain also can contribute to brand growth and cohesiveness among stakeholders.

Asserting that "'The Devil's in the details': contested standards of corporate social responsibility in social media," Robert L. Heath, Adam J. Saffer, and Damion Waymer note that of the various approaches to corporate social responsibility communications, one of them views the discourse as a dialogic contest, with contextually relevant levels of corporate social responsibility and strategies. The unique structural and functional networks of social media facilitate discourse, because many voices express different, conflicting judgments of corporate social responsibility, without gatekeeping. The network connections provide conduits through which discourse flows, but they also can build siloes in which identities and opinions form and get reinforced. Accordingly, textual and visual messages, which create simulated realities, can reframe disputed issues of policy and reputation. With three cases, this chapter emphasizes how social media reveals "the devil in the details," because competing voices add authenticity and transparency to corporate social responsibility discourses. A Netflix case reveals how one concerned person can pressure a company to raise its corporate social responsibility performance; a pork producers' reputation case focuses on pig waste as an environmental and animal health issue, together with the humane crating of sows, which generates debates and marketing challenges; and an IRATE 8 case demonstrates how students can take over established social media networks and use their networks to pressure a university to respond to an emotional issue.

Moving toward symmetry and interactivity in digital corporate social responsibility communication

In this section, Urša Golob and Klement Podnar start by "Exploring corporate social responsibility communication patterns in social media: a review of current research." Their chapter focuses on growing literature on corporate social responsibility communication in social media and explores how this particular topic has been studied and presented previously. The review of papers indexed in the Scopus database is thematic in its organization, using a co-word and co-citation approach to determine the main themes and research foci. An idealistic perception of social media with regard to corporate social responsibility communication is the starting point for most empirical research; however, an overview of published empirical evidence suggests that the reality is not necessarily in line with this dialogic "ideal." The theoretical underpinnings of corporate social responsibility communication in social media thus might benefit from a more realistic view of the power of social media, as a platform for symmetrical, two-way corporate social responsibility communication.

In the second chapter in this section, Ralph Tench and Mavis Avo-Mensah proclaim "The death of transmission models of corporate social responsibility communication," with their finding that the rapid rise of new technologies has rendered transmission modes of communication out of date. This chapter therefore highlights the relevance of constitutive approaches and their relationship with corporate social responsibility communication; the observed trends in web-based corporate social responsibility communication research also suggest a dialogic construction. With an exploratory study in Ghana, these authors demonstrate the practical challenges that companies face with regard to their use of modern methods of communication. The insights derived from this research imply that companies should redesign their corporate social responsibility communication strategies and adapt to new technologies by leveraging the novel opportunities that they create for stakeholder engagement.

The third chapter in this section, "Social media: from asymmetric to symmetric communication of corporate social responsibility" by Swaleha Peeroo, Martin Samy, and Brian Jones, suggests organizations already have adopted social media as a cost-effective corporate communication tool that can add value through the use of interactive platforms. However, the shift from asymmetric to symmetric communication, facilitated by social media, represents both opportunities and threats to corporations and stakeholders, including the wider public. For example, with the expansion of the social web, business reputation no longer is solely the responsibility of a corporate team. This new era of "socialcasting" allows empowered stakeholders to enhance or damage corporate reputations easily, due to the polyphony of corporate social responsibility on social media. Despite the interactive capacity of social media, companies still mainly apply a broadcasting strategy for their corporate social responsibility communication though, such that they are missing some benefits of social media, such as symmetrical communication and relationship building.

In their chapter, Zhifeng Chen and Haiming Hang assert that for "Communication corporate social responsibilities in the digital media: interactivity is key." With a thematic review of previous research, these authors consider whether the interactive nature of digital media allows organizations to engage more fully with stakeholders, which could transform the effectiveness of corporate social responsibility communication. According to this review, organizations mainly engage in one-way communication on digital media, focused on disseminating their corporate social responsibility information, rather than fully engaging with stakeholders. Extant literature also is unbalanced, dominated by descriptive research that details how organizations communicate about their corporate social responsibility in digital media. Few studies examine the impact of interactivity though. Noting the existing conceptualizations of interactivity in marketing, information systems, and media studies, the authors criticize the failure to address the multidimensional nature of interactivity and also call for further research into the implications of this multidimensional nature of interactivity for transforming corporate social responsibility communication in digital media.

Fostering stakeholder engagement in and through digital corporate social responsibility communication

Moving on to studies of how to foster stakeholder engagement, Keith J. Perks, Mónica Recalde Viana, Francisca Farache, and Jana Kollat offer "A critical reflection on the role of dialogue in communicating ethical corporate social responsibility through digital platforms." Recognizing that organizations are under increasing pressure to communicate their positions while more critical citizens expand their uses of digital platforms to express their opinions, the authors argue that these changes demand a corporate culture of listening, management commitment, responsible action, and more effective corporate social responsibility communication with stakeholders. Digital platforms such as Facebook and Twitter provide a mechanism for dialogue with stakeholders, yet despite its potential for helping corporations listen and respond to stakeholder concerns in an open and honest discourse, such communication often is perceived to serve only instrumental goals. If corporate social responsibility communication through digital platforms was grounded in the ethical premise of responsibility and the concept of dialogue, it could change this perception. This chapter recommends that organizations should enact an ethical premise by adopting a dialogic mind-set in which they listen and respond to the views of stakeholders. This critical reflection also suggests a conceptual lens for continued empirical studies.

To examine the interaction of corporate social responsibility with public relations and other forms of professional communication, Isabel Ruiz-Mora and Jairo Lugo-Ocando contribute "The imperative needs of dialogue between corporate social responsibility departments and PR practitioners: empirical evidence from Spain." The authors investigate the top listed companies in Spain, which also have invested more resources in corporate social responsibility than other firms in that country. To triangulate the data, they combine semi-structured interviews with analyses of annual reports, communication strategies, and digital ethnographic observations of digital platforms (websites and social networks). The findings suggest the scarcity of public relations practitioners responsible for formulating or communicating corporate social responsibility policies in major Spanish companies, whether in digital or non-digital spaces. Thus, an important gap exists: corporate social responsibility departments recognize their communication needs, but they fail to acknowledge the ability of their communication colleagues to address these needs. The resulting communication strategies are peripheral, performative exercises in the organization, rather than core elements of the corporate social responsibility strategy.

In the next contribution, Augustine Pang, Angela Mak, and Wonsun Shin consider the potential pitfalls of relying on the mainstream media as a sole agent and engine of corporate social responsibility communication, with their chapter "Integrated corporate social responsibility communication: toward a model encompassing media agenda building with stakeholder dialogic engagement." Therefore, they integrate research that suggests digital media (online, mobile, and social) are critical platforms for organizations to not just disseminate information but also interact with stakeholders through feedback or dialogic loops. Organizations can integrate their media agenda building with stakeholder engagement, using both mainstream media and digital platforms to communicate their corporate social responsibility activities, according to the corporate social responsibility – integrated media model that the authors propose.

Christian Fieseler, Kateryna Maltseva, and Christian Pieter Hoffmann advance the notion that corporate efforts to engage stakeholders in social, ecological, and governmental issues are unbalanced and unrepresentative, such that they are dominated by elite users, with their chapter "Hedonic stakeholder engagement: bridging the online participation gap through gamification." Therefore, they propose lower-threshold modes of participation to enlarge the potential circle of contributors, based on hedonic gratification as opposed to the more common utilitarian motives mostly employed today. Using input from gamification research, the authors investigate narrative-, reward-, and technology-enabled elements as worthwhile routes to corporate online stakeholder engagement. Although challenges remain for gamifying corporate social responsibility efforts, the benefits of speaking to a larger stakeholder base and familiarizing them with corporate social responsibility policies and deliberations through gamified approaches, are substantial as well.

Leveraging effective digital corporate social responsibility communication

The first contribution in this section, "Social media concepts for effective corporate social responsibility online communication," is by Lina M. Gómez, who notes that social media platforms provide interactive richness for two-way conversations, yet communication on these platforms still tends to be treated as a one-way approach. Of the many empirical studies of corporate social responsibility communication and social media, none has discussed the importance of using social media concepts for interactive corporate social responsibility communication, including dialogue, engagement, transparency, authenticity, influence, and mobilization. By considering how these innate social media concepts have been used by various entities that communicate about social responsibility issues on Twitter (e.g., companies, media, non-profits, influencers, advocates, professionals, citizens/consumers), according to a quantitative content analysis of a random sample of 1,000 public tweets that feature the hashtag "#CSR," the author reveals that social media platforms can engage stakeholders to commit to responsible practices. However, some users do not leverage all the unique elements that these platforms have to offer. The proposed corporate social responsibility communication framework can help managers design effective messages to promote stakeholder engagement and participation.

Next, Shuili Du and Kun Yu propose a contingency model in their chapter, "Effectiveness and accountability of digital corporate social responsibility communication: a contingency model." By drawing on different literature streams pertaining not only to corporate social responsibility but also institutional legitimacy, digital communication, and accountability, this chapter provides an in-depth discussion of the unique characteristics of digital corporate social responsibility communication, the array of techniques managers could employ to enhance the effectiveness of such communication, and metrics they can use to assess the accountability of their digital corporate social responsibility communication. Rich media, encouraging interactivity, and active participation by stakeholders emerge as critical to digital corporate social responsibility communication. Yet the effectiveness of digital corporate social responsibility communication also is contingent on several factors, including the accessibility of the corporate social responsibility message, media richness, level of stakeholder participation, and the perceived credibility of the messages. Accountability also is a critical issue; this chapter accordingly outlines several corporate social responsibility – related, stakeholder-related, and firm performance – related metrics that managers should monitor continuously to gauge the accountability of their digital corporate social responsibility communications.

The next chapter, by Claudia E. Henninger and Caroline J. Oates, instead considers "The role of social media in communicating corporate social responsibility within fashion micro organizations." That is, this chapter investigates how sustainable fashion micro-organizations understand and communicate about their corporate social responsibility activities through digital platforms, with a particular focus on social media, such as Twitter, Facebook, and blogs. The qualitative research, based on semi-structured interviews, semiotics, and Twitterfeed analyses, provides insights into three micro-organizations. The findings suggest that though social media has an increasingly important role for promoting a company's products and services, not all platforms are appropriate for communicating about corporate social responsibility activities. Blogs emerge as valuable means to gain stakeholder engagement, which allow organizations to communicate their corporate social responsibility activities to a wider audience.

The last chapter in this section, by Ezgi Akpinar, discusses "Corporate social responsibility and word of mouth: a systematic review and synthesis of literature." Given the era of more connected consumers, it has become much more important for companies to take advantage of word of mouth for their corporate social responsibility. Positive word of mouth (e.g., sending a viral video to collect donation, talking about a social cause to raise awareness) can benefit companies. On the other hand, negative word of mouth (e.g., sending news about a product harm crisis, talking about environmental concerns about production facilities) can harm companies' status greatly. This chapter presents a systematic review and synthesis of corporate social responsibility and word of mouth literature based on 71 studies. The chapter explores 1) the role of potential drivers that could make corporate social responsibility activities propagate, 2) the consequences of corporate social responsibility activities in terms of word of mouth, and 3) the role of four components of communication (sender, receiver, content and channel) that could make corporate social responsibility activities propagate.

Digital activism and corporate social responsibility

Three chapters focus on digital activism. First, Vidhi Chaudri and Asha Kaul contribute "Digital activism: NGOs leveraging social media to influence/challenge corporate social responsibility." They note how extant scholarship privileges a managerial perspective and situates corporations as key actors in business–society relations, without including non-profit organizations as influential institutional actors. This gap may not be surprising, considering the managerial bias in corporate social responsibility scholarship and the unequal, often hostile relationship among corporations and non-profit organizations. Yet the growing influence of social media and the digitalization of communication represent game changers, so this chapter uses illustrative cases to discover how traditionally marginalized stakeholders (e.g., NGOs) leverage new social media to effect change. Traditional forms of activism may persist, but the uncensored, instantaneous, widespread reach of new media amplify stakeholder concerns and offer unprecedented potential for collective action. In turn, advocacy groups gain a new source of leverage and new opportunities to be heard and noticed. These social-mediated developments suggest several ethical and pragmatic implications.

Second, Majia Nadesan investigates a notable industrial crisis in "Catastrophe, transparency, and social responsibility on online platforms: contesting cold shutdown at the Fukushima nuclear plant." To determine whether social media activism can increase democratic responsiveness and corporate social responsibility, this chapter focuses on the March 2011 Fukushima Daiichi nuclear disaster. With participatory action research, the author examines whether social media successfully challenged TEPCO's narrative of control regarding reactor conditions, using corporate webcam and government radiation monitoring data. The analysis of webcam watchers' efforts to contest official accounts of a "cold shutdown" reveal two specific time periods, which are significant for coinciding with TEPCO's reassurances that the fuel had cooled, despite unusual activity on the webcams.

Third, Angela Mak and Suwichit Chaidaroon consider the situation surrounding another tragic event, the collapse of Rana Plaza in 2013, in "Plotting corporate social responsibility narratives: corporate social responsibility stories by global fashion brands after the collapse of Rana Plaza in Bangladesh." Many global fashion brands that had outsourced to Bangladesh's garment factories initiated corporate social responsibilities to help victims and local communities, as well as to restore their brand images, considering that they arguably were responsible. Two interrelated textual analysis approaches examine the corporate social responsibility videos of involved fashion brands. First, an analysis of narrative plots and characters identifies how heroes and dilemmas (or social issues) are framed. Second, a multimodal discourse analysis reveals how meanings are constructed and made salient through multimodal features. Three distinct narrative patterns emerge among the corporate social responsibility stories told by fashion brands involved directly in Rana Plaza (wrongdoers), brands that were not involved directly (malefactors), and brands that were not involved at all (heroes). These interpretations suggest that digital media serve as a multimodal communication platform for corporate social responsibility narratives and reach their maximum dramatic effect from constructing heroes and framing the dilemmas that the Bangladeshi victims faced, especially when the narratives are authentic, transparent, and engaging.

Digital methodologies and corporate social responsibility

The final section contains two chapters. Edward T. Vieira Jr. and Susan Grantham suggest "A new content analysis methodology appropriate for corporate social responsibility communication." A text network analysis approach may complement traditional content analysis methods by distilling content into a more manageable amount of text and providing a textual structure. In addition, text network analysis is unsupervised and employs network analysis betweenness centrality and degree principles to identify influential words and word clusters. With this information, various content analysis strategies can be applied, including analyses that incorporate individual and contextual-related nontextual factors. Furthermore, text network analysis is informed by the landscape model of reading comprehension, which is a reader-focused framework. Because text network analysis is unsupervised, it is not very labor intensive or time consuming. Finally, text network analysis provides a graphical visualization and overview of the entire text, indicating keywords and themes. The authors illustrate the proposed approach by analyzing corporate social responsibility introductory letters written in 2002 and 2012 by the ExxonMobil CEO.

Finally, Ana Adi considers the emerging discourses and themes associated with the corporate social responsibility hashtag on Twitter as a way to discover concerns, issues, and key conceptual associations in "#CSR on Twitter: a hashtag oversimplifying a complex practice." The sample of 15,000 tweets collected over three different periods (23–29 August 2015, 14–21 December 2015, and 23–29 January 2016) reveals automatically reported hashtag frequencies, most active and most influential accounts, a user network visualization, and hashtag network visualization. The resulting conceptual associations indicate that tweets referring to #CSR include information relevant to the profession and the field, which often is reiterated, repeated, and repackaged across a few accounts responsible for the greatest bulk of information. The corporate social responsibility hashtag also is closely associated with #sustainability, #green, and #jobs, suggesting that wider approaches to corporate social responsibility receive less attention and support than the triple bottom line approach that centers specifically on people, planet, and profit. This trend misleads users into associating corporate social responsibility primarily with profit-enhancing and environment-saving (or maybe just greenwashing) practices.

Closing remarks

We extend a special thanks to Routledge and its staff, who have been most helpful throughout this entire process. Equally, we warmly thank all of the authors who submitted their manuscripts for consideration for this book. They have exhibited the desire to share their knowledge and experience with the book's readers – and a willingness to put forward their views for possible challenge by their peers. We also thank the reviewers, who provided excellent, independent, and incisive consideration of the anonymous submissions.

We hope that this compendium of chapters and themes stimulates and contributes to the ongoing debate surrounding the optimal communication of corporate social responsibility in an ever-more digitalized world. The chapters in this book can help fill some knowledge gaps, while also stimulating further thought and action pertaining to the multiple aspects surrounding communication through digital means.

Adam Lindgreen, Ph.D.
Copenhagen, Denmark
Joëlle Vanhamme, Ph.D.
Lille, France
François Maon, Ph.D.
Lille, France
Rebecca Mardon, Ph.D.
Cardiff, Wales

Part 1

Challenges and opportunities for communicating corporate social responsibility through digital platforms

1.1 CSR engagement via social media

In theory and practice

Sarah Glozer and Sally Hibbert

Introduction

Corporate social responsibility (CSR) communication is often understood as a process of anticipating stakeholders' expectations to provide true and transparent information on economic, social and environmental concerns.[1] Traditionally, the primary platforms for CSR communications were CSR reports, public relations and website content. Today, the ever-increasing capabilities of information and communication technology (ICT) bring the opportunity to not only adopt social media (SM) as a channel for communicating CSR[2] but also to invite stakeholders into communicative processes, empowering and connecting them as active collaborators and 'co-creators' of CSR.[3]

SM are defined as, "a group of Internet-based applications that build on the ideological and technological foundations of Web 2.0, and that allow the creation and exchange of User Generated Content".[4] Recent literature explores the potential of SM to facilitate more fluid, collaborative[5] and dialogical[6] engagement between organisations and stakeholders around CSR activities.[7] Yet there is limited practical insight into the different approaches adopted by organisations in communicating CSR through SM and the degree of integration with other (non-CSR) communications. Traditionally dominated by the marketing function, SM are being used as contemporary channels through which to build relationships with customers, as well as non-commercial stakeholders (e.g., charities, the media). Integration across these stakeholder groups poses challenges because marketing and CSR are rooted in different management traditions, producing tensions, which are well rehearsed in debates of marketing's impacts on society.[8] Stakeholders, however, tend to view their relationship with the organisation holistically, and they are largely unconcerned with internal functional boundaries and difficulties that arise from incompatibility across principles and practices.

In this chapter, we examine practitioners' views on, and approaches to, implementing CSR communications via SM, with particular consideration of whether CSR can (and should be) integrated with marketing communications. We address this issue by adopting the lens of engagement. Engagement has emerged as a key concept in both CSR and marketing fields, as part of a broader shift towards collaborative perspectives on management.[9,10] However, there are marked differences in how engagement is conceptualized and practiced. In the following pages we examine the challenges that this creates for practitioners facing a shift towards more interactive relationships with customers and stakeholders.

The CSR-marketing interface and the integration of social media communications

Research into CSR implementation highlights that in the majority of organisations, CSR initiatives are introduced alongside routine business functions, particularly at the early stages of CSR integration.[11,12] As CSR activities are expanded over time, managers are faced with decisions on whether and how to integrate CSR activities with those carried out by other functions. Studies that have looked at CSR integration generally adopt the perspective of leadership and organisational change,[13] examining the broad business context[14,15] and specific areas of activity, such as human resource (HR) management.[16] Yet, there is a lack of attention to the interface of marketing and CSR.

This volume focuses on communications, which is a central activity for both marketing and CSR. In the following pages we make two assertions. First, while marketing and CSR both espouse relational modes of interaction, there are differences in the purpose and principles of these two fields, giving rise to areas of incompatibility within communications practices. Secondly, SM allow organisations to speak to consumers and/or broader stakeholders and enable individuals to communicate with each other.[17] The prominence and potential of SM is such that organisations are under pressure to incorporate them within their communications mix. Yet there is considerable uncertainty on how best to use such tools given that they afford low levels of organisational control, contrasting markedly with traditional communications tools. Below, we contrast relational approaches in marketing and CSR by reference to the concept of engagement to illuminate the differences between the two fields.

Consumer engagement: the marketing perspective

Consumer engagement has gained traction in marketing theory and practice, with the shift towards relationship perspectives,[18] as an approach to building sustainable competitive advantage through satisfaction, loyalty[19] and, in particular, enabling consumers to play an active and collaborative role in their relationships with organisations.[20] Customer-based metrics such as trust commitment, brand experience and customer equity have become increasingly commonplace,[21] replacing firm-focused metrics such as sales and market share. While conceptualisations suggest that engagement reflects cognitive, affective and behavioural dimensions of consumers' experiences with an entity,[22] there is some discrepancy in how these elements feature in definitions of the construct.[23,24] The extant literature, however, largely distinguishes between engagement as a motivated volitional interaction or a psychological state associated with co-creative experiences.[25]

To date, most attention has been devoted to organisation-to-customer interactions to promote consumer engagement at a firm or brand level.[26,27] However, the importance of consumers' interactions with one another is widely recognised, based on the theoretical influence of service perspectives that espouse a network view of value creation.[28,29] Scholars have investigated how to encourage engagement through experiences and interactions, focusing upon single platforms (e.g., SM)[30,31,32] and combinations of on and offline platforms, representing the multiple touch points or ecosystem of consumer experiences.[33] Research into the consumers perspective has revealed that consumer are willing to invest greater effort in their relationship with an organisation and other stakeholders because they derive a range of benefits, including functional and hedonic benefits[34] and, where there are interactions with third parties (e.g., via SM), social benefits.[35] In essence, then, engagement reflects a consumer's willingness to contribute to and collaborate with a focal entity. The acknowledgement that consumer engagement takes place within network contexts has the potential to bring a societal perspective through attention to organisational activities that affect other stakeholders. However, there is a lack of consumer engagement research that examines value outcomes beyond the self-interested benefits of individual consumption.

Interactions that contribute to consumer engagement are not limited to communications. SM contribute to the communications mix but are distinctive in that they facilitate high levels of interconnectivity and interactivity and, as such, are more dynamic and egalitarian.[36] The novelty of these platforms has led to considerable experimentation as practitioners attempt to navigate the risks and opportunities that they afford. Many organisations adhere to traditional practices of managing inside-out communications (e.g., creating messages, controlled by the organisation and distributing them to consumers) and privilege simple cognitive and behavioural aspect of engagement captured by metrics such as 'likes', 'follows' and 'views'.[37,38] Others are making the cultural shift to outside-in modes of communications that involve listening, responsive approaches and engaging in conversation and dialogue with consumers.[39] But the apparent simplicity of cultivating conversations is deceptive, and understanding interactive communications amongst multiple actors and across networks is complex. There is no shortage of either qualitative or quantitative data, rather it is so plentiful that it is overwhelming and organisations have insufficient resources to analyse it.

Stakeholder engagement: the CSR perspective

CSR scholarship focuses upon the relationships between organisations and a wider range of individuals and groups that affect and are affected by the organisation's activities.[40] Building upon stakeholder theory[41] the concept of stakeholder engagement has been defined as the process for developing, "trust-based collaborations between individuals and/ or social institutions with different objectives that can only be achieved together".[42] Akin to conceptions of consumer engagement, the extant literature on stakeholder engagement has focused upon strategic and 'trust' based relationship development. Therein, it is 'primary' stakeholders that directly interact with organisations (e.g., consumers, employees, investors) who remain at the forefront of discussions of stakeholder engagement, often to the detriment of 'secondary' stakeholders who operate at the periphery and potentially beyond the organisational boundary (e.g., regulators, pressure groups, media).[43]

CSR literature on stakeholder engagement has been primarily concerned with presenting normative views of what stakeholder engagement *should* look like.[44] Given the confluence of corporate and societal perspectives in this domain, political science has been particularly influential in the debates around the conceptualisation of stakeholder engagement. Scholars distinguished between processes of moral engagement and ethical strategic engagement.[45] The moral engagement perspective draws on Habermasian philosophy on discourse ethics and deliberative democracy to identify procedural guidelines to enable moral engagement with stakeholders and facilitate consensus, avoiding power imbalances.[46] Ethical strategic engagement represents a more managerial perspective that similarly seeks to facilitate honest and open dialogue with stakeholders, but it is resistant to claims that corporate strategic interests corrupt engagement. The latter approach has been dominant; thus approaches to engagement have tended to seek effective means by which stakeholders can be 'managed' as resources, in the pursuit of achieving maximum cooperation between multiple stakeholder groups.[47,48]

In contrast to consumer engagement, which emanates from various forms of interaction, communication activities are central to stakeholder engagement. The approaches adopted have traditionally been initiated by the organisation and have taken place in offline settings. As in marketing, the received view of communications is that it is a transmissional exercise: a one-way process of information dissemination from organisational encoders to passive stakeholder recipients.[49] SM offer more fluid forms of engagement and can appeal to a broader range of constituent audiences, challenging the dominant normative and prescriptive perspectives that focus upon CSR communication as an exercise in informing and responding to stakeholders.[50] Indeed, as stakeholders are increasingly *involved* in CSR communication,[51] interest in the formative role of CSR communication as a two-way exercise is burgeoning within the CSR literature,[52] particularly in digital contexts.[53] Recently, there has been some take up of SM tools to complement traditional forms of CSR communication (e.g., CSR reports developed by internal managers), such as Starbucks''My Starbucks Idea'[54] forum or E.On UK's 'Talking Energy' YouTube channel,[55] both of which allow stakeholders to contribute consumer experience and CSR ideas.

The need to understand how organisations reconcile varied, competing and, at times, discordant interests in SM, is increasingly capturing scholarly attention.[56] As a result, more network-based, relational and process-orientated views of company–stakeholder engagement are evolving to better account for mutuality, interdependence and power relations between organisations and stakeholders.[57] It is argued that these SM platforms open up more dialogical and dialectical 'arenas of citizenship', online spaces wherein CSR knowledge is cultivated, sustained and challenged.[58] Recent research explores corporate–civil society online engagement practices through the lens of political and civic participation,[59] illuminating the collaborative, but also conflictual processes inherent in SM interactions.[60] The democratic potential of SM engagement has come to the fore through exploration of broader empirical contexts such as e-government[61] and not-for-profit practices in SM settings.[62] Yet despite the richness of scholarly research into stakeholder engagement via SM, empirical research suggests that practitioners lack knowledge of how to deploy SM in ways that is appropriate for CSR and often apply traditional communicative principles (i.e., information dissemination) to SM platforms.[63] There is also a fear that CSR communications may be exposed to questions of authenticity, legitimacy and integrity if core

Table 1.1.1 Characteristics of consumer engagement and stakeholder engagement

	Consumer engagement	*Stakeholder engagement*
Participants	• *Major:* Consumers • *Minor:* Other actors	• Major: Primary stakeholders • Minor: Secondary stakeholders
Motives	• Building trust & relationships • Influencing consumer choice, value creating activities & contributions	• Building trust & relationships • Democratic participation
Processes	• Consumer interactions & experiences via multiple platforms within service ecosystem	• Multi-stakeholder dialogue via offline or online platforms
Outcomes	• Increased long term competitive advantage & revenue (economic & strategic value)	• Co-operation & consensus (social value), • Coordination with organisational objectives & business sustainability (economic and strategic value)

principles of clarity, consistency and continuity within an integrated approach to CSR communication are not upheld.[64]

The lack of an amalgamated scholarship that explores the integration of marketing *and* CSR domains of engagement has not helped to address this problem. In response, Table 1.1.1 sets out key features of both fields to illustrate similarities and differences likely to affect consideration of whether and how to adopt an integrated approach to SM communications across CSR and marketing. The review of literature on SM as a platform for engagement suggests that there are attempts in both fields to move away from inside-out communications practices towards more interactive approaches, but that this is hampered in practice by the lack of insight available to managers and the risks of making mistakes in this relatively unchartered territory.

Methodology

To gain insights into practitioner views on whether on how to implement SM as a means to engaging consumers and stakeholders in CSR communication, 48 industry CSR 'experts' were contacted in accordance with convenience and snowball sampling techniques.[65] A total of 39 individuals agreed to participate in the research across a range of industries including: marketing/PR agency, banking and finance, consultancy, consumer goods, engineering, insurance, leisure and hospitality, charity, policy and retail. Data were collected by the first author through asynchronous email interviews defined as, "semi-structured in nature and involv[ing] multiple email exchanges between the interviewer and interviewee over a period of time".[66] Email interviews were chosen to expand the reach of data collection (i.e., it created opportunities to contact geographically dispersed participants and those with major time constraints).[67] We note, however, that there are shortcomings of this approach (e.g., loss of contextual richness) with implications for the limitations of the research. Data were thematically coded and iteratively analysed between the authors, tacking back into the engagement literature akin with recommendations for interpretive research.[68]

Findings and discussion

The analysis of practitioner views of the use of SM as an element of CSR communications and its integration with marketing revealed three different views, which we label as avoidance, convergence and divergence.

Avoidance

The first group of informants is of the view that SM is not currently well geared to corporate–stakeholder communications. This stance is generally observed in contexts where CSR is integrated at the corporate level but does not permeate into marketing activities, which emanate from competitive strategies at a brand level. The primary use of SM is the marketing function, which is disconnected from CSR strategy.

Our informants who witness the use of SM by marketing managers to develop consumer–brand relationships consider it unsuitable for CSR engagement, arguing that there are stark contrasts between consumer and stakeholder engagement; the latter being considered as a more formal process. This is illustrated in the quote below, which contrasts CSR and marketing interactions in terms of their depth of engagement, indicating that such variance has consequences for the participants, content and process of each form of communication.

> Consultancy: To be honest, based on my experience, I get the sense that social media use among my clients so far seems to be around soft CR branding – or to complement traditional media (e.g., TV ads). The people whose opinions actively shape their CSR debate tend to engage with the issues raised a bit more formally. Social media seem to be used more for engaging the general public. In many such cases, the media do not get into the core of the issues as that might make the material too heavy and uninteresting for social media audiences.

In terms of participants in engagement activities via SM, there is a widespread view that consumer stakeholders are dominant. The quote above reflects a broadly held sentiment that few of these participants are sufficiently interested in organisations' CSR to explore the issues in depth. By contrast, the informant infers that people involved in CSR debates have a well-informed perspective (e.g., non-governmental organisations [NGOs], community representatives), which grants them a role with influence to, 'actively shape' organisations' CSR. While these observations are valid and may even reflect a scenario that is currently most common, this stance underestimates consumers as active stakeholders. There are plenty of cases to demonstrate the considerable scope for SM interactions around CSR either facilitated by the organisation (e.g., 'Join the Revolution' campaign by The Co-operative (retailer) in the UK; or cosmetics company 'Lush's' blog site) or stimulated by other parties (e.g., activist groups).[69] Research that has examined stakeholder dialogue via SM clearly challenges a view that CSR engagement online lacks depth.[70,71]

In relation to process, this group suggest that the use of SM by marketing has cultivated roles and practices (e.g., consumers engage in frequent and rapid interactions such as 'liking' or 'sharing' responses to organisational posts or brief comment) that serve marketing objectives such as reinforcing brand commitment amongst a target market or stimulating sales. Yet they neglect the evidence that consumer engagement, for example, in brand communities, is often highly involved, whether in support of or opposition to the organisation.[72] However, the main comparison drawn is that CSR engagement, in working towards consensus across a range of stakeholder groups, requires more 'formal' processes, which normally involve planned consultations, allowing organisations to address issues at times and in ways that are compatible with their resources. They also use language such as 'professional practice' to describe typical activities, and normative processes of stakeholder engagement, whether moral[73] or managerial,[74] espoused by CSR professionals.

This group recognise that it is not only marketing communications practices that are discordant with stakeholder engagement but other forms of CSR communication (e.g., press releases, company reports, labelling) also. For these activities, a traditional model of information dissemination; informing and responding to stakeholders,[75] persists, and informants suggest that digital platforms have been harnessed to extend this activity. They expressed a discomfort with the use of SM and other digital channels as a 'push' rather than a 'pull' medium.

> Insurance: I do however believe that the website is used purely as a knowledge-sharing site: more of a push than a pull. I do not believe that, even though it publishes articles/thought pieces on climate change and sustainability, that these are linked – or comments directed to – the company's own sustainability strategy.

Engineering: the majority of our engagement is providing comments, information i.e., telling, rather than asking.

This approach to CSR communications has long been regarded with scepticism,[76] but the risks are seen to be augmented when it is deployed in channels that are highly interactive (by comparison to advertising or press coverage), where there is clear potential to actively involve stakeholders in CSR but organisational processes are such that inputs are often ignored.

Additionally, this group of informants are concerned about the lack of organisational resources and know-how to exploit the interactive potential of SM.[77] Specific concerns related to feeling 'exposed' through fluid SM interactions and corporate risk management:

Brand agency: Typically the clients we work with are trying to get their heads around social media generally so are less likely to be engaging with these stakeholders online, although they may be monitoring what's being said and by whom on a rudimentary basis. These are not small clients either! Unless they are actually politically active they're unlikely to be actively engaging in these areas of CSR publically.

Consultancy: I think themes of trust, transparency and authenticity will/are driving digital communication. However companies are handcuffed by legal – so comments often need to be approved by legal teams before being posted. How can companies overcome this to have meaningful relationships on-line?

The concerns expressed by this group reveal anxieties about the fit of SM with current communications practices, established ideas on good practice for stakeholder engagement, the organisational competence and structures to implement CSR communications well and potential reputational risks. In light of these challenges, their own inclination and observation of client behaviour errs towards avoidance of using SM to facilitate interactive communications on CSR.

Divergence

A second group recognised an approach of divergence, that is, SM communications are used for both marketing and CSR purposes but within two separate streams of activity rather than a unified function.

Brand agency: SM's not about a channel it's about the content. Development of that content requires integration of corporate and brand worlds, which are normally non-communicative in client organisations.

This group's discussion of engagement via SM channels reflects observations similar to those seen in the avoidance group, in that corporate-led CSR is not seen to be fully integrated within the marketing function. However, these informants are distinct in that they believe that SM interactions with consumers *can* be a means to engage on CSR issues and standards, especially amongst those who are interested and active. They reiterate the argument advanced by the avoidance group, that there are different drivers of engagement for marketing and CSR, and highlight that SM is deployed by the marketing function as a customer relationship tool, by contrast to the democratic processes of CSR engagement. For these practitioners, however, this is not a reason to avoid the use of SM, rather it justifies their separation of engagement into discrete streams of communication. This divergence approach is relatively common in practice, where separate CSR channels often complement mainstream organisational SM sites. The informants are clear that attention centres on 'primary' consumer stakeholders[78] when communicating via online platforms and they emphasise that few organisations take advantage of opportunities to interact with broader stakeholder communities online.

> Consultancy: I think most companies engage with active consumers and drive brand loyalty. But I am not sure that many think about broader stakeholder segments. So for example, development experts and groups; governments/donors; customers. I think this is an interesting emerging area – as it's niche conversations that will drive these conversations forward.

A number of informants expressed that they have limited knowledge of who actually gets involved in their SM-based CSR communication platforms:

> Charity: It would be interesting to map different types of audience for SM/CSR communication with different channels. Which channels and platforms are working best for reaching different audiences?

Despite the limitation concerning the scope of stakeholder engagement online, it is suggested that 'listening to' and having 'conversations with' consumers and other stakeholders on SM is prioritised, as opposed to simply transmitting positive messages.

> Retail: Listening to stakeholders (especially customers) is extremely important.

This apparent openness to stakeholders' views has the potential to enhance the organisation's legitimacy, if the interaction is facilitated to enable learning and change, exploring rather than suppressing dissensus as integral to a process of co-operation. However, few informants backed up their advocacy for 'listening' with evidence that their resources, especially staff competencies, and internal structures supported deep engagement. Where there is an internal process, it typically involves feeding back into the organisation should there be a 'ground swell' of comment around a particular issue that posed threat (mostly to reputation, hence the response is often handled through public relations), but many claimed that these incidents are rare. Recent scholarship suggests that external stakeholders detect when SM interactions are inadequately resourced and are dissatisfied when their contributions are not taken seriously.[79] Thus, superficial efforts to engage with stakeholders online are unlikely to cultivate consensual views on CSR issues and contribute to organisations' quest for legitimacy as they risks stoking critical SM conversations about the process of stakeholder engagement. In sum, while CSR and marketing engagement remain distinct endeavours, informants within the divergence group are cognisant of the benefits and challenges of SM in communication activities.

Convergence

Finally, a third group of informants reported that their organisations, or clients, integrate CSR into their strategy across activities, involving both primary and secondary stakeholders.[80] Within this context, CSR is integrated with corporate and brand communications, of which SM interactions are one element of the mix. Informants who reported this convergent approach generally work for organisations that have well-developed CSR strategies or charities, whose strategy is inherently focused upon social goals.

> Consumer goods: Companies with great CSR have this as an intrinsic part of their strategy and it flows naturally through key initiatives both internal and external.

In such organisations, internal structures and processes had been adapted to enable communications to be driven by one aligned team, rather than being managed separately.

> Consumer goods: Our brand SM is managed by our digital agency, with guidance from brand marketing. We would consult corporate affairs with any challenges.

These findings are consistent with research that suggests that extensive integration between core commercial functions and CSR is characteristic of organisations at advanced stages of CSR development.[81] The literature also suggests that these organisations pursue stakeholder relationships and interactions that are collaborative or even aim for joint innovation. Yet when the informants refer to SM interactions, and broader communications strategies, the predominance of distributing 'news' and unidirectional 'messaging'[82] is evident, reflecting anxieties voiced by the avoidance group. It seems that the principle that interaction is central to engagement via SM, whether for marketing and/or CSR purposes, is yet to be realised. Instead we have further evidence that communications traditionally used at corporate and brand levels to support strategic goals (e.g., reputation, brand image, market share) are being extended to incorporate SM, with little transformation of the dominant unidirectional communications model.

> Consumer goods: We communicate about CSR at both a corporate and brand level. . . . When we have had sufficient news we have done this through a fully integrated campaign, including TV. . . . Most of the time we do this through our website, Facebook and our CRM email programme.

> Consultant: For consumer marketing, they use SM platforms regularly (apps, Facebook page, Twitter, Pinterest). They are monitored every day by the digital team. . . [it is] used more to push information out to consumers than to respond to stakeholder comments.

The integration of CSR into marketing communications belies the assumption that recipients of communications perceive there to be a comfortable fit between organisational and social/environmental goals and a view that legitimacy has been 'achieved'.[83] Informants clearly indicate the dominance of a strategic motive for CSR, for instance, one noted 'there was never any question of whether it was *worth* communicating". This infers a belief that posting messages on CSR activities will strengthen organisation–stakeholder relationships, reinforcing the consensus on CSR and delivering benefits for marketing/ corporate reputation. The potential for CSR communications via SM to contribute to strategic goals is further emphasised below in the report from a retail informant on the ways that feedback is used:

> Retail: On a daily basis Tweets, blog responses etc. are looked at, sent to relevant people across the business and will be fed into a range of meetings including strategy development including product development.

Research suggests that promoting a consensual view of CSR can be commercially ben-eficial, hence the adage 'doing well by doing good',[84] but a call for caution comes from the growing body of research that challenges managed approaches to legitimacy that are geared towards solely meeting organisational objectives.[85] Recent scholarship highlights that interactive SM platforms facilitate forms of stakeholder engagement characterised by opportunities for agency and forms of influence and control that contrast starkly with organisational-led forms of communication.[86] Stakeholders are surrounded by a plural-ity of voices, involved in processes of consensus or dissensus around issues that relate to organisational activities. Against this backdrop, where organisations sideline disputes, there is a risk that stakeholders will perceive their CSR messages as a public relations exercise.[87]

A notable exception to this broader pattern is evident in the experience of an inform-ant working for a charitable organisation. The quote below reveals a more adaptive and collaborative approach in which stakeholder views are sought and used to inform changes to organisational activity.

> Charity: Yes, comments do sometimes impact strategies and also help us to improve execution of our SM activity. We have changed and improved what sits on our web-site as a result of comments from members of the public or stakeholders e.g., where information has not been available, or is not clear enough. We have also created new assets online (e.g., downloadable documents) or improved our Q+A. We have used comments as part of formal evaluations . . . we opened up space for comment from stakeholders [on a new venture] and used this as part of assessment of what went well, and what we could do differently in communicating company commitments in the future. Comments made regarding individual company engagement with [charity] are often referred to commercial colleagues and passed on to companies we work with.

This is much closer to the interactional model of communications promised by organisa-tions' SM activity. Social goals are inherent to the charity's organisational purpose, which may mean that it typically encounters less tension in stakeholder engagement and sees SM as less risky. It is, however, encouraging to see examples of organisations that are open to and actively facilitate the influence of stakeholders within their organisation, hence sup-porting the view that SM can indeed be seen as tools for converging CSR and marketing engagement.

Conclusions and implications

For both marketing and CSR, engagement is recognised as an interactive process that enables the building of trust and relationships.[88,89] SM platforms afford technical capabil-ity for organisations and other actors to share ideas and get involved in dialogue on CSR. This chapter draws upon 39 interviews with practitioners who were asked about the experiences and observations of the use of SM in engaging stakeholders and consum-ers. Our informants' accounts reveal three perspectives on whether and how to adopt SM for stakeholder engagement. Those most sensitised to the barriers and anxious about the (in)compatibility of SM with normative principles of stakeholder engagement err towards *avoidance*. A second group suggest that CSR communication is being developed as a separate stream of engagement activity, which we label as a *divergence* approach. A third group report that SM is being integrated with marketing engagement, which we label as *convergence*. The experiences of these latter two groups afford some indication of a trend towards SM interactions on CSR and occasional instances (especially in non-profit organisations) of real openness and responsiveness to stakeholder contributions. However, the weight of evidence suggests that progress is slow; organisations continue to place greater emphasis on internally constructed, strategic rather than moral communications that they 'push' out to stakeholders, while efforts to promote in-depth dialogue appear to be limited. It seems that the promise of SM to transform social relations and increase engagement amongst organisational and stakeholder constituents[90] is far from being fulfilled in practical contexts.

Against a backdrop of growing investment in CSR and some impressive corporate programmes, the overall picture of engagement we reveal via SM is disappointing. Surveys reveal that many people believe that organisations should communicate about their CSR activities,[91] but discomfort arises when it becomes only a celebration of achievement without any critical reflection. Stakeholder engagement plays a key role in generating, sustaining and challenging CSR knowledge.[92] There will inevitably be areas of tension, and consensus and co-operation will not always be possible. However, transparent and honest engagement is critical in creating trust in CSR and as a basis for collaborative action.[93,94] To pursue this only in contexts carefully controlled by the organisation is a risky endeavour; SM engagement is becoming inevitable as the momentum of SM interaction grows. If organisations shun opportunities to engage with consensual and dissensual voices online, then discordant voices may simply move into forums controlled by others, with the risk that conversations take place about but not with organisations. Existing studies of CSR integration are concentrated at the corporate level, but this study highlights the importance of also understanding how CSR communications can be integrated at a functional (marketing) level.[95] The integration with marketing is due particular attention given that it is at the fore of income generating activities and, as such, is closely associated with aspects of corporate activity that are detrimental to society.[96]

A primary limitation of this research relates to the method of conducting interviews by email, which constrains the depth of insight around particular issues raised by informants. A further research avenue may be to interrogate the themes of convergence, divergence and avoidance in more depth through face-to-face interviews with industry informants, as well as observation of interactions within the SM settings themselves. Additionally, we advocate further conceptual work into the aligning of consumer and stakeholder literatures to better account for the networked nature of much of today's communication, particularly in online environments.

Notes

1 Podnar, K. (2008). Guest Editorial: Communicating Corporate Social Responsibility. *Journal of Marketing Communications*, *14*(2), 75–81.

2 Birth, G., Illia, L., Lurati, F., and Zamparini, A. (2008). Communicating CSR: Practice Among Switzerland's Top 300 Companies. *Corporate Communications: An International Journal*, *13*(2), 182–196; Dawkins, J. (2005). Corporate Responsibility: The Communication Challenge. *Journal of Communication Management*, *9*(2), 108–119.

3 Bhattacharya, C., Sen, S., and Korschun, D. (2011). *Leveraging Corporate Responsibility: The Stakeholder Route to Maximizing Business and Social Value*. New York: Cambridge.

4 Kaplan, A. M., and Haenlein, M. (2010). Users of the World, Unite! The Challenges and Opportunities of Social Media. *Business Horizons*, *53*(1), 59–68.

5 Whelan, G., Moon, J., and Grant, B. (2013). Corporations and Citizenship Arenas in the Age of Social Media. *Journal of Business Ethics*, *118*(4), 777–790.

6 Morsing, M., and Schultz, M. (2006). Corporate Social Responsibility Communication: Stakeholder Information, Response and Involvement Strategies. *Business Ethics: A European Review, 15*(4), 323–338.

7 Korschun, D., and Du, S. (2013). How Virtual Corporate Social Responsibility Dialogues Generate Value: A Framework and Propositions. *Journal of Business Research, 66*(9), 1494–1504.

8 Sheth, J. N., and Sisodia, R. S. (2005). A Dangerous Divergence: Marketing and Society. *Journal of Public Policy and Marketing, 24*(1), 160–162.

9 Vargo, S. L., and Lusch, R. F. (2004). Evolving to a New Dominant Logic for Marketing. *Journal of Marketing, 68*, 1–17.

10 Windahl, C., and Lakemond, N. (2006). Developing Integrated Solutions: The Importance of Relationships Within the Network. *Industrial Marketing Management, 35*(7), 806–818.

11 Zadek, S. (2004). The Path to Corporate Responsibility. *Harvard Business Review, 82*(12), 125–132.

12 van Marrewijk, M., and Werre, M. (2003). Multiple Levels of Corporate Sustainability. *Journal of Business Ethics, 44*(2), 107–119.

13 Werre, M. (2003). Implementing Corporate Responsibility: The Chiquita Case. *Journal of Business Ethics, 44*(2–3), 247–260.

14 Maon, F., Lindgreen, A., and Swaen, V. (2009). Designing and Implementing Corporate Social Responsibility: A Framework Grounded in Theory and Practice. *Journal of Business Ethics, 87*(Suppl.1), 71–89.

15 Maon, Lindgreen and Swaen (2010) op cit.

16 Gond, J.-P., Igalens, J., Swaen, V., and El Akremi, A. (2011). The Human Resources Contribution to Responsible Leadership: An Exploration of the CSR – HR Interface. *Journal of Business Ethics, 98*, 115–132.

17 Mangold, W. D., and Faulds, D. J. (2009). Social Media: The New Hybrid Element of the Promotion Mix. *Business Horizons, 52*, 357–365.

18 Gummesson, E. (1994). Making Relationship Marketing Operational. *International Journal of Service Industry Management, 5*(5), 5–20.

19 Brodie, R. J., Ilic, A., Juric, B., and Hollebeek, L. D. (2013). Consumer Engagement in a Virtual Brand Community: An Exploratory Analysis. *Journal of Business Research, 66*(1), 105–114.

20 Prahalad, C. K., and Ramaswamy, V. (2000). Co-Opting Customer Competence. *Harvard Business Review, 78*(January), 79–90.

21 van Doorn, J., Lemon, K., Mittal, V., Naas, S., Pick, D., Pirner, P., and Verhoef, P. (2010). Consumer Engagement Behaviour: Theoretical Foundations and Research Directions. *Journal of Service Research, 13*(3), 253–266.

22 Brodie, J. R., Hollebeek, L., Juric, B., and Ilic, A. (2011). Consumer Engagement: Conceptual Domain, Fundamental Propositions and Implications for Research. *Journal of Service Research, 14*(3), 252–271.

23 Bowden, J. L. H. (2009). The Process of Consumer Engagement: A Conceptual Framework. *Journal of Marketing Theory and Practice, 17*(1), 63–74.

24 van Doorn, Lemon, Mittal, Naas, Pick, Pirner, and Verhoef op cit.

25 Brodie, Hollebeek, Juric, and Ilic op cit.

26 van Doorn, Lemon, Mittal, Naas, Pick, Pirner, and Verhoef op cit.

27 Hollebeek, L., and Chen, T. (2014). Exploring Positively versus Negatively-Valenced Brand Engagement: A Conceptual Model. *Journal of Product & Brand Management, 23*(1), 62–74.

28 Chandler, J. D., and Vargo, S. L. (2011). Contextualization and Value-in-context: How Context Frames Exchange. *Marketing Theory, 11*(1), 35–49.

29 Wirtz, J., den Ambtman, A., Bloemer, J., Horváth, C., Ramaseshan, B., Van De Klundert, J., Gurhan Canli, Z., and Kandampully, J. (2013). Managing Brands and Consumer Engagement in Online Brand Communities. *Journal of Service Management, 24*(3), 223–244.

30 Chu, S.-C., and Kim, Y. (2011). Determinants of Consumer Engagement in Electronic Word-of-mouth (eWOM) in Social Networking Sites. *International Journal of Advertising, 30*(1), 47–75.

31 Mollen, A., and Wilson, H. (2010). Engagement, Telepresence, and Interactivity in Online Consumer Experience: Reconciling Scholastic and Managerial Perspectives. *Journal of Business Research, 63*(9–10), 919–925.

32 Calder, B. J., Malthouse, E. C., and Schaedel, U. (2009). An Experimental Study of the Relationship Between Online Engagement and Advertising Effectiveness. *Journal of Interactive Marketing, 23*(4), 321–331.

33 Breidbach, C. F., Brodie, R., and Hollebeek, L. (2014). Beyond Virtuality: From Engagement Platforms to Engagement Ecosystems. *Managing Service Quality, 24*(6), 592–611.

34 Calder, Malthouse, and Schaedel op cit.
35 Dholakia, U. M., Bagozzi, R. P., and Pearo, L. K. (2004). A Social Influence Model of Consumer Participation in Network- and Small-Group-Based Virtual Communities. *International Journal of Research in Marketing*, *21*(1), 241–263.
36 Peters, K., Chen, Y., Kaplan, A. M., Ognibeni, B., and Pauwels, K. (2012). Social Media Metrics – A Framework and Guidelines for Managing Social Media. *Journal of Interactive Marketing*, *27*, 281–298.
37 Peters, Chen, Kaplan, Ognibeni, and Pauwels op cit.
38 Gummerus, J., Liljander, V., Weman, E., and Pihlstrom, M. (2012). Customer Engagement in a Facebook Brand Community. *Management Research Review*, *35*(9), 857–877.
39 Drury, G. (2008). Social Media: Should Marketers Engage and How Can It Be Done Effectively? *Journal of Direct, Data and Digital Marketing Practice*, *9*, 274–277.
40 Burchell, J., and Cook, J. (2008). Stakeholder Dialogue and Organisational Learning: Changing Relationships Between Companies and NGOs. *Business Ethics: A European Review*, *17*(1), 35–46.
41 Freeman, R. E. (1984). *Strategic Management: A Stakeholder Approach*. Boston: Pitman.
42 Andriof, J., and Waddock, S. (2002). Unfolding stakeholder engagement. In J. Andriof, S. Waddock, B. Husted and S. Sutherland Rahman (Eds.) *Unfolding Stakeholder Thinking: Theory, Responsibility and Engagement* (pp. 19–43). Sheffield: Greenleaf.
43 Clarkson, M. E. (1995). A Stakeholder Framework for Analysing and Evaluating Corporate Social Performance. *Academy of Management Review*, *20*(1), 92–117.
44 Burchell and Cook op cit.
45 Noland, J., and Phillips, R. A. (2010). Stakeholder Engagement, Discourse Ethics and Strategic Management. *International Journal of Management Reviews*, *12*(1), 39–49.
46 Zakhem, A. (2007). Stakeholder Management Capability: A Discourse-Theoretical Approach. *Journal of Business Ethics*, *79*, 395–405.
47 Emshoff, J. R., and Freeman, R. E. (1978). *Stakeholder Management*. Philadelphia: Wharton Applied Research Centre.
48 Lawrence, A. T. (2002). The Drivers of Stakeholder Engagement. *Journal of Corporate Citizenship*, *6*, 71–85.
49 Axley, S. R. (1984). Managerial and Organizational Communication in Terms of the Conduit Metaphor. *Academy of Management Review*, *9*(3), 428–437.
50 Morsing and Schultz op cit.
51 Morsing and Schultz op cit.
52 Crane, A., Morsing, M., and Schoeneborn, D. (2015). *CSR and Communication: Examining How CSR Shapes, and Is Shaped by, Talk and Text, Call for Papers: Special Issue or Business and Society*. Retrieved from http://bas.sagepub.com/site/includefiles/CSR_Communication.pdf (accessed 30 December 15)
53 Illia, L., Romenti, S., Rodríguez-Cánovas, B., Murtarelli, G., and Carroll, C. E. (2015). Exploring Corporations' Dialogue About CSR in the Digital Era. *Journal of Business Ethics*, (October), 1–20.
54 Retrieved from http://mystarbucksidea.force.com/ (accessed 30 December 15).
55 Retrieved from www.youtube.com/user/talkingenergy/ (accessed 30 December 15).
56 Castelló, I., Morsing, M., and Schultz, F. (2013). Communicative Dynamics and the Polyphony of Corporate Social Responsibility in the Network Society. *Journal of Business Ethics*, *118*(4), 683–694; Schultz, F., Castelló, I., and Morsing, M. (2013). The Construction of Corporate Social Responsibility in Network Societies: A Communication View. *Journal of Business Ethics*, *115*(4), 681–692.
57 Andriof, J., and Waddock, S. (2002). Unfolding stakeholder engagement. In J. Andriof, S. Waddock, B. Husted and S. Sutherland Rahman (Eds.) *Unfolding Stakeholder Thinking: Theory, Responsibility and Engagement* (pp. 19–43). Sheffield: Greenleaf; Schultz, F., and Wehmeier, S. (2010). Institutionalization of Corporate Social Responsibility Within Corporate Communications: Combining Institutional, Sensemaking and Communication Perspectives. *Corporate Communications: An International Journal*, *15*(1), 9–29.
58 Whelan, Moon, and Grant op cit.
59 Hoffmann, C. P., and Lutz, C. (2015). The Impact of Online Media on Stakeholder Engagement and the Governance of Corporations. *Journal of Public Affairs*, *15*(2), 163–174.
60 Whelan, Moon, and Grant op. cit.
61 Ho, A, T.-K. (2002). Reinventing Local Governments and the e-Government Initiative. *Public Administration Review*, *62*(4), 434–444.
62 Quinton, S., and Fennemore, P. (2013). Missing a Strategic Marketing Trick? The Use of Online Social Networks by UK Charities. *International Journal of Nonprofit and Voluntary Sector Marketing*, *18*(1), 36–51.

63 Capriotti, P. (2011). Communicating corporate social responsibility through the internetand social media. In Ø. Ihlen, J. L. Bartlett, and S. May (Eds.), *The Handbook of Communication and Corporate Social Responsibility* (pp. 358–378). Sussex: John Wiley and Sons.

64 Christensen, L. T., Firat, A. F., and Torp, S. (2008). The Organisation of Integrated Communications: Toward Flexible Integration. *European Journal of Marketing, 42*(3-4), 423–452.

65 Denzin, N. K., and Lincoln, Y. S. (2011). Introduction. In N. K. Denzin and Y. S. Lincoln (Eds.), *Handbook of Qualitative Research* (pp. 1–30). London: Sage.

66 Meho, L. I. (2006). E-Mail Interviewing in Qualitative Research: A Methodological Discussion. *Journal of the American Society for Information Science and Technology, 57*(10), 1284–1295.

67 Meho op. cit.

68 Spiggle, S. (1994). Analysis and Interpretation of Qualitative Data in Consumer Research. *Journal of Consumer Research, 21*(3), 491–503.

69 Illia et al. op cit.

70 Morsing and Schultz op cit.

71 Du, S., and Vieira, E. T. (2012). Striving for Legitimacy Through Corporate Social Responsibility: Insights from Oil Companies. *Journal of Business Ethics, 10*(4), 413–427.

72 Wirtz et al., op cit.

73 Phillips op cit.

74 Payne and Calton op cit.

75 Morsing and Schultz op cit.

76 Schlegelmilch, B. B., and Pollack, I. (2005). The Perils and Opportunities of Communicating Corporate Ethics. *Journal of Marketing Management,* 21(3), 267–290.

77 Capriotti op cit.

78 Clarkson op cit.

79 Illia et al. op cit.

80 Clarkson op cit.

81 Maon et al. op cit.

82 Axley op cit.

83 Barron, D. N. (1998). Pathways to Legitimacy Among Consumer Loan Providers in New York City, 1914–1934. *Organisation Studies, 19*(2), 207–233.

84 Chernev, S., and Blair, S. (2015). Doing Well by Doing Good: The Benevolent Halo of Corporate Social Responsibility. *Journal of Consumer Research, 41*(6), 1412–1425.

85 Lozano, J. M. (2005). Towards the Relational Corporation: From Managing Stakeholder Relationship to Building Stakeholder Relationships (Waiting for Copernicus). *Corporate Governance, 5*(2), 60–77.

86 Schultz, F., and Wehmeier, S. (2010). Institutionalization of Corporate Social Responsibility Within Corporate Communications: Combining Institutional, Sensemaking and Communication Perspectives. *Corporate Communications: An International Journal, 15*(1), 9–29.

87 Colleoni, E. (2013). CSR Communication Strategies for Organizational Legitimacy in Social Media. *Corporate Communications, 18*(2), 228–248.

88 Brodie et al. op cit.

89 Andriof and Waddock op cit.

90 Andriof and Waddock op cit.

91 Morsing and Schultz op cit.

92 Whelan et al. op cit.

93 Podnar op cit.

94 Chaudhri, V., and Wang, J. (2007). Communicating Corporate Social Responsibility on the Internet: A Case Study of the Top 100 Information Technology Companies in India. *Management Communication Quarterly, 21*(2), 232–247.

95 Gond et al. op cit.

96 Sheth and Sidosia op cit.

1.2 Unlocking corporate social responsibility communication through digital media

Mark Anthony Camilleri

Introduction

The general public is continuously being presented with content marketing, as corporate communication has become a valuable tool for the promotion of social and environmental responsibility. When businesses share non-financial information on their stakeholder engagement with online communities, they may find out that their followers (or friends) could also share their passion for good causes. Digital communication could create a ripple effect that grows as it has potential to reach wider audiences. Therefore, it is in the companies' interest to strike a balance in satisfying numerous stakeholders' expectations[1] and to engage in collaborative working relationships with people. Dialogue often leads to improvements in mutual trust and understanding.[2] Hence, ongoing communications with stakeholders could also translate into tangible benefits for a company's reputation, brand image, customer loyalty and investor confidence.[3,4,5] For these reasons, companies cannot afford to overstate or misrepresent their corporate social responsibility (CSR) reporting. Although they often manage to control their internal communication paths, it is much harder to control external media.[6] As a result, it has never been more necessary to turn stakeholders into advocates for both the cause and the company.[7] Indeed, this can happen if CSR initiatives are a good fit for the firms' mission and vision.[8] Relevant theoretical underpinnings suggest that CSR communication often reflects the ethos of the practicing organisations.[4] Therefore, environmental, social and governance disclosures should be presented in a fair manner in all material respects for the benefit of all stakeholders. Businesses are expected to disclose relevant information that reflects their accountability and transparency credentials.[9]

CSR reporting may cover areas like training and development opportunities for employees; employee consultation and dialogue; health, safety and security; and also measures for work-life balance among other issues.[10] Very often, business organisations also pledge their commitment on environmental matters and sustainability issues. For instance, innovative practices in environmental responsibility may include: energy and water conservation; waste minimisation and recycling; pollution prevention by reducing emissions; increasing environmental protection and using sustainable transportation options.[10] Such innovative sustainability investments could bring strategic benefits such as operational efficiencies and cost savings in the long run. Several empirical studies have indicated that discretionary investments in CSR, whether they are driven from strategic intents or from posturing behaviours, often result in improved relationships with internal and external stakeholders.[10] Arguably, legitimate companies are in a position to prevent third-party pressures through societal engagement, as they lower the criticisms from the general public. At the same time, they could minimise legal cases through compliance with regulations.[11,12]

The research question

The purpose of this study is to examine the owner-managers' attitudes on digital media to promote their social responsibility and sustainability practices. Therefore, this research unlocks the potential of the ubiquitous technologies as a vehicle for CSR communication. Specifically, this study uses the 'pace of technological innovativeness';[13,14,15] 'the technological acceptance model'[16,17,18,19] and the 'technological anxiety'[15,20] measures to explore the respondents' attitudes on web technologies. In addition, it also uses the CSR measures that relate to commercial, ethical and social responsibility.[21,22,23] This contribution examines the owner-managers' perceptions on the use of technology to communicate with stakeholders. At the same time, it extends the results of extant theoretical underpinnings and prior studies, particularly those which have already explored the subject of CSR reporting and environmental, social and governance disclosures in other contexts.

The conceptual framework

CSR communication is produced, translated, and integrated according to specific reality constructions.[24] Strategic manipulation and isomorphic adaptation strategies tend to be organised by the firm in one-way communication events with selected stakeholders.[4] Traditional media are based on a hierarchical one-to-many communication, with a clear distinction between producer and consumer of information.

There are many communication channels that may not always be entirely controlled by the company as networked strategies favour dialogic and contextual engagements in two-way communications between the firm and its stakeholders.[4,25] In this case, there is likely to be a trade-off between the issues of controllability and credibility of CSR communications. The stakeholders will probably perceive corporate messages that come from sources that are biased or subjective. CSR communications via corporate sources could trigger scepticism among stakeholders, as they may have less credibility than non-corporate sources.[7] For instance, consumers react more positively to a company's CSR activities when they learn about its CSR activities from a neutral source (e.g., an independent organisation that provides unbiased evaluations of corporate activities) rather than from a corporate source.[26]

Although getting media co-operation is often difficult, companies should try hard to get positive media coverage from independent, objective sources, such as editorial coverage on television or in the press. It would greatly enhance a company's reputation if corporate news were reported positively by specialty publications such as *Business Ethics*, or if a business received a good CSR rating by independent organisations such as *Fortune* magazine. Companies should try to encourage informal yet credible communication channels such as word of mouth by stakeholders.

Evidently, the internet has reshaped communication at different levels. It has enabled the emergence of a new participatory public sphere that is based on a many-to-many communications where everybody can dialogically and publicly interact and collaborate in the creation of content and the definition of the agenda.[27] In a relatively short period of time, the internet has become an essential tool for organisational communication.[28] For this reason, businesses are encouraged to become more proficient in the use of online media in addition to the traditional media in order to increase their impact of their corporate communication.

Moreover, in today's digital era, the engagement between the public and the organisation is one of the main characteristics of the internet.[29] Web pages are a vehicle for the marketing communications of CSR policy and practices. The general public is continuously being presented with the companies' content marketing of social and environmentally-responsible behaviours on the web. Many businesses are increasing presenting CSR and sustainability content that is readily available on websites.[7] This content is often being presented directly on corporate websites or through reports that are made available through links to other pages. However, there is little research that has been dedicated to analysing how such content is organised and structured.[29] Of course, the organisation and presentation of information on corporate websites is of great relevance to stakeholders. Different stakeholders expect comprehensive information on environmental, social and governance behaviours in CSR reports. Therefore, the quality of the CSR reporting relies on adequate web architecture and on the organisation of information.[30,31]

The presentation of the website is defined by organisation schemes and structures.[7] Organisation schemes define the shared characteristics of the units of content and influence its logical grouping.[29] The organisational structures define the types of relationships that exist between different units (and groups), whilst also establishing the basic routes through which users may navigate the website.[29] The information that is related to a single theme needs to be structured and ordered vertically in a hierarchical sequence. The hierarchy can be structured to move from the most general or important topics to the most specific or detailed ones. Therefore, the themes' topics could also link to other sub-topics or related aspects. This way, online users could easily locate and consult the themes they are searching for. The manner in which the information is organised on a website will determine the usability and accessibility of its contents to visitors.[18,19] Hence, the stakeholders could easily access the CSR themes through the organisational schemes and structures in corporate websites.[29]

Many corporate websites already possess a high degree of interactivity; including their ability to disseminate information and to generate relationships between the different publics and the organisation.[28] In the first approach, the level of interactivity is low, and the use of the Internet is unidirectional; as its essential objective is to diffuse information and to try to improve the corporate image of the business. However, in the second approach, the degree of interactivity is high, and the Internet is used to facilitate bidirectional communication and to nurture relationships by allowing dialogue and interaction between the organisation and its stakeholders.

Interactive communication is becoming one of the most important information channels for corporations as it is changing the social dynamics.[32] Web-based co-operation and data exchanges have empowered the communication between businesses and their stakeholders.[33,34] It enables them to engage with online users and to take advantage of positive publicity arising from word-of-mouth marketing and digital platforms. As a result, it has never been more necessary to turn stakeholders into advocates for both the cause and the company.[7] Therefore, environmental, social and governance disclosures should be presented in a fair and transparent manner for the benefit of all stakeholders. Corporations can engage with stakeholders via digital media and take on the gatekeeping function of traditional media.[34]

Businesses are currently undergoing a fundamental transformation towards globally networked societies.[35] The public relations and corporate communications of business are increasingly using social networking software. These technological advances may have positive implications for CSR communication, as companies can reach out to stakeholders in a more interactive way. The use of social networks has offered the businesses new forms of interactivity that enable them to address the CSR information toward a variety of stakeholders.[4] This recent development has inevitably empowered the stakeholders as they are in a position to disrupt the corporations' legitimacy by using social media.[35] The consumers are a powerful stakeholder group, as they are a highly credible source of CSR communication. In particular, the consumers' word of mouth has been greatly magnified given the popularity and the vast reach of interactive communication channels though web technologies.

Communication through social media is dynamic in relation to traditional media.[34] The global diffusion of social software like blogs, RSS feeds, wikis, electronic fora, social networks have facilitated companies to attract prospects and consumer groups. Social media has the technological potential to speed up communication processes[36] and to increase direct interaction, dialogue and participation across organisations and various audiences.[27,37] Such interactive communications are referred to as 'viral' because ideas and opinions spread like epidemic diseases through the network via word of mouth. These channels are perceived as highly trustworthy sources.[24,38] When businesses share information on their stakeholder engagement and CSR engagement with online communities, they may find out that their followers (or friends) could also share their passion for good causes. Hence, online communication could create a ripple effect that grows as it has potential to reach wider audiences.

Social media has transformed the communicative dynamics within and between corporations and their environment. These online networks are effective monitoring tools as they could also signal trending topics. Digital media may help business communicators and marketers to keep themselves up to date on the latest sustainability issues. CSR influencers are easily identified on particular subject matters or expertise. For example, businesses and customers alike have learned how to use the hashtag (#) to enhance the visibility of their shareable content[16] (Some of the most popular hashtags comprise: #CSR #ESG #StrategicCSR, #sustainability, #susty, #CSRTalk, #Davos2016, #KyotoProtocol, #SharedValue, etc.). Hashtags could be used to raise awareness on charities, philanthropic institutions and green non-governmental organisations. They may also help during fund raising events. Thus, businesses could raise their profile through social networks as they engage with influencers and media.

The ubiquity of Facebook, Twitter and Google Plus over the past years has made them familiar channels for many individuals and businesses around the globe. These networks have become very popular communication outlets for brands, companies and activists alike. Twitter, in particular, has become one of the most popular tools, used by millions of people to publish messages and interact with strangers in conversations through computers and mobile phones. Twitter provides a variety of ways for users to become interactive.[38]

Moreover, LinkedIn is yet another effective tool, particularly for personal branding. However, this social network also helps users identify and engage with influencers. Companies can use this site to create or join their favourite groups on LinkedIn (e.g., GRI, FSG, Shared Value Initiative, among others). They may also use this channel for CSR communication as they promote key initiatives and share sustainability ideas. Therefore, LinkedIn connects individuals and groups as they engage in fruitful conversations with academia and CSR practitioners.

In addition, Pinterest and Instagram enable their users to share images and ideas with their networks. These social media could also be relevant in the context of the sustainability agenda. Businesses could illustrate their CSR communication to stakeholders through visual and graphic content. Evidently, these innovative avenues provide sharable imagery, infographics or videos to groups who may be passionate on certain issues, including CSR.

Moreover, digital marketers are increasingly uploading short, fun videos which often turn viral on internet. YouTube, Vimeo and Vine seem to have positioned themselves as important social media channels for many consumers. These sites offer an excellent way to humanise or animate CSR communication through video content. These digital media also allow their users to share their video content across multiple networks. For instance, videos featuring university resources may comprise lectures, documentaries, case studies and the like.

In sum, the digital media provides access to multiple stakeholders. Its open platforms has facilitated symmetric two-way communication between participants without formal hierarchies.[35,39] In addition, there is a lack of gatekeeping in social media.[4,40] Hence, web technologies may be considered as suitable platforms for undertaking a corporate–public dialogue.[32,41] Online platforms can also increase the complexity of the debates[42] and decrease the level of institutionalisation of the interaction between the stakeholders and the firms.[43]

The formulation of hypotheses

Corporate communications managers and executives are in a position to amplify the effectiveness of their company's CSR communication efforts. They should decide what to communicate (i.e., message content) and where to communicate (i.e., message channel) to reach out to different stakeholders. However, despite the premise that social media improves the efficiency of the engagements between the firms and their publics, recent studies have shown that the implementation of the engagement is neither automatic nor easy.[34,44,45] The dialogic features that are enabled by web pages, blogs, and other social media, for instance, may prove difficult to apply.[41,45] Although recent communication research has developed indicators to measure the dialogic level of online stakeholder engagement,[41] little research has attempted to identify the legitimacy constraints on managing CSR communication through digital media. Therefore, this study investigates the owner–managers' stance on 'technology acceptance' for marketing communications.[13,14,15] The respondents will be expected to indicate whether they perceive the use (or ease of use) of online technologies, including WEB2.0. This study has adapted "the pace of technological innovativeness" measure as it involves continuous engagement with ubiquitous technologies, including new emerging innovations. It presumes that practitioners keep themselves up to date with the latest innovations,[13] including digital media, to promote their companies' activities. This argumentation leads to the first two hypotheses:

1   *There is a relationship between 'the pace of technological innovation' and 'the technological acceptance' of digital media.*
2   *There is a relationship between the pace of technological innovation of digital media and online CSR reporting.*

The technology acceptance model (TAM) has often explained the users' adoption behaviours of technology.[16,17,18,19] It suggests that there is a causal relationship between the users' internal beliefs, attitudes, intentions and their use of technology (for CSR communication). In the past, TAM sought to explain why people accept or reject a particular technological innovation.[18] In this light, this model has been purposely chosen to determine why businesses were accepting or rejecting the use of digital media for stakeholder engagement and CSR disclosures. The perceived usefulness (variable) of digital media is the degree to which a person believes that using this technology would enhance their job performance in marketing communications.[18,19] From the outset, the researcher presumed that the owner-managers would perceive the usefulness and the ease of use of digital media (to communicate their CSR credentials to stakeholders).

Notwithstanding, this model also comprises the perceived ease of use variable (PEOU), which is the degree to which a person believes that using a particular system (including websites, search engine optimisation, social media, blogs etc.) would be free of effort.[18] The usage of such online technologies is influenced by the perceived ease of use. In this case, the researcher has investigated whether the owner-managers were (or were not) proficient in the use of digital media. Hence, this study hypothesised:

3   *There is a positive relationship between perceived usefulness and the perceived ease of use of digital media for CSR reporting (this hypothesis investigates the technological acceptance model).*

Although potential users may believe that a given innovation is useful, they may, at the same time be wary of digital media. The owner-managers may not be proficient enough, or may not possess adequate digital skills. They may perceive that online technologies may be too hard to use and that the performance benefits of usage are outweighed by the effort of using such applications.[15,20] Alternatively, they could not dedicate sufficient time and resources to use web technologies. As a result, companies may not always report enough information on their social, ethical and environment-related activities.[21,22,23] Relevant academic literature suggested that there is scope for companies to engage in continuous online communication with stakeholders including suppliers and consumers.[1,4,5,7,10] Well-known brands are usually visible online and they even communicate about their CSR engagement. Yet, there are still a number of companies' that are not reaching their target audience through digital media.[21] This leads to the fourth hypothesis that aims to identify the possible antecedents (by using stepwise regression) of CSR reporting on digital media:

4   *The technological innovation of digital media (that is represented by: perceived usefulness, perceived ease of use, the pace of technological innovativeness and/or technological anxiety) and the enterprises' CSR ethos (in terms of commercial responsibility, ethical responsibility and social responsibility) are the antecedents for the online disclosures of corporate social and environmental responsibility (CSER).*

Methodology

This empirical study targeted owner-managers of small and medium-sized enterprises in the retail and trading industry. The survey questionnaires were distributed by email to all business owners who were members in a trade union representing importers, retailers, wholesalers, manufacturers and service providers. Subsequently, the completed surveys were either submitted online or printed by the owner-managers and returned to the researcher. There was a total of 202 (N=202) out of 395 responses (which represented 51% of the total population) from all the targeted enterprises in a small European Union country. The rationale behind the selection of the designated profile of owner-managers

Table 1.2.1 Socio-demographic profile of the survey participants

Age		Gender	
Less than 19 years	2	Male	87
Between 20 to 29 years	47	Female	115
Between 30 to 39 years	57		
		n=202	
Between 40 to 49 years	43	**Firm Size**	71
Between 50 to 59 years	27		
Between 60 to 69 years	17	1 to 10 Employees	92
Over 70 years	8	11–50 Employees	39
mean:	*37.1 years*	51–250 Employees	
n=201		*n=202*	
Education			
Secondary	13		
Post-secondary/vocational	123		
Undergraduate	45		
Postgraduate	18		
n=199			

was to gain a good insight into their ability to make evaluative judgments in making decisions regarding stakeholder engagement as well as on the CSER communications through digital media. Table 1.2.1 presents the socio-demographic profile of the sample:

Digital media

The web is currently advancing at an unprecedented pace of technology. Its online communities have already transformed the internet through innovative, highly scalable social media networks and product recommendation systems. Notwithstanding, there have been significant developments in web analytics, cloud computing and digital platforms. The emergence of user-generated content in fora, newsgroups, social media and crowdsourcing have offered endless opportunities to both researchers and practitioners to 'listen' to marketplace stakeholders, including customers, employees, suppliers, investors and the media. Therefore, the researcher has adapted six items from the 'pace of technological innovation' that were intended to measure the practitioners' attitude toward technological change in marketing. Originally, this scale reported a construct reliability of 0.97[14] and used confirmatory factor analysis to provide evidence to support the scales' convergent and discriminant validities.

This study has also used the technology acceptance model to explore the respondents' attitudes on web technologies.[18,19,33] This model has become a popular means by which to evaluate the users' attitudes on their 'perceived ease of use' and 'perceived usefulness' towards technological innovations, as well as their behavioral intention.[18] Originally, the PU six-item scale attained a construct reliability of 0.97, while PEOU six-item scale achieved a reliability of 0.91.[18] These scales were considered acceptable, as the factor loadings were reported to be significant and the evidence of discriminant validity were provided for each construct.

Four items relating to 'technological anxiety' were used to measure the degree to which an owner-manager could (or could not) be apprehensive about the usage of digital media.[20,34] This construct is synonymous with the term 'technophobia'.[35] The original measure reported an alpha of 0.93.[20] The authors tested a measurement model containing all of their constructs and indicators. This measure was acceptable as the factor loadings were reported to be significant. There was evidence of discriminant validity for each construct using different tests (the confidence interval as well as the variance were extracted).

Corporate Social Responsibility Communication

Many companies are increasingly following an ethical code of conduct. Very often, they may disclose non-financial information on their web pages relating to socially responsible behaviours, as they give a breakdown of all the actions they undertake toward their stakeholder groups.[21] In addition, they may report other information on issues relating to environmental sustainability and governance behaviours. Therefore, this study has adapted Singh and Del Bosque's 'commercial', 'ethical', 'social' and 'support' dimensions that consist of 3 items each. With respect to scale reliability, the Cronbach alpha and composite reliability coefficients[36] were, in all cases, above the minimum acceptance value of 0.7. Moreover, all standardised lambda values were statistically significant and above 0.5.

The commercial dimension measured the owner-managers' perceptions about their economic strategy. The ethical dimension featured items on ethics and regulatory matters as it explored the respondents' attitudes about honesty, integrity and moral principles. The social dimension referred to environmental protection and to discretionary investments in the community, at large. These reference variables were tried and tested in previous empirical studies.[37,38,39] The fourth dimension sought to discover how the respondents' perceived corporate communications on commercial, ethical and social issues.[21]

Data analysis

Firstly, the descriptive statistics illustrate the means and standard deviations for all variables. Secondly, a principal component analysis (PCA) has been chosen to obtain a factor solution of a smaller set of salient variables. Thirdly, a multivariate regression analysis has investigated the hypothesised associations by using the stepwise method.

Descriptive statistics

All responses were coded using a five-point Likert scaling mechanism. The values ranged from 1 (strongly disagree) to 5 (strongly agree), whereas 3 signaled an indecision. The scale items used in this study included 'the pace of technological innovativeness', 'perceived ease of use', 'perceived usefulness', 'technological anxiety', 'commercial responsibility', 'ethical responsibility' and 'social responsibility' and are presented in Table 1.2.2.

This study is consistent with the extant literature on the 'technology acceptance model'.[18,20] As a matter of fact, there were high mean scores of near 4, which reflected the respondents' stance on the use of digital media. Moreover, the survey participants have indicated their strong agreement with the 'pace of technological innovativeness'.[14] The owner-managers suggested that digital media is continuously changing; the mean score was 4.03 and there was a standard deviation of 0.87. They also suggested that integrated marketing communications relies on technological innovation (in the negatively worded item). More importantly, these research participants were not apprehensive towards digital technology.[20] They indicated that they do not hesitate to use most forms of technology for fear of making mistakes; the mean was 1.9, and the standard deviation was 0.29.

Table 1.2.2 Complete list of measures and their descriptive statistics

Pace of technological innovativeness	Items	Mean	Std dev.
Grewal, Mehta and Kardes (2004)	Digital media is changing at a very fast pace.	4.03	0.53
	Compared to other integrated marketing communication, digital media is changing fast.	3.42	0.46
	I have consistently seen new digital media technologies for some time.	3.95	3.37
	Innovations in digital media are frequent.	3.68	3.53
	The pace of technological innovations in digital media is high.	3.2	0.47
	Technological innovations and integrated marketing communications don't go hand in hand.	2.19	0.71
Perceived ease of use	**Items**	**Mean**	**Std dev.**
	Learning to operate digital media would be easy for me.	3.82	0.58
Davis (1989); Meuter, Bitner, Ostrom and Brown (2005)	I would find it easy to use digital media for corporate communication.	3.21	0.53
	My interaction with the digital media would be clear and understandable for my stakeholders.	3.86	0.34
	I would find digital media to be flexible to interact with.	3.81	0.4
	It would be easy for me to become skillful at using digital media.	3.86	0.53
	I would find digital media resources easy to use.	3.95	0.39
Perceived usefulness	**Items**	**Mean**	**Std dev.**
	Using digital media would enable me to accomplish corporate communication tasks more quickly.	3.78	0.41
Davis (1989); Meuter, Bitner, Ostrom and Brown (2005)	Using digital media would improve my communication.	3.96	0.38
	Using digital media would enhance my effectiveness in integrated marketing communication.	3.91	0.28
	Using digital media would make it easier to do my corporate communications.	3.99	1.25
	I would find digital media resources useful in my job.	3.95	0.34
	Learning to operate digital media resources would be easy for me.	3.78	1.41
Technological anxiety	**Items**	**Mean**	**Std dev.**
	I feel apprehensive about using digital media.	2.71	0.45
Meuter, Bitner, Ostrom and Brown (2005)	Technical terms sound like confusing jargon to me.	2.88	0.44
	I have avoided digital media because it is unfamiliar to me.	2.34	0.53
	I hesitate to use most forms of technology for fear of making mistakes I cannot correct.	1.9	0.29

Table 1.2.3 Complete list of measures and their descriptive statistics

Measure			
Commercial responsibility	*Items*	*Mean*	*Std dev.*
(Singh and Del Bosque, 2008)	My company is an innovator and continuously launches new products (or service) into the market.	4.23	0.87
	My company's products (or service) always maintain good quality.	4.65	1.77
	My company informs its stakeholders in a correct and truthful way about the characteristics/properties of its products (or services).	4.46	0.58
	My company behaves ethically/honestly with its customers.	4.07	1.19
Ethical responsibility	**Items**	**Mean**	**Std dev.**
(Singh and Del Bosque, 2008)	My company is concerned to fulfil its obligations vis-à-vis its shareholders, suppliers, distributors and other agents with whom it deals.	4.12	0.88
	My company is concerned to respect the human rights when carrying out its activities.	4.02	1.13
	My company always respects the norms defined in the law when carrying out its activities.	4.25	1.15
	My company's respects ethical principles in its stakeholder relationships, this respect has priority over achieving superior economic performance.	3.94	1.22
Social responsibility	**Items**	**Mean**	**Std dev.**
(Singh and Del Bosque, 2008)	My company is concerned about protecting its natural environment.	3.46	1.64
	My company directs part of its budget to donations and social works favouring the disadvantaged individuals and groups.	2.43	0.47
	My company supports the development of the society financing social and/or cultural activities.	2.56	0.94
	My company is concerned to improve general well-being of the society.	3.34	1.24
Support	**Items**	**Mean**	**Std dev.**
(Singh and Del Bosque, 2008)	I avoid buying products from suppliers that don't have an ethical and socially responsible behaviour.	3.37	0.95
	If the price and quality of two products are the same, I would buy from a firm that has an ethical and socially responsible reputation.	4.02	0.45
	I would pay more to buy products from an ethical and socially responsible company.	2.12	0.87
	I consider the ethical reputation of businesses when I buy.	2.54	1.21
	I consider the social activities of businesses when I buy.	3.21	0.65

The participants strongly agreed with the statements pertaining to the commercial responsibility of their business. The mean scores were all higher than four. This finding suggests that the owner-managers felt that they were providing a high-quality service to their customers. They also indicated that they were acting fairly and honestly with stakeholders, where the mean was 4.07, and the standard deviation was 1.19. The survey participants were committed to fulfilling their legal obligations. The results suggest that they respected the human rights and ethical norms. Apparently, this respect had priority over achieving superior economic performance, where the mean was 3.94, and the standard deviation was 1.22. Moreover, these owner-managers were also concerned about social issues (mean was 3.34 and standard deviation was 1.24) and environmental responsibility (mean was 3.46, standard deviation was 1.64). Yet there were low attitudinal scores on philanthropy and stewardship towards disadvantaged groups and individuals (mean was 2.43 and standard deviation was 0.47). The results also indicated that the owner-managers were not so committed to financing social and cultural activities (mean was 2.56 and the standard deviation was 0.94). The survey respondents indicated that they would try to support responsible suppliers. However, they were not willing to pay more to buy products from ethical and socially responsible companies (where the mean was 2.12, and the standard deviation was 0.87).

This study investigated how 'gender' and 'age' could influence the frequency of use of digital media. The results suggested that gender did not influence this choice, as there was no statistically significant difference between the groups' means as determined by the Chi square tests. This study indicated that 83 males and 113 females (there were six missing values) used digital media on a daily basis. Pearson's chi-square, χ^2, was 1.150, Df 2. $p = 0.563$. This finding suggested that gender did not significantly influence the frequency of use of digital media. There were no statistically significant differences between different age groups and the frequency of use of digital technology. However, the results showed that the survey participants who were between 30 to 39 years of age (where n=57), followed by those who were between 20 to 29 years old (where n=47), were more likely to use digital media than other groups. Pearson's chi-square, χ^2, was 3.803, Df 6 and $p = 0.703$. Surprisingly, there were also a few owner-managers who have never used digital media in the past (n=5).

Data reduction

Bartlett's test of sphericity also revealed sufficient correlation in the dataset to run a principal component analysis (PCA) since $p < 0.001$. PCA has identified the patterns within the data and expressed it by highlighting the relevant similarities (and differences) in each and every component. In the process, the data has been compressed, as it was reduced in a number of dimensions without much loss of information. PCA has produced a table which illustrated the amount of variance in the original variables (with the respective initial eigenvalues) which were accounted for by each component. A varimax rotation method was used to spread variability more evenly amongst the constructs. There was a percentage of variance column which indicated the expressed ratio as a percentage of the variance (accounted for by each component in all of the variables). Only principal components with eigenvalues greater than one were extracted. Table 1.2.4 illustrates the number

Table 1.2.4 Data reduction through principal component analysis

Original number of variables		Cumulative percentage of variance %	Loss of information %	Components extracted
Use of digital media	22	62	38	6
Corporate social responsibility	12	74	26	4

Table 1.2.5 Extracted factor components of digital media variables

Use of digital media		Initial eigenvalues	
		Total	% of variance
1	Perceived usefulness of digital media	5.533	25.152
2	Pace of technological innovation	2.378	10.809
3	Technological anxiety	1.846	8.391
4	Easy interaction with digital media	1.662	7.553
5	Perceived ease of use of digital media	1.192	5.418
6	Effective digital media	1.119	5.085

Extraction method: PCA

Alpha = 0.802; KMO = 0.792; Sig:000

Table 1.2.6 Extracted factor components

Corporate social and environmental responsibility (CSER) communication		Initial eigenvalues	
		Total	% of variance
1	Engagement with marketplace stakeholders	8.874	35.024
2	Valuing online corporate social responsibility disclosures	4.654	20.119
3	Valuing online environmental sustainability reporting	1.846	13.454
4	Engagement with human resources	1.162	5.403

Extraction method: PCA

Alpha = 0.845; KMO = 0.812; Sig: 0.000

of extracted components from the original number of variables and presents the resulting cumulative percentage of variance for the group of variables (and also reports the related 'loss of information').

All constructs were analysed for internal consistency by using Cronbach's alpha. There were excellent measures that exceeded the recommended reliability estimates. The value of the Kaiser Meyer Olkin (KMO) measure of sampling adequacy was also very acceptable at 0.8. The factors accounted for more than 62% variance before rotation for the digital media variables, whereas there was 74% of the variance explained before rotation for the CSR measure. There were ten extracted components from the original 39 variables for the digital media and CSR variables. A brief description of the extracted factor components, together with their eigenvalue and respective percentages of variance is provided in Tables 1.2.5 and 1.2.6.

The factor components were labelled following a cross-examination of the variables with the higher loadings. Typically, the variables with the highest correlation scores had mostly contributed towards the make-up of the respective component. The underlying scope of combining the variables by using component analysis was to reduce the data and make it more adaptable for the regression analysis.

Regression analysis

This section examines the four hypothetical relationships by using multivariate regression analysis. A stepwise procedure was chosen to select the most significant predictive variables in the regression equations. Therefore, the *p*-value was less than the 0.05 bench-mark. This also resulted in adequate F-ratios, implying that only the significant amounts of variation in regression were accounted for. More importantly, in the stepwise procedure the insignificant variables were excluded without appreciably increasing the residual sum of squares. The regression models produced the regression coefficients which represented the strength and the significance of the relationships. Moreover, the socio-demographic control variables were also entered into the regression equations.

H1: The first hypothesis indicated that there was a relationship between 'the pace of technological innovation' and 'technological acceptance' on the use of digital media. The results indicated that there was a positive and significant relationship between per-ceived usefulness of digital media and the pace of technological innovation where Spear-man's rho, adj r2 = 0.173. This relationship was significant at (p <0.05). It transpired that the 'perceived usefulness' was dependent on the pace of technological innovation (t–value = 4.457).

H2: The second hypothesis explored the correlation between the technological innova-tion of digital media with the factor component, namely, 'valuing online CSR disclosures'. The results indicated that there were positive and very significant relationships (p <0.01), where Spearman's rho, adj r2 = 0.296. It transpired that CSR disclosures were correlated with the technological innovation of digital media (t–value = 2.53) and also with firm size (t–value = 1.87).

H3: In a similar vein, there was a positive correlation between perceived usefulness of digital media and valuing CSR disclosures where adj r^2 = 0.128. In this case, the measure-ment of significance has an indicated a confidence level of 94%. The perceived usefulness of digital media was correlated to CSR disclosures (t = 3.337) and negatively correlated to 'age' (t–value = −1.202). However, the stepwise regression results were inclusive between perceived ease of use of digital media and valuing CSR disclosures.

H4: The last hypothesis investigated whether the use of digital media and the compa-nies' ethos on responsible behaviours would have an effect on their CSR communication. Therefore perceived usefulness, perceived ease of use, the pace of technological innovation and technological anxiety, as well as commercial responsibility, ethical responsibility and social responsibility variables were all considered as plausible independent variables in the regression equation. 'Valuing CSR disclosures' was inserted as the outcome variable. There was a positive and significant relationship where Spearman's rho, adj r2 was 0.230. The regression equation indicated that online CSR communication was dependent on easy interaction with digital media (perceived ease of use) where t = 6.501; the users' digital skills (pace of technological innovativeness) where t = 4.022; stakeholder relationships (commercial responsibility) where t = 1.855; firm size, where t = 0.877; and apprehension of digital media (technological anxiety) where t = −0.126 and age, where t = −0.114.

Discussion

A communications platform can be finely tuned to share relevant information on cor-porate responsible behaviours that are directed at diverse audiences through interactive channels.[38] This chapter reported how businesses are increasingly embracing the dynamics of new online technologies, as they communicate meaningful content (including poli-cies, case studies, stories et cetera) on their responsible initiatives through corporate web-sites and other digital channels including social media and blogs. This empirical study has addressed its research objectives and its implicit hypotheses by using quantitative techniques to unfold the costs and benefits of utilising digital technologies to promote CSR communication. This empirical study has applied valid and reliable measures from the 'pace of technological innovativeness',[14] 'technology acceptance'[18,20] and 'technology anxiety', as well as previously tested CSR dimensions.[21] The quantitative results have indicated that the survey participants recognised that digital media could help them promote their social and environmental behaviours. Apparently, the owner-managers perceived the usefulness of digital media, as this technological innovation has helped them to engage with stakeholders. In fact, the businesses' CSR disclosures were correlated with the technological innovation of digital media. This study also indicated that larger businesses were more likely to use online media than their smaller counterparts. Another finding revealed that younger owner-managers were more adept and proficient in the use of digital media. In sum, it may appear that CSR communication is facilitated when the businesses perceive the ease of use and the usefulness of online media. Notwithstanding, this research has shown that the owner-managers or their staff members need to possess relevant digital skills to communicate about CSR engagement with stakeholders.

Very often, the stakeholders' first point of interaction with the business happens online. Hence, it is in the businesses' interest to make a positive impact through their website or social media platforms. This study suggests that most owner-managers were already resorting to digital marketing tactics on the web. Apparently, online media has enabled these businesses to engage with stakeholders as it exposed them to those beyond their geographic area. In the main, the owner-managers indicated that they were using digital media and they perceived its usefulness. Yet there were a few participants who were still apprehensive toward this technological innovation. Over time, engaging with the people who matter most (i.e., the stakeholders) will pay off in terms of corporate reputation, customer loyalty and market standing.[5,7,10,12,46] Therefore, marketers need to possess relevant stakeholder-specific information as this will impact on the effectiveness of their CSR communication.[4,40] The value of their communications lies in their ability to open up lines of dialogue through stories and ideas that reflect their stakeholders' interests.[32,41,42,43] For these reasons, companies cannot afford to overstate or misrepresent CSR communications that could ultimately foster positive behaviours or compel remedial action.[4,7,45,47,48,49,50,51,52]

Implications and conclusions

Corporate communications managers and executives are in a position to amplify the effectiveness of their company's CSR communication efforts. They should decide what to communicate (i.e., message content) and where to communicate (i.e., message channel) to reach out to different stakeholders.

This study has identified and analysed the determinants which explain the rationale for the utilisation of digital media for CSR reporting. Previous academic research may have paid limited attention to the engagement of ICT among small businesses within the retail industry. In this case, the research findings suggest that digital technologies and applications were found to be useful for the promotion of social and sustainable activities. This implies that the use of digital media can be viewed as a critical success factor that may lead to an increased engagement with stakeholders.

In the past, CSR practices have provided a good opportunity for businesses to raise their profile in the communities around them. Very often, businesses have communicated their motives and rationales behind their CSR programmes in conventional media.

Today, companies have additional media outlets at their disposal. Savvy businesses are already promoting their CSR initiatives as they are featured in different media outlets (e.g., *The Guardian Sustainability Blog, CSRwire, Triple Pundit* and *The CSR Blog in Forbes*). In addition, there are instances where consumers themselves, out of their own volition, are becoming ambassadors of trustworthy businesses. On the other hand, there are stakeholders who are becoming skeptical on certain posturing behaviours and greenwashing.[40]

Generally, digital communications and traditional media will help to improve the corporate image and reputation of firms. Moreover, positive publicity may lead to forging long lasting relationships with stakeholders. Hence, corporate websites with user-centred designs that enable interactive information-sharing possibilities including widgets and plugins will help to promote the businesses' CSR credentials. Inter-operability and collaboration across different social media outlets may help businesses to connect with all stakeholders. This contribution suggests that there is potential for marketers to create an online forum where prospects or web visitors can engage with their business in real time. These days, marketing is all about keeping and maintaining a two-way relationship with consumers, by listening to their needs and wants. Digital marketing is an effective tool for consumer engagement. A growing number of businesses have learnt how to collaborate with consumers on product development, service enhancement and promotion. Successful companies are increasingly involving their customers in all aspects of marketing. They join online conversations as they value their stakeholders' attitudes, opinions and perceptions. Today, ubiquitous social media networks are being used by millions of users every day. In a sense, it may appear that digital media has reinforced the role of public relations. These contemporary marketing communications strategies complement well with CSR communication and sustainability reporting. In conclusion, this contribution encourages businesses to use digital channels to raise awareness of their societal engagement, environmentally sustainable practices and governance procedures among their stakeholders.

Limitations of study and future research avenues

Recently, there have been a few studies that have explored the entrepreneurial attitudes on CSR reporting.[47,53,54] Previous studies have considered different sampling frames, research designs, methodologies and analyses which have produced different outcomes. This research project has investigated the owner-managers' perceptions of CSR reporting through digital media. Although the number of survey participants were sufficient in drawing conclusions about their online CSR reporting, this study is not amenable in drawing general conclusions in other contexts. Moreover, the researcher believes that there is scope in undertaking qualitative studies to explore the participants' in-depth opinions and perceptions on the subject. A longitudinal study in this area of research could possibly investigate the opportunities and threats of consistent disclosures of social and environmental behaviours through digital media and to establish its reputational effects in the long run. Perhaps, further research can specifically investigate the quality and relevance of online content.

Diverse stakeholders may have different expectations on what information ought to be given in the realms of environmental, social and governance reporting. The author acknowledges that there is a managerial bias in this research, as the chosen sample did not focus on the marketplace or regulatory stakeholders' expectations.

Notes

1 Lindgreen, Adam, and Valerie Swaen. "Corporate Social Responsibility." *International Journal of Management Reviews* 12, no. 1 (2010): 1–7.
2 Kanter, Rosabeth Moss. "Collaborative Advantage." *Harvard Business Review* 72, no. 4 (1994): 96–108.
3 Deephouse, David L. "Media Reputation as a Strategic Resource: An Integration of Mass Communication and Resource-Based Theories." *Journal of Management* 26, no. 6 (2000): 1091–1112.
4 Morsing, Mette, and Majken Schultz. "Corporate Social Responsibility Communication: Stakeholder Information, Response and Involvement Strategies." *Business Ethics: A European Review* 15, no. 4 (2006): 323–338.
5 Camilleri, Mark A. "The Business Case for Corporate Social Responsibility" (Paper presented at the American Marketing Association in collaboration with the University of Wyoming, Oklahoma State University and Villanova University: *Marketing & Public Policy as a Force for Social Change Conference.* Washington D.C., 5th June 2014): 8–14, Accessed June 26, 2015. www.ama.org/events-training/Conferences/Documents/2015-AMA-Marketing-Public-Policy-Proceedings.pdf
6 Vanhamme, Joëlle, and Bas Grobben. "Too Good To Be True!": The Effectiveness of CSR History in Countering Negative Publicity." *Journal of Business Ethics* 85, no. 2 (2009): 273–283.
7 Du, Shuili, Chitrabhan B. Bhattacharya, and Sankar Sen. "Maximizing Business Returns to Corporate Social Responsibility (CSR): The Role of CSR Communication." *International Journal of Management Reviews* 12, no. 1 (2010): 8–19.
8 Kotler, Philip, and Nancy Lee. *Corporate Social Responsibility: Doing the Most Good for Your Company and Your Cause.* John Wiley and Sons, Hoboken, New Jersey, 2008.
9 Adams, Carol A. "Internal Organisational Factors Influencing Corporate Social and Ethical Reporting: Beyond Current Theorising." *Accounting, Auditing & Accountability Journal,* 15, no. 2 (2002): 223–250.
10 Camilleri, Mark A. "Unlocking Shared Value Through Strategic Social Marketing" (Paper presented at the American Marketing Association and the University of Massachusetts Amherst: Marketing & Public Policy Conference, Boston, 6th June 2014): 60–66. Accessed June 26, 2015.
11 Porter, Michael E., and Mark R. Kramer. "Creating Shared Value." *Harvard Business Review* 89, no. 1/2 (2011): 62–77.
12 Camilleri, Mark A. "Creating Shared Value Through Strategic CSR in Tourism." Saarbrucken: Lambert Academic Publishing, 2013.
13 Greenhow, Christine, and Beth Robelia. "Old Communication, New Literacies: Social Network Sites As Social Learning Resources." *Journal of Computer-Mediated Communication* 14, no. 4 (2009): 1130–1161.
14 Grewal, Rajdeep, Raj Mehta, and Frank R. Kardes. "The Timing of Repeat Purchases of Consumer Durable Goods: The Role of Functional Bases of Consumer Attitudes." *Journal of Marketing Research* 41, no. 1 (2004): 101–115.
15 Garcia, Rosanna, and Roger Calantone. "A Critical Look at Technological Innovation Typology and Innovativeness Terminology: A Literature Review." *Journal of Product Innovation Management* 19, no. 2 (2002): 110–132.
16 Ayeh, Julian K., Norman Au, and Rob Law. "Predicting the Intention to Use Consumer-Generated Media for Travel Planning." *Tourism Management* 35 (2013): 132–143.
17 Rauniar, Rupak, Greg Rawski, Jei Yang, and Ben Johnson. "Technology Acceptance Model (TAM) and Social Media Usage: An Empirical Study on Facebook." *Journal of Enterprise Information Management* 27, no. 1 (2014): 6–30.
18 Davis, Fred D. "Perceived Usefulness, Perceived Ease of Use, and User Acceptance of Information Technology." *MIS Quarterly* 13, no. 3 (1989): 319–340.
19 Davis, Fred D., Richard P. Bagozzi, and Paul R. Warshaw. "User Acceptance of Computer Technology: A Comparison of Two Theoretical Models." *Management Science* 35, no. 8 (1989): 982–1003.
20 Meuter, Matthew L., Mary Jo Bitner, Amy L. Ostrom, and Stephen W. Brown. "Choosing Among Alternative Service Delivery Modes: An Investigation of Customer Trial of Self-service Technologies." *Journal of Marketing* 69, no. 2 (2005): 61–83.
21 Singh, Jaywant, and Ignacio Rodriguez Del Bosque. "Understanding Corporate Social Responsibility and Product Perceptions in Consumer Markets: A Cross-Cultural Evaluation." *Journal of Business Ethics* 80, no. 3 (2008): 597–611.

22 Jamali, Dima, and Ramez Mirshak. "Corporate Social Responsibility (CSR): Theory and Practice in a Developing Country Context." *Journal of Business Ethics* 72, no. 3 (2007): 243–262.

23 Carroll, Archie B. "Corporate Social Responsibility Evolution of a Definitional Construct." *Business & Society* 38, no. 3 (1999): 268–295.

24 Schultz, Friederike, and Stefan Wehmeier. "Institutionalization of Corporate Social Responsibility Within Corporate Communications: Combining Institutional, Sensemaking and Communication Perspectives." *Corporate Communications: An International Journal* 15, no. 1 (2010): 9–29.

25 Castelló, Itziar, Michael Etter, and Finn Årup Nielsen. "Strategies of Legitimacy Through Social Media: The Networked Strategy." Journal of Management Studies 53, no. 3 (2016): 402–432. doi: 10.1111/joms.12145

26 Yoon, Yeosun, Zeynep Gürhan-Canli, and Norbert Schwarz. "The Effect of Corporate Social Responsibility (CSR) Activities on Companies with Bad Reputations." *Journal of Consumer Psychology* 16, no. 4 (2006): 377–390.

27 Colleoni, Elanor. "CSR Communication Strategies for Organizational Legitimacy in Social Media." *Corporate Communications: An International Journal* 18, no. 2 (2013): 228–248.

28 Capriotti, Paul, and Angeles Moreno. "Corporate Citizenship and Public Relations: The Importance and Interactivity of Social Responsibility Issues on Corporate Websites." *Public Relations Review* 33, no. 1 (2007): 84–91.

29 Capriotti, Paul, and Angeles Moreno. "Communicating Corporate Responsibility Through Corporate Web Sites in Spain." *Corporate Communications: An International Journal* 12, no. 3 (2007): 221–237.

30 Adams, Carol A., and Geoffrey R. Frost. "Integrating Sustainability Reporting into Management Practices." *Accounting Forum*, 32, no. 4 (2008): pp. 288–302. 2008.

31 Idowu, Samuel O., and Brian A. Towler. "A Comparative Study of the Contents of Corporate Social Responsibility Reports of UK Companies." *Management of Environmental Quality: An International Journal* 15, no. 4 (2004): 420–437.

32 Fieseler, Christian, and Matthes Fleck. "The Pursuit of Empowerment Through Social Media: Structural Social Capital Dynamics in CSR-Blogging." *Journal of Business Ethics* 118, no. 4 (2013): 759–775.

33 Buhalis, Dimitrios, and Rob Law. "Progress in Information Technology and Tourism Management: 20 Years on and 10 Years After the Internet – The State of eTourism Research." *Tourism Management* 29, no. 4 (2008): 609–623.

34 Fieseler, Christian, Matthes Fleck, and Miriam Meckel. "Corporate Social Responsibility in the Blogosphere." *Journal of Business Ethics* 91, no. 4 (2010): 599–614.

35 Castelló, Itziar, Mette Morsing, and Friederike Schultz. "Communicative Dynamics and the Polyphony of Corporate Social Responsibility in the Network Society." *Journal of Business Ethics* 118, no. 4 (2013): 683–694.

36 Kaplan, Andreas M., and Michael Haenlein. "Users of the World, Unite! The Challenges and Opportunities of Social Media." *Business Horizons* 53, no. 1 (2010): 59–68.

37 Schultz, Friederike, Sonja Utz, and Anja Göritz. "Is the Medium the Message? Perceptions of and Reactions to Crisis Communication via Twitter, Blogs and Traditional Media." *Public Relations Review* 37, no. 1 (2011): 20–27.

38 Hansen, Lars Kai, Adam Arvidsson, Finn Årup Nielsen, Elanor Colleoni, and Michael Etter. "Good Friends, Bad News-Affect and Virality in Twitter." In J. J. Park, L. T. Yang, and C. Lee (Eds.), *Future Information Technology*, pp. 34–43. Springer, Berlin Heidelberg, 2011.

39 Briones, Rowena L., Beth Kuch, Brooke Fisher Liu, and Yan Jin. "Keeping up with the Digital Age: How the American Red Cross Uses Social Media to Build Relationships." *Public Relations Review* 37, no. 1 (2011): 37–43.

40 Vorvoreanu, Mihaela. "Perceptions of Corporations on Facebook: An Analysis of Facebook Social Norms." *Journal of New Communications Research* 4, no. 1 (2009): 67–86.

41 Moreno, Angeles, and Paul Capriotti. "Communicating CSR, Citizenship and Sustainability on the Web." *Journal of Communication Management* 13, no. 2 (2009): 157–175.

42 Whelan, Glen, Jeremy Moon, and Bettina Grant. "Corporations and Citizenship Arenas in the Age of Social Media." *Journal of Business Ethics* 118, no. 4 (2013): 777–790.

43 Schultz, Friederike, Itziar Castelló, and Mette Morsing. "The Construction of Corporate Social Responsibility in Network Societies: A Communication View." *Journal of Business Ethics* 115, no. 4 (2013): 681–692.

44 Besiou, Maria, Mark Lee Hunter, and Luk N. Van Wassenhove. "A Web of Watchdogs: Stakeholder Media Networks and Agenda-Setting in Response to Corporate Initiatives." *Journal of Business Ethics* 118, no. 4 (2013): 709–729.

45 Etter, Michael. "Reasons for Low Levels of Interactivity:(Non-) Interactive CSR Communication in Twitter." *Public Relations Review* 39, no. 5 (2013): 606–608.

46 Rodrigo, Pablo, and Daniel Arenas. "Do Employees Care About CSR Programs? A Typology of Employees According to Their Attitudes." *Journal of Business Ethics* 83, no. 2 (2008): 265–283.

47 Golob, Urša, Klement Podnar, Wim J. Elving, Anne Ellerup Nielsen, and Christa Thomsen. "CSR Communication: quo vadis?" *Corporate Communications: An International Journal* 18, no. 2 (2013): 176–192.

48 Nielsen, Anne Ellerup, and Christa Thomsen. "Investigating CSR Communication in SMEs: A Case Study Among Danish Middle Managers." *Business Ethics: A European Review* 18, no. 1 (2009): 83–93.

49 Dawkins, Jenny. "Corporate Responsibility: The Communication Challenge." *Journal of Communication Management* 9, no. 2 (2005): 108–119.

50 Lewis, Stewart. "Reputation and Corporate Responsibility." *Journal of Communication Management* 7, no. 4 (2003): 356–366.

51 Bruning, Stephen D., and John A. Ledingham. "Relationships Between Organizations and Publics: Development of a Multi-Dimensional Organization-Public Relationship Scale." *Public Relations Review* 25, no. 2 (1999): 157–170.

52 Manheim, Jarol B., and Cornelius B. Pratt. "Communicating Corporate Social Responsibility." *Public Relations Review* 12, no. 2 (1986): 9–18.

53 Fassin, Yves. "SMEs and the Fallacy of Formalising CSR." *Business Ethics: A European Review* 17, no. 4 (2008): 364–378.

54 Murillo, David, and Josep M. Lozano. "SMEs and CSR: An Approach to CSR in Their Own Words." *Journal of Business Ethics* 67, no. 3 (2006): 227–240.

1.3 Strategic imperatives of communicating CSR through digital media

An emerging market perspective

Prashant Mishra and Madhupa Bakshi

Researchers have contended that by engaging in CSR activities firms obtain a wide range of business benefits such as positive attitudes towards the firm and its activities, favourable brand image and advocacy behaviours.[1] However, scholars further noted that these benefits are linked to the stakeholder's awareness and their favourable attribution of the firm's CSR activities. In order to achieve these, it is imperative for the organization to communicate about CSR with diverse stakeholders. Communication is also acknowledged as central to the CSR activity because CSR is acknowledged as a discourse constructed through the constant dialogue and negotiation between corporations and their different stakeholders.

In line with this perspective coupled with other factors, such as the impact of global stakeholder activism, and the extant information age requires that companies conduct their businesses in a socially responsible and transparent manner and subsequently make an effort, through the right means, to communicate to its stakeholders to satisfy their expectations and achieve the expected goals of CSR initiatives.[2] Hence it is seen as critical to examine how firms communicate their CSR activities, even though their CSR communication might be decoupled from their actual CSR practices. The context of globalization further requires an exploration of how firms in different countries with different cultures and political-economic systems communicate about CSR as such comparisons may allow alternative CSR paradigms to emerge.[3]

With the onset of the digital revolution in communication and media realm, the whole landscape of communication tools have undergone a dramatic change. In recent times, companies have increasingly used the internet for CSR communication.[4] Researchers noted that the main advantage of online communication is that it enables two-way communication among an unlimited number of individuals[5] and makes it possible for organizations to develop and sustain relationships. However, in practice, symmetric communication and relationship building have hardly been embraced for CSR communication online. Whereas public relations theory emphasizes the importance of interaction between organizations and their stakeholders,[6] a number of studies in recent past show that the opportunities to interact with stakeholders about CSR issues are hardly exploited through websites.[7]

The recent emergence of social media as an interactive tool has changed the face of communication and interaction between businesses and their stakeholders.[8] With social media, there are new opportunities for symmetric communication and for relationship management online because social media tools "have almost no gatekeeping mechanism, enabling conversation without formal hierarchies".[9] For example, Twitter, a popular social media tool, provides several ways for companies to interact with their stakeholders and vice versa.[10]

Despite the heightened attention on the role of online communication in CSR, there are few empirical studies about practitioner perspective on the CSR communication through digital media. In this study, using an exploratory framework we attempt to fill this gap by extending the research to a non-Western emerging market context, that is, India. This is in line with the emerging trend of examining CSR and its communication realm using digital platforms in other cultural contexts (non-Western), particularly emerging economies, such as India. Based on the interviews of senior executives responsible for CSR/corporate communication in medium to large public/private sector firms in India, we explore practitioner's perspective on the role of communication in CSR in general and to understand the potential motivators and inhibitors of use and strategic imperative of digital platforms in their overall CSR communication strategy. The objective is to investigate the current state of digital platform usage in CSR communication and, secondly, how these fit into the firm's overall strategic perspective about CSR activities and its communication in furthering their business agenda. With the above research objectives in mind, this study provides a qualitative analysis of the rationale behind organizations' use of digital media for communicating CSR initiatives. In addition, the study also explores the organisational strategic imperatives of CSR digital outreach by the firms. This chapter seeks to build upon the existing body of knowledge in trying to explain how businesses engage with different stakeholders regarding their CSR initiatives.

Corporate social responsibility and stakeholders' engagement and communication

Most of today's leading corporations acknowledge the importance of CSR and include it as part of their day-to-day activities. CSR has been seen as an organization's obligation to meet a diverse array of needs of its stakeholders. Additionally, CSR has also been considered in academic research as a key stakeholder relationship building activity with subsequent relationship benefits for the firms involved in such activities. Though the roots of CSR lie in the philanthropic activities (such as donations, charity, relief work, etc.) of corporations, globally, the concept of CSR has evolved and now encompasses all related concepts such as triple bottom line, corporate citizenship, philanthropy, strategic philanthropy, shared value, corporate sustainability and business responsibility.[11,12]

Companies are increasingly engaging in and communicating about CSR activities. Communicating about CSR is no longer optional but actually mandatory in some countries, including India. Thus, companies have to meet not only societal but also legal demands for CSR communication. The approach to disclosure is by no means uniform and is changing only slowly as the communication of CSR is perceived to be difficult because of the complexity of fitting multiple stakeholders' expectations while providing a concise and credible message. In the academic world too, many theorists and researchers have contributed to the field of CSR, without paying much attention to the rhetorical and discursive challenges of CSR.[13]

In the recent past, driven by concerns of transparency and the need to build trust and confidence of its stakeholders, CSR communication and reporting has acquired an important role as a management function. In its conceptualization as "the stated commitments of an organization" to go beyond economic priorities, to foster relationships with stakeholders, and to maintain transparency and ethical behaviour, communication is central to the practice of CSR.[14] Considerable attention had been given in the past about corporate social disclosures and communication through annual or social environmental reports in the form of descriptive analysis.[15] It has been observed that organizations communicate their corporate social responsibility (CSR) efforts to a varied, influential, and alert audience.[16]

With a reactive strategy, the firm communicates CSR information in reaction to any event or crisis facing the industry and/or the firm,[17] increasing legitimacy through the quality of the response. With a proactive strategy, a company's CSR communications are designed to prevent any legitimate concerns that may arise. Interestingly, though, regardless of which type of strategy a brand or firm chooses, overall awareness of the firms' CSR activities is generally low among both internal stakeholders (employees) and external stakeholders (consumers).[18]

Many researchers have used legitimacy theory to explain how companies deal with voluntary disclosure,[19] while another set[20] take recourse to stakeholder theory to explain such actions. The methods applied by these researches to study CSR communication has been varied from cases and content analysis to large sample size quantitative research.[21] There are a series of studies that look into the CSR communication practices of large multinational firms in developed countries[22] another set of studies compares the practices of different developing nations;[23] while there are also country specific studies that report on the extent to which CSR is put in the public domain.[24] These studies are mainly a report of the communication done by the companies through different media. In the Indian context, there are several studies[25] which found that CSR communication was far from being proactive and more driven by regulatory pressure in reporting matters.

Researchers have noted that stakeholders perceive company-controlled information channels to be hypocritical because companies are believed to perform CSR for their own advantage instead of to benefit the community or society at large.[26] Furthermore, these studies highlight how companies replace stakeholder information strategies with stakeholder involvement strategies in which dialogue is instrumental for their organizational image.[27] Moreover, such studies mainly analyse antecedents and outcomes of dialogue, such as facilitators of dialogue,[28] barriers to dialogue,[29] pillars and outcomes of a good dialogue,[30] and the functionality of dialogue for the CSR reporting activity.[31]

Previous studies on CSR and the use of the Internet and social media have focused on how new media have changed in the way the different stakeholders engage with corporations.[32] These studies have looked at diverse issues, for example, how new digital forms of organizing and deliberation have empowered networks of activists to contest CSR policies, bringing institutional change on CSR issues;[33] how Twitter has changed the way communication flows and brings dissent into CSR discussions;[34] how blogging decreases corporations' 'greenwashing' of their actions;[35] and how social media contributes to changes in corporate–society citizenship relations.[36] Despite the heightened research interest, what is yet unknown is how new digital media driven communication platforms have been embedded into corporate communication strategies and how they has enhanced the transparency of corporate dialogue about CSR. Recent research has called for re-considering how companies might incorporate dialogue into their activities.[37] Specifically, many scholars have shown interest in exploring the role of both instrumental (e.g., corporate websites) and deliberative (e.g., social media, blogs) communication tools.

The CSR communication and digital media

Digital media makes CSR information accessible to more people more of the time. Additionally, digital media can encourage 'citizen philanthropy', a movement where consumers connect with all types of organizations through meaningful social networking. Hence, corporations are increasingly intensively utilizing it for creating dialogues that debate issues related to CSR. This is in tune with the current practice of the younger generation, who have a fragmented way of using different communication platforms, thus utilizing Facebook, Myspace, and Twitter every day and viewing public disclosure of their personal lives in these spaces as natural behaviour.[38] Therefore for corporations, digital media may represent powerful tools of corporate communication about CSR at different levels. Bringing in the consumer angle, researchers have observed that compared to traditional communication tools, social media allow firms to engage in timely and direct end consumer contact at relatively low cost and higher levels of efficiency.[39] In fact the efficacy of social media for communication is further demonstrated by the previous research of Lee et al., which points out that the more socially responsible a company is, the more the intensive use of social media to discuss CSR issues is beneficial for the company itself and for the success of related social causes.[40]

When selecting media channels, one important factor is the degree of control the channel allows. Some channels have a high level of control, giving the firm complete or near complete control of the message. Such channels include official CSR reports and press releases, brand-based websites, television commercials, and product packaging. Other channels offer less control as consumers and other communicators interact with, adapt, or respond to the message. Such channels include word of mouth, consumer forums and rating sites, and social media such as Facebook, Twitter, and blogs. Whereas many firms prefer a high degree of control, reduced control has benefits. Messages delivered from low control channels tend to be more credible than messages from high control channels, as individuals are more likely to trust these messages.[41] Given this focus on community engagement, it would seem CSR messages would be a clear fit with digital media.

Digital media outlets offer a varying level of control as firms can post messages, videos, images, and the like on a social network site and allow consumers and other stakeholders to participate in a dialogue with the firm. Stakeholders become a key element in the firm's external environment that can affect the organization.[42]

Two spaces have been identified by previous studies as potential areas where a company can initiate CSR dialogues.[43] While one is deliberate like blogs, forums, social media accounts, the other is instrumental like corporate websites, micro websites. The latter allows the company to initiate dialogues which are closed than being open-ended and gives them a chance to push information which they choose. The deliberate one allows active participants to discuss more actively, thus giving the stakeholders a chance to think that the content of the messages are manipulated. Therefore, user generated content, which happens within online communities and stakeholder groups, lends more credibility to the word of mouth that is generated about CSR activities.

The paradox of digital media is that the degree of controllability of a dialogue leads to the credibility of communication; hence a communicator's credibility depends upon the extent to which they are controllable.[44] The CSR dialogue created between the company and the stakeholders has different forms and understanding as it happens in different settings, spaces or timeframes.[45] This dialogue creates stakeholder engagement and relationships in CSR communication[46] and becomes suspect if the stakeholders view it as messages that the corporate is promoting because of its self-interest.

Research methodology

We followed a qualitative approach to achieve the research objectives. The objective was to understand how the CSR Communication strategies of the selected organizations in

India are conducted and the strategic imperatives of use of digital media tools for such communication. In addition, the study explores the drivers and inhibitors of the adaptation of the digital media tools in CSR communication. In-depth interviews were considered as a method for research as they combine structure and flexibility with a structure to permit topics to be covered at the convenience of the interviewee so that responses can be fully probed and explored. Interviews have been criticized by social researchers as a form of data gathering and the extent to which they can reveal 'data' or 'facts' about the area of interest; however, the technique is useful for gaining in-depth insights, and it is subjective information that cannot be gleaned from other sources.[47] The interviews were undertaken between November 2015 to January 2016 and covered companies with CSR programmes and individuals who were connected with the initiatives. Twenty-one companies were contacted either through email or telephone requesting them to be part of the study. The companies were located in different geographic regions of India, and in choosing them, we made sure that all practiced CSR and had some form of digital presence. Table 1.3.1 gives the anonymized descriptions of companies that were interviewed in this research. We first contacted the companies mentioned below by email and when they agreed we took interviews. The respondents were all responsible for the CSR programmes of the company and sometimes were the highest person in that area. Efforts were made to interview companies from diverse business areas so that they were representative of the business scenario in India.

A semi-structured questionnaire was followed so that the respondents had the opportunity to give as much detail as possible and create a narrative that was not dictated by just the research objectives. Therefore, the organizations were broadly asked: 'How do organizations communicate CSR activities', 'Is your CSR communication strategy aligned to their business goals', 'How does your CSR communication strategy engage with different stakeholders of the CSR initiatives', 'Is CSR communication effectiveness measured? How?', 'How is the stakeholder's perspective taken into account in such initiatives?', 'What are the impediments?' and 'What factors drive adaptation of digital tools for communicating with CSR stakeholders?' Some of the interviews were telephonic, while

Table 1.3.1 Descriptions of the firms covered in the study

Organizations in India (pseudonym)	Nature and description of business
Firm 1	Indian arm of a multinational consumer goods company which meets the need of nutrition, hygiene and personal care
Firm 2	Indian industrial conglomerate
Firm 3	World's largest chain of hamburger fast food restaurants
Firm 4	One of the largest banking and financial services organisations in the world
Firm 5	Private sector Indian infrastructure financing bank
Firm 6	Multi-business conglomerate, has diversified presence in FMCG, hotels, paperboards and packaging, agribusiness and information technology
Firm 7	One of the largest suppliers of breast pumps
Firm 8	Indian mobile network operator
Firm 9	Leading global professional services company
Firm 10	One of the world's leading nutrition, health and wellness companies
Firm 11	Global car manufacturing company

others answered by email. The telephone interviews were transcribed and then subject to analysis. The evidence collected in these interviews is presented in the next section.

Findings and discussion

This section focuses on presenting the kernel of the interviews that focussed on finding the drivers of digital media usage in the dissemination of CSR information. We analysed whether this form of communication fits the strategic objective of CSR activities for furthering business agenda. The transcripts, as a whole, represented a collection of stories and discussions about the utilization of social media. On the basis of the literature reviewed, we identified certain themes from the transcripts. The summary of this analysis is shown in Table 1.3.2.

Digital media reaches out to stakeholders

According to previous research when social media is used, the applications are varied, most of them being related to marketing or communications.[48] It has been explained that they cover both internal and external communication and include knowledge transfer, internal crowdsourcing, enhancing communication related to the company brand and enabling dialogue with customers.[49] In our research, we found that the interviewed companies were definitely using it for communicating CSR initiatives to various stakeholders.

The private sector bank (Firm 5) which was part of the research interview, during the recent floods in Chennai, utilized digital media to mobilize stakeholders to collect relief

Table 1.3.2 Different primary and secondary themes emerging from the interview data

Primary themes	Secondary themes	Organizations
Digital media reaches out to the stakeholders who are affected by the CSR efforts	1 Communicating initiatives 2 Mobilizing stakeholders	Firm 2, Firm 5, Firm 3, Firm 10
Digital media creates a platform for two way communication the organization	1 Involving the employees 2 Using digital efforts to facilitate integration of the firms with the stakeholders	Firm 7, Firm 11, Firm 1, Firm 2, Firm 9
Measurability of CSR communication	1 Using software to measure the effectiveness of campaigns 2 Digital campaigns specific to CSR are not measured as of now	Firm 5, Firm 7, Firm 8, Firm 1
Digital media and other traditional media in communicating CSR	1 Digital media remains the preferred medium 2 Traditional media is more for stakeholders who are beyond the scope of digital media 3 Digital media is cheaper than traditional media	Firm 2, Firm 5, Firm 6, Firm 10
Digital media as part of strategic communication for CSR	1 Creates a strategic positioning 2 Stakeholder engagement	Firm 1, Firm 2, Firm 6, Firm 11

material for the flood victims. According to the spokesperson for the bank, this effort enabled them to muster concerned citizens in Chennai to come and participate and help in the entire effort. The bank posted regularly in social media during this period about what they were doing and why they were doing it which resulted in garnering the support of the stakeholders. For the industrial manufacturing giant (Firm 2), much of the digital media effort concentrated on getting volunteers for the CSR programs. Housewives, students and all sorts of volunteers, according to the company spokesperson, were being enlisted as teachers for the volunteer teaching program it runs through digital media. The spokesperson was very specific in saying that unlike the other firms for getting support

> We have our Facebook page which is continuously updated and we encourage our employees to like it, share it among friends and communities. We have a very large website, through which we communicate all the initiatives that are under CSR. So it is a mix of classic social media, which is Facebook, Twitter; our internal mobile app, and the email which lands in every employee's box; and when it comes to investors and external stakeholders we share through the newsletters, the annual report and website.

For the multi business conglomerate (Firm 6), digital media was an essential part of the CSR communication, as farmers accessed the company sites and the special platforms made for them and became aware of the various advantages waiting for them. The multinational bank (Firm 4) representative was very clear in laying down the role of digital media when the spokesperson said that it is

> really very important part of the communication strategy, and we make it a point to bring all stakeholders on our website to accept all our initiatives and then we leverage Twitter handle and Facebook to reach out to people, where we almost have hundred thousand followers, and immediately it goes to them.

Similar leveraging of social media and company website was also done by the car manufacturing company.

For the next set of companies, though digital media was an integral part of communication, CSR communication was not the priority. The fast food company (Firm 3) representative pointed out that CSR initiatives were being communicated to the stakeholders through digital media; however, the main purpose for usage of the media was brand communication rather than such initiatives. On the other hand, for the telecom company (Firm 8), related marketing initiatives were the main focus of digital media, and CSR communication remained much more confined to just reporting of such actions rather than garnering stakeholder attention. The same was true for the breast pump company (Firm 7), the health and nutrition giant (Firm 10) and the professional services company (Firm 9).

This finding that companies were using digital media for CSR communication, albeit in a limited fashion, is consistent with that of earlier studies.[50] It also supports the previous research which studied the corporate websites of 100 information technology companies in India for CSR communication and found that companies lack proactive CSR communication in terms of information, creativity in presentation and interactivity.[51]

Two-way communication

Previous studies[52] have already advanced the idea that corporations use deliberative spaces in the wrong way – not to deliberate but to inform. These studies have shown that corporations are missing a valuable opportunity to engage in conversations with civil society. As a result, external stakeholders still view corporations' CSR initiatives skeptically.[53] In the literature review section, we cited Kent to highlight the power of social media to maintain sustainable relationships between an organization and its stakeholders through dialogue Therefore, we looked at the transcript for evidence of two-way communication of the companies. The best example came from the industrial goods manufacturing company (Firm 2), when the representative said that

> Even in e-mailers, people respond, because there is a response mechanism where they hit the reply button and you get feedback right away. Hence we know that something has been liked, or they want more of it or want to volunteer more, or they want to donate more, or what they thought of the programme, so we find it very immediate.

As mentioned earlier, this organization has an app that gives the employees an opportunity for immediate feedback; therefore, they were expecting that CSR efforts streamed in the app would bring immediate response. The consumer goods manufacturing giant (Firm 1) utilized the interactivity of the media by sharing CSR movies in their YouTube channel, and this sharing had garnered responses in the form of likes. An anthem on 'Swatcha Bharat' (Clean India Mission) had more than 600,000 likes, whereas another educational video teaching children the advantages of washing hands had little more than 100,000 likes. The spokesperson also outlined that yearly efforts to create two communication were being made. The spokesperson mentioned that

> From a purely digital point of view what I am doing is meeting a group of people who have never thought of our brand and now actually we have brands which are developing relationships with existing customers as well.

The same company was also utilizing two-way communication internally to advance sustainability goals. They had carried out three awareness programs around sustainable development goals, and 30 factories communicated those sustainable development goals to the employees by uploading pictures and messages on the Whatsapp channel. As the directors or leaders commented on the photographs and messages came from employees, there was stakeholder engagement in real time.

This effort to create dialogue with stakeholders for CSR was also seen in the car manufacturing company (Firm 11) through the various digital platforms; the employees are asked to participate in the annual global caring program, by which they engage in environmental, sustainable and infrastructural development. The breast pump (Firm 7) company also emphasized that they had feedback from stakeholders through Twitter and Facebook about their CSR programme which promoted breastfeeding. However, for most of the organizations, digital media remained a one way street as what they updated was mostly in the form of reports, facts and figures and videos rather than content that could inspire feedback. The other reason for not actively utilizing the interactivity of the medium was the philosophy of keeping CSR programmes essentially internal and not content that can be branded. The telecom company (Firm 8) and the consulting firm both echoed similar sentiments. Also, since digital media is essentially urban, the multi-business company executive felt that for reaching out to the rural poor about CSR issues it was still not the best medium. In sum, most of the companies were not utilizing the full potential of the interactivity of the medium. Hence, we can say that, as outlined in the theoretical portion, digital media was being used by companies to forge two-way communications; however, the number of companies doing that is few. The reason can be that they still do not know the efficacy of digital media in creating a two-way dialogue, or they still believe that CSR is an internal effort.

Measurability of digital media

In a study of 50 companies across seven Asian countries, researchers found a culture where dedicated CSR reports are rare,[54] though India is the country that most extensively reports its CSR; hence, it has been argued that this represents a low level of CSR institutionalization.[55] It is thus natural that attempts to measure the effects of such communication would be minimal. The companies when questioned on this were more focussed on the measurement of effectiveness of social media than the effectiveness of the CSR campaigns. The private bank (Firm 5) spokesperson pointed out that measurement of effectiveness of digital campaigns was a new initiative, and while it was done for the corporates, now it was being done at the retail level. Various software were being put into use to generate data about the effectiveness of the campaigns; however, it was not clear as to whether CSR campaigns were segregated. Similarly for the telecom company (Firm 8), all digital campaigns were being measured, but as the company did not highlight their CSR efforts, the results remained unaccounted.

The consumer goods (Firm 1) manufacturing giant pointed out that the digital media measurement tools were at nascent stage. They gave numbers, but the quality of the engagement was still missing, and therefore, they optimized the usage of digital media measurement tools. There were certain text analysis programs which told the company the nature of the engagement; however, they were yet to be applied to different social media platform. For the breast pump company (Firm 7) and the multi-business organization, there were various digital media tools which were being utilized; however, for the others, there was nothing which told them about how they were effective for CSR campaigns. It can be said that for the companies studied here that CSR efforts in the digital media are not being measured, but the various digital effort measurement tools give an idea about the awareness of the various CSR digital media efforts.

Digital versus traditional media

Social media is the 'people's media' and has the ability, if used properly, to turn 'window dressing' CSR into being the 'window to a firm's soul'.[56] Social media, therefore, will become more than the message of CSR, it will become the soul of CSR and, therefore, be embedded as part of the brand and its message.[57] This sentiment is echoed by the respondents of this study when we have the spokesperson of the industrial conglomerate (Firm 2) saying

> In the old fashioned way, you would create a whole template for the communication and you would have a printed and would distribute it and who knows whether anyone will read it or not. But digital is fast, there we can run a teaser campaign, a

really effective volunteering campaign, which can land in your mailbox and can lead to immediate action. So I think digital is a really exciting tool for CSR and it is a fraction of the cost, So I think digital is way ahead of the old fashioned media way of communicating, from the cost, impact, sort of drives immediate action that can be taken.

At the same time, as pointed out by the consumer giant (Firm 1) representative, the role for social media has more to do with a particular brand, and it is more about communicating with people who have not thought about the brand. The spokesperson continues "it has been extremely strenuous to think whether the entire strategy needs a rethink and to move into social media in an even bigger way; and whatever we decide there, social media is a critical challenge". This is further elaborated when the role of social media versus traditional media is outlined: while social media helps in "providing the scale and reach and it really conveys what you want to convey to your stakeholders and channels like Whatsapp are very effective in reaching specific groups", traditional media as pointed out by the bank representative demands

> The quality of attention, which is of a completely different nature and intensity. So I think firms need to target both ends while social media is more sensory, traditional media is more of the intellect. Also traditional media is for the older generation and the newer generation is more for the millennials.

Another factor relating to the usage of digital media is the connectivity issue. In rural areas digital media has not penetrated, so when the nutrition, health and wellness company has to campaign for water conservation, traditional media is the means to communicate. Similarly the breast pump organization (Firm 7), in promoting the values of breastfeeding in rural areas, has to resort to traditional media for creating awareness. The multi-business organization (Firm 6) also agreed that digital media is not a panacea for all stakeholders. Annual reports and sustainability reports were still targeted to investors and the people with different queries visited the websites. The farmers were being mobilized through specialized digital platforms which were made accessible to them. Hence our finding supports earlier research,[58] which showed that it enabled people to be increasingly involved in communities that (co-)create, modify, and share information.

Strategic CSR communication through digital media

While CSR messages indeed communicate to external stakeholders, they also forcefully (yet often unnoticed by marketers) serve internal purposes, such as reinforcing corporate identity and building identification among organisational members.[59] This strategic role of CSR is emphasized through digital media, as we see several of the interviewees mentioning that employees rally around CSR issues because of the buzz created in digital media. The representative of the industrial conglomerate (Firm 2) mentioned instances where because of digital media a brand which was doing CSR gave the opportunity of visibility to another brand. According to her

> We were doing this programme for malnourishment at the tyre plant, when the email went out we talked about how many children were being helped and the food interventions we were doing, and the health check-ups that were being organized.

Someone in the sister energy organization immediately said that they have this health tonic booster for malnourishment and they were launching this product, so why could it not be given to the children. Hence digital media becomes a launch pad, where cross fertilization of ideas of employees happen which helps to make CSR not only better but more enriched. This and other efforts certainly inspire more employees to connect for CSR and contribute to the strengthening of the brand.

In the same vein, the car manufacturing company (Firm 11) said that communicating social messages through digital media to the target audience has a strong relevance in developing the brand image in the market. According to the multi-business representative (Firm 6), brands communicate about sustainability issues over social media, therefore, aligning the product with such causes in the mind of the consumer. A strong company–stakeholder relationship often results from stakeholder identification with a company identity that matches their own sense of who they are.[60] In other words, if important stakeholders such as managers, employees, opinion leaders and consumers identify with a company, it is more likely that they will contribute in a positive and active way and provide organisational support.[61]

This is furthermore articulated by the consumer goods manufacturing (Firm 1) representative, when the spokesperson says that the digital campaign must be appealing and reach out to different groups of people. The spokesperson elaborated that from a purely digital point of view what we are doing is meeting a group of people who have never thought of our brand and now, actually, we have brands which are developing relationships with existing customers as well. In fact, it was pointed out that initially the digital strategy was to just test the waters; now it is part of the business strategy and they are not only able to reach out to the consumer, but increasingly more and more consumers are coming in to it. That digital media was being leveraged is evident from the health and nutrition food giant's (Firm 10) effort in communicating to youth. The representative elaborated that in this age, it is vital to maintain a transparent mode of communication. CSR is definitely propagated through all channels; however, it is prioritized as per the campaign and its social and demographic relevance.

Implications and conclusions

Two factors emerge from the discussion: 1) digital media for CSR can mobilize stakeholders meaningfully, and 2) strategically, such communication in the digital domain can contribute towards brand growth and cohesiveness among stakeholders. It also endorses previous research that in advancing the communication imperative for CSR, participants in this study position communication primarily in terms of an instrumental approach aimed at building awareness, sharing information and garnering support for their respective CSR activities. Thus, it can be concluded that emerging market firms tend to follow an integrated approach towards CSR communication – focussing on both external and internal stakeholders. This can be viewed as an inside-out approach also targeting employees who would act as credible endorsers of the company's sustainability practices. It is also evident that compared to the Western world, Indian firms are at an early stage of evolution in leveraging digital media for CSR communication. Given that social media today can touch a definite set of stakeholders and can consistently portray a definite image, it is necessary that it is leveraged properly. At the same time, as pointed out by previous research, it cannot be a blind aping of Western communication practices instead developing realistic models based on the developing nature of the business scenario.

Research has shown that CSR communications contribute to the brand image; hence, Indian companies must highlight such efforts when they use the digital platform. The greatest advantage of digital media is a two-way dialogue which, theoretically, in marketing communications literature has been regarded as the core value of company communications. Such communications contribute towards crowdsourcing and creating efforts that have consumer interests at the core. As evidenced from the interviews, Indian firms need to strengthen their efforts towards this end. They are yet to take into account that such consumer focussed efforts can create far more consumer connections that are actually measurable. The accountability factor of digital media also remains unutilized. Going beyond just 'likes', the communication efforts need to be measured in terms of quality of connect and the type of connect. When these analyses are available, only then CSR communication in digital media can create a meaningful dialogue. The strategic use of communication has been long understood, but in the context of CSR it remains a fuzzy area for corporations. The philanthropic philosophy and its confusion with cause-related marketing makes CSR communication knee-jerk reactions. No consistent policy is followed about how it has to be conveyed; as a result, it depends on the whims of the brands or individual managers.

The study has some limitations too. As the firms covered in this study are large firms, it would be interesting to see whether similar themes emerge for small and medium enterprises too. The study can also be extended further by bringing other stakeholders' perspectives into analysis. Today all digital communication is measurable. The present study was focused on strategic aspects of CSR communication and did not measure issues related to reach or depth, which can be a potential area for further research.

Notes

1   Fombrun, C. J., Gardberg, N. A., and Sever, J. M. (2000). The Reputation QuotientSM: A Multi-Stakeholder Measure of Corporate Reputation. *Journal of Brand Management*, 7(4), 241–255; Lichtenstein, D. R., Drumwright, M. E., and Braig, B. M. (2004). The Effect of Corporate Social Responsibility on Customer Donations to Corporate-Supported Nonprofits. *Journal of Marketing*, 68(4), 16–32; Du, S., Bhattacharya, C. B., and Sen, S. (2010). Maximizing Business Returns to Corporate Social Responsibility (CSR): The Role of CSR Communication. *International Journal of Management Reviews*, 12(1), 8–19.
2   Clark, C. E. (2000). Differences Between Public Relations and Corporate Social Responsibility: An Analysis. *Public Relations Review*, 26(3), 363–380; Podnar, K. (2008). Guest Editorial: Communicating Corporate Social Responsibility. *Journal of Marketing Communications*, 14(2).
3   Palazzo, G., and Scherer, A. G. (2008). Corporate Social Responsibility, Democracy, and the Politicization of the Corporation. *Academy of Management Review*, 33(3), 773–775.
4   Birth, G., Illia, L., Lurati, F., and Zamparini, A. (2008). Communicating CSR: Practices Among Switzerland's Top 300 Companies. *Corporate Communications: An International Journal*, 13(2), 182–196.
5   Kent, M. L., and Taylor, M. (1998). Building Dialogic Relationships Through the World Wide Web. *Public Relations Review*, 24(3), 321–334; Hallahan, K. (2001). The Dynamics of Issues Activation and Response: An Issues Processes Model. *Journal of Public Relations Research*, 13(1), 27–59.
6   Grunig, J. E., and Hunt, T. (1984). *Managing Public Relations*. Vol. 343. New York: Holt, Rinehart and Winston; Taylor, M., Kent, M. L., and White, W. J. (2001). How Activist Organizations Are Using the Internet to Build Relationships. *Public Relations Review*, 27(3), 263–284; Kelleher, T. (2009). Conversational Voice, Communicated Commitment, and Public Relations Outcomes in Interactive Online Communication. *Journal of Communication*, 59(1), 172–188.
7   Angeles, M, and Capriotti, M. (2009). Communicating CSR, Citizenship and Sustainability on the Web. *Journal of Communication Management*, 13, 157–175; Ingenhoff, D., and Koelling, A. M. (2009). The Potential of Web Sites as a Relationship Building Tool for Charitable Fundraising NPOs. *Public Relations Review*, 35(1), 66–73; Insch, A. (2008). Online Communication of Corporate Environmental

Citizenship: A Study of New Zealand's Electricity and Gas Retailers. *Journal of Marketing Communications*, 14(2), 139–153.

8 Etter, M., and Fieseler, C. (2010). On relational capital in social media. *Studies in Communication Sciences*, 10(2), 167–190.

9 Fieseler, C., Fleck, M., and Meckel, M. (2010). Corporate Social Responsibility in the Blogosphere. *Journal of Business Ethics*, 91(4), 599–614; Boyd, D., Golder, S., and Lotan, G. (2010, January). Tweet, tweet, retweet: Conversational aspects of retweeting on twitter. In *System Sciences (HICSS), 2010 43rd Hawaii International Conference on* (pp. 1–10). IEEE Press.

10 Honey, C., and Herring, S. C. (2009, January). Beyond microblogging: Conversation and collaboration via Twitter. In *System Sciences, 2009. HICSS'09. 42nd Hawaii International Conference on* (pp. 1–10). IEEE Press.

11 Clarkson, M. E. (1995). A Stakeholder Framework for Analyzing and Evaluating Corporate Social Performance. *Academy of Management Review*, 20(1), 92–117; Waddock, S. A., Bodwell, C., and Graves, S. B. (2002). Responsibility: The New Business Imperative. *The Academy of Management Executive*, 16(2), 132–148.

12 Waddock, S., and Smith, N. (2000). Corporate Responsibility Audits: Doing Well by Doing Good. *MIT Sloan Management Review*, 41(2), 75.

13 Schmeltz, L. (2012). Consumer-oriented CSR Communication: Focusing on Ability or Morality? *Corporate Communications: An International Journal*, 17(1), 29–49.

14 Capriotti, P., and Moreno, A. (2007). Communicating Corporate Responsibility Through Corporate Web Sites in Spain. *Corporate Communications: An International Journal*, 12(3), 221–237.

15 Patten, D. M. (1991). Exposure Legitimacy, and Social Disclosure. *Journal of Accounting and Public*, 10, 297–308.

16 Perks, K. J., Farache, F., Shukla, P., and Berry, A. (2013). Communicating Responsibility-Practicing Irresponsibility in CSR Advertisements. *Journal of Business Research*, 66(10), 1881–1888.

17 van Staden, C. J., and Hooks, J. (2007). A Comprehensive Comparison of Corporate Environmental Reporting and Responsiveness. *The British Accounting Review*, 39(3), 197–210. Chicago.

18 Du, Bhattacharya and Sen 2010. op. cit.

19 Cormier, D., and Gordon, I. M. (2001). An Examination of Social and Environmental Reporting Strategies. *Accounting, Auditing & Accountability Journal*, 14(5), 587–617.

20 Ruf, B. M., Muralidhar, K., Brown, R. M., Janney, J. J., and Paul, K. (2001). An Empirical Investigation of the Relationship Between Change in Corporate Social Performance and Financial Performance: A Stakeholder Theory Perspective. *Journal of Business Ethics*, 32(2), 143–156. Adams, C. A., and Frost, G. R. (2006). Accessibility and Functionality of the Corporate Web Site: Implications for Sustainability Reporting. *Business Strategy and the Environment*, 15(4), 275–287. Haddock-Fraser, J., and Fraser, I. (2008). Assessing Corporate Environmental Reporting Motivations: Differences Between "Close-to-Market" and "Business-to-Business" Companies. *Corporate Social Responsibility and Environmental Management*, 15(3), 140–155.

21 Amaladoss, M. X., and Manohar, H. L. (2013). Communicating Corporate Social Responsibility – A Case of CSR Communication in Emerging Economies. *Corporate Social Responsibility and Environmental Management*, 20(2), 65–80.

22 Esrock, S. L., and Leichty, G. B. (1998). Social Responsibility and Corporate Web Pages: Self-Presentation or Agenda-Setting? *Public Relations Review*, 24(3), 305–319; Adams, C. A., and Frost, G. R. (2006). Accessibility and Functionality of the Corporate Web Site: Implications for Sustainability Reporting. *Business Strategy and the Environment*, 15(4), 275–287; Capriotti, P., and Moreno, A. (2007). Corporate Citizenship and Public Relations: The Importance and Interactivity of Social Responsibility Issues on Corporate Websites. *Public Relations Review*, 33(1), 84–91; Tagesson, T., Blank, V., Broberg, P., and Collin, S. O. (2009). What Explains the Extent and Content of Social and Environmental Disclosures on Corporate Websites: A Study of Social and Environmental Reporting in Swedish Listed Corporations. *Corporate Social Responsibility and Environmental Management*, 16(6), 352–364.

23 Thompson, P., and Zakaria, Z. (2004). Corporate Social Responsibility Reporting in Malaysia: Progress and Prospects. *The Journal of Corporate Citizenship*, 13, 125–136; b Tang, L., Gallagher, C. C., and Bie, B. (2015). Corporate social responsibility communication through corporate websites: A comparison of leading corporations in the United States and China. *International Journal of Business Communication*, 52(2), 205–227.

24 Wang, J., and Chaudhri, V. (2009). Corporate Social Responsibility Engagement and Communication by Chinese Companies. *Public Relations Review*, 35(3), 247–250; Vural, Z. A. B., and Öksüz, B.

(2009). Communicating Corporate Social Responsibility Through Corporate Web Sites: A Research on Turkish GSM Operators. *Journal of Yasar University*, 4(13), 1047–1065; Kuo, L., Yeh, C. C., and Yu, H. C. (2012). Disclosure of Corporate Social Responsibility and Environmental Management: Evidence from China. *Corporate Social Responsibility and Environmental Management*, 19(5), 273–287.

25 Chaudhri, V., and Wang, J. (2007). Communicating Corporate Social Responsibility on the Internet a Case Study of the Top 100 Information Technology Companies in India. *Management Communication Quarterly*, 21(2), 232–247; Lattemann, C., Fetscherin, M., Alon, I., Li, S., and Schneider, A. M. (2009). CSR Communication Intensity in Chinese and Indian Multinational Companies. *Corporate Governance: An International Review*, 17(4), 426–442; Lattemann, C., Fetscherin, M., Alon, I., Li, S., and Schneider, A. M. (2009). CSR Communication Intensity in Chinese and Indian Multinational Companies. *Corporate Governance: An International Review*, 17(4), 426–442. Amaladoss and Manohar 2013. op. cit.

26 Illia, L., and Lurati, F. (2006). Stakeholder Perspectives on Organizational Identity: Searching for a Relationship Approach. *Corporate Reputation Review*, 8(4), 293–304; Susanne, J. T., and Nielsen, E. A. (2011). Strategic Stakeholder Dialogues: A Discursive Perspective on Relationship Building. *Corporate Communications: An International Journal*, 16(3), 204–217; Morsing, M., and Schultz, M. (2006). Corporate Social Responsibility Communication: Stakeholder Information, Response and Involvement Strategies. *Business Ethics: A European Review*, 15(4), 323–338.

27 Eisenegger, M., and Schranz, M. (2011). Reputation Management and Corporate Social Responsibility. *The Handbook of Communication and Corporate Social Responsibility*, 128–146.

28 Burchell, J., and Cook, J. (2008). Stakeholder Dialogue and Organisational Learning: Changing Relationships Between Companies and NGOs. *Business Ethics: A European Review*, 17(1), 35–46; Kuhn, T., and Deetz, S. (2008). Critical Theory and Corporate Social Responsibility: Can/should We Get Beyond Cynical Reasoning. *The Oxford Handbook of Corporate Social Responsibility*, 173–196.

29 Etter, M. (2013). Reasons for Low Levels of Interactivity: (Non-) interactive CSR Communication in Twitter. *Public Relations Review*, 39(5), 606–608.

30 Burchell and Cook 2008. op. cit; Golob, U., and Podnar, K. (2011). Corporate Social Responsibility Communication and Dialogue. *The Handbook of Communication and Corporate Social Responsibility*, 231–251; Pedersen, E. R. (2006). Making Corporate Social Responsibility (CSR) Operable: How Companies Translate Stakeholder Dialogue into Practice. *Business and Society Review*, 111(2), 137–163.

31 Hess, D. (2008). The Three Pillars of Corporate Social Reporting As New Governance Regulation: Disclosure, Diablogue, and Development. *Business Ethics Quarterly*, 18(4), 447–482.

32 Castelló, I., Morsing, M., and Schultz, F. (2013). Communicative Dynamics and the Polyphony of Corporate Social Responsibility in the Network Society. *Journal of Business Ethics*, 118(4), 683–694.

33 De Bakker, F. G., and Hellsten, I. (2013). Capturing Online Presence: Hyperlinks and Semantic Networks in Activist Group Websites on Corporate Social Responsibility. *Journal of Business Ethics*, 118(4), 807–823.

34 Schoeneborn, D., and Trittin, H. (2013). Transcending Transmission: Towards a Constitutive Perspective on CSR Communication. *Corporate Communications: An International Journal*, 18(2), 193–211.

35 Lee, E. M., Park, S. Y., and Lee, H. J. (2013). Employee Perception of CSR Activities: Its Antecedents and Consequences. *Journal of Business Research*, 66(10), 1716–1724.

36 Whelan, G., Moon, J., and Grant, B. (2013). Corporations and Citizenship Arenas in the Age of Social Media. *Journal of Business Ethics*, 118(4), 777–790.

37 Fieseler, C., and Fleck, M. (2013). The Pursuit of Empowerment Through Social Media: Structural Social Capital Dynamics in CSR-Blogging. *Journal of Business Ethics*, 118(4), 759–775, Seele, P., and Lock, I. (2015). Instrumental and/or Deliberative? A Typology of CSR Communication Tools. *Journal of Business Ethics*, 131(2), 401–414.

38 Rasmussen, S. E. (2009). *Kan universitet rumme Generation Mig?* Copenhagen: Universitetsavisen.

39 Kaplan, A. M., and Haenlein, M. (2010). Users of the World, Unite! The Challenges and Opportunities of Social Media. *Business Horizons*, 53(1), 59–68.

40 Lee, K., Oh, W. Y., and Kim, N. (2013). Social Media for Socially Responsible Firms: Analysis of Fortune 500's Twitter Profiles and Their CSR/CSIR Ratings. *Journal of Business Ethics*, 118(4), 791–806.

41 Du, Bhattacharya, and Sen 2010. op. cit.

42 Murray, K. B., and Vogel, C. M. (1997). Using a Hierarchy-of-effects Approach to Gauge the Effectiveness of Corporate Social Responsibility to Generate Goodwill Toward the Firm: Financial versus Nonfinancial Impacts. *Journal of Business Research*, 38(2), 141–159.

43 Seele, P., and Lock, I. (2014). Deliberative and/or instrumental? A Typology of CSR Communication. *Journal of Business Ethics, 131*(2), 401–414.

44 Du, Bhattacharya, and Sen (2010) op cit.

45 Romenti, S., Murtarelli, G., and Valentini, C. (2014). Organisations' Conversations in Social Media: Applying Dialogue Strategies in Times of Crises. *Corporate Communications: An International Journal, 19*(1), 10–33.

46 Kent, M. L., and Taylor, M. (1998). Building Dialogic Relationships Through the World Wide Web. *Public Relations Review, 24*(3), 321–334; Wigley, S., and Lewis, B. K. (2012). Rules of Engagement: Practice What You Tweet. *Public Relations Review, 38*(1), 165–167.

47 MacDonald, D. H., et al. (2013). An Interview Methodology for Exploring the Values That Community Leaders Assign to Multiple-Use Landscapes. *Ecology and Society, 18*(1), 29.

48 Stelzner, M. A. (2012). Marketing Industry Report: How Marketers are Using Social Media to Grow Their Business. *Social Media Examiner*. Retrieved from www.socialmedia examiner.com/SocialMe diaMarketingIndustryReport2012.pdf

49 Vuori, M. (2012). Exploring Uses of Social Media in a Global Corporation. *Journal of Systems and Information Technology, 14*(2), 155–170.

50 Amaladoss, M. X., and Manohar, H. L. (2013). Communicating Corporate Social Responsibility – A Case of CSR Communication in Emerging Economies. *Corporate Social Responsibility and Environmental Management, 20*(2), 65–80. Adams, C. A., and Frost, G. R. (2006). Accessibility and Functionality of the Corporate Web Site: Implications for Sustainability Reporting. *Business Strategy and the Environment*, 15(4), 275–287; Morsing et al., op. cit.

51 Chaudhri, V., and Wang, J. (2007). Communicating Corporate Social Responsibility on the Internet a Case Study of the Top 100 Information Technology Companies in India. *Management Communication Quarterly, 21*(2), 232–247.

52 Etter et al. 2011. op. cit.; Fieseler and Fleck (2013) op cit.

53 Illia et al. 2013. op. cit. Johansen and Ellerup Nielsen (2011) op cit; Scherer and Palazzo, 2011. op. cit.

54 Chapple, W., and Moon, J. (2005). Corporate Social Responsibility (CSR) in Asia a Seven-Country Study of CSR Web Site Reporting. *Business & Society, 44*(4), 415–441.

55 Jayakumar, T. (2013). MNC CSR in Emerging Economy Conflict Zones-A Case Study of HUL's North-East Operations in India. *VIKALPA, 38*(4), 69.

56 Kesavan, R., Bernacchi, M. D., and Mascarenhas, O. A. (2013). Word of Mouse: CSR Communication and the Social Media. *International Management Review, 9*(1), 58.

57 Briones, R. L., Kuch, B., Liu, B. F., and Jin, Y. (2011). Keeping up with the Digital Age: How the American Red Cross Uses Social Media to Build Relationships. *Public Relations Review, 37*(1), 37–43.

58 Kietzmann, J. H., Hermkens, K., McCarthy, I. P., and Silvestre, B. S. (2011). Social Media? Get Serious! Understanding the Functional Building Blocks of Social Media. *Business Horizons, 54*(3), 241–251.

59 Morsing and Schultz, 2006. op. cit.

60 Dutton, J. M., Dukerich, J. M., and Harquail, C. V. (1994). Organizational Images and Member Identification. *Administrative Science Quarterly, 39*(2), 239–263.

61 Morsing and Schultz, 2006. op. cit.

1.4 "The Devil's in the details"

Contested standards of corporate social responsibility in social media

Robert L. Heath, Adam J. Saffer, and Damion Waymer

Introduction

This chapter focuses on how social media give voice to critics who demand higher corporate social responsibility (CSR) standards and question organizations' and industries' willingness and abilities to meet those standards. Supporters of CSR standards and organizational performance also have access to social media. This dialogue increases the dimensionality of traditional media by adding networks of supportive and critical voices that otherwise may not be heard in traditional discourse networks. This participatory complexity of social media networks increases the turbulence organizations experience as they navigate the straits of stakeholder judgments.

This dialogic approach to CSR threshold standards and performance measures produces robust arguments regarding the roles and norms organizations, especially businesses, should fulfill in society to achieve legitimacy. Reflective approaches to CSR have refuted Milton Friedman's precarious claim that profit/revenue managerial efficiency metrics sufficiently integrate CSR into strategic management.[1] Critics press executives to think in ways that serve society, not the other way around. Strident voices call for corporate initiatives to raise performance expectations to gain reputational return on financial and social investments.

We begin by reviewing theory and research on CSR to propose a paradigm that discusses how social media allow for participative engagement by many voices that support and challenge managements' operational preferences and messages. We offer network theory as a framework to investigate nine social media challenges. Three case studies are used to examine the turbulence of social media CSR discourse arenas as network functions and legitimacy issue contests. Such discourse demonstrates the participatory richness of networks. Social media may champion an organization's CSR performance with the purpose of enhancing its reputation as a broker of the public interest. Likewise voices challenge organizations' legitimacies by demanding strategic management changes needed to close legitimacy gaps.

Rather than taking an organization-centric approach to social media CSR discourse, this chapter demonstrates how CSR dialogue occurs in social media arenas. Social media's unique structural and functional networks facilitate discourse; many voices express different and conflicting CSR judgements. Traditional media facilitate CSR discussions as gatekeepers that allow or bring divergent views into the discourse. Social media operates without such gatekeeping. In one sense, network connections provide the conduits through which discourse flows while fostering siloes in which identities and opinions are formed and reinforced. Issues of policy and reputation are disputed and reframed in text and by visual messages that create simulated realities.[2] This chapter emphasizes how social media challenges reveal that the devil is in the details when competing voices add authenticity and transparency to CSR discourse.

CSR expectations: communicative contests in social media networks

CSR is instrumental to societal productivity because stakeholder expectations challenge organizations to meet interdependent normative/evaluative (moral legitimacy) and cognitive/pragmatic (financial/material legitimacy) standards. By this logic, organizations (artificial citizens) are authorized to operate for reward if they add moral and pragmatic value that exceeds the costs (financial and moral equity – for instance, health and safety) of their presence in a community.[3]

Whether adversarial, collaborative, reactionary, or proactionary, CSR discourse occurs in many arenas. Not all stakeholders hold the same CSR standards, so each discourse arena(s) becomes a place to ask what standards are held by which stakeholders (stakeholder attributes of power, legitimacy, urgency, and salience).[4] The complexity within these arenas poses substantial uncertainty for those who manage organizations, shape industries, and engage in CSR communications. Which stakeholders are critical? Why are they critics? What standards do they propose? How influential are their arguments?

When organizations fail to meet legitimacy standards set by one – or more – stakeholder group(s), a legitimacy gap occurs. When an organization narrows one gap, another may open with another stakeholder group. Take for instance an industrial farming corporation that establishes its economic legitimacy by providing consistent returns to stockholders. Stockholders may be pleased that industrial farming reduces costs (thus raising profits), but animal rights groups may be displeased. If the industry raises its operational standards to be more humane to animals, stockholders will complain if costs increase and profits drop. Legitimacy gaps are dynamic, not static or one-dimensional.

Stakeholders' debate whether organizations are legitimate brokers of others' interests.[5] The alignment of such interests establish the core of corporate legitimacy, as Suchman[6] reasoned, "a generalized perception or assumption that the actions of an entity are desirable, proper, or appropriate within some socially constructed system of norms, values, beliefs and definitions." Given this legitimacy rationale of CSR, strategic management is expected to align missions, visions, and operations with stakeholders' CSR expectations.

CSR expectations – legitimacy tug of wars between organizations and stakeholders – may be the same and well aligned, but they may be in conflict. This is the case because CSR standards are neither universal nor stable – righteous nor binary.[7] How the standards are developed and applied to support or oppose organizations' managerial decisions can test and strain but also strengthen stakeholder relationships as a means of aligning interests.[8]

Legitimacy is a counterpart to CSR; both concepts frame threshold tests of the fit between organizations' operations and community standards, prevailing and relevant CSR expectations.[9] This multifaceted sense of CSR accounts is why so many definitions of CSR exist and why so much confusion surrounds CSR studies.[10] Legitimacy debates and CSR contests provide substantial content for the analysis of how social media discourse arenas operate as organizations present their CSR cases and users respond, and as users make their cases and organizations respond.[11,12,13]

Especially in social media, many voices compete to set threshold standards by which organizations gain (or fail to gain) stakeholders' approval. Social media lacks certain controlling factors of traditional media, such as journalistic gatekeeping, editorial commentary, balanced coverage, and third-party confirmation. Thus, CSR judgments can become magnified due to discussant's ease of access to this discourse arena. If an organization or industry does meet stakeholders' standards – or does not – challengers can magnify their perspective via social media discourse. Critics keep issues alive that otherwise might fade by injecting perspectives, agenda, facts, values, and motives that create more turbulence than typically occurs during the filtering by traditional media gatekeepers. This multidimensionality presumes, from the organization's perspective, that CSR legitimacy communications is like the dike into which the little Dutch boy had to insert all of his fingers to prevent a breach.

Such CSR thresholds and legitimacy contests 1) debate standards that focus on issues of fact, value, policy, and identification, 2) textually enunciate normative standards, and 3) contest whether organizations (or collectively as industries) meet or violate those standards. These dynamics demonstrate the continual challenge organizations face to be judged legitimate, a topic elaborated in the next section.

CSR legitimacy standards and practices in social media

Social media creates a participatory culture as messages are introduced by many voices in a self-selective discourse arena facilitated by virtually instantaneous co-constructed communication. This discourse exhibits immediacy and infuses thoughts about whose identities and interests are served. As they function in this participatory manner, social media pose opportunities, but it also challenge organizations' CSR communications.[14,15]

The unlimited access interested parties have to these participative arenas creates an ebb and flow of legitimacy gaps. An organization-centric approach to such discourse can feature monologue while assuming dialogue. Even if statements produce counter statements, the interaction may be more indirect or oblique than engaged dialogue: statement, refutation, and counter refutation to consensus or concurrence. Likewise, the "social-media-as-a-communication-tool" paradigm falsely proclaims that organizations' interactions with stakeholders can be used to strategically converge or co-create meaning between stakeholders' expectations and organizations' practices.[16,17] As Colleoni[18] explained,

> establishing an interactive and engaging approach is not enough to align to stakeholders' social expectations. The idea that the more the dialog, the more the communality seems to fail to portray the complexity of the communication dynamics, such as the persistence of different vocabulary within the same discourse or simply a dialog without alignment.

The dynamic nature of social media foils the organization-centric or social-media-as-an-organizational communication-tool perspectives to analyzing CSR discourse. The discourses in social media arenas are shaped by the digital functionalities and the structures of networks.

Reflecting on the complexity of discourse arenas, Schultz, Castello, and Morsing[19] reasoned that CSR communications, especially in social media, require "a multi-faceted understanding of many concerns, voices, and conceptions of truth, and an ability to engage across independent and conflicting interpretations of the intricate issues related to corporate behavior." This network perspective accounts for the multidimensionality, multifacetedness, and multitextual issues of CSR legitimacy gaps and threshold standards.

A network perspective, which includes network theories and methods, focuses on the connections among individual units (i.e., individuals, groups, organizations, artifacts). Whereas traditional social science examines the attributes of units that are often assumed to have autonomous independence, a network perspective specifically focuses on how units are connected and interdependent.[20] Yang and Taylor[21] argued that a network perspective captures the "the understanding of multiple, simultaneous, and diverse communicative relationships and increasing complexities in organizations' environments." Indeed, this perspective is apt for CSR communications, legitimacy gaps, and threshold standards in social media arenas.

Social media arenas create a multitude of networks from the connections among individuals, organizations, media types (social v. traditional), and topics of discussion. Most apparent in social media arenas are the networks of individuals and organizations conversing about a topic in a social media arena. When communicators discuss their dissatisfaction (or satisfaction) with an organization's behaviors in a social media arena, they create a network by co-mentioning the same topic. From the co-mentioning connections, communicators can have more interactions and develop relationships (online or offline) to create a social network. Within the social network, a network (or sub-network) of communicators can form among those who share a common understanding or interpretation of information.[22] All the while, connections are being formed among communicators who can connect topics by bringing together otherwise separate issues or connecting types of media by sourcing or sharing information from different outlets/formats. Thus, the network perspective explains how connections form around one topic and evolve to connect topics.

Our review of the literature reveals nine challenges facing organizational CSR communications and the management and communication efforts to align CSR threshold standards within networks. The following principles offer insights into the nature and use of social media for CSR communications, while serving as hypotheses that can be illustrated by the three cases:

1　*Because of their unique network structures and functions, social media is discourse arenas*: social media may be conduits through which organizations share information about their CSR performance. As networks, social media allow stakeholders participative opportunities to promote, challenge, and reframe CSR standards and performance:[23] the more dialogue, the more communality.[24]

2　*In such arenas, organizations' images can fragment*: in social media discourse arenas, organizations' image constructions encounter unlimited and unfiltered criticism. Terms that are preferred and used by a business – whole foods and organic for example – can differ by venue and lead to conflicting narratives that fracture images.[25,26]

3　*Social media discourse networks allow discussants to connect to and comment on others' commentary*: discussants comment without restraint or filter and can connect to and comment on others' commentaries. Discourse turbulence increases when trust does not exist and ambiguity prevails. Statements intended to demonstrate environmental responsibility, for example, can be interpreted, translated, and transmitted as greenwashing.[27,28]

4　*Within networks of connections, reputation damage becomes a contagion as critics comment on and share comments in ways that find organizations guilty by association*: reputational damage becomes a social network contagion when the damage suffered by a sponsoring organization (BP, for instance) spreads to the recipient (Tate Modern) of its philanthropy.[29,30,31]

5   *Social media users' communicative behaviors are motivated by their idiosyncratic identities and identifications:* network connections and demographics of readers, listeners, viewers of standard media influence how they receive and interpret stories about organizations' CSR. The same factors are amplified in social media as users' self-interested identities and identifications, which can be formed by their network connections, predict the stories they receive, and how they interpret, comment, and share such stories with others of similar identities and identifications. Whereas user bias is inherent to their discourse, organizations are expected to mute their self-interested identity and achieve a truly shared-interest identity to establish trust.[32,33]

6   *As they participate in discourse arenas, organizations seem more credible and trustworthy when they demonstrate commitment to responsible communication processes more than preferred outcomes:* corporate communications is traditionally goal oriented, but organizations' credibility becomes discredited if messages are interpreted as designed to achieve self-serving goals.[34]

7   *Social media allow power and knowledge to be blended and shared:* in an era sensitive to power/knowledge balance and authenticity, social media is a daunting means for collaboratively blending power and knowledge rather than using knowledge to achieve/exert power.[35]

8   *Social media arenas compel organizations to be transparent and authentic:* because social media arenas are multidimensional, multivocal, and consist of webs of connections, social media make it hard for organizations to hide, mask, or spin information or fake transparency and authenticity.[36] Stakeholders form watchdog webs (social media networks) to monitor organizational practices.[37]

9   *Discourse on social media is affected by visualized, simulated reality:* CSR social media discourse is full of pictures and video and other forms of visual communication that simulate reality. Multilayered and multitextual discourse can enhance and question organizations' authenticity, transparency, and rhetorical evidence. Pictures, videos, and graphics provide visual impact; seeing is believing. Users add this content and comment on it. Rhetorical evidence becomes more layered and complex in social media, because user groups' visual lexicons are enculturated into their identities and identifications.[38] The social media communicative model of participatory collaboration can simultaneously address group, organizational, and public frames (judgments, expectations, and points of view).[39]

Method: case studies of CSR

The three cases below illustrate the challenges of social media CSR. Case 1 (Netflix) examines business challenges executives face as they encounter critics of their CSR performance. Social media networks can grow to give voice to and empower like-minded CSR critics whose identities and interests are inadequately served by current business practices. Case 2 (Pig Raisers' CSR reputation management) demonstrates the peril of failing industry responses to critics' discussions on social media. Pro-industry voices talk to one another, as critics talk to one another by adding visual impact by showing lagoons of pig waste and "neurotic" sows. The CSR issue of environmentally sound and humane pork production plays out on networks that often are like trains passing in the night. Disputation over normative/evaluative (moral legitimacy) and cognitive/pragmatic CSR principles and practices occurs to the advantage of industry critics who convince companies to buy "humane" and environmentally responsible pork. Many voices within the industry and by critics become entropic and fracture an industry's image and voice rather than resolve the CSR controversy in favor of the industry. Case 3 (The IRATE 8) examines how universities, if reactionary rather than proactionary, can have their reputations challenged by activists armed with cell phones and the eternal memory of digital platforms. Even though student protest might be short-lived, it occurs by self-empowerment in social media by which a group of students reach extended audiences through social media networks. The cases emphasize the participatory turbulence social media creates in CSR communication.

Netflix: CSR expectations for closed captioning

In 2010, the National Association for the Deaf (NAD) filed suit against Netflix for failing to provide closed captions in its streaming videos. Arguing for higher CSR standards, the NAD claimed that the deaf and hard of hearing, approximately 48 million Americans, were unable to adequately use the streaming service, a violation of the Americans with Disabilities Act (ADA). The filing marked the beginning of CSR legitimacy gap court battles between Netflix and stakeholder groups.

This case especially demonstrates three of the nine social media challenges when CSR communications is seen through the lens of network theory. As mentioned above, network theory identifies a set of social actors and examines how relationships among them form a network. Each network provides the potential for an interactive, even dialogic, framework for tracking and examining what is achieved (or has failed to be achieved) by the presentation and analysis of information within a network.

The first challenge this case illustrates is that social media creates a turbulent network in which multiple stakeholders stated their expectations for Netflix's CSR.[40,41] Second, network relationships formed among individuals (e.g., stakeholders) on social media provided deaf and hard of hearing Netflix users the conduits – a network – to express their identity and find other stakeholders with whom they identify.[42,43] Third, the network created a web of watchdogs[44] that made Netflix's CSR efforts more transparent and illuminated its inauthentic efforts.

Prior to litigation, Amy Cohen Efron posted on her blog, *Deaf World as Eye See It*, her email conversation with Netflix representatives about getting closed captioning for *Wizard of Oz*. A longtime subscriber to Netflix, Efron simply wanted to enjoy watching *Wizard of Oz* as a streaming video, with closed captioning, with her friends and family. Initially, Netflix contended that the Microsoft Media Player, the mechanism for delivering instant videos, could not display closed captioning – a claim some contested. Efron's blog posts gained traction. Many in the deaf and hard of hearing community found it, shared it, and linked to it in their own posts. A network emerged as the issue became more visible to others who also shared the same expectation. Yet, Netflix abjured the issue and broadened the legitimacy gap.

Capitalizing on the cacophony emerging on social media networks, the NAD challenged the legality of Netflix's inaction. The network of conversations in the social media arenas moved the issue to the judicial arena, where Netflix was forced to respond. Netflix posed two arguments. Instead of maintaining the original argument that it was a technological issue, Netflix focused on the economic impact claiming that providing closed captioning would require considerable labor costs to manually write and rewrite programing code. Netflix unsuccessfully attempted to crowdsource the coding. Then, to get the lawsuit dismissed, Netflix claimed that as an Internet-only business it was outside the ADA's parameters of being a *physical* place of public accommodation. The NAD maintained that Netflix was not providing the same experience for deaf and hard of hearing viewers. In 2012, the two parties settled out of court; Netflix agreed to provide closed captioning on 100% of its streaming videos by 2014.[45,46]

Still, the CSR battle did not end for Netflix. Nor did the networked connections fade. The connections transitioned to a new topic. While Netflix promised to provide adequate captioning for 100% of its streaming videos, it failed to do so and took a number of shortcuts. One shortcut was poor quality captions. For instance, when a character spoke in another language, the caption would read, "Speaking in Japanese." Netflix and other steaming video providers took a shortcut by not captioning song lyrics. For deaf or hard of hearing users, the contextual information or mood state of characters is missed without song captions. Failing to meet stakeholder expectations, again, and in what some might consider an inauthentic way, Netflix inadvertently reactivated the web of watchdogs.

One watchdog catalogued numerous examples of the poor, sometimes humorous, captioning errors on a Tumblr page, while others contributed to or shared the Tumblr page. Collectively the stakeholders challenged Netflix and others to improve the quality of the captioning of all content including song lyrics. In late 2015, the Alexander Graham Bell Association for the Deaf and Hard of Hearing filed a class action lawsuit against Netflix and other media providers for not captioning song lyrics in their streaming videos. Their claim was that Netflix, again, did not provide a sufficiently similar experience to deaf and hard of hearing users – a violation of the ADA and earlier court rulings.

Networks of stakeholder groups – individuals and associations that have taken the issues to court – have kept the issues alive. Social media arenas have provided a space without gatekeepers (e.g., traditional media) for users to share their CSR criticisms of Netflix. In this space, individuals reinforced their identities and identified with others to solidify their CSR expectations. Netflix had multiple opportunities to hear and respond to these expectations in what might have narrowed the legitimacy and structural gaps. Instead, organizations like the NAD and the Alexander Graham Bell Association took the discourse from social media arenas to the judicial arena.

Overall, the Netflix case emphasizes how one person, or a limited number of persons, empowered by the network nature of social media can expand voice in such a way as to pressure a large organization to take a higher standard of CSR: that is, the one person wrote about this issue and others shared the issue and even more became aware of the issue. In short, the blog post flipped the switch that turned on that network. Hence, this case demonstrates how social media can be a turbulent and enduring arena that fractures a company's image and tests its CSR communications for transparency and authenticity. The networks of concerned stakeholders were an opportunity for Netflix to demonstrate its CSP. Just as these networks of stakeholders challenged Netflix's CSR and CSP, they *could* have championed Netflix's efforts. However, Netflix dismissed the legitimacy of these stakeholders' concerns and has not engaged the network. In fact, it does not address closed captions on its FAQ webpage or in its CSR communications, only in its help center. Thus, the network of stakeholders is left to fester and speak poorly of Netflix, when they could be promoting Netflix's CSR. Netflix's reputation management seems to be more reactive than proactive; it has received a 46 out of 100 score from CSRHUB.46.

Pork raisers' CSR reputation management

Although Americans like pork, most do not think much about pork production; but raisers and critics do – and passionately. CSR challenges have led to legislative and regulatory changes. Networks of critics as well as producers, industry groups, and agricultural scientists have developed. Pig producers' reputational and public policy challenges motivate their social media use, including attaching or linking to scientific documents that are online and easy to share on Facebook and Twitter. The conversation expresses identities and identifications relevant to this CSR challenge, including personal stories by producers and critics. The analysis that follows features two major themes of this CSR battle: pig waste material and crating to control sows' movement to conserve energy and maximize production.

Whether in traditional or social media, pig production CSR discourse is detailed, loud, pointed, values-driven, and visual, especially in terms of environmental impact, animal health, and humane treatment of sows. Raisers and critics believe that pigs deserve humane treatment; humanely raised and slaughtered pigs add value to society (even brand value for a nation as in the case of Denmark). For example, Estabrook[47] recently critiqued US pork production's use of growth hormones and steroids, the relative isolation of intelligent animals whose lives and growth are enhanced by activity and sociality, and environmental damage created by concentrated amounts of pig waste. Balanced reporting (in mediated controversies balance is always questionable), such as that by Bob Segall[48] of WTHR television, emphasizes that on this, as most stories, there are two (or more) sides as many voices engage. Such engagement is the essence of the structural and functional network relationships made easy on social media.

Several social media CSR communications challenges noted above are evident in this case, especially arena complexity, visually simulated reality, and visual lexicons (happy pigs versus sad, neurotic pigs). Pork industry discourse defends key issues by using raisers' personal comments and veterinarian science; it demonstrates that they understand the CSR virtue of strategic management changes to narrow legitimacy gaps. The industry seeks a single reputational image, but individual voices (critics as well as raisers) fracture the wholeness of that image when the industry does not speak with one voice. Critics' arguments are often experientially based on simulated reality and visual lexicons which counter industry (power/knowledge) claims that production practices conform to sound veterinarian science and environmental responsibility.

Pig waste

Pig manure really stinks and can damage the environment; both challenge CSR thresholds! Concentrated production facilities produce a lot of waste, and the EPA regulates how it is disposed. "Toxic manure lagoons" reek, according to Halverson.[49] When powerful sprayers broadcast the manure produced by thousands of pigs, the mist drifts. To live near large pig raising facilities requires tolerance and coping abilities.

Some industry spokespersons demonstrate empathy for neighbors, but one company, Smithfield Foods, fractures that reputational image. Operating 2,700 pork-producing factories in 12 states, it was recently purchased by a Chinese company, WH Group, to produce pork for China. Neighbors complain of odor, manure and sewage sludge, and "mist" that redistributes the waste beyond plant facility boundaries. The company has sought injunctions against complaining neighbors.

Pig waste is contained on-site through specially designed pig production barns, stored in waste fields near barns, and sprayed or otherwise dispersed onto the land of or near each farm. Some passes beyond farm boundaries and finds its way into streams. Prior to the purchase of Smithfield Foods, Maron[50] predicted an environmental quality battle. In 2013, Smithfield facilities produced 4.7 billion gallons of pig manure. In addition to the odor and environmental damage of that much waste, regulators worry about antibiotic-resistant bacteria, and the environmental impact of concentrated amounts of pig waste contained within the buildings, where it enters pigs' lungs, especially those of piglets. Studies reveal that people who live and work near waste lagoons suffer respiratory problems, including asthma. Concentrated farming requires ever-greater quantities of antibiotics.

Such CSR battles are less likely to occur in Denmark and Switzerland, for instance, which prohibit massive pig farms. Defenders of the industry in the United States claim that foreign countries have smaller populations to feed and therefore need less concentrated pig production. They argue that by concentrating production, as in the United States, producers have fewer neighbors. Techniques are in place or will be implemented to abate waste problems. Waste can be composted, a remediating technology industry leaders propose to solve this CSR problem.

Social media (see for instance social media reports through Pork Checkoff, www.youtube.com/user/PorkCheckoff) carry reputational presentations of proud owners showing off the construction of new pig facilities to contain and manage pig waste and advisory commentary on waste management. But critics point out that pig waste explosions result from gas build up. Internal circulation systems can spread disease among pigs housed in barns. A trade association, National Hog Farmer[51] offered advice on the matter: "Long-term manure storage (six months or longer) under the barn contributes significantly to barn emissions and air quality. Safety risks during pump-out and, more recently, manure foaming and explosion hazards led the advisory group to recommend that future designs should focus on storing manure outside of the building."

Environmental impact regulations change, thereby creating or expressing CSR stakeholder standards. Cheryl Day[52] wrote in *National Hog Farmer* about recent EPA and Army Corps of Engineers interpretations of the Clean Water Act based on Supreme Court rulings. Day's commentary featured comments by Bob Stallman, American Farm Bureau president: "This rule was never really about protecting water sources: It's about giving EPA and the U.S. Army Corps of Engineers the power to regulate any activity on the land that they choose to regulate." He further explained, "The definitions were so broad-reaching and vague about what would constitute a 'water of the U.S.' we pretty much deemed it a regulatory mechanism by which the EPA could effectively control land use."

Reactionary comments, identification battles, and a commitment to outcomes rather than fact and value-driven change can fracture CSR images and miss threshold levels of acceptability. Social media allow watchdogs to monitor industry performance.

Sow crating

Sow crating is another CSR flash point. Sows, averaging 300 pounds, are kept in 2-foot by 7-foot enclosures where they live most of their lives to give birth and nurture their litters. Social media carry pictures of "neurotic," sad sows chewing iron bars of crates that define their life-space (simulated reality and visual lexicons). An alternative is to pen sows into small groups allowing them more movement and contact with other sows. A third alternative is free range.

About sows' "isolation," Segall[53] quoted Dr. Thomas Parsons, director of the University of Pennsylvania School of Veterinary Medicine's Swine Teaching and Research Center: "One of the challenges we face is we don't have an accepted single measure of animal welfare. There's [*sic*] many different competing agendas." Proponents and critics go online to battle (power/knowledge) each other over animal welfare with text, pictures and video.

One rejoinder to critics is the happy pig raiser posting on social media how personal contact with sows makes them quite happy, even with some sows seeming to smile from the contact. Networks of simulated reality (pigs like personal contact) ostensibly "proves" raisers' and critics' cases while raising the question: if we want to see what makes sows happy, let them decide between crating and penning.

The Humane Society of America[54] condemns putting sows into "jail" where they lack social contact with nothing to occupy their minds. This story claims that better times are coming for sows. In 2012, McDonalds[55] condemned crating as "not a sustainable production system for the future." Costco, Oscar Mayer and food service giants Sodexo, ARAMARK, and Compass Group have pledged to stop buying gestation crate pork. Chipotle, Whole Foods, Cysco and Wolfgang Puck sell higher welfare pork. So, the pork battle has marketing and reputational consequences.

US pork producers use social media, including the PorkNetwork to combat critics' social media campaigns (www.porknetwork.com/pork-news/Pork-Checkoff-launches-social-media-blitz-267173801.html, accessed January 28, 2016). Supporters of crating claim that it reduces the number of piglets that are crushed by their mothers, keeps the mothers safe from dominant sows, allows for individual health and feed monitoring, and is not jail or isolation but allows limited, but safe, social contact.

Members of the industry use social media to provide text, pictures, and videos regarding the normative advantages of happy pig production. Pork Checkoff (www.pork.org/features/pork-producers-join-realpigfarming-mission/, accessed January 28, 2016) states its mission: "Consumers continue to have questions about how pigs are raised, and no one knows the answers better than pork producers. Pork Checkoff's social media outreach program is helping real farmers share real stories with consumers through #RealPigFarming." The American Association of Swine Veterinarians claimed, "Sows housed in groups at weaning and regrouped after insemination experienced higher stress than sows housed in individual stalls at weaning and mixed in groups after insemination." Pork Checkoff (www.youtube.com/user/PorkCheckoff) uses social media to present and track engagement on issues and to help producers present their cases.

The site presents power/knowledge and identity/identification commentary, such as that by Tom Burkgren, DVM, executive director of American Association of Swine Veteranians (www.youtube.com/watch?v=EoiOT3gO1HI, accessed April, 6, 2016):

> The outright ban of gestation stalls will not result in better welfare for sows, but it is sure to deprive farmers and veterinarians of the option to choose the type of housing that best fits a specific farm and production system. As swine veterinarians, it is up to us to continue to advocate, as much as possible, for the pig. Doing what is right for the pig never goes out of style. It is not an effort for promoting political or social change, nor is it a fund-raising or marketing campaign. Pig welfare is a fundamental duty and responsibility of the farmers and veterinarians who provide daily care of the animals entrusted to them. It breaks my heart to think that large corporations and animal rights organizations will dictate production practices on the farm, needlessly threatening the welfare of pigs and putting farmers out of business.

With such statements, the pork industry takes an issue management approach to CSR legitimacy battles in a digital platform.

The debate between pork producers and critics reveal support for all of the challenges of social media and CSR presented above. For examples of the primary challenges, consider that supporters and opponents of these issues are siloed and networked into same-opinion camps on social media. The industry's social mediated CSR communications features themes (with text, video, and pictures) to gain reach by being shared and retweeted. Expert opinions about facility design and operation improvements include pictures (visual simulation) of clean and happy pigs in the care of attentive farm personnel. Reputational messages conflict with anecdotal claims (including pictures and video) of sad (neurotic) pigs in cramped spaces and ponds of foul-looking pig waste.

Overall, this case on pork emphasizes how one interest (the pork industry) cannot control the discussion and its outcome regarding CSR because multiple networks and network users voice opinions, including nonverbal lexicons, that empower different standards of CSR and CSR performance. Even though some might argue that the network component for the pork industry is less tangible, the ramifications of the network are quite tangible – for this case is a collision of networks and practices. The case represents a collision of networks in the sense that the connections the pork industry has, and those connected to the pork industry, are limitless. The case represents a collision of practices too, because networks that may have been once separate are now coming together, and that collision is melding practices. Hence, what is evident in this case is that the pork industry engages the CSR expectations regarding its production practices by offering what it believes to be sound scientific arguments. Such CSR communications may be more of a holding pattern, trains passing in the night, than a legitimacy slam dunk, insofar as arguments can seem more self-justifying rather than societally responsible engagement. Such dialogue demonstrates that arenas enlarge the number of voices included, but they do not inherently achieve consensus. How pork is produced depends on the expectations of retailers and critics. Industry images fracture, because there is not one unified industry voice and because critics' messages have strong authenticity and transparency. Industry efforts to join power and knowledge is fractured by counter argument, and especially by the visual presentation of information that can be interpreted in ways that do not support industry preferences.

College/university cultures of diversity

University administrations welcome dialogue, but social media can shift the power/knowledge tone of discourse arenas when student activists make personal statements and include videos that justify their grievances and demonstrate their passionate engagement. Currently some students are challenging administrators to pay close attention to the mix, diversity and harmony of campus cultures. As protests occur and administrators soothingly promise changes, social media reporting can track and challenge such claims in ways that fragment an administrator's reputation.

Student activist thorns appear among the ivy of university reputation and identity building. Armed with cell phones and nimble social media access, students evaluate administrators' comments in layers and with links. Reputational damage can become a contagion as images, comments, critiques, and rejoinders fly throughout digital space across a campus, state, nation, and the globe. Such voices emphasize the participatory nature of social media expressions of identity, identification, and credible complaints that can reshape traditional power/knowledge relationships.

Student activists raise difficult questions, such as: What is the social responsibility of a university? Conventional answers include excellence in creative research and teaching and community outreach and service, even social uplift. While these may be traditional measures of university CSR, the groundswell of protest happening across the United States on college campuses makes it clear that students are challenging the CSR diversity and harmony of higher education. The latest layer of CSR criticism calls for universities to be welcoming places of inclusive excellence and serve as societal change agents. For instance, Libresco[56] reported that students from more than 50 universities across the country have issued demands protesting racism on their campuses. TheDemands.org (www. thedemands.org/) lists schools and links to the demands students of specific colleges and universities have made. Social media allow this arena to be functionally and structurally linked because of network capabilities and students' social media proficiency.

However general, such criticisms can become more specific and focused as flashpoints occur. One such student-inspired CSR campaign resulted from digital media advocacy by students at the University of Cincinnati (UC); in minutes they became widely known as The IRATE 8. The name stems from "the fact that black students comprise 8% of UC [in Cincinnati which is 44% black] and the frustration we have about our quality of life on this campus." Specific claims were sparked by the shooting death of Samuel DuBose, an unarmed black motorist killed by a UC police officer. DuBose is one of at least three black men who have died at the hands of or in UC police custody.

Seeking their own identity, identification, and CSR standards, The IRATE 8, stated their mission:

> to raise awareness of the experiences of Black students at the University of Cincinnati, and how they connect with the #BlackLivesMatter movement nationally. We are also moving to reform some of the institutionalized policies that result in a negative and unsafe experience for a number of Black students on the University of Cincinnati campus.

Frustration about police violence against black men and the sense of being treated unjustly as black students on the campus motivated The IRATE 8 to launch a multifaceted social media campaign against the University of Cincinnati.

On August 31, 2015, the IRATE 8 hijacked the University of Cincinnati's #THE-HOTTESTCOLLEGEINAMERICA – a hashtag then-President Santa J. Ono coined and which has garnered national attention.[57] The IRATE 8 used Twitter and Instagram, activist/digital social advocacy vehicles[58] to challenge UC and President Ono, whose image, ironically, is strongly tied to his social media presence. According to The IRATE 8 website (www.theirate8.com):

> On August 31, over 250 posts flooded the feeds of President Ono and the #hottest-collegeinamerica. The posts stated our unity statement:
>
>> We, the black leadership at the University of Cincinnati, stand in solidarity with each other and the greater community in a demand for change on this campus effective immediately.
>> To the family of Samuel Dubose we offer our support, our prayers, and deepest condolences. To the black students here at UC, we offer empowerment and our commitment to ensure the inclusion of and safety of black students on this campus. To the community we offer our service, our resources, and a bridge into the University of Cincinnati. To UC, we do not offer, but we DEMAND reform."

The students then posted on September 1, 2015 the following:

> On Monday, August 31st we took to social media to post our Unity Statement. In a little over 3 hours 240+ posts of our Unity Statement were posted to Instagram. We tagged Ono in the hopes that he would solidify the fact that black lives indeed, do matter. Okay he said it, now what? Now we make our campus reflect that statement. If UC truly believes that black lives matter, then why have multiple unarmed black individuals been killed by the University of Cincinnati Police Department? Why have the two officers who corroborated Ray Tensing's lies not been fired? Why are the retention and graduation rates lowest for black males and females on this campus? . . . Why is funding so scarce for initiatives and offices that directly support the black student population? Why is there such a large disparity in the percentage of black individuals in Cincinnati and the percentage of black students at UC?

Since September 2015, students have hosted a series of campus events including "teach ins" and speaker series. They launched YouTube videos explaining what it is like being a black student on Cincinnati's campus and "why" they are "IRATE." Contests between students and administrators test each other's commitment to engage in discourse to solve problems and make change. Universities admire free expression, but often combine power and knowledge to narrowly advance their images.

The demands of The IRATE 8 have been heard by President Ono and senior administrators. Ono assembled a task force to work in concert with representatives from The IRATE 8 to address each issue brought forth by the group. Ono set deadlines, many of which occur in 2016, for plans to be in place for implementation to resolve the challenges raised by The IRATE 8.

Social media networks allow the students to engage in discussions and to plan for the future. The IRATE 8 implements succession planning by recruiting freshmen to continue this advocacy as seniors graduate. The IRATE 8 tries to ensure that gains achieved via its advocacy can be permanently archived for instant retrieval. The IRATE 8's website (www. theirate8.com) chronicles each of its moves against the university, including its list of ten demands and the university's responses. The IRATE 8's digital advocacy demonstrates how powerful social media networks empower stakeholders to provide alternative voices that judge legitimacy and influence improved organizational CSR performance.

In sum, turbulent social media discourse critiques the university's legitimacy, transparency, and authenticity. Watchful eyes bring knowledge of events, opinions, and actions into public display. Social media create a simulated reality of calls for change; CSR-oriented change reshapes the brand of universities in general and UC in particular. Social media networks provide student critics, university supporters, and administrators the space to define and judge individual universities' legitimacy. CSR image and issue battles occur under the watchful eye of social media networks.

Overall, The IRATE 8 case emphasizes how grassroots activism gains presence and voice by enacting their own network, but more importantly, the case emphasizes how grassroots activism gains voice and presence by connecting it with an establishment network which tightens and narrows the social media discourse arena. Most importantly, this case demonstrates the import of grassroots activism to seize and connect with a network of events. Oftentimes, networks are thought of exclusively for their social connections, but this case is a prime example of how events are connected to one another. The events that occurred around The IRATE 8 are part of a large network of nationally known activist events. Individuals and other social actors make connections from previous events by drawing on the tactics, strategies and rhetoric from other events that can be associated.

Conclusions and final thoughts

This chapter embraces the CSR logic of societal productivity through self-governance: normative/evaluative (moral legitimacy) and cognitive/pragmatic (financial/material legitimacy) standards. Social media arenas facilitate networked discourses by which organizations and their critics and supporters contest organizational performance and legitimacy. CSR debates focus on cost-benefit ratios to determine whether an organization's contributions outweigh its multidimensional, contextual, and layered costs to society. The cases explored in this study lend support for this paradigm by demonstrating how external influences impinge on operations and organizational communication.

The three cases discussed above demonstrate how social media networks allow organizations to take public stands on CSR principles and accomplishments. They also allow otherwise relatively mute individuals and organizations participatory access to networks with powerful messages that critique organizational performance. In such arenas, organizational images can fragment. Discussants comment on commentaries. Discussion can create a contagion whereby critical voices attract like-minded voices. With the click of a mouse, discussants share verbal and visual (simulated reality) comments (lexicon). These comments have impact as they simulate reality relevant to the identities and identifications of like-minded persons. Credibility, transparency, and authenticity depend on the ability to sustain constructive deliberative processes rather than merely support predetermined outcomes. Thousands of voices seek to right imbalances of societal productivity.

This adversarial paradigm of CSR explains how and why social media allow organizations the means by which to reach targeted stakeholders, but also give stakeholders easy means of raising issues and making responses that can significantly increase the size and complexity of each discourse arena. In social media, timeframes of reporting, digesting, and responding become shortened, even virtually instantaneous and contagious. Corporate spokespersons can lose the trajectory of an issue if they do not respond quickly and adequately with communication and strategic management legitimizing corrections.

Specifically, the Netflix case demonstrates how social media allow otherwise mute but highly motivated voices to improve corporate behavior when they might never gain visibility in traditional media to challenge Netflix's performance. The voices attracted the attention of others that led to relationships, shared identities, and a collective effort to challenge (and re-challenge) Netflix. The pork raisers case demonstrates the power of social media and how it is used to address the need to continually refine farming policies and scientific justification to legitimatize CSR practices. Years of serious and committed pork production improvement can suffer a fractured image if it does not have coordinated management and effective CSR messaging to engage the network of stakeholders. Third, students who pack tools of social media activism in their pockets and can become connected to national networks of activism can challenge universities' CSR. A click of a camera and a post send images around a campus, nation, and world gaining critical awareness and shaping opinions of interconnected stakeholders in milliseconds.

Voices use social media to participate in CSR contests that judge organizational performance without the gatekeeping and clearinghouse functions of standard media; many voices compete to define legitimacy and determine whether legitimacy gaps exist. Stakeholders interrogate what strategic management changes may be needed to satisfy critical stakeholder expectations. Stakeholders also grant their support; they reward managements' initiatives and communicative investments if stakeholders deem such activities legitimate. Social media users do not merely find themselves attracted to discourse but become part of it.

CSR communications is issues and image based, relevant to reputation, and subject to opinions of those stakeholders whose comments center on the societal productivity model of legitimacy: costs versus benefits. In such arenas, order can quickly become turbulent and entropic.

Notes

1 Beliveau, B., Cottrill, M., and O'Neill, H. M. (1994). Predicting Corporate Social Responsiveness: A Model Drawn from Three Perspectives. *Journal of Business Ethics*, 13, 731–738.
2 Griffin, M. (2008). Visual communication. In Donsbach, W. (Gen. Ed.), *International Encyclopedia of Communication* (pp. 5304–5316). Malden, MA: Blackwell Publishing.
3 Golant, B. D., and Sillince, J. A. A. (2007). The Constitution of Organizational Legitimacy: A Narrative Perspective. *Organization Studies*, 28(8), 1149–1167.
4 Agle, B. R., Mitchell, R. K., and Sonnenfeld, J. A. (1999). Who Matters to CEOs? An Investigation of Stakeholder Attributes and Salience, Corporate Performance, and CEO Values. *Academy of Management Journal*, 42(5), 507–525.
5 Heath, R. L., and McComas, K. (2015). Interest, interest, whose interest is at risk? Risk Governance, issues management, and the fully functioning society. In Fra.Paleo, U. (Ed.), *Risk Governance: The Articulation of Hazard, Politics, and Ecology* (pp. 117–133). Heidelberg: Springer Dordrecht.
6 Suchman, M. C. (1995). Managing Legitimacy: Strategic and Institutional Approaches. *Academy of Management Review*, 20(3), 574.
7 Heath, R. L., and Waymer, D. (2015). Corporate social responsibility and corporate social performance: Neither binary nor righteous. In Stachowicz-Stanusch, A. (Ed.), *Corporate Social Performance: Paradoxes, Pitfalls and Pathways to the Better World* (pp. 189–210). Charlotte, NC: Information Age Publishing.
8 Sen, S., Bhattacharya, C. B., and Korschun, D. (2006). The Role of Corporate Social Responsibility in Strengthening Multiple Stakeholder Relationships: A Field Experiment. *Journal of the Academy of Marketing Science*, 34(2), 158–166.
9 Heath, R. L. (2011). External Organizational Rhetoric: Bridging Management and Sociopolitical Discourse. *Management Communication Quarterly*, 25, 415–435.
10 Dahlsrud, A. (2008). How Corporate Social Responsibility Is Defined: An Analysis of 37 Definitions. *Corporate Social Responsibility and Environmental Management*, 15, 1–13.
11 Capriotti, P. (2011). Communicating corporate social responsibility through the Internet and social media. In Ø. Ihlen, J. Bartlett, and S. May (Eds.), *The Handbook of Communication and Corporate Social Responsibility* (pp. 358–378). West Sussex, UK: John Wiley and Sons.
12 Colleoni, E. (2013). CSR Communication Strategies for Organizational Legitimacy in Social Media. *Corporate Communications: An International Journal*, 18(2), 228–248.
13 Fieseler, C., Fleck, M., and Meckel, M. (2010). Corporate Social Responsibility in the Blogosphere. *Journal of Business Ethics*, 91(4), 599–614.
14 Motion, J., Heath, R. L., and Leitch, S. (2016). *Social Media and Public Relations: Fake Friends and Powerful Publics*. London: Routledge.
15 Ott, L., and Theunissen, P. (2015). Reputations at Risk: Engagement During Social Media Crises. *Public Relations Review*, 41, 97–102.
16 Dawkins, J. (2004). Corporate Responsibility: The Communication Challenge. *Journal of Communication Management*, 9(2), 108–119.
17 Morsing, M., Schultz, F., and Nielsen, K. U. (2008). The 'Catch 22' of Communicating CSR: Findings from a Danish Study. *Journal of Marketing Communication*, 14(2), 97–111.
18 Colloeni, op cit., p. 241.
19 Schultz, F., Castelló, I., and Morsing, M. (2013). The Construction of Corporate Social Responsibility in Network Societies: A Communication View. *Journal of Business Ethics*, 115(4), 681.
20 Marin, A., and Wellman, B. (2011). Social network analysis: An introduction. In J. Scott and P. J. Carrington (Eds.), *The SAGE Handbook of Social Network Analysis* (pp. 11–25). Thousand Oaks, CA: Sage.

21 Yang, A., and Taylor, M. (2015). Looking over, Looking out, and Moving Forward: Positioning Public Relations in Theorizing Organizational Network Ecologies. *Communication Theory*, 25(1), 110.

22 Saffer, A. J. (2016). A Message-Focused Measurement of the Communication Dimension of Social Capital: Revealing Shared Meaning in a Network of Relationships. *Journal of Public Relations Research*, 28(3–4).

23 Aula, P. (2011). Meshworked Reputation: Publicists' Views of the Reputational Impacts of Online Communication. *Public Relations Review*, 37, 28–36.

24 Colloeni, op cit.

25 Gilpin, D. (2010). Organizational Image Construction in a Fragmented Online Media Environment. *Journal of Public Relations Research*, 22, 265–287.

26 Aula, P. (2010). Social Media, Reputation Risk and Ambient Publicity Management. *Strategy & Leadership*, 38(6), 43–49.

27 Beder, S. (2002). *Global Spin: The Corporate Assault on Environmentalism*. Devon, UK: Green Books.

28 Schultz, F., Utz, S., and Goritz, A. (2011). Is the Medium the Message? Perceptions of and Reactions to Crisis Communication via Twitter, Blogs, and Traditional Media. *Public Relations Review*, 37, 20–27.

29 *Tate* (2014). Corporate Social Responsibility. Retrieved from www.tate.opg/join-support/corporate-support/sponsorship/corporate social responsibility (accessed 12 February 2015).

30 Motion et al., op cit.

31 van der Meer, T. G. L. A., Verhoeven, P., Beentjes, H., and Vliegenthart, R. (2013). Public Framing Organizational Crisis Situation: Social New Media. *Public Relations Review*, 39, 229–231.

32 Barker, V. (2009). Older Adolescents' Motivations for Social Network Site Use: The Influence of Gender, Group Identity, and Collective Self-Esteem. *CyberPsychology & Behavior*, 12, 209–213.

33 Motion et al., op cit.

34 Motion et al., op cit.

35 Ibid.

36 Coombs, W. T., and Holladay, S. (2011). The Pseudo-panopticon: The Illusion Created by CSR-related Transparency and the Internet. *Corporate Communications: An International Journal*, 18(2), 212–227.

37 Besiou, M., Hunter, M. L., and Van Wassenhove, L. N. (2013). A Web of Watchdogs: Stakeholder Media Networks and Agenda-setting in Response to Corporate Initiatives. *Journal of Business Ethics*, 118(4), 709–729.

38 Griffin, op cit.

39 Keyton, J., Ford, D. J., and Smith, F. I. (2008). A Mesolevel Communicative Model of Collaboration. *Communication Theory*, 18(3), 376–406.

40 Aula (2011), op cit.

41 Colleoni, op cit.

42 Barker, op cit.

43 Motion et al., op cit.

44 Besiou, et al., op cit.

45 Kerr, D. (2012, October 11). Netflix and Deaf-rights Group Settle Suit over Video Captions. *CNET*. Retrieved from www.cnet.com/news/netflix-and-deaf-rights-group-settle-suit-over-video-captions/

46 *CSRHUB*. Netflix, Inc. CSR Ratings. (Retrieved from www.csrhub.com/CSR_and_sustainability_information/Netflix-Inc/ (accessed 1 February 2016).

47 Estabrook, B. (2015). *Pig Tales: An Omnivore's Quest for Sustainable Meat*. New York: W. W. Norton and Company.

48 Segall, B. (2015, February 23). *Crate Controversy: Pig Farmers Face Growing Pressure*. Retrieved from www.wthr.com/story/28182789/gestation-crate-controversy-indiana-pig-farmers-face-growing-pressure/ (accessed 21 January 2016).

49 Halverson, N. (2015, March 10). Toxic Manure Lagoons Stir Battle over Chinese-Owned Pigs in the US. *Reveal*. Retrieved from www.revealnews.org/article/north-carolinians-say-expansion-of-chinese-owned-pig-farms-stinks/

50 Maron, D. F. (2013, July 12). Defecation Nation: Pig Waste Likely to Rise in U.S. from Business Deal. *Scientific American*. Retrieved from www.scientificamerican.com/article/smithfield-pig-waste/

51 Miller, D. (2011, September 19). Designing 'Greener' Pit Barns. *National Hog Farmer*. Retrieved from http://nationalhogfarmer.com/facilities-equipment/designing-greener-pig-barns-0919/ (accessed 27 January 2016).

52 Day, C. (2015, September 17). WOTUS: A Mucky Mess. *National Hog Farmer*. Retrieved from http://nationalhogfarmer.com/environment/wotus-mucky-mess/ (accessed 23 January 2016).

53 Segall, B. (2015, February 23). Crate Controversy: Pig Farmers Face Growing Pressure. Retrieved from www.wthr.com/story/28182789/gestation-crate-controversy-indiana-pig-farmers-face-growing-pressure/ (accessed 21 January 2016).

54 *Humane Society of America* (2014, February 19). Crammed into Gestation Crates. Retrieved from www.humanesociety.org/issues/confinement_farm/facts/gestation_crates.html/ (accessed 21 January 2016).

55 *McDonalds*. Retrieved from www.aboutmcdonalds.com/content/dam/AboutMcDonalds/Newsroom/HUSUS%20McD%20gestation%20stall%20release%20FINAL.pdf/ (accessed 19 February 2016).

56 Libresco, L. (2015, December 3). *Here Are the Demands from Students Protesting Racism at 51 Colleges*. Retrieved from http://fivethirtyeight.com/features/here-are-the-demands-from-students-protesting-racism-at-51-colleges/

57 Riddell, R. (2014, February 28). 6 University Presidents to Watch in 2014. *Education Dive*. Retrieved from www.educationdive.com/news/6-university-presidents-to-watch-in-2014/232082/

58 Hon, L. (2015). Digital Social Advocacy in the Justice for Trayvon Martin Campaign. *Journal of Public Relations Research, 27*, 299–321.

Part 2

Toward symmetry and interactivity in digital corporate social responsibility communication

2.1 Exploring CSR communication patterns in social media

A review of current research

Urša Golob and Klement Podnar

Introduction

This chapter focuses on the role of social media in corporate social responsibility (CSR) communication by reviewing current academic research. Social media has recently become an important part of CSR communication. Commercial surveys show that expectations of consumers and other stakeholders regarding CSR communication in social media is rising and that companies are increasingly using social media to communicate about these topics. This reality is reflected in academic publications as well. On the one hand, they explore ideas about how CSR communication should emerge in social media; on the other hand, they want to determine whether these perspectives are indeed reflected in everyday interactions between companies and their stakeholders.

Alongside the expansion of CSR triggered by increasing expectations of stakeholders in a globalized world, the issue of CSR communication has emerged as an important focus of companies and stakeholders worldwide.[1] CSR communication reflects not only how firms communicate about CSR but also how the meanings of the messages are construed and shared among firms and stakeholders. The communication perspective therefore influences how stakeholders and organizations think about CSR.[2] KPMG's 2013 study on global CSR presented more evidence that CSR communication in different forms is on the rise and has become mainstream for more than 90% of the world's biggest corporations.[3] Data from a 2015 study[4] on CSR communication through corporate reporting also showed a significant increase in the quality of CSR reporting among the 250 biggest global companies. Another global study on CSR communication in 2015 conducted by CONE Communications[5] reported that CSR expectations of global consumers are rising; 88% are eager to hear about the CSR practices of companies. By seeking more options to engage in CSR-related behaviors, consumers are increasingly expecting to become partners in the CSR endeavors of companies and brands. Companies are also expected to find creative ways to communicate CSR and to approach consumers; the report suggests that many of the consumers are unwilling to spend their time searching for relevant information. Consumers prefer to obtain information about CSR from brief written summaries of reports, interactive websites, videos, and infographics.[6]

In addition to what is known from practice, several recent scholarly publications have shown that CSR communication is gaining more attention and is emerging as a field of study[7] including a variety of different topics. Researchers are concerned with questions of transparency in communicating, establishing dialogues with stakeholders, and the usage of communication tools, media, genres, and new media technologies to better reach and engage stakeholders in the communication process as well as to better negotiate and develop the meanings of CSR.[8]

Social media is growing more popular in CSR communication with stakeholders (and consumers in particular): Global studies on CSR communication have shown that from around 2010 onward, social media has been leading CSR conversations. The data show that three in five global consumers use social media with regard to CSR topics to learn about CSR, to voice their opinions, or to talk directly to companies about CSR issues.[9]

Social media, often characterized as new media that has a tendency to complement or even replace more traditional outlets, has emerged within the last decade and has started to change how people organize their lives and how they interact with each other.[10] These changes are emerging from a new set of "technological, economic, and socio-cultural mechanisms" and platforms labeled as *social media logic*, which refers to the "processes, principles, and practices through which these platforms process information."[11] Social media encompasses "a group of Internet-based applications that build on the ideological and technological foundations of Web 2.0, and that allow the creation and exchange of user-generated content."[12] It is also defined as two-way media that allows for two-way communication using self-presentations and dialogue.[13]

Social media has brought about new challenges for firms communicating with their stakeholders. Some of the established patterns of communication are no longer suited to and need to be aligned with the changed nature of communication and information processes. Social media appears to have caused a shift in the power held by corporations and has democratized corporate communications.[14] Communication about corporations and brands can happen without firms having control over the information available about them. The process can be initiated by other stakeholders rather than by corporations themselves, and it is up to firms to decide whether they want to be a part of these conversations.[15]

The participation of different actors thus seems to be intrinsic to social media, along with the connectivity that emphasizes the mutual shaping of users, platforms, and firms.[16] This further leads to a "mixture" of collective and *connective action* "in which formal organizations are losing their grip on individuals, and group ties are being replaced by large-scale, fluid social networks."[17]

These new networked conditions of social life are aligned with the emerging trends in CSR and CSR communication not just in terms of adjusting to the new communicative conditions of social media, but also concerning the recent attempts to construct and conceptualize CSR and CSR communication in the literature. Social media has opened up space for a variety of voices and discursive struggles on CSR that produce alternative CSR meanings that go beyond the instrumental "business case."[18] The alternative voices reflect "higher-order" interests of various stakeholders, forcing corporations to operate under a broader understanding of responsibility,[19] which demands a more interactive CSR discourse that is not necessarily dominated and controlled by the business community.[20] Taking these different voices about CSR into account, Scherer and Palazzo suggested a shift toward the social connectedness model, which uses a network logic to tackle CSR-related problems.[21] The social connectedness model goes hand in hand with the new stream of thought that poses the question of what communication does to CSR; thus, it sees CSR communication in "a broader sense as an arena where social standards and expectations for corporate social responsibility are constantly articulated, negotiated and developed."[22] This calls for a different perspective on CSR communication as well: from a control-oriented and persuasive one to a consensus-oriented, dialogic, and discursive or even conflicted, aspirational, and co-constructed one.[23] Social media operates as an organizing agent[24] and, thus, seems to offer a solid ground for implementing such a changed perspective of CSR communication.

The aims of this chapter are to map scholarly articles that deal with CSR communication in social media and to provide a framework for making sense of the different concepts and research foci that scholars use when writing about CSR communication in social media. Our review should matter both to scholars who wish to further advance this field of study and to practitioners who are interested in the practical aspects of social media for CSR communication.

The review that evaluates the body of literature on CSR communication in social media is thus based on two questions. First, what is the approach to understanding the role of social media in CSR communication, or what kinds of theoretical underpinnings do authors tend to use for examining CSR communication in social media? Second, what do empirical findings of published studies show on how social media is used for CSR communication in practice? Based on the review, we also explore the potential gap between the theoretical underpinnings and the empirical evidence on practical aspects of using social media in CSR communication.

Method

Our approach to the literature review was built on a summary of the main characteristics of the literature. Our analysis of CSR communication and social media was thematically driven and performed in two steps.[25] To explore the literature on social media and CSR communication, we used two content analysis techniques: co-word analysis (based on the co-occurrence of terms) and co-citation analysis. Concept-centric and co-citation analyses were performed using VOSviewer software, which combines the most advanced techniques for the field mapping process in different steps including concept selection and relatedness mapping.[26] The aim of co-word analysis this first step was to determine a set of themes and research foci in the area of CSR communication and social media. We then based our further analysis on this previously defined set of themes to explore the understanding of the nature and methods of CSR communication in social media.

Other thematic analyses in the CSR literature, such as the one recently done by Crane and Glozer,[27] considered the time component, the range of scholarly articles, and relevant search terms as criteria for including papers in the review. Setting the period was not particularly relevant to our analysis, since CSR communication in social media is a fairly recent research phenomenon. The first article on the topic listed in the Scopus database, which is the database used in our review, was published in 2009. Hence, we did not limit our search to a specific time frame. Rather, all the papers from 2009 onward were included in both steps of our overview. The literature search was conducted using the digital search engine Scopus, which offers one of the most comprehensive databases of journals with CSR and CSR communication papers. We searched for the terms "corporate social responsibility" or "CSR" and "social media" or "new media" in the title, keywords, or abstract. Our search on the Scopus database yielded 106 hits, from which we selected 40 papers that met all the inclusion criteria (see Appendix for a more detailed description of the methods and sample).

Themes and knowledge base of literature on CSR communication and social media

The focus of our preliminary literature overview is thematic (word co-occurrence analysis). However, to fully address our question regarding the approach to studying CSR communication in social media and to complement the thematic clusters, we also identified the points of connection in the corpus of literature on CSR communication and social media (co-citation analysis). This showed us to what extent and in what ways scholars writing about these topics use the same earlier literature that indicates their research foci.[28] We thus clustered highly co-cited documents to identify the knowledge base for CSR communication and social media.

The first two sub-sections that follow summarize the results on the themes and research foci in CSR communication and social media papers. In the subsequent sub-sections, we present a narrative synthesis of the papers based on the qualitative thematic analysis.

Thematic clusters

The relevant terms (each with at least two occurrences) were grouped into six clusters (see Figure 2.1.1). Three clusters (blue, red, and green) appear to be the most central ones. The more distant ones contain concepts that do not co-occur frequently with the concepts in the three central clusters.

The first cluster (red), *interactivity and outcomes of CSR communication in social media*, is reflected by terms such as "interactive channel," "interactivity," "CSR Twitter network," "corporate reputation," and "effectiveness." "Twitter" and "tweet" appear as relevant words, putting Twitter in the spotlight among social media. The words in the second cluster (green), such as "CSR issue," "CSR activity," "campaign," "online presence," and

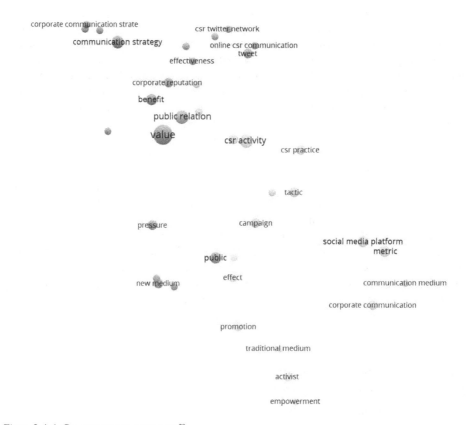

Figure 2.1.1 Co-occurrence term map[29]

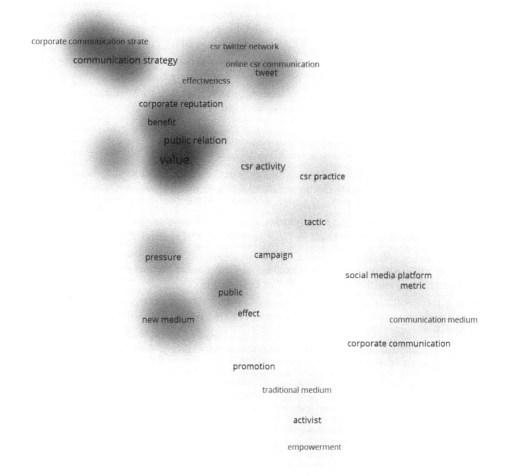

Figure 2.1.2 Cluster density map

"stakeholder relationship," connote *practical aspects of using social media in CSR communication*. Scholars using these terms research and discuss different aspects of actual CSR campaigns in social media. Figure 2.1.1 shows that the second cluster (green) also acts as a connection between the central clusters (1–3) and the more distant clusters (4–5). This has some merit: The terms in the second cluster reflect practical cases of CSR communication that are common to most publications, notwithstanding their conceptual focus (see Figure 2.1.2 for cluster density).

The third cluster (blue) has the highest density; concepts in this cluster are more closely grouped together compared with those of other clusters. Terms such as "benefit," "dialogue," "stakeholder expectations," "communication strategy," and "value" are related in a conceptual manner. Conceptually, this cluster most closely matches the idea of two-way symmetrical communication and the power of dialogue in social media. We labeled this cluster as the *value and nature of social media in CSR communication*.

Clusters 4 and 5 deal with the dangers and uses of social media in relation to CSR communication. Cluster 4 (yellow), labeled as *perils and facets of social media*, also deals with the idea of empowerment of stakeholders in social media compared with traditional media and the perils of activism and negative comments in social media. It is conceptually close to cluster 5 (pink), labeled as *uses of social media*, with such terms as "new medium," "public," "individual," "voice," and "pressure" also connoting how the non-corporate side makes use of social media in CSR communication. The last, most distant, and smallest cluster (turquoise) was left unlabeled, as it does not suggest any conceptual clarity.

Research foci

The results of the co-citation analysis of references with a citation threshold of at least three occurrences show three distinct clusters. After examining these clusters, we assigned them labels reflecting the knowledge base of the area they represent. These labels are as follows: *strategic and managerial focus* (cluster 1), *CSR reflections in new media* (cluster 2), and *communicative and dialogic potentials in CSR* (cluster 3; see Figure 2.1.3). The labels are not meant as strict denominators of all papers in a particular cluster, but they can give us an idea of the direction of the knowledge base in each cluster related to key concepts, epistemological roots, and methods that researchers build on.

The cluster with a *strategic and managerial focus* contains mainly references linked to management and marketing roots. These sources are considered fairly instrumentally oriented in their core assumptions and emphasize strategic elements of CSR-related thinking. They are organization centered and organization oriented and normally not focused on the notion of new or social media.

A common denominator of references in the second cluster, labeled as *CSR reflections in new media*, is the use of new (social) media in relation to CSR. This cluster addresses the issues of selecting messages and encouraging the engagement of stakeholders in new media. Finally, the last cluster reflects a strong communicative "research front" and is labeled as *communicative and dialogic potentials in CSR*. Most of the papers in this cluster are concerned with dialogic potential and two-way symmetrical communication in general and digital environments/social media in particular; they were published in communication or public relations journals. The last two clusters are very close to one another and thus conceptually similar (Figure 2.1.3).

Having set out thematic and knowledge-based clusters in the existing literature, we now turn to the thematically driven analysis of CSR communication in social media. Our synthesis in this next step is informed by the set of themes identified in the previous sections. Based on the results of the word co-occurrence analysis, we decided to combine clusters into three sets of relevant main themes that served as pointers of relevance for our thematic overview.

Clusters were joined based on a qualitative review of terms combined in each cluster as well as on the cluster density map (Figure 2.1.2), where clusters with greater conceptual proximity can be identified. The themes emerging from the combined clusters were as follows: the interactive nature and value of CSR communication in social media, uses and perils of social media for CSR communication, and practical aspects of CSR communication in social media.

These three themes that represent basic components for understanding the nature of CSR communication in social media were further informed by the findings of the

Figure 2.1.3 Co-citation analysis of cited references

co-citation analysis. Co-citation analysis helped us add aspects of the cognitive structure shared by publications on CSR and social media. When we compared these results with those of the co-word analysis, both "new media" and "communication" co-citation clusters appeared to be rather closely reflected in the themes we identified. This indicates coherence between the sets of publications from our corpus file that were used in co-word analysis and the references cited in these publications that were subjected to co-citation analysis. Such coherence suggests that papers sharing a focus on a set of common concepts also tend to share a focus on intellectual base literature.[30]

The third cluster, which shares references with a strategic and managerial focus, does not appear to be as closely reflected in the themes. However, it seems to be relevant as a point of departure for analyzing distinct topics (e.g., effects of CSR communication in social media) that a number of scholars in the social media and CSR communication literature seem to be focusing on.[31]

The interactive nature and value of CSR communication in social media

As suggested by the word co-occurrence analysis (see Figures 1 and 2), the theme focusing on the interactive nature of CSR communication in social media appears to be at the forefront of the papers we examined.

Interactivity refers to changes in "traffic": Within social media logic, one-way traffic is replaced with two-way traffic. The examined papers suggest that interactivity, a characteristic of social media platforms and Web 2.0 environments, can have a positive effect on the perceived quality and quantity of CSR-related messages. Eberle and colleagues, for example, suggested that interactivity offers an opportunity for establishing dialogue and has a positive impact on message credibility and perceptions of trust.[32] Furthermore, as Fieseler and Fleck noted, interactivity has the potential to connect seemingly marginalized users who collectively promote their issues and to put a wider range of social and environmental concerns on the agenda.[33]

Although interactivity also suggests that content is no longer just programmed and controlled by a central agent/provider and that users are also able to influence content, the agent can still to some extent retain control over the content by directly placing it in media. Thus, other favorable characteristics of social media examined within CSR and CSR communication, such as the possibility for companies to fully control the communicated content they place in the social media and an opportunity for users to better measure and demand authenticity of information, are also mentioned in the literature.[34]

The notion of symmetrical communication based on the relationship perspective of social media is addressed in several examined papers and emphasizes the role of users who are not viewed as a passive audience but rather as active co-creators of value.[35] Hence, they are co-creators of the content of CSR-related activities performed by companies.[36] The possibilities of co-creation offered by social media platforms supposedly lead to more credibility. Stakeholder-generated messages should be more effective and could break through the social media clutter. Such messages are perceived as more credible and therefore have greater potential for engaging stakeholders compared with company-generated messages.[37]

Several papers tend to theoretically discuss the potential of bidirectional and symmetrical communication channels offered by the new media platforms; they use previous literature on dialogue and symmetrical communication to support their claims about the importance of the normative ideal of symmetric communication.[38] There appears to be a tendency to idealize the notion of two-way symmetrical communication and the power of unrestrained dialogue in social media together with its communicative potential. Social media is perceived as a platform offering perfect conditions for CSR-related dialogue with stakeholders,[39] where communication is viewed as a mechanism for transparency.[40] Social media platforms are unique spaces for diversity and plurality, facilitating two-way communication without gatekeeping,[41] allowing motivated organizations and individuals to create and react to messages in new ways due to the networked and multidirectional nature of social media.[42]

Uses and perils of social media for CSR communication

The literature on CSR communication in social media is also concerned with how social media is used by different actors and the potential risks of social media for actors engaged in CSR-related communication online.

The authors of the examined papers agree that the use of social media ensures an immediate response from stakeholders.[43] Social media is thus seen as an enabler of stakeholder empowerment; as Lee and colleagues argued, stakeholders using social media are more aware and more willing to mobilize themselves and take action.[44] As Boyd et al. pointed out, this seems to be especially evident in the context of stakeholder (and particularly consumer) CSR activism.[45] Although the idea behind empowerment is positive and based on democratic (horizontal) communication, where everybody can collaborate in setting the agenda,[46] scholars are bringing attention to the dark side of social media for CSR-related activism as well. Social media can be dysfunctional in its impact on CSR activism.[47] One of the examined papers, for example, showed that CSR activists are sometimes faced with frustration over not having enough impact through social media or with the risk of being exposed to social judgment by other actors.[48] Possibilities of empowerment are particularly ascribed to micro-blogging platforms such as Twitter.[49]

Despite the seemingly democratic and egalitarian character of social media, which should enable greater empowerment of users on one side and opportunities for firms to directly reach stakeholders on the other, it seems that even in social media, actors (either corporate or individual) are increasingly faced with different mechanisms that platforms such as Twitter are putting in place. These mechanisms are used to select and advance more popular or powerful themes and promote particular users, while others often remain passive receivers of information.[50]

The idea of selecting and promoting certain themes or social media users is related to what van Dijck and Poell referred to as popularity, one of the four main strategies that define the social media logic.[51] The mechanism of popularity in social media explains how social media has become an extension of mass media. For example, journalists from news media often quote influential Twitter users alongside other "traditional" media celebrities.[52] Hence, with the ever-increasing amount of information flowing through social media, members of networks must gain attention by relying on other users to spread their message.[53] This is a challenge that even firms are facing with regard to their CSR communication. As Castelló, Morsing, and Schultz argued, there is evidence that social media users tend to rely on content provided via traditional media organizations online, as such sources are perceived as more neutral and credible.[54]

Discussing the potential uses and risks of social media for CSR communication further, Lee et al.[55] and Etter[56] referred to social media as potentially the best outlet that firms can use to advance their CSR-related issues. Following this line of thought, public endorsement and support have been established as prerequisites for making CSR communication successful.[57] It is crucial to have stakeholders as supporters and followers and to build an extensive social presence in social media to secure one-to-one attention and enforce positive relationships with stakeholders.[58] On the other hand, it has been suggested that companies must "let go" of exercising control over interactions and move toward nonhierarchical, non-regulated participatory relationships to secure legitimacy.[59]

Practical aspects of CSR communication in social media

Social media is mainly being used to build successful CSR communication campaigns[60] or to debate CSR issues.[61] Studies in the papers we examined revealed that firms tend to employ social media for CSR communication rather frequently, but they approach it mostly through one-way communication.[62] Firms remain at the basic levels of interaction with their stakeholders[63] and fail to fully engage with the networks of stakeholders; thus, firms do not exploit the potential of social media platforms.[64] Studies examining the character and openness of dialogue on CSR-related themes in social media have concluded that firms tend to "facilitate dialogue processes that have a low degree of openness."[65] The spaces for "real" collaboration and two-way interaction therefore remain empty. Companies appear to be more self-centered than dialogical, and even those who open up for dialogue and establish an interactive approach are not necessarily meeting stakeholders' social expectations.[66]

Studies have also pointed out that when stakeholders have mixed or negative feelings about CSR messages, this decreases message credibility and effectiveness.[67] The issue of message quality is thus of bigger concern than the quantity of messages that firms are sending to their stakeholders via social media.[68] One of the studies also raised concern about the quality of the messages and how messages should be construed; the study found that stakeholders do not engage in dialogues because they feel that companies fail to address CSR-related problems that are personally relevant to them.[69] Tailoring the CSR messages to be of interest to relevant stakeholders is thus related to the notion of "effectiveness" of CSR communication in social media. With regard to effectiveness, the studies presented mixed signals. One of the studies showed that social media rewards socially responsible firms with "greater output" for the "same amount of input" compared with traditional media.[70] However, the authors of another study argued that consumers tend to "discredit or even ignore positive CSR information shared by firms" because they believe that firms use social media primarily for promotional purposes.[71]

Despite the seemingly low impact of CSR communication efforts, the rewards and benefits of social media for companies are seen as purely instrumental. Rewards are related to the issue of control mentioned in several studies. As noted earlier, the majority of papers on social media and CSR communication that we reviewed based their ideas on theoretical assumptions of the dialogic nature of social media. However, idealistic assumptions such as openness, interaction, and transparency seem to prevent the companies from being more engaged in dialogues with stakeholders in practice.[72] The more the spaces for dialogue are open, the more companies face the risk of attracting criticism and endangering their reputations.[73] Companies therefore tend to communicate in a less interactive way, mostly sharing positive messages to boost their reputation.[74] By doing so, they use the so-called broadcasting strategy to communicate – they inform and promote instead of deliberate. The studies in the examined papers showed a general trend reflecting the reluctance and anxiety of the firms to be more open and interactive about CSR issues in the social media environments.[75]

Conclusions and managerial implications

CSR communication in social media is still on the rise, and the research on this topic is rather scarce. Nevertheless, the term "co-occurrence map" indicates that several themes on social media and CSR have been researched. Identified as distinctive themes, they represent potential conceptual building blocks of this particular area. We identified three relevant themes and research foci: the interactive nature and value of CSR communication in social media, uses and perils of social media for CSR communication, and practical aspects of CSR communication in social media. They are informed by three clusters of literature that scholars use to back up their arguments: The first contains literature representing the baseline for CSR research, and the other two represent literature strongly related to the communication research front, either emphasizing the different aspects of new media use for CSR communication or reflecting the communicative and dialogic possibilities of CSR communication.

Our overview suggests that the theoretical frameworks of the papers we examined view social media through idealized lenses and that a critical assessment of the complexity of social media logic and the changes affecting its strategies is mostly absent. The area of reference of most scholars remains the dialogic "ideal," a normative position that appears increasingly unsynchronized with the complex reality of social media logic as presented in the broader communication literature on social media.[76] The authors of some of the examined papers acknowledge that social media does have a few paradoxes that may hinder empowerment, dialogue, and efficiency of communication. However, these paradoxes are rarely mentioned and elaborated on. Hence, an idealistic perception of social media with regard to CSR communication is a starting point for most empirical research in this area, as shown by the examined papers.

Empirical studies on CSR communication in social media – most of which have been conducted on blogging[77] or micro-blogging platforms[78] – are mostly exploratory; while there are some exceptions, they do not offer in-depth insights about social media and CSR communication. The practice of CSR communication in social media shows that new communicative environments do not allow companies to shield themselves from stakeholder involvement.[79] However, companies need to consider the mechanisms of social media logic that influence the ways in which relationships are built. The question arises as to what ways both practice and research can challenge high expectations related to two-way communication and dialogue – conceptual ideals that are supposed to guide the reality of social media CSR communication. Although evidence gathered by one of the examined papers indicates that this could be possible when the approach to engagement is decentralized and control over communication flows is released,[80] several other studies show that relationships are exposed to rather strong tensions hindering dialogues. This suggests a reality different from the theoretical ideals of transparent and agenda-free dialogues.

Our review thus offers some insights for managers dealing with CSR communication in social media. One insight is related to the gap between theoretical propositions on how to use social media dialogically and effectively and the actual documented practices among companies and stakeholders in the literature. Managers and stakeholders need to be aware that the "optimal" use of social media for CSR communication depends on an understanding of social media logic with all its possibilities and risks, as well as an understanding of the participants in social media and the nature of CSR communication.

If communication is only seen as a means for *promoting CSR efforts* and *raising awareness about CSR actions*, then the pursuit of dialogic CSR is not necessarily consistent with these purposes. Our review shows that motives seem to be an important part of social media CSR conversations. In some studies, stakeholders expressed unwillingness to interact with companies whose messages were perceived as too promotional; dialogic CSR in such cases could be counterproductive. As one of the studies suggested,[81] fostering non-hierarchical and non-regulated conversations is not necessarily the ideal way, especially when a firm-centric perspective on communication prevails.[82] Although social media is characterized by loose ties between users and relatively decentered networks, not all online communication works this way. Companies can still build Facebook profiles and blogs and reproduce the logic of the organization-centered brick-and-mortar world while retaining control firmly in their own hands.[83]

When following this path, to enhance the effects of social media over traditional outlets, companies can rely on one of the characteristics of social media: automated personalization, defined as commercially and technologically steered activities using online content calibration based on supposed users' needs and interests and companies' interests.[84] This way, they can build so-called exchange relationships based on "interest matching" – both companies and users are prepared to offer benefits because they expect comparable benefits in return.[85] Such types of communication are legitimate and may be accepted by the users provided that corporate motives about CSR communication are transparent. When CSR messages are relevant and aligned with users' agendas, some users will be willing to engage in the co-production and sharing of content, motivated by personal expression.

Companies should also be aware that dialogic CSR does not necessarily relate to communication between a firm and other users, as suggested by some studies.[86] If *CSR communication* is seen as *constitutive* and formative for CSR,[87] companies could engage in dialogic communication as affiliates. This approach assumes a role as a facilitator of conversations, offering users "personal options in ways to engage and express themselves."[88] However, under this approach, companies also avoid branding the issues around themselves or their corporate brands, despite feeling the need to own the messages or control the understanding of participants.[89] Such an approach to CSR communication in social media means less control over the conversations. This does not suggest that organizations are not allowed to pursue their own agendas through communicating via social media. However, they need to become equal members of issue networks and suppress the need for projecting strong agendas or their corporate brands in favor of enabling personal engagement.[90] Such an approach to CSR communication can mean more success in terms of sharing and impact; actions and content can be distributed widely across social networks.[91] Nevertheless, managers need to be aware that using social media for the sole purpose of "opening up" spaces for CSR-related conversations is insufficient for companies to be perceived as dialogic and transparent; deliberative conversations also need to perform the function of determining individual and shared outcomes.

Future research directions

The literature review in this chapter revealed a gap between practice and the theoretical propositions of the dialogic ideal that most of the examined papers presented in their theoretical frameworks, as several studies showed how this ideal is not really practiced and how CSR communication meets reluctance and distrust among social media users. Thus, CSR communication in social media is caught between idealized belief and reality. One theoretical implication for CSR communication research is thus to acknowledge this tension and interpret it using a more realistic picture of the power of social media as a platform for symmetrical two-way CSR communication. Theoretical underpinnings of CSR communication in social media could also benefit from a refinement based on current and future empirical research. They could focus on addressing the unspoken premises of CSR communication in social media, such as motives, (hidden) agendas of social media users, and users' different roles in such interactions. They could also explore the notion of connective action[92] as a suitable base for advancing CSR communication as a constitutive force for CSR.

Although the analysis presented in this chapter offers sufficient insight into the dynamics of the literature on social media and CSR communication, we recommend that future research widens the scope of the literature to include book chapters and other publications not accessible in Scopus and World of Science. A structural approach to determine additional sources for review could be used based on a "go backward – go forward" approach, examining the references of selected papers to enlarge the corpus file of publications.

Appendix
Methods and sample

For our literature search, we searched for the terms "corporate social responsibility" or "CSR" and "social media" or "new media" in the title, keywords, or abstract. The initial search yielded 106 hits. Two researchers simultaneously performed a refinement of the results. The three main reasons for excluding papers were as follows: 1) the paper was not published in a peer-reviewed journal, 2) the language was not English, or 3) the content was irrelevant (similar keywords but the paper did not contain social media and/or CSR content). Although some book chapters were also published covering these topics, we excluded them from further analysis because only a few of them are indexed in Scopus. The final selection resulted in 40 publications.

Our search was not time-restrained because social media is a relatively recent phenomenon in the academic literature. The first paper on CSR and social media in a peer-reviewed journal was published in 2009; none were published in 2010 and 2011, and two were published in 2012. In 2013, 15 papers on the topic were published, followed by six in 2014, 13 in 2015, and three by March 2016. In all, papers on CSR and social media were published in 21 different journals. The most important outlet for these topics seems to be the *Journal of Business Ethics* (11 papers), followed by *Public Relations Review* (5 papers) and *Journal of Communication Management* (3 papers). *Corporate Communications* and *Journal of Business Research* each published 2 papers, while the rest of the journals each had only one paper covering this particular topic.

For our analysis, the VOSviewer program was used. The program allows for the creation of two-dimensional concept maps where the frequency of occurrence of a concept is defined by the label size and distance. The distance represents the relatedness between terms based on the number of co-occurrences of terms in the corpus file; thus, the terms that frequently co-occur are positioned closely to one another in the map. VOSviewer also groups terms by clusters, which represent sets of terms that are considered conceptually related to one another. Words of the same color in the term map belong to the same cluster.

In creating the concept map, we selected terms with at least two occurrences. Based on relevance scores computed by the software, 60% of those terms were selected (131 terms). Relevant terms selected by the natural language processing algorithm of VOSviewer were then edited. We deleted terms that were not appropriate for our analysis goals (e.g., general or ambiguous terms with low relevance, section titles of structured abstracts). The final map documents 38 terms.

The co-citation clusters were constructed from the reference lists of 1,806 cited references in the examined publications, taking into account all documents that were cited more than three times, which was our citation threshold. Out of these documents, pairs that co-occur relatively frequently in the reference lists of the examined publications were then selected for clustering.

The aim of the qualitative analysis was to see in what ways and to what extent social media logic is reflected on the theoretical and empirical levels of CSR communication. We used a purposive method based on a thematically driven approach to select the articles. Thus, only those papers that are directly related to these aspects were included and examined more closely.

Notes

1 Du, S., Bhattacharya, C. B., and Sen, S. (2010). Maximizing Business Returns to Corporate Social Responsibility (CSR): The Role of CSR Communication. *International Journal of Management Review*, 12(1), 8–19.
2 Elving, W. J., Golob, U., Podnar, K., Ellerup-Nielsen, A., and Thomson, C. (2015). The Bad, the Ugly and the Good: New Challenges for CSR Communication. *Corporate Communications: An International Journal*, 20(2), 118–127.
3 KPMG. (2013). *Corporate Responsibility Reporting Survey 2013*. Retrieved from www.kpmg.com/au/en/issuesandinsights/articlespublications/pages/corporateresponsibility-reporting-survey-2013.aspx/ (accessed 23 May 2014).
4 KPMG. (2015). *Currents of Change: The KPMG Survey of Corporate Responsibility Reporting 2015*. Retrieved from http://assets.kpmg.com/content/dam/kpmg/pdf/2015/11/kpmg-international-survey-of-corporate-responsibility-reporting-2015.pdf (accessed 14 January 2016).
5 CONE Communications. (2015). Press Release: *CONE Releases the 2015 CONE Communication/Ebiquity Global CSR Study*. Retrieved from www.conecomm.com/2015-global-csr-study-press-release (accessed 14 January 2016).
6 Ibid.
7 Golob, U., Podnar, K., Elving, W. J., Ellerup Nielsen, A., and Thomsen, C. (2013). CSR Communication: quo vadis? *Corporate Communications: An International Journal*, 18(2), 176–192; Crane, A., and Glozer, S. (2016). Researching CSR Communication: Themes, Opportunities and Challenges. *Journal of Management Studies*, 53(7), 1223–1252.
8 Crane and Glozer, op cit.
9 CONE, op cit.
10 van Dijck, J., and Poell, T. (2013). Understanding Social Media Logic. *Media and Communication*, 1(1), 2–14.
11 Cited on p. 5 in: van Dijck and Poell, op cit.
12 Cited on p. 60 in: Kaplan, A. M., and Haenlein, M. (2010). Users of the World, Unite! The Challenges and Opportunities of Social Media. *Business Horizons*, 53(1), 59–68.
13 Smith, B. G. (2010). Socially Distributing Public Relations: Twitter, Haiti, and Interactivity in Social Media. *Public Relations Review*, 36(4), 329–335.
14 Kietzmann, J. H., Hermkens, K., McCarthy, I. P., and Silvestre, B. S. (2011). Social Media? Get Serious! Understanding the Functional Building Blocks of Social Media. *Business Horizons*, 54(3), 241–251.
15 Ibid.
16 van Dijck and Poell, op cit.
17 Cited on p. 748 in: Bennett, W. L., and Segerberg, A. (2012). The Logic of Connective Action. *Information, Communication & Society*, 15(5), 739–768.
18 Scherer, A. G., and Palazzo, G. (2011). The New Political Role of Business in a Globalized World: A Review of a New Perspective on CSR and Its Implications for the Firm, Governance, and Democracy. *Journal of Management Studies*, 48(4), 899–931.
19 Scherer and Palazzo, op cit.
20 Burchell, J., and Cook, J. (2006). Confronting the "Corporate Citizen" Shaping the Discourse of Corporate Social Responsibility. *International Journal of Sociology and Social Policy*, 26(3-4), 121–137.
21 Scherer and Palazzo, op cit.
22 Cited on p. 494 in: Christensen, L. T., and Cheney, G. (2011). Interrogating the communicative dimensions of corporate social responsibility. In Ø. Ihlen, J. Bartlett, and S. May (Eds.), *Handbook of Communication and Corporate Social Responsibility*. Malden, MA: Wiley-Blackwell, 491–504.

23 Schultz, F., Castelló, I., and Morsing, M. (2013). The Construction of Corporate Social Responsibility in Network Societies: A Communication View. *Journal of Business Ethics*, 115(4), 681–692.

24 Bennett, and Segerberg, op cit.

25 Grant, M. J., and Booth, A. (2009). A Typology of Reviews: An Analysis of 14 Review Types and Associated Methodologies. *Health Information & Libraries Journal*, 26(2), 91–108.

26 Lee, C. I. S., Felps, W., and Baruch, Y. (2014). Mapping Career Studies: A Bibliometric Analysis. *Academy of Management Proceedings*, 1, Academy of Management. doi:10.5465/AMBPP.2014.284

27 Crane and Glozer, op cit.; Golob et al., op cit.; Scherer and Palazzo, op cit.

28 Braam, R. R., Moed, H. F., and Van Raan, A. F. (1991). Mapping of Science by Combined Co-citation and Word Analysis I: Structural Aspects. *Journal of the American Society for Information Science*, 42(4), 233.

29 Figure 2.1.1 shows a co-occurrence term map in VOSviewer. Each term or concept is a circle. The size of the circle indicates the frequency of the word, the proximity of one word to another represents the degree of relatedness of the two concepts and the color is a cluster to which the word conceptually belongs.

30 Braam, op cit.

31 Ibid.

32 Eberle, D., Berens, G., and Li, T. (2013). The Impact of Interactive Corporate Social Responsibility Communication on Corporate Reputation. *Journal of Business Ethics*, 118(4), 731–746; Haigh, M. M., and Wigley, S. (2015). Examining the Impact of Negative, User-Generated Content on Stakeholders. *Corporate Communications: An International Journal*, 20(1), 63–75.

33 Fieseler, C., and Fleck, M. (2013). The Pursuit of Empowerment Through Social Media: Structural Social Capital Dynamics in CSR-blogging. *Journal of Business Ethics*, 118(4), 759–775.

34 Lyon, T. P., and Montgomery, A. W. (2013). Tweetjacked: The Impact of Social Media on Corporate Greenwash. *Journal of Business Ethics*, 118(4), 747–757.

35 See for example: Etter, M. (2014). Broadcasting, Reacting, Engaging – Three Strategies for CSR Communication in Twitter. *Journal of Communication Management*, 18(4), 322–342; Korschun, D., and Du, S. (2013). How Virtual Corporate Social Responsibility Dialogs Generate Value: A Framework and Propositions. *Journal of Business Research*, 66(9), 1494–1504.

36 Korschun and Du, op cit.

37 Ibid.

38 Etter, 2014, op cit.

39 Bonsón, E., and Ratkai, M. (2013). A Set of Metrics to Assess Stakeholder Engagement and Social Legitimacy on a Corporate Facebook Page. *Online Information Review*, 37(5), 787–803.

40 Stohl, C., Etter, M., Banghart, S., and Woo, D. (2015). Social Media Policies: Implications for Contemporary Notions of Corporate Social Responsibility. *Journal of Business Ethics*, 1–24.

41 Castelló, I., Etter, M., and Årup Nielsen, F. (2015). Strategies of Legitimacy Through Social Media: The Networked Strategy. *Journal of Management Studies*, 53(3), 402–432.; Etter, op cit.

42 Whelan, G., Moon, J., and Grant, B. (2013). Corporations and Citizenship Arenas in the Age of Social Media. *Journal of Business Ethics*, 118(4), 777–790.

43 Lee, K., Oh, W. Y., and Kim, N. (2013). Social Media for Socially Responsible Firms: Analysis of Fortune 500's Twitter Profiles and Their CSR/CSIR Ratings. *Journal of Business Ethics*, 118(4), 791–806.

44 Ibid.

45 Boyd, D. E., McGarry, B. M., and Clarke, T. B. (2015). Exploring the Empowering and Paradoxical Relationship Between Social Media and CSR Activism. *Journal of Business Research*, 69(8), 2739–2746.

46 Colleoni, E. (2013). CSR Communication Strategies for Organizational Legitimacy in Social Media. *Corporate Communications: An International Journal*, 18(2), 228–248.

47 Boyd et al., op cit.

48 Ibid.

49 Colleoni, op cit.

50 van Dijck and Poell, op cit.

51 Ibid.

52 Ibid.

53 Romero, D. M., Galuba, W., Asur, S., and Huberman, B. A. (2011). Influence and passivity in social media. In Gunopulos, D. et al. (Eds.), *Machine Learning and Knowledge Discovery in Databases, Part III: European Conference, ECML PKDD 2010, Athens, Greece, September 5–9, 2011, Proceedings (Vol. 6913)*. Berlin, Heidelberg: Springer, 18–33.

54 Castelló, I., Morsing, M., and Schultz, F. (2013). Communicative Dynamics and the Polyphony of Corporate Social Responsibility in the Network Society. *Journal of Business Ethics*, 118(4), 683–694.
55 Lee et al., 2013, op cit.
56 Etter, M. (2013). Reasons for Low Levels of Interactivity (Non-)interactive CSR Communication in Twitter. *Public Relations Review*, 39(5), 606–608.
57 Lee et al., 2013, op cit.
58 Ibid.
59 Castelló et al., 2015, op cit.
60 Fieseler, C., Fleck, M., and Meckel, M. (2010). Corporate Social Responsibility in the Blogosphere. *Journal of Business Ethics*, 91, 599–614.
61 Illia, L., Romenti, S., Rodríguez-Cánovas, B., Murtarelli, G., and Carroll, C. E. (2015). Exploring Corporations' Dialogue About CSR in the Digital Era. *Journal of Business Ethics*, 1–20.
62 Etter, 2014, op cit.
63 Bonsón and Radkai, op cit.
64 Fieseler and Fleck, op cit.
65 Cited on p. 18 in: Illa et al., op cit.
66 Colleoni, op cit.
67 Eberle et al., op cit.
68 Lee et al., 2013, op cit.
69 Illa et al., op cit.
70 Lee et al., 2013, op cit.
71 Cited on p. 7 in: Boyd et al., op cit.
72 Etter, 2013, op cit.
73 Etter, 2014, op cit.
74 Colleoni, op cit.
75 Etter, 2014, op cit.
76 van Dijck and Poell, op cit.
77 Fieseler and Fleck, op cit.
78 Colleoni, op cit.; Etter, op cit.
79 Etter, 2014, op cit.
80 Castelló et al., 2015, op cit.
81 Illa et al., op cit.
82 Boyd et al., op cit.
83 Bennett and Segerberg, op cit.
84 van Dijck and Poell, op cit.
85 Kelleher, T., and Miller, B. M. (2006). Organizational Blogs and the Human Voice: Relational Strategies and Relational Outcomes. *Journal of Computer-Mediated Communication*, 11(2), 395–414.
86 Lee et al., 2013, op cit.
87 Golob et al., op cit.; Schultz et al., op cit.
88 Cited on p. 760 in: Bennett and Segerberg, op cit.
89 Ibid.
90 Bennett and Segerberg, op cit.
91 Ibid.
92 Bennett and Segerberg, op cit.

2.2 The death of transmission models of CSR communication

Ralph Tench and Mavis Amo-Mensah

Introduction

The literature suggests that companies have been too slow in adjusting to the changing circumstances in the technological realm and to the innovations that are ultimately relevant in today's world of business.[1] A recent comprehensive review of the multidisciplinary areas of CSR communication by Crane and Glozer for example revealed that the literature has mainly focused on "communication to audiences from companies rather than with them".[2] In the context of online CSR communication, studies have found that companies predominantly adopt a transmission approach, where the web is constructed in a way that seeks to influence stakeholders.[3] Thus, companies primarily control the content of information and how this should be disseminated or accepted by potential stakeholders. Significantly, the so-called 'linguistic turn' in twentieth century philosophy drew into focus more theoretical and methodological approaches in interdisciplinary research.[4] Within this domain, the traditional transmission models of communicating CSR have undergone profound shifts towards a more constitutive approach, which views communication as a social construction or meaning negotiation.[5] In its essence, constitutive perspectives permit both companies and their stakeholders to have greater input into CSR related activities.[6] Moreover, the global economic crises coupled with various scandals like Enron and the latest Volkswagen emissions deception have generally undermined public trust and confidence in business. The 2016 Trust Barometer, for instance, affirms that businesses around the world continue to suffer a general mistrust.[7] According to the Edelman report, trust is below 50% for the broader population in more than 60% of the countries surveyed.[7] The report further revealed that 80% of those surveyed have CSR expectations of companies to improve communities besides increasing company profits. Responding to such demands, many companies both large and small have made CSR an integral part of the way they do business in an attempt to improve their public image.[8,9] Research suggests that, not only are companies striving to adopt sustainable business practices, they are also faced with the complexity of communicating their efforts in a variety of ways.[10,11]

On the other hand, the role of dialogue in the implementation of CSR communication practices has greatly been emphasized in the literature.[5,11,12,13,14,15] Indeed, broader technological developments have given rise to new forms of media which presents unique opportunities for companies to engage with their stakeholders on a daily basis. Although, the use of the web has been rapidly growing, and many researchers have analyzed online CSR communications content in different corporate contexts,[3,16,17,18,19,20,21,22,23,24] the many potential opportunities of this medium for effective two-way dialogue and exchange about social and environmental issues have not yet been fully maximized.[3,21]

As Isenmann and Lenz succinctly describe, "the evident benefit of internet use for integrated, efficient, dialogue-oriented, hypermedia-featured, interactive and customized environmental reporting have hardly been exploited yet".[25] According to Isenmann and Lenz, online push and pull technologies provide an efficient tool for companies to adapt their CSR communications to the diverse information requirements of all target groups.[25] In other words, the web proves useful by enabling customized and adept information that supports multiple stakeholders' preferences, engagement and dialogue.[26] The rapid rise of Web 2.0 and the resulting 3.0 signal the beginning of the death of transmission models of CSR communication. The question is, are CSR communication strategies changing with the current technological revolution? This chapter seeks to challenge CSR communication practitioners and researchers still living in the transmission world. It argues that recent technological trends foretell the end of one-way communication, making it imperative to refresh current CSR communication approaches. We also highlight strategies that companies can adopt to improve their online CSR engagements. The chapter has implications for companies in terms of media for communicating CSR, stakeholder engagement processes and for researchers in their attempt to devise models or concepts for CSR communication. In the remainder of the chapter, we first provide an overview of the interrelationship between CSR, communication and web environments as a context to understanding constitutive perspectives in the literature. We then discuss how a constitutive approach shapes online CSR disclosure by contrasting it with the traditional monological or one-way form of communication. A report on our empirical research is presented next, after which some conclusions are drawn.

Corporate social responsibility, communication and the internet

In this section, we discuss the nature of the relationship between CSR and its communication on the web to provide sufficient background information that helps to illuminate constitutive perspectives in the literature. While some scholars describe CSR as actions that go beyond legal requirements,[27] others view it from the notion of sustainable development,[8] corporate citizenship[28] or the triple bottom line.[29] On the other hand, CSR has also been examined in terms of the 'business case' impact[30,31] or the dimensions that characterize the concept including economic, social, environmental, stakeholder and voluntarism.[32,33] Whichever perspective is used to describe companies' responsibilities towards society, research suggests concerns in these areas continue to grow.[34] A survey by Cone Communications[35] shows the importance global consumers attach to companies' responsible activities and how their being informed about such actions influence their perceptions and behaviors.[11,36] On the other side, the literature suggests that CSR is 'problematic'[8] due to the lack of agreement of how the concept should be specifically defined.[37] It is observed that the context-specific nature of CSR, along with evolving practices has contributed in part to the debates surrounding CSR.[38]

   The controversial nature of CSR has led to the growing challenges in its implementation and the further confusion surrounding the strategies to communicate such achievements.[39,40] Studies have revealed that companies face many difficulties in determining how to disseminate and manage CSR information due to growing skepticisms.[41,42] The literature suggests that most companies spin around their communications to look more committed to their responsibilities than they actually are, which often tends to raise stakeholders' doubts about companies' real intentions when CSR efforts are communicated.[43] Accordingly, companies face a "general perception of hypocrisy with the paradoxical consequences that sincerity of company managers' motives are questioned even when their CSR efforts are genuine".[44] The problem, of course is that, although stakeholders must definitely be told the CSR story to make them understand companies' actions, this must be done carefully in a way that resonates with the various groups to make it a fruitful experience.

The dilemma for companies is that overemphasizing CSR activities may undermine their credibility.[45,42] Morsing et al. capture this paradoxical nature of CSR communication as 'catch 22' and propose two communication frameworks to help companies achieve favorable reputation: the expert CSR communication process, where specialists and experts become the main communicators of CSR through the second framework which is the 'endorsed' communication process.[42] In Morsing et al.'s view, stakeholders are more inclined to believe messages from third parties rather than from corporate sources.[42] Although relying on intermediaries is useful, studies suggest that unless stakeholders are engaged in the CSR communication process, efforts about communications are likely to be perceived as mere acts of greenwashing.[40] The literature suggests various strategies to limit the difficulties confronting companies in skeptical environments. While some scholars propose companies align their CSR messages with their main objectives,[41] others have developed evaluation frameworks that aim to show inconsistencies between corporate CSR rhetoric and reality.[44] On the other hand, others have argued for CSR as 'aspirational talk', where disparities between talk and action are seen as important resource to trigger critical developments in CSR communication.[46]

In spite of stakeholder attributions, "Communication is inescapable – it is implicated in CSR and business strategies".[10] Interactive communication about CSR is essential to changing stakeholders' attitudes, since it clarifies organizational decision-making processes to resolve any ensuing controversies and disagreements. Stakeholder involvement techniques from the onset of CSR communication processes and joint decision-making help to build trust, confidence and mutually beneficial relationships that can minimize, if not curtail, negative stakeholder reactions.[47] At the same time, there is considerable evidence that higher levels of genuine CSR disclosure lead to good corporate reputation which can further benefit a company in many ways including enhancing customer loyalty, employees' commitment and purchase decisions.[12,39,48]

Today, new technologies have offered a myriad of ways for communication, and as part of the overall CSR communication strategy, the online medium is seen as an unavoidable platform. As already noted, there has been valuable work on CSR in web environments. Studies have, for instance, shown that the web is one of the most popular and widely used channels for CSR communication.[49] Some recent studies have also examined information in annual, sustainability and other non-financial reports that companies make available online,[50] as well as social networking sites such as Facebook and Twitter,[12,49,51,52,53] All these studies demonstrate there is an increasing interest in the use of online media to discuss socially responsible initiatives. Park et al.[54] examined how Fortune 500 companies use the web to disseminate their social behaviors particularly focusing on the major rhetorical themes adopted. The study found that although the companies communicate to their stakeholders via online, economic and corporate-centric orientations were dominant similar to the finding by Crane and Glozer.[2] Recent findings from the European Communication Monitor[1] also suggest that, only a few companies (21%) have incorporated big data platforms, albeit the majority of the respondents surveyed believed this technology will have a dramatic impact on the communication profession in the future. The study, which mirrored perspectives from 2,710 communicators across 43 countries, further revealed that, many communication professionals required analytic capabilities to derive relevant information from big data. Similarly, Adam and Frost compared how three countries: Australia, Germany and the United Kingdom use the website as a medium for sustainability reporting highlighting the advantages and challenges that arise when using such a medium.[3] Moreno and Capriotti[17] explored how CSR issues are presented and organized on the websites of companies listed on IBEX 35 in Spain. The study found that CSR reporting practices are higher, however, more in-depth and interactive engagements with stakeholders were lacking. The survey of Birth et al. in the Swiss context suggests online communications about CSR need to be effective.[16] McCorkindale[53] examined how the top 50 Fortune 500 companies use their Facebook pages to talk about CSR and found that, only few of the companies (less than a quarter) effectively utilized this medium. In the Indian context, Chaudhri and Wang[19] found that very few leading companies proactively use the web as a tool to present their social engagements. According to the most recent KPMG survey[34] on trends in corporate responsibility reporting, 92% of the world's largest 250 companies now issue reports up from 12% in 1993, and since 2013, there has been a steady growth in the number of companies producing non-financial information. The report also suggests corporate reporting has become a mainstream practice (among many of the 45,000 companies studied), guided by the Global Reporting Initiative (GRI), which came through as the leading standard for reporting. The KPMG[34] report, however, indicated that companies could strengthen non-financial reporting through stakeholder engagements. In a related development, a global survey of websites of 150 leading companies showed that less than 50% provided opportunities for engagement.[55]

These findings are consistent with many other recent research that suggests that constitutive approaches have had limited impact in the CSR management literature.[6,56] The opportunity for collaboration, particularly in online CSR communication, remains fairly underdeveloped; there is limited stakeholder inclusion, thereby reducing communication processes to a one-way dissemination of information.[57] From company perspectives, insights from the studies above reveal various limitations in companies' abilities to utilize the many probable advantages of the web in stakeholder dialogic communication. At the same time, very few studies in the academic literature focus on how web-based stakeholder dialogue can play an integral part in a mutual consideration of CSR disclosure.[58] Many of the studies focus on the degree of information on CSR activities in online environments,[22] the readability of such information,[59] how accessible it is to locate CSR information,[3] the range of CSR issues addressed,[20,60] and how CSR issues are organized and structured.[18,61] Taken together, an organization's reputation as reflected in all areas of the business includes its representations on the web in terms of not only structure, placement, readability and content, but also opportunity for interaction,[5] which means that companies that focus on joint decision-making processes may derive much greater value than those that only provide their stakeholders a say.[62]

As noted earlier, the significance of the web as an ideal tool for communicating CSR primarily lies in its possibility to enhance interactive dialogue, offering companies the chance to move beyond static self-presentations.[39,63] Along with these, the web is also associated with many other advantages that include its 24/7 availability,[24] versatility,[25] incredible reach[17] and powerful influence in agenda setting, in terms of which CSR related content to make salient, particularly when there is the need for instantaneous communication with stakeholders.[19] Given this, we argue in line with recent scholars who view CSR communication as a constitutive process. Through the framework suggested, we aim to stimulate constitutive perspectives in online CSR discourses, and contend that web environments make such an approach more profound for an engagement in stakeholder dialogue. We highlight this approach by contrasting it with its opposing stance, the traditional monological communication process, which is discussed in the following section.

A transmission view of CSR communication

This section examines transmission models and highlights its limitations in contemporary CSR communication. There are still ongoing debates in the management literature between classical economic theorists claiming, on one hand, that organizations should seek to maximize profits for shareholders in their social responsibilities[64,65] and stakeholder theorists, on the other hand, that as far as companies CSR is concerned, claiming that there are other groups who have legitimate claims of the firm.[66,67,68] Typically, the transmission view of communication is defined by the classical economic theory, and it is deeply rooted in one of the earliest communication models developed by Shannon and Weaver, where communication messages basically move from a sender to a receiver.[69] Essentially, communication is described in terms of the 'conduit metaphor',[70] which presupposes meanings are transmitted in a linear informational approach only giving sense to receivers.[11] Such perspectives conform to positivist approaches to CSR where profit is the primary motivation for business, operated within the domain of 'enlightened self-interest'.[71] Most research that exemplifies this stance aim to substantiate the claim that the adoption of CSR leads to financial benefits,[72,73] with communication about CSR perceived as a way of influencing stakeholders' attitudes and behaviors in terms of the reactions of information.[5]

In web environments, transmission orientations manifest within the earliest conventional static form of the web, referred to as Web 1.0, where companies basically predict the demands of stakeholders and make the required information online available.[74] Typically, companies who recognize CSR information from the old Web 1.0 view use 'push' mechanisms such as emails, advertising, CSR links, e-newsletters, press releases and reports. Along these lines, messages about CSR are formulated and 'pushed' to stakeholders in a unidirectional process with little room for updates.[75] Some scholars have classified mainstream media such as TV and radio as 'push' content, with claims that new internet-based media beat traditional modes as stakeholders' primary source of information.[63] Longitudinal data from the European Communication Monitor[1] reinforce digital growth and traditional demise in communication related practices. Various studies, for instance, also show a significant drop in global newspaper revenue and circulation.[76] To survive, many newspaper industries (e.g., *The New York Times*, *The Washington Post*, *Daily Mail*) now have online presence to be able to reach stakeholders through digital platforms. Television is also gradually being taken over by online video content. All these developments show that one-way Web 1.0 CSR communication is no longer a viable option, but the more current active Web 2.0 based applications with 'pull' strategies that allow users to co-create and share information, along with the emerging Web 3.0, described as the semantic web which promises more compelling innovations for the future.[75,77]

Many scholars have criticized one-way transmission models for a failure to recognize the complexities of communication systems in reality.[6,11,56,57] Golob et al., for example, note that such conceptualizations are 'functionalistic'[5] and reflect a view of CSR communication that has ability to "conceal and confuse".[78] Schultz et al., on the other hand, observe more specifically that these "corporate goal-driven self-presentations" neglect the dynamics of communication "for the constitution of CSR and legitimacy".[56] What these authors suggest is that, functionalist viewpoints only lead to short-term results and sometimes negative consequences that may create difficulties for companies to maintain legitimacy. Clearly, the dominance of this view has contributed to the lack of corporate ethical practices in recent times, as witnessed from the Volkswagen case.[79] The limitations in transmission models lie in what Ashcraft et al. describe as 'partial truth' one-way of understanding communication.[78] Currently, most CSR communication scholars agree on a constitutive approach on the basis that stakeholders today want stronger forms of engagements and more symmetrical relations with companies, rather than 'strategic' motives.[80] This alternative view justifies a major priority in CSR communication which co-creates information in a way that balances the interests of both stakeholders and organizations. The next section discusses constitutive approaches in more detail and demonstrates how companies can make use of the constitutive or two-way capabilities of the web.

A constitutive approach to online CSR communication

Constitutive approaches, as explained earlier, have long established traditions in the 'linguistic turn', which recognizes language as the underling system of the real world.[4] This line of argument is grounded in the transactional model of communication,[81] primarily focusing on dialogue.[80] For such thinkers, communication constructs social realities[82] where organizational objectives and outcomes are determined in such communicative events.[78] Based on the CSR communication literature, two main constitutive schools of thought can be highlighted: the first orientation is held by scholars,[10,83,84] who draw insights from the social constructivist stance.[85] From a social constructionist orientation, CSR communication is jointly produced by companies and their stakeholders in an on-going interactive process.[56] The second constitutive theorizing[6] is influenced by the Communication Constitutes Organization (CCO) perspective, an emerging area of CSR communication, which is founded in organization studies (see for example[78,82,86,87,88,89] for critical discussions). The basic premise of the CCO perspective is that communication is the most important element of organizations.[89] Koschman et al.[26] note that in the CCO approach "actors use symbols and interpretations to create the meanings that coordinate and control activity and knowledge". In spite of the various manifestations of these two perspectives, advocates agree on the basic premise that the relationship between organizations and their stakeholders is mutually constitutive in dialogue.[10,56,82] Proponents also provide various views to challenge functionalist or transmission conceptions (see Table 2.2.1), drawing largely on the stakeholder concept which clearly justifies notions of CSR and its communication strategies.[13,15,68]

Table 2.2.1 Transmission and constitutive approaches to CSR communication

Characteristic	Functionalist approach (Web 1.0)	Constitutive approach (Web 2.0 and beyond)
Conceptualisation	messaging	interaction
Objective	transparency	co-creation
Metaphor	conduit	connectedness
Channel	monological	dialogical
Perspective	sequential	holistic
Application	content-driven	user-generated
Content	pushed	pulled

(Source[5])

In contrast to the shareholder view, stakeholder theory suggests that companies must be accountable to a wide range of groups,[66] and the legitimate ones ought to experience some form of corporate benefit as a direct result of companies actions, often in collaborative agreements.[56] These stakeholder groups ought to be identified and prioritized based on their characteristics, their relationship to the firm and to the situation, and in line with the communication strategy to be adopted.[90] In summing up the arguments and concepts in the stakeholder literature, Donaldson and Preston[67] argue that, the normative base of the theory is morally tenable and seeks to restrict as much as possible self-serving company behaviors as reflected in functionalistic perspectives. Constitutive approaches are also shaped by ideas from Weick,[91] which in the context of online CSR communication, helps companies to negotiate communication by combining both sense-giving and sense-making processes for desired results.[11,84, 92]

From constitutive perspectives, companies negotiate CSR communication processes with their stakeholders through concurrent input and output processes (See Figure 2.2.1). The dynamic nature of the web assures a democratic process of dialogue where stakeholders such as customers, employees and others can play an active role in a mutual realization of CSR communication goals. In particular, the new version of online applications, or Web 2.0 technologies, has many innovative features that encourage company–stakeholder interactions via blogs, social networks, podcasts, chat rooms, wikis, Google Docs or other web services and collaborative websites.[74]

For example, its live online chat system create unique avenues for various company groups from different locations and countries to simultaneously interact on CSR through text-based messages and, in some cases, audio or video calls. Companies can also share videos on CSR with stakeholders through channels like YouTube. Through crowdsourcing, companies can obtain feedback from stakeholders to improve CSR communication processes. These opportunities for co-creation promote transparency and help to overcome the many challenges associated with the conventional offline CSR communication approaches. A global survey by McKinsey & Company shows that companies that strategically adopt Web 2.0 applications gain significant benefits from the expenditure they plunge in the web: 69% of the over 1,700 managers surveyed in different industry sectors

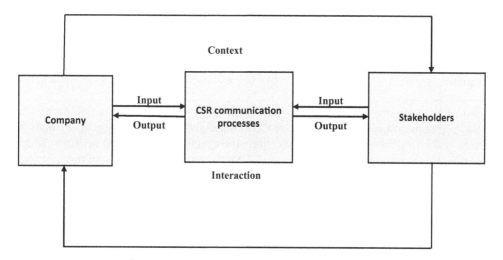

Figure 2.2.1 A constitutive framework of CSR communication

revealed significant value generated in various relevant areas of business, including better relationships with stakeholders.[93] The literature, however, suggests that the evolving nature of the new online technologies and the many options guaranteed can be overwhelming for companies.[74] Consequently, an understanding of how these technologies work and in what way or manner they can be effectively incorporated into CSR is necessary to derive successful outcomes. In this regard, a clear strategy that determines the purpose for CSR communication, users and their characteristics, scope in terms of the platforms and open directives that facilitate a mutual culture of collaboration is critical to engage stakeholders the right way.[39]

In a review of various dialogic frameworks O'Riordan and Fairbrass[14] outline four mutually determining factors that support a comprehensive and systematic stakeholder dialogue: context (operating environment of companies and their stakeholders); events (importance of key events within the context); stakeholders (the nature and aspirations of various groups) and management response (the myriad ways in which stakeholders' expectations are potentially addressed). Pedersen,[15] on the other hand, identifies four dimensions that determine the effectiveness of stakeholder dialogue in CSR decision-making processes. According to Pedersen,[15] successful implementation of participatory dialogue necessitates consciousness, capacity, commitment and consensus. First, an organizational consciousness reflects a thorough knowledge and awareness (consciousness) of key CSR communication issues and how they are embedded in all facets of the business. This is to avoid ad hoc initiatives that become dissociated from company's daily operating practices[13] given the various complexities encircling how best to engage in stakeholder dialogical communication and the fact that an ideal dialogue is not also always achievable.[80]

In the second dimension, Pedersen[15] notes that, it is practically difficult for organizations to co-create effective CSR plans and strategies without the needed available resources. In his view, companies that have the necessary capacities (in terms of organizational and human resources) in developing good relationships with stakeholders make a great difference in their stakeholder relationships. Nevertheless, these resources may not be enough to secure companies the possibility of engaging successfully with various individuals and societal groups. Genuine commitment (of financial and non-financial resources) from management and other employees in companies' stakeholder interactions is important when dealing with CSR issues as these have crucial effects in the implementation of stakeholders.[11] Finally, there is also the need for consensus which Pedersen[15] describes as "the level of harmony between the parties involved in the dialogue and between those parties and the implementing agents". Due to corporate deception in recent times, however, robust periodic assessments and evaluation of CSR communication strategies and programs ought to be done to determine the extent to which these meet anticipated outcomes.[13]

From a constitute view, it is important to know much more about the context in which communication is embedded, as O'Riordan and Fairbrass[14] suggest, in order to better understand the processes that determine the overall success of such activities. Much research shows context affects approaches to CSR communication and resulting relationships with stakeholders.[60,94] The implicit and explicit CSR approach which Matten and Moon use to describe practices in the European and American contexts respectively show how institutional frameworks affect social responsibility issues and outcomes, and for that matter the media for communicating such activities.[16,94] Visser also shows how the nature of CSR practices differ in developed and developing country contexts.[95] To this end, both Ashcraft et al. and Craig have suggested a pragmatic interpretation of constitutive approaches to open up different conceptualizations in unique contexts.[78, 96] Thus, constitutive orientations should be recognized as a 'meta model' or an 'umbrella' concept that helps to examine the different ways online CSR communication can be co-created and how these lead to novel developments in unique regions.[78,96] In this regard, contextual considerations can either inhibit or promote companies' ability to effectively use the web as a channel to convey socially responsible issues. In the section that follows, we seek to demonstrate practical challenges companies face applying modern methods of communication using our research from a developing country perspective as a case in point.

Illustrative case: the Ghana Club 100

In this section, we briefly report on our exploratory study which aimed at providing initial insights of how top companies in Ghana (companies listed on the Ghana Club 100) communicate their CSR activities online. Specifically, we employed content analysis looking at which social issues are described on companies' web pages and how these are discussed. Our research concentrated on the Ghana club 100 (GC100), which is an annual ranking of top 100 Companies in Ghana. Criteria for eligibility onto the GC100 include size, return on equity and growth where a weighted average is determined.[97] CSR is also incorporated as part of the criteria, with discretionary awards given to companies who have performed exceptionally in this area.

The study was based on all the companies listed on the 2013 ranking, compiled by the International Accounting firm Ernst & Young. GC 100 companies are acknowledged for corporate excellence and, therefore, have the potential to communicate about their social issues.[34] The 2013 ranking comprised companies in 15 different industry sectors. The websites of 21 companies could not be located despite repeated attempts to locate these. Four other companies (multinationals) were excluded from the study since they did not have local Ghanaian websites (each had a main website for all operating counties). The websites of the final sample of 75 companies were content analyzed consistent with previous studies,[60] excluding links to reports made available online. Drawing on the literature and prior studies, we found it important to develop and categorize our own set of themes (economic, social, ethical, environmental, philanthropic and stakeholder) based on information on corporate websites for the dimensions of CSR communication, and using an unweighted binary scoring scheme to calculate the presence or absence of these categories.[17] Through qualitative content analysis procedures, we coded and classified CSR information on websites into the themes identified. Two independent coders were used to ensure the trustworthiness of the study.[98]

In summary, the high number of companies without websites shows that these companies did not have the most basic core of an online presence. Obviously, the companies have not yet adapted to the technological realm or see the web as the right channel for CSR communication. As a World Bank Development Report notes, many communities in Africa have an adaptation challenge in terms of the new technological developments, with some plagued with limited internet access.[99] Observations from our study also indicated that although top companies in Ghana showed an awareness of the importance of communicating CSR, web CSR contents were very limited and unstructured, consistent with previous researches by Hinson et al. and Hinson.[100, 101] Only 32 (43%) of the 75 companies had fully devoted sections on their websites for CSR, 12 (16%) companies did not discuss any CSR issue, while 31 (41%) detailed information about CSR in other sections such as the 'About us' column, general news and/or press, including references to CSR commitments in mission and vision statements. Companies' use of the website was significantly lower, since CSR issues were not sufficiently elaborated. Cumulatively, only a few of the companies 5 (8%) had several pages of CSR information (11 pages and beyond), with as many as 36 (57%) having just up to a page of information on CSR. This finding contrasts the studies by Capriotti and Moreno[18] and Esrock and Leichy[21] who found high CSR disclosures of companies' websites. Generally, it appeared the web was not used to prominently address social and environmental issues in Ghana. Thus, companies still relied on Web 1.0 techniques, without taking advantage of the current technological revolution in their CSR communication agendas. The study also found that, in many of corporate websites, stakeholder engagement strategies were inadequate, in terms of how to prioritize and reach out to a range of groups and using feedback systems, suggesting various limitations in dialogic communication. Our findings suggest that the use of the web to communicate CSR in Ghana is still at a developing stage, since many of the companies tended to be more passive in their use of this medium. To this end, corporate managers in the top 100 companies in Ghana ought to improve and make effective use of the web in their CSR communications online.

The study basically highlights the need for companies to consider the role of new media for CSR communication. The global big data market, the changes in lifestyle, the rise in smartphone usage, the increasing prevalence of social networking sites, the range of broadband services, the time spent online and the enhanced web browsers, all indicate Web 2.0 technologies have come to stay.[74,77] Nokia, Blackberry, Eastman Kodak, Motorola are all great examples of companies whose failure to embrace changing technology and consumer trends have been displaced. In 2013, Microsoft acquired Nokia, a company which was the mobile industry leader in the early 2000s. Similarly, Eastman Kodak was very slow to adjust to the digital photography advancements and filed for bankruptcy in 2012. In a related development, Netflix's new approach in the video rental industry led to the collapse of the then leading video rental retailer, Blockbuster. These trends show that stakeholders require companies to be adaptive and constantly innovate. Companies like Google, Amazon, Netflix, Facebook, Apple and YouTube have seen tremendous progress in that direction. Of course, a shift to interactive virtual technologies will not be effortless. But, ultimately, a better understanding of these new technologies could prompt improvements in companies' CSR communication.

Conclusions

Clearly, rapid technological innovations have spelled the death of transmission models of CSR communication. It is therefore time companies shifted their focus to dialogic perspectives. This chapter has provided an overview of constitutive approaches and how this shape online CSR communication. We emphasize that the web has many benefits that companies can exploit in their CSR interactions in an attempt to gain moral legitimacy in the wake of the many cynical stakeholder attributions. The current Web 2.0 and the resulting Web 3.0 technologies create avenues for all stakeholders to hold companies answerable for adhering to their economic objectives in a more responsible and ethical manner.[63] Our research findings from Ghana also provoke thoughts about the importance of context in the choice of media for CSR communication and the need for companies to adapt their strategies to reflect the pace of technological developments. Indeed, given the complexity of CSR communication issues as we have seen, no peculiar kind of channel could be adequate. The success of companies' communications largely lies on how well several channels are combined and tailored to meet the needs of specific stakeholders. Of course, traditional media (e.g., prints such as annual and sustainability reports and broadcast such as radio) are valuable, since some stakeholders still rely on these conventional sources. In practice, there may be more overlaps across the traditional and the new modes of communication, and given the inherent benefits of each, we suggest these should be seen as complementary. It is quite obvious, however, that with the ongoing technological developments, the new forms of media are receiving increasing attention and becoming the dominant way information is shared, given the myriad intrinsic and extrinsic benefits. The future, therefore, is for companies to transform mainstream media into 'pull' content. We suggest that the constitutive assumption as a 'meta theory'[96] deserve further research attention in CSR communication. The foregoing discussions show that it can contribute to the effectiveness of companies' interactions with their stakeholders, which makes it imperative to develop more theoretical arguments. The use of the web to engage in direct dialogue with stakeholders also requires further examination as well as an assessment of the areas that impact on effective company–stakeholder relationships. Credible communications about social issues emanate from the company itself through the means and strategies it seeks to convey these messages.[11] We emphasize that CSR communication pays off only if companies have genuine communications and have also done substantive CSR projects. When companies' online CSR communication largely reflect the reality, only then can it present successful factors or advantages for companies.

Notes

1 A. Zerfass, P. Verhoeven, A. Moreno, R. Tench, and D. Verčič, *European Communication Monitor 2012: Challenges and Competencies for Strategic Communication: Results of an Empirical Survey in 42 Countries*, Brussels: EACD/EUPRERA, Quadriga Media Berlin, 2016.

2 A. Crane, and S. Glozer, "Researching Corporate Social Responsibility Communication: Themes, Opportunities and Challenges", retrieved from www.online.wiley.com/doi/10.1111/joms.12196/epdf (accessed April 10, 2016), 2016.

3 C.A. Adams, and G.R. Frost, "Accessibility and Functionality of the Corporate Website: Implications for Sustainability Reporting", *Business Strategy and the Environment*, 155 (2006): 275–287.

4 R.M. Rorty, *The Linguistic Turn: Essays in Philosophical Method*, Chicago: University of Chicago Press, 1967.

5 U. Golob, K. Podnar, W.J. Elving, A.E. Nielsen, C. Thomsen, and F. Shultz, "CSR Communication: Quo vadis?", *Corporate Communications: An International Journal*, 18/2 (2013): 176–192.

6 D. Schoeneborn, and H. Trittin, "Transcending Transmission: Towards a Constitutive Perspective on CSR Communication", *Corporate Communications: An International Journal*, 18/2 (2013): 193–211.

7 Edelman, "Edelman Trust Barometer: Annual Global Survey", retrieved from www.edelman.com/insights/intellectual-property/2016-edelman-trust-barometer/, (accessed January 28, 2016), 2016.

8 G. Aras, and D. Growther, "Corporate Sustainability Reporting: A Study in Disingenuity?", *Journal of Business Ethics*, 87 (2009): 279–288.

9 S. Arvidsson, "Communication of Corporate Social Responsibility: A Study of the Views of Management Teams in Large Companies", *Journal of Business Ethics*, 96/3 (2010): 339–354.

10 Ø. Ihlen, J.L. Barlett, and S. May, "Corporate Social Responsibility and Communication", In Ø. Ihlen, J. L. Barlett, S. May (Eds.), *The Handbook of Communication and Corporate Social Responsibility*, West Sussex, UK: Wiley, 2011, 1–22.

11 M. Morsing, and M. Schultz, "Corporate Social Responsibility Communication: Stakeholder Information, Response and Involvement Strategies", *Business Ethics: A European Review*, 5 (2006): 323–338.

12 D. Korschun, and S. Du, "How Virtual Corporate Social Responsibility Dialogs Generate Value: A Framework and Propositions", *Journal of Business Research*, 66/9 (2013): 1494–1639.

13 F. Maon, V. Swaen, and A. Lindgreen, "Designing and Implementing Corporate Social Responsibility: A Framework Grounded in Theory and Practice", *Journal of Business Ethics*, 87 (2009): 71–89.

14 L. O'Riordan, and J. Fairbrass, "Corporate Social Responsibility (CSR): Models and Theories in Stakeholder Dialogue", *Journal of Business Ethics*, 83/4 (2008): 745–758.

15 E.R.G. Pedersen, "Making Corporate Social Responsibility (CSR) Operable: How Companies Translate Stakeholder Dialogue into Practice", *Business and Society Review*, 11/2 (2006): 137–163.

16 G. Birth, L. Illia, F. Lurati, and A. Zamparini, "Communicating CSR: Practices Among Switzerland's Top 300 Companies", *Corporate Communications: An International Journal*, 13/2 (2008): 182–196.

17 M.C. Branco, and L.L. Rodrigues, "Communication of Corporate Social Responsibility by Portuguese Banks: A Legitimacy Theory Perspective", *Corporate Communication: An International Journal*, 11/3 (2006): 232–248.

18 P. Capriotti, and A. Moreno, "Communicating Corporate Responsibility Through Corporate Web Sites in Spain", *Corporate Communications: An International Journal*, 12/3 (2007): 221–237.

19 V. Chaudhri, and J. Wang, "Communicating Corporate Social Responsibility on the Internet: A Case Study of Top 100 Information Technology Companies in India", *Management Communication Quarterly*, 21/2 (2007): 232–247.

20 S. Du, and E.J. Vieira, "Striving for Legitimacy Through Corporate Social Responsibility: Insights from Oil Companies", *Journal of Business Ethics*, 10/4 (2012): 413–427.

21 S.L. Esrock, and G.B. Leichty, "Corporate World Wide Web Pages: Serving the News Media and Other Publics", *Journalism and Mass Media Quarterly*, 78 (1999): 456–467.

22 A. Moreno, and P. Capriotti, "Communicating CSR, Citizenship and Sustainability on the Web", *Journal of Communication Management*, 13/2 (2009): 157–175.

23 I. Pollach, "Communicating Corporate Ethics on the World Wide Web: A Discourse Analysis of Selected Company Websites", *Business and Society*, 42/2 (2003): 227–287.

24 L. Wanderley, R. Lucian, F. Farache, and J. Sousa Filho, "CSR Information Disclosure on the Web: A Context Based Approach to Analysing the Influence of Country of Origin and Industry Sector", *Journal of Business Ethics*, 82/2 (2008): 369–378.

25 R. Isenmann and C. Lenz, "Customized Corporate Environmental Reporting by Internet-Based Push and Pull Technologies", *Eco-management and Auditing*, 8 (2001): 100–110

26 M. Koschmann, T.R. Kuhn, and M.D. Pfarrer, "A Communicative Framework of Value in Cross-Sector Partnerships", *Academy of Management Review*, 37/3 (2012): 332–354.

27 A. McWilliams, D.S. Siegel, and P.M. Wright, "Corporate Social Responsibility: Strategic Implications", *Journal of Management Studies*, 43/1 (2006): 1–18.

28 D. Windsor, "The Future of Corporate Social Responsibility", *The International Journal of Organizational Analysis*, 9/3 (2001): 225–256.

29 J. Elkington, *Cannibals with Forks: The Triple Bottom Line of the 21st Century Business*, Gabriola Island: New Society Publishers, 1998.

30 A.B. Carroll and K.M. Shabana, "The Business Case for Corporate Social Responsibility: A Review of Concepts, Research and Practice", *International Journal of Management Review*, 12/1 (2010): 85–105.

31 M.E. Porter and M.R. Kramer, "Strategy & Society: The Link Between Competitive Advantage and Corporate Social Responsibility", *Harvard Business Review*, 84/2 (2006): 78–92.

32 A.B. Carroll, "The Pyramid of Corporate Social Responsibility: Toward the Moral Management of Organisational Stakeholders", *Business Horizons*, July/August (1991): 30–48.

33 A. Dahlsrud, "How Corporate Social Responsibility Is Defined: An Analysis of 37 Definitions", *Corporate Social Responsibility and Environmental Management*, 15 (2008): 1–13.

34 KPMG, "The KPMG Survey of Corporate Responsibility Reporting 2015", retrieved from www.kpmg.com/CN/en/IssuesAndInsights/ArticlesPublications/Documents/kpmg-survey-of-corporate-responsibility-reporting-2015-O-2 (accessed January 4, 2016), 2015.

35 Cone Communications, "Cone Communications/Ebiquity Global CSR Study", retrieved from www.conecomm.com/2015-global-csr-study-press-release (accessed November 2, 2015), 2015.

36 K. Podnar, "Guest Editorial: Communicating Corporate Social Responsibility", *Journal of Marketing Communications*, 14/2 (2008): 75–81.

37 A. Crane, A. McWilliams, D. Matten, J. Moon, and D. Siegel, "Introduction: The Corporate Social Responsibility Agenda", In A. Crane, A. McWilliams, D. Matten, J. Moon, and D. Siegel (Eds.), *The Oxford Handbook of Corporate Social Responsibility* (pp. 3–18), Oxford: Oxford University Press, 2008.

38 A. Okoye, "Theorizing Corporate Social Responsibility as an Essentially Contested Concept: Is a Definition Necessary?", *Journal of Business Ethics*, 89/4 (2009): 613–627.

39 S. Du, C.B. Bhattacharya, and S. Sankar, "Maximizing Business Returns to Corporate Social Responsibility (CSR): The Role of CSR Communication", *International Journal of Management Reviews*, 12 (2010): 8–19.

40 B.B. Schlegelmilch, and I. Pollach, "The Perils and Opportunities of Communicating Corporate Ethics", *Journal of Marketing Management*, 21 (2005): 267–290.

41 W.J.L. Elving, "Skepticism and Corporate Social Responsibility Communications: The Influence of Fit and Reputation", *Journal of Marketing Communication*, 19/4 (2013): 277–292.

42 M. Morsing, M. Schultz, and K.U. Nielsen, "The 'Catch 22' of Communicating CSR: Findings from a Danish Study", *Journal of Marketing Communications*, 14/22 (2008): 97–111.

43 W.J.L. Elving, and M. Van Vuuren, "Beyond Identity: Corporate Social Responsibility in the Age of Skepticism", *Slovenian Scientific Journal of Marketing*, 17 (2011): 49–56.

44 Y. Fassin, and M. Buelens, "The Hypocrisy-Sincerity Continuum in Corporate Communication and Decision-Making: A Model of Corporate Social Responsibility and Business Ethics", *Journal of Corporate Citizenship*, 42 (2011): 73–91.

45 S.K. May, G. Cheney, and J. Roper (Eds.), *The Debate over Corporate Social Responsibility*, New York, NY: Oxford University Press, 2007.

46 L.T. Christensen, M. Morsing, and O. Thyssen, "CSR as Aspirational Talk", *Organization*, 20/3 (2013): 372–393.

47 S.A. Waddock, and B.K. Googins, "The Paradoxes of Communicating Corporate Social Responsibility", In Ø. Ihlen, J.L. Bartlett, S. May (Eds.), *The Handbook of Communication and Corporate Social Responsibility*, West Sussex, UK: Wiley, 2011, 23–44.

48 C.B. Bhattacharya, D. Korschun, and S. Sen, "Strengthening Stakeholder-Company Relationships Through Mutually Beneficial Corporate Social Responsibility Initiatives", *Journal of Business Ethics*, 85/2 (2009): 257–272.

49 W. Tao, and C. Wilson, "Fortune 1000 Communication Strategies on Facebook and Twitter", *Journal of Communication Management*, 19/3 (2015): 208–223.

50 D. Waller, and R. Lanis, "Corporate Social Responsibility (CSR) Disclosure of Advertising Agencies: An Exploratory Analysis of Six Holding Companies' Annual Reports", *Journal of Advertising*, 38/1 (2009): 109–112.

51 J. Dawkins, "Corporate Responsibility: The Communication Challenge", *Journal of Communication Management*, 9/2 (2004): 108–119.

52 S. Kim, S-Y. Kim, and K.H. Sung, "Fortune 100 Companies' Facebook Strategies: Corporate Ability Versus Social Responsibility", *Journal of Communication Management*, 18/4 (2014): 343, 362.

53 T. McCorkindale, "Can You See the Writing on My Wall? A Content Analysis of the Fortune 50's Facebook Social Networking Sites", *Public Relations Journal*, 4/3 (2010): 1–10.

54 J. Park, H. Lee, and H. Hong, "The Analysis of Self-presentation of Fortune 500 Corporations in Corporate Web Sites", *Business and Society*, 55/5 (2016): 706–737.

55 Sustainability – UNEP, "The *Internet Reporting Report*", London: Sustainability-UNEP, 1999.

56 F. Schultz, I. Castelló, and M. Morsing, "The Construction of Corporate Social Responsibility in Network Societies: A Communication View", *Journal of Business Ethics*, 115/4 (2013): 681–692.

57 S. Deetz, "Corporate Governance, Corporate Social Responsibility and Communication", In S.K. May, G. Cheney, J. Roper (Eds.), *The Debate over Corporate Social Responsibility*, Oxford: Oxford University Press, 2007, 267–278.

58 J. Unerman, and M. Bennett, "Increased Stakeholder Dialogue and the Internet: Towards Greater Corporate Accountability or Reinforcing Capitalist Hegemony?", *Accounting, Organizations and Society*, 29 (2004): 685–707.

59 A.S. Abu Bakar, and R. Ameer, "Readability of Corporate Social Responsibility Communication in Malaysia", *Corporate Social Responsibility & Environmental Management*, 18/1 (2011): 50–60.

60 I. Maignan, and D.A. Ralston, "Corporate Social Responsibility in Europe and US: Insights from Businesses' Self-presentations", *Journal of International Business Studies*, 33/3 (2002): 497–514.

61 M. Frostenson, S. Helin, and S. Andström, "Organising Corporate Responsibility Communication Through Filtration: A Study of Web Communication Pattern in Swedish Retail", *Journal of Business Ethics*, 100/1 (2011): 31–43.

62 J. Lange, "Environmental Collaboration and Constituency Communication", In L. Frey (ed.), *Group Communication in Context*, Hillsdale, NJ: Erlbaum, 2003, 209–234.

63 P. Capriotti, "Communicating Corporate Social Responsibility Through Internet and Social Media", In Ø. Ihlen, J. L. Barlett, S. May (Eds.), *The Handbook of Communication and Corporate Social Responsibility*, West Sussex, UK: Wiley, 2011, 358–378.

64 M. Friedman, "The Social Responsibility of Business Is to Increase Its Profits", *The New York Times Magazine*, September 13, 1970.

65 A.K. Sundaram, and A.C. Inkpen, "The Corporate Objective Revisited", *Organization Science*, 15 (2004): 350–363.

66 M.B.E. Clarkson, "A Stakeholder Framework for Analysing and Evaluating Corporate Social Performance", *Academy of Management Review*, 20(1995): 92–117.

67 T. Donaldson, and L.E. Preston, "The Stakeholder Theory of the Corporation: Concepts, Evidence and Implications", *Academy of Management Review*, 20(1995): 65–91.

68 R.E. Freeman, *Strategic Management: A Stakeholder Approach*, Boston: Pitman, 1984.

69 C.E. Shannon, and W. Weaver, *The Mathematical Theory of Communication*, Urbana, IL: University of Illinois Press, 1948.

70 M. Reddy, "The Conduit Metaphor: A Case of Frame Conflict in Our Language About Language", In A. Ortony (Ed.), *Metaphor and Thought*, Cambridge: Cambridge University Press, 1979, 285–324.

71 A.G. Scherer, and G. Palazzo, "Toward a Political Conception of Corporate Social Responsibility: Business and Society Seen from a Habermasian Perspective", *Academy of Management Review*, 32/4 (2007): 1096–1120.

72 M. Porter, and M. Kramer, "Creating Shared Value", *Harvard Business Review*, 89, 1/2 (2011): 66–77.

73 M. Orlitzy, F.L. Schmidt, and S.L. Rynes, "Corporate Social and Financial Performance: A Meta-analysis", *Organisational Studies*, 24/3 (2003): 404–441.

74 J. Macnamara, "New Media: How Web 2.0 Is Changing the World", retrieved from www.archipe/agopress.com/images/ResearchPapers/New%20Media%20-%20Web%202.0%20Paper.pdf (accessed July 6, 2016).

75 J. Macnamara, "Public Communication Practices in the Web 2.0–3.0 Mediascape: The Case for PRevolution", *PRism*, 7/3 (2010): 1–13.

76 Pew Research Center, "State of the News Media 2016", retrieved from www.journalism.org/2016/06/15/newspapers-fac=sheet/ (accessed June 30, 2016), 2016.

77 T. O'Reilly, "What Is Web 2.0: Design Patterns and Business Models for the Next Generation of Software", retrieved from www.oreilly.com/pub/a/web2/archive/what-is-web-20.html (accessed May 30, 2016), 2015.

78 K.L. Ashcraft, T.R. Kuhn, and F. Cooren, "Constitutional Amendments: 'Materializing' Organizational Communication", *Academy of Management Annals*, 3/1 (2009): 1–64. 4.

79 K.R. Gray, L.A. Frieder, and G.W. Clark, *Corporate Scandals-The Many Faces of Greed*, St. Paul, MN: Paragon House, 2005.

80 U. Golob, and K. Podnar, "Critical Points of CSR-Related Dialogue in Practice", *Business Ethics: A European Review*, 23/3 (2014): 248–257.

81 D.C. Barnlund, "A Transactional Model of Communication", In K.K Sereno and C.D. Mortensen (Eds.), *Foundations of Communication Theory*, New York: Harper and Row, 1970, 83–102.

82 F. Cooren, T.R. Kuhn, J.P. Cornelissen, and T. Clark, "Communication, Organizing, and Organization: An Overview and Introduction to the Special Issues", *Organization Studies*, 32/9 (2011): 1149–1170.

83 L.T. Christensen, and Cheney, G., "Integrating the Communicative Dimensions of Corporate Social Responsibility", In Ø. Ihlen, J. L. Barlett, and S. May (Eds.), *The Handbook of Communication and Corporate Social Responsibility*, West Sussex, UK: Wiley, 2011, 491–504.

84 F. Schultz, and S. Wehmeier, "Institutionalization of Corporate Social Responsibility Within Corporate Communications: Combining Institutional, Sensemaking and Communication Perspectives", *Corporate Communication: An International Journal*, 15/1 (2010): 9–29.

85 P.L. Berger and T. Luckmann, *The Social Construction of Knowledge: A Treatise in the Sociology of Knowledge* (Kindle Ed.), London, UK: Penguin Books, 1966.

86 B. Brummans, F. Cooren, D. Robichaud, and J.R. Taylor, "Approaches in Research on the Communicative Constitution of Organizations", In L. L. Putnam, D. Mumby (Eds.), *SAGE Handbook of Organizational Communication* (3rd ed.), Thousand Oaks, CA: Sage, 2013, 173–194.

87 T.R. Kuhn, "A Communicative Theory of the firm: Developing an Alternative Perspective on Intra-organizational Power and Stakeholder Relationships", *Organization Studies*, 29, 8/9 (2008): 1227–1254.

88 N. Luhmann, *Social Systems*, Stanford, CA: Standford University Press, 1995.

89 D. Schoeneborn, S. Blaschke, F. Cooren, R.D. McPhee, D. Seidl, and J.R. Taylor, "The Three Schools of CCO Thinking: Interactive Dialogue and Systematic Comparison", *Management Communication Quarterly*, 28/2 (2004): 285–316.

90 B. Rawlins, "Prioritizing Stakeholders for Public Relations", *Peer Reviewed Published White Paper for Institute for Public Relations, PR and Management Section*, March 2006, retrieved from http: www.instituteforpr.org/wp-content/uploads/2006_Stakeholders_1.pdf (accessed June 25, 2015), 2006.

91 K.E. Weick, *The Social Psychology of Organizing*, Reading, MA: Addison-Wesley, 1979.

92 K. Basu, and G. Palazzo, "Corporate Social Responsibility: A Process Model of Sensemaking", *Academy of Management Review*, 33/1 (2008): 122–136.

93 McKinsey and Company, "How Companies Are Benefiting from Web 2.0: McKinsey Global Survey Results", retrieved from http://McKinsey.com/business-functions/business-technology/our-insights/how-companies-are-benefiting-from-web-20-mckinsey-global-survey (accessed January 10, 2016), 2009.

94 D. Matten, and J. Moon, "Implicit" and "Explicit" CSR: A Conceptual Framework for a Comparative Understanding of Corporate Social Responsibility", *Academy of Management Review*, 33/2 (2008): 404–424.

95 W. Visser, "Revisiting Carroll's CSR Pyramid: An African Perspective", In E. P. Rahbek, M. Huniche (Eds.), *Corporate Citizenship in a Development Perspective*, Copenhagen Business School Press, Copenhagen, 2006, 29–56.

96 R.T. Craig, "Communication Theory as a Field", *Communication Theory*, 9/2 (1999): 119–161.

97 GIPC, "Ghana Club 100", retrieved from www.gipcghana.com/about-gc-100, (accessed January 5, 2016), 2016.

98 J.W. Creswell, *Research Design: Qualitative, Quantitative and Mixed Methods Approaches*, (4th Edn.), Thousand Oaks, CA: Sage, 2014.

99 Internet World Stats, "World Internet Users and 2015 Population Stats", retrieved from http://ww.internetworldstats.com/stats.htm (accessed January 8, 2016), 2016.

100 R. Hinson, R. Boateng, and N. Madichie, "Corporate Social Responsibility Activity Reportage on Bank Websites in Ghana", *International Journal of Bank Marketing*, 28/7 (2010): 498–518.

101 R. Hinson, "Online CSR Reportage of Award-winning versus Non Award-winning Banks in Ghana", *Journal of Information, Communication and Ethics in Society*, 9/2 (2011): 102–115.

2.3 Social media

From asymmetric to symmetric communication of CSR

Swaleha Peeroo, Martin Samy, and Brian Jones

Introduction

A 'social media revolution'[1] comparable to the monumental industrial revolution[2] is underway. Facebook, the most popular social media platform, has one billion users and this represents nearly 50% of the world population.[3] Increasingly, organizations are adopting social media as an effective tool of corporate communication. Social media use by companies is rising in America: 77% of Fortune 500 companies use Twitter, 70% have a Facebook page, and 69% harness a YouTube account.[4] Hence, social media is transforming the nature of the relationship between organizations and their stakeholders.

The advent of Web 2.0 provides an array of social media platforms to customers, organizations and their stakeholders, enabling innovative forms of connection, interaction, and sharing through the Internet.[5] Technological and social tools such as wiki pages, online petitions, blogs, Twitter, and Facebook are shaping interactions between corporations and civil society in a number of areas.[6]

Corporations use social media to respond to customer queries, ranging from store operating hours to job postings, to increase awareness and demand for products through targeted brand-specific marketing, and to educate stakeholders about corporate social responsibility (CSR) initiatives by the parent company.[7] Additionally, companies have included social media in their marketing communications mix for their corporate communication about sustainability to their internal and external publics.[8,9] Moreover, 71% of the Fortune Global 500 firms dedicated a separate section of their corporate website to environmental responsibility and 75% of these CSR sections gave users the opportunity to react to the information provided.[10]

With unprecedented access to networks and information, both customers and activists have found a new voice in their interactions with organizations.[5] Organizations aim to add value to corporate communication strategies about CSR by using interactive platforms. However, the shift from asymmetric to symmetric communication facilitated by social media for CSR reporting represents both opportunities and challenges for corporations and stakeholders, including the wider public. Increasingly companies are concerned about the consequences of the use of social media on their reputations.[8]

Several studies have covered the field of CSR communication and reporting;[11] however, there is a dearth of research in the academic field on the use of social media as a CSR communication tool and its impact on corporate reputation. This chapter addresses this research gap and furthers the debate on the themes of social media, corporate reputation and CSR. The social media, CSR and corporate reputation interface is a contested and complex area, and because of this, there is a need for greater insight and more research.

With the pervasiveness of social media, it is crucial for organizations to understand how social media could be used as a CSR communication tool and the implications that symmetric communication would have on their corporate reputation. To remain competitive, organizations need to adapt to the new realities of the marketplace.[12] Therefore, the aim of this chapter is to provide insights into the role social media play in the communication of CSR initiatives and how these link with corporate reputation. In this chapter, we provide a brief overview of social media, stakeholder empowerment, corporate reputation, and CSR and conclude by considering some of the managerial implications as well as the theoretical contribution. We explore the challenges and opportunities that these phenomena present to corporations and their CSR communication strategies in particular.

Social media in the corporate world

Social media is defined as the tools, platforms and applications that enable users to connect, communicate, and collaborate with others.[13] One of the most cited definitions of social media is that of Kaplan and Haenlein, who define social media as a collection of Internet-based applications that build on the ideological and technological underpinnings of Web 2.0, which allows the creation and exchange of user-generated content.[14] The definition of social media was further enriched when social media were linked to mobile technology; "Social media employ mobile and web-based technologies to create highly interactive platforms via which individuals and communities share, co-create, discuss, and modify user-generated content."[15]

In the recent past, websites were mainly personal, static, and published by the website owner in such a way that visitors could only view the web content, that is, Web 1.0.[16] However, in Web 2.0, websites are collaborative, dynamic, and interactive, and users actively participate in the generation or enrichment of content.[14,16] A detailed illustration of Web 2.0 along three main dimensions is proposed: application types, social effects and enabling technologies.[17] The five application types include blogs, social networks, communities, forums/bulletin boards, and content aggregators. The social effects dimension embraces the concepts of empowerment, participation, conversation, democratization and, among other things, networking. The enabling technologies dimension comprises of the equipment and software necessary to create an interactive platform.

With Web 2.0 technology, users create, share and disseminate information to other users or communities of special interests.[17] User-generated content (UGC) is defined as the aggregation and leveraging of users' content on the Internet and is the foundation of social media.[18] Users are now adding content in blogs, mashups, podcasts, videos, online social networks, online games, and user reviews.[19] Although UGC can be developed for any purpose, increasingly people create UGC about brands, companies, products, and services.[20] This has led companies to leverage social media to reach their publics and achieve their corporate goals.

The most popular social media platforms for organizations to use in the United States are company websites, Facebook, Twitter, LinkedIn, StockTwits, YouTube, Pinterest, Reddit, SlideShare, Google Plus, and Instagram.[21] Since more users are moving towards social media, the largest web presence of organizations are their Facebook fan pages and corporate communications posted on Facebook obtain a higher click-through rate than messages posted on corporate websites.[22] Studies have found that several corporations use more than one social media channel, which makes it more complex for both users and providers of corporate information who need to ensure that a consistent message is being sent to stakeholders.[21]

Another major challenge facing organizations is that social media has changed the communications landscape, since users have the ability to create messages and send these messages to other individuals, with or without the consent of the organization.[15] Customers on Web 2.0 are referred as 'Real-Time Customers' to whom communication cannot be made only through traditional broadcast media.[17] Similarly, some authors contend that marketers can no longer speak at their audience, but they must speak with them.[17,23] The most common use of social media among businesses is to communicate and engage in conversation with their customers.[15,24,25,26,27,28,29]

Conceivably the most meaningful advantages of harnessing social media is the opportunities for organizations to interact directly with customers, investors, suppliers and other stakeholders, thus facilitating a global dialogue between stakeholders.[21] Social media offers a public platform to an increasing number of 'influencers', such as financiers and activists who may wish to push a specific agenda.[21] Social media has not only shifted communication from monologue to dialogue, but it has also given rise to a new phenomenon, trialogue, where customers also engage in conversations with other customers.[30]

With social media there is co-creation of the brand.[14,20,28,29,31,32,33,34,35] For example, Amazon, the largest global online retailer, has established its success on the trust engendered by product reviews from its customers.[36] Social media can provide valuable tools for the brand, as they allow the organization to communicate its brand identity, its brand image, and values.[28] Corporations are using social media to achieve their goals by communicating with stakeholders, trying to better understand them, and creating a connection with their brands. In the same vein, online communication is growing to be one of the most essential information channels for organizations aspiring to increase awareness of stakeholders about their CSR activities.[36] The Internet has remodeled communication at different levels by virtue of different avenues due to increase real time technological advances.

Undeniably, traditional broadcast media is founded on a hierarchical one-to-many communication, clearly differentiating between producer and user of information and an audience that does not contribute in the selection and creation of content. On the contrary, the Internet has facilitated the emergence of a new public sphere built on a many-to-many communication where everybody can participate, interact publicly, and collaborate in the production of content and the establishment of the agenda.[37] With the pervasive nature of social media such as Facebook and Twitter, attracting individuals and creating an active community is now an easy and inexpensive task for companies. Furthermore, a growing number of corporations have adopted social media as a cost effective channel of corporate communication.[9]

Kaplan and Haenlein reported that "social media allow firms to engage in timely and direct end-consumer contact at relatively low cost and higher levels of efficiency than can be achieved with more traditional communication tools".[14] However, within the realm of social media, where relationships are developed around a network of individuals sharing similar interests, organizations no longer have total control of corporate communications, as members of the online community also drive the conversation.[36] Within these new media, communications are 'viral', because opinions and ideas spread like a virus via the social network through word of mouth and are perceived as highly trustworthy by the members because they are centered on group similarities.[38]

Social media has transformed the communication landscape for organizations and their stakeholders owing to its interactive capabilities.[39,40] The social web offers new possibilities for symmetric communication and relationship building, as social media tools "have almost no gatekeeping mechanism, enabling conversation without formal hierarchies".[6] For instance, Twitter, a popular social media platform, provides several avenues for corporations to interact with their stakeholders and vice versa.[41,42] Additionally, with the expansion and development of the social web, business reputation no longer lies solely in the hands of the corporate team. In this new era of blogs, podcasts, social networks, wikis, newsgroups, forums, chat rooms, and mail groups, corporate reputation can be easily improved or damaged permanently by empowered stakeholders.[43]

Social media and stakeholder empowerment

Social media has unfolded new possibilities for content creation and increased sharing and participation among Internet users. This gives rise to the concept of socially shared meaning, which is critical and central to the whole aspect of Web 2.0, where broadcasting that is, one-to-many communication is replaced by participation, exchange, and collaboration, which could now be termed as 'socialcasting'.[44]

The development of UGC via social media channels from the Web 2.0 era is reshaping the marketing landscape as business-to-consumer (B2C) marketing is being replaced by consumer-to-consumer (C2C) marketing.[45] Customers are no longer content to select goods produced, distributed, and promoted by companies, which determined what customers wanted and needed. In C2C marketing, consumers are increasingly taking control of the marketplace and they take a more active role in marketing functions, such as the creation or modification of products.[45] These empowered customers have a voice through their user-generated content, which can spread virally on the web.[17]

Customers are increasingly exploiting social media to gain reviews, recommendations, and opinions from friends, family, experts, and the collective social community before buying products and services.[46] Numerous studies have shown that more people are relying on sources they trust such as social media reviews made by their family, friends and colleagues rather than trusting commercial messages.[19,47] However, customers do still consider information obtained from traditional media before making purchases.

Customers too recognise that they wield more power over brands and organizations than before and that they can make or break a brand through word of mouth and word of mouse.[34] So, businesses that adopt social media as a strategy must accept that they are losing an element of control to the consumer.[48] However, social media adds value to the relationship, since prosumers feel empowered.[13] Similarly, stakeholder awareness has been considerably enriched by the advent of the Internet, which empowers people, to share to other 'connected' users wherever they are in an unprecedented scale.[38]

With the rapid expansion of social networking sites, such as Twitter and Facebook, stakeholders are no longer passive receivers of messages; they engage increasingly in the creation, assessment, and judgement of content.[49] For instance, the fast-food giant McDonald's experience with Twitter serves as a salutary lesson about the power of social media. When the fast-food company launched a campaign on Twitter with the hashtag #McDStories, it wanted to give customers a platform to share positive stories about the cultivators and suppliers who produce and grow the ingredients for Big Macs and Chicken McNuggets. The first tweet read "when u make something w/pride people can taste it. McD potato supplier #McDStories." Almost instantaneously, the tweet generated a huge flow of negative #McDStories about animal welfare concerns, low labor standards, and food poisoning at the fast-food chain. McDonald's had no other choice than to stop the campaign within hours. This example of 'tweetjacking' (turning the initial tweets to suit one's own purposes) is one of the biggest corporate social media disasters of 2012.[50] The McDonald's case offers a vibrant example of the speed and impact with which users of social media can create a backlash when organizations try to create an image, which stakeholders consider being hypocritical.[5] Confronted by these new challenges, organizations have now to adapt and reconsider their communication strategies and branding management practices, together with online corporate reputation management.[43]

CSR and corporate reputation

In the past ten years, there have been a growing number of companies involved in socially responsible activities, such as charitable deeds, which can promote various social causes that are totally distinct from the core business of the company.[51] CSR is defined as efforts to "integrate social, environmental, ethical, human rights and consumer issues into their business operations and core strategy".[52] According to the World Bank, CSR is an organizational commitment to contribute to sustainable economic development by engaging with employees and their families, the society at large, and the local community with a view of improving quality of life, in ways that benefit the business.[53] Therefore, CSR is "the voluntary integration of social and environmental concerns in the enterprises' daily business operations and in the interaction with their stakeholders".[54]

The study of CSR has been associated with the general stakeholder theory, maintaining that companies make decisions and assign their resources in order to satisfy stakeholders (e.g., stockholders, customers, suppliers, employees, the local community).[54] CSR activities embrace all of the various corporate social initiatives implemented so as to increase the congruence between organizational behavior and social expectations of stakeholders and, as a result, increasing their legitimacy within society.[36] Legitimacy is defined as a widespread perception or belief that the actions of an organization are appropriate, proper and desirable within a socially constructed system of beliefs, norms, values, and definitions.[55]

So, this raises the question of what motivates organizations to be involved in socially responsible activities. Researchers have found that socially responsible organizations tend to generate superior financial performance, which is positively linked to the level of investment in CSR.[56,57] Additionally, studies unearthed that CSR increased brand loyalty and decreased the price sensitivity of customers.[58,59] Furthermore, customers were more willing to recommend products and services of socially responsible firms.[60] Consumers tended to defend socially responsible organizations against criticism.[61,62] It has also been claimed that the socially responsible behavior of a company tends to increase the level of sales by motivating buyers to reward the organization for its prosocial behavior.[63]

The socially responsible behavior of a company can change perceptions of consumers' on the performances of products.[51] These authors showed that products produced by socially responsible firms are perceived as performing better. However, the positive impact of CSR is mitigated when customers believe that the actions of the company are driven by self-interest rather than by generosity and goodwill. Therefore, the prosocial behavior of a firm is more likely to impact positively on perceived product performance when it is consistent with the moral values of consumers.[51] Organizations also aim to foster relationships with their publics through CSR.[64] Most researchers agree CSR is about 'doing good' within the community,[65] which leads to more favorable corporate reputations.[66,67] When organizations communicate CSR activities, perceptions of corporate reputation, image and credibility are strengthened.[68] McKinsey carried out its annual executive survey and reported that company executives ranked managing corporate reputation as the first and foremost reason for carrying out CSR projects.[69]

Corporate reputation is defined as the "perceptions of how the firm behaves towards its stakeholders and the degree of informative transparency with which the firm develops relations with them".[70] Likewise, Fombrun describes corporate reputation as the immediate mental image of an organization that develops over time as a consequence of consistent performance, strengthened by effective communication.[71] Hence, corporate reputation possesses a behavioral and an informative component.

The legitimate behaviour, which the organization exhibited in the past while establishing and distributing value, will allow stakeholders to expect legitimate behavior by the corporation in the future. Also, sharing asymmetric information decreases the likelihood of managerial opportunism and, consequently, increases the satisfaction and trust of stakeholders and, thus, corporate reputation.[72] For example, "Unilever seeks to maintain its strong CSR reputation by prominently highlighting via the company website its long list of high-profile corporate awards, including Fortune magazine's World's Most Admired Companies, the Reputation Institute's Global RepTrak1 100, the Global 1000 Sustainable Performance Leaders, and 14 consecutive years with the Dow Jones Sustainability Index."[9]

Companies are increasingly focussing on corporate reputation management owing to the characteristics of the existing competitive markets.[73] Globalisation, innovation, deregulation, disintermediation, and the advent of new technologies and electronic distribution channels have transformed the key characteristics of the corporate environment, which is determined by intense competition, standardisation, overcapacity, uncertainty, hostility, and anxiety.[74] Corporate reputation is an effective tool in highly competitive markets. It is argued that intangible attributes of organizations such as corporate reputation are more lasting and resistant to competitive forces than product and service attributes.[73] Similarly, corporate reputation may assist companies better in their quest for competitive advantage.[70] Melo and Garrido claim that "the benefits driven by accrued positive reputation represent a potential path to sustained competitive advantage",[75] as it is harder for competitors to imitate or duplicate corporate reputation because of its intangible form.[76] In markets where competition is rife, building, refining, and even mending the reputation of companies with stakeholders is key to success.[77]

One way of enhancing the corporate reputation of companies is to engage in CSR reporting with its stakeholders. Perez linked CSR reporting and corporate reputation based on five theoretical approaches: institutional/legitimacy theory, impression management theory, reputation risk management theory, agency theory and signalling theory.[72] Most of these perspectives emphasise the benefits of CSR reporting for corporations when they endeavor to enhance their reputation.[78] Companies are less keen to report on acts of corporate social irresponsibility (CSI).[79,80]

CSR reporting contributes to strengthening corporate reputation when stakeholders do not perceive economic incentives or corporate opportunities for engaging in CSR efforts. Conversely, greenwashing communications, that is, the practice of making an uncorroborated or misleading claim about the environmental benefits of a product or service, result in growing social cynicism and loss of trust, which is harmful to corporate reputation.[81]

Du, Bhattacharya, and Sen opine that if there is no communication about the type and the number of CSR initiatives organizations develop, there will be no or even negative influence of CSR on perceptions of stakeholders.[82] CSR reporting refers to the disclosure of corporate initiatives that exhibit the inclusion of environmental and social concerns in business operations as well as interactions with stakeholders[72] and "is designed and distributed by the company itself about its CSR efforts".[83] Based on the institutional/ legitimacy and agency theories, researchers have argued that the CSR disclosure is part of the conversation between an ethical organization and its stakeholders that assists to legitimise corporate behaviour and consequently contributes to engender a positive corporate reputation.[36] Centred on this idea, a growing number of CSR reports have been published in recent years.[72]

CSR reporting can mirror three approaches closely linked to corporate reputation.[84] Firstly, the reputation management approach focuses "on the basic requirements of conducting a responsible business to obtain and maintain a license to operate from society".[84] Secondly, the approach of building a virtuous corporate brand by making an "explicit promise to the stakeholders and the general public that the corporation excels with respect to their CSR endeavours".[84] Thirdly, the ethical product differentiation approach is about "differentiating a certain product or service on the basis of an environmental or social quality"[84] in such a way that corporate reputation is linked not only to the organization but also to its products and services. However, it is very challenging for organizations to be perceived as socially responsible, as companies must match the social expectations of stakeholders, which may at times be a difficult task.[36] For corporations to derive beneficial relationships from their CSR initiatives, they must communicate them to appropriate stakeholders in a symmetric, that is, two-way communication approach.[6, 85]

CSR communication and social media

Academics tackle the concept of CSR communication from different standpoints, namely, corporate communication and public relations, promotion, organizational studies, and organizational communication.[86] Owing to differences in epistemological stances, scholars have different perceptions on the role of CSR communication.

Positivists, who support the idea of a positive relationship between business revenues and social activities, view CSR communication as a means to create awareness of CSR efforts through the use of promotional tools.[85] This was evident from studies of the top 20 UK corporations, which readily communicated positive impacts on a number of environmental and labor initiatives.[87] Thus, CSR communication aims to generate CSR-based brand identity and corporate reputation and favorably influence perceptions of stakeholders. However, positivist views of CSR communication ignore the role of communication for negotiation between expectations of stakeholders and environmental conditions influencing organizations.[88]

Social constructivists hold an alternative view of CSR communication in which corporations connect and interact with stakeholders with the intent to negotiate and discuss CSR initiatives so as to achieve mutual understanding.[88, 89,90] To build positive relationships, CSR efforts are increasingly being communicated to relevant stakeholders.

Morsing and Schultz developed three types of stakeholder relations' strategies in terms of how corporations engage in CSR communication with their stakeholders.[85] Organizations use the stakeholder information strategy, which is based on one-way communication to disseminate information to the public to create awareness of the CSR efforts. However, both the stakeholder response strategy and the stakeholder involvement strategy are established on a two-way communication system. In the stakeholder response strategy, there is a greater proportion of communication in favor of the company, for example, through the use of public relations.

In contrast, the stakeholder involvement strategy assumes a more balanced communication between the company and its stakeholders, whereby both parties mutually persuade and influence each other. This two-way balanced communication of the stakeholder involvement strategy gives rise to the concepts of symmetry and relationship management, thus resulting in favorable outcomes for both parties.[85]

Formerly, the main objective of organizations was to communicate their financial performance.[91] However, nowadays demonstrating and communicating corporate commitment to CSR initiatives has become important to build and maintain corporate reputation. The perceived benefits of CSR disclosure and reporting include improved corporate reputation and financial results, with the capability to attract foreign investors and gain greater employee commitment and customer satisfaction.[91,92]

However, perceptions of corporate behaviour by stakeholders are not solely built from information disclosed by the company and mass media but increasingly from information shared with peers within social networks.[36] Consequently, corporations have increasingly utilized the Internet for CSR communication.[93]

The major advantage of online communication is two-way communication among a large audience, enabling organizations to develop and sustain relationships.[36] As compared to static websites, Web 2.0 technology offers significantly greater potential for symmetric communication and for managing relationships, because on social media platforms, there are no gatekeeping mechanisms, facilitating conversation without hierarchical barriers.[6] Information about corporations can be aired and made quickly available on social media platforms such as Twitter and Facebook before being reported by journalist gatekeepers and traditional mass media channels.[94]

A study carried out in 2012 identified the usage of social media for CSR communication as one of the top ten trends in CSR.[95] Social networking sites are valuable in CSR communication, as they make it easier to gain public engagement and collaboration.[40] Fortune 500 companies consider shareholders as the most important stakeholder with whom to engage, with respect to CSR communication, followed by customers, community members, local and national government bodies, and activists.[10] Among the most noteworthy advantages of social media are the opportunities for organizations to interact directly with customers, investors, suppliers, and other stakeholders and the ability to have a worldwide dialogue among stakeholders.[36]

Social media provides a public forum to an increasing number of 'influencers' who may wish to push a particular agenda.[21] So, how are corporations using social media for CSR communication, reporting, and disclosure? Several scholars have examined the use of social media as a tool to communicate about CSR activities. Twitter is one of the most popular social media tools for communication, through which corporations distribute CSR information to an anonymous public, but also to 'followers', that is, interested individuals.[96] Several stakeholders with a keen interest in CSR activities use Twitter, for example, for consumers,[97] politicians,[98] investors,[99] journalists,[100] activists,[101] or non-governmental organizations.[102]

Etter carried out a study to examine how organizations use Twitter to communicate CSR initiatives to embrace the opportunities of symmetric communication and relationship management.[96] He developed three CSR communication strategies on Twitter: the broadcasting strategy, the reactive strategy, and the engagement strategy.

The broadcasting strategy uses one-way communication to inform stakeholders about CSR initiatives with no intention of interacting about CSR on Twitter. For example, the Microsoft Citizenship account just diffuses information about CSR initiatives toward an anonymous audience and its followers: "Microsoft has launched an online donations page built with the American Red Cross: https://donate.microsoft.com/" (Twitter/msftciti-zenship,13.1.2010). Companies using the broadcasting strategy can achieve benefits such as improved corporate reputation, but they miss out on the opportunity to create mutual understandings and build relationships with stakeholders.[96] Companies mainly apply the broadcasting strategy for their CSR communication.[36,97,103] In reports that online communication, despite its interactive capacity, is often used as traditional mass media for corporate reputation, owing to the fear of sceptic stakeholders.[104]

The reactive strategy uses two-way communication in which organizations mainly respond to queries and remarks related to CSR issues and is characterized by low proactive communicative behaviour. For example, when Twitter users voice out their concerns about the environmental foot print of a particular product, Starbucks replies to these questions: "@jenville @mriggen Hey-Check out our Shared Planet site that talks about our recycling efforts: http://bit.ly/AIyLs" (Twitter/MyStarbucksIdea, 23.7.2009). The reactive strategy enables organizations to partly establish symmetric communication and build relationships, to some extent.[96]

Finally, corporations with an engagement strategy disseminate CSR information towards targeted members, proactively address Twitter members, and respond to questions and comments. These organizations make the best use of the potential of Twitter to enable symmetric two-way interactions for building and enhancing stakeholder relationships. For example, Green Mountain Coffee applies an engagement strategy, which actively approaches other Twitter users: "Looks like @fairtradeboston has a spectacular Fair Trade Crawl planned for tomorrow-fun! http://bit.ly/bkuRBV" (GreenMtncoffee, 7.5.2010). Consequently, with the engagement strategy, trust and commitment of stakeholders can be enhanced, and this may lead to favorable outcomes for both the corporation and the public.[96]

This study reveals that most companies use Twitter as a broadcasting strategy whereas only a minority (4 out of 30) use the engagement strategy. Therefore, Etter argues that Twitter primarily offers a platform to increase awareness of CSR efforts of companies, but it can also provide opportunities for communication symmetry and relationship building when an engagement strategy is used.[96]

Researchers have also studied the use of Facebook as a CSR platform to engage stakeholders. Kim, Kim and Sung examined how Fortune 100 companies are using communication strategies through Facebook to meet expectations of stakeholders.[105] They explored three main corporate communication strategies used on corporate websites, namely, a corporate ability strategy in which the company stresses its expertise of its products and services, a CSR strategy in which the company informs of its CSR efforts, and a hybrid strategy, that is, combination of corporate ability and CSR strategy.[106,107] On corporate websites, companies have employed a CSR strategy to generate strong CSR associations among their stakeholders.[107] They also uncovered that larger corporations tend to adopt a CSR strategy on their websites, whereas the bottom Fortune 100 companies highly emphasized a corporate ability strategy. This may be explained by the high expectations the public has of big companies regarding their corporate social responsibilities.[107] Another explanation for favoring a CSR strategy is that well-known companies already have a strong reputation regarding corporate ability.

Kim, Kim and Sung examined the three communication strategies on Facebook and found that unlike corporate websites where companies adopted more the CSR strategy, on Facebook, Fortune 100 companies use mostly the corporate ability strategy.[105] The difference in strategy adoption between corporate websites and Facebook pages may be explained by the expectations of the public of the presence of a company on social media.[105] Another study found that 54% of people surveyed were for the presence of companies on Facebook and that 58% expected to get product or service promotional deals.[108] Also, Facebook was initially created to connect friends and build relationships. So for these reasons, companies may prefer to use a corporate ability strategy, that is, to communicate on its products and services, focus on customer needs and wants and provide customer services than adopting a CSR strategy.

Eberle, Berens, and Li carried out an experiment to assess whether using social media to communicate CSR related messages is beneficial to corporate reputation and word of mouth intentions.[8] They found that when stakeholders perceive a higher degree of interactivity, there is higher message credibility and stronger brand identification, resulting in strengthened corporate reputation and greater word of mouth. This study also reveals that negative word of mouth has a greater impact on corporate reputation than favorable word of mouth.

Similarly other researchers found that negative user-generated comments on Facebook about CSR initiatives of companies tended to damage the perceptions of stakeholders on the organization – public relationship, corporate social responsibility, and corporate reputation.[109] This phenomenon has been referred as the polyphony of CSR on social media.[110] As a result of polyphony, several voices can be heard while individual voices can remain separate identities instead of being merged into one common voice.[111] Conflicting voices on CSR efforts challenge the claims made by organizations about their CSR commitments.[111] Castelló, Morsing, and Schultz write, "This dynamization of communication changes the relationship between business and society, thus leading to a higher plurality and potential polarization of voices, which dynamically interact and can lead to new forms of legitimacy." Additionally businesses often have to face alternative reality constructs about their products and services or operations. Activists criticize actions of corporations and morally pressurize them when there is no alignment with environmental and societal norms.[90]

Concluding remarks: managerial implications and theoretical contribution

As outlined in the introduction, the aim of this chapter was to review the literature on the relationship between CSR, corporate reputation, and social media. By drawing together disparate strands of argument, it has grown knowledge of CSR communication, corporate reputation and social media. This chapter has contributed to knowledge by providing a comprehensive review of the role of social media in CSR communication and how this impacts corporate reputation. It has sought to highlight the value that CSR communication can have for communication and management research. From the extant literature, it is clear that social media is influencing corporate reputation and the way businesses are being managed today.

Increasingly corporations are adopting social media for CSR reporting and disclosure as they acknowledge that on social media, they can observe public opinion and communicate and engage with multiple stakeholders. The literature review found that though social media is an interactive medium, most organizations still tend to use the broadcasting strategy, that is, one-way communication to convey information on CSR initiatives. Reinforcing a point made in the introduction, without greater engagement, businesses of all types and sizes are likely to miss out on the beneficial outcomes of social media, such as symmetrical communication and relationship building.

Social media can increase the level of interaction, facilitating the diffusion of CSR-related information with stakeholders and the development of relationships. The public expect companies to be socially responsible and transparent.[106] Those companies that are transparent and socially responsible gain public trust. Part of the winning of public trust can be garnered by their increased engagement with CSR through social media.

CSR strategy and corporate reputation need to be continually monitored, reviewed, and built on social media platforms. In a quickly changing social media landscape for CSR, referred as the 'Wild West',[112] continual vigilance is needed. Companies should carefully consider which social media platforms to use for CSR communication and assess which platforms to add or drop. Companies no longer have to only address the questions of 'how' and 'what' but also 'to whom' and 'with whom' they communicate. For good or ill, corporate reputation is today in part shaped by social media. Future research in this area might look to better understand, theoretically deconstruct, explore and report on the complex and constructed concepts of asymmetric and symmetric communication. The CSR social media landscape is prone to shift beneath companies' feet. Those that are communication savvy, social media agile, and reputation fit are likely to prosper and succeed. Those companies that are not savvy, agile and fit are likely to fall through the cracks opened up by the shifting CSR social media landscape.

Notes

1 Dubose, C., (2011), "The social media revolution", *Radiologic Technology*, Vol. 12, No. 1, pp. 30–43.

2 Choi, J.H., and Scott, J.E., (2013), "Electronic word of mouth and knowledge sharing on social network sites: A social capital perspective", *Journal of Theoretical and Applied Electronic Commerce Research*, Vol. 8, No. 1, pp. 69–82.

3 Nair, A., (2012), 'Facebook for businesses', *Vikalpa: The Journal for Decision Makers*, Vol. 37, No. 4, pp. 85–90.

4 Barnes, N. G., Lescault, A. M., and Wright, S., (2013), "Fortune 500 are bullish on social media: Big companies get excited about Google+, Instagram, Foursquare and Pinterest." Available at www.umassd.edu/cmr/socialmediaresearch/2013 fortune500/ [accessed 27 May 2015].

5 Lyon, T.P., and Montgomery, A.W., (2013), "Tweetjacked: The impact of social media on corporate greenwash", *Journal of Business Ethics*, Vol. 118, pp. 747–757.

6 Fieseler, C., Fleck, M., and Meckel, M., (2010), "Corporate social responsibility in the blogosphere", *Journal of Business Ethics*, Vol. 91, pp. 599–614.

7 DeMers, J., (2013), "The top 7 social media marketing trends that will dominate 2014", *Forbes*. Available at www.forbes.com/sites/jaysondemers/2013/09/24/the-top-7-social-media-marketing-trends-that-will-dominate-2014/2/ [accessed 26 May 2015].

8 Eberle, D., Berens, G., and Li, T., (2013), "The impact of interactive corporate social responsibility communication on corporate reputation", *Journal of Business Ethics*, Vol. 118, pp. 731–746, doi: 10.1007/s10551–013–1957-y

9 Reilly, A.H., and Hynan, K.A., (2014), "Corporate communication, sustainability, and social media: It's not easy (really) being green", *Business Horizons*, Vol. 57, pp. 747–758.

10 Kim, D., Nam, Y., and Kang, S., (2010), "An analysis of corporate environmental responsibility on the global corporate web sites and their dialogic principles", *Public Relations Review*, Vol. 36, pp. 285–288.

11 Tench, R., Sun, W., and Jones, B., (Ed.) (2014) "*Communicating Corporate Social Responsibility: Perspectives and Practice*" (*Critical Studies on Corporate Responsibility, Governance and Sustainability, volume 6*), Emerald Group Publishing Limited.

12 Dijkmans, C., Kerkhof, P., and Beukeboom, C.J., (2015), "A stage to engage: Social media use and corporate reputation", *Tourism Management*, Vol. 47, pp. 58–67.

13 Williams, J., and Chinn, S.J., (2010), "Meeting relationship-marketing goals through social media: a conceptual model for sport marketers", *International Journal of Sport Communication*, Vol. 3, pp. 422–437.

14 Kaplan, A., and Haenlein, M., (2010), "Users of the world, unite! The challenges and opportunities of social media", *Business Horizons*, Vol. 53, pp. 59–68.

15 Kietzmann, Jan H., Hermkens, Kristopher, Mccarthy, Ian P., and Silvestre, Bruno S., (2011), "Social media? Get serious! Understanding the functional building blocks of social media", *Business Horizons*, Vol. 54, pp. 241–251.

16 Adebanjo, D., and Michaelides, R., (2010), 'Analysis of Web2.0 enabled e-clusters: A case study', *Technovation*, Vol. 30, No. 4, pp. 238–248.

17 Constantinides, E., Romero, C., and Boria, M., (2008), "Social media: A new frontier for retailers?", *European Retail Research*, Vol. 22, pp. 1–28.

18 Hvass, K. A., and Munar, A. M., (2012), "The takeoff of social media in tourism", *Journal of Vacation Marketing*, Vol. 18, No. 2, pp. 93–103.

19 Liu-Thompkins, Y., and Rogerson, M., (2012), "Rising to Stardom: An Empirical Investigation of the Diffusion of User-generated Content", *Journal of Interactive Marketing*, Vol. 26, pp. 71–82.

20 Vanden Bergh, B., Lee, M., Quilliam, E., and Hove, T., (2011), "The Multidimensional Nature and Brand Impact of User-Generated Ad Parodies in Social Media", *International Journal Of Advertising*, Vol. 30, No. 1, pp. 103–131, Business Source Premier, EBSCO*host*, viewed 30 October 2012.

21 Alexander, R.M., and Gentry, J.K., (2014), "Using social media to report financial results", *Business Horizons*, Vol. 57, pp. 161–167.

22 Champoux, V., Durgee, J., and McGlynn, L., (2012), "Corporate Facebook pages: when 'fans' attack", *Journal of Business Strategy*, Vol. 33, No. 2, pp. 22–30.

23 Mills, A. J. (2012), "Virality in social media: The SPIN Framework", *Journal of Public Affairs*, Vol. 12, No. 2, pp. 162–169.

24 Kwok, L., and Yu, B., (2012), "Spreading social media messages on Facebook: An analysis of restaurant business-to-consumer communications", *Cornell Hospitality Quarterly*, pp. 1–11.

25 Linke, A., and Zerfass, A., (2012), "Future trends in social media use for strategic organisation communication: Results of a Delphi study", *Public Communication Review*, Vol. 2, No. 2, pp. 17–29.

26 Lipsman, A., Mudd, G., Rich, M., and Bruich, S., (2012), "The power of 'like' how brands reach (and influence) fans through social-media marketing", *Journal of Advertising Research*, Vol. 52, No. 1, pp. 40–52.

27 Rao, S., (2012), "Facebook for businesses", *Vikalpa: The Journal for Decision Makers*, Vol. 37, No. 4, pp. 90–92.

28 Yan, J., (2011), "Social media in branding: Fulfilling a need", *Journal of Brand Management*, Vol. 18, No. 9, pp. 688–696.

29 Zauner, A., Koller, M., and Fink, M., (2012), "Sponsoring, brand value and social media", *RAE: Revista De Administração De Empresas*, Vol. 52, No. 6, pp. 681–691, Academic Search Complete, EBSCO*host*, viewed 11 November 2012.

30 Porter, C., Donthu, N., MacElroy, W., and Wydra, D., (2011), "How to foster and sustain engagement in virtual communities", *California Management Review*, Vol. 53, No. 4, pp. 80–110.

31 Asur, S., (2012), "The economics of attention: Social media and businesses", *Vikalpa: The Journal for Decision Makers*, Vol. 37, No. 4, pp. 77–85.

32 Fournier, S., and Avery, J., (2011), "The uninvited brand", *Business Horizons*, Vol. 54, pp. 193–207.

33 Lim, Y., Chung, Y., and Weaver, P., (2012), "The impact of social media on destination branding: Consumer-generated videos versus destination marketer-generated videos", *Journal of Vacation Marketing*, Vol. 18, No. 3, pp. 197–206.

34 Ramsay, M., (2010), "Social media etiquette: A guide and checklist to the benefits and perils of social marketing", *Database Marketing and Customer Strategy Management*, Vol. 17, pp. 257–261.

35 Singh, S., and Sonnenburg, S., (2012), "Brand performances in social media", *Journal of Interactive Marketing*, Vol. 26, pp. 189–197.

36 Colleoni, E., (2013), "CSR communication strategies for organizational legitimacy in social media", *Corporate Communications: An International Journal*, Vol. 18, No. 2, pp. 228–248.

37 Jenkins, H., (2006), *Convergence Culture: Where Old and New Media Collide*, New York University Press, New York, NY.

38 Colleoni, E., Arvidsson, A., Hansen, L.K., and Marchesini, M., (2011), "Measuring corporate reputation using sentiment analysis", paper presented at the 15th *International Conference on Corporate Reputation, Brand, Identity and Competitiveness*, New Orleans, LA, May 18–20.

39 Etter, M., and Fieseler, C., (2010), "On relational capital in social media", *Studies in Communication Sciences*, Vol. 10, No. 2, pp. 167–189.

40 Capriotti, P., (2011), "Social responsibility through the internet and social media", in Ihlen, Ø., Bartlett, J., and May, S. (Eds), *The Handbook of Communication and Corporate Social Responsibility*, Vol. 16, Oxford: Wiley-Blackwell.

41 Boyd, D., Scott, G., and Gilad, L., (2010), "Tweet, tweet, retweet: Conversational aspects of retweeting on twitter," presented at the System Sciences (HICSS), 43rd Hawaii International Conference on IEEE, January 17.

42 Honeycutt, C., and Herring, S.C., (2009), "Beyond microblogging: Conversation and collaboration via twitter", Proceedings of The 42nd Hawaii International Conference on System Sciences HICSS, IEEE Computer Society, Washington, DC, January, pp. 1–10.

43 Jones, B., Temperley, J., and Lima, A., (2009), "Corporate reputation in the era of Web 2.0", *Journal of Marketing Management*, Vol. 25, No. 9–10, pp. 927–939.

44 Greaves, M., and Mika, P., (2008), "Semantic Web and Web 2.0", *Journal of Web Semantics*, Vol. 6, January, pp. 1–3.

45 Kimmel, A., (2010), *Connecting with Consumers: Marketing for New Marketplace Realities*, University Press, Oxford.

46 Baird, C.H., and Parasnis, G., (2011), "From social media to social customer relationship management", *Strategy and Leadership*, Vol. 39, No. 5, pp. 30–37.

47 Villanueva, J., Yoo, S., and Hanssens, D.M., (2008), "The impact of marketing-induced versus word-of-mouth customer acquisition on customer equity growth," *Journal of Marketing Research*, Vol. 45, No. 1, pp. 48–59.

48 O'Brien, C., (2011), "The emergence of the social media empowered consumer", *Irish Marketing Review*, 21, 1/2, pp. 32–40, Business Source Premier, EBSCO*host*, viewed 5 November 2012.

49 Dellarocas, C., (2003), "The digitization of word of mouth: Promise and challenges of online feedback mechanisms", *Management Science*, Vol. 49, No. 10, pp. 1407.

50 Thomases, H., (2012), "McDonald's twitter mess: What went wrong", *From Inc.* Available at www.inc. com/hollisthomases/ mcdonalds-mcdstories-twitter-mess.html [accessed 26 May 2015].

51 Chernev, A., and Blair, S., (2015), "Doing well by doing good: The benevolent Halo of corporate social responsibility", *Journal Of Consumer Research*, Vol. 41, pp. 1412–1425.

52 European Commission, (2011), "A renewed EU strategy 2011–2014 for corporate social responsibility", available at http://eur-lex.europa.eu/LexUriServ/LexUriServ. do?uri=COM:2011:0681:FIN: EN:PDF, [accessed 26 May 2015], p. 6.

53 Petkoski, D., and Twose, N., (Eds.), (2003), "Public policy for corporate social responsibility", available at http://info.worldbank. org/etools/docs/library/57434/publicpolicy_econference.pdf [accessed 26 May 2015].

54 Benoit-Moreau, F., and Parguel, B., (2011), "Building brand equity with environmental communication: an empirical investigation in France", *EuroMed Journal of Business*, Vol. 6, No. 1, pp. 100–116.

55 Matejek, S., and Göosling, T., (2014), "A case study in BP's 'green lashing'", *Journal of Business Ethics*, Vol. 120, No. 4, pp. 571–584.

56 Orlitzky, M., Schmidt, F.L., and Rynes, S., (2003), "Corporate social and financial performance: A meta-analysis", *Organization Studies*, Vol. 24, No. 3, pp. 403–411.

57 Russo, M.V., and Fouts, P.A., (1997), "A resource-based perspective on corporate environmental performance and profitability," *Academy of Management Journal*, Vol. 40, June, pp. 534–559.

58 Green, T., and Peloza, J., (2011), "How does corporate social responsibility create value for consumers?" *Journal of Consumer Marketing*, Vol. 28, No. 1, pp. 48–56.

59 Marin, L., Ruiz, S., and Rubio, A., (2009), "The role of identity salience in the effects of corporate social responsibility on consumer behavior," *Journal of Business Ethics*, Vol. 84, January, pp. 65–78.

60 Du, S., Bhattacharya, C. B., and Sen, S., (2007), "Reaping relational rewards from corporate social responsibility: The role of competitive positioning," *International Journal of Research in Marketing*, Vol. 24, September, pp. 224–241.

61 Klein, J., and Dawar, N., (2004), "Corporate social responsibility and consumers' attributions and brand evaluations in a product-harm crisis," *International Journal of Research in Marketing*, Vol. 21, September, pp. 203–217.

62 Murray, K.B., and Vogel, C.M., (1997), "Using a hierarchy-of-effects approach to gauge the effectiveness of corporate social responsibility to generate goodwill toward the firm: Financial versus nonfinancial impacts," *Journal of Business Research*, Vol. 38, February, pp. 141–159.

63 Mohr, L.A., Webb, D.J., and Harris, K.E., (2001), "Do consumers expect companies to be socially responsible? The impact of corporate social responsibility on Buying Behavior," *Journal of Consumer Affairs*, Vol. 35, No. 1, pp. 45–72.

64 Kim, S., and Reber, B.H., (2008), "Public relations' place in corporate social responsibility: Practitioners define their role", *Public Relations Review*, Vol. 34, No. 4, pp. 337–342.

65 Werther, W.B., and Chandler, D., (2006), *Strategic Corporate Social Responsibility: Stakeholders in a Global Environment*, Sage, Thousand Oaks, CA.

66 Fombrun, C.J., (2005), "Building corporate reputation through CSR initiatives: Evolving standards", *Corporate Reputation Review*, Vol. 8, No. 1, pp. 7–11.

67 Bhattacharya, C.B., and Sen, S., (2004), "Doing better at doing good: When, why, and how consumers respond to corporate social initiatives", *California Management Review*, Vol. 47, No. 1, pp. 9–24.

68 Pfau, M., Haigh, M., Sims, J., and Wigley, S., (2007), "The influence of corporate front-group stealth campaigns", *Communication Research*, Vol. 34, No. 1, pp. 1–27.

69 Bonini, S., (2012), "The business of sustainability", *McKinsey on Sustainability and Resource Productivity*, Summer, pp. 96–105.

70 De la Fuente, J.M., and de Quevedo, E., (2003), "The concept and measurement of corporate reputation: An application to Spanish financial intermediaries", *Corporate Reputation Review*, Vol. 5, No. 4, pp. 280–230.

71 Fombrun, C., (1996), *Reputation: Realizing Value from the Corporate Image*, Harvard Business School Press, Boston, MA.

72 Pérez, A., (2015), "Corporate reputation and CSR reporting to stakeholders", *Corporate Communications: An International Journal*, Vol. 20, No. 1, pp. 11–29.

73 Illia, L., and Balmer, J.M.T., (2012), "Corporate communication and corporate marketing", *Corporate Communications*, Vol. 17, No. 4, pp. 415–433.

74 Aaker, D.A., (2005), *Strategic Marketing Management*, 7th ed., John Wiley, New York, NY.

75 Melo, T., and Garrido, A., (2012), "Corporate reputation: A combination of social responsibility and industry", *Corporate Social Responsibility and Environmental Management*, Vol. 19, No. 1, pp. 11–31.

76 Surroca, J., Tribó, J.A., and Waddock, S., (2010), "Corporate responsibility and financial performance: The role of intangible resources", *Strategic Management Journal*, Vol. 31, No. 5, pp. 463–490.

77 Ellen, P.S., Webb, D.J., and Mohr, L.A., (2006), "Building corporate associations: Consumer attributions for corporate socially responsible programs", *Journal of the Academy of Marketing Science*, Vol. 34, No. 2, pp. 147–157.

78 Connelly, B.L., Ketchen, D.J., and Slater, S.F., (2010), "Towards a 'theoretical toolbox' for sustainability research in marketing", *Journal of the Academy of Marketing Science*, Vol. 39, No. 1, pp. 86–100.

79 Jones, B., Bowd, R., and Tench, R., (2009), "Corporate irresponsibility and corporate social responsibility: Competing realities", *Social Responsibility Journal*, Vol. 5, No. 3, pp. 300–310.

80 Tench, R., Sun, W., and Jones, B., (Ed.) (2012), *Corporate Social Irresponsibility: A Challenging Concept (Critical Studies on Corporate Responsibility, Governance and Sustainability, Volume 4)*, Bingley, UK: Emerald Group Publishing Limited.

81 Jahdi, K.S., and Acikdilli, G., (2009), "Marketing communications and corporate social responsibility (CSR): Marriage of convenience or shotgun wedding", *Journal of Business Ethics*, Vol. 88, No. 1, pp. 103–113.

82 Du, S., Bhattacharya, C.B., and Sen, S., (2010), "Maximizing business returns to corporate social responsibility (CSR): The role of CSR communication", *International Journal of Management Reviews*, Vol. 12, No. 1, pp. 8–19.

83 Morsing, M., (2006), "Corporate social responsibility as strategic auto-communication: On the role of external stakeholders for member identification", *Business Ethics: A European Review*, Vol. 15, No. 2, pp. 171–182.

84 Van de Ven, B., (2008), "An ethical framework for the marketing of corporate social responsibility", *Journal of Business Ethics*, Vol. 82, No. 2, pp. 339–352.

85 Morsing, M., and Schultz, M., (2006), "Corporate social responsibility communication: Stakeholder information, response and involvement strategies", *Business Ethics: A European Review*, Vol. 15, No. 4, pp. 323–338.

86 Golob, U., Podnar, K., Elving, W.J., Nielsen, A.E., Thomsen, C., and Schultz, F., (2013), "CSR communication: quo vadis?", *Corporate Communications: An International Journal*, Vol. 18, No. 2, pp. 176–192.

87 Samy, M., Odemilin, G., and Bampton, R., (2010), "Corporate social responsibility: Strategy for sustainable business success- an analysis of 20 selected British companies", *Corporate Governance, The International Journal of Business in Society*, Vol. 10, No. 2, pp. 203–217.

88 Christensen, L.T., and Cheney, G., (2011), "Interrogating the communicative dimensions of corporate social responsibility", in Ihlen, Ø., Bartlett, J., and May, S. (Eds), *The Handbook of Communication and Corporate Social Responsibility*, Wiley, Oxford, pp. 491–504.

89 Schultz, F., (2013), "Corporate social responsibility, reputation, and moral communication: A constructivist view", in Carroll, C.E. (Ed.), *The Handbook of Communication and Corporate Reputation*, Wiley, Hoboken, NJ, pp. 362–75.

90 Schultz, F., and Wehmeier, S., (2010), "Institutionalization of corporate social responsibility within corporate communications: Combining institutional, sensemaking and communication perspectives", *Corporate Communications: An International Journal*, Vol. 15, No. 1, pp. 9–29.

91 Bayoud, N.S., and Kavanagh, M., (2012), "Corporate social responsibility disclosure: Evidence from Lybian managers", *Global Journal of Business Research*, Vol. 6, No. 5, pp. 73–83.

92 Varenova, D., Samy, M., and Combs, A., (2013), "Corporate social responsibility and profitability: Trade-off or synergy, perceptions of executives of FTSE all-share companies", *Sustainability Accounting, Management and Policy Journal*, Vol. 4, No. 2, pp. 190–215.

93 Birth, G., Illia, L., Lurati, F., and Zamparini, A., (2008), "Communicating CSR: Practices among Switzerland's top 300 companies", *Corporate Communications: An International Journal*, Vol. 13, No. 2, pp. 182–196.

94 Castells, M., (2008), "The new public sphere: Global civil society, communication networks, and global governance", *The Annals of the American Academy of Political and Social Science*, Vol. 616, No. 1, pp. 78–93.

95 Mohin, T., (2012), "The top 10 trends in CSR for 2012", *Forbes*, available at www.forbes.com/sites/forbesleadershipforum/2012/01/18/the-top-10-trends-in-csr-for-2012/ [accessed 26 May 2015].

96 Etter, M., (2014), "Broadcasting, reacting, engaging – three strategies for CSR communication in Twitter", *Journal of Communication Management*, Vol. 18, No. 4, pp. 322–342.

97 Burton, S., and Soboleva, A., (2011), "Interactive or reactive? Marketing with twitter", *Journal of Consumer Marketing*, Vol. 28, No. 7, pp. 491–499.

98 Golbeck, J., Grimes, J.M., and Rogers, A., (2010), "Twitter use by the US congress", *Journal of the American Society for Information Science and Technology*, Vol. 61, No. 8, pp. 1612–1621.

99 Arvidsson, A., Etter, M., and Colleoni, E., (2012), "General sentiment and value: how does online sentiment affect financial evaluations?", presented at The 28th EGOS Colloquium, Aalto University, Helsinki, June 7.

100 Ahmad, A.N., (2010), "Is twitter a useful tool for journalists?", *Journal of Media Practice*, Vol. 11, No. 2, pp. 145–155.

101 Christensen, C., (2011), "Discourses of technology and liberation: State aid to net activists in an era of 'twitter revolutions'", *The Communication Review*, Vol. 14, No. 3, pp. 233–253.

102 Segerberg, A., and Bennett, W.L., (2011), "Social media and the organization of collective action: Using Twitter to explore the ecologies of two climate change protests", *The Communication Review*, Vol. 14, No. 3, pp. 197–215.

103 Waters, R.D., and Jamal, J.Y., (2011), "Tweet, tweet, tweet: A content analysis of nonprofit organizations' twitter updates", *Public Relations Review*, Vol. 37, No. 3, pp. 321–324.

104 Insch, A., (2008), "Online communication of corporate environmental citizenship: A study of New Zealand's electricity and gas retailers", *Journal of Marketing Communications*, Vol. 14, No. 2, pp. 139–153.

105 Kim, S., Kim, S.-Y., and Sung, K.H., (2014), "Fortune 100 companies' Facebook strategies: corporate ability versus social responsibility", *Journal of Communication Management*, Vol. 18, No. 4, pp. 343–362.

106 Kim, S., (2011), "Transferring effects of CSR strategy on consumer responses: The synergistic model of corporate communication strategy", *Journal of Public Relations Research*, Vol. 23, No. 2, pp. 218–241.

107 Kim, S., and Rader, C.S., (2010), "What they can do versus how much they care: Assessing corporate communication strategies on Fortune 500 websites", *Journal of Communication Management*, Vol. 14, No. 1, pp. 59–80.

108 Beauchamp, M.B., (2013), "Don't invade my personal space: Facebook's advertising dilemma", *Journal of Applied Business Research*, Vol. 29, No. 1, pp. 91–96.

109 Haigh, M.M., and Wigley, S., (2015), "Examining the impact of negative, user-generated content on stakeholders", *Corporate Communications: An International Journal*, Vol. 20, No. 1, pp. 63–75.

110 Castello, I., Morsing, M., and Schultz, F., (2013), "Communicative dynamics and the polyphony of corporate social responsibility in the network society", *Journal of Business Ethics*, Vol. 118, pp. 683–694.

111 Christensen, L. T., Morsing, M., and Thyssen, O., (2011), "The polyphony of corporate social responsibility: Deconstructing accountability and transparency in the context of identity and hypocrisy", in Cheney, G., May, S., and Munshi, D. (Eds.), *Handbook of Communication Ethics*, Routledge, New York, pp. 457–474.

112 Tench, R., and Jones, B., (2015), "Social media: The Wild West of CSR communications", *Social Responsibility Journal*, Vol. 11, No. 2, pp. 290–305.

2.4 Communicating corporate social responsibilities (CSR) in digital media

Interactivity is key

Zhifeng Chen and Haiming Hang

During the past few decades, CSR has become one of the central constructs in business and management literature describing the social responsibilities of business, firms and their managers.[1] One of the key assumptions in the literature is that CSR can enhance firms' competitive advantages and their financial performance.[2] However, in order for firms to fully benefit from their CSR activities, the importance of effective CSR communication cannot be underestimated.[3]

With the increasing popularity of digital media, the Internet and social media have become key platforms for firms to communication their CSR activities with stakeholders.[4] As a result, research on CSR communication in the digital arenas is emerging. One of the key assumptions in the literature is that the interactive nature of the digital media allows organizations to fully engage with their stakeholders, potentially transforming CSR communication effectiveness.[5] Thus, the main purpose of this chapter is to thematically review previous research to determine whether this assumption is supported by extant literature.

The remainder of the chapter is organized as follows: we will first emphasize CSR is a moral coloured concept, reflecting a firm's character that is not directly observable. Thus, effective CSR communication is crucial for firms to benefit from their CSR activities. Then we present our research questions developed from the literature. After that, we review existing conceptualisations of interactivity in marketing, information system and media studies, proposing it is a multidimensional construct. This is followed by a thematic review of CSR communication in the digital media. In particular, we argue that the extant literature on this topic is limited and only provides a partial understanding of interactivity in digital CSR communication. Then our chapter concludes with recommendations for future research.

CSR communication

Although CSR has attracted researchers' attention for decades, no consensus has been reached regarding the best way to conceptualize it.[6] However, scholars in general do agree CSR is a moral coloured concept. It leads to character reputation judgement of a firm.[7] In other words, due to its moral-coloured nature, stakeholders cannot directly observe a firm's CSR but can use its CSR activities to infer its moral reputation.[8] Therefore, CSR communication has been widely acknowledged as an essential element for firms to benefit from their CSR activities.

However, extant literature on CSR communication is embryonic and fragmented, lacking a unified conceptual framework.[9] In addition, research on CSR communication is unbalanced, dominated by a functionalist approach examining external stakeholders' responses to and judgment of organizations' CSR.[10] As a result, the 4Is framework is developed to integrate current diverse literature. According to this framework, CSR communication can be classified as CSR integration, CSR interpretation, CSR identity and CSR image. While CSR integration and CSR interpretation focus on internal stakeholders (e.g., employees), CSR identity and CSR image direct towards external stakeholders (e.g., consumers). Different Is reflect different approaches, with CSR integration and CSR identity guided by a functionalist approach while CSR interpretation and CSR image guided by a constitutive approach.[11]

CSR communication can be used for different purposes such as stakeholder management, image enhancement and identity creation.[12] But low awareness of and unfavourable attributions towards CSR activities are the key obstacles for a firm to maximize these business benefits from its CSR engagement. For example, the business case of CSR is built on the assumption that stakeholders reward good corporate citizens while punishing bad ones.[13] This, therefore, requires stakeholders to at least be aware of a firm's CSR activities. However, research has repeatedly reported stakeholders tend to have low awareness of a firm' CSR activities.[14]

In addition, stakeholders' scepticism towards a firm's CSR activities is another key challenge for it to maximize business benefits.[15] Stakeholders tend to react positively towards a firm that shows a genuine concern about societal well-being (intrinsic motives) while reacting negatively towards a firm that engages CSR for ulterior, self-serving purposes (extrinsic motives).[16]

Thus, the extant CSR communication literature suggests a successful CSR communication campaign needs to raise awareness and generate favourable CSR attribution (intrinsic motives).[17] In order to achieve these objectives, when a firm disseminates its CSR activities, it needs to choose a social cause that fits with the company's business.[18] In addition, it needs to demonstrate its commitment and actual contribution to the social cause.[19]

Research questions

A firm can disseminate its CSR engagement via different media such as TV commercials, magazine, websites or social media. A recent excellent review of CSR communication literature points out the interactive nature of digital media can offer bidirectional and symmetrical communication, potentially transforming organization-stakeholder interaction.[20] In other words, the interactive nature of the digital media can provide stakeholders more control about the way they process a firm's CSR activities. This, in turn, will increase their elaboration and favourable attribution of a firm's CSR.[21] As a result, scholars in general assume interactive digital media can increase CSR communication effectiveness. Thus, the main purpose of this book chapter is to thematically review extant literature on CSR communication in digital media to see whether this assumption is supported by existing scientific evidence. Since one of the defining features of digital media is interactivity, our literature review will focus on the following two questions:

RQ1: How is interactivity used by organizations to communicate their CSR in digital arenas?
RQ2: How does interactivity influence the effectiveness of digital CSR communication?

The interactive nature of digital media

During the past few decades, interactivity has become a central construct in marketing,[22] information system[23] and media studies[24] to understand activities in digital media. However, various approaches are used to underpin this construct. The following paragraphs discuss this in detail.

A mechanical perspective

A mechanical perspective defines interactivity as "the extent to which users can participant in modifying the form and content of a mediated environment in real time" (p. 84).[25] In particular, a mechanical perspective suggests that interactivity includes three key components: speed, range and mapping. Speed refers to whether users can manipulate content in a fast or slow way.[26] Relating to CSR communication, this can be interpreted as the pace (fast or slow) firms allow stakeholders to provide feedback to their CSR activities. Range focuses on the way users can manipulate content.[27] In terms of CSR communication, this can be reflected as the number of options stakeholders can assess to provide feedback to firms' CSR activities, with more options indicating higher interactivity. As for mapping, it refers to the extent to which the control used in the mediated environment is similar to a real environment.[28] In other words, in the context of CSR communication, mapping focuses on whether online CSR communication can provide a realist way for firms to communicate their CSR activities to stakeholders. However, the mechanical perspective assumes interactivity derives from the structure or design of a medium.[29] Thus, it does not take the communication process and users' perceptions into consideration.

A communication process perspective

Media studies scholars define interactivity as "the extent to which messages in a sequence relate to each other, and especially the extent to which later messages recount the relatedness of earlier messages"(p. 3).[30] In a similar way, in marketing, interactivity is defined as "the degree to which two or more communication parties can act on each other, on the communication medium, and on the messages and the degree to which such influences are synchronized" (p. 54).[31] A communication process further argues interactivity has three dimensions: active control, two-way communication and synchronicity. Active control refers to the abilities users can have to customize information flow and influence their own experiences.[32] In the CSR communication context, active control can be interpreted as whether stakeholders can browse and comment on firms' CSR activities based on their own goals and wishes. Two-way communication refers to "the ability for reciprocal communication between companies and users and users and users" (p. 56).[33] Applying this to CSR communication, two-way communication reflects whether firms offer any feedback to stakeholders when they interact via digital media. As for synchronicity, it refers to the speed and effectiveness of message exchange, with quick and effective responses indicating higher interactivity.[34] However, "the experiential aspect of interactivity is the interactivity of the communication process as perceived by the communication parties" (p. 55).[35] This leads to some researchers arguing for a user perception perspective of interactivity.[36]

A user perception perspective

A central argument of a user perception perspective is that interactivity should not be defined by counting medium features or analysing processes. Rather, interactivity exists in the minds of medium users.[37] This, therefore, implies interactive medium features do not automatically lead to interactivity. Existing empirical evidence does support this.[38] For example, there is a low correlation between perceived interactivity and interactive features available on the websites. In addition, adding an interactive feature to a websites does not automatically enhance interactivity perception.[39] Thus, a user perception perspective argues perceived interactivity and objective interactivity (number of interactive features) are two distinct concepts.[40]

The essence of interactivity

Although there are different perspectives on the best way to conceptualize interactivity, they all agree interactivity is a multidimensional construct.[41] In addition, different perspectives are not mutually exclusive. Interactive features may facilitate the communication process, leading to higher interactivity. Alternatively, interactive features may make users perceive the medium as highly interactive. This has important implications for research on CSR communication via digital media. The following section provides a thematic review of CSR communication in digital media to see how interactivity is used by organizations to transform their CSR communication and whether interactivity can enhance their CSR communication effectiveness.

A thematic review of CSR communication in digital media

Based on the above research questions, a literature review was used to reveal the key patterns and themes across a wide range of settings and empirical methods. This is more robust than a single empirical study whose results may be limited to its research contexts (e.g., its sample and research methods). Indeed, if studies give consistent results, a literature review can provide evidence that the phenomenon is robust and transferable. If the studies give inconsistent results, sources of variation can be studied.[42]

The high heterogeneity of current CSR communication research makes it difficult to determine the boundaries of what should or should not be included in a literature review.[43] This, therefore, implies it may be impossible for any researchers to do a systematic literature review on the topic. Thus, following a recent literature review on CSR communication,[44] this chapter adopts a thematic approach, pinpointing and recording key themes in the literature to address our two research questions. A thematic approach is appropriate because it is widely used to pinpoint, examine, and synthesise patterns within data.[45] The following sections discuss our inclusion criteria and analytical process.

Inclusion criteria

Time period and research domains: academic research on digital CSR communication starts from 1998, when digital media was reported to be used widely by Fortune 500 companies to communicate their CSR.[46] Thus, our thematic review only focuses on research from 1998, covering a period of 18 years (1998–2016). Due to the multidisciplinary nature of CSR and interactivity, we did not limit our search in business and management literature. Rather, we also searched literature in computer science and media studies to provide a comprehensive coverage.

Search terms: following a recent literature review,[47] we used various terms to search extant literature. For example, for CSR, we used terms 'CSR', 'corporate sustainability', 'corporate responsibility', 'corporate citizenship' and 'stakeholder management'. For communication, we used the terms 'communication', 'public relations', 'advertising', 'disclosure', and 'stakeholder management'. For digital media, we used terms 'Internet', 'website', 'social media' and 'digital media'. The different combinations of these terms (e.g., corporate citizenship + communication + website) were used to retrieve extant literature.

Databases used: we did not limit our search to particular management and business journals or books/book chapters. Rather, we chose to use various databases to identify the key literature relating to our topic. The databases we searched were: EBSCO Business Source Premier, ABI/INFORM Global (ProQuest), Scopus, Emerald, Web of Science, PubMed and Google Scholar. In addition, we reviewed the bibliographies of the retrieved literature and checked their citations using Web of Knowledge and Google Scholar to identify additional sources relevant to our review. However, we excluded articles published in trade magazines and conferences. Thus, our review only included articles published in peer-reviewed journals or books and book chapters.

Analytical process

Following a recent literature review,[48] we determined research that offered direct insights to our two research questions as a priori and used them as indicators of relevance in informing our analysis. Previous research also suggests theoretical saturation may be reached when data adds nothing new to the current understanding of a topic.[49] However, this approach has been criticized for its reliability because of the wide variety of interpretations that arise from the themes, as well as applying themes to large amounts of text.[50] Thus, we adopted an iterative approach, identifying commonalities and divergence across and between different sources till the research team reached a consensus that no more new theoretical insights were added. Following this procedure, we found extant literature focuses on two different themes, each addressing one of our key research questions.

Theme 1: Documenting interactivity of CSR communications in digital media

Since extant literature on digital CSR communication tends to focus on either websites or social media, our review discusses them separately.

Websites: Only limited studies have examined interactivity of online CSR communication. One of the early articles on this topic suggested activist organizations acknowledged the importance of using websites to build relationships with publics. However, they did not engage in two-way communication with the public, even though they had relevant technical and design expertise to do so.[51] In a similar view, the majority of New Zealand's electricity and gas retailers did report their environmental initiatives on their websites. But they did not employ interactive features to encourage dialogue with stakeholders.[52] This is the same for firms taking part in the Global Reporting Initiatives. Through content analysis, previous research criticized these firms for the low levels of interactivity in their digital CSR communication. They argued that those websites failed to fully engage relevant stakeholders, as they mainly focused on presenting information rather than collecting feedback.[53] This is echoed in later research. For example, although Fortune 500 firms differed on the prominence of CSR sections on their websites, in general they failed to interact with stakeholders to establish effective dialogues.[54] Other research reported online CSR reports use rhetorical strategies of ethos, pathos, and logos to disseminate information to stakeholders without actively engaging with them.[55]

More recent research has tried to provide some explanations about the low levels of interactivity in online CSR communication. Some scholars suggested the Internet was not considered as an important medium for universities to communicate their CSR with stakeholders.[56] However, these articles only focus on higher education. Thus, whether their findings can be generalized to other sectors is debatable. For example, other studies found firms acknowledged the importance of using digital media to communicate CSR. They further believed digital media needed to be integrated with other media to develop coherent CSR communication campaigns.[57]

Social media: While early digital CSR communication literature mainly focuses on websites, more recent research has shifted their attention to social media. These studies underpin the types of firms that use social media to engage stakeholders,[58] key CSR issues disseminated via social media,[59] stakeholders' perceptions of and response to CSR communication via social media[60] and key constrains of using social media to disseminate CSR activities.[61]

A common finding of these studies is the low interactivity of CSR communication in social media. For example, by analysing Twitter accounts of multinational firms and NGOs, previous research found a key pattern for these institutions to engage stakeholders via Twitter was one-way communication.[62] Through coding 40,000 tweets, another study found a dominant CSR communication strategy in social media was broadcasting, focusing on disseminating information rather than relationship building.[63] A most recent research provides further support to this, pointing out interactivity is very low among eight global firms' Twitter CSR accounts.[64] This is evident in both emerging markets[65] and more developed ones.[66] But others reported firms with high CSR ratings and high corporate social irresponsibility ratings were more likely to engender user-driven communications in social media than their counterparts. However, their research mainly focused on what types of firms were more likely to use social media to communication their CSR activities.[67] Thus, their research does not provide direct evidence on the high (or low) interactivity of CSR communication in this medium.

Other scholars aim to underpin the key reasons for low interactivity in social media. By content analysis of social media policies of 112 largest firms in the world, some scholars argued existing policies constrained rather than facilitated employees' participation in social media CSR communication. They reasoned that these policies hindered employees' free speech rights and collective information sharing because those guidelines blurred the boundaries among firm, private and public spheres.[68] Others attributed low interactivity to a reactive approach widely adopted by firms in different sectors.[69] In other words, these researchers argued firms did not want to seek interaction with stakeholders via Twitter. Rather the main purpose of Twitter was to respond to other Twitters users.[70] From a stakeholder' perspective, recent studies suggested there was a little interaction via social media among different stakeholders. This, therefore, makes firms feel no pressure to interact with them.[71]

Another key focus of the literature is the impact of interactivity on CSR communication effectiveness. The next theme addresses this in detail.

Theme 2: Examining the impact of interactivity on CSR communication in digital media

Websites: Compared with social media, only limited studies have investigated the impact of interactivity on CSR communication on websites. For example, previous research demonstrates that allowing stakeholders to interact with company website messages can enhance message credibility and identification with the company. This, in turn, can have a positive impact on company reputation, positive word of mouth, stakeholder expectation and establishing legitimacy.[72] However, previous research has also found companies cannot benefit from stakeholders' positive comments posted on websites. But mixed or mostly negative comments can have a detrimental impact.[73] One thing to note is that interactivity is defined as two-way communication in this research. This is consistent with a communication process perspective of interactivity. But a communication process perspective of interactivity includes active control, two-way communication and synchronicity.[74] Thus, previous research only provides a partial picture of interactivity in digital media.

Using the notion of dialogue, other scholars suggest an organization can use digital media to help stakeholders to learn its CSR activities (co-learning), generate new meanings (co-innovating) and decide next steps (co-deciding). Through a two-year three-stage qualitative study, their research proposes organizations can use four types of dialogues (directing conversations, moderating conversations, building open script conversations and crowdsourcing conversations) to interact with stakeholders. They further argue only when organizations use all types of dialogues then they can engage with stakeholders in digital media.[75] By focusing on dialogue, their research also adopts a communication process perspective of interactivity to examine digital CSR communication. This is consistent with other research focusing on the same topic.[76]

Social media: The majority of previous studies on the impact of interactivity on CSR communications focus on social media. Some scholars found that in social media, food companies tended to report product-related CSR initiatives and promotion-related CSR initiatives. They defined promotion-related CSR initiatives as those CSR activities that were not related to firms' core business. In contrast, product-related CSR initiatives related to firms' products, thus relating to their core business.[77] Their results suggested stakeholders tended to respond more positively towards product-related CSR initiatives, while responding negatively towards promotion-related CSR initiatives.[78] In a similar vein, other scholars argue corporate communications via social media can be classified as three types: corporate ability, CSR or a hybrid approach.[79] Their research suggests that exposure to CSR communication can lead to more positive attitudes and higher purchase intents than other two types of communication approaches.[80] More importantly, these scholars claim interactivity on social media can increase all positive outcomes. In their study, when participants are provided with an opportunity to click different tabs in Facebook to search information, it can lead to more positive outcomes such as more positives attitudes and higher purchase intents.[81] Other scholars support this.[82] For example, when organizations respond to bloggers' comments, it can lead to more positive attitudes towards and perceptions of CSR motives. In contrast, when organizations do not respond to blogger's comments and have a negative reputation, bloggers have the worst judgements towards the firm.[83] Other research further suggests interactive CSR communication can increase young adult consumers' emotional brand value and knowledge.[84] Although these studies focus on the different dimensions of interactivity (e.g., two-way communication vs. active control), they all suggest interactivity can lead to positive outcomes.[85] Recent research provides further evidence on this.[86] Using a longitudinal case study, recent research finds organizations can gain legitimacy via participation in non-hierarchical open platforms in social media. This offers them the opportunity to co-construct their agendas with stakeholders.[87]

However, the above results should be interpreted with caution. First, CSR topics in social media were mostly ignored. Only a minority of people pay attention to CSR related messages.[88] This is perhaps because, compared with news media, social media such as Facebook has relatively limited power to shape public interpretations of a corporate crisis.[89] Second, stakeholders mainly used social media to ask their peers about information and opinions about different CSR topics. Thus, engaging stakeholders by opening dialogs with them did not produce any positive effects. This was mainly due to the fact that stakeholders considered CSR communication in social media as a marketing practice and therefore not credible.[90] This makes some scholars argue that when engaging stakeholders via social media, organizations should focus on popularity, commitment and vitality.[91]

Rather than focus on organizations, some scholars examine the impact of interactive social media on stakeholders.[92] In general, these studies all suggest that social media empowers stakeholders. For example, some scholars suggested social media provided a powerful platform for them to negotiate and influence firms' CSR initiatives. In particular, they suggested if stakeholders made CSR-related issues salient in their own social media, it would increase the likelihood for other stakeholders to comment on the issues. This, in turn, would pose pressure for firms to respond to stakeholders' expectations.[93] This thesis is supported by recent case studies.[94] For example, social media allows stakeholders to publicly challenge organization's irresponsible behaviour.[95] In the case of China, social media was used by Chinese stakeholders to spark criticism towards Conoco Phillips after its oil spill incident.[96] Other research suggests the transparency of information posted on social media may reduce firms' tendency of 'greenwash', as stakeholders can use social media to disclose and criticize any inconsistency between what firms do and what they say.[97] However, this does not mean social media makes the public more powerful than corporations. Rather, social media potentially enables individual citizens to influence and negotiate with corporations.[98] Indeed, while some consumers felt empowered by social media to promote their CSR agendas, other consumers felt they were negatively judged by others. For these consumers, social media was not an efficient method for CSR activism.[99]

General discussion and conclusions

While scholars and managers agree digital media offer unique opportunities for firms to interact with stakeholders, research so far has repeatedly suggested low levels of interactivity in both websites and social media. In particular, the main criticism from previous research is that organizations only engage in one-way communication with stakeholders. This is an argument built on the two-way communication dimension in the communication process perspective of interactivity. Thus, it may provide a narrow understanding of interactivity because, as discussed above, interactivity can also be conceptualised from a mechanical perspective and a use-perception perspective.

Our review further suggests only a few studies have examined the impact of interactivity on CSR communication effectiveness. This is perhaps because extant literature tends to treat CSR communication as an instrument, disseminating a firm's CSR activities to the wide public.[100] Thus, descriptive studies explaining how organizations disseminate their CSR in the digital arenas dominate current research; in addition, since current research mainly takes a firm's perspective to explore CSR communication,[101] it ignores the unique features of digital media – interactivity.

However, among those limited studies that do focus on the impact of interactivity on CSR communication, they all reported interactivity could lead to positive outcomes.[102]

But they either focus on two-way communication[103] or active control.[104] None of them focus on how the different dimensions of interactivity can jointly influence CSR communication effectiveness. Neither does research adopt a mechanical perspective and/or a use-perception perspective of interactivity to examine its impact.

Our review has also identified that the interactive nature of digital media can empower the public, allowing them to influence and negotiate organizations' CSR.[105] Thus, a key challenge for firms to communicate their CSR via digital media is how to fully engage with stakeholders to benefit their own CSR activities. Focusing on the construct of interactivity may provide some useful insights. The following section discusses this in detail.

Recommendations for future research

Since CSR is a moral-coloured concept that is not directly observable, CSR communication is essential for firms to benefit from their own CSR activities.[106] However, as discussed above, our thematic review suggests that firms currently fail to fully interact with their stakeholders in the digital media. Thus, in the final part of this chapter, we use the construct of interactivity to underpin the key areas for future research that can help organizations to fully engage with stakeholders and increase their CSR communication effectiveness. Since interactivity is conceptualised in different ways, our discussion will cover them in turn.

A mechanical perspective assumes the structure or design of a medium decides interactivity.[107] Previous research suggests that digital media has the technological capabilities to increase the dynamics of CSR communication by enhancing speed and connectivity.[108] Thus, from a mechanical perspective, future research needs to identify key features of digital media to fully engage with stakeholders. For example, a mechanical perspective proposes speed, range and mapping are the three key elements of interactivity.[109] Thus, future research can test whether increased speed will help firms to fully engage with their stakeholders, which, in turn, increases their CSR communication effectiveness. In other words, a key question for future research to address is whether responding to stakeholders' comments more promptly will increase stakeholders' awareness of and positive attribution towards firms' CSR activities. In a similar way, future research can also explore whether increased range in digital media will enhance CSR communication effectiveness. For example, one key difference between social media and corporate websites is that social media allows users to create and share information among their own networks. Thus, from a mechanical perspective, social media can have higher range than corporate websites, enabling stakeholders to fully express their values. This, in turn, will increase the richness of information flow, leading to higher awareness and positive attribution. But whether this is true awaits future research.[110]

A communication perspective of interactivity proposes the defining feature of interactivity is whether later messages are built on and feed back to earlier ones.[111] It further proposes that interactivity entails both two-way communication and active control.[112] However, our thematic review suggest extant literature mainly focus on two-way communication while ignore active control. Thus, from a communication process perspective, future research can explore the impact of active control on digital CSR communication. Some scholars argue that autonomy reduces stakeholders' perceptions of uncertainty, which, in turn, increase message believability.[113] However, others suggest active control can have detrimental effects as it creates demand on information processing resources.[114] This is particularly evident when stakeholders work under time pressure. Thus, future research is needed to identify when active control can lead to positive outcomes and when it can lead to negative outcomes.

A user perception perspective suggests interactivity exists in the minds of medium users.[115] Thus, from a user perception perspective, future research needs to take stakeholders' characteristics and responsibilities into consideration when investigating digital CSR communication effectiveness. For example, previous research has documented that the effectiveness of CSR communication depends on stakeholders' own values and lifestyles.[116] Thus, future research can explore other factors such as stakeholders' online information search styles to understand digital CSR communication effectiveness. In addition, the stakeholder theory[117] proposes that each corporation has a wide range of stakeholders (e.g., government, suppliers and customers) who have different interests and responsibilities in the same organization. This, therefore, suggests different stakeholders may have different preferences on how an organization implements and communicates its CSR. Thus, future research is needed to see how stakeholders' roles and responsibilities may influence their judgment of an organization's digital CSR communication. One way to address this is to focus on the democratic potential of digital public.[118] One key argument in this literature is that the digital arenas have the potential to increase political participation of the general public.[119] Thus, stakeholders with different responsibilities may use digital arenas to negotiate and influence a firm's CSR differently. Recent research has provided some initial evidence on this.[120] But more research is needed to see how interaction between organizations and the general public in the digital arenas shapes a firm's CSR.

Finally, as CSR is a multidimensional and multi-level construct,[121] future research needs to focus on different dimensions and different levels to see how the construct of interactivity will influence digital CSR communication effectiveness. For example, future research can compare different dimensions of CSR to see whether interactivity will influence them in the same way. Alternatively, future research can compare the impact of interactivity on CSR communication at different levels (e.g., individual vs. organizational) to see whether they will differ. In addition, since CSR communication can be studied with different approaches (i.e., constructivist approach and functionalistic approach),[122] we also encourage future research to take different approaches to underpin how interactivity may transform CSR communication.

Limitations and contributions

Similar to other research, our research also has some limitations: first of all, a recent book chapter suggests the unique features of the digital arenas pose several challenges to CSR communication in this media.[123] Interactivity is just one of the unique features differentiates digital arenas from other medium. However, digital arenas can also have other unique features. For example, very recently digital platforms have become the most important source for collecting large amounts of data (i.e., big data) to identify trends and moods.[124] Since this book chapter only focuses on interactivity, it does not underpin how digital arenas may transform data collection and analysis for CSR communication. Future research can explore how the large amount of data collected via digital media can help organizations effectively communicate their CSR. Secondly, extant literature tends to treat CSR communication as an instrument while it ignores the formative role of communication for CSR.[125] Since our thematic review is built on extant literature, our review may be biased towards the instrumental approach of CSR communication while it ignores its formative role. Thus, we encourage future research to take a constitutive perspective[126] to further explore how the meaning of CSR is continuously shaped by new communication technologies/platforms. Thirdly, a recent book suggests integrated CSR communication is more effective than uncoordinated efforts.[127] Our review only focuses on digital arenas. Thus, it provides few insights about how organizations can integrate their digital CSR communications with other media. Therefore, we encourage future research to identify the key mechanisms organizations can use to integrate their CSR communication across media.

Despite these limitations, by addressing our two key research questions, our book chapter makes several contributions to the CSR communication literature. First, we highlight that one defining feature of digital media is interactivity. Thus, more research is needed to understand how interactivity can transform CSR communication. Second, we criticize extant literature for ignoring the multidimensional nature of interactivity as they only provide a partial understanding of interactivity in digital media. Third, our review suggests that currently CSR communication in digital media is dominated by one-way communication, focusing on disseminating CSR information rather than fully engaging with stakeholders. Thus, based on the current conceptualisations of interactivity, we identify key research areas that can help firms transform their CSR communication in digital media.

Notes

1 For reviews see Aguinis, H. and Glavas, A. (2012), What we know and don't know about corporate social responsibility: A review and research agenda, *Journal of Management, 38*(4), 932–968; Carroll, A. B. (1999), Corporate social responsibility: Evolution of a definitional construct, *Business and Society, 38*, 268–295; Carroll, A. B. (2008), A history of corporate social responsibility: Concepts and practices, in Crane, A., McWilliams, A., Matten, D., Moon, J. and Siegel, D. (Eds.), *The Oxford Handbook of Corporate Social Responsibility*. Oxford: Oxford University Press, pp. 19–46; Wood, D. J. (1991), Corporate social performance revisited, *Academy of Management Review, 16*, 691–718; Wood, D. J. (2010), Measuring corporate social performance: A review, *International Journal of Management Reviews, 12*, 50–84.
2 For a meta-analysis see Orlitzky, M., Schmidt, F. L. and Rynes, S. L. (2003), Corporate social and financial performance: A meta-analysis, *Organization Studies, 24*, 403–441.
3 Du, S., Bhattacharya, C.B. and Sen, S. (2010), Maximizing business returns to corporate social responsibility (CSR): The role of CSR communication, *International Journal of Management Reviews, 12*(1), 8–19.
4 Examples see Bravo, R., Matute, J. and Pina, J. M. (2012), Corporate social responsibility as a vehicle to reveal the corporate identity: A study focused on the websites of Spanish financial entities, *Journal of Business Ethics, 107*, 129–146; Smith, K. T. and Alexander, J. J. (2013), Which CSR-related headings do Fortune 500 companies use on their websites, *Business Communication Quarterly, 76*(2), 155–171.
5 Crane, A. and Glozer, S. (2016), Researching Corporate Social Responsibility Communication: Themes, Opportunities and Challenges, *Journal of Management Studies, 53*, 1223–1252.
6 Carroll, 1999; 2008.
7 Godfrey, P. C. (2005), The relationship between corporate philanthropy and shareholder wealth: A risk management perspective, *Academy of Management Review, 30*, 777–798.
8 Jones, T. M. (1995), Instrumental stakeholder theory: A synthesis of ethics and economics, *Academy of Management Review, 20*(2), 404–437.
9 Crane and Glozer, 2016.
10 Crane and Glozer, 2016.
11 Crane and Glozer, 2016.
12 Crane and Glozer, 2016.
13 Du et al., 2010.
14 Bhattacharya, C.B., Sen, S. and Korschun, D. (2008), Using corporate social responsibility to win the war for talent, *Sloan Management Review, 49*, 37–44.
15 Du et al., 2010.

16 Yoon, Y., Gurhan-Canli, Z. and Schwarz, N. (2006), The effect of corporate social responsibility (CSR) activities on companies with bad reputations, *Journal of Consumer Psychology, 16*, 377–390.

17 Du et al., 2010

18 Menon, S. and Kahn, B.E. (2003), Corporate sponsorships of philanthropic activities: When do they impact perception of sponsor brand? *Journal of Consumer Psychology, 13*, 316–327.

19 Du et al., 2010.

20 Crane, A. and Glozer, S. (2016), Researching corporate social responsibility communication: Themes, opportunities and challenges, *Journal of Management Studies, 53*, 1223–1252.

21 Du et al., 2010.

22 Liu, Y. and Shrum, L. J. (2002), What is interactivity and is it always such a good thing? Implications of definitions, person, and situation for the influence of interactivity on advertising effectiveness, *Journal of Advertising, 31*(4), 53–64.

23 Steuer, J. (1992), Defining virtual reality: Dimensions determining telepresence, *Journal of Communication, 42*(Autumn), 73–93.

24 Rafaeli, S. (1988), Interactivity: From new media to communication, in R. P. Hawkins, J. M. Wiemann and S. Pingree (Eds.), *Sage Annual Review of Communication Research: Advancing Communication Science: Merging Mass and Interpersonal Processes*, Beverly Hills: Sage, pp. 110–134

25 Steuer, 1992.

26 Steuer, 1992.

27 Steuer, 1992.

28 Steuer, 1992.

29 Ha, L. and James, E. L. (1998), Interactivity reexamined: A baseline analysis of early business web sites, *Journal of Broadcasting and Electronic Media, 42*(4), 457–469.

30 Rafaeli, op. cit; Rafaeli, S. and Sudweeks, F. (1997), Networked interactivity, *Journal of Computer-Mediated Communication, 2*.

31 Liu and Shrum, 2002.

32 Liu and Shrum, 2002.

33 Liu and Shrum, 2002.

34 Liu and Shrum, 2002.

35 Liu and Shrum, 2002.

36 Voorveld, H. A. M., Neijens, P. C., and Smit, E. G. (2011), The relation between actual and perceived interactivity: What makes the web sites of top global brands truly interactive. *Journal of Advertising, 40*, 77–92.

37 Voorveld et al., 2011.

38 Song, J. and Zinkhan, G. (2008), Determinants of perceived web site interactivity, *Journal of Marking, 72*, 99–113; Voorveld et al., op. cit.

39 Voorveld et al., 2011.

40 Voorveld et al., 2011

41 Johnson, G., Bruner II, G., and Kumar, A. (2006), Interactivity and its facets revisited, *Journal of Advertising, 35*, 35–52.

42 Thomas, J. and Harden, A. (2007), Methods for the thematic synthesis of qualitative research in systematic reviews, *ESRC National Centre for Research Methods NCRM Working Paper Series Number (10/07)*

43 Crane and Glozer, 2016

44 Crane and Glozer, 2016

45 Thomas and Harden, 2007

46 Crane and Glozer, 2016

47 Crane and Glozer, 2016

48 Crane and Glozer, 2016

49 Crane and Glozer, 2016

50 Braun, V. and Clarke, V. (2006), Using thematic analysis in psychology, *Qualitative Research in Psychology, 3*, 77–101.

51 Taylor, M., Kent, M., and White, W. (2001), How activist organizations are using the internet to build relationships, *Public Relations Review, 27*, 263–284.

52 Insch, A. (2008), Online communication of Corporate Environmental Citizenship: A study of New Zealand's electricity and gas retailers, *Journal of Marketing Communications*, 14, 139–153.

53 Capriotti, P. and Moreno, A. (2007), Corporate citizenship and public relations: The importance and interactivity of social responsibility issues on corporate websites, *Public Relations Review, 33,* 84–91.

54 Kim, S., Kim, S., and Sung, K. H. (2014), Fortune 100 companies' Facebook strategies: corporate ability versus social responsibility, *Journal of Communication Management, 18,* 343–362.

55 Feldner, S. B. and Berg, K. T. (2014), How corporations manage industry and consumer expectations via the CSR report, *Public Relations Journal, 8.*

56 Sanchez, R. G., Bolivar, M.P.R., and Hernandez, A.M.L. (2015), Are Australian universities making good use of ICT for CSR reporting? *Sustainability, 7,* 14895–14916; Bolivar, M.P.R., Sanchez, R. G., and Hernandez, A. M. J. (2013), Online disclosure of corporate social responsibility information in leading Anglo-American universities, *Journal of Environmental Policy and Planning, 15,* 551–575.

57 Tomaselli, G. and Melia, M. (2014), The role of interactive technologies for CSR communication, *Journal of International Scientific Publications, 8,* 324–340.

58 Bonson, E. and Bednarova, M. (2015), YouTube sustainability reporting: Empirical evidence from Eurozone-listed companies, *Journal of Information Systems, 29*(3), 35–50; Lee, K., Oh, W., and Kim, N. (2013), Social media for socially responsible firms: Analysis of Fortune 500's Twitter profiles and their CSR/CSIR ratings, *Journal of Business Ethics, 118,* 791–806; Lyon, T. P. and Montgomery, A. W. (2013), Tweetjacked: The impact of social media on corporate greenwash, *Journal of Business Ethics, 118,* 747–757.

59 Lee et al., 2013

60 Besiou, M., Hunter, M. L., and Wassenhove, L. (2013), A web of watchdogs: Stakeholder media networks and agenda-setting in response to corporate initiatives, *Journal of Business Ethics, 118,* 709–729; Colleoni, E. (2013), CSR communication strategies for organizational legitimacy in social media, *Corporate Communications: An International Journal, 18*(2), 228–248; Lee et al., 2013.

61 Stohl, C., Etter, M., Banghart, S., and Woo, D. (2015), Social media policies: Implications for contemporary notions of corporate social responsibility, *Journal of Business Ethics,* forthcoming.

62 Inauen, S., Schoeneborn, D. and Scherer, A. G. (2011), Twitter and its usage for dialogic stakeholder communication by MNCs and NGOs, in Ralph Tench, William Sun, Brian Jones (ed.) *Communicating Corporate Social Responsibility: Perspectives and Practice (Critical Studies on Corporate Responsibility, Governance and Sustainability, Volume 6)* Emerald Group Publishing Limited, pp. 283–310.

63 Etter, M. (2014), Broadcasting, reacting, engaging – three strategies for CSR communication in Twitter, *Journal of Communication Management, 18,* 322–342.

64 Okazaki, S. and Menendez, H. D. (2017), Virtual corporate social responsibility dialog: seeking a gap between proposed concepts and actual practices, in *Handbook of Integrated CSR Communication,* 225–234.

65 Serban, A. D. (2016), CSR as corporate power, a communication view Facebook approach: An exploratory study, *Management Dynamics in the Knowledge Economy, 4,* 31–61.

66 Cortado, F.J. and Chalmeta, R. (2016), Use of social networks as a CSR communication tool, *Cogent Business and Management, 3,* 1–18.

67 Lee et al., 2013

68 Stohl et al., 2015

69 Etter, M. (2013), Reasons for low levels of interactivity (non-) interactive CSR communication in twitter, *Public Relations Review, 39,* 606–608.

70 Etter, 2013

71 Di Bitetto, M., Pettineo, S. and D'Anselmi, P. (2015), Dear brand of the world: CSR and the social media, in Ana Adi, Georgiana Grigore, David Crowther (ed.) *Corporate Social Responsibility in the Digital Age (Developments in Corporate Governance and Responsibility, Volume 7)* Emerald Group Publishing Limited, pp. 39–61.

72 Feldner and Berg, 2014

73 Eberle, D., Berens, G. and Li, T. (2013), The impact of interactive corporate social responsibility communication on corporate reputation, *Journal of Business Ethics, 118,* 731–746.

74 Liu and Shrum, 2012

75 Illia, L., Romenti, S., Rodriguez-Canovas, B., Murtarelli, G. and Carroll, C. E. Exploring corporations' dialogue about CSR in the digital era, *Journal of Business Ethics,* forthcoming.

76 Eberle et al., 2013

77 Lee, H. M., Van Dolen, W. and Kolk, A. (2013), On the role of social media in the 'responsible' food business: Blogger buzz on health and obesity issues, *Journal of Business Ethics, 118,* 695–707.

78 Lee et al., 2013

79 Haigh, M. H., Brubaker, P. and Whiteside, E. (2013), Facebook: Examining the information presented and its impact on stakeholders, *Corporate Communications: An International Journal, 18,* 52–69; Fraustino, J. D. and Connolly-Ahern, C. (2015), Corporate associations written on the wall: Publics' responses to Fortune 500 ability and social responsibility Facebook posts, *Journal of Public Relations Research, 27,* 1–23.

80 Haigh et al., 2013

81 Haigh et al., 2013

82 Rim, H. and Song, D. (2013), The ability of corporate blog communication to enhance CSR effectiveness: the role of prior company reputation and blog responsiveness, *International Journal of Strategic Communication, 7,* 165–185.

83 Rim and Song, 2013

84 Lauritsen, B.D. and Perks, K. J. (2015), The influence of interactive, non-interactive, implicit and explicit CSR communication on young adults' perception of UK supermarkets' corporate brand image and reputation, *Corporate Communications: An International Journal,* 20, 178–195.

85 Rim and Song, 2013; Haigh et al., 2013

86 Castelló, I., Etter, M. and Nielsen, F. N. (2016), Strategies of legitimacy through social media: The networked strategy, *Journal of Management Studies, 53,* 402–432.

87 Castelló, I. et al., 2016

88 Pavlicek, A. and Doucek, P. (2015), Corporate social responsibility in social media environment, *Information and Communication Technology, 9357,* 323–332.

89 Etter, M. A. and Vestergaard, A. (2015), Facebook and the public framing of a corporate crisis, *Corporate Communications: An International Journal,* 20, 163–177.

90 Colleoni, 2007

91 Bonson, E. and Ratkai, M. (2013), A set of metrics to assess stakeholder engagement and social legitimacy on a corporate Facebook page, *Online Information Review, 37,* 787–803.

92 Besiou et al., op. cit.; Boyd, D. E., McGarry, B. M. and Clarke, T. B. (2016), Exploring the empowering and paradoxical relationship between social media and CSR activism, *Journal of Business Research, 69,* 2739–2746; McQueen, D. (2015), CSR and new battle line in online PR war: A case study of the energy sector and its discontents, in Ana Adi, Georgiana Grigore, David Crowther (ed.) *Corporate Social Responsibility in the Digital Age (Developments in Corporate Governance and Responsibility, Volume 7)* Emerald Group Publishing Limited, pp. 99–125; Lyon and Montgomery, op. cit.; Whelan, G., Moon, J. and Grant, B. (2013), Corporate and citizenship arenas in the age of social media, *Journal of Business Ethics, 118,* 777–790; Yin, J. L., Feng, J. Y. and Wang, Y. Y. (2015), Social media and multinational corporations' corporate social responsibility in China: The case of ConocoPhillips oil spill incident, *IEEE Transactions On Professional Communication, 58,* 135–153.

93 Besiou et al., 2016

94 McQueen, 2015; Yin et al., 2015

95 McQueen, 2015

96 Yin et al., 2015

97 Lyon and Montgomery, 2013

98 Lyon and Montgomery, 2013; Whelan et al., 2013

99 Boyd et al., 2016

100 Crane and Glozier, 2016

101 Du et al., 2010

102 Rim and Song, 2013; Haigh et al., 2013

103 Haigh et al., 2013

104 Rim and Song, 2013

105 Besiou et al., 2016; Boyd et al., 2016; McQueen, 2015; Lyon and Montgomery, 2013; Yin et al., 2015

106 Du et al., 2010

107 Ha and James, 1998

108 Castello, I., Morsing, M. and Schultz, F. (2013), Communicative dynamics and the polyphony of corporate social responsibility in the network society, *Journal of Business Ethics, 118,* 683–694.

109 Steuer, 1992

110 Korschun, D. and Du, S. (2013), How virtual corporate social responsibility dialogs generate value: A framework and propositions, *Journal of Business Research, 66,* 1494–1504.

111 Rafaeli and Sudweeks, 1997

112 Liu and Shrum, 2002

113 Korschun and Du, 2013
114 Ariely, D. (2000), Controlling information flow: Effects on consumers' decision-making and preference, *Journal of Consumer Research, 27,* 233–248.
115 Song and Zinkhan, 2008; Voorveld et al., 2011
116 Kim et al., 2014
117 Donaldson, T. and Preston, L. E. (1995), The stakeholder theory of the corporation: concepts, evidence, and implications, *Academy of Management Review, 20,* 65–91.
118 Hague, B. N. and Loader, B. (1999), *Digital Democracy: Discourse and Decision Making in the Information Age,* Routledge New York, NY; Papacharissi, Z. (2004), Democracy online: civility, politeness, and the democratic potential of online political discussion groups, *New Media and Society, 6,* 259–283.
119 Hague, B. N. and Loader, 1999; Papacharissi, 2004
120 Illia et al., 2015
121 Aguinis and Glavas, 2012
122 Crane and Glozer, 2016
123 Capriotti, P. (2017), The World Wide Web and the Social Media as Tools of CSR Communication, in *Handbook of Integrated CSR Communication,* 193–210.
124 Reichert, R. (2017), Big Data and CSR Communication, in *Handbook of Integrated CSR Communication,* 211–224.
125 Crane and Glozer, 2016; Crane et al., 2016
126 Schoeneborn, D. and Trittin, H. (2013) Transcending transmission: Towards a constitutive perspective on CSR communication, *Corporate Communications: An International Journal,* 18, 193–211.
127 Diehl, S., et al. (2017), *Handbook of Integrated CSR Communication,* Springer.

Part 3

Fostering stakeholder engagement in and through digital corporate social responsibility communication

3.1 A critical reflection on the role of dialogue in communicating ethical CSR through digital platforms

Keith J. Perks, Mónica Recalde Viana,
Francisca Farache, and Jana Kollat

Introduction

Organizations are under increasing pressure to communicate to stakeholders their position and policies on social responsibility, informing them about the corporation's good intentions and actions. This pressure has intensified in a global context marked by constant change and whereby more critical, demanding citizens using emerging new technologies. This context has been cited by the Melbourne Mandate of the Global Alliance (MMGA)[1] as signaling a need for changes in organizational approaches to CSR communication. The changes, according to the MMGA, demand a corporate culture of listening, management commitment and responsible action if organizations are to retain or restore their social legitimacy. Hence corporations' dissemination and communication of CSR information needs more effective forms of engagement with stakeholders through symmetrical relations.[2] In initiating a two-way symmetrical dialogue with stakeholders, organizations have an opportunity to understand their perspective, respond to criticism[3] and reduce stakeholder scepticism.[4] Dialogue is "a process in which parties with different interests and values at stake in a particular issue work together towards mutually acceptable solutions".[5] Thus, a dialogue is essential for someone or an entity to speak and listen to the thoughts, opinions and responding to the interlocutor to meet the ethical premise for responsibility.[6] The emergence of digital hardware and software platforms such as Facebook or Twitter provides managers with mechanisms that have the potential for a dialogue with stakeholders to communicate their CSR initiatives and policies. These digital platforms allow managers and corporations to listen and respond to stakeholders and their concerns in an open and honest discourse. Through this connection of digital platforms and dialogue, corporations have an opportunity to meet the ethical premise of responsibility. On the other hand, the notion that digital platforms are an opportunity for organizations to interact with stakeholders, transforming a passive observer into an active participant, has been challenged.[7] Rather, in this view, digital platforms result not in interactivity but interpassivity (a combination of interactive and passive), and the illusion of being empowered, which is, however, a deferral of the interaction to the device or the digital platform to act or interact on our behalf with the participation of an automated 'like' or 'dislike' response rather than a dialogue. This critique suggests that digital platforms are the mechanism but not the foundation for an ethical premise for CSR whereby people and entities participate in an active dialogue. Given this critique, we probe whether or not organizations are able to satisfy and enact the ethical premise of CSR. Our contextual emphasis is on the potential for implementing the ethical premise of CSR in large organizations, which due to more scrutiny by governments, NGOs and other publics, are more likely to use a wide range of one-way or two-way interactive tools to communicate their corporate social responsibility to a varied audience.[8]

To achieve the central aim of the chapter, we explore the ethical premise of responsibility and its connection to the concept of dialogue as a basis for assessing if, how and why digital platforms can or cannot meet the ethical premise and dialogic prerequisite for CSR. We then discuss the implications and make recommendations for implementing the ethical premise of CSR into an organization. In the first section of the chapter, we define and clarify the ethical premise of CSR.

The ethical premise of CSR

According to Gibb, responsibility is asymmetric because I, nor another party, can be held responsible for the actions of each other and "this ethics requires me to respond for the actions of others, actions I could neither cause nor control".[9] The ethical premise for responsibility rests not only on entering a discourse but that I also listen and expose myself to the other person. "In discourse I expose myself to the interrogation of the Other Person and this urgency of response – the sharp point of the present – engenders me for responsibility".[10] Ethical responsibility comes from someone or an entity listening to the thoughts and opinions and responding to the interlocutor – "we listen in order to gain responsibility; by making ourselves vulnerable to questioning, we become responsible".[11] Habermas[12] extends the ethical premise of responsibility to a discourse among all those affected "in a cooperative search for truth, in which they may come to the conclusion by the force of a better argument . . . on which rests the fundamental principle of discourse ethics". The capacity to listen, a sense of openness and being vulnerable to questioning and responsiveness necessitates establishing a moral legitimacy of conforming to the norms of society through a deliberative discourse with internal and external publics.[13] In the corporate context, moral legitimacy is where stakeholders' views reflect a normative and positive evaluation of a corporation and its activities on the basis of what they see as the "right thing to do"[14] as an outcome of "explicit public discussion".[15] Corporations bear the political responsibilities[16] through discourse in the four Habermasian validity claims of communicative action, which are truth, sincerity, understandability and appropriateness. Further, discourse also meets the political CSR criteria of open discourse, participation, transparency and accountability.[17]

In the next section, we discuss CSR communication theory, the connection of the concept of dialogue with the ethical premise of responsibility.

CSR communication theory, dialogue and the ethical premise

Organizations signal their economic, social and environmental initiatives through CSR communication,[18] which is a tool to enhance their corporate and public image[19] and to gain legitimacy and support from different stakeholder groups.[20] Here we define stakeholders as "any group or individual who can affect or is affected by the achievement of the organization's objectives",[21] who are located internally (owners, managers, employees) or externally (government, competitors, customers, consumer advocates, environmentalists, media, NGOs, and activists). Companies use a range of channels in their CSR communication with stakeholders, such as social reports, codes of conduct, CSR websites, stakeholder consultations, internal channels, awards and events, cause-related marketing, product packaging, advertising and its own social media channels.[22] Further, interactive

CSR communication, allowing for stakeholder involvement in a common setting of a CSR agenda with organizations, contributes to a feeling of self-enhancement and the belief that companies engage in CSR for responsible and societal reasons.[23] For external stakeholders', independent media coverage of CSR is more credible than what corporations say about their CSR initiatives,[24] as such information helps them to make a balanced assessment and gain a sense of an organizations social responsibility claims.[25] Proactive CSR communication strategies use expert opinion, third party endorsements and substantiation in the form of CSR investments, for example, financial and in-kind contributions, or employee volunteering, have been found to mitigate the levels of perceived hypocrisy in a reactive strategy.[26]

While organizations have made use of such policies to gain legitimacy, a few have gone further to embed the ethical premise of CSR into their core mission. This has been achieved through listening to and having an open, honest conversation with stakeholders and responding to their concerns. This requires corporations to adopt a 'dialogic mindset'[27] to express a manifestation of inner thoughts and exploration of understanding each other which is "itself more as a stance, orientation, or bearing in communication rather than as a specific method, technique or format". Dialogue transcends the view that is limited to particular interests and endeavors to seek for "a persistent effort to reach the truth"[28] "whereby parties with different interests and values at stake on a particular issue work together towards mutually acceptable solutions".[29] This we argue, is a fundamental element of the ethical premise of responsibility connecting dialogue and ethical CSR.

A pioneer in and exemplar of the dialogic 'conversational corporation'[30] and participatory approaches before the emergence of digital platforms was the Body Shop. Their Social Statement 95 was "one of the most sensitive in feeding stakeholder concerns into the design of the survey and other dialogic tools".[31] There are several decades of experience in developing participatory approaches, which pass through evolutionary stages in a laddering from 'dialogue shifts' at the bottom to higher levels "that involves the exploration, appreciation and in some instances acceptance of the interests of others".[32] Achieving an effective dialogue at the higher levels requires a shift from a give-and-take debate to one of dialogue and learning, which leads to understanding something differently and an evolution of purpose beyond what is currently possible. For example, the Body Shop's definition of stakeholder dialogue is "a genuine process of sharing each other's perspectives with a view to tackling a joint issue. It assumes you are willing to change your views. It is the spirit of seeking out and valuing the views of others".[33] As digital platforms are widely acknowledged as an interactive media, there is potential to use them as a mechanism for a dialogue, in a participatory communication process[34] to meet the ethical premise for CSR, which we explore in the next section.

Digital platforms as a dialogical mechanism for the ethical premise of CSR

Digital platforms such as blogs, Facebook, wikis, Twitter or Instagram[35] enable users to interact and connect with each through user-generation, information sharing, and collaboration. Corporations, including Ford, have set up corporate CSR blogs to engage with opinion leaders on the issue of sustainability; McDonald's manages a blog whereby employees blog and respond to users' comments openly and transparently, which is highly interactive;[36] Starbucks uses a Twitter account to respond to consumers CSR comments; and Cisco Systems focus on NGOs, with CSR bloggers using a Twitter account created to engage with highly interested stakeholders.[37] However, while corporate blogs encourage a dialogue, it is dedicated to a corporation's key constituents with the purpose of informing and persuading them.[38] Other digital platforms, such as wikis, which are administered and edited by any user, mean that the corporation is not in control of who participates (for example, see Apple www.apple.wikia.com).[39] However, such dialogue-based blogs face the criticism that they are instrumental, company-centric and biased, rather than deliberative and largely conducted with groups of experts or individuals rather than a wider audience.[40] Despite this view, the exploration of digital platforms as a dialogic medium has intensified in the literature on public relations and corporate communication over the course of the last ten years.[41] To date there has been a focus on two approaches: one is the dissemination of information, and the other is the generation of a dialogue between the different publics and the organization.[42] In the first approach, the level of interactivity is low, and a digital platform is used as a monological mechanism to communicate fixed information to influence the image of the company amongst its various publics.[43] In the second approach, a digital platform has the potential to be a mechanism for an organizational dialogue to maintain an open-ended conversation with the public. Further, it is also a space where stakeholders have opportunities to share their opinions about corporate initiatives, decisions and activities. Hence, digital platforms have the potential to be a mechanism for a dialogue discourse between the organization and its different stakeholders if the discourse is based on openness, listening, responding and a change in ideas,[44] which is the ethical premise of CSR.

Despite examples of organizations engaging in a dialogue with stakeholders about CSR issues, extant research depicts a situation whereby organizations are practicing a one-way transmission, public information and transactional model of communication.[45] In taking this approach, organizations are not opening an opportunity for dialogue with the public;[46] instead they are using digital platforms for dissemination purposes.[47] Posting content on digital platforms "does not mean that those contents created conversations among the followers of organizations' social media, or that organizations have a dialogue or, still less a relationship with their followers", rather "conversations emerge as a result of sharing information that arouses interest in someone, but also from the presentation of content that stimulate an individuals' interest and curiosity, or that simply respond to information-seeking needs".[48] Neither conversations, nor two-way communications, can take place if individuals do not create, share content, or respond to existing content with comments. In digital platforms, information is available from the moment it is created and often transmitted by the participants themselves or by eyewitnesses. This acceleration has driven organizations, advised by digital agencies, to respond to comments immediately with limited time for reflection. Such an approach may not establish the basis for a CSR dialogue with stakeholders, as it places a greater emphasis on response than responsibility.[49]

Digital platforms, which are not administered and set up by corporations, have three main characteristics: the de-institutionalization of communication, the evolution of users as producers, and interactivity in networks.[50] Digital platforms can, in this context, empower users to create and filter content according to their own interests and share them within their own networks. Through digital platforms, organizations have the opportunity to communicate directly and mutually with their stakeholders[51] in an involvement strategy,[52] changing the landscape for organizational communication of CSR which:

> sketches an inherent double-sidedness in user participation and associated patterns and values of 'produsage' in social media: the user is simultaneously an empowered, productive agent.[53]

As a first step, organizations can use digital platforms to deliver information to their relevant stakeholder groups as they are actively looking for it,[54] and that "the thirst for information facilitated by digital platforms asks for more ongoing and regular engagement in CSR will expose business to a much more direct and visible scrutiny by the general publics".[55] Through a lack of transparency and substantial information in communication, an organization could face accusations of greenwashing, spread virally in a short space of time. Consequently, organizations are under more pressure to be socially responsible in digital platforms,[56] resulting in decreasing organizational power to control public opinion.[57] The diversity of digital platforms fragments audiences, making it difficult for organizations to identify and engage with relevant interest groups.[58] Conversely, digital platforms give stakeholders access to information they could not reach before,[59] and organizations may establish a much more intense and interactive CSR communication network with them, resulting in higher levels of belief in the commitment to CSR activities.[60] But organizations tend to use digital platforms like other mass communication channels and mainly distribute information in a one-way communication approach.[61] Interactivity levels of digital CSR communication are generally low, as organizations behave passively on digital platforms and only react when directly addressed.[62] Furthermore, higher levels of corporate dialogue do not necessarily lead to diverse networks with high densities of dialogue about CSR; instead, organizations tend to develop their own audiences fostering an interest in specific organizational content.[63] Research to evaluate three communication strategies (information, response, involvement)[64] in the context of digital platforms identified the three strategies used on Twitter as broadcasting, reactive and engagement, revealing that most organizations follow a broadcasting strategy and only few communicate according to the engagement strategy.

We argue that for corporations to meet the ethical premise for CSR set out in our chapter, organizations have to adopt new approaches in their communication processes to remove the conditions of structural power[65] by taking a deliberative approach towards CSR communication, meaning "consideration, discussion, and weighting of ideas with multiple actors (in digital platforms) implies a balance of power of actors involved and democratic will formation based on ethical discourse combined with economic bargaining".[66] Thus, deliberative CSR communication is seen less as an instrument of organizational self-serving goals but more of a situation where "people organize collectively to regulate or transform some aspects of their social conditions, along with the communicative activities in which they try to persuade one another to join such collective actions or decide which direction they wish to take".[67] The deliberative rather than the instrumental approach is a more appropriate basis for meeting the ethical premise (capacity to listen, sense of openness, being vulnerable to questioning and responsiveness) for CSR communication in digital platforms. However, not all digital "tools of CSR communication take into account . . . the normative demands of open discourse".[68]

While digital platforms are a potential mechanism for establishing a dialogic discourse with others in order to meet the ethical premise of CSR, other factors have to be taken into consideration, which we discuss in the next section.

Implications: meeting the ethical premise of CSR communication in digital platforms

In our introduction to this chapter, we argued that while there was potential for digital platforms to satisfy the conditions of the ethical premise of CSR, other factors have to be taken into consideration. Organizations using digital platforms for automated CSR messages to stakeholders without recognising the importance of a dialogical mind-set at the top management level will, we argue, fail to meet the requirements for the ethical premise of CSR. While there are instances of where corporations are willing to hold an open and responsive dialogue with a wider audience, digital platforms as a mechanism for establishing the ethical premise for CSR and how such an approach could be adopted in organizations is still unclear.[69] Prior research suggests that stakeholders are sceptical about the CSR efforts of organizations seeing this as part of an attempt to appear responsible while continuing to practice irresponsibility.[70] If organizations are genuinely interested in overcoming such scepticism, top managers need to re-think their approach towards CSR communication through embracing a spirit of openness, dialogue and responsiveness to establish an ethical premise of responsibility set out in this chapter. Digital platforms provide a basis for ethical CSR, in a dialogue and response communication between the corporation and its stakeholders. Achieving this goal is a significant challenge for organizations and communication managers who adopt an instrumental digital CSR communication approach of information dissemination rather than a dialogical and response approach. Organizations are, understandably, reluctant to open up dialogues with stakeholders to expose the corporation in all their areas of business. However, they need to respond, as digital platforms are exposing corporations to high levels of scrutiny beyond their control. A proactive approach acknowledging that mistakes are made in their business operations and communicating and discussing these issues through digital platforms signals a serious attempt to listen and respond to criticism.

There are, however, no easy solutions, single schemas or 'dashboards' to be offered to meet the requirements of the ethical premise of CSR. However, digital platforms in conjunction with setting specific CSR objectives, and managers adopting a dialogic mind-set, listening to the view of others about their concerns on a specific issue would fulfil the ethical premise of responsibility. As a starting point for our recommendations, we propose that communication managers address two fundamental questions they need to consider and answer, which are:

1   *To what extent do we as an organization and management team believe in the ethical premise of CSR that by listening to the thoughts, opinions and responding to the interlocutor – 'we listen in order to gain responsibility; by making ourselves vulnerable to questioning, we become responsible'?*
2   *If we accept this ethical premise, are we willing to incorporate it into our strategy and organizational practices?*

If managers believe in the ethical premise of CSR and are willing to introduce this into their organizational practices, then the next step is how would this approach be implemented?

It is to this question that we now turn to make practical recommendations for implementing an ethical premise of CSR in an organization. In Table 3.1.1, we summarise our recommendations into five stages. In stage 1, we recommend that organizations take into consideration structural issues, such as who would be responsible and at what levels? In our judgement to achieve the ethical premise of CSR, there has to be a commitment to a digital platform as mechanism for a dialogic listening and responding approach at the top management level. This could mean allocation of responsibility to an existing communication director or if there is no appropriate board member to recruit externally. Whoever is delegated or recruited would need to have the appropriate sensitivity and commitment to the ethical premise of a dialogic listening and response mind-set. Further,

Table 3.1.1 Recommendations for implementing the ethical premise of CSR into an organization[71]

Stage 1: Structural considerations – who would be responsible for implementing a ethically based digital CSR approach and at what level(s)?
Inclusion of ethical intrapreneurs – brokers between the inside and outside of the organization.

Stage 2: Inclusiveness – who is to be included in the digital CSR dialogue?

Stage 3: What would be the most appropriate digital platform?

Stage 4: Responsiveness – degree to which the various stakeholder parties respond to the dialogue (not exclusively internal parties).

Stage 5: Outcomes – what actually happens as a consequence of the dialogue?

the communication director should also have an understanding of how this dialogue with stakeholders would be deployed through digital platforms. The director of communication would then be responsible for taking this strategy forward with the communication manager and their team. If outside expertise in the area of digital platforms is lacking, then the organization should recruit people with the necessary skills and experience into the team. The communication director, manager and their team would need to ensure that the policy and approach continues to have the attention of the board members and has 'political' weight at the top level. A corporate wide commitment to ethical CSR should be diffused and cascaded to employees through internal events and meetings to embed the approach into the practices of the organization. We also recommend that as digital platforms span and blur the lines between the organization and the external environment that an ethical intrapreneur be identified. This would be someone within the organization who would act as a 'broker', taking direct responsibility for initiatives to sustain the ethical premise of CSR through a dialogic discourse with the stakeholders. Further, we would recommend an organization develops a systematic cooperation with groups who represent the central CSR issues facing the corporation who are situated outside of the organization.[72] In stage 2, we recommend connecting the specific CSR issue and objective to the identification of the appropriate stakeholders with which to have a dialogue.

In stage 2, 'decisions' would have to be made as to which stakeholders would be included in the CSR dialogue. We recommend primary research to identify the specific stakeholders and the levels of their involvement with CSR, such as lobby groups, forums, individuals, and the areas and societal issues where they have the most involvement and motivation. This same exercise would be carried out with internal employee stakeholders. We recommend this approach so that organizations would be able to have some initial scope and boundaries to launch and implement the ethical premise for CSR in digital platforms. This can then be extended in an iterative and dynamic manner in response to events and issues that occur in their business environment.

In stage 3, we recommend an audit is carried out to determine how and why stakeholders use digital platforms to select the most appropriate means of communication and digital platforms for different stakeholders and levels of engagement.

Stages 4 and 5 are essential for the implementation of the ethical premise of CSR, as there should be a response from an individual or entity as the basis for a dialogue. Whilst stakeholders may have the intention to respond, this may not occur with a high degree of frequency and intensity. Therefore, we recommend that organizations use a hybrid of digital platforms and offline communications through meetings and events, inside and outside of the organization with stakeholders to stimulate interest and intensity of dialogue. Stage 5 is where the organization has to demonstrate to stakeholders that they have listened to and made changes in response the dialogue. This could take many forms, in terms of, for example, organizational change, initiatives and actions.

Conclusions

The aim of this chapter was to examine and probe the ethical premise of CSR communication, which requires a corporation to listen to and respond to the questioning of an interlocutor in a dialogue. The emergence of digital platforms has changed the landscape of CSR communication from one in which the corporation is in control of the communication through dissemination of information to stakeholders, to one wherein stakeholders communicate with each other out of the control of organizations. In this more open environment organizations are challenged and questioned about their CSR performance and called upon to respond through digital platforms. In this new, challenging environment, the practice and research of how organizations cope with the pressures of digital communication of CSR is only just emerging. We argue that organizations should take a step back to apply the ethical premise of CSR communication based on a dialogue and response to stakeholders. Through such an approach of open dialogue, accepting criticism, responding to questioning and action based on the outcome of the discourse, organizations could fundamentally change the self-serving and instrumental public perception of corporations.

Limitations and future research

Our chapter is a conceptual piece, and therefore, we have not sought to explore the ethical premise of CSR through, for example, case studies, which is a limitation. Future research could explore the challenges of operationalizing the ethical premise of CSR through case studies and interviews with communication managers. However, we have provided a critical perspective grounded in the ethical premise of responsibility for future researchers to use as a basis for an empirical study. This would help further our understanding of the nuances and challenges of implementing the ethical premise of CSR and dialogical mindset through digital platforms within organizations. A further limitation of the chapter is that we have explored the ethical premise of CSR in large organizations and hence do not claim to generalize our findings to other contexts, such as SMEs. Hence, future research could explore the ethical premise of CSR, dialogue and digital platforms in the context of SMEs.

Notes

1 Global Alliance for Public Relations and Communication Management (2012). The Melbourne Mandate http://melbournemandate.globalalliancepr.org/wp-content/uploads/2012/11/Melbourne-Mandate-Text-final.pdf [Accessed 26 January 2017].
2 Lauritsen, B. D. and Perks, K. (2015). The influence of interactive, non-interactive, implicit and explicit CSR communication on young adults' perception of UK supermarkets' corporate brand image and reputation. *Corporate Communications: An International Journal*, 20(2), 178–195; Morsing, M., and Schultz, M. (2006). Corporate social responsibility communication: Stakeholder information, response and involvement strategies. *Business Ethics: A European Review*, 15(4), 323–338.
3 Golob, U., and Podnar, K. (2014). Critical points of CSR-related stakeholder dialogue in practice. *Business Ethics: A European Review*, 23(3), 248–257.

4 Maon, F., Lindgreen, A., and Swaen, V. (2009). Designing and implementing corporate social responsibility: An integrative framework grounded in theory and practice. *Journal of Business Ethics*, 87(1), 71–89.

5 Perret, A. (2003). BNFL national stakeholder dialogue: A case study in public affairs. *Journal of Public Affairs*, 3(4), 383–391.

6 Gibbs, R. (2000). *Why Ethics? Signs of Responsibilities*. Princeton, NJ: Princeton University Press.

7 Zizek, S. (2009). The Interpassive Subject Lacan Turns a Prayer Wheel www.lacan.com/essays/?p=143 interpassive subject. [Accessed 30 March 2016].

8 Perks, K., Farache, F., Shukla, P., and Berry, A. (2013). Communicating responsibility-practicing irresponsibility in CSR advertisements. *Journal of Business Research*, 66(10), 1881–1888.

9 Gibbs, op. cit. Page 4.

10 Levinas, E. (1969). *Totalite et Infini*. 4th ed. The Hague: Martinus Nijhoff, 1971 (1st ed., 1961). Trans. Alphonso Lingis as *Totality and Infinity*. Pittsburgh: Duquesne University Press, 1969. Pages 178–179.

11 Gibbs, op. cit. Page 30.

12 Habermas, J. (1993). *Erläuterungen zur Diskursethic*. Frankfurt: Suhrkamp, 1991. Trans. Ciaran P. Cronin as *Justification and Application*. Cambridge, MA: MIT Press, 1993. Pages 49–50.

13 Habermas, J. (1984). *The Theory of Communicative Action*. 2 vols. Boston: Beacon Press.

14 Suchman, M.C. (1995). Managing legitimacy: Strategic and institutional approaches. *Academy of Management Review*, 20(3), 571–610. Page 579.

15 Suchman, op. cit. Page 585.

16 Scherer, A., and Palazzo, G. (2011). The new political role of business in a globalized world: A review of a new perspective on CSR and its implications for the firm, governance, and democracy. *Journal of Management Studies*, 48(4), 899–931.

17 Seele, P., and Lock, I. (2015). Instrumental and/or deliberative? A typology of CSR communication tools. *Journal of Business Ethics*, 131(2), 401–414.

18 Ihlen, Ø., Bartlett, J. L., and May, S. (2011). Corporate social responsibility and communication. In Ihlen, Ø., Bartlett, J. L. and May, S. (Eds.), *The Handbook of Communication and Corporate Social Responsibility*. Sussex: John Wiley and Sons, 3–22.

19 Mark-Herbert, C. and Von Schantz, C. (2007). Communicating CSR responsibility – brand management. *Electronic Journal of Business Ethics and Organization Studies*, 12(2), 4–11: Bhattacharya, C. B., Sen, S. and Korschun, D. (2008). Using corporate social responsibility to win the war for talent. *MIT Sloan Management Review*, 49(2), 37–44.

20 Du, S., Bhattacharya, C. B., and Sen, S. (2007). Reaping relational rewards from corporate social responsibility: The role of competitive positioning. *International Journal of Research in Marketing*, 24(3), 224–241: Golob, U., and Bartlett, J. L. (2007). Communicating about corporate social responsibility: A comparative study of CSR reporting in Australia and Slovenia. *Public Relations Review*, 33(1), 1–9: Bueble, E. (2009). *Corporate Social Responsibility: CSR Communication as an Instrument to Consumer Relationship Marketing*. München: GRIN Verlag.

21 Freeman, R.E. (1984). *Strategic Management: A Stakeholder Approach*. Pitman series in business and public policy. Page 46.

22 Farache, F., and Perks, K.J. (2010). CSR advertisements: A legitimacy tool? *Corporate Communications: An International Journal*, 15(3), 235–248.

23 Kent, M.L., and Taylor, M. (1998). Building dialogic relationships through the worldwide web. *Public Relations Review*, 24(3), 321–334: Lauritsen and Perks, op. cit.

24 Goodman, M.B. (1998). *Corporate Communications for Executives*. Albany: State University of New York Press.

25 Parguel, B., Benoît-Moreau, F., and Larceneux, F. (2011). How sustainability ratings might deter 'greenwashing': A closer look at ethical corporate communication. *Journal of Business Ethics*, 102(1), 15–28.

26 Wagner, T., Lutz, R. J. and Weitz, B. A. (2009). Corporate hypocrisy: Overcoming the threat of inconsistent corporate social responsibility perceptions. *Journal of Marketing*, 73(6), 77–91: Morsing, M., Schultz, M. and Nielsen, K.U. (2008). The 'Catch 22' of communicating CSR: Findings from a Danish study. *Journal of Marketing Communications*, 14(2), 97–111: Perks et al., op. cit.: Du, S., Bhattacharya, C. B. and Sen, S. (2010). Maximizing business returns to corporate social responsibility (CSR): The role of CSR communication. *International Journal of Management Reviews*, 12(1), 8–19: Polonsky, M., and Jevons, C. (2009). Global branding and strategic CSR: An overview of three types of complexity. *International Marketing Review*, 26(3), 327–347.

27 Zadek, S. (2007). *The Civil Corporation*. London: Earthscan; Gutiérrez-García, E., Recalde, M. and Piñera, A. (2015). Reinventing the wheel? A comparative overview of the concept of dialogue. *Public Relations Review*, 41(5), 744–753.

28 Gutiérrez-García, et al. op. cit.; Kierkegaard, S. (1971). *Concluding Unscientific Postscript*. Princeton: Princeton University Press. Page 110.

29 Perret op. cit. Pages 383–391.

30 Zadek op. cit. chapter 10.

31 Zadek op. cit. Page 220.

32 Zadek op. cit. Page 224.

33 The Body Shop (1996). The Body Shop Social Statement 95, Body Shop, Littlehampton, UK.

34 Seele and Lock op. cit.

35 Jansen, B.J., Zhang, M., Sobel, K. and Chowdury, A. (2009). Twitter power: Tweets as electronic word of mouth. *Journal of the American Society for Information Science and Technology*, 60(11), 2169–2188.

36 Seele and Lock op. cit.

37 Etter, M. (2014). Broadcasting, reacting, engaging – three strategies for CSR communication in Twitter. *Journal of Communication Management*, 18(4), 322–342. Page 335.

38 Fleck, M., Kirchhoff, L., Meckel, M., and Stanoevska-Slabeva, K. (2007). Applications of Blogs in Corporate Communication. *Studies in Communication Sciences*, 7(2), 227–246: Fieseler, C., Fleck, M. and Meckel, M. (2010). Corporate social responsibility in the blogosphere. *Journal of Business Ethics*, 91(4), 599–614.

39 Seele and Lock, op. cit.

40 Fieseler et al., op. cit.

41 Verčič, D., Verčič, A.T., and Sriramesh, K. (2015). Looking for digital in public relations, *Public Relations Review*, 41(2), 142–152: Zerfass, A., Tench, R., Verčič, D., Verhoeven, P., and Moreno, A. (2014). *European Communication Monitor 2014. Excellence in Strategic Communication Key Issues, Leadership, Gender and Mobile Media. Results of a Survey in 42 Countries*. Brussels: EACD/EUPRERA, Helios Media.

42 Capriotti, P. and Moreno, A. (2009). Communicating CSR, citizenship and sustainability on the web. *Journal of Communication Management*, 13(2), 157–175.

43 Bakhtin, M.M. (1986). *Speech Genres and Other Late Essays* (Y. McGee, trans.). Austin: University of Texas Press.

44 Connor, C., and Michaels, S. (2007). When Is Dialogue 'Dialogic'? *Human Development* 50 (5), 275–285.

45 Yang, A., and Kent, M. (2014). Social media and organizational visibility: A sample of Fortune 500 corporations. *Public Relations Review*, 40(3), 562–564: Carim, L., and Warwick, C. (2013). Use of social media for corporate communications by research-funding organisations in the UK. *Public Relations Review*, 39(5), 521–525: Valentini, C. (2015). Is using social media "good" for the public relations profession? A critical reflection. *Public Relations Review*, 41(2), 170–177.

46 Diga, M., and Kelleher, T. (2009). Social media use, perceptions of decision-making power, and public relations roles. *Public Relations Review*, 35(4), 440–442.

47 Larrson, A., and Moe, H. (2012). Studying political microblogging: Twitter users in the 2010 Swedish election campaign. *New Media and Society*, 14(5), 729–747.

48 Valentini, op. cit. Pages 174 and 154.

49 Ackerman, R.W. (1973). How companies respond to social demands. *Harvard University Review*, 51(4), 88–98.

50 Bechmann, A. and Lomborg, S. (2013). Mapping actor roles in social media: Different perspectives on value creation in theories of user participation. *New Media and Society*, 15(5), 765–781.

51 Grunig, J. E. (2009). Paradigms of global public relations in an age of digitalisation. *Prism*, 6(2), 1–19.

52 Morsing and Schultz, op. cit.

53 Bechmann and Lomborg, op. cit. page 767.

54 Bonsón, E. and Flores, F. (2011). Social media and corporate dialogue: The response of global financial institutions. *Online Information Review*, 35(1), 34–49; Colleoni, E. (2013). CSR communication strategies for organizational legitimacy in social media. *Corporate Communications: An International Journal*, 18(2), 228–248.

55 Crane, A. and Matten, D. (2013). The Top 5 CSR Trends for 2013 http://craneandmatten.blogspot.de/2013/01/the-top-5-csr-trends-for-2013.html [Accessed 1 March 2016].

56 Lee, K., Oh, W.-Y., and Kim, N. (2013). Social media for socially responsible firms: Analysis of fortune 500's Twitter profiles and their CSR/CSIR ratings. *Journal of Business Ethics*, 118(4), 791–806.

57 Castelló, I., Etter, M. and Årup Nielsen, F. (2016). Strategies of legitimacy through social media: The networked strategy. *Journal of Management Studies*, 53(3), 402–432: Castelló, I., Morsing, M., and Schultz, F. (2013). Communicative dynamics and the polyphony of corporate social responsibility in the network society. *Journal of Business Ethics*, 118(4), 683–694.

58 Pope, S., and Wæraas, A. (2016). CSR-Washing is rare: A conceptual framework, literature review, and critique. *Journal of Business Ethics*, 137(1), 173–193.

59 Fieseler, et al., op. cit.

60 Saffer, A.J., Sommerfeldt, E.J., and Taylor, M. (2013). The effects of organizational Twitter interactivity on organization-public relationships. *Public Relations Review*, 39(3), 213–215.

61 Lovejoy, K., Waters, R.D., and Saxton, G.D. (2012). Engaging stakeholders through Twitter: How nonprofit organizations are getting more out of 140 characters or less. *Public Relations Review*, 38(2), 313–318.

62 Etter, M. (2013). Reasons for low levels of interactivity. *Public Relations Review*, 39(5), 606–608.

63 Colleoni, op. cit.

64 Morsing and Schultz, op. cit.

65 Castelló et al., op. cit.

66 Seele and Lock op.cit. Page 404.

67 Young, I. (2004). Responsibility and global labor justice. *Journal of Political Philosophy*, 12(4), 365–388.

68 Seele and Lock, op cit. Page 405.

69 Mulhern, F. (2009). Integrated marketing communications: From media channels to digital connectivity. *Journal of Marketing Communications*, 15(2–3), 85–101.

70 Perks et al., op. cit.

71 Zadek op. cit. page 226 adaptation and extension of four dimensions of dialogue in quality assessment.

72 Grayson, D., McLaren, M., and Spitzeck, H. (2011). Social intrapreneurs – an extra force for sustainability. A Doughty Centre for Corporate Responsibility Occasional Paper.

3.2 The imperative needs of dialogue between CSR departments and PR practitioners

Empirical evidence from Spain

Isabel Ruiz-Mora and Jairo Lugo-Ocando

Introduction

Recent research carried out in Spain[1] suggests that corporate social responsibility (CSR) departments tend to downplay existing and potential contributions from public relations professionals. Accordingly, public relations practitioners are not sufficiently involved in the conceptualization, designed and implementation of CSR programs.[2,3] This lack of input from PR professionals, in our view, accounts for some of the most important operational deficiencies and accountability deficits of CSR programs. To be sure, public relations practitioners' involvement in CSR has traditionally been limited to assistance in the production of the annual reports[4,5] or just seeking ways of using CSR as a peripheral activity for reputation management purposes.[6] This has become bluntly obvious in current times, when social media and interactive technologies are re-configuring the relationship and landscape between companies, institutions and their stakeholders. It is in the face of this scenario of transformational communications that many CSR departments within large, medium and small organizations find themselves deprived from the necessary expertise to address the challenges of the digital age.

Indeed, many of those managing CSR, for example, still see annual reports as the main tool for transparency and accountability in relation to the performance and the politics of the companies and organizations for which they work.[7] Consequently, not only these reports continue to be at the core of reputation management in relation to CSR, but they also continue to consume a disproportionate amount of time and resources from the organization. All of which have meant neglecting other areas of public engagement such as dialogue building with stakeholders in times of increasing digitalization, interconnectivity and interactivity. The end result is that CSR continues to be mostly a 'performative exercise',[8,9] one that fails to engage with stakeholders and the public in general in the boarder sense.

Moreover, in this digital era, when stakeholders seem to be more proactive and constantly demanding and looking for information[10] regarding the organizations performance and wider impact upon society, some of the most traditional approaches towards CSR have become outdated or at least insufficient to comply with normative requirements regarding transparency and accountability. Indeed, the increasing use by stakeholders, NGOs, activists and journalists of social media and other interactive communication technologies present important challenges and opportunities that do not currently seem to be properly addressed by CSR departments in Spain.

To be sure, digital platforms and all their applications are creating new ways in which stakeholders, pressure groups and the public at large are engaging with the organizations and companies, flattening traditional hierarchical relations and bringing about a further degree of complexity. Contrary to the past, an organization cannot decide nowadays to restrict its channels of communication nor predict with certainty the ultimate outcomes of its engagement strategy. Organizations no longer can avoid public criticism of their brands on Facebook,[11] and people can share on Twitter or Instagram pictures about the effects of their commercial activities on the environment, upload a video on YouTube of a major corporation that can wipe out the share price value in seconds or create a Whats-App group to mobilize local people in favor or against that organization. All in all, the digital era has brought about a forced reality of hectic and complex engagement for all companies and organizations from around the globe,[12] which now operate in the context of the so-called 'risk society'.[13]

It is because of this context of increasing interconnectivity and risk that CSR has to be understood and examined in terms of the larger spectrum of communicative action theory.[14] Despite this, many of those studying, conducting and implementing CSR programs continue to display a lack of engagement with areas such as political communication and professional communication. Indeed, CSR tends to be seen and treated from a theoretical perspective and an empirical standpoint as an empty concept – loosely based on moral communication – which is "filled with different meanings".[15] It is a concept that in practice tends to accommodate to the strategic priorities of each organization and it is often devoid of wider societal considerations and critical thinking.

Moreover, the prevalent meanings given to CSR by practitioners tend to be articulated without a proper contextualization within political communication. This is a gap that we ourselves have found among practitioners in the case of Spain, as we observed the gaps between the communication requirements of modern CSR and its actual engagement with the organization's own departments of PR and public affairs.[16] This, we argue, is not only due to managerial perception towards what PR is and does (or in that effect what it can do for CSR) but also fundamentally a product of a misconception of what CSR is about in this day and age.

This all is aggravated by the very naïve assumptions around the role of social media and digital technologies in the practices of CSR and PR. These assumptions, we found, tend to embrace a techno-determinist view that 'symmetrical communication'[17] can be achieved by pure technological means, while downplaying the role of human agency and political context. According to this premise, the new technologies themselves would facilitate a process of dialogue and democratization of corporate communication and enable further accountability of corporate actions. A view, of course, that tends to ignore issues such history and organizational prerogatives.

Instead, as we suggest here, the configuration of new 'media ecology' for PR[18] has exacerbated in many cases the fundamental dilemma in CSR; its prevalent functionalistic assumption that is there to address issues on the periphery of the organization and that it should be subordinated to managerial prerogatives, which is something that public relations practice also assumed for years in its own deontological realm, but that many now have come to question.[19,20] By doing this, CSR ends up reacting to issues management and reputation management, rather than using the new technologies to constitute itself as a space for stakeholders, the public and the organization to deliberate on equal terms.

It is because of this that we propose to examine how CSR engages with PR and other forms of professional communication in the context of the digital age as an urgent need. The chapter is based on an empirical study investigating, why do CSR practitioners fail to understand that political communication and stakeholder engagement are at the core of what they do? In order to answer this question, we have carried out semi-structured interviews with those in charge of CSR in the top Spanish organization and companies. We also included the analysis of communication strategies, annual reports and most commonly used digital platforms among these companies.

Our overall suggestion is that CSR needs to engage with professional communication in the same way that natural science organizations and researchers have been engaging with professional communications over the past few decades.[21] To us this benchmarking is urgently needed to enable CSR departments to develop their full potential in an age in which virtual and interactive communications foster meta-geographic communities around the organizations. However, this engagement cannot be carried out just in the traditional terms of 'communicative action',[22] that is, as propaganda (or pure dissemination of messages).

To be sure, CSR and PR departments can no longer be fixate with issues of propaganda and reputation, but instead, they need to advance towards establishing and consolidating horizontal relational networks that bring about true accountability and dialogue between the organization and the stakeholders. To do so, CSR departments will have to embrace professional communication and place it, as social practice, at the core of its own activities. Only in that manner, we argue, can CSR departments use the new technologies to create spaces for a none-hierarchical dialogue between organizations and the rest of society.

Failed mutual engagement

The professional definitions of PR[23,24,25] and CSR[26,27] are closely related. This is because accountability to the public is a capital premise for both,[28] as they are seen as an opportunity for transparency and accountability in the face of managing relations between the organization and its stakeholders. Otherwise, as some authors point out, CSR and PR efforts are in danger of becoming just a 'greenwashing reputation' exercise.[29,30] This point has been embraced by several authors. Gonzalez-Herrero, for example, studies this relation from a crisis communication perspective and argues how responsible companies are in a stronger position to avoid crisis when they are managing the relations with their public in a proactive manner, particularly in relation to issues management.[31]

Castillo-Esparcia, on the other hand, has examined this relation from the need to achieve equality among stakeholders, the public and organizations and the necessity to recognize each other. For him a "permanent dialogue with the publics", where all the stakeholders are participating in the decision-making process, is crucial in modern times.[32] L'Etang, also follows a similar approach when she affirms that PR and CSR are closely linked as professional disciplines as they both are strategic for the organization.[33] She states that PR implies communication and exchange of ideas to generate a change in the organization,[34] while issues management is related with CSR, because emerging issues normally have a social background.[35]

Moreover, Daugherty considers public relations practitioners as the "corporate conscience" suggesting that "public relations are the practice of social responsibility".[36] This concept of 'corporate conscience' may sound moral and seductive, maybe because of the idealistic role given to PR as a peacemaker, breaking the barriers between organizations and publics.[37] However, as L'Etang cautiously reminds us, in reality these 'conscience efforts' end up focusing, too often, on protecting the organization's reputation from external threats[38] rather than providing organizational accountability to publics and stakeholders.

Putting L'Etang's well-reasoned reservations to one side, there are nevertheless very convincing arguments to support the incorporation of public relations professionals in

CSR policy planning and execution,[39,40] particularly in an era in which information and communication technologies are fostering and extended realm of influence and social responsibilities for all organizations. Daugherty, in fact, regrets the limited participation of public relations professionals in the design and implementation of CSR, since its functions,

> are increasingly being placed in the hands of others individuals because many public relations practitioners are unprepared to handle the responsibilities of continuously monitoring attitudes and expectations of stakeholders, preparing executives to develop strong relationships with stakeholders and truly understanding the relationship between and organization and its many constituents.[41]

Contrary to this view, Signitzer and Prexl, in their own research about sustainable communication, stated that "public relations practitioners do have the necessary expertise and competence to communicate on issues of corporate sustainability and CSR". This, according to them, happens especially in the area of sustainability issues, where "professional communication skills are urgently needed".[42] In this sense, these authors state that CSR and PR must have a close relationship in the organization, while advising that CSR and professional communication managers should work closely together.

This above is even more the case in a scenario in which CSR departments not only need to communicate what they do but are required to integrate communities and stakeholders in general into the process of design and implementation of organizational policy. To do so, one should ask: who is better placed than communicational professionals? Who is capable and has sound expertise in dealing with external and internal publics? Who would be better placed to develop the relational platform for CSR department than those who know how to create content and develop social media provisions in ways that are accessible and relevant for the variety of publics and stakeholders?

Having said that, CSR and PR departments have rarely walked hand in hand.[43,44] Furthermore, different organizations have different approaches to CSR. Some of them assume that CSR is a unidirectional exercise and they decide when, what and how they communicate with the public in relation to their own organizational efforts. They practice an approach to CSR from business-centrism,[45] one that maintains a relation with the publics from the economic/profit point of view.[46] These organizations tend to altogether overlook stakeholder approaches to CSR;[47,48] therefore, they do not take into account approaches that perhaps would allow them to understand their impact upon society and solve more structural issue,[49,50]

Overall, as some authors suggest, public relations practitioners lead or are involved in CSR efforts, even in those cases in which organizations depart from the stakeholders' perspective.[51] In the cases in which public relations practitioners are not involved, dialogue seems to be absent from the communication process relating to CSR, which tends to be instead unidirectional and hierarchical. Therefore, any possibility of fulfilling the potential of social media and digital technologies to develop a relational platform with the variety of publics and stakeholders of the organization is mostly hindered by the inability of both disciplines to talk to each other.

Social media and dialogue

There are, however, many cases from around the world when organizations have undertaken a distinctive approach, one defined by 'open and interactive communication'.[52] In these cases, this relation of dialogue with the stakeholders and the public becomes an opportunity for organizations to use CSR programs to create spaces for mutual under-standing and accountability. This model to which Grunig and Hunt[53] referred to as 'sym-metrical' assumes that the public has some effect upon the organization's policy and actions. In it, stakeholders can be engaged and take part in shaping and evaluating the agenda of the organization, offering the possibility of implementing a creative problem-solving pro-cess[54] in which the public in general and stakeholders in particular become active actors.

In this sense, social media represents an opportunity to initiate transcendental organi-zational changes. By introducing new ways of dialogue these organizations can foster a relational approach that would help them achieve a two-way symmetrical public relations model.[55] However, it is beyond the scope of this chapter to discuss whether this is really happening on the ground yet; moreover, there is already a comprehensive body of litera-ture that has presented a set of criticisms toward some of the assumptions around sym-metrical models of communication.[56,57,58] As Yang and Kent have highlighted in their own research about social media use in Fortune 500 corporations, the evidence indicates that social media is still mostly used as one-way messaging tools by most organizations, rather than as relationship building tools.[59]

Likewise, let us be clear in our own position, it is not the technologies themselves that have catalyzed dialogue and relational networks in those cases where it has effectively hap-pened but the fact that these organizations decided to embraced a model that privileges dialogue as they consider it "an efficient and ethical way for organizations to communi-cate with their publics in the social network and maintain corporate legitimacy".[60] This is not to say that information and communication technologies have not played any role whatsoever. On the contrary, it is precisely because of them that dialogical spaces have become so important nowadays, but rather they have had a 'facilitating' role. This because the age of digital and interactive media has incentivized new types of behaviors, both from the publics and the organizations. As Charest, Bouffard and Zajmovic state,

> The listening strategy[61] . . . assumes that new technologies, and particularly the Inter-net, make it possible to invent new ways of sharing knowledge faster. It is therefore important to listen to the conversations that take place on social platforms and ana-lyze them in order to stay abreast of public opinion and, through this, to recruit col-laborators, or even create partnerships with influencers.[62]

In the digital age, stakeholders are more active in their behavior towards companies and organizations, and organizations are constantly under pressure to maintain their reputation and strengthen their brands[63] in a way that was not that common in the past. Social media has changed the way people relate and participate in their communities by allowing them to create and share content. The new digital media ecology has reinforced the ability of stakeholders to express their identity, provoking co-creation, and also facilitating the stake-holders' identification with the company and with the community.[64] Indeed, this new media ecosystem – also referred to as new 'media ecology'[65] – is creating further demands for transparency, accountability and dialogue. The public in general and stakeholders in particular can now manage their own relations with the organizations while these last can no longer avoid interaction or prevent public exposure.

Therefore, what we want to rescue from this 'symmetrical' approach is not its techno-deterministic assumptions but its premise that communication professionals need to truly engage with horizontal platforms to foster dialogue and that fact that the approach aspires to see the organization, the stakeholders and the public at large as equals. CSR departments have to face to the fact that public relations professionals have become increasingly important in "creating, cultivating, and managing online brand communities, as well as of establishing and maintaining the relationships created by active, engaged publics",[66] something that is becoming increasingly important.

Indeed, if building, maintaining and enhancing relationships with the stakeholders has always been a function of public relations professionals, this has now extended to a global scale[67] thanks to the new technologies, which facilitate global interconnectivity and exposure. This can create, nevertheless, a 'risky environment'[68] for those companies with CSR programs that stand away from transparency and a stakeholder approach. Research in the context of Spain indicates that CSR organizational programs that are not managed by public relations professionals tend to present important deficiencies when trying to engage stakeholders into the process of corporate decision-making (this might be of course a deliberated effort, but it is not a sensible strategy).[69]

In the majority of these cases, dialogue is absent and CSR becomes a cynical and futile performative exercise to preserve reputation and branding at all cost, with subsequent backlash on the long term. The recent history of CSR is filled with the graveyards of those who failed in the attempt to reach out by means of unsatisfactory compromises between the corporative prerogatives and societal demands.[70] It is precisely in this context in which we need to raise the question about why companies are not exploring and incorporating the ability of public relations professionals to promote this engagement and why it has become such a missed opportunity, particularly in the light of the rise of social media and digital technologies?

Research approaches

To answer these questions, we have carried out semi-structured interviews to those in charge of CSR in top Spanish organization of companies, as well as public relations professionals also working for them. We also included the examination of communication strategies, annual reports and most commonly used digital platforms among these companies. In doing so, we wanted to explore why particular companies and organizations are not making full use of the possibilities offered by the new media technologies. The key thesis is that the lack of communication professional, by which we mean individuals who have studied and prepared themselves to design and implement communication policy within organizations, in CSR departments hinders their ability to appropriate and use the relatively new wave of communication technologies.

To do so, we looked at the top companies listed in the IBEX 35 in Spain, which happen to be the ones that have invested more resources in CSR in that country. Our sample, however, included only 28 companies in total. This because one company (Acerol Mittal) cannot really be considered Spanish, while six others declined to take part in the study (Inditex, Bankia -Caja Madrid-, Amadeus IT Holding, Grifols, EbroFoods, Bolsas y Mercados Españoles). At the time of the fieldwork, the companies in our study included, among others, Telefónica, Santander, Iberdrola, BBVA, Repsol, Gas Natural, Abertis Infraestructuras, Ferrovial, ACS Construcción, Caixa Bank, Red Eléctrica Corporación, Banco Popular, Iberia, Banco Sabadell, Acciona, Mapfre, Enagas, Bankinter, Indra A, FCC, Endesa, Técnicas Reunidas, OHL, Mediaset España, Acerinox, Abengoa, and Gamesa y Sacyr Vallehermoso.

We triangulated the data to examine a) the relationship between CSR and professional communication and b) how these companies engage with stakeholders and publics in general by means of digital platforms. In so doing, we were trying to better understand not only the existing gaps between moral communication, normative claims and CSR practice, but also we intend to seek ways in which this gap can be addressed. We are fully aware of the limitations that these types of approaches carried out, particularly in relation to the performative aspects of the semi-structured interviews (that is, between what people say they do and what they actually do). We triangulated the different sets of data by combining semi-structured interviews with the close reading of annual reports, communication strategies and digital ethnographic observations of the digital platforms (such as websites and social networks).

What the data say

Firstly, we map the professional profile of the CSR departments of these companies. They are, on average, small, as 71% of them have five or less employees. There is also a particular imbalance in terms of gender, despite the fact that 93% of their employees are women, 61% of the managers are men. This, however, is not different from the national trends in Spain in which similar levels of inequality can be observed[71,72] in other areas of these same organizations. Secondly, almost a third of all employees in these CSR departments have a business background (32%), followed by environmental (16%), then information/computing and communication – but none in PR – (14%), quality and engineering (9%) and, finally, human resources (6%).

Overall, the semi-structured interviews suggest that part of the activities of CSR managers in the companies included in the study relate to PR. However, those interviewed confirmed that most of these managers do not have any professional training in PR or background in professional communication. They are, in other words, professionals who lack adequate training around professional communication, which is – paradoxically – an area that they themselves recognize as 'key' part of their own work. Only in one case did we find a person with a communications background. This was, nevertheless, someone with a background in journalism not in PR.

The data obtained from the semi-structured interviews also highlight the low opinion that CSR managers have of public relations professionals: 64% of them think they "do not need any professional communication expertise in their departments". They justify this because 1) their companies have already a general communication department and 2) communication in CSR is only for "doing reports" so "you can outsource" that task. It is worth highlighting that there were specific cases in which CSR managers had opted to incorporate temporarily communications professionals in their departments. They did so, according to the interviews, for two main reasons, 1) to manage relations with stakeholders and 2) to communicate CSR policies.

Nevertheless, our data shows that there is scarcity of public relations practitioners responsible for the formulation or communication of CSR policies in major Spanish companies. When we asked about the ideal professional profile for a CSR manager, not in one single case were public relations professionals mentioned. Moreover, one of the managers went out of his way to say that he "never would choose a public relations practitioner to fill that post". This reluctance to employ public relations professionals happens, despite the fact that 46% of the staff in CSR departments seems well aware of the links with communications departments as 'strategic'. Moreover, 64% of the interviewees think that "communication" is "fundamental" for CSR programs.

The way we interpret these results is that there is an important gap between the aware-ness of CSR departments in relation to communication needs and the view they have about the ability of communication professionals to deliver these goals. These findings correspond to similar studies that have also indicated negative perceptions around public relations practitioners.[73,74] In any case, further research is needed to understand better the bureaucratic and organizational barriers imposed to communication professionals in CSR departments.

We do know, however, that this dichotomy is not only about assigning importance to communication while downplaying the role of professional communication, but it also reflects a wider paradox between theory and practice within CSR departments. Indeed, when asked about the need to engage the public in the process of designing CSR polices, 97% responded that it was in fact "very important". Moreover, many of the same respond-ents added how digital technologies had enabled the possibility of ample consultation and dialogue. However, when the responses from the semi-structured interviews were contrasted against the actual digital records of the companies, we found that in only a few cases had the organization actually used these technologies to open bidirectional channels of communications with its stakeholders and the public. Moreover, in most cases in the sample, there was no evidence that any feedback had been incorporated or even taken into account in the design or evaluation of any of the CSR programs in question. In other words, there is a big disparity between the normative claims of communication engagement and the actual practice on the ground. Rather than inclusive consultation, the communication provisions – both organizational and digital – are in fact set in a very traditional hierarchical form by the top managers of the organizations.

The data also suggests that despite normative claims of symmetrical approaches and the rise of the interactive and digital technologies, the predominant channels of communica-tion continue to be used in very unidirectional ways from the top to the bottom. To be sure, the main channels used by CSR staff to engage with stakeholders and the public are annual reports (93%), traditional corporate website (86%), email (82%) and questionnaires (79%). Other channels used include discussion fora (64%) and group meetings (86%), but this – for what we observed – are performed in controlled environments, and none of its contents or outputs seem to permeate into CSR policy or actions.

To make matters worse, there seems to be an important gap in the understanding of what dialogue in the digital era means. Indeed, while 57% of the interviewees claim to use Facebook or LinkedIn, 32% use blogs and 32% use Twitter as channels to communi-cate with the public, our own ethnographic observations found no conversations at all. Instead, what we were able to observe were very 'standardized' messages with little or no interaction between the publics and the organizations. In other words, these technologi-cal platforms are mostly used as channels for top-to-bottom dissemination rather than as a space for conversation. This top-to-bottom dissemination is even more prevalent in the way these organizations understand and manage their annual reports.

What CSR reports say

From previous research, we know that companies claim to have different reasons for issuing CSR reports but that, in practice, those who do so mainly see these reports as being 'good for business'.[75] Therefore, despite the fact that an annual CSR report should be an instrument to engage with the general public in general and stakeholders in particular, it is not surprising to see how in 61% of cases there is a clear focus on internal stakeholders. Moreover, 100% of companies included employees, and a very large proportion of these reports were dedicated to shareholders and investors (97%), while 94% of these reports dedicated sections to customers (94%). In other words, CSR reports have effectively become an instrument for the company to talk to itself and to its clients rather than with society at large.

Indeed, only in 33% of these reports we were able to find references to 'other' stakeholders such as foundations, regulators, indigenous communities and media. The content analysis found relatively low frequency in the use of words relating to corporate governance, analysts and experts, opinion leaders and external bloggers. What our content analysis highlights is that CSR reports tend to leave aside what Burson-Marsteller call 'e-influential' or 'techno-influential' stakeholders,

> A new breed of opinion leaders, influential and focused on technology, seamlessly connecting their work and personal lives while transmitting information on companies, brands and products.[76]

This again happens despite explicit normative claims made around communication. Indeed, 85% of the CSR reports provided information about the tools of dialogue and participation that are used in the organization, both in the area of CSR and in business in general. These reports make explicit claims about external communication tools, which are said to be both bidirectional and unidirectional. These claims seem to be based on the notion that traditional websites and microblogging are per se interactive and bidirectional and the belief that this in itself is sufficient to create spaces for symmetrical dialogue. In 100% of cases, the reports claim to use online tools such as corporate websites, emails and online documentation available on the web to engage with the public, while in 67% of the cases similar claims are made in relation to the use of specific microsites.

In these reports, the CSR departments claim to use other digital spaces such as e-conferences and e-meetings (61%), followed by face-to-face meetings with different stakeholders (58%). But contrasting this with the semi-structured interviews and the observations, it became clear that the use of these spaces was heavily controlled and not entirely open. With a lower frequency in their use, we find a mailbox for suggestions and complaints (36%), online newsletters (27%), email services (email or mobile message) and online forums, with 24% in both cases. In all, 21% turn to blogs and to a lesser degree, corporate publications, such as corporate magazines (18%) and institutional magazines (15%).

Finally, social networks (15%) and subscription services or RSS (6%) score at the bottom of our analysis. In this sense, social networks appearing in CSR reports as channels with stakeholders are Twitter (36%), Facebook (36%) and YouTube (33%). Those that appear less prominently are Flirk (21%), LinkedIn (9%), Tuenti (9%) and Slideshare (6%). Other social networks are appearing, such as Xing (6%), Picassa (3%) and Google+ (3%), particularly as these companies expand in other markets. Interestingly, all these forms of social media and networking scored way below very traditional channels such as the corporate magazines, which are still used in 58% of the cases to deliver the message to the stakeholders as the preferred channel to communicate with stakeholders.

CSR on PR

The close reading of CSR reports can also help elucidate how those producing the report – staff in CSR departments – see the issues concerning to PR. The results point out different categories. On a first instance (Level A), we find that an overwhelming majority of the reports deal with risk management (85%), relationships with stakeholders (76%), the production itself of CSR reports (76%), ethical codes (70%), corporate image and reputation (61%), internal communication management (61%), CSR training (61%), communication channels and face-to-face contact with the public (58%) and external communication management (52%). In other words, CSR staff in their own annual reports recognized these areas – associated with PR – as priorities in their day-to-day work.

On a second level (which we will call B), we found that 33% of the reports deal with communication channels online 2.0. These included issues relating to transparency, such as CSR redemption accounts (33%), marketing and/or advertising responsible (33%) and research on CSR (6%). On a third level (called C), we found CSR agendas by countries and topics such as education, health, productivity and energy efficiency, the resolution of conflicts through approved systems, communication and crisis management, code of ethics in advertising and suppliers, measuring 2.0 environments reputation and credibility. All of these are issues that demand professional communication expertise. Therefore, the absence of public relations professionals in CSR departments is even more striking.

Conclusions

The case remains that many CSR departments underperform in relation to extracting the full potential of professional communication approaches in general, and in particular, they fail in taking advantage of the wide set of possibilities offered by new digital and interactive media technologies. We can only speculate as to why these departments are so reluctant to engage in a more comprehensive manner with PR as a professional discipline and as to why public relations practitioners tend to seem systematically excluded from CSR. Moreover, when it is perfectly clear to us that by developing these bridges between CSR departments and public relations professionals they could become an 'ombudsmen'[77] for both stakeholders and the public at large and therefore fulfill their potential as a space for transparency and accountability in a complex and challenging era in which social media and digital technologies are creating a set of new demands.[78]

Examining the interviews responses to this lack of recognition of and cooperation with PR, it is clear that professional boundaries and protection of 'guilds' seem to play an important part in creating barriers against these professionals. Not only because of what the interviewees and their CSR report said, but also because of what they did not say. That is, a lack of reasonable justification as to why they are reluctant to employ more public relations professionals. These silences perhaps also help explain, in part, the gender imbalances at the top of the managerial scale, which no doubt are a key component in these attitudes towards PR.

Indeed, being small departments within large organizations, people might become very protective of their working space and jobs. In these cases, managers tend to act as a Pretorian Guard for vested interests and traditional organizational arrangements. However, this has tremendous organizational and ethical implications as the incorporation of public relations professionals into CSR departments could also help close the gender gap. After all, it is a unique professional area overwhelmingly pursued by women who tend to occupy leadership and managerial roles, something desperately needed in CSR departments.[79]

Our data, at least in the case of Spain, challenge in part the findings of other authors in relation to how in European companies CSR and communication departments seem to frequently engage and cooperate in the continent. According to these authors, referring to other countries in Europe, these are the two departments that tend to more frequently cooperate and are more likely to have formalized their cooperation.[80] This regrettably does not seem to be the case of Spain, where instead the biggest companies' CSR and communication departments appear to be living in almost parallel universes. Nevertheless, against this seemly distinctiveness of Spain let us not forget – and warn – that the variety of studies around CSR departments in Europe and the United States have been mostly based on perceptions derived from interviews, therefore dominated by normative claims rather than by empirical observations.

If anything, by triangulating different approaches and research strategies, our findings show the lack of professionalization for communication in CSR on an empirical level. This applies well in Spain and perhaps also in other countries. It would advisable for researchers of these societies to examine factual empirical evidence beyond the normative claims made in semi-structured interviews. Moreover, as Russo and Perrini[81] have stated, when we have seen globally how "large firms still lack the ability to integrate the management of these specific relationships into their corporate strategy".

If this gap is to be filled, then CSR departments ought to consider the incorporation of professional communication practitioners at the core of their strategy, something that at the moment is not happening. Perhaps, in all justice to the CSR departments, there seems to be a generalized distrust against PR, not because of their professional capacity but instead because communication departments are generally perceived to be "aligned to the strategic management of the organization, whereas this is not always the case for the CSR departments".[82] In other words, it is not so much the professional capacities of those individuals which are in question, but the ethical reservations around their ability to detach themselves sufficiently from the core objectives of the organization. Public relations professionals are in fact seen as prone to 'contaminate' or 'hinder' the ability of CSR departments to communicate effectively and transparently with the stakeholders given these ethical reservations. Sadly, in these cases, the tradition of PR is seen as too 'rotten' and too 'compromised' by many.[83]

This presents an important paradox, given the need of organizations to improve dialogue with stakeholders and to show how companies are genuinely interested in working with the community to mitigate, if not eliminate, negative societal impacts. In today's digital era, these companies have to demonstrate how they are working to introduce the stakeholder's point of view in their agenda. They need to prove how committed they are with CSR and society and, on top of that, be able to communicate this message effectively, particularly in the light of unfulfilled promises and mistakes made in the past. But how to do this without a close collaboration and engagement with professional communication? Particularly in light of the emergence of a multiplicity of 2.0 tools, which so far – as we have seen here – have been mostly sub-utilized. These questions, in our sample of companies, remain wide open and in need of further research. Nevertheless, these are issues, which urgently need to be addressed.

Notes

1 Ruiz-Mora, I., Lugo-Ocando, J. and Castillo, A. (2016). Reluctant to talk, reluctant to listen: Public relations professionals and their involvement in CSR programmes in Spain. *Public Relations Review*, 42(3), 402–407.

2 Benn, S., Todd, L. R., and Pendleton, J. (2010). Public relations leadership in corporate social responsibility. *Journal of Business Ethics*, 3(96), 403–423.

3 Kim, S.Y. and Reber, B. H. (2008). Public relations' place in corporate social responsibility: Practitioners define their role. *Public Relations Review*, 34(4), 337–342.

4 Hou, J. and Reber, B. H. (2011). Dimensions of disclosures: Corporate social responsibility (CSR) reporting by media companies. *Public Relations Review*, 37(2), 166–168.

5 Neu, D., Warsame, H. and Pedwell, K. (1998). Managing public impressions: environmental disclosures in annual reports. *Accounting, Organizations and Society*, 23(3), 265–282.

6 Munshi, D. and Priya, K. (2005). Imperializing spin cycles: A postcolonial look at public relations, greenwashing, and the separation of publics. *Public Relations Review*, 31(4), 513–520.

7 Zadek, S., Evans, R. and Pruzan, P. (2013). *Building corporate accountability: Emerging practice in social and ethical accounting and auditing*. London: Routledge.

8 Morsing, M., Majken, S. and Kasper-Ulf, N. (2008). The 'Catch 22' of communicating CSR: Findings from a Danish study. *Journal of Marketing Communications*, 14(2), 97–111.

9 Zhang, J. and Swanson, D. (2006). Analysis of news media's representation of corporate social responsibility (CSR). *Public Relations Quarterly*, 51(2), 13–17.

10 McKie, D. and Willis, P. (2012). Renegotiating the terms of engagement: Public relations, marketing, and contemporary challenges. *Public Relations Review*, 38(5), 846–852.

11 Ott, L. and Theunissen, P. (2015). Reputations at risk: Engagement during social media crises. *Public Relations Review*, 41(1), 97–102.

12 Merrill, T., Latham, K., Santalesa, R. and Navetta, D. (2011). *Social media: The business benefits may be enormous. But can the risks – reputational, legal, operational – be mitigated?* (p. 7). Available from: Http://www.acegroup.com/us-en/assets/ace-progress-report-social-media.pdf [Accessed 1 December 2015].

13 Beck, U. (1998). *La Sociedad del Riesgo*. Barcelona: Paidos.

14 Lehman, G. (2001). Reclaiming the public sphere: Problems and prospects for corporate social and environmental accounting. *Critical Perspectives on Accounting*, 12(6), 713–733.

15 Schultz, F. and Wehmeier, S. (2010). Institutionalization of corporate social responsibility within corporate communications: Combining institutional, sensemaking and communication perspectives. *Corporate Communications: An International Journal*, 15(1), 9–29 (p. 28).

16 Ruiz-Mora et al., op.cit.

17 Grunig, J. E. (2013). *Excellence in public relations and communication management*. Abingdon, Oxon: Routledge.

18 Kietzmann, J. H., Hermkens, K., McCarthy, I. P. and Silvestre, B. S. (2011). Social media? Get serious! Understanding the functional building blocks of social media. *Business Horizons*, 54(3), 241–251.

19 L'Etang, J., Lugo-Ocando, J. and Ahmed, Z. (2011). Ethics, CSR, power and strategic communication. In Ø. Ihlen, J. Bartlett and S. May (Eds.), *Handbook of communication and corporate social responsibility* (pp. 170–187). Oxford: Wiley-Blackwell.

20 Lugo-Ocando, J. and Hernandez-Toro, M. (2016). Public relations and humanitarian communication: From persuasion to the creation of a community of equals. In J. L'Etang, D. McKie, N. Snow, and J. Xifra (Eds.), *The Routledge Handbook of Critical Public Relations*. Abingdon, Oxon: Routledge.

21 An, N. and McIlwaine, S. (2011). Who wants a voice in science issues – and why? A survey of European citizens and its implications for science journalism. *Journalism Practice*, 5(2), 210–226.

22 Habermas, J., Lenhardt, C. and Nicholsen, S. W. (1990). *Moral consciousness and communicative action*. Cambridge, MA: MIT press.

23 Black, S. (2011). *ABC de las Relaciones Públicas*. Barcelona: Gestion 2000.

24 Cutlip, S.M., Center, A.H. and Broom, G.M. (2001). *Relaciones Públicas eficaces*. Barcelona: Gestión 2000.

25 Seitel, F. (2002). *Teoría y práctica de las Relaciones Públicas*. Madrid: Pretencie Hall.

26 European Comission. (2011). *A renewed EU strategy 2011–14 for corporate social responsibility*. Brussels: European Comission.

27 European Comission. (2001). *Green paper: Promoting a european framework for corporate social responsibility*. European Commission. Brussels: European Commission.

28 Grunig, J. and Hunt, T. (2003). *Direccion de Relaciones Publicas*. Barcelona: Gestion 2000 (p. 241).

29 Greenland, S., Bainbridge, J., Galloway, Ch. and Gill, R. (2012). *Strategic communication: Cases in marketing, public relations, advertising and media*. Sydney: Pearson Higher Education.

30 Willers, Ch. and Kulik, A. (2013). CSR as corporate strategy vs."Greenwashing": CSR as a new paradigm of brand management? In R. A. Conrady (Ed.), *Trends and issues in global tourism* (pp. 301–313). Berlin: Springer.

31 Gonzalez-Herrero, A. (2006). Comunicación de Crisis y Responsabilidad Social Corporativa. En *Capriotti, P. y Garrido, F.J. Guía de la Responsabilidad Social Empresarial, Fascículo 4* (pp. 8–11). Santiago (Chile): Universidad del Desarrollo/Diario Financiero (p. 8).

32 Castillo-Esparcia, A. (2009). *Relaciones Públicas. Teoría e Historia.* Barcelona: UOC (p. 225).

33 L'Etang, J. (2006). Corporate responsibility and public relations ethics. En L'Etang, J. y Pieczka, M. (Eds.), *Public relations: Critical debates and contemporary practice* (pp. 405–422). Mahwah, NJ: Erlbaum (p. 409).

34 L'Etang, J. (2009). *Relaciones Públicas. Conceptos, práctica y crítica.* Barcelona: UOC (p. 25).

35 L'Etang (2006), op-cit.

36 Daugherty, E. (2001). Public relations and social responsibility. En Heath, R.L. (Ed.), *Handbook of public relations* (pp. 389–401). Thousand Oaks, CA: Sage (pp. 390–292).

37 L'Etang (2006), op. cit. (p. 417).

38 L'Etang (2006), op. cit. (p. 417).

39 Soo-Yeon, K. and Reber, B.H. (2008). Public relations' place in corporate social responsibility: Practitioners define their role. *Public Relations Review*, 34(4), 337–342.

40 Ruiz-Mora et al., op. cit.

41 Daugherty, op. cit (p. 401).

42 Signitzer, B. and Prexl, A. (2008). Corporate sustainability communications: Aspects of theory and professionalization. *Journal of Public Relations Research* 20, 1–19 (p. 12).

43 Clark, C. E. (2000). Differences between public relations and corporate social responsibility: An analysis. *Public Relations Review*, 26(3), 363–380 (p. 376).

44 Kim, S.Y. and Reber, B.H. (2008). Public relations' place in corporate social responsibility: Practitioners define their role. *Public Relations Review*, 34(4), 337–342 (p. 341).

45 Mayes, R., Pini, B. and McDonald, P. (2012). Corporate social responsibility and the parameters of dialogue with vulnerable others. *Organization*, 20(6), 840–859 (p. 841).

46 Plowman, K., Ostrom-Blonigen, J. and Bornsen, S. (2008). Stakeholder theory: Antidote to a drug company's market health? A case study of Synthroi. *Journal of Communication Management*, 12(1), 5–17 (p. 8).

47 Freeman, R. E., Harrison, J. S., Wicks, A.C., Parmar, B. and Colle, S. (2010). *Stakeholder theory. The state of the art.* Nueva York: Cambridge University Press.

48 Freeman, R. E. (1984). *Strategic management: A stakeholder approach.* Boston: Pitman Publishing.

49 Freeman (1984), op. cit.

50 Plowman et al., op. cit.

51 Soo-Yeon, K. and Reber, B.H. (2008). Public relations' place in corporate social responsibility: Practitioners define their role. *Public Relations Review, 34*(4), 337–342.

52 Mayes et al., op. cit (p. 841).

53 Grunig, J. E. and Hunt, T. (1984). *Managing public relations.* Holt, Rinehart and Winston, New York.

54 Deetz, S. (2007). Corporate governance, corporate social responsibility, and communicatio. En S. May, G. Cheney, and J. Roper (Eds.), *The debate over corporate social responsibility* (pp. 267–278). Oxford: Oxford University Press.

55 Grunig, J. E. (2001). Two-way symmetrical public relations: Past, present, and future. In R. L. Heath (Ed.), *Handbook of public relations* (pp. 11–30). Thousand Oaks, CA: Sage.

56 Kent, M. L. and Taylor, M. (2002). Toward a dialogic theory of public relations. *Public Relations Review*, 28(1), 21–37.

57 Murphy, P. (1991). The limits of symmetry: A game theory approach to symmetric and asymmetric public relations. *Journal of Public Relations Research*, 3(1–4), 115–131.

58 Roper, J. (2005). Symmetrical communication: Excellent public relations or a strategy for hegemony? *Journal of Public Relations Research*, 17(1), 69–86.

59 Yang, A. and Kent, M. (2014) Social media and organizational visibility: A sample of Fortune 500 corporations. *Public Relations Review*, 40(3), 562–564 (p. 563) DOI: 10.1016/j.pubrev.2014.04.006

60 Gonçalves, G. (2012). Who's afraid of social media? A normative approach to corporate discourse on the Web. En Gonçalves, G. (org). *The dialogue imperative. Trends and challenges in strategic and organisational communication* (pp. 33–45). Covilhã: LabCom (p. 41).

61 A Listening strategy allows for interaction with different audiences to elicit first the "conversations market" in Balagué, C. and Fayon, D. (2012). Quelle est l'utilité des réseaux sociaux pour les entreprises? In *Facebook, Twitter et les autres. Intégrer les réseaux sociaux dans une stratégie d'entreprise* (pp. 75–114). Paris: Éditions Pearson, Collection Mondial.

62 Charest, F., Bouffard, J. and Zajmovic, E. (2016) Public relations and social media: Deliberate or creative strategic planning. *Public Relations Review*, 42(4), 530–538. http://dx.doi.org/10.1016/j.pubrev.2016.03.008.

63 Jones, B., Temperley, J. and Lima, A. (2009). Corporate reputation in the era of Web 2.0: The case of Primark. *Journal of Marketing Management*, 25(9–10), 927–239.

64 Korschun, D. and Du, S. (2013). How virtual corporate social responsibility dialogs generate value: A framework and propositions. *Journal of Business Research*, 66, 1494–1504. (p. 1146).

65 Lundby, K. (2009). *Mediatization: Concept, changes, consequences*. New York: Peter Lang.

66 Hutchins, A. and Tindall, N. (2016). *Public relations and participatory culture fandom, social media and community engagement*. London: Routledge (p. 4).

67 Hutchins and Tindall, op. cit. (p. 4).

68 Jones et al., op. cit. (p. 931).

69 Ruiz-Mora, I., Lugo-Ocando, J. and Castillo, A. (2016). Reluctant to talk, reluctant to listen: Public relations professionals and their involvement in CSR programmes in Spain. *Public Relations Review*, 42(3), 402–407.

70 An example of this being the case of the CSR programme of Royal Dutch Shell in Nigeria and the criticism it has drawn to it. See Marchant, M. (2014). *Corporate social responsibility and oil in the Niger Delta: Solution or part of the problem?* United Nations Research Institute for Social Development www.unrisd.org/UNRISD/website/newsview.nsf/(httpNews)/F338B68CE5C7D543C1257D1E00411594?OpenDocument [Accessed 2 March 2016].

71 Martín, M. T. T. and Recio, C. (2012). Desigualdades de género en el mercado de trabajo: entre la continuidad y la transformación. *Revista de economía crítica*, 14(1), 178–202.

72 Simón, H. (2009). La desigualdad salarial en España: Una perspectiva internacional y temporal. *investigaciones económicas*, 33(1), 439–471.

73 Grunig, L. A. (1990). Power in the public relations department. *Journal of Public Relations Research*, 2(1–4), 115–155.

74 Pincus, J. D., Rimmer, T., Rayfield, R.E. and Cropp, F. (1993). Newspaper editors' perceptions of public relations: How business, news, and sports editors differ. *Journal of Public Relations Research*, 5(1), 27–45.

75 Idowu, S. O. and Papasolomou, I. (2007). Are the corporate social responsibility matters based on good intentions or false pretences? An empirical study of the motivations behind the issuing of CSR reports by UK companies. *Corporate Governance: The International Journal of Business in Society*, 7(2), 136–147 (p. 136).

76 Burson-Marsteller. (2005). *Los tecnoinfluenciadores, una nueva generación de líderes de opinión*. (Burson-Marsteller, Ed.) (p. 2). Available from: http://issuu.com/burson-marsteller-emea/docs/e_fluenciadores [Accessed 9 January 2016].

77 An official appointed to investigate individuals' complaints against a company or organization, especially a public authority.

78 Lugo-Ocando, J. and Hernández-Toro, M. (2015). Public relations and humanitarian communication: From persuasion to the creation of a community of equals. In J. L'Etang, D. McKie, N. Snow and J. Xifra (Eds.), The *Routledge handbook of critical public relations* (pp. 226–234). New York: Routledge.

79 Salzman, M. (2014, 23 September). *Why are there so many women in PR? – PRSAY*. Available from: http://prsay.prsa.org/index.php/2014/09/23/why-are-there-so-many-women-in-pr/ [Accessed 9 January 2016].

80 Pollach, I., Johansen, T. S., Ellerup Nielsen, A. and Thomsen, C. (2012). The integration of CSR into corporate communication in large European companies. *Journal of Communication Management*, 16(2), 204–216 (p. 215).

81 Russo, A. and Perrini, F. (2010). Investigating stakeholder theory and social capital: CSR in large firms and SMEs. *Journal of Business Ethics*, 91, 207–221 (p. 217).

82 Pollach et al., op.cit (p. 216).

83 Miller, D. and Dinan, W. (2007). *A century of spin: How public relations became the cutting edge of corporate power*. London: Pluto Press.

3.3 Integrated CSR communication

Toward a model encompassing media agenda building with stakeholder dialogic engagement

Augustine Pang, Angela Mak, and Wonsun Shin

Introduction

With corporate social responsibility (CSR) increasingly gaining prominence as a key component of corporate governance (Lau, Lu, & Liang, 2016; Shaukat, Qiu, & Trojanowski, 2016), CSR needs to be communicated effectively. One way is through the media. With their enlarged digital platforms, the media[1] can influence corporate behavior to a large extent and CSR in particular (Baron, 2005). Organizations depend on what the media report about them because the media is the main source of information for many stakeholders (Pang, 2010; Pang, Chiong, & Nasrath, 2014). Publicity of CSR activities is critical, as it informs the organization's stakeholders of its business decisions and processes (Fassin, 2008).

CSR has been defined in many ways. The most widely used definition is by the Commission of the European Communities (2001): "A concept whereby companies integrate social and environmental concerns in their business operations and in their interaction with their stakeholders on a voluntary basis" (Dahlsrud, 2006, p. 7). Matten and Moon (2005) attempted to offer an overarching definition: CSR is a cluster concept that overlaps with business ethics, corporate philanthropy, corporate citizenship, sustainability, and environmental responsibility. Carroll (1991) asserted that the four kinds of CSR are economic, legal, ethical, and philanthropic. Thus, CSR encompasses a wide range of commitments to both internal and external stakeholders. However, CSR communication research has overlooked an important player in the process of communication – the public relations (PR) practitioners who provide information subsidies to the media on their organizations' behalf and, in the process, shape the media's agenda and possibly public opinion (Turk 1985). The important role of PR practitioners in affecting what is ultimately said to the public is represented by information in press releases, which makes up approximately half of news content (Wilcox & Cameron, 2009).

However, many noteworthy events – even when the activity is a topic of public significance – do not get covered by the media. The lack of media coverage, in this case CSR, could be due to the historical and perennial tension between journalists and public relations practitioners of the respective organizations (Pang, 2010). Another reason is that while journalists might be familiar with the concept of CSR, the extent of CSR activity in the corporate, community, and government sectors is less known in the everyday exigencies of journalistic practice (Pang, Mak, & Lee, 2015). Signitzer and Prexl (2008) argued that if the media understood the concept better and could elicit from organizations the newsworthy elements of their CSR activities, the coverage could lead to greater public awareness of socially, culturally, economically, and environmentally sustainable policies.

Additionally, Pang, Mak, and Lee (2011) argued that political, social, economic, and cultural factors adversely influence CSR communication through the media, with its attendant digital platforms. Lee, Mak, and Pang (2013) argued there are four impediments on why organizations have challenges relating to the media. First, media shyness. Organizations may shun media spotlight for fear that the gatekeepers (i.e., journalists) will view CSR engagement with cynicism or construe it as corporate social irresponsibility (CSI) (Dickson & Eckman, 2008). Second, media style. The amount of time and money needed to meet formal, internationally recognized reporting standards, such as the Global Reporting Index, may deter organizations from taking steps to communicate their CSR efforts. Depending on how extensive the CSR communication is going to be, extra organizational resources to facilitate the coverage are needed. This may be more than what the organization can afford or is willing to allocate in lieu of other operational priorities. Third, cultural factors. Communicating CSR efforts might lower the moral status of the action, and this in turn might prohibit organizations from communicating them (Ihlen, 2011). Fourth, lack of newsworthiness. The traditional news values of human interest, geographical and cultural proximity, relevance, impact, and extent of impact need to be evident to the journalist to prevent them from binning the PR message at the point of media contact. Tench, Bowd, and Jones (2007) found that one of the major grouses journalists had about CSR communication from organizations was that the PR messages had little news value, seemed overtly self-serving, or were pitched to the wrong media.

There are, thus, potential pitfalls relying on the media as the sole agent and engine of CSR communication. For instance, Stoll (2008) warned of possible public backlash in media reporting against the organization's CSR efforts. The industry has both good and poor examples of how CSR is communicated.

Exemplar of good CSR communication: Google

Since 2013, Google has maintained its CSR reputation at the number 1 position (Miceli, 2015; Reputation Institute, 2015). While Google does not communicate its CSR efforts in annual reports, stakeholders can access Google's CSR information on its website (Dudovskiy, 2015). However, Google is not impervious to bad press. For instance, it was fined US$22.5 million for its attempt to track its competitors' users by bypassing privacy settings (Gaudin & Perez, 2012). Despite that, Google's image remains intact (Gillett, 2016). Reputation Institute posited that "Google has been successful in building a perception of caring around the world" (Smith, 2013). Google is a good example of how CSR communications work – it is transparent in managing information by posting it on its own site; it ensures its own stakeholders and customers are happy, and it engages the press effectively, even when its actions are called into question (Smith, 2013).

Exemplar of poor CSR communication: Volkswagen

The Volkswagen (VW) emissions crisis came to light on 18 September 2015. Just before the crisis, VW had announced that it had topped the Dow Jones Sustainability Index (DJSI) (Hardyment, 2015). Lynn (2015) pointed out VW's annual report was full of "lovingly described projects it backed and charities it supported". On social media, VW USA went dark the day the scandal broke, while its global Twitter account was used only to broadcast (Davis, 2015). The silence was interrupted only when US CEO Michael Horn's statement was posted a week later (Davis, 2015). VW's communication was a massive fail. For a start, the company could not live up to its CSR claims that it has "a modern understanding of responsibility and sustainability with the traditional values of running a business" (Adams, 2015).

Given that digital platforms are increasingly accessed by different stakeholders as sources of information (Mak, Pang, & Hart, 2015), besides relying on the media, organizations should also harness various digital platforms to communicate their CSR activities. Instead of going through a gatekeeper, organizations have the opportunity to connect directly with stakeholders using their own digital communication platforms, such as corporate websites and blogs and social media profiles.

Researchers argued that digital media (online, mobile, and social) are critical platforms not just for organizations to disseminate information but also for interaction with stakeholders through feedback or dialogic loops (Kent & Taylor, 1998; Lillqvist & Louhiala-Salminen, 2014). An increasing number of stakeholders expect organizations to listen and respond (Lillqvist & Louhiala-Salminen, 2014), and such communication between organizations and the public in digital media is considered "conversation" (Spinuzzi, 2009, p. 257). In fact, the interactivity of digital media, which allows organization–public interactions, conversations, and user engagement, is associated with positive outcomes (Yang, Kang, & Johnson, 2010), including consumers' enhanced knowledge of the organizations (Melton & Hicks, 2011; Sundar, Xu, & Dou, 2012; Wu, Hu, & Wu, 2010). Digital media provide a great opportunity for organizations to generate two-way, dialogic communication and build relationships with the public (Bortree & Seltzer, 2009: Briones, Kuch, Liu, & Jin, 2011; Park & Reber, 2008; Waters, Burnett, Lamm, & Lucus, 2009).

This chapter argues how organizations can integrate both media agenda building with stakeholder engagements using both mainstream media and digital platforms to communicate their CSR activities. The chapter has four sections:

- Entrenching CSR communication: The first section discusses how CSR communication has been entrenched between the organization and journalists.
- Engaging in CSR communication: The second section discusses how this entrenchment is observed through organization engagement in CSR communication through the lens of Qiu and Cameron's (2008) Media Agenda model.
- Enlarging CSR communication: The third section examines how CSR communication can be enlarged by integrating digital media tools.
- Encompassing CSR communication: The final section proposes an integrated model that extends the Media Agenda model with stakeholder dialogic engagement.

Entrenching CSR communication

By most measures, CSR communication has been very much entrenched in seeking publicity through the media. However, for all the connotations of altruism associated with CSR, one would imagine organizations would not have problems sharing their efforts publicly via the media. While organizations are free to publicize their work using their own digital media platforms, top management still defines the effectiveness of communication by the amount of positive media coverage generated (Pang & Yeo, 2009). From a societal point of view, if the media can increase public understanding of the concept and drive organizations to be more involved, the increased participation can potentially move a society toward the greater awareness of sustainable development and be more "future-oriented" (Signitzer & Prexl, 2008, p. 7). This could lead to shifts in the publics' attitudes and behaviors such as more informed purchasing decisions and greater empowerment.

CSR coverage in the media

Dickson and Eckman (2008) analyzed media events of companies that were accredited to Fair Labor Association (FLA), a non-profit organization (NPO). The results were encouraging. Contrary to the organizations' fear of receiving bad press, coverage was mostly positive. However, the positive coverage may stem from the accreditation by the FLA and results may differ for organizations who are directly communicating their CSR efforts to the media. Another notable point is that most of the coverage followed a certain format: information about FLA, information about the organization that is quoted from the FLA reports, and interviews with extremists who were cynical about CSR. This seems to suggest the media is keen to provide opposing points of views to make the story balanced as seen from how extremists rather than experts were interviewed.

In their analysis of 33 US newspapers and 18 international newspapers, Zhang and Swanson (2006) devised a typology of media's use of the term CSR into the following: objective use, social achievement of corporations, a necessary business function, social expectation for corporations, and spin. They found that 29% of the stories used the term objectively, 18% as an endorsement, 27% as a social expectation, 5% as a specialty, 6% as a necessary business function, and 15% as spin. Considering that only 15% of coverage is negative (spin), it shows that the media largely accepts the idea of CSR.

Carroll (2011) argued that how the media reports on CSR can be examined on three levels. First, content. This includes the volume of coverage, the tone of coverage, and the topics covered. Second, production. Drawing on Shoemaker and Reese's (1996) seminal work on news production, Carroll (2011) argued that there are several layers of influences on CSR coverage: a) the individual journalist level; b) news routines; c) the workings of the news organization; d) extra-media influences; and e) ideology. All these in turn influence CSR behavior. The effects can be seen in three ways: a) greater CSR coverage leads to higher attention from the public; b) greater coverage may also lead to greater pressures from stakeholder groups; and c) public scrutiny increases.

Tench et al. (2007) surveyed the UK media practitioners and found that 66% of practitioners indicated they would report CSR from a positive angle, although 32% said they most frequently cover negative angles. What was interesting was that while 45% of the journalists interviewed felt that organizations were engaging in CSR purely for profits, 56% felt that the media, as a whole, would hold such a view. This shows that the tendency to magnify cynicism of CSR engagement exists even among journalists. The researchers also broke down the type of CSR angles, and journalists were asked to indicate the type of stories they would cover positively, negatively, or not at all. CSR activities such as obeying law and order, adapting to changing stakeholder needs, and fulfilling obligations to the society were not likely to be covered, whereas environmental efforts, community work, and philanthropic projects were likely to be covered. This supports Zerk's (2008) assertion that the media is contributing to the formation of an incorrect conception of CSR as comprising of caring for the environment and the community to a large extent. Issues related to corporate governance, quality of products, and ethical work operations were likely to be covered negatively.

Besides having an exaggerated fear of media backlash, organizations' fear of public backlash seems to be unfounded, as the MORI survey also found that 60% of the British public said they would trust CSR communication originating from the organization, thus making organization-disseminated information almost as trustworthy as those originating from NPOs (66%). MORI also surveyed several opinion leaders on the importance they accrued to organizations' CSR communication. Results showed that editors were most concerned, with 80% of those surveyed indicating that they were looking for proof of organizations' social responsibility.

The media, thus, remain a credible platform to communicate CSR communication. Pang, Chiong, and Nasrath (2014) argued that even with the proliferation of alternative media such as online and mobile media, engaging the mainstream media remains critical. This is because there is credibility in the news covered by mainstream media. George (2012) argued that the credibility comes from the "discipline of verifying information with multiple sources, institutional memory to sense when things are more complex than they seem, and higher order judgment honed by experience and specialized beat knowledge" (p. 179).

Therein, however, is the problem. How do PR practitioners build good relations with journalists when there is a historical root of distrust?

Challenges in media relations

According to Pang (2010), influencing the media in the news production process through information subsidy function has long been the modus operandi in media relations (Bland, Theaker, & Wragg, 2005; Lerbinger, 2006; Wilcox & Cameron, 2009). Public relations' influence on news content is dominant (Gandy, 1982), which researchers estimate ranges from 25% to 50% (Cameron, Sallot, & Curtin, 1997). Journalists recognize that PR practitioners serve as one of the most important sources of news (*Media relations and Europe*, 2008; Shin & Cameron, 2003). PR's influence on news is so important that issues that suffer poor news coverage were managed by those practitioners who were poorly skilled or had no skills whatsoever (Cameron, Sallot, & Curtin, 1997). Yet this process is fraught with challenges faced by PR practitioners: why do journalists dislike them?

To unearth the roots of deep-seated antagonism that journalists have of PR practitioners (Tilley & Hollings, 2008), scholars found that journalists often treat PR practitioners "with contempt" (DeLorme & Fedler, 2003, p. 99). This is "puzzling" as journalists have "rarely, if ever, expressed a similar contempt for related fields" (p. 114). The long-held and innate dislike journalists have for PR practitioners stem from historical roots, DeLorme and Fedler (2003) argued. Consistently, it appears to revolve around the idea that PR practitioners do not understand what journalists want.

The argument is that even though journalists recognize that PR practitioners serve an important information-subsidy function, those who do not know how to perform this function found little favor with journalists. In a survey among European journalists, more than two-thirds of PR practitioners were found to lack understanding of what journalists needed ("Media relations and Europe", 2008). The deficiencies appear to fall in the area of news sense. Sallot and Johnson (2006) found 78% of journalists surveyed said PR practitioners offered information that was "overtly and overly self-serving" (p. 84) on behalf of their organizations. Kopenhaver (1985) found 78% of journalists surveyed said that news releases were "publicity disguised as news" (p. 40). The top six reasons why editors rejected news releases were first, lack of news value; second, lack of local news angle; third, lack of information; fourth, lack of timeliness; fifth, poorly written; and sixth, grammatical errors. Supa and Zoch (2009) replicated a study by Kopenhaver, Martinson, and Ryan (1984) on how PR practitioners and editors in Florida viewed each other 23 years later. As far as how PR practitioners disseminate information to journalists, Supa and Zoch (2009) concluded PR practitioners still do not know how to present relevant information to journalists.

Engaging in CSR communication

Despite that, PR practitioners continue to seek media coverage. Agenda building is one plausible way where journalists and PR practitioners can find common ground. Qiu and Cameron (2008) examined the determinants of agenda building effectiveness.

Agenda building

The relationship between the PR practitioners and journalists has been intensely discussed in agenda-setting studies (Curtin, 1999; Turk, 1985; Zoch & Molleda, 2006), whereby PR practitioners can help set the agenda on behalf of their organizations through their information subsidy functions (Kiousis, 2005; Turk, 1985). The agenda building framework (Cobb & Elder, 1971; Kiousis & Wu, 2008; Qiu & Cameron, 2008) examines the process by which PR practitioners attempt to influence press agenda (see Figure 3.3.1).

Figure 3.3.1 shows the interaction among the three key elements in the agenda building model (Qiu & Cameron, 2008): PR practitioners and the PR materials they disseminate that contains source agenda, journalists and their gatekeeping function, and the use of PR-disseminated information in media content.

In the process of building the media agenda, PR practitioners approach journalists with subsidized materials and, in the course of interaction with journalists, attempt to have their PR stories covered (arrow a). Ultimately, journalists still have the autonomy to decide how much and how the PR material is used (arrow b). Other than interaction with PR practitioners, journalists' editorial decisions are influenced by news values, comprehension of the issue, newsroom schedules, and the organization they belong to and society, among others (Shoemaker, 1991). Hence, the influence PR practitioners have on news content is mediated through journalists, and the level of agenda building is determined by how much the media uses PR materials (arrow c). This model posits that the effectiveness of

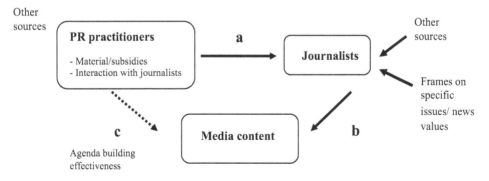

Figure 3.3.1 Agenda Building model (adapted from Qiu & Cameron, 2008)

agenda building is affected by the degree to which PR practitioners and journalists share news values and understanding of a specific issue (Qiu & Cameron, 2008).

CSR reporting is a suitable context for the agenda building process to be studied as the current level of CSR knowledge among journalists is suspected to be rather dismal, with most journalists equating it to philanthropy and going green (Pang, Mak, & Lee, 2015). In addition, most aspects of CSR concern internal stakeholders and business processes, which are most likely to remain confidential unless the organization decides otherwise. What this means for journalists is that organizations may be the main source of information, thus putting the latter in a better position to influence media content.

Findings from application of model

A total of 13 interviews with media professionals and 20 CSR practitioners in Singapore and Australia (Lee, Mak, & Pang, 2013; Mak, Pang, & Hart, 2015) were conducted to examine the relationships, tensions, and challenges in the media agenda building process in communicating CSR. Findings indicated that agenda building is somewhat ineffective, as journalists were largely not paying much heed to organization-disseminated CSR information. In particular, CSR practitioners viewed CSR as part of their organizations' business operation whereas journalists regarded organizations doing CSR as beyond the profit motive (e.g., philanthropy and environmental concerns). In addition, journalists see organizational materials as triggers for their news reporting because of the quest of independence and cynicism towards the CSR motives.

How much of CSR news makes it to print depends on the ideology of news selection (Phillips, 2015). Journalists, while understanding the concept of CSR, might dismiss a CSR story because of time constraints, prevalence of other news, wariness of commercialism, lack of interest in pursuing the details, or mistrust of public relations as a source of information. Findings also suggested that while CSR activities are newsworthy to journalists, PR practitioners seeking publicity for CSR activities should refrain from using the term CSR, find tailored news angles, show support from top management as spokespersons, and develop symbiotic relationships with the media to find a place in the journalism source hierarchy.

Revised agenda building model for CSR communication

Figure 3.3.2 shows the modification of Qiu and Cameron's (2008) model based on the CSR studies conducted in Singapore and Australia.

The solid and dotted arrows at "a" signify the two-way communication between PR practitioners and journalists. However, the CSR studies revealed that PR practitioners are much more proactive than journalists in information sharing (Mak, Pang, & Hart, 2015). While journalists would sometimes take the initiative to ask PR practitioners for information, it is usually to cite the organization as an example in a more generic story or to get additional contacts to write up their own stories. The dotted arrow also signifies the indirect way journalists obtain CSR information about companies. It may be through consulting firms, PR agencies, and even archives to search out companies previously featured for their CSR and to attempt to contact them again (Mak, Pang, & Hart, 2015).

Arrow "b" shows the direct control and autonomy journalists have in deciding media content. Arrow "c" shows how PR practitioners indirectly influence media content (1) through press releases sent out by their partnering organizations; (2) via social media to

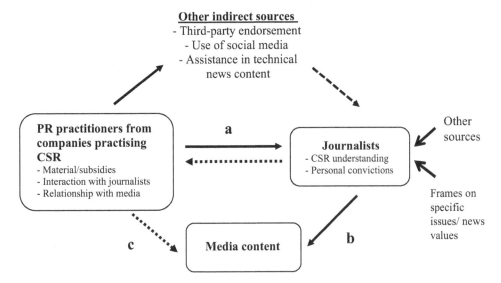

Figure 3.3.2 Modified Agenda Building model toward CSR communication

provide shareable stories; and (3) by building good relationships with the media through frequent meetings to update the media as well as providing assistance in technical content (Lee, Mak, & Pang, 2013; Mak, Pang, & Hart, 2015). This indirect control of news content is also what makes success in agenda building so precious, since controllability and credibility often work against each other; hence, the lack of control PR practitioners have over media content makes CSR covered by the media more credible to the audience (Du, Bhattacharya & Sen, 2010).

Enlarging CSR communication

Instead of solely relying on journalists to disseminate information via mainstream media, organizations can also use digital communication platforms as additional information dissemination and dialogic tools to provide feedback on the effectiveness of their CSR programs.

The prevalence of digital media, which are online, social, and mobile, allows stakeholders to easily access a wide range of information and to share their views on organizational practices with other stakeholders. These digitally empowered stakeholders also expect organizations to actively listen and respond to their needs (Lillqvist & Louhiala-Salminen, 2014). In response to the global spread of digital media and changing stakeholder expectations, organizations now heavily rely on various digital communication platforms to build strong relationships with stakeholders (Shin, Pang, and Kim, 2015).

Traditional mainstream media permit organizations to fulfill the stakeholders' informational or relational needs by disseminating information on organizational practices such as CSR activities. However, information dissemination via traditional media is mostly unidirectional, from organizations to stakeholders. Using digital media, organizations now can go beyond one-way information dissemination. Corporate websites, for example, allow organizations to obtain feedback on stakeholders' requests and embrace their inputs using interactive communication features (Chiou, Lin, & Perng, 2010; Pollach, 2005). Organizations also use social media such as Facebook, Twitter, and Instagram to join in on the conversations, interact with stakeholders, and facilitate positive word of mouth (Moran, Muzellec, & Nolan, 2014; Whiting & Deshpande, 2014). Using mobile and behavioral targeting technologies, organizations can reach individual target stakeholders with content customized to their current context and enable them to immediately provide feedback to organizations (Kang, Shin, and Tam, 2016).

Overall, digital media facilitates dialogic communication between organizations and stakeholders. Dialogic communication refers to "any negotiated exchange of ideas and opinions" (Kent & Taylor, 1998, p. 325). From an organization's perspective, dialogic communication encompasses an organization's efforts to engage in an open, honest, and ethical relationship with its stakeholders and adapt to their needs (Hong, Yang, & Rim, 2010; Taylor, Kent, & White, 2001). As public relations practices have become more centered on relationship building, the importance of dialogic communication in digital media has increased in public relations and organizational communication research (De Bussy, 2010; Shin et al., 2015).

To engage CSR stakeholders in the digital media, Schultz, Castello, and Morsing (2013) emphasized the importance of a multi-faceted understanding of different concerns, voices, and beliefs, and an ability to engage across various interpretations of the complicated issues related to corporate behaviors. Wehmeier and Schultz (2011) proposed a storytelling perspective on CSR communication where sense-giving and sense-making in social reality can be negotiated and organized through the interplay of different actors.

Incorporating relationship cultivation theories (Hon & Grunig, 1999) and Kent and Taylor's (1998) five dialogic communication principles, Shin et al. (2015) proposed four dimensions of relationship cultivation and dialogic communication applicable to various forms of digital communication platforms: (1) disclosure (i.e., the extent to which an organization discloses information about the nature of the organization); (2) access (i.e., an organization's availability to its publics); (3) information dissemination (i.e., the extent to which an organization provides useful information to its publics about what it offers); and (4) engagement (i.e., the extent to which an organization actively engages in conversations with its publics and embraces their input) (p. 191).

Although different researchers have used different terms and dimensions to examine dialogic communication, research suggests that organizations' efforts in engaging in dialogues with stakeholders using interactive and digital media result in positive outcomes such as positive attitudes toward organizations (Seltzer & Zhang, 2011) and increased profits (Sundar et al., 2012). However, studies also show that many organizations do not fully harness the potential of digital media to facilitate dialogic communication and cultivate relationships with stakeholders (Vernuccio, 2014; Waters & Lemanski, 2011). In addition, many organizations still use digital media more for one-way than two-way communication (Shin et al., 2015).

Encompassing CSR communication

Utilizing insights from studies of both the Agenda Building model and dialogic communication, this study proposes an integrated framework that encompasses engaging the media while simultaneously harnessing digital platforms to directly connect with stakeholders.

Building on the Agenda Building model, the solid and dotted arrows at "a" between the journalists and practitioners signifies the two-way communication. While journalists

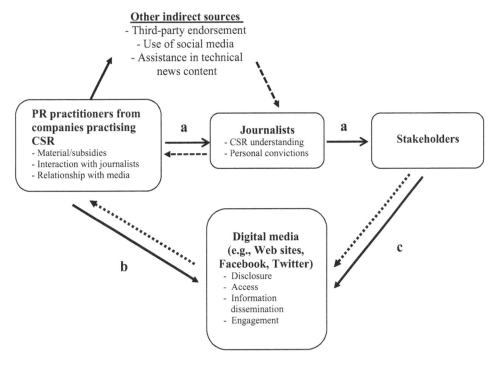

Figure 3.3.3 Encompassing CSR communication

would sometimes take the initiative to ask practitioners for information, it is usually to cite the organization as an example in a more generic story or to get additional contacts to write up their own stories. The dotted arrow also signifies the indirect way journalists obtain CSR information about companies. It may be through consulting firms, PR agencies, and even archives to search out companies previously featured for their CSR and to attempt to contact them again. The solid "a" between the journalists and stakeholders shows that ultimately, the information must reach the stakeholders. The arrows at "b" show the possible digital communication platforms that organizations can use to build dialogic communication with stakeholders. These include corporate websites, blogs, and multiple types of social and mobile media. We only discuss three types of digital communication platforms – websites, Facebook, and Twitter – due to their popularity and widespread use in both interpersonal and public relations (Shin et al., 2015).

Websites: Websites are used by organizations to disseminate information across the globe and to cultivate relationships with stakeholders (Chiou et al., 2010; Park & Reber, 2008). Park and Reber (2008) argued that websites could incorporate various dialogic communication features that facilitate ease of interface to promote mutuality, trust, openness, and intimacy with stakeholders. Organizations can upload stories, information, photos and videos to enhance their CSR communication efforts. However, as pointed out earlier, websites are more often used for one-way rather than two-way communication (Shin et al., 2015).

Facebook: Facebook, with 1.59 billion monthly active users (Facebook, 2015), is the world's most popular social media platform. Many organizations have their own "Facebook page" where they upload news, share stories, and engage in conversations with their stakeholders (Chu, 2011). Users can connect with an organization by "following" its Facebook page, "liking", "sharing", or commenting on its newsfeeds. Organizations can also respond to the comments, engage in direct two-way conversations, and interact with stakeholders using such features as polling, contest, and idea solicitation (Chu, 2011; Lillqvist & Louhiala-Salminen, 2014; Men & Tsai, 2011). However, scholars argue that hosting a Facebook page alone would not automatically generate dialogic communication (Water et al., 2009) and that more could be done to fully utilize Facebook's potential as a dialogic communication platform (Bortree & Seltzer, 2009; Shin et al., 2015).

Twitter. Twitter is a microblogging social networking service that allows its 320 million active monthly users to broadcast short text-based status updates (up to 140 characters), called "tweets". Users "follow" or "retweet" the tweets of others to share information, highlight their interest, or agree with the issue presented (Twitter.com, n.d.). Tweets are shared and spread using such features as hashtags and hyperlinks (Strachan, 2009), and they foster user-to-user interactions at a rapid pace (Jones, 2013). Twitter allows organizations to disseminate useful information about their CSR programs to their followers and allow for one-on-one communication with individual followers. Similar to Facebook, Twitter is an excellent communication platform that provides organizations with opportunities to engage in dialogic communication and cultivate relationships with stakeholders (Kwon & Sung, 2011; Rybalko & Seltzer, 2010).

The features of (1) disclosure; (2) access; (3) information dissemination; and (4) engagement could be featured in the above platforms and other digital communication platforms to encourage conversation with stakeholders.

The arrows at "c" show how organizations should seek feedback from stakeholders via digital platforms. Since there is direct access to stakeholders, organizations should do more to encourage feedback. The feedback can be channeled back to PR practitioners.

How the model can work – and overcoming challenges

This model calls for organizations to engage in a two-step simultaneous process of communication:

* Step 1: Even as PR practitioners from organization remain active in engaging with journalists and providing information about their CSR efforts, they should at the same time upload the information in text, photo and/or video formats on their digital media platforms.
* Step 2: Information provided in digital platforms would be accessed by stakeholders, particularly those who have interests in how the organization is performing. Organizations by and large do not have issues in disclosing or disseminating information (Shin et al., 2015). They would have to be cognizant in providing access to stakeholders and engaging stakeholders, additional tasks which they should make efforts to cultivate. The dotted lines in "b" and "c" back to the organization demonstrate the feedback loop available to stakeholders. Kent & Taylor (1998) posit that one of the strategies in building dialogic communication is to establish a dialogic loop that allows publics to query organizations and for organizations to respond.

As it stands, the challenges of the Agenda Building model have been documented above. The challenges facing organizations in instituting dialogic communication via digital media are also well documented. Shin et al. (2015) argued that even though organizations practiced integrated use of websites, Facebook, and Twitter, the use has largely been unidirectional. On websites, disclosure and information dissemination features were more prevalent than engagement features. The access features seemed to lack the interactivity that could potentially stimulate quality conversations between members of the organization and its stakeholders. Overall, websites appeared to be a useful source for stakeholders to obtain information about an organization, but they did not appear to be useful for stakeholders to engage and interact with its representatives. The findings are consistent with what previous studies have demonstrated (see Park & Reber, 2008; Taylor et al., 2001; Waters, Friedman, Mills, & Zeng, 2011). Facebook and Twitter were also found to be used in similar ways: more for information dissemination than for user engagement, and one-way communication to convey news or an announcement about the organization than for two-way communication with stakeholders. Additionally, neither Facebook nor Twitter appeared to be useful sources for stakeholders who wished to access (i.e., physically talk to or meet with) people at an organization. Although users could post messages or tweet the organizations, these organizations did not actively use these platforms to stimulate conversations with stakeholders.

A second challenge appears to be that while organizations have begun using digital communication tools, they are still not fully embracing them. They have expressed common concerns regarding: a) difficulty in controlling the message (DiStaso, McCorkindale, & Wright, 2011, 2011; Seo, Kim, & Yang, 2009); b) difficulty in determining the scope of online audiences (Seo et al., 2009); c) ability to connect effectively with stakeholders (DiStaso et al., 2011; Lovejoy, Waters, & Saxton, 2012); and d) difficulty in finding the most effective mix of digital tools and traditional media (DiStaso et al., 2011; Elling, Lentze, & de Jong, 2012).

A third challenge is the fast-paced media environment. There is now a wider range of social and digital media including Instagram, LinkedIn, Google +, Snapchat, and Pinterest. Although Facebook and Twitter are still considered the "must-have" social media due to their influence and prevalence, they may not be sufficient to reach "all" target segments. For instance, Pinterest, an image-sharing web and mobile application that allows users to sort and manage images, is considered an ideal platform to reach females in the 30s who are interested in fashion, cooking, and home decoration (Delzio, 2015). Snapchat is the most popular social media platform among US teenagers, making it an important medium for PR practitioners to consider if they wish to reach young stakeholders (Beck, 2016). Each digital media offers different features and benefits, requiring media practitioners to catch up with the trends and understand the nature of emerging media platforms and constant changes in the media environment.

A fourth challenge is that political, social, economic, and cultural factors adversely influence CSR communication through the media (Pang et al., 2011), especially with its presence in the digital platforms. The same media strategy in one country for integrating traditional and new media in CSR engagement may not be fully applicable to another country due to its business environment. Also, with digital platform, and a fast-changing media culture, a local CSR issue could easily grab the attention of the international media.

How then can practitioners integrate the use of mainstream media with digital platforms strategically? Some suggestions are proffered. First, PR practitioners must engage in proactive media relations by understanding the sets of influences on news production discussed earlier. One way is to refer to Carroll's (2011) and Pang's (2010) models, which were both inspired by Shoemaker and Reese's (1996) mediating the message model. Second, be proactive and comprehensive in disclosing and disseminating information about the organization's CSR efforts. Since not all of the organization's efforts would be covered by the media, digital platforms would be critical avenues to demonstrate efforts. Third, be willing to engage stakeholders. Stakeholders may have their ideas about the organization's CSR efforts, and some may have suggestions on how to deepen and expand these efforts. This calls for organizations to listen to and interact with stakeholders. Fourth, use digital platforms to galvanize stakeholders into participating in the organization's CSR efforts. Beyond sharing information and interacting with stakeholders, the platforms can serve as calls to service by organizations. Fifth, media monitoring and understanding the idiosyncrasies of cultural issues in CSR through a dialectical model are essential to form effective CSR dialogues for stakeholder engagement (Mak, Chaidaroon, & Pang, 2015). This will increase collaboration between stakeholders and organizations. Regardless of how organizations utilize online platforms, Shin et al. (2015) argued that success in such online media initiatives must begin with the objective of building relationships and enabling conversations with stakeholders (Booth & Matic, 2011; Waters et al., 2009) and of "grow(ing) virtual communities with stakeholders" (Lovejoy et al., 2012, p. 316). Once this motivation is entrenched in the organizational psyche, the activation and use of the tools will follow.

Despite the challenges, we believe that organizations that are able to integrate both agenda building and dialogic communication would be able to communicate CSR in a holistic manner. What is lacking in one would be compensated by the other. For instance, if seeking media coverage is less adequate, organizations would still have direct access to stakeholders. The reverse holds true as well.

Conclusions

This chapter begins by arguing that the current state of communicating CSR via the mainstream media, though prevalent, may not be adequate. Besides the inability of some organizations to effectively communicate in a manner journalists understand, there are also historical and perennial tensions and issues between journalists and practitioners. Despite that, the chapter argues that the Agenda Building model, which describes how practitioners reach out to journalists, remains relevant. This chapter goes on to examine how it is increasingly important to build relationships with stakeholders using digital communication tools. It culminates in how organizations can integrate both media agenda building with stakeholder engagements using both mainstream media and digital platforms to communicate their CSR activities. A CSR integrated media model is proposed.

The next step is to examine how this model can be used by organizations. One limitation of the study is that this model has yet to be tested. Future studies can examine cases involving organizations on how they can integrate both mainstream media and digital platforms to communicate their CSR activities. Another area of future research is to examine which platform is used more frequently compared to the other platforms and why. Insights can help refine the model further.

In an increasingly fragmented marketplace and media environment, organizations should leverage on both the mainstream media and digital platforms to ensure that their CSR messages are communicated via multiple contact points. Past research in CSR communication either studied the traditional media or new media. Few have offered an integrated approach that could bring CSR communication to the next level. This chapter seeks to address this gap. At the heart of it, it is making the organization's good works known – in the most expedient, balanced, accessible, and effective manner.

Note

1 The media used in this chapter refers to mainstream media and their complement of digital platforms.

References

Adams, C.A. (2015, October 28). The Art of Communicating Corporate Social Responsibility – and Some Learnings from VW. *Caroladams.net*. Retrieved September 12, 2016 from http://drcaroladams. net/the-art-of-communicating-corporate-social-responsibility-and-some-learnings-from-vw/

Baron, D. P. (2005). Competing for the public through the news media. *Journal of Economics and Management Strategy, 14*, 339–376.

Beck, K. (2016) Snapchat is now the most popular social network among teens, according to new study. *Mashable*.com. Retrieved September 12, 2016 from http://mashable.com/2016/04/14/ snapchat-teens-winner/#0ZyUF7j9xSqg

Bland, M., A. Theaker and D.W. Wragg. (2005). *Effective media relations: How to get results.* Kogan Page, Sterling, VA.

Booth, N., and Matic, J.A. (2011). Mapping and leveraging influencers in social media to shape corporate brand perceptions. *Corporate Communications: An International Journal, 16*, 184–191.

Bortree, D. S., and Seltzer, T. (2009). Dialogic strategies and outcomes: An analysis of environmental advocacy groups' Facebook profiles. *Public Relations Review, 35*, 317–319.

Briones, R. L., Kuch, B., Liu, B. F., and Jin, Y. (2011). Keeping up with the digital age: How the American Red Cross uses social media to build relationships. *Public Relations Review, 37*, 37–43.

Cameron, G. T., Sallot, L. M., and Curtin, P. A. (1997). Public relations and the production of news: A critical review and a theoretical framework. In B. R. Burleson (Ed.), *Communication Yearbook 20* (pp. 111–155). Thousand Oaks, Sage.

Carroll, A. B. (1991). The pyramid of corporate social responsibility: Toward the moral management of organizational stakeholders. *Business Horizons, 34*(4), 39–48.

Carroll, C. (2011). Media relations and corporate social responsibility. In O. Ihlen, J. L. Bartlett, and S. May (Eds). *Handbook of communication and corporate social responsibility* (pp. 423–444). Malden, MA: Wiley-Blackwell.

Chiou, W.-C., Lin, C.-C., and Perng, C. (2010). A strategic framework for Website evaluation based on a review of the literature from 1995–2006. *Information and Management, 47*, 282–290.

Chu, S.-C. (2011). Viral advertising in social media: Participation in Facebook group and responses among college-aged users. *Journal of Interactive Advertising, 12*, 30–43.

Cobb, R.W., and Elder, C. D. (1971). *The politics of agenda-building: An alternative perspective of foreign nations.* Paper presented at the Annual Conference of the International Communication Association, New York.

Commission of the European Communities. (2001). *Promoting a European framework for corporate social responsibility – Green Paper.* Luxembourg: Office for Official Publications for the European Communities.

Curtin, P. A. (1999). Reevaluating public relations information subsidies: Market driven journalism and agenda-building theory and practice. *Journal of Public Relations Research, 11*(1), 53–90.

Dahlsrud, A. (2006). How corporate social responsibility is defined: An analysis of 37 definitions. *Corporate Social Responsibility and Environmental Management, 15*(1), 1–13.

Davis, B. (2015, September 29). Social media and crisis management: A Volkswagen case study. *EConsultancy*. Retrieved September 12, 2016 from https://econsultancy.com/blog/66972-social-media-and-crisis-management-a-volkswagen-case-study/

De Bussy, N. M. (2010). Dialogue as a basis for stakeholder engagement. In R. L. Heath (Ed.), *The SAGE handbook of public relations* (pp. 127–144). Thousand Oaks, CA: Sage.

DeLorme, D. E., and Fedler, F. (2003). Journalists' hostility toward public relations: A historical analysis. *Public Relations Review, 29*, 99–124.

Delzio, S. (2015). Pinterest set to surge in 2016: New research. *Social Media Examiner*. Retrieved September 12, 2016 from www.socialmediaexaminer.com/pinterest-set-to-surge-in-2016-new-research/

Dickson, M., and Eckman, M. (2008). Media portrayal of voluntary public reporting about corporate social responsibility performance: Does coverage encourage or discourage ethical management? *Journal of Business Ethics, 83*(4), 725–744.

DiStaso, M. W., McCorkindale, T., and Wright, D. K. (2011). How public relations executives perceive and measure the impact of social media in their organizations. *Public Relations Review, 37*, 325–328.

Du, S., Bhattacharya, C. B., and Sen, S. (2010). Maximizing business returns to corporate social responsibility: The role of CSR communication. *International Journal of Management Reviews, 12*(1), 8–19.

Dudovskiy, J. (2015, Jun 23) Google Corporate Social Responsibility (CSR). *Research-Methodology.net*. Retrieved September 12, 2016 from http://research-methodology.net/google-corporate-social-responsibility-csr/

Elling, S., Lentz, L., and de Jong, M. (2012). Users' abilities to review Website pages. *Journal of Business and Technical Communication, 26*, 171–201.

Facebook (2015). Facebook Q4 2015 Results. Retrieved April 5, 2016 from http://files.share holder.com/downloads/AMDA-NJ5DZ/1416036400x0x871917/922D0DF8-A983-42F9-98E3-23370A29381F/FB_Q4_15_Earnings_Slides.pdf

Fassin, Y. (2008). SMEs and the fallacy of formalizing CSR. *Business Ethics: A European Review, 17*(4), 364–378.

Gandy, O. H., Jr. (1982). *Beyond agenda setting: information subsidies and public policy*, Norwood, NJ: Albex.

Gaudin, S., and Perez, J. C. (2012, Aug 27). Google hit with fine, bad press for tracking users. *Computerworld*. Retrieved September 12, 2016 from www.computerworld.com/article/2491531/security0/google-hit-with-fine – bad-press-for-tracking-users.html

George, C. (2012). *Freedom from the press*. Singapore: NUS Press.

Gillett, R. (2016, April 28). Why Google is the Best Company to Work for in America. *Business Insider*. Retrieved September 12, 2016 from www.businessinsider.sg/google-is-the-best-company-to-work-for-in-america-2016-4/?r=USandIR=T#OhTHdvApVVhcdeiu.97

Hardyment, R. (2015, Oct 28). CSR after the Volkswagen Scandal. *Triplepundit.com*. Retrieved September 12, 2016 from www.triplepundit.com/2015/10/csr-volkswagen-scandal/

Hon, L. C., and Grunig, J. E. (1999). *Guidelines for measuring relationships in public relations*. Gainesville, FL: Institute for Public Relations.

Hong, S. Y., Yang, S., and H. Rim (2010). The influence of corporate social responsibility and customer-company identification on publics' dialogic communication intentions. *Public Relations Review, 36*, 196–198.

Ihlen, O. (2011). Rhetoric and corporate social responsibility. In O. Ihlen, J. L. Bartlett, S. May (Eds.), *The handbook of communication and corporate social responsibility* (pp. 147–166). Hoboken, NJ: Wiley-Blackwell.

Jones, J. (2013). Switching in Twitter's hashtagged exchanges. *Journal of Business and Technical Communication, 28*, 58–82.

Kang, H., Shin, W., and Tam, L. (2016). Differential responses of loyal versus habitual consumers towards mobile site personalization on privacy management. *Computers in Human Behavior, 56*, 281–288.

Kent, M. L., and Taylor, M. (1998). Building dialogic relationships through the World Wide Web. *Public Relations Review, 24*, 321–334.

King, A. (2015, September 27). Volkswagen launches website to help consumers with its diesel crisis. *Jalopnik.com*. Retrieved September 12, 2016 from http://jalopnik.com/volkswagen-launches-website-to-help-consumers-with-its-1733263492

Kiousis, S. (2005). Compelling argument and attitude strength: Exploring the impact of second-level agenda-setting on public opinion of presidential candidate images. *Harvard International Journal of Press/Politics, 10*(2), 3–27.

Kiousis, S., and Wu, X. (2008). International agenda-building and agenda-setting: Exploring the influence of public relations counsel on US news media and public perceptions of foreign nations. *International Communication Gazette, 70*(1), 58–75.

Kopenhaver, L. L. (1985). Aligning values of practitioners and journalists. *Public Relations Review, 11*, 38–42.

Kopenhaver, L. L., Martinson, D. L., and Ryan, M. (1984). How public relations practitioners and editors in Florida view each other. *Journalism Quarterly, 61*, 860–884.

Kwon, E. S., and Sung, Y. J. (2011). Follow me! Global marketers' Twitter use. *Journal of Interactive Advertising, 12*, 4–16.

Lau, C., Lu, Y., and Liang, Q. (2016). Corporate social responsibility in China: A corporate governance approach. *Journal of Business Ethics, 136*(1), 73–87.

Lee, M. H., Mak, A. K. Y., and Pang, A. (2013). *Communicating corporate social responsibility: agenda building process in news reporting*. Australia and New Zealand Association of Management annual conference. Hobart, TAS.

Lerbinger, O. (2006), *Corporate public affairs*. Mahwah, NJ: Lawrence Erlbaum.

Lillqvist, E., and Louhiala-Salminen, L. (2014). Facing Facebook: Impression management strategies in company – consumer interactions. *Journal of Business and Technical Communication, 28*, 3–30.

Lovejoy, K., Waters, R. D., and Saxton, G. D. (2012). Engaging stakeholders through Twitter: How non-profit organizations are getting more out of the 140 characters or less. *Public Relations Review, 38*, 313–318.

Lynn, M. (2015, September 28). Corporate Social Responsibility has Become a Racket – and a dangerous one. *The Telegraph*. Retrieved September 12, 2016 from www.telegraph.co.uk/finance/newsbysector/industry/11896546/Corporate-Social-Responsibility-has-become-a-racket-and-a-dangerous-one.html

Mak, A. K. Y., Chaidaroon, S., and Pang, A. (2015). MNCs and CSR engagement in Asia: A dialectical model. Asia Pacific Public Relations Journal, *16*(1), 31–60.

Mak, A. K. Y., Pang, A., and Hart, E. (2015). Communicating corporate social responsibility: Agenda building in Australia. *Australian Journalism Review, 37*(1), 149–163.

Matten, D., and Moon, J. (2005). A conceptual framework for understanding CSR. In A. Habisch J. Jonker, M. Wegner and R. Schmidpeter (Eds.), *Corporate social responsibility across Europe* (pp. 335–356). Berlin/Heidelberg: Springer.

Media relations and Europe – from the journalist's perspective (2008, May). APCO Worldwide.

Melton, J., and Hicks, N. (2011). Integrating social and traditional media in the client project. *Business Communication Quarterly, 74*, 494–504.

Men, L. R., and Tsai, W. S. (2011). How companies cultivate relationships with publics on social networking sites: Evidence from China and United States. *Public Relations Review, 38*, 723–730.

Miceli, M. (2015, September 17). Google tops reputation rankings for corporate responsibility. *US News and World Report*. Retrieved September 12, 2016 from www.usnews.com/news/articles/2015/09/17/google-tops-reputation-rankings-for-corporate-responsibility

Moran, G., Muzellec, L., and Nolan, E. (2014). Consumer moments of truth in the digital context: How "search" and "e-word of mouth" can fuel consumer decision-making. *Journal of Advertising Research, 54*(2), 200–204.

Moreno, C. (2015). Doing their part: 3 Excellent examples of corporate social responsibility. *Redshift*. Retrieved September 12, 2016 from https://redshift.autodesk.com/doing-their-part-3-excellent-examples-of-corporate-social-responsibility/

Pang, A. (2010). Mediating the media: A journalist-centric media relations model. *Corporate Communications: An International Journal, 15*(2), 192–204.

Pang, A., Mak, A., and Lee, M. H. (2011). Significance of sector-specific corporate social responsibility initiatives: Status and role of CSR in different sectors. In O. Ihlen, J. Bartlett and S. May (Eds.), *Handbook of communication and corporate social responsibility* (pp. 295–315). Malden, MA: Wiley-Blackwell.

Pang, A., Chiong, V., and Nasrath, B. (2014). Media relations in an evolving media landscape. *Journal of Communication Management, 18*(3). 271–294.

Pang, A., Mak, A. K. Y., and Lee, M. H. (2015). Communicating corporate social responsibility in Singapore: Towards more effective media relations. In P. Ng and C. Ngai (Eds.), *Role of language and corporate communication in Greater China: From academic to practitioner perspectives* (pp. 127–148). New York: Springer.

Pang, A., and Yeo, S. L. (2009). Winning respect: Transformation to professionalization of public relations in Singapore. *Media Asia, 36*(2), 96–103.

Park, H., and Reber, B. H. (2008). Relationship building and the use of Websites: How Fortune 500 corporations use their Websites to build relationships. *Public Relations Review, 34*, 409–411.

Phillips, A. (2015). *Journalism in context: Practice and theory for the digital age*. NY: Routledge.

Pollach, I. (2005). Corporate self-presentation on the WWW: Strategy for enhancing usability, credibility and utility. *Corporate Communication: An International Journal, 10*, 285–301.

Pristin, T. (2011, January 25). Who invests in low-income housing? Google, for one. *New York Times*. Retrieved September 12, 2016 from www.nytimes.com/2011/01/26/realestate/commercial/26credits.html?_r=2

Reputation Institute (2015). Global CSR RepTrak 100. Retrieved September 12, 2016 from www.reputationinstitute.com/CMSPages/GetAzureFile.aspx?path=~%5Cmedia%5Cmedia%5Cdocuments%5C2015-global-csr-reptrak-results.pdfandhash=f3758543515765441ae88db1e043e7417e9f057f83955bb3768454dd8e0417353andext=.pdf

Rybalko, S., and Seltzer, T. (2010). Dialogic communication in 140 characters or less: How Fortune 500 companies engage stakeholders using Twitter. *Public Relations Review, 36*, 336–341.

Qiu, Q., and Cameron, G. T. (2008). *Communicating health disparities: building a supportive media agenda*. Saarbruecken, Germany: VDM Verlag.

Sallot, L. M., and Johnson, E. A. (2006). Investigating relationships between journalists and public relations practitioners: Working together to set, frame and build public agenda, 1991–2004. *Public Relations Review, 32*, 151–159.

Schultz, F., Castelló, I., and Morsing, M. (2013). The construction of corporate social responsibility in network societies: A communication view. *Journal of Business Ethics, 115*(4), 681.

Seltzer, T., and Zhang, W. (2011). Toward a model of political organization – public relationships: Antecedent and cultivation strategy influence on citizens' relationships with political parties. *Journal of Public Relations Research, 23*, 24–45.

Seo, H., Kim, J.Y., and Yang, S. (2009). Global activism and new media: A study of transnational NGOs' online public relations. *Public Relations Review, 35*, 123–126.

Shaukat, A., Qiu, Y., and Trojanowski, G. (2016). Board attributes, corporate social responsibility strategy, and corporate environmental and social performance. *Journal of Business Ethics, 135*(3), 569–585.

Shin, J., and Cameron, G.T. (2003). The interplay of professional and cultural factors in the online source-reporter relationship. *Journalism Studies, 4*(2), 253–272.

Shin, W., Pang, A., and Kim, H. J. (2015). Building relationships through integrated online media: Global organizations' use of brand websites, Facebook, and Twitter. *Journal of Business and Technical Communication, 29*(2), 184–220.

Shoemaker, P. J. (1991). *Gatekeeping*. Thousand Oaks, CA: Sage.

Shoemaker, P., and Reese, S. D. (1996). *Mediating the message*. New York, NY: Longman.

Signitzer, B., and Prexl, A. (2008). Corporate sustainability communications: Aspects of theory and professionalization. *Journal of Public Relations Research, 20*(1), 1–19.

Smith, J. (2013, October 2). The companies with the Best CSR Reputations. *Forbes.com*. Retrieved September 12, 2016 from www.forbes.com/sites/jacquelynsmith/2013/10/02/the-companies-with-the-best-csr-reputations-2/#5e6b4ff622bc

Spinuzzi, C. (2009). Starter ecologies: Introduction to the special issue on social software. *Journal of Business and Technical Communication, 23*, 251–262.

Stoll, M. L. (2008). Backlash hits business ethics: Finding effective strategies for communicating the importance of corporate social responsibility. *Journal of Business Ethics, 78*, 17–27.

Strachan, D. (2009, February 16). *Twitter: How to set up your account*. Retrieved November 1, 2013, from www.telegraph.co.uk/travel/4698589/Twitterhow-to-set-up-your-account.html

Sundar, S. S., Xu, Q., and Dou, X. (2012). Role of technology in online persuasion: A MAIN Model perspective. In S. Rodgers and E. Thorson (Eds.), *Advertising theory* (pp. 355–372). New York, NY: Routledge.

Supa, D. W., and Zoch, L. M. (2009). *Maximizing media relations through a better understanding of the public relations-journalist relationship: A quantitative analysis of changes over 23 years*. Paper presented at the International Public Relations Research Conference, Miami, FL.

Taylor, M., Kent, M., and White, W. (2001). How activist organizations are using the Internet to build relationships. *Public Relations Review, 27*, 263–284.

Tench, R., Bowd, R., and Jones, B. (2007). Perceptions and perspectives: Corporate social responsibility and the media. *Journal of Communication Management, 11*(4), 348.

Tilley, E., and Hollings, J. (2008). *Still stuck in a "love-hate relationship": Understanding journalists' enduring and impassioned duality towards public relations.* Proceedings of the ANZCA 2008 conference, Wellington, NZ.

Turk, J.V. (1985). Information subsidies and influence. *Public Relations Review, 11*(3), 1–14.

Twitter.com (n.d.). *Help Center.* Retrieved November 30, 2013 from https://support.twitter.com/

Twitter.com (2015). Retrieved April 5, 2016 from https://about.twitter.com/company

Vernuccio, M. (2014). Communicating corporate brands through social media: An exploratory study. *International Journal of Business Communication, 3*, 211–233.

Waters, R. D., Burnett, E., Lamm, A., and Lucas, J. (2009). Engaging stakeholders through social networking: How non-profit organizations are using Facebook. *Public Relations Review, 35*, 102–106.

Waters, R. D., Friedman, C. S., Mills, B., and Zeng, L. (2011). Applying relationship management theory to religious organizations: An assessment of relationship cultivation online. *Journal of Communication and Religion, 34*, 88–104.

Waters, R. D., and Lemanski, J. L. (2011). Revisiting strategic communication's past to understand the present. *Corporate Communications: An International Journal, 16*, 150–169.

Wehmeier, S., and Schultz, F. (2011). Communication and corporate social responsibility: A storytelling perspective. In Ø. Ihlen, J. Bartlett, and S. May (Eds.), *The handbook of communication and corporate social responsibility* (pp. 467–488). Malden, MA: John Wiley and Sons.

Whiting, A., and Deshpande, A. (2014). Social media marketing: A myth or a necessity. *Journal of Applied Business and Economics, 16*(5), 74–81.

Wilcox, D. L., and Cameron, G. T. (2009), *Public relations strategies and tactics* (9th ed.). New York: Pearson Allyn and Bacon.

Wu, G., Hu, X., and Wu, Y. (2010). Effects of perceived interactivity, perceived Web assurance and disposition to trust on initial online trust. *Journal of Computer-Mediated Communication, 16*, 1–26.

Yang, S.-U., Kang, M., and Johnson, P. (2010). Effects of narratives, openness to dialogic communication, and credibility on engagement in crisis communication through organizational blogs. *Communication Research, 37*, 473–497.

Zerk, J. A. (2008). *Multinationals and corporate social responsibility, limitations and opportunities in international law.* Cambridge: Cambridge University Press.

Zhang, J., and Swanson, D. (2006). Analysis of news media's representation of corporate social responsibility (CSR). *Public Relations Quarterly, 11*, 13–17.

Zoch, L. M., and Molleda, J. C. (2006). Building a theoretical model of media relations using framing, information subsidies and agenda building. In C.H. Botan and V. Hazleton (Eds.). *Public Relations Theory II* (pp. 279–309). Mahwah, NJ: Lawrence Erlbaum.

3.4 Hedonic stakeholder engagement

Bridging the online participation gap through gamification

Christian Fieseler, Kateryna Maltseva, and Christian Pieter Hoffmann

Introduction

Digital media provides easy access to an unprecedented wealth of information, facilitates the association with like-minded citizens, and supports the organization and coordination of interest groups.[1] Social media, particularly, reduces barriers to public self-expression and provides access to the public agenda for non-elite citizens.[2] At the same time, research on online political participation consistently shows that while digital media exert an overall positive influence on citizen engagement,[3] only few actually take advantage of the opportunities provided by new communication technologies: When it comes to online participation, a noticeable gap remains between those who participate and those who do not. In recent years, therefore, the notion of a 'digital divide' has expanded to include participatory Internet uses, that is, the 'participation divide'.[4] Van Dijk[5] notes that many users lack the material requirements, the skills or the motivation to employ digital media for participatory purposes.

We propose that novel ways of engaging stakeholders online might help close this 'participation divide' and engage broader audiences. To date, CSR efforts often implicitly assume that engagement is driven by utilitarian motives. We, in contrast, posit that framing stakeholder engagement as only a utilitarian endeavor will often result in a sizeable participation/engagement divide, with specific organized interests taking advantage of the opportunities of digital media while the larger populace abstains from any substantial engagement. From political economy theory, we already know that specific organized rational interests are easier to organize and mobilize and are more likely to affect decision-making processes, frequently at the cost of a disorganized general public.[6]

Given that both political and corporate governance processes share structural similarities, we would expect the same social dynamic to apply to (online) stakeholder engagement. Thus, in order to overcome this motivational divide in online CSR engagement and to engage larger segments of their stakeholder base, corporations should look beyond mere utilitarian incentives and also address hedonic motives for online engagement.

One of such techniques is to address the hedonic motives of stakeholders via gamification. Gamification is the use of game-like elements in non-game settings.[7] Emerging research is showing that enriching communication messages with such game elements may lead to more engagement.[8] In this chapter, we want to explore why and when gamification may be an effective tool to minimize online participation gaps in CSR engagement.

Past, present and future of stakeholder engagement

Companies are increasingly expected to assume responsibility for a broad range of social and environmental concerns. Apart from adhering to laws and regulations, as well as behaving ethically, they are asked to tangibly contribute to the solution of a number of social and environmental challenges.[9] As Clarkson[10] pointed out, in order to address complex social or environmental tasks, it is crucial for corporations to manage relationships with governments and civil society. In fact, interactions of businesses and various stakeholders are inevitable, as BSR[11] points out: "whether they like it or not they will have to engage with stakeholders, be it in conflict or consensus". Pedersen[12] argues against this background that the concept of CSR can only be made operable in the context of stakeholder management.

Freeman[13] defined stakeholders as "any group or individual who can affect or is affected by the achievement of the organization's objectives". Companies interact with stakeholders in the context of various market or non-market transactions. Individuals can become stakeholders in a company voluntarily or involuntarily.[14] A range of models has been proposed to analyze and differentiate stakeholder groups. Mitchell and colleagues,[15] for instance, suggested ranking stakeholders by the power, legitimacy and urgency of their demands. The perspective of stakeholder management extends the understanding of companies beyond their primary business responsibilities towards more comprehensive ethical, social or environmental responsibilities.[16]

Krick and colleagues[17] differentiate three generations of stakeholder engagement: in the first generation, companies are primarily responding to specific interest groups that exerted pressure on them. This reactive approach is intended to prevent bad publicity and protests, trying to soothe critical voices. The second generation is characterized by a more pro-active and strategic approach – companies strive to increase their understanding of relevant competitive forces through stakeholder engagement. The third generation of stakeholder engagement, in turn, is focused on creating and maintaining strategic competitiveness by aligning social, environmental and economic performance, that is, by focusing on issues of corporate responsibility.[18]

SustainAbility[19] points out that without a proper differentiation of relevant stakeholders, companies run the risk of a familiarity bias, that is, continually engaging the 'usual suspects'. Also, rather than weighing the legitimacy and urgency of stakeholder demands, corporations may become distracted by stakeholders noise, and ultimately focus on those interests most accomplished in garnering attention. Pedersen[20] therefore describes the engagement of stakeholders as a process involving several 'filters' – such as choosing the adequate interaction partners, defining necessary decisions and adequate responsibilities and finally selecting effective implementations.

In summary, in order to manifest their corporate responsibilities, businesses have to engage relevant stakeholder groups in their communication, decisions and actions. BSR[21] characterizes stakeholder engagement as "a way of gathering important inputs and ideas, anticipating and managing conflicts, improving decision-making, building consensus amongst different views, strengthening relationships, and enhancing corporate reputation". Of course, such a characterization puts a strong emphasis on corporate action – in reality, stakeholder engagement on CSR issues may just as well be initiated by stakeholder demands. Just because corporations begin to understand the value of strategic and systematic stakeholder engagement does not mean that stakeholders will cease to strive for attention or demand corporate action.

A new avenue for stakeholder engagement: digital platforms

Some have argued that online media may invigorate stakeholder engagement and further solidify its strategic importance: numerous digital platforms facilitate two-way symmetrical communication[22] and dialogue between corporations and stakeholders,[23] driving organizations to apply more participative communication approaches.[24] Social media has been particularly powerful in connecting like-minded individuals, providing an infrastructure for communities of interest.[25] Applications like social network services allow pursuers of common interests to join conversations[26] and to bond with peers sharing similar views.[27] Also, social media is used to reduce transaction and coordination costs, making it easier for like-minded individuals to organize.[28]

A large majority of studies on online engagement and participation focus on political participation.[29] Research on the potential of digital media to facilitate stakeholder engagement in corporate affairs largely focuses on the engagement of customers in designing tailored services or in open innovation projects.[30] Only a few studies analyze online engagement or participation in the context of sustainability issues or corporate social responsibility. In a systematic literature review of online participation, Hoffmann and Lutz[31] argue that findings on online political participation may well be applied to the corporate context as "both are characterized by hierarchical decision-making processes, a delegation of power to professionals and select committees, and a strong asymmetry of power between professional decision-makers and members of various interest groups". Stakeholders struggling for influence on the corporate agenda[32] may thereby be attracted to the participatory opportunities provided by online platforms – if corporations actually extend such opportunities.

In an early study of the use of blogs for CSR communications, Fieseler, Fleck and Meckel[33] highlight the opportunities provided by social media to engage audiences on a variety of sustainability topics. Schultz, Castello and Morsing[34] argue that social networks create a more level playing field, facilitating more deliberative forms of CSR communication. At the same time, empirical studies find that corporate outreach efforts in social media show little interactivity or dialogue.[35] This finding can be contrasted with recent evidence that more interactive forms of CSR communication may positively affect corporate perceptions and reputation.[36] Strategies suggested for more deliberative forms of CSR engagement tend to apply insights from political theory.[37]

Yet in political theory, the notion that social media may actually contribute to more participatory discourses is heavily contested. While the 'mobilization thesis' proposes that Internet use will increase citizens' propensity to become engaged across the board,[38] the 'reinforcement thesis' holds that those citizens already more prone to participate will disproportionally benefit from the affordances of online platforms.[39] This discussion is of significant importance to the corporate context as well, as it raises the question of which stakeholders will most benefit from engagement opportunities provided by corporate outreach in online media.[40]

The participation divide

Digital divide research suggests that 'offline' inequalities are replicated online. Research has found ample evidence for a socio-demographic stratification of online participation. Users of high socio-economic status (SES), as measured by income or education, are held to more easily take advantage of digital media, because they command the necessary resources (material, human and social capital) allowing better access to modern information and communication technologies (ICT)[41] –for example, broadband Internet connection, smartphones or tablets. They also possess the necessary skills to use new media.[42] Hargittai and Walejko[43] found that higher social status is associated with more expressive Internet uses. Compared with low SES users, those with high SES are expected to use the Internet in more capital-enhancing ways.[44]

Besides socio-economic status, age and gender have been shown to affect online participation. Although gender differences in access to the Internet have almost leveled out in many Western countries, differences in Internet uses remain.[45] Online games or sexual content, for example, tend to be male-dominated uses, while online health information seems to be more popular among female users.[46] Overall, studies find that men are more active and eager to participate online than women.[47] Younger individuals are consistently shown to be more active and skillful Internet users than their older counterparts.[48]

The digital and participation divide literature has differentiated a number of 'gaps' between those who achieve to reap the benefits of digital platforms and those who do not: Van Dijk[49] points out that, aside from resources (material access) and use skills (skills access), users also require the adequate motivation to apply online media in a capital-enhancing capacity (motivational access). Again, in the domain of political participation, the beneficial effect of young users' superior use skills tend to be moderated by political interest, with older users generally reporting higher levels of interest in political affairs.[50] Thereby, while digital platforms have the potential to facilitate the political engagement of youth, their overall effect remains questionable due to a lack of user motivation (in line with the 'reinforcement thesis').

Online participation has been defined as "the creation and sharing of content on the Internet addressed at a specific audience and driven by a social purpose".[51] Thereby, the motivation to affect other users is implied in the concept. As Jenkins[52] points out, online participants need to believe that their contribution matters, that someone or something will be affected by their contribution. Given that material and skills access are becoming ever less relevant as an obstacle to online participation in the West, attention increasingly needs to be focused on user motivation to ensure beneficial Internet uses. We propose that this key insight from the participation divide literature needs to be taken into consideration when pondering the impact of online media on stakeholder engagement.

In other words: just because online media affordances have the potential to facilitate broader and more dialogic stakeholder engagement does not mean that corporations will, in fact, be able to generate more lively and insightful interactions. Even more: rather than broadening the scope and base of stakeholder engagement, digital platforms may well play into the hands of those interest groups already skilled at attracting attention and capturing corporate resources (i.e., reinforce the influence of those already engaged). To overcome the 'reinforcement trap' and both qualitatively and quantitatively improve stakeholder engagement efforts and effects, companies should think about new approaches to overcome the 'motivation gap' in the digital sphere.

Introducing hedonic stakeholder engagement

Literature on stakeholder engagement is frequently based on the assumption that interactions are primarily driven by utilitarian motives. Stakeholders are held to compete for consideration on the corporate agenda and, ultimately, corporate resources.[53] Thereby, stakeholders are willing to engage companies if they can hope to gain some more or less tangible benefit from the interaction. However, based on related research in the domain of consumer behavior, it may be more adequate to assume that stakeholder interest in ecological, social and governance issues are also driven by more hedonic factors. Such hedonic motives may prove especially conducive to overcoming the 'motivation gap' in online stakeholder engagement.

Many acts of consumption are in fact driven by some combination of utilitarian and hedonic motives.[54] Aside from pleasure and thrill-seeking, consumption is motivated by a need for group membership or a sense of community, self-expression and personal growth and achievement.[55] Research by Caruana and Chatzidakis,[56] for instance, describes conscious consumption as a conduit of social bonding, similar to other research in eco-communities that implicitly employ sustainable consumption practices to cement relationships.[57]

Next to the social aspect, Schaefer and Crane[58] identify the element of exploration as a motivation to buy organic products. Some sustainable forms of consumption, as well as getting involved in the overall lifestyle of being interested and contributing to sustainability may fulfill certain hedonic motives such as aesthetic, experiential, and enjoyment-related benefits.[59] Associated with hedonic experiential behaviors is the desire to be entertained, have fun and to be immersed in the experience,[60] which may be a conduit for gamified experiences.

As was previously mentioned, social media facilitates the connection to like-minded individuals. Global access to information and the ease of producing and sharing online content also facilitates a need for self-expression. Being a passive recipient of information can be insufficient to "fill in" an emotional component of an experience. Activities that are laborious can be emotionally satisfying if imbued with meaning and a sense of progress.[61] We can conclude that for some people, in order to like an experience, it should require some efforts, cognitive skills and be reasonably challenging.

As to the inherent benefit of the hedonic approach, with regards to products, Chitturi, Raghunathan and Mahajan[62] find that as long as certain basic functional and hedonic requirements are exceeded, the hedonically superior option is favored. Thus, an engagement effort hedonically imbued with gamified elements may thus be the more appealing option. With regard to marketing communications, research by Lucassen and Jansen[63] concludes that gamification's goals align with core marketing concepts such as brand awareness, customer engagement and loyalty. For non-profit marketing, Freudmann and Bakamitsos[64] consider gamification a powerful tool for reaching out to stakeholders by delivering communication messages in a "palatable, digestible and enjoyable way". Seiffert and Nothhaft[65] propose that public relations and marketing practitioners can benefit from implementing the procedural rhetoric of computer games into their communication strategies to reach stakeholders.

Motivating stakeholder engagement through gamification

In order to stay relevant and to create awareness or even engagement among its constituencies, organizations have to look for new ways to engage their stakeholder bases. Among these, there is a new approach, gamification, emerging, that builds on audiences' hedonic drive. Some initiatives such as Community PlanIt and Civic Seed, developed by Engagement Lab at Emerson College,[66] or the Nissan Leaf Challenge powered by CARWINGS point to the potential of such an approach. In principle, gamified messages about corporate social responsibility (CSR) could become a helpful complement to more traditional, utilitarian communication efforts, intended to safeguard awareness and understanding of social responsibility efforts even in a changing media environment.

Gamification targets various groups of stakeholders – employees, clients, shareholders, community members, suppliers, public or market. Its primary purposes are in line with existing marketing and public relations (PR) metrics, for example, facilitating engagement, increasing loyalty or conveying favorable associations.[67] Gamification design strategies vary in their content and structure; however, what unites these strategies is an intention to develop an intervention that conveys a strategic message that leads to desirable cognitive or behavioral outcomes. Gamification is proposed as an effective tool to reach different groups of stakeholders, as it offers diverse social, hedonic and utilitarian benefits that are appealing and valuable for different groups of stakeholders.[68] For instance, there are different dimensions of fun that are associated with the process of playing video games, or in other words, with intrinsic motivation to play video games. These dimensions are: sensation, fantasy, narrative, challenge, competence, fellowship, discovery, expression, submission and autonomy.[69] Because game elements vary in their purpose, gamification does not only address hedonic motives, the implementation of gamification may also have implications for self-efficacy, sense of self-worth, and social cohesion. We believe that by implementing gamification interventions for communicating messages, organizations may increase the effectiveness of their messages and reach out to their shareholders better.

There are a number of definitions of gamification. The focus of these definitions comprises various game elements, application purpose and context, intended cognitive and behavioral outcomes. The definitions of gamification in the literature are presented below.

The most comprehensive definition is the one suggested by Deterding and colleagues[70] who define gamification as "the use of design elements characteristic for games in non-game contexts". As this definition focuses on the underlying mechanism of gamification, rather than its purpose and application context, we deem it most suitable for the purposes of the research at hand. It has to be noted that the principles of gamification are universal and not solely bound to the mechanics of digital games but an attempt to utilize the human ludic drive. Each game has a set of game elements that constitutes a unique game experience and that drives different behavioral outcomes. For this reason, depending on

Table 3.4.1 Definitions of gamification

Author	Definition
Deterding et al.[71]	Gamification is the use of design elements characteristic for games in non-game contexts.
Hamari & Huotari[72]	Gamification is a process of enhancing a service with (motivational) affordances for gameful experiences in order to support the user's overall value creation.
Zichermann[73]	Gamification is the employment of game logic or mechanics with the aim of motivating people and changing behavior, rather than existing for the sake of pure entertainment.
Seaborn & Fels[74]	Gamification has two key ingredients: it is used for non-entertainment purposes, and it draws inspiration from games, particularly the elements that make up games, without engendering a fully fledged game.
Roth et al.[75]	Gamification is the use of game design methods as a means to leverage games for business benefit.
Robson et al.[76]	Gamification is the application of the lessons from gaming domain to change behavior in non-game situations.

the type of desired behavioral outcomes, any game element or a combination of games elements may potentially serve as a platform for gamifying an experience.

Despite its relatively recent nature, gamification research has been applied in various fields and contexts, such as education,[77] health and wellness,[78] crowdsourcing[79] transportation,[80] civic learning,[81] sustainability,[82] as well as online communities and social networks.[83]

Both artifactual and social game elements may contribute to a gamified experience. Leaderboards, challenge structures, badges, avatars are examples of artifactual game elements. The need for achievement, curiosity and team play are related to social game elements. Deterding and colleagues[84] highlight that the difference between a fully fledged game and an artifact with game elements is a very subjective, empirical and social one. For this reason, it is essential to understand that gamification is not an end in itself, but serves as a means to an end. This is a very important notion, because it points out that gamification is a complex process, rather than static usage of game elements. Deterding and colleagues[85] developed a classification of game design elements from concrete to abstract level, displayed in table 3.4.2 below.

According to Robson and colleagues,[86] gamification is built on three concepts of game design: mechanics that embrace goals, rules and rewards; dynamics that reflect how players enact mechanics; and emotions that players feel towards the gamified experience. In addition to the MDE (mechanics–dynamics–emotions) approach to gamification, the element of involvement plays an important role in designing a gamified experience (Robson et al., 2015). Players (participants, users exposed to the gamified experience) are a target group of gamification; however, they are not the only group that is involved in a gamified experience. Besides players who compete, Robson and colleagues[87] define three other groups involved in a gamified experience, first, designers who are developing, designing and managing the gamified experience, second, the spectators who contribute to the general atmosphere but who do not participate directly, and third, observers, who are passively involved and do not affect the gamified experience directly; however, their numbers signals the popularity of the experience.

Table 3.4.2 Classification of game design elements

Level	Description	Examples
Concrete		
Game interface design patterns	Common, successful interaction design components and design solutions for a known problem in a context, including prototypical implementations	Badge, leaderboard, level
Game design patterns and mechanics	Commonly reoccurring parts of the design of a game that concern gameplay	Time constraint, limited resources, turns
Game design principles and heuristics	Evaluative guidelines to approach a design problem or analyze a given design solution	Enduring play, clear goals, variety of game styles
Game models	Conceptual models of the components of games or game experiences	Challenge, fantasy, curiosity, game design atoms
Abstract		
Game design methods	Game design-specific practices and processes	Playtesting, playcentric design, value conscious game design

As game mechanics are a fundamental pillar of gamification, we will next focus on their components. Mechanics includes all rules, organizational as well as managerial technologies that may be used in order to induce some intended behavioral and cognitive outcomes. Ašeriškis and Damaševičius[88] specify that game mechanics describe the particular game components at the level of algorithms and data representation. Game components, depending on their purpose, are classified within three groups: setup mechanics, rule mechanics and progression mechanics. Setup mechanics consists of considerations that shape an environment of an experience. Decisions on who is going to compete against whom, or whether the settings will be based within the real or virtual world are part of developing setup mechanics. Rules, constraints, possible game actions and corresponding consequences are elements of rule mechanics. Progression mechanics include mechanisms that affect reinforcement and experience while it happens. Reward systems such as badges and scores, levels and ranks are examples of progression mechanics.

As previously discussed, game elements can be categorized into artifactual and social, and there is a certain level of abstraction present for each game element. For instance, reward systems are a rather abstract game element because they may include various mechanisms and ways of rewarding progress. Virtual scores are more tangible and concrete examples of game elements, as one may receive a specific score for completing tasks or following rules. In addition, reward systems are part of game mechanics, specifically, progression mechanics, and are intended to affect reinforcement.

There are several classifications of the most characteristic game elements that constitute the platform for a gamified experiments. We synthesized the conclusions of several studies[89] to create a list of elements that are used to create a gamified experience. These are first, the possibility to create a legend, for instance through the explanation of rules, the setting of goals, the personalization of the experience through for instance avatars or nicknames, and through the addition of a meaningful narrative. Second, the tracking of progress to maintain motivation – this may be achieved through for instance the design of achievable tasks, manageable constraints, or the adjustment of difficulty levels, as well as the provision of instant feedback or assistance, if needed. Third, reward systems and recognition, in the form of, for instance, badges, leaderboards or financial gains. Fourth, the creation and maintenance of social bonds, through, for instance, team-play of the integration of social media. Fifth, follow-up activities and future engagement that contribute to a gamified experience.

Gamification taps into the motivational drivers of human behavior such as reinforcements and emotions; therefore, it may change stakeholders' behavior. For this reason, the implementation of gamification may result in desired cognitive and behavioral outcomes. Numerous research documents a positive effect of gamification: gamification helps to increase awareness in environmental issues, to facilitate sustainable behavior,[90] to increase motivation for leaning,[91] increase public awareness and contribute to the development of lateral trust while participating in civic learning,[92] to improve group reflection at early stages of innovation development processes,[93] to increase productivity and to contribute to social bonding.[94] Gamification is also implemented in order to increase user activity and retention;[95] increase user motivation to engage with a product or service;[96] enhance employees' productivity, efficiency, engagement and innovation potential.[97]

Gamification as a tool may achieve some behavioral or cognitive outcomes. Designers of gamified experiences do not aim at engaging people to play for the sake of play. As was previously mentioned, gamification is used to increase motivation and improve awareness as a result of being exposed to a gamified experience. Hamari and Koivisto[98] investigated the motives of people to use gamification services. Utilitarian, hedonic and social benefits were associated with the attitude towards gamification services and potential continued use of these services. Specifically, social and utilitarian aspects positively affect attitude formation, whereas the intention to revisit the gamified experience is more dependent on the service's hedonic benefits.

Outlook: gamifying CSR

Implementing gamification on digital platforms to facilitate stakeholders' participation and engagement in CSR requires an understanding of techniques that are commonly used to motivate individuals to engage in prosocial behavior. Froehlich[99] summarizes several intervention techniques used in environmental psychology to motivate and promote proenvironmental and prosocial behavior.

Information techniques are the most commonly used. They comprise presenting information to stakeholders about certain CSR efforts to increase stakeholders' knowledge, however, they may have a minimal effect on their further interest or engagement. Some studies[100] even show that in some cases, being ignorant about certain socio-economic problems, for example, climate change or resource depletion, may lead to avoiding information about these issues in contrast to stimulating interest for these issues.

Comparison between individuals or groups of individuals is another intervention technique. Comparison stimulates competition between individuals and groups and aims to activate a need for achievement that fuels further participation and engagement. In the context of game studies and behavioral psychology, rewards are examples of progression mechanics that are responsible for positive reinforcement. Scores, badges, and points are game elements that serve as stimuli that follow appropriate (in this case prosocial and environmental) behavior in order to make such behavior more likely to occur.

Goal setting intervention techniques may serve as triggers to increase attention, effect and persistence in achieving goal-relevant activities. The complexity and difficulty level of goals determines the level of engagement. Goals should be perceived as meaningful, moderately difficult, or in other words, achievable, in order to motivate individuals to achieve them.

Feedback generally enhances these intervention techniques. Combining goals and feedback is a common practice to improve performance. Research on sustainable consumption shows that sustainable consumption improves as a result of the joint effects of goal setting and feedback. For instance, when consumers were provided with goals to reduce electricity consumption and received feedback on their consumption rate, they consumed significantly less, in comparison to consumers that did not receive feedback.[101]

There are examples for applying all these techniques in unison, such as the online platform "Community PlanIt" which aims to engage local community members to contribute to the community development of their neighborhood. The platform relies firstly on information intervention in form of advertising campaigns, launched by local authorities, addressing community-related problems and encouraging people to join the platform to work on solutions.

Moderators of the platform set goals for platform members to achieve. Members are, for instance, asked to explore their city and write about problems or issues they encounter, such as broken traffic lights and incorrect bus schedules. Afterwards, members are asked to critically evaluate each other's posts. For being an active member of the platform, members receive points. Community problems that are discussed by platform members the most then are acknowledged to be the most important. In order to address them, moderators of the platform set a second set of goals.

Members are then asked to come up with solutions that may help solve the problems of their local community. Each solution can be endorsed via members' accumulated points – the projects that collects the most points receives a share of the community's budget in order to execute the project. What we see in this example is that relevant information, goals, feedbacks, comparisons (in form of competitions) and rewards are combined and presented in a non-game context in order to drive psychological and behavioral reactions as if people were playing a game for the sake of entertainment.

By making stakeholder engagement feel more fun, digital platforms may be one measure to engage broader audiences on social and ecological sustainability issues. Provided that this form of engagement is at this point in time still tailored to very specific situations and within very managed frameworks for deliberation, an argument can still be made that gamification allows for low-threshold forms or participation that can potentially open engagement to previously underrepresented demographics. Thus, going forward, hedonic approaches to engagement might become one supplement to more traditional approaches to broaden the participation in, and eventually the impact of, stakeholder engagement.

What gamification adds to CSR

In conclusion, gamification may open new avenues for engagement efforts around ecological, social and governmental issues by providing new forms of communicating with stakeholders, and by enriching CSR campaigns through narrative-, reward-, and technology-enabled elements. In the consumer space, consumption experiences enhanced through gamification may raise greater awareness and understanding for a product's ecological and social footprint. For communities, gamification might make collaboration in decision-making more open, even for those less engaged or utilitarian-motivated, and foster a greater sense of coherence and belonging throughout the community. For organizations, gamification might simply be a way of telling their story better and more engaging, or an avenue for tapping into the wisdom, or least the behavioral data, of the crowds.

In practical terms, designing a gamified experience for stakeholders is a process that requires strategic planning. A starting point in creating such an experience, may it be a marketing campaign, a promotion event, or some other type of communication, is the identification of a problem that the company is trying to solve. Sophisticated game elements will not compensate for the lack of a value proposition; therefore, strategists, developers and designers must agree on the metrics they are trying to improve beforehand, may they be stakeholders' participation, engagement, interest, awareness, or word of mouth.

The next step comprises accounting for the motivation to play games. People play games for various reasons: rewards (extrinsically driven motivation), fun, or excitement (intrinsically driven motivation). To succeed in designing a gamified experience, one must account for the drivers of both: extrinsic and intrinsic motivation. Broadly speaking, the experience itself (playing) is as important as the outcome (rewards). Thus, implementing gamification should not be associated with pointification (providing points in form of rewards for certain behavior), instead, the gamified experience in itself and the outcomes of this experience should be meaningful and relevant for stakeholders. Finally, using gamification calls for the careful study of every stakeholder group that is targeted by gamified communications and to customize the gamified experience respectively.

Still, the main challenge that developers and designers of gamified experiences face is the measurement of the effects created by gamified experiences. From a theoretical perspective, it might be interesting to look whether hedonic approaches might bring any further insights for the debate on the attitude-behavior gap in ethical consumption, which recently sees renewed interest.[102] Imagine an NGO creating a gamified app to collect donations for a good cause. In this case, the main purpose of implementing gamification is to induce behavioral change that can be easily tracked by comparing the amount of collected donations after the campaign to the amount of donations collected on average without using gamification. However, such an effect measurement plan neglects tracking changes of the psychological effects of gamification, such as the change of attitude or opinions about the NGO. As gamification affects comparatively many psychological processes (e.g., competitiveness, need for achievement, need for cognition) there are certain limitations with regards to evaluating the effects of gamification.

Another limitation of implementing gamification is associated with the effectiveness of gamification seen from a long-term perspective. Gamified experiences may be a novelty for stakeholders. However, with time, the effectiveness may drop, as people might get used to the gamified features they are exposed to. One solution to that problem could be investing in constant innovation in order to keep up with stakeholders' expectations. However, that solution breeds another issue: gamification is a resource-intensive tool. It requires certain level of skills related to technology development and certain financial resources.

Still, we argue that these challenges might be overcome, and that exploring the hedonic mechanism for engaging stakeholder might be an interesting additional avenue for future research and practice. With social media becoming an increasingly dominant channel for engagement efforts, coupled with an overabundance of competing communication offerings, and the will to open these efforts for wider, maybe less engaged audiences, engaging stakeholders via play might sound like a fun diversion at first. A diversion however, that if managed right, might lead to tangible benefits and greater participation in deliberating social and environmental issue on a wider, and more participative, scale.

Notes

1 Wilson, S. M., and Peterson, L. C. (2002). The anthropology of online communities. *Annual Review of Anthropology*, 31(1), 449–467; Woodly, D. (2007). New competencies in democratic communication? Blogs, agenda setting and political participation. *Public Choice*, 134(1–2), 109–123; Steinfield, C., Ellison, N., and Lampe, C. (2008). Social capital, self-esteem, and use of online social network sites: A longitudinal analysis. *Journal of Applied Developmental Psychology*, 29(6), 434–445; Gil De Zuniga, H., Veenstra, A., Vraga, E., and Shah, D. (2010). Digital democracy: Reimagining pathways to political participation. *Journal of Information Technology* Politics, 7(1), 36–51.

2 Pasek, J., More, E., and Romer, D. (2009). Realizing the social internet? Online social networking meets offline civic engagement. *Journal of Information Technology Politics*, 6(3), 197–215; Foot, K. A., and Schneider, S. M. (2002). Online action in campaign 2000: An exploratory analysis of the U.S. political web sphere. *Journal of Broadcasting Electronic Media*, 46(2), 222–244. Towner, T. L., and Dulio, D. A. (2011). An experiment of campaign effects during the YouTube election. *New Media and Society*, 13(4), 626–644; Wattal, S., Schuff, D., Mandviwalla, M., and Williams, C. B. (2010). Web 2.0 and politics: The 2008 US presidential election and an e-politics research agenda. *MIS Quarterly*, 34(4), 669–688.

3 Boulianne, S. (2009). Does internet use affect engagement? A meta-analysis of research. *Political Communication*, 26(2), 193–211.

4 Blank, G. (2013). Who creates content? *Information, Communication and Society*, 16(4), 590–612; Blank, G., and Reisdorf, B. C. (2012). The participatory web. *Information, Communication and Society*, 15(5),

537–554; Correa, T. (2010). The participation divide among 'online experts': Experience, skills and psychological factors as predictors of college students' web content creation. *Journal of Computer-Mediated Communication*, 16(1), 71–92; Hargittai, E., and Walejko, G. (2008). The participation divide: Content creation and sharing in the digital age. *Information, Communication and Society*, 11(2), 239–256; Schradie, J. (2011). The digital production gap: The digital divide and Web 2.0 collide. *Poetics*, 39(2), 145–168.

5 Van Dijk, J. (2005). Skills access. In J. Van Dijk (Ed.), *The deepening divide: Inequality in the information society* (1st ed., pp. 71–94). London: Sage.

6 Buchanan, J. M., and Tullock, G. (1962). *The calculus of consent: Logical foundations of constitutional democracy*. Ann Arbor: University of Michigan Press; Di Gennaro, C., and Dutton, W. (2006). The Internet and the public: Online and offline political participation in the United Kingdom. *Parliamentary Affairs*, 59(2), 299–313; Smith, A. (2013). *Civic engagement in the digital age*. Pew Internet American Life Project (p. 59). Retrieved from http://pewinternet.org/Reports/2013/Civic-Engagement.aspx

7 Deterding, S., Dixon, D., Rilla, K., and Lennart, N. (2011). From game design elements to gamefulness: defining "gamification". In *Proceedings of the 15th International Academic MindTrek Conference: Envisioning Future Media Environments* (pp. 9–15). Tampere: ACM.

8 Seaborn, K., and Fels, D. I. (2014). Gamification in theory and action: A survey. *International Journal of Human-Computer Studies*, 74, 14–31; Ašeriškis, D., and Damaševičius, R. (2014). Gamification patterns for gamification applications. *Procedia Computer Science*, 39, 83–90.

9 Carroll, A. B. (1979). A three dimensional model of corporate social performance. *Academy of Management Review*, 4, 497–505; Carroll, A. B. (1991). The pyramid of corporate social responsibility: Toward the moral management of organizational stakeholders. *Business Horizons*, 34(4), 39–48; Carroll, A. B. (1999). Corporate social responsibility – evolution of a definitional construct. *Business and Society*, 38(3), 268–295.

10 Clarkson, M. B. E. (1995). A stakeholder framework for analyzing and evaluating corporate social performance. *The Academy of Management Review*, 20(1), 92–117.

11 Business for Social Responsibility (BSR). (2003). *Overview of corporate social responsibility issue brief*. Retrieved from www.bsr.org/insight/issue-brief-details.cfm?DocumentID=48809

12 Pedersen, E. R. (2006). Making corporate social responsibility (CSR) operable: How companies translate stakeholder dialogue into practice. *Business and Society Review*, 111(2), 137–163.

13 Freeman, R. E. (1984). *Strategic management – a stakeholder approach*. Boston: Pitman.

14 Cornell, B. and Shapiro, A. C. (1987). Corporate stakeholders and corporate finance. *Financial Management*, 16(1), 5–14; Hatch, M. J. (1997). *Organization theory – modern, symbolic, and postmodern perspectives*. Oxford: Oxford University Press; Clarkson, M. B. E. (1995). A stakeholder framework for analyzing and evaluating corporate social performance. *The Academy of Management Review*, 20(1), 92–117; Post, J. E., Preston, L. E. and Sachs. S. (2002). Managing the extended enterprise: The new stakeholder view. *California Management Review*, 45(1), 6–28.

15 Mitchell, R. K., Agle, B. R., and Wood, D. J. (1997). Toward a theory and a principle of stakeholder identification and salience. Defining the principle of who and what really counts. *Academy of Management Review*, 22(4), 835–896.

16 Freeman op. cit; Donaldson, T. and Preston, L. E. (1995). The stakeholder theory of the corporation: Concepts, evidence and mplications. *The Academy of Management Review*, 20(1), 65–91.

17 Krick, T., Forstater, M., Monaghan, P., Silannpää, M., Van der Lugt, C., Patridge, K., Jackson, C. and Zohar, A. (2005). *From words to action. The stakeholder engagement manual. Volume 2: The practitioner's handbook on stakeholder engagement*. Retrieved from www.unep.fr/outreach/home/SE%20 Handbook(sm).pdf

18 Andriof, J. and Waddock, S. (2002). Unfolding stakeholder engagement. In J. Andriof, S. Waddock, B. Husted and S. Sutherland Rahman (Eds.), *Unfolding stakeholder thinking – theory, responsibility and engagement* (pp. 19–42). Sheffield: Greenleaf; Fombrun, C., Gardberg, N. A. and Barnett, M. L. (2000). Opportunity platforms and safety nets: Corporate citizenship and reputational risk. *Business and Society Review*, 105(1), 85–106; Lawrence, A. (2002). The drivers of stakeholder engagement. Reflections on the case of royal Dutch / Shell. In J. Andriof, S. Waddock, B. Husted, S. Sutherland Rahman (Eds.), *Unfolding stakeholder thinking – theory, responsibility and engagement* (pp. 185–199). Sheffield: Greenleaf Publishing Ltd.; Burchell, J. and Cook, J. (2008). Stakeholder dialogue and organisational learning: Changing relationships between companies and NGOs. *Business Ethics: A European Review*, 17(1), 35–46.

19 SustainAbility, op. cit.

20 Pedersen, op. cit.

21 Business for Social Responsibility (BSR), op. cit.

22 Grunig, J. E. and Hunt, T. (1984). *Managing public relations*. New York, NY: Holt Reinhart and Winston.

23 Kent, M. L. and Taylor, M. (1998). Building a dialogic relationship through the World Wide Web. *Public Relations Review*, 24(3), 321–340; Kent, M. L. and Taylor, M. (2002). Toward a dialogic theory of public relations, *Public Relations Review*, 28(1), 21–37.

24 Castello, I., Morsing, M. and Schultz, F. (2013). Communicative dynamics and the polyphony of corporate social responsibility in the network society. *Journal of Business Ethics*, 118, 683–694; Colleoni, E. (2013). CSR communication strategies for organizational legitimacy in social media. *Corporate Communications: An International Journal*, 18(2), 228–248; Schultz, F., Utz, S., and Göritz, A. (2011). Is the medium the message? Perceptions of and reactions to crisis communication via Twitter, blogs and traditional media. *Public Relations Review*, 37(1), 20–27.

25 Wilson, S. M. and Peterson, L. C. (2002). The anthropology of online communities. *Annual Review of Anthropology*, 31(1), 449–467.

26 Woodly, D. (2007). New competencies in democratic communication? Blogs, agenda setting and political participation. *Public Choice*, 134(1–2), 109–123; Gil de Zúñiga, H., Veenstra, A., Vraga, E., and Shah, D. (2010). Digital democracy: Reimagining pathways to political participation. *Journal of Information Technology and Politics*, 7(1), 36–51.

27 Steinfield et al., op. cit.

28 Nie, N., Miller, D., Golde, S., and Butler, D. (2010). The World Wide Web and the U.S. political news market. *American Journal of Political Science*, 54(2), 428–439.

29 Hoffmann, C. P.; Lutz, C. and Meckel, M. (2014). Beyond just politics: A systematic literature review of online participation. *First Monday*, 19(7), doi: http://dx.doi.org/10.5210/fm.v19i7.5260.

30 Hoffmann, C. P., and Lutz, C. (2015). The impact of online media on stakeholder engagement and the governance of corporations. *Journal of Public Affairs*, 15(2), 163–174.

31 Hoffmann and Lutz op cit., p. 163

32 Noda, T. and Bower, J. L. (1996). Strategy Making as Iterated Processes of Resource Allocation. *Strategic Management Journal*, 17(Special Issue), 159–192.

33 Fieseler, C., Fleck, M., and Meckel, M. (2010). Corporate social responsibility in the blogosphere. *Journal of Business Ethics*, 91(4), 599–614.

34 Schultz, F., Castelló, I., and Morsing, M. (2013). The Construction of Corporate Social Responsibility in Network Societies: A Communication View. *Journal of Business Ethics*, 115(4), 681–692.

35 Etter, M. (2013). Reasons for low levels of interactivity: (Non-)interactive CSR communication in Twitter. *Public Relations Review*, 39(5), 606–608; Etter, M. (2014). Broadcasting, reacting, engaging – three strategies for CSR communication in Twitter. *Journal of Communication Management*, 18(4), 322–342; Colleoni, E. (2013). CSR communication strategies for organizational legitimacy in social media. *Corporate Communications: An International Journal*, 18(2), 228–248.

36 Eberle, D., Berens, G., and Li, T. (2013). The impact of interactive corporate social responsibility communication on corporate reputation. *Journal of Business Ethics*, 118(4), 731–746.

37 Seele, P., and Lock, I. (2015). Instrumental and/or deliberative? A typology of CSR communication tools. *Journal of Business Ethics*, 131(2), 401–414.

38 De Vreese, C. H. (2007). Digital renaissance: Young consumer and citizen? *The Annals of the American Academy of Political and Social Science*, 611(1), 207–216; Shah, D. V., Cho, J., Eveland, W. P. Jr. and Kwak, N. (2005). Information and expression in a digital age: Modeling Internet effects on civic participation. *Communication Research*, 32(5), 531–565; Wellman, B., Quan-Haase, A., Witte, J. and Hampton, K. (2001). Does the Internet increase, decrease, or supplement social capital? Social networks, participation, and community commitment. *American Behavioral Scientist*, 45(3), 436–455.

39 Jennings, M. K. and Zeitner, V. (2003). Internet use and civic engagement: A longitudinal analysis. *Public Opinion Quarterly*, 67(3), 311–334; Norris, P. (2001). *Digital divide: Civic engagement, information poverty, and the Internet worldwide*. Cambridge University Press, Cambridge, UK.

40 Taylor, M., Kent, M. L. and White, W. J. (2001). How activist organizations are using the Internet to build relationships. *Public Relations Review*, 27, 263–284.

41 DiMaggio, P., Hargittai, E., Celeste, C., and Shafer, S. (2003). *From unequal access to differentiated use: A Literature review and agenda for research on digital inequality*. Princeton; Van Dijk, J. (2006). Digital divide research, achievements and shortcomings. *Poetics*, 34(4–5), 221–235.

42 Hargittai, E. (2002). Second-level digital divide: Differences in people's online skills. *First Monday*, 7(4). Online: http://firstmonday.org/article/view/942/864; Hargittai, E. (2010). Digital na(t)ives?

Variation in Internet skills and uses among members of the net generation. *Sociological Inquiry*, 80(1), 92–113; Hargittai, E., and Shafer, S. (2006). Differences in actual and perceived online skills: The role of gender. *Social Science Quarterly*, 87(2), 432–448; Van Deursen, A., and Van Dijk, J. (2010). Internet skills and the digital divide. *New Media and Society*, 13(6), 893–911.

43 Hargittai and Walejko op.cit.

44 Hargittai, E., and Hinnant, A. (2008). Digital inequality: Differences in young adults' use of the Internet. *Communication Research*, 35(5), 602–621; Zillien, N., and Hargittai, E. (2009). Digital distinction?: Status-specific types of Internet usage. *Social Science Quarterly*, 90(2), 274–291.

45 Helsper, E. (2010). Gendered internet use across generations and life stages. *Communication Research*, 37(3), 352–374; Li, N., and Kirkup, G. (2007). Gender and cultural differences in Internet use: A study of China and the UK. *Computers and Education*, 48(2), 301–317; Ono, H., and Zavodny, M. (2003). Gender and the Internet. *Social Science Quarterly*, 84(1), 111–121.

46 Helsper, op. cit., 356–357

47 Calenda, D., and Meijer, A. (2009). Young people, the Internet, and political participation. *Information, Communication and Society*, 12(6), 879–898.; Di Gennaro and Dutton, op. cit.

48 Hargittai, 2002, 2010 op. cit.

49 Van Dijk, J. (2005). Skills Access. In J. Van Dijk (Ed.), *The deepening divide: Inequality in the information society* (1st ed., pp. 71–94). London: Sage.

50 Gibson, R. K., Lusoli, W., and Ward, S. (2005). Online participation in the UK: Testing a 'contextualised' model of Internet effects. *The British Journal of Politics and International Relations*, 7(4), 561–583; Wang, S.-I. (2007). Political use of the Internet, political attitudes and political participation. *Asian Journal of Communication*, 17(4), 381–395.

51 Lutz, C., Hoffmann, C. P., and Meckel, M. (2014). Beyond just politics: A systematic literature review of online participation. *First Monday*, 19(7). Online: http://firstmonday.org/ojs/index.php/fm/article/view/5260/4094

52 Jenkins, H. (2006). Confronting the challenges of participatory culture: Media education for the 21st century. *MacArthur Foundation Report*. Online: www.macfound.org/media/article_pdfs/ JENKINS_WHITE_PAPER.PDF

53 Freeman, op. cit.; Noda and Bower, op. cit.

54 Alba, J.W., and Williams, E.F. (2012). Pleasure principles: A review of research on hedonic consumption. *Journal of Consumer Psychology*. http://dx.doi.org/10.1016/j.jcps.2012.07.003

55 Alba and Williams, op. cit.

56 Caruana, R. and Chatzidakis (2014). Consumer Social Responsibility (CnSR): Toward a Multi-Level, Multi-Agent Conceptualization of the "Other CSR". *Journal of Business Ethics*, 121, 577–592.

57 Etzioni, A. (1998). Voluntary simplicity: Characterization, select psychological implications, and societal consequences. *Journal of Economic Psychology*, 19(5), 619–644; Kozinets, R.V. (2002). Can consumers escape the market? Emancipatory illuminations from burning man. *Journal of Consumer Research*, 29, 20–38.

58 Schaefer and Crane (2005) Schaefer, A., and Crane, A. (2005). Addressing sustainability and consumption. *Journal of Macromarketing*, 1, 76–92.

59 Batra, R., and Ahtola, O.T. (1991). Measuring the hedonic and utilitarian sources of consumer attitudes. *Marketing Letters*, 2, 159–170; Chitturi, R., Raghunathan, R., and Mahajan, V. (2007). Form versus function: How the intensities of specific emotions evoked in functional versus hedonic trade-offs mediate product preferences. *Journal of Marketing Research*, 44, 702–714; Dhar, R. and Wertenbroch, K. (2000). Consumer Choice Between Hedonic and Utilitarian Goods. *Journal of Marketing Research*, 37 (February), 60–71; Strahilevitz, M., and Myers, J. G. (1998). Donations to charity as purchase incentives: How well they work may depend on what you are trying to sell. *Journal of Consumer Research*, 24, 434–446.

60 Wolfinbarger, M. and Gilly, M.C. (2001). Shopping online for freedom, control and fun. *California Management Review*, 43(2), 34–55.

61 Amabile, T. M., and Kramer, S. J. (2011). The power of small wins. *Harvard Business Review*, 89, 71–80.

62 Chitturi et al., op. cit.

63 Lucassen G. and Jansen S. (2014). Gamification in marketing – future of fallacy? *Procedia – Social and Behavioral Sciences*, 148, 194–202.

64 Freudmann, E. A., and Bakamitsos, Y. (2014). The role of gamification in non-profit marketing: an information processing account. *Procedia-Social and Behavioral Sciences*, 148, 567–572.

65 Seiffert, J., and Nothhaft, H. (2015). The missing media: The procedural rhetoric of computer games. *Public Relations Review*, 41(2), 254–263.

66 Gordon, E., and Baldwin-Philippi, J. (2014). Playful civic learning: enabling reflection and lateral trust in game-based public participation. *International Journal of Communication*, 8, 759–786.

67 Freudmann and Bakamitsos, op. cit.; Seiffert and Nothhaft, op. cit.

68 Lucassen and Jansen, op. cit.; Robson, K., Plangger, K., Keitzmann, H., J., McCarthy, I. and Leyland, P. (2015). Is it all a game? Understanding the principles of gamification. *Business Horizons*, 58(4), 411–420.

69 Hunicke, R., LeBlanc, M., and Zubek, R. (2004, July). MDA: A formal approach to game design and game research. In *Proceedings of the AAAI Workshop on Challenges in Game AI* (Vol. 4, p. 1).

70 Deterding et al., op. cit.

71 Deterding et al., op. cit.

72 Huotari, K., and J. Hamari (2012). Defining gamification – a service marketing perspective. In *Proceedings of the 16th International Academic MindTrek Conference*, Tampere, Finland, 3–5 October 2012.

73 Zichermann, G. (2013). The power of play. *IESE Insight*, 18, 69–73.

74 Seaborn and Fels, op. cit.

75 Roth, S., Schneckenberg, D., and Tsai, C.-W. (2015). The ludic drive as innovation driver: Introduction to the gamification of innovation. *Creativity and Innovation Management*, 24(2), 300–306.

76 Robson et al., op. cit.

77 Seaborn and Fels, op. cit.; Robson et al., op. cit.

78 Seaborn and Fels, op. cit.; Robson et al., op. cit.

79 Roth et al. op. cit.; Seaborn and Fels, op. cit.

80 Robson, et al., op. cit.

81 Gordon, E., and Baldwin-Philippi, J. (2014). Playful civic learning: enabling reflection and lateral trust in game-based public participation. *International Journal of Communication*, 8, 759–786.

82 Lee, J. J., Matamoros, E., Kern, R., Marks, J., de Luna, C., and Jordan-Cooley, W. (2013). Greenify: fostering sustainable communities via gamification. *CHI '13 Extended Abstracts on Human Factors in Computing Systems* (pp. 1497–1502). Paris: ACM; Robson et al., op. cit.; Roth et al., op. cit.

83 Seaborn and Fels, op. cit.

84 Deterding et al., op. cit.

85 Deterding et al., op. cit.

86 Robson, et al., op. cit.

87 Robson, et al., op. cit.

88 Ašeriškis and Damaševičius, op. cit.

89 Deterding et al., op. cit.; Mavletova, A. (2015). A gamification effect in longitudinal web surveys among children and adolescents. *International Journal of Market Research*, 57(3), 413–438; Hamari, Koivisto, and Sarsa, 2014 Hamari, J., Koivisto, J., and Sarsa, H. (2014). Does gamification works? – A literature review of empirical studies on gamification. *System Sciences (HICSS), 47th Hawaii International Conference on System Sciences* (pp. 3025–3034). Washington: IEEE Computer Society.

90 Lee, et al., op. cit.; Seaborn and Fels, op. cit.

91 Seaborn and Fels, op. cit.

92 Gordon and Baldwin-Philippi, op. cit.

93 Roth et al., op. cit.

94 Seaborn and Fels, op. cit.

95 Deterding et al., op. cit.

96 Ašeriškis and Damaševičius, op. cit.

97 Maan, J. (2013). Social business transformation through gamification. *International Journal of Managing Information Technology*, 5(3), 9–16.

98 Hamari and Koivisto (2015) Hamari, J., and Koivisto, J. (2015). Why do people use gamification services? *International Journal of Information Management*, 35(4), 419–431.

99 Froehlich (2014) Froehlich, J. (2015). Gamifying green: gamification and environmental sustainability. *The Gameful World: Approaches, Issues, Applications*, 563–596

100 Shepherd, S., and Kay, A. C. (2012). On the Perpetuation of Ignorance: System Dependence, System Justification, and the Motivated Avoidance of Sociopolitical Information. *Journal of Personality and Social Psychology*, 102(2), 264–280.

101 Becker, L. J. (1978). Joint effect of feedback and goal setting on performance: a field study of residential energy conservation. *Journal of Applied Psychology*, 63(4), 428–433.

102 Caruana, R., Carrington, M. J., and Chatzidakis, A. (2016). Beyond the Attitude-Behavior Gap: Novel Perspectives in Consumer Ethics. *Journal of Business Ethics*, 135(2); 215–218.

Part 4

Leveraging effective digital corporate social responsibility communication

4.1 Social media concepts for effective CSR online communication

Lina M. Gómez

Introduction

Literature on CSR and social media is still scarce. Although there are few studies on CSR and social media, none of them have addressed the importance of social media concepts for CSR communication. Some have indicated that corporations are increasing social media usage for CSR communication,[1] but further studies, especially empirical ones, are needed to support this hypothesis. This chapter will elucidate how CSR messages are constructed and communicated through social media among different types of users or stakeholders.

Previous work (focused on CSR communication through corporate websites) has found that CSR is communicated using a one-way approach. In fact, studies in the US non-profit sector have noted that organizations' overall use of social media platforms are focused on one-way communication strategies.[2] Information dissemination through social media still predominates when promoting products and services instead of using a two-way communication approach.[3] However, what remains unclear is if this pattern is persistent on discussions about CSR among different users (professionals, citizens/consumers, NGOs, companies, universities, etc.) where all actors can assume the role of transmitters and receivers.

This chapter focuses on how different actors (companies, media, NGOs, influencers, advocates, professionals, and citizens/consumers) are communicating CSR issues on social media, specifically Twitter. It analyses how innate social media concepts are employed by different users for designing CSR messages. This work argues that content that use social media concepts will achieve greater resonance with people. In order to examine this proposition, specific concepts or elements for CSR social media communication were identified and adapted from the literature. Social media data was also analyzed inductively to find additional features for CSR communication.

This study particularly addresses the following research questions:

RQ1: What are the most common social media concepts employed in CSR online communication? In other words, what kinds of elements are adopted by users on social media for CSR communication and who are those users?

RQ2: Is social media used for interaction and mobilization regarding CSR issues? Are social media platforms used for interaction between users or for mobilizing users to do something in favor of the sender?

RQ3: What kind of topics (i.e., CSR core areas) are communicated and discussed among users on social media?

For answering these questions, a quantitative content analysis was performed in a random sample of 1,000 public tweets that contained the CSR hashtag (#CSR). Categories were developed from the literature and used to code the tweets. The empirical analysis draws that social media is a suitable platform for engaging audiences in contributing and committing to responsible practices. This chapter provides new approaches and practical insights on the importance of crafting effective CSR content for promoting proactive stakeholder engagement and participation. This study hence proposes and develops a theoretical framework for effective CSR communication through social media, so practitioners and organizations can learn what other organizations and actors are doing for enriching the practice of CSR communication.

The next section begins with a theoretical background of social media for CSR communication.

The role of social media in CSR communication

Social media platforms are widely used among people to access news, share information, and comment on different situations as they occur in their lives. Social media is an influential platform where consumers get their voices heard;[4] people love to share thoughts, opinions, and experiences, and this in turn impacts significantly what things people read, buy or do. In fact, individuals are sharing more than 16,000 words per day, with many of them being about brands.[5]

Social media is a group of formalized social networks based on communications that promote information, interactivity, knowledge sharing, collaboration, user-generated content, and participation.[6] Social media, then, is dialogic and interactive, which differentiates it from traditional media.[7] However, social media is uncontrollable due to its inherent interactive features. The information flow through social media is multidirectional, interconnected, and sometimes difficult-to-predict.[8]

Social media includes social networks sites (e.g., Facebook, LinkedIn, Google+), microblogs (Twitter), photo sharing sites (Instagram, Pinterest), video sharing sites (YouTube, Vimeo), virtual worlds (Second Live), and live streaming video and audio (Periscope, Zcast). Twitter, specifically, has become the scenario for breaking news at such high speed that when stories reach the mainstream media, they are already trending on Twitter.[9] Retweets and mentions are two of the most important features of Twitter. Retweets are forwarded messages, while mentions refer to replies or simply mentioning other users in the tweet. Both retweets and mentions are indicators of audience engagement.[10] While the number of retweets indicates the ability of a person to share content that is valuable, both replies and mentions are an indication of audience engagement.[11]

The rise of social media has brought unprecedented opportunities for companies to increase public awareness and engagement[12] for CSR efforts.[13] CSR communication is a proactive social process[14] where multiple actors (corporations, government, media, NGOs, consumers, citizens) talk, negotiate, and engage in topics and issues[15] through complex and dynamic networks,[16] such as social media and Internet. CSR makes and gives sense as actors produce and integrate CSR into their personal and specific realities.[17]

Literature about online CSR communication has focused mostly in the analysis of corporate websites, especially in United States and Europe. Studies have come to the conclusion that companies are using a one-way communication approach in the communication of CSR practices through corporate websites.[18] This unidirectional pattern is also present on social media channels due to corporate fear of potential stakeholders' skepticism.[19] However, people are living in a globally scaled networked society where anyone with Internet access can create and share content (text, audio and/or video) and participate in conversations arising in the social media world. This has permitted an increment of proactive consumers (prosumers) pressuring companies to be transparent and responsible with their operations. This new 2.0 *active stakeholder scenario* has impacted in the way CSR communication is developed and presented. Effective CSR communication must include audiences' interests, needs, and expectations, in order to promote awareness and engagement.[20] One form of interactive communication helping to pass along value content is stakeholder dialogue and engagement.[21] This form of interactive communication, especially on social media, engages stakeholders in two-way symmetrical communication. This kind of interactive communication helps build and maintain relationships that are based on truth and understanding,[22] differing from traditional ways where audiences were managed and controlled by corporate media structures.[23]

Social media concepts for CSR communication

Information is the basic function of any social media platform,[24] which is based on a one-way communication approach. The next function, communication, encompasses messages that foster relationships and build communities through the promotion of dialogues and interactions.[25] Besides these two basic functions, social media includes particular concepts or elements that enable content to resonate with audiences. CSR communication through social media is conceived and developed through the employment of unique concepts such as dialogue and engagement, transparency, authenticity, influence,[26] and mobilization.[27] These social media concepts are taken into account for the development of the theoretical framework and the data analysis.

Dialogue and engagement are two of the most important social media concepts in the construction of an effective CSR communication process using social media channels. Engagement is part of dialogue, and through dialogue, both organizations and stakeholders can create and contribute to social capital.[28] Companies learn through dialogue which issues are important to stakeholders and how to attach their needs and expectations to CSR strategies.[29] Through engagement, stakeholders are co-constructing messages with the purpose of reaching a mutual understanding with organizations.[30] The ultimate goal of dialogue and engagement is to build and maintain relationships with stakeholders.[31] A message that includes dialogue and engagement encourages stakeholders to participate in conversations. Messages that promote dialogue (like casual conversations, advice, and problem solving) and engagement are designed to create fruitful discussions that could lead to relationship building with stakeholders in the long term.

Another social media concept is transparency, which includes openness and honesty, reporting (disclosing the good and the bad), and providing information on time.[32] Transparency involves the process of looking within.[33] Being transparent can inhibit stakeholder's skepticism and lead to the acceptance of CSR reporting and communication.[34] A message that promotes transparency presents useful information (including hyperlinks to more information) so audiences can make important decisions. It also includes messages aiming to resolve stakeholder issues or problems. If content helps people to save time, improve their lives or save money, people will spread the word, and in turn, they will be helping others.[35]

Authenticity in social media equates to having a sincere and human voice in contrast to a faceless/institutional voice.[36] Authenticity is an important factor in CSR social media communication because "lies or wrong communication are discovered very fast".[37] Another social media element, influence, is based on the higher use of public reaction indicators that promote message resonance with audiences, such as retweets and mentions (including replies). Influencers are important actors in CSR communication because they help to spread the message (both positively and negatively)[38] and mobilize stakeholders. Influential messages can be: 1) positive, 2) negative or 3) neutral. Positive content relates to achievements, acknowledgements, relevant projects, or initiatives, and overall, they have a positive tone and the use of words denotes positivism. Negative content includes messages that have a negative tone and the choice of words denotes negativism. It can enclose messages regarding bad news and poor service. Neutral content includes messages that are not neither positive nor negative. These messages present information regarding news, announcements, or other neutral information.

Lastly, mobilization includes content that encourage and engage users to do something in favor of someone (e.g., a person, organization, or cause),[39] for example, share information, like a post, attend an event, buy a product, donate. This social media concept is very powerful because it can help an organization to fulfil its mission and strategic goals[40] regarding CSR issues.

Table 4.1.1 includes the different social media concepts proposed for effective CSR online communication.

This work also proposes that in order for CSR online communication to be effective, social media innate indicators and supportive features must be used.[41] First, social media innate indicators promote stakeholder engagement/influence which are divided in low influencer and high influencer. On one hand, low influencer indicators, such as liking a post, sharing or retweeting information or using hashtags, promote minimal stakeholder

Table 4.1.1 Theoretical framework of social media concepts for CSR online communication

Social media concept	Definition	Theoretical support
Transparency	Content that is useful, valuable and includes key supportive resources (such as hyperlinks)	42
Authenticity	Content that poses a human and sincere tone	43
Influence	Content that makes people talk about other people (e.g., influencers or advocates) to achieve desired impressions	44
Dialogue and engagement	Content that drives conversations and engages or attracts audiences to dialogue and care for others	45
Mobilization	Content that drives or triggers people to do something in favor of someone (person, company or organization), e.g., share information, attend an event, learn something, donate, and buy a product	46
Emotions	Content that makes people feel something (positive or negative). Some emotions increase sharing while others decrease it	47
Storytelling	Content that tells stories that are valuable and integral	48
Social media innate indicators that promote dialogic engagement and influence	Low influencer indicators: liking, sharing/retweeting, and hashtags	49
	High influencer indicators: replies and mentions	
Social media supportive features	Photos, videos, hyperlinks	50

involvement because people are passively participating. On the other hand, high influencer indicators, such as replying to messages or mentioning other users in order to engage in conversations and dialogues, encourage stakeholders to actively participate. Second, social media supportive features are elements that must be used in messages for supporting the effectiveness of social media concepts, for example, photos, videos, and hyperlinks. Therefore, CSR content should include at least one social media indicator (low or high influence) and the use of at least one supportive feature (photos, videos, hyperlinks).

Emotions and storytelling are other two social media concepts that are not widely used at the moment of crafting CSR messages. For example, awe, which is a complex emotion that frequently involves a sense of surprise, greatness, mystery or unexpectedness, can boost people to share content.[51] Other positive emotions responsible for audience engagement are excitement and amusement (humor), while negative emotions can include anger and anxiety. Storytelling which transmits helpful information to others through improvisation or embellishment.[52] Emotions and storytelling are used for promoting dialogue, engagement, influence, authenticity, transparency, and mobilization. Therefore, both emotions and storytelling are necessary elements for achieving audience acceptance, commitment, and participation regarding CSR issues.

Method

A random sample of 1000 tweets with the hashtag #CSR from 2015 and 2016 was collected and analyzed quantitatively. The sample chosen surpasses statistical sampling standards set for content analysis.[53] A Python code was written to access the Twitter application programming interface (API) to download tweets with the hashtag #CSR.

To address the question of how social media concepts are employed on Twitter by different users, a codebook was developed. This codebook included specific variables for the quantitative content analysis. Each tweet was coded using the following variables or criteria: 1) type of Twitter user, it includes different Twitter users that posted messages using the hashtag #CSR, such as: NGOs, educational institutions, media, companies, influencers (they have information on their Twitter bio profiles that they have or had work on CSR), other professionals (they do not particularly work or have strong interest on CSR but they display their profession or work in their Twitter profiles), advocates (they display their passion and commitment with CSR in their Twitter profiles), and citizens/consumers (they do not display their profession or work); 2) type of social media concept (engagement and dialogue, transparency, authenticity, influence, and mobilization); and 3) topic of the tweet.

The variable "topic of the tweet" refers to the subject of the message. Tweets were coded according to the seven core subjects defined by the ISO 26000 in social responsibility. These were: organization governance, human rights, labor practices, environment, fair operating practices, consumers issues, and community involvement and development. Tweets that did not fit in any of these categories, because of their broad and general nature, were coded as CSR/sustainability broad topic. The CSR/sustainability broad topic was categorized in the following sub variables: events, news, announcements, education messages, annual reports, achievements, opinions/testimonials, acknowledgments, partnerships, chats, and marketing. Examples for each sub category are included in Appendix 4.

Examples of the variable "type of social media concept" are presented in Appendix 5. Emotions and storytelling (introduced in the literature and included in the framework) were not used for the data analysis. If a message did not present social media concepts, it was categorized as disclosure. Influence was subcategorized as positive, negative, and neutral (as explained in the literature review). Mobilization was subcategorized as: 1) liking/sharing/retweeting: encourages users to like, share or retweet; 2) learning: encourages users to learn about something in a website, blog, or any kind of social media platform; 3) participation: engages users to participate in conversations and dialogues, and also to participate in events, including chats; and 4) others: encloses messages that market services related to CSR or non-CSR products and it also encourages users to make donations.

Persuasion was another feature coded. However, it was not included in the theoretical framework. Persuasion includes two-way asymmetrical communication messages, which encourage fans to give feedback or suggestions regarding CSR (the company has the only purpose of using this feedback for its improvement). However, persuasion is considered as an informational approach. While multiple social media concepts (transparency, dialogue/engagement, mobilization, authenticity, influence) can occur in any message, the variable "disclosure" is mutually exclusive.

Content was also categorized for the inclusion of *supportive features* such as photos, videos, hashtags, and hyperlinks. Inter-coder reliability tests were conducted to check the validity of the manual coding schemes. Specifically, the author, with the help of a colleague, independently coded 100 tweets. The inter-coder reliability tests conducted on each variable indicated Cohen's kappa (κ) scores ranging from 0.90 to 0.95, indicating a high level of inter-coder reliability. The remaining tweets were coded by the author.

Findings

Table 4.1.2 includes a summary of statistics for all the social media supportive features and indicators. Social media indicators (both low and high) help to boost audience engagement, resonance, and influence regarding CSR. Low indicators are retweets and hashtags, and high indicators are mentions. Supportive features refer to elements that support the content such as photos, videos, and hyperlinks. As observed, low indicators (such as hashtags) and supportive features (such as hyperlinks) are highly used, while photos and videos are the least employed for message support.

To start, 42% of the messages contained retweets. On average, each message presented two retweets. This points out that half of the CSR messages promoted pass-along value. In other words, content was designed with the inclusion of different indicators and features that encouraged users to share it. Hashtags were the indicator most employed. Each tweet presented an average of three hashtags per message, which is adequate. Users included hashtags to help messages reach outside their network of followers. Hashtags help to track conversations about a certain topic. As presented in Figure 4.1.1, most of the hashtags are about broad topics such as CSR, sustainability, green, sustainable, environment, responsible,

Table 4.1.2 Variables – social media indicators and features

Use of social media features/indicators	Count	Mean	Min.	Max
Retweets	417	0.42	0	100
Mentions	457	0.46	0	10
Hashtags	1000	1.00	1	12
Hyperlinks	794	0.79	0	2
Photos	195	0.20	0	1
Videos	6	0.01	0	1

supply change, socent (social enterprise), among others. Two findings curiously stand out. First, tweet topics categorized as others were mostly related to jobs as customer service representatives, not corporate social responsibility. There is a CSR automated account (@ CSRRT) that retweets information that contains CSR hashtags, and this account includes content that is not related to corporate social responsibility. Second, it was found that a few media platforms related to CSR and sustainability, such as *triplepundit*, are using their company name as a hashtag.

Mentions (including both mentions and replies) were employed in 46% of the messages. An average of one mention per message was found. As shown in Figure 4.1.2, most

Figure 4.1.1 Word cloud of hashtags

Figure 4.1.2 Word cloud of mentions

of the users tagged or mentioned on messages were media platforms such as *CaelusGreen-Room*, *CSRwire*, *EthicalCorp*, *TriplePundit*, *CSRRT*, *Justmeans*, or *3BLMedia*. Most of the tweets contained hyperlinks (20%), while 20% included photos and 1% videos. Supportive features are important elements that help the content of the message to have more resonance. People live in an era where video is the dominant resource for audience engagement, so organizations should include video content that is visually attractive and valuable to engage audiences.

Figure 4.1.3 shows the different types of users mostly found in conversations related to CSR. Thirty percent of the messages were sent by media outlets, 20% by companies, and 16% by professionals. Government and educational institutions were the absent users in conversations. A summary statistics table and examples for each user are included in Appendix 3. In addition, Appendix 1 and Appendix 2 present a word cloud of users' locations and descriptions. The majority of the users are located in Berlin, London, New York, Washington, Los Angeles, and Toronto. Most of them care about CSR and sustainability, as disclosed in the bio description. They like to share news, and they favor social, service, and green causes.

The content disclosed on Twitter was mainly about CSR/sustainability as a broad topic (58% of the messages). This means that content was not explicit about a particular CSR-narrow area, such as environment. As presented on Figure 4.1.4, community (6%), environment (4%) and labor practices (4%) were the CSR core areas most discussed on Twitter. This is consistent with other studies where societal and environmental issues were the most discussed.[54] The topics least discussed were regarding fair operating practices (1%) and human rights (2%). Appendix 4 presents summary statistics for all core areas and examples for each sub variable. It is important to notice that 16% of the messages were

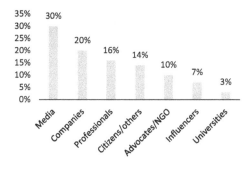

Figure 4.1.3 Most popular Twitter users

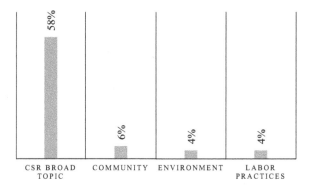

Figure 4.1.4 Most popular CSR topics

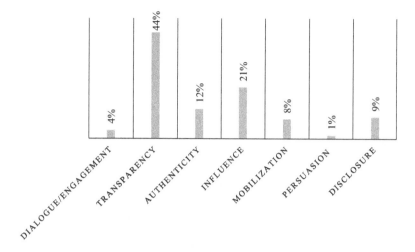

Figure 4.1.5 Use of social media concepts

coded in the others category. These were the tweets that either were nonsensical or were about customer service representative (#csr) jobs.

Messages that were categorized as CSR/sustainability broad topic were mostly about announcements (26%), news (23%), and educational messages (17%). Examples of each subcategorization, plus a word cloud about the content of the tweet's sample, are located in Appendix 4. It is noted that most of the content included the words CSR and sustainability. The least discussed CSR/Sustainability broad topics were related to acknowledgments (1%), annual reports, chats, and partnerships (2%).

As shown in Figure 4.1.5, the most used social media concept was transparency (44%), followed by influence (21%). Nine percent of the messages were about disclosure, which means that 9% of the messages did not include social media innate elements. The least employed concepts were dialogue, engagement (4%) and mobilization (8%). Even though persuasion was not analyzed as a concept, only 1% of the messages included two-way asymmetrical communication.

Findings are consistent with this study,[55] which found that some of the strategies used by companies to convey messages on social media is related to conventional politeness (greeting, thanking) and diversion (not promoting feedback, not responding to comments). Little dialogue and engagement were found, and companies were concerned only to disclose information that is transparent while being polite. Most of the messages were unidirectional. Although users were transparent in their messages by disclosing relevant and valuable content, they were not promoting mobilization, dialogue, and engagement. Influential tweets included more mentions (tagging) than replies. However, influence was also unidirectional, users were tagging other users but they were not encouraging these tagged users to act or to discuss a particular issue. Most of the influential tweets were neutral (58%), while 38% were positive. Only 4% were negative. Tweets that included mobilization (8% of the messages) were about learning (51%) and encouraging users to participate in an event or a chat/discussion (32%). This also indicates that mobilization was also unidirectional and for marketing purposes, because users were encouraging other users to learn about something by visiting a webpage or social platform, reading a report or news, or doing some other activity. After users were mobilized to learn something, there is no encouragement for dialogue or relationship-building. A summary of statistics for all social media concepts variables and examples of each one are included in Appendix 5.

Discussion

In 1984, 50% of companies engaged in one-way communication (information dissemination) while only 35% performed two-way communication.[56] Unfortunately, this unidirectional pattern still predominates in this networked and digital era where interactivity and participation are key. Companies are still using social media platforms as black boxes when it comes to stakeholder dialogue and engagement.[57] However, users are employing social media platforms for getting their voices heard, creating and sharing content, and participating in conversations. Different groups of stakeholders are communicating about diverse CSR issues (e.g., environmental issues) before companies talk about them. Social media has also helped to mobilize public opinion and shape a new global solidarity,[58] which causes new challenges for companies.

In spite of these new challenges, companies are not using all the concepts, elements, and features that social media platforms bring for stakeholder dialogue, engagement, and mobilization.[59] Findings agree with this viewpoint, and reaffirm that different users (especially companies) are failing to take into account the different innate concepts and supportive resources that social media platforms provide for communication and participation. This is due to the fact that social media is still perceived as another unidirectional disclosure channel for marketing purposes, even when engaging in dialogues.[60] Results indicate that users were encouraging other users to engage in dialogue and actions, but they were short-termed and did not promote follow-up (e.g., ask a question or visit a page). Findings are also in line with a study[61] that found that dialogue and engagement is used, but they are not quite ideal, because they tend to be asymmetrical, usually for information giving and gathering and a particular user is the stronger party.

Among the social media concepts analyzed, transparency was the most employed, but transparency is innate in any form of information and communication. Companies, organizations, journalists, and advocates, in other words, any person in social media, must be transparent and disclose relevant and valuable information to others. Transparency is categorized as content that is valuable, relevant, and includes social media supportive features like hyperlinks, so it can point out where that valuable information is located. If companies are disclosing valuable information on Twitter, they must provide a link with further information. Tweets that include hyperlinks or URLs spread faster through the network.[62]

Influence was another social media concept used frequently. As explained in the results, most of the tweets included mentions rather than replies. This means that users where tagging or mentioning other users in most of cases to let them know about information they have found that may be valuable to them. This is again consistent with another study,[63] where most relevant topics for audiences are related to information seeking or peer-to-peer information sharing. However, tagging/mentioning another user (no matter the type of user: media, advocate, company) indicates that the user is building and reinforcing its online ties and relations with another user, thus increasing awareness and thereby influence.[64] Most influential tweets were neutral and positive; this is consistent with other studies of online communities.[65] Tweets that present a positive or negative sentiment tend to receive more retweets than neutral.[66] This suggests that social media content that is both influential and positive can resonate better with audiences and boost sharing. Further studies should include other categorizations, besides positive, negative, and neutral, such as anger, anxiety, sadness, awe, excitement, amusement, contentment, and emotions,[67] because these are the principal motors in content to gone viral. More research is needed to see variations between groups,[68] for instance, to see if companies promote more positive and influential tweets than advocates.

The majority of users discussed CSR and sustainability broad topics regarding announcements, news, and educational messages. These broad topics are related to disclosure and information seeking. Narrow CSR topic areas are related to society and environment and using keywords such as green energy, social, and people. Findings indicate that some CSR topics and situations are more interactive than others, and organizations and companies need to increase their participation when these situations occur. Additionally, media outlets, companies, and professionals were the leaders in the CSR Twitterverse. These results are consistent with a study[69] which explained that CSR dialogues are constructed and practiced mostly by companies (including media), NGOs and consultants. Consultants and media were discussing CSR topics via Twitter, but only corporations, with solid CSR programs, disclosed information on Twitter.[70] Findings also answer why most of the topics are related to announcements, news, and educational messages about CSR and sustainability broad topics. Media companies (including those specialized in CSR like *Triplepundit, CSRWire, Justmeans,* etc.) are focused on disclosing information (in the form of news, announcements, and educational messages), the same applies to companies and professionals. It is easier to retweet or to share information that was found on a page, than designing, writing, and crafting a message that involves social media concepts. People live in a networked era where immediacy is the norm, and sometimes quality and valuable content is sacrificed.

This chapter proposed a theoretical framework for effective CSR communication through social media, using different concepts, indicators, and features that are fundamental for designing content that adds value for audiences. Companies need to develop strategies for communicating CSR messages and promote stakeholder commitment and support through social media. In order to achieve this, it is necessary to identify the different innate concepts and supportive features that social media has for CSR communication (as the ones proposed in this chapter in the theoretical framework). It is said that each social media platform is different, and what works on Facebook may not work on Twitter and so on. Marketers asseverate that business must use a specific approach on each social network and recognize the differentiating factor in their social media efforts.[71] However, the theoretical framework presented and developed in the literature section can be applied to any social media platform for different types of messages, not only CSR ones. All the concepts and features included in this framework are the basis for communicating and interacting in social media platforms.

The model proposed was not built on an existing framework. However, it was built deductively using elements and concepts from different published studies regarding CSR online communication and social media, as shown in Table 4.1.1 in the literature review section. This theoretical framework can be used as a guideline for companies or organizations when designing CSR communication plans and messages (both day-to-day communication and issue-related communication messages). Scholars and practitioners in the field of CSR, public relations, and marketing can use the theoretical framework proposed in this chapter and apply or evaluate it in other different types of real time social media data.

After reviewing literature and collecting and analyzing social media data, this chapter proposes that in order to be effective and boost audience engagement, CSR messages must comprise: 1) two or more social media concepts (transparency must be one of them); 2) one or more social media indicators (both low and high influence); and 3) one or two social media supportive features. In addition, CSR effective communication should be crafted with emotions and incorporate storytelling elements. Both principles are important for a message to be contagious or motivator[72] to cause things to be talked about, shared, and imitated. Although emotions and storytelling were not included in the empirical analysis, more research studies are needed to address the inclusion of these principles as vessels of audience engagement in social media.

As explained before, more than one social media concept can be included in any message. This chapter proposes that including at least two concepts can be sufficient for boosting audience engagement. However, situations can occur when all the concepts can be presented. In that particular scenario, it is proposed that messages should be crafted in the following order as shown in Figure 4.1.6. Transparency should be innate in any message, as it is the first concept to be considered. Next, the message must be authentic and present a sincere and human tone. Then, in order to engage in dialogue and mobilize others, the message has to promote influence; in other words, it has to mention other users to engage them in dialogues, and finally mobilize others to do something and continue promoting conversations about it. But above all, emotions and content that promotes storytelling should be included so messages can help to boost audience resonance, engagement, and participation.[73]

The practice of CSR online communication, especially through social media, is very complex and dynamic. Therefore, businesses and stakeholders must fully understand the dynamics[74] and the innate concepts and features that are at play in the social media world. With this notion, users can make sense of the messages they are constructing, deconstructing, liking, spreading, and commenting within their network so real dialogues, engagement, influence, and mobilization can take place.

Conclusions and managerial implications

This chapter has highlighted the importance of using social media concepts, indicators, and supportive features for effective CSR communication that enhances stakeholder relationships. This study proposes a theoretical model for designing CSR messages that resonate and engage with stakeholders. Although some of the concepts presented in this framework were applied to social media data, as explained in the results and discussion sections, more research is needed in order to validate the framework with other kinds of samples.

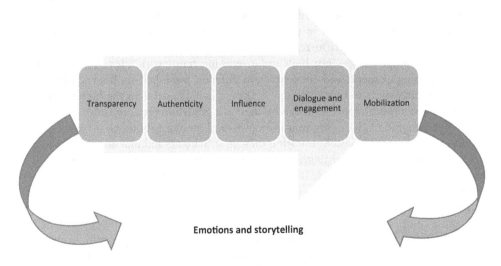

Figure 4.1.6 Social media concepts sequence for crafting messages

This work also elucidates how different users (companies, NGOs, advocates, influencers, CSR researchers, and professionals), interested in CSR issues, use social media for CSR information, discussion, engagement, and mobilization. Companies, organizations, and consultants, specifically, can take into account the results and the theoretical framework discussed in this chapter, so they can understand the importance of using social media concepts, elements and features when creating CSR content for their respective audiences. However, it is not enough to take an interactive and engagement posture for aligning stakeholders needs and expectations into messages.[75] It is also needed the employment of social media concepts, indicators, and supportive features on messages that will help to build and nurture authentic relationships. The proposed framework fills a void in the literature about CSR communication's effectiveness from the stakeholders' point of view,[76] because it includes all the actors' perspectives involved in CSR communication.

Limitations and recommendations for further research

This work presents some limitations that can be avenues for further research. For instance, this study only focuses on Twitter. Future studies can analyze (both quantitatively and qualitatively) data from different social media accounts like Facebook, LinkedIn, and Instagram, and the use of other CSR-related hashtags like sustainability, society, environment. Further studies can build upon this model and adapt it for different social media platforms, and perform empirical studies that include all the elements presented in the framework. This model can also be applied to specific groups like corporations or NGOs (for example, a sample of the top 50 Fortune companies) in different countries.

People use social media for different reasons. One is to be informed, however, with massive amounts of information and resources presented online, individuals need valuable content that they can use. If information is relevant and useful for individuals, they will care about it and share it with their network.[77] The way users in social media (including companies) design messages is the key to effectiveness. CSR messages impact audiences not because of random luck, but because they contain certain elements to make content more likely to be talked about and shared. The Internet and social media world is inundated with information lacking social media concepts. We need to craft CSR communication messages that are "positively contagious" and effective for social transmission, opinion formation, and mobilization.

Notes

1 Capriotti, P. (2011), Communicating Corporate Social Responsibility Through the Internet and Social Media, in O. Ihlen, J.L. Barlett and S. May (Eds.), *The Handbook of Communication and Corporate Social Responsibility*, Oxford: Wiley-Blackwell, 358–378; Etter, M. (2013), Reasons for low levels of interactivity: (Non-) interactive CSR communication in twitter, *Public Relations Review*, 39(5), 606–608.

2 Waters, R.D., Burnett, E., Lamm, A., and Lucas, J. (2009), Engaging Stakeholders Through Social Networking: How Nonprofit Organizations Are Using Facebook. *Public Relations Review*, 35(2), 102–106; Lovejoy, K., and Saxton, G.D. (2012), Information, Community, and Action: How Nonprofit Organizations Use Social Media, *Journal of Computer-Mediated Communication*, 17(3), 337–353.

3 Gomez, L., and Soto, I. (2011), Social Media as a Strategic Tool for Corporate Communication, *Revista Internacional de Relaciones Públicas*, 1(2), 157–174; Shin, W., Pang, A., and Kim, H.Y. (2015), Building Relationships Through Integrated Online Media Global Organizations' Use of Brand Web Sites, Facebook, and Twitter, *Journal of Business and Technical Communication*, 29(2), 184–220.

4 Lillqvist, E., and Louhiala-Salminen, L. (2014), Facing Facebook Impression Management Strategies in Company – Consumer Interactions, *Journal of Business and Technical Communication*, 28 (1), 3–30.

5 Berger, J. (2013), *Contagious Why Things Catch On*, New York, NY: Simon and Schuster.

6 Kaplan, A.M., and Haenlein, M. (2010), Users of the World, Unite! The Challenges and Opportunities of Social Media, *Business Horizons*, 53(1), 59–68.

7 Schultz, F., Castelló, I., and Morsing, M. (2013), The Construction of Corporate Social Responsibility in Network Societies: A Communication View, *Journal of Business Ethics*, 115(4), 681–692.

8 Friedman, T. L. (2006), *The World Is Flat [Updated and Expanded]: A Brief History of the Twenty-First Century*. New York: Farrar, Straus and Giroux.

9 Oh, O., Hazel Kwon, K., and Raghav Rao, H. (2010), An Exploration of Social Media in Extreme Events: Rumor Theory and Twitter During the Haiti Earthquake, in: *Proceedings of the International Conference on Information Systems*, St. Louis, Missouri, 12–15 December 2010.

10 Lee, K., Oh, W.Y., and Namhyeok, K. (2013), Social Media for Socially Responsible Firms: Analysis of Fortune 500's Twitter Profiles and Their CSR/CSIR Ratings, *Journal of Business Ethics*, 118(4), 791–806.

11 Ibid.

12 Kaplan and Halein, op. cit.

13 Colleoni, E. (2013), CSR Communication Strategies for Organizational Legitimacy in Social Media, *Corporate Communications: An International Journal*, 18(2), 228–248.

14 Golob, U., and Podnar, K. (2011), Corporate Social Responsibility Communication and Dialogue, in O. Ihlen, J.L. Barlett and S. May (Eds), *The Handbook of Communication and Corporate Social Responsibility*, Oxford: Wiley-Blackwell, 231–251.

15 Wehmeier, S., and Schultz, F. (2013), Communication and Corporate Social Responsibility: A Storytelling Perspective, in O. Ihlen, J.L. Barlett and S. May (Eds), *The Handbook of Communication and Corporate Social Responsibility*, Oxford: Wiley-Blackwell, 467–490.

16 Schultz et al., op cit.

17 Wehmeier and Schultz, op cit.

18 Capriotti, P., and Moreno, A. (2007), Communicating Corporate Responsibility Through Corporate Web Sites in Spain. *Corporate Communications: An International Journal*, 12(3), 221–237; Basil, D.Z., and Erlandson, J. (2008), Corporate Social Responsibility Website Representations: A Longitudinal Study of Internal and External Self-Presentations, *Journal of Marketing Communications*, 14(2), 125–137; Gomez, L., and Chalmeta, R. (2011), Corporate Responsibility in U.S. Corporate Websites: A Pilot Study, *Public Relations Review*, 37(1), 93–95.

19 Insch, A. (2008), Online Communication of Corporate Environmental Citizenship: A Study of New Zealand's Electricity and Gas Retailers", *Journal of Marketing Communications*, 14(2), 139–153.

20 Colleoni, op. cit.

21 Morsing, M., and Schultz, M. (2006), Corporate Social Responsibility Communication: Stakeholder Information, Response and Involvement Strategies, *Business Ethics: A European Review*, 15(4), 323–338.

22 Taylor, M., and Kent, M.L. (2014), Dialogic Engagement: Clarifying Foundational Concepts, *Journal of Public Relations Research*, 26(4), 384–398.

23 Lee et al., op. cit.

24 Lovejoy and Saxton, op. cit.

25 Ibid.

26 McCorkindale, T., and DiStaso, M.W. (2014), The State of Social Media Research: Where Are We Now, Where We Were and What It Means for Public Relations, *Research Journal of the Institute for Public Relations*, 1(1), 1–17.

27 Lovejoy and Saxton, op. cit.

28 Taylor and Kent, op. cit.

29 Golob and Podnar, op. cit.

30 Morsing and Schultz, op. cit.

31 McCorkindale and DiStaso, op. cit.

32 Ibid.

33 Coombs, W.T., and Holladay, S. (2013), The Pseudo-Panopticon: The Illusion Created by CSR-Related Transparency and the Internet, *Corporate Communications: An International Journal Corporate Communications An International Journal*, 18(2), 212–227.

34 Coombs and Holladay, op. cit.; Forehand, M.R., and Grier, S. (2003), When Is Honesty the Best Policy? The Effect of Stated Company Intent on Consumer Skepticism, *Journal of Consumer Psychology*, 13(3), 349–356.

35 Berger, op. cit.

36 McCorkindale and DiStaso, op. cit.

37 Etter, M., and Fieseler, C. (2010), On Relational Capital in Social Media, *Studies in Communication Sciences*, 10(2), 167–189, page cited: 178.

38 McCorkindale and DiStaso, op. cit.

39 Lovejoy and Saxton, op. cit.

40 Ibid.

41 Cha, M., Haddadi, H., Benevenuto, F., and Gummadi, K. (2010), Measuring User Influence in Twitter: The Million Follower Fallacy, in: *Proceedings Fourth International AAAI Conference on Weblogs and Social Media*, Washington, DC, 23–26 May 2010; Saxton, G.D., and Waters, R.D. (2014), What Do Stakeholders Like on Facebook? Examining Public Reactions to Nonprofit Organizations' Informational, Promotional, and Community-Building Messages, *Journal of Public Relations Research*, 26(3), 280–299; Gomez and Chalmeta, op. cit.

42 McCorkindale and DiStaso, op. cit.; Berger, op.cit.; Kent, M.L., and Taylor, M. (1998), Building Dialogic Relationships Through the World Wide Web, *Public Relations Review*, 24(3), 321–334.

43 McCorkindale and DiStaso, op. cit.; Etter and Fieseler, op. cit.

44 McCorkindale and DiStaso, op. cit.; Berger, op. cit.

45 McCorkindale and DiStaso, op. cit.; Taylor and Kent, op. cit.

46 Lovejoy and Saxton, op. cit.

47 Berger, op. cit.

48 Ibid.

49 Cha et al., op cit.; Saxton and Waters, op. cit.

50 Gomez and Chalmeta, op. cit.

51 Berger, op. cit.

52 Ibid.

53 Krippendorff, K. (2012), *Content Analysis: An Introduction to Its Methodology*, Third edition, Sage Publications: Thousand Oaks, CA.

54 Gomez-Vasquez, L. (2013), Me gusta o te sigo: Análisis de la comunicación de prácticas de Responsabilidad Social Corporativa a través de los medios sociales, *Correspondencias and Análisis*, 3, 89–109; Maignan, I., and Ralston, D.A. (2002), Corporate Social Responsibility in Europe and the US: Insights From Businesses Self-Presentations, *Journal of International Business Studies*, 33(3), 97–514.

55 Lillqvist and Louhiala-Salminen, op. cit.

56 Grunig, J.E., and Hunt, T. (1984), *Managing Public Relations*. Orlando, FL: Harcourt Brace Jovanich.

57 Riu, H., Liu, Y., and Whinston, A.B. (2010), Chatter matters: How Twitter Can Open the Black Box of Online Word-of-Mouth, in: *Proceedings of the International Conference on Information Systems*, St. Louis, Missouri, 12–15 December 2010.

58 Aras, G., and Crowther, D. (2011), Commentary: The View From Management, in O. Ihlen, J.L. Barlett and S. May (Eds.), *The Handbook of Communication and Corporate Social Responsibility*, Oxford: Wiley-Blackwell, 516–533.

59 Lovejoy and Saxton, op.cit.; Waters et al., op cit.; Rybalko, S., and Seltzer, T. (2010), Dialogic communication in 140 characters or less: How Fortune 500 companies engage stakeholders using Twitter, *Public Relations Review*, 36(4), 336–341.

60 Colleoni, op. cit.

61 Golob, U., and Podnar, K. (2014), Critical Points of CSR-Related Stakeholder Dialogue in Practice, *Business Ethics: A European Review*, 23(3), 248–257.

62 Park, J., Cha, M., Kim, H., and Jeong, J. (2012), Managing Bad News on Social Media: A Case Study of Domino's Pizza Crisis, in: *Proceedings of the International AAAI Conference on Weblogs and Social Media*, Dublin, Ireland, 4–8 June 2012.

63 Colleoni, op. cit.

64 Lovejoy, K., Waters, R.D., and Saxton, G.D. (2012), Engaging Stakeholders Through Twitter: How Nonprofit Organizations Are Getting More Out of 140 Characters or Less, *Public Relations Review*, 38(2), 313–318.

65 Berger, J., and Milkman, K. (2012), What Makes Online Content Viral?, *Journal of MarketingResearch*, 49(2), 192–205; Hansen, L.K., Arvidsson, A., Nielsen, F., Colleoni, E., and Etter, M., (2011), Good Friends, Bad News – Affect and Virality in Twitter, in: *Proceedings of the International Workshop on Social Computing, Network, and Services*, Crete, Greece, 28–30 June 2011.

66 Stieglitz, S., and Dang-Xuan, L. (2012), Impact and Diffusion of Sentiment in Public Communication on Facebook, in: *Proceedings of the European Conference on Information Systems*, Barcelona, Spain, 10–13 June 2012.

67 Colleoni, op. cit.

68 Berger, op. cit.

69 Golob and Podnar, 2014, op. cit.

70 Gomez, L., Vargas Preciado, L., Cea Moure, R., and Adelopo, I. (2014), CSR Dialogue on Social Media Platforms: An Analysis of CSR Tweets, in: *Proceedings 17th International Public Relations Research Conference*, Miami, USA, 5–9 March 2014.

71 Hutchinson, A. (2016), Facebook Releases New Data on What Users Are Looking for on Facebook and Instagram. *Social Media Today*. Available from, www.socialmediatoday.com/social-business/facebook-releases-new-data-what-users-are-looking-facebook-and-instagram [Acessed July 14, 2016].

72 Berger, op. cit.

73 Ibid.

74 Nitins, T., and Burgess, J. (2014), Twitter, Brands, and User Engagement, in K. Weller, A. Bruns, J. Burgess, M. Mahrt, and C. Pushmann (Eds.), *Twitter and Society*, New York: Peter Lang, 293–304.

75 Colleoni, op. cit.

76 Kim, S., and Ferguson, M.A. (2014), Public Expectations of CSR Communication: What and How to Communicate CSR, *Public Relations Journal*, 8(3), pp. 1–22.

77 Berger, op. cit.

Appendix 1 – User location word cloud

Appendix 2 – User description word cloud

Appendix 3 – Type of Twitter user descriptive statistics table and example

Table 4.1.3 and Table 4.1.4 Type of Twitter user descriptive statistics table and example

Type of Twitter user	Count	Mean	Min.	Max.
Company	196	0.20	0	1
Media	297	0.30	0	1
NGO	48	0.05	0	1
Government	2	0.00	0	1
Education	30	0.03	0	1
Influencer	72	0.07	0	1
Advocate	53	0.05	0	1
Professional	159	0.16	0	1
Citizen/consumer	70	0.07	0	1
Others	73	0.07	0	1

Type of Twitter user	Example (user description)
Company	*Official account of @EdelmanPR's Business + Social Purpose practice, tweeting about #CSR and #Sustainability	tweets by @DrewTMitch and @Katherine_CSR*
Media	*A globally-read online publication on CSR, social entrepreneurship, green jobs, and the triple bottom line in sustainable business. A Certified B Corp.*
NGO	*Womankind Worldwide is a UK charity working in partnership with women's rights organisations in Africa, Asia & Latin America to help women transform their lives*
Government	*Embassy of Sweden, Doha, Qatar @SwedenDoha (Retweet does not equal endorsement) H.E. Ambassador Ewa Polano tweets from @SwedenInDoha*
Education	*The official Twitter for The University of Nottingham Libraries*
Influencer	*I'm a #csrnative working in #CSR #Sustainability and #developmenteconomics. #beyondGDP #sosteniAMOilgreen #smartcities #ecodesign*
Advocate	*Management Specialist with OMAFRA. Strong supporter of sustainable practices, healthy living and good science. Tweets are my own*
Professional	*Communication Executive: Browning Dudley, Corporation, Broadcast Journalist, White House Correspondent*
Citizen/consumer	*I Tweet/Re-Tweet good deeds of the mankind :)*

Appendix 4 – Tweet topic descriptive statistics table and example

Table 4.1.5 and Table 4.1.6 Tweet topic descriptive statistics table and example

Tweet topic	Count	Mean	Min.	Max
Organizational governance	34	0.03	0	1
Human rights	22	0.02	0	1
Labor practices	40	0.04	0	1
Environment	42	0.04	0	1
Community development and engagement	61	0.06	0	1
Consumer issues and product responsibility	49	0.05	0	1
Fair operating practices	9	0.01	0	1
Others	164	0.16	0	1
CSR broad topic	579	0.58	0	1
Events	59	0.07	0	1
News	196	0.23	0	1
Announcements	219	0.26	0	1
Education messages	147	0.17	0	1
Annual reports	18	0.02	0	1
Achievements	36	0.04	0	1
Opinions/testimonials	107	0.13	0	1
Acknowledgments	12	0.01	0	1
Partnerships	20	0.02	0	1
Chats	15	0.02	0	1
Marketing	22	0.03	0	1

Tweet topic	Example
Organizational Governance	
Human rights	RT @amolmehra: Ruggie urges #business leaders #SDGs to do more than #CSR – focus on #humanrights in own operations #bizhumanright
Labor practices	RT @ Causecast: Ensure your #EmployeeGiving #CSR programs are keeping pace w/ industry trends. Join AmerCharities â€¦ https://t.co/L2zUt5i7VI
Environment	U.S. files civil lawsuit against Volkswagen for environment violations https://t.co/fNB6m7oRiI #corpgov #csr
Community development and engagement	.@KeyBank provides $28.67M investment to affordable housing development for seniors in St. Lawrence County https://t.co/2UuspyRcRy #CSR
Consumer issues and product responsibility	RT @ greeneconpost: Monsanto, Novozymes Product Increases Crop Yields Using Microbes https://t.co/T70iZHEm0dÂ #sustainability #csr

Tweet topic	Example
Fair operating practices	*RT @CSRCommunicator:. @thomaskolster We need more responsible #supplychain stories which are engaging, actionable, and simple*
Others	*RT @ jobofthehut: #Call Center #LasVegas – #CSR #LasVegas #NV Apply: https://t.co/y6kZdA9adp*
CSR broad topic	*Just a fifth of companies believe that their impacts are understood https://t.co/gp4UgAx4pr via CCitizenship #CSR #sustainability*
Events	*Trends in #CSR plus #sustainability careers. Excellent panel! EVENT: 3/16 #NYC REGISTER HERE: https://t.co/uc5V21ToUD via @cbsacny $20*
News	*All @MillerCoors Major Breweries Reach Landfill-Free Milestone: https://t.co/ilUSStXw7Z #CSR https://t.co/9DEROQkjGE*
Announcements	*RT @CaelusGreenRoom: Inspiring Future Engineers – #green #sustainability #csr https://t.co/38qveIwLa6*
Educational messages	*7 benefits of integrated thinking #CSR #sustainability #sharedvalue thanks @TriplePundit https://t.co/ydObsmBQ7F*
Annual reports	*U.S. Chamber Foundation Issues New Report on the Business Value of Circular Economy https://t.co/U726tvblck #csr*
Achievements	*@Humana named No. 1 U.S. #HealthCare Company for #CSR Efforts by @RobecoSAM https://t.co/Z3lLD8168F #HUMemployee https://t.co/TaDHI8KdtF*
Opinions/testimonials	*RT @bpowernyc:Well said @frankirmser "Equity is so much a part of #SocialResponsibility" #NYUSRS #CSR*
Acknowledgments	*RT @ GlueTalk: CSR_RT Thank you for sharing! #CSR*
Partnerships	*RT @Justmeans:. @vitalvoices & @BankofAmerica partner to host #Women, Progress and the Global Economy https://t.co/faaZykM2oh #CSR #socent*
Chats	*RT @GreatPositive:Take a coffee break with us & @causeartist next week for a tweet chat on #csr #socent #nonprofits #socialgood*
Marketing	*RT @ CrediblyGreen: Our clients value #CrediblyGreen as a means of quantifying #CSR, monitoring business performance https://t.co/CpEY7bVkhq*

Appendix 5 – Social media concepts descriptive statistics table and examples

Table 4.1.7 and 4.1.8 Social media concepts descriptive Statistics table and example

Type of social media concept	Count	Mean	Min.	Max
Dialogue/engagement	44	0.04	0	1
Transparency	552	0.44	0	1
Authenticity	153	0.12	0	1
Influence	267	0.21	0	1
Positive	102	0.38	0	1
Neutral	155	0.58	0	1
Negative	7	0.04	0	1
Mobilization	101	0.08	0	1
Like, share, retweet	10	0.10	0	1
Learning	52	0.51	0	1
Participation	32	0.32	0	1
Others (marketing, donations)	7	0.07	0	1
Persuasion (two-way asymmetrical com)	17	0.01	0	1
Disclosure	114	0.09	0	1

Type of social media concept	Example
Dialogue/engagement	*@jododds @Engage4Success do you think sustainability makes employees more entrepreneurial? https://t.co/kSlAv4iCu7 #EmployeeEngagement #CSR*
Transparency	*RT @AAInsights: AccountAbility Releases Global Standard in Stakeholder Engagement #AA1000SES #CSR #sustainability https://t.co/HbsBP8eJKY*
Authenticity	*Great to hear all about the benefits of @TradingforGood this morning @ StaffsChambers #Staffordshire businesses – Get Involved! #CSR*
Influence	*#NAPWsummit2015 when you educate a community you educate the world @ StarJonesEsq about #girlsinc #diversity #CSR https://t.co/6emc8hvVEN*
Positive	*#Heineken USA embraces #sustainability to brew a better world https://t.co/kGF2QHGZem #CSR #SocialEntrepreneurship https://t.co/MMoNF9EYdg*
Neutral	*What happens when you combine #EmergingMarkets, #innovation & #CSR. How @Uber's competitor in India broke the mould.https://t.co/IJ7AW4WbFY*
Negative	*@DrNicholasLord RT AU bank $CBA CEO Ian Narev behind $8.2 billion banking fraud https://t.co/GmKePj5taq #CSR*
Mobilization	*RT @CSRwire: Find out how @Cigna is improving affordability and lowering costs of #health care. Read the 2014 #CSR Report https://t.co/FguVâ*

Type of social media concept	Example
Like, share, retweet	*RT @ blogaffinity: Share your #CSR story without bragging too much: https://t. co/7ANVMCzsEk*
Learning	*RT @WhitbreadPLC: Our latest #CSR report highlights continued progress towards our 2020 #targets. Find out more https://t.co/p46s6ARW50*
Participation	*RT @Sust_Train: Join the COP21 Conversation at #GoParis! via @ triplepundit https://t.co/1DESiFHY4F #sustainability #csr*
Others (marketing, donations)	*RT @ RubenBrunsveld: Join me in our #leadership and #csr training for #asia. Application now open! https://t.co/6IpyXxx4eCÂ*
Persuasion (two-way asymmetrical com)	*RT @ TriplePundit: If your business is looking for #branding insights, this video with ALongsworth. https://t.co/LQXujiGoiqÂ Earth2017*
Disclosure	*Why #Yemen Under Attack by #Saudi?#KSA#csr#LabaykYaHussain#foodsecu rity#hrc23#ibelong#onu#al_saud_crimes#UN*

4.2 Effectiveness and accountability of digital CSR communication

A contingency model

Shuili Du and Kun Yu

Digital corporate social responsibility (CSR) communication, referring to a firm's utilization of Internet and social media technologies to communicate its CSR activities to various stakeholders, is rapidly gaining popularity, with a growing number of forward-looking companies actively utilizing digital platforms, such as corporate websites, Facebook, Twitter, YouTube, Instagram, and so on, to communicate their CSR activities and performance to stakeholders. As an example, Proctor & Gamble not only comprehensively presents its corporate sustainability report on the corporate website (us.pg.com/sustainability), but also communicates its various sustainability initiatives to its stakeholders using social media platforms including Facebook, Twitter, LinkedIn, YouTube, and Instagram. Similarly, in addition to using a variety of social media channels, General Electric has a dedicated website, www.gesustainability.com, aimed at boosting communication with its stakeholders on issues related to human rights, community work, environment, and corporate governance.

However, little is known about the effectiveness and accountability of digital CSR communication (Korschun and Du 2013; Peloza et al. 2012). This chapter seeks to advance current knowledge on this important topic by addressing the following key questions. First, what are the unique, fundamental characteristics of digital CSR communication? What are different types of digital CSR communication commonly used by firms? Second, what are key methods for enhancing the effectiveness of such communication? And third, how could firms assess the effectiveness and accountability of digital CSR communication? What are the key metrics that firms should monitor and track in order to assess the effects of their digital CSR communication? In addressing these important questions, this chapter synthesizes different streams of literature on CSR, institutional legitimacy, digital communication, and accountability and offers a conceptual framework (see Figure 4.2.1) for better understanding the effectiveness and accountability of digital CSR communication. In a nutshell, our model suggests that the ability of digital CSR communication in generating positive business outcomes is contingent on the effectiveness of such communication. We first review key characteristics and types of digital CSR communication, then discuss various methods for enhancing communication effectiveness, followed by a section on assessment metrics companies could use to gauge the effectiveness and accountability of their digital CSR communication efforts.

Digital CSR communication: key characteristics and types

CSR, a firm's commitment to maximize long-term economic, societal and environmental well-being through business practices, policies and resources (Kotler and Lee 2005), is a

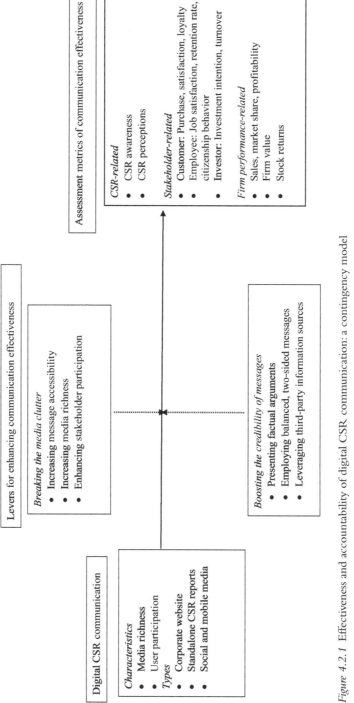

Figure 4.2.1 Effectiveness and accountability of digital CSR communication: a contingency model

strategic imperative in today's socially conscious world. Companies, such as Procter & Gamble and Unilever, that envision CSR as an integral part of their business strategy are at the forefront of the global tilt towards sustainable business (GlobeScan/SustainAbility 2014). A vast body of research has documented the numerous business benefits that accrue to companies engaging in socially responsible business practices. Socially responsible firms generate more favorable stakeholder reactions such as greater purchase (Brown and Dacin 1997; Sen and Bhattacharya 2001), higher employment likelihood (Du et al. 2015), more investments and lower cost of equity capital (Dhaliwal et al. 2011). Over the long term, socially responsible firms enjoy great corporate reputation and higher stakeholder trust and loyalty (Sen et al. 2016). However, for companies to reap these coveted business benefits, they need to communicate their CSR-related efforts and achievements to their stakeholders. Indeed, more and more companies are communicating their CSR efforts and performance, particularly through various digital platforms (Cone 2015; Du and Vieira 2012). Most prior research has focused on CSR communication on traditional media (e.g., company-centric, one-way messages on TV, print ads; Wagner et al. 2009; Yoon et al. 2006). On the other hand, digital CSR communication, due to its ability to accommodate rich, multimedia technologies and stakeholder participation, allowing two-way and even multi-way conversation, can enhance communication effectiveness. This chapter focuses on digital CSR communication, not CSR communication on traditional media, due to the increasing importance of the former, as well as the lack of research on this topic.

CSR communication on various digital platforms (e.g., corporate websites, Facebook, Twitter, Instagram) has grown dramatically. The increasing popularity of the Internet and social media is transforming the way companies interact with their stakeholders. Across the globe, there are over 3 billion active Internet users and over 2 billion active social media accounts (Kemp 2015). A recent industry survey conducted by Social Media Examiner (2014) shows that a significant 92% of marketers indicate that social media is important for their business, up from 86% in 2013. Not surprisingly, companies are actively utilizing these Internet and social media platforms to communicate their CSR efforts to stakeholders. According to the latest study by Cone (2015), Internet and social media channels have become one of the most important sources of CSR information; stakeholders are leveraging various digital technologies to learn about and share information about specific companies' CSR initiatives and even contribute directly to a social effort led by a company (e.g., pledge, volunteer, donate). These digital media, due to their unique characteristics, have dramatically altered the media landscape facing companies that seek to communicate their CSR information to stakeholders.

Key characteristics of digital CSR communication

Digital CSR communication is different from CSR communication via traditional media because the former involves the active and purposeful utilization of advanced web technologies and Web 2.0 platforms such as social networking sites (e.g., Facebook, LinkedIn), media sharing sites (e.g., YouTube, Instagram), and sharing sites (e.g., user-sponsored or company-sponsored blogs). While the traditional media are primarily characterized by the company-centric, one-way conversation, digital CSR communication offers stakeholders the opportunity to engage in two-way conversation with the company as well as with other stakeholders (Kaplan and Haenlein 2010). Specifically, two key features of digital media technologies, media richness and user participation, are particularly relevant for CSR communication (Kaplan and Haenlein 2010; Korschun and Du 2013; Mangold and Faulds 2009).

Media richness

Internet and social media technologies enable companies to use a variety of multimedia techniques when communicating their CSR activities, enhancing the media richness of digital CSR communication. According to media richness theory (Daft & Lengel, 1986), utilization of various multimedia technologies (e.g., text, videos, graphics, animation) raises the media richness of information and enhances the effectiveness of communication. "Rich" media are not only vivid and attention-grabbing but also more effective in the transmission of highly complex information (Kaplan & Haenlein, 2010; Vickery et al. 2004). Since CSR information tends to be complex due to its multi-faceted and long-term-oriented nature (e.g., impact on environment and community, changes in stakeholder welfare; Du et al. 2010), rich media are particularly suited for communication of such information. It is worth pointing out that different types of digital CSR communication vary in terms of media richness; for example, communicating CSR via corporate blogs is generally low in media richness, while communicating CSR via a company's official YouTube channel or Instagram site is likely to be high in media richness.

User participation

Digital CSR communication provides greater opportunity for stakeholders (e.g., consumers, employees, community members, NGOs) to participate in two-way stakeholder-company, and multiple-way stakeholder-stakeholder conversation. User-generated content is the hallmark of social media platforms; through user-generated content, stakeholders are no longer passive recipients of information initiated by companies but actively engage in conversations with the company and peers. On social media platforms (e.g., Facebook, YouTube, Twitter, and Instagram), content is not single-handedly created by companies, but instead could be modified and shaped by users in a participatory and collaborative fashion. To illustrate, on a company's Facebook page, stakeholders could like, share, or comment on the company's postings; similarly, on a company's Twitter account, stakeholders could like, retweet, share, or reply to the company's tweets. Research suggests that stakeholders are not content being passive recipients of CSR messages, but instead desire to be enactors and enablers of CSR activities (Bhattacharya et al. 2010). Digital CSR communication allows stakeholders to actively participate in CSR communication and get their voices heard. Different digital communication platforms vary in the level of user participation, or the amount of user generated content it accommodates. For example, blogs and collaborative projects tend to be high in user generated content, whereas corporate websites tend to be low in user generated content (Korschun and Du 2013).

Different types of digital CSR communication

There are different types of digital CSR communication. Some commonly employed types include (a) CSR information disclosure on corporate websites, (b) standalone CSR reports available digitally through a link on corporate websites, and (c) CSR communication using social media and mobile platforms. In general, firms need to consider a variety of digital communication media and employ a portfolio approach, using multiple types of digital CSR communication to reach various stakeholders and convey CSR messages that vary in depth and breadth.

CSR disclosure on corporate websites

CSR communication through corporate websites has become increasingly widespread and popular (Du and Vieira 2012; Maignan & Ralston, 2002; Moreno & Capriotti, 2009). According to Esrock and Leichty (2000), 85% of the Fortune 500 address CSR issues on their websites. Large scale studies conducted by KPMG (2013) and Cone (2015) also indicate that a majority of companies utilize their corporate websites to communicate CSR information. In particular, research suggests that the likelihood of CSR communication on corporate websites increases as the firm size increases (Branco and Rodrigues 2008).

Compared to traditional media, corporate websites allow a company to comprehensively communicate CSR information in a way that is less expensive and faster, as well as being available 24 hours a day and 7 days a week. Furthermore, research suggests that the target audiences of corporate websites are more active in how they seek and process information than the more passive publics who are reached via traditional mass media (Esrock & Leichty, 1998). Finally, those web audiences tend to come from a variety of stakeholder groups, including customers, employees, government officials, news media, and issue activists (Lee et al. 2009); thus, a company can reach a diverse set of stakeholders with its corporate website. Due to the above characteristics, companies consider corporate websites to be an important platform for CSR communication (Wanderley et al. 2008).

Standalone CSR report available digitally through a link on corporate websites

Standalone CSR reports, often available in pdf format via a hyperlink on corporate websites, are rapidly gaining momentum (Dhaliwal et al. 2011; Dhaliwal et al. 2012; Perrini 2006; Tschopp and Huefner 2015). Research by KPMG (2013) shows that, of the 4,100 companies surveyed globally, 71% engage in CSR reporting. Standalone CSR reports provide the most comprehensive content of a firm's CSR activities and performance, containing a much higher level of details relative to other forms of CSR communication (e.g., CSR advertising, press releases, corporate websites; Perrini 2006). For instance, Intel's 2014 Corporate Social Responsibility Report, published in May 2015, has 116 pages, containing six main chapters, which detail not only Intel's strategic approach to CSR initiatives and corporate governance structure but also the company's programs and performance in taking care of its key stakeholders (e.g., employees, the environment, communities, and supply chain partners). The Intel report follows the Global Reporting Initiatives (GRI) G4 Sustainability Reporting Guidelines, covers numerous specific social and environmental initiatives, performance statistics and trends, graphs, and case studies, and importantly, was reviewed and assured by an independent accountant, Ernst & Young LLP.

Stakeholders such as socially responsible investment (SRI) fund managers and institutional investors prefer standalone CSR reports because these reports systematically and comprehensively communicate a firm's CSR performance. Research by Ernst & Young and Boston College (2013) shows that firms publish standalone CSR reports to cater to the demand for increasing amounts of social and environmental data from not only (SRI) funds, but also mainstream investors and large institutional investors. Dhaliwal et al. (2011, 2012) find that CSR reports help reduce information symmetry between the firm and its investors, lowering the cost of equity capital and increasing analyst forecasting accuracy.

CSR communication on social media and mobile platforms

For stakeholders such as consumers and employees, CSR communication on social media and mobile platforms is likely to be more effective (Cone 2015; Du et al. 2010). CSR messages on social and mobile media tend to be concrete and engaging (e.g., utilizing multimedia technologies), and conveyed in a way to which individual stakeholders could relate. On social and mobile media, firms' complex CSR strategies and data have often been distilled into bite-sized, meaningful content to which stakeholders could relate. CSR communication on social and mobile platforms often take place via firm's official (a) social networking sites such as Facebook, LinkedIn, (b) media sharing sites such as YouTube channel, Instagram, Flickr, and (c) thought sharing sites such as corporate blog or Twitter. To illustrate, Proctor & Gamble uses its Facebook page, which has over 5 million likes, to communicate its various social initiatives, such as its global clean water initiatives and its efforts to celebrate and support women and girls. Being the corporate partner of "Love Has No Label," an award-winning community activism campaign, the company posted a "Love Has No Label" video, which has gathered 1.69 million views, testifying to the enormous reach of social media. Dove, a personal care brand, has a signature Real Beauty campaign, which celebrates the natural physical variation embodied by all women and inspires them to be confident in themselves. To spread the positive message of real beauty, Dove leverages the YouTube channel to present a series of profoundly touching videos. By September 2016, Dove's "Real Beauty Sketch" video has been viewed more than 67 million times on YouTube since its debut in April 2013, and another Dove film "Choose Beautiful," released in April 2015, has over 7.6 million views.

CSR communication on mobile platform is of increasing importance due to the ubiquitous existence and explosive usage of mobile devices (e.g., smartphones and tablets). Forward-looking companies are using mobile technologies to spread the message about their CSR initiatives and engage with their consumers. Chipotle Mexican Grill, a global fast-food restaurant specializing in burritos and tacos, communicates its social values and CSR engagement not only on social media (e.g., Facebook, YouTube), but also through smartphone apps and a mobile game. The company's "Scarecrow" video, which criticizes the conventional, large-scale industrial production method of food, has garnered over 15 million views on YouTube. Furthermore, the company seeks to increase consumer awareness of and support for social issues (i.e., supporting real and healthier food) through the "Scarecrow" mobile game, where consumers go on a journey to bring real food back to people. As Chipotle's spokeswomen stated, "A mobile game is also a way to engage and entertain people, making them curious about Chipotle while also teaching them where their food comes from and why that's important" (QSR Magazine 2013).

Importantly, social media also constitutes valuable, and perhaps more effective, platforms to address CSR-related problems and crises due to its ability to engage stakeholders in the conversation. Reacting to its food contamination crisis in 2015, Chipotle used Facebook, among other platforms, to post messages about how the company is taking various measures to increase food safety. For example, its 16 January 2015 Facebook post displayed a personal statement from its founder Steve Ells, "As a chef, nothing is more important to me than serving my guests food that is safe, delicious, and wholesome," and included a letter from the founder where Chipotle laid out its comprehensive food safety plan. The company followed up with additional posts to communicate its determinations and actions to increase food safety (e.g., its 8 Februrary 2016 post announced that the company was having a national employee meeting to discuss food safety changes it has deployed and talk about additional steps they are taking for the future; and its spokesperson on Facebook replied to individual consumers' food safety concerns). Chipotle's communication efforts on Facebook seem to be well received, with these posts generating thousands of likes, shares, and positive comments from its customers (e.g., one customer stated, "I applaud your efforts. . . . You've handled everything with humility, and the public's interests have always come first").

Levers for enhancing the effectiveness of digital CSR communication

Not all CSR communication is created equal (Dawkins 2004; Du et al. 2010). Prior research suggests that firms face two key challenges in communicating their CSR messages to stakeholders. First, in today's era of information overload, managers need to make CSR messages easily accessible, attention-grabbing, and engaging to break the media clutter, so that stakeholders have the opportunity to process a firm's CSR messages. Second, stakeholders do not always accept CSR messages at face value, instead, they may doubt the credibility of such messages. Research shows that stakeholders are often skeptical of firm's motivation for engaging in social initiatives (Sen et al. 2016) or doubt the truthfulness of the messages (e.g., greenwashing; Parguel, Benoît-moreau, and Larceneux, 2011). Therefore, to increase the overall effectiveness of digital CSR communication, firms need to break the media clutter to engage their targeted stakeholders, and enhance the perceived credibility of their CSR messages. Next we talk about ways to effectively break the media clutter, followed by ways to enhance perceived credibility of CSR communication.

Breaking the media clutter

Increasing the accessibility of CSR messages

It is important to increase the accessibility of CSR messages on digital platforms so that it is easy for stakeholders to obtain and locate the information. Accessibility, referring to how easy it is for stakeholders to locate or access CSR related information on digital media platforms, is an important mechanism to break the media clutter (Du and Vieira 2012). On corporate websites, hierarchization is an effective way to organize information, with the most general or important topics on the main page and then moving towards more specific and detailed sub-topics via hyperlinks. Thus, for CSR communication on corporate websites, prominently featuring CSR-related headlines or CSR/sustainability-related sections on the main pages of corporate websites enhances the accessibility of CSR messages (Du and Vieira 2012).

With regard to standalone CSR reports, a good practice is to first issue a press release announcing the issuance of the company's annual CSR report. Circulating the press release to websites specialized in CSR communication (e.g., www.csrwire.com, www.corporateregister.com, www.prweb.com) as well as the general business websites (e.g., www.reuters.com, www.businesswire.com) serves to significantly increase the accessibility a firm's CSR report, leading to greater awareness of this important event among key stakeholder groups (e.g., the media, business partners, institutional investors). To increase accessibility of such reports among consumers, companies could use social media, such as Twitter and Facebook, to announce the availability of their CSR reports and provide hyperlinks for download. Importantly, the company should include news about the release of its CSR report in the newsroom section or investor relations section of its corporate website to make it widely accessible to the visitors of its website. A digital copy of the annual CSR report in its entirety should be made publicly available and easy to find on its corporate website as well, so that interested parties or individuals could download the report and read it carefully.

For CSR messages on social/mobile media, due to the way messages/posts are organized (e.g., latest messages and stories appear at the top of the page), it is important for a company to regularly update the content of its communication by posting new CSR messages and feeds, adding new videos and stories. This way, relevant CSR messages will stay on the top page and are more likely to be noticed and processed by stakeholders.

Increasing media richness

Rich media are more effective for CSR communication because they are not only attention grabbing but also entertaining and engaging; thus all else equal, individuals have greater motivation to process the targeted message if presented via rich media. Rich media are capable of transmitting both formal and informal cues rapidly and effectively and reducing uncertainty and ambiguity (Daft and Lengel 1986; Vickery et al. 2004). Vickery et al. (2004) find that, in a business-to-business service environment characterized by complexity and uncertainty, media richness has a positive impact on relational performance and customer satisfaction and loyalty. Media richness is a particularly pertinent issue for CSR communication, because relative to non-CSR, product-related information, CSR information is often value-laden and highly complex (Dawkins 2004; Korschun and Du 2013), thus necessitating rich communication media to convey complex messages through the usage of compelling images, text, and audio and video files. Rich media enhance stakeholders' motivation and ability to process the CSR messages.

To enhance media richness of digital CSR communication, managers should supplement textual information with highly engaging, vivid graphics, videos, and games. Internet and social media platforms can easily accommodate pictures, graphs, and videos. Leveraging rich media such as establishing a YouTube channel or an Instagram page and embedding videos and pictures on corporate websites, corporate blogs, and Twitter pages are great ways to attract and engage stakeholders.

One unique way of employing rich media is to present individual stories or case studies of a company's social involvement in the format of an interview or embedded video. CSR stories are easy to absorb and memorable. In contrast to "hard," fact-based presentations of CSR information, these "soft," personal stories put a "human face" on CSR activities, and thus are effective in capturing audience attention, as well as in conveying, vividly and concretely, the societal impact of their CSR initiatives (Du and Vieira 2012; Henderson & Kitzinger, 1999). Furthermore, relative to argument-based advertising, narrative- or drama-based advertising (i.e., story-based communication) reduces counterargument and is processed empathically, resulting in greater persuasion effectiveness (Deighton et al. 1989).

Therefore, to enhance communication effectiveness, in addition to presenting statistics or textual information on CSR initiatives, firms can present an in-depth story or interview featuring beneficiaries of a specific initiative, illustrating the social impact from the personal perspective of beneficiaries. Such a personal angle adds depth and meaningful content to which stakeholders can relate (Escalas 2004; van Laer and de Ruyter 2010).

Increasing stakeholder participation in CSR communication

Research shows that stakeholders, particularly primary stakeholders such as customers and employees, want to be involved in co-creating social initiatives with corporate decision-makers (Bhattacharya et al. 2010). Digital platforms, facilitated by technological drivers (e.g., increased broadband availability and hardware capacity, and greater availability of tools), allow users to engage in a variety of two-way or multi-way dialogs and value co-creation activities (Kaplan and Haenlein 2010), enabling users to contribute their expertise/knowledge, voice their opinions, share information with peers, and so on (Chakravorti 2010). The participatory and collaborative nature of social media-based communication turns stakeholders from passive recipients of information to enablers and enactors of CSR communication. The greater the level of stakeholder participation in digital CSR communication, the more likely they are to have a close connection with the company's CSR initiatives and identify with the firm and its social initiatives (Bhattacharya et al. 2010; Korschun and Du 2013).

Using social media and mobile technologies, firms could initiate dialogues with stakeholders and incorporates representative stakeholder input as early as possible in the formulation and implementation process of a CSR initiative. To illustrate, Starbucks has been empowering stakeholders to co-create its social initiatives through the digital platform: www.mystarbucksidea.com, where individuals propose ideas on social initiatives the company could embark on, such as increasing in-store recycling and more fair trade and non-GMO options. By engaging stakeholders in a two-way conversation, companies not only harness their knowledge and expertise but also create a highly attentive audience who is familiar with the company's CSR initiatives and act as company/brand ambassadors spreading word of mouth, both online and offline, about its CSR to peer stakeholders.

Boosting credibility of CSR messages

Research has shown that stakeholders tend to be skeptical of companies' CSR claims (Du et al. 2010; Sheehan and Atkinson 2012). While stakeholders want to know about companies' social initiatives (Cone 2015), they also easily become leery of the CSR motives when companies aggressively promote their CSR efforts (Yoon et al. 2006). Indeed, many consumers consider that companies engage in CSR communication mainly for image management and self-serving reasons – a practice often referred to as *greenwashing* (Parguel, Benoît-moreau, and Larceneux, 2011). There are several ways that firms could use to boost the credibility of CSR messages, including using factual arguments, using balanced, two-sided messages, and leveraging third-party information sources.

Presenting factual arguments

To raise the credibility of CSR messages, companies need to be factual and emphasize key information (e.g., the level of CSR investment, the importance of the issues, and the societal impact of their CSR programs) in a straightforward and engaging way (Du et al. 2010). Credible CSR messages are often characterized by factual arguments on central aspects of a company's CSR engagement, particularly factual information (e.g., statistics, trends, key performance indicators, etc.) about the level of its CSR commitment and the societal impact of its CSR initiatives (Bhattacharya and Sen 2004). Factual information presents central cues about a company's social involvement and is hard to counter-argue.

Of course, the factual information should be presented through rich media utilizing pictures, graphs, tables, and should be supplemented with in-depth individual stories or case studies. In particular, for stakeholder groups such as investors, financial analysts, and business partners, factual data allow them to conduct in-depth analysis based on credible objective evidence and incorporate such data in their quantitative investment and decision models. For stakeholder groups including consumers, employees, and local communities, showcasing awards and certificates that a company has won is a highly effective way to increase the credibility of its CSR messages.

Using balanced, two-sided messages

In contrast to one-sided messages containing only positive information about the company, two-sided messages include both positive and negative information. CSR performance is complex, pertaining to multiple social, environmental, and governance domains (e.g., product safety, employee interests, environment, and community involvement); thus, it is not uncommon to occasionally witness negative behaviors or accidents by even good corporate citizens (Klein and Dawar 2004). For example, Chipotle positions its brand as organic and healthy (i.e., Food with Integrity); yet in 2015, it encountered a severe food contamination crisis. Such negative accidents or inconsistent CSR behaviors could trigger perceptions of corporate hypocrisy (Wagner et al. 2009) and greenwashing (Parguel et al, 2011). Rather than communicating a "perfect CSR record," companies need to acknowledge the negative aspects of their CSR performance (Hahn and Lülfs 2014) and demonstrate the progress they have made over the years. Research has found that including negative or qualifying information about a brand can be more effective than a one-sided message, where only positive information is presented (Pechmann, 1992). Two-sided messages can enhance message credibility, leading the receiver of the message to conclude that the company is "telling the truth" and are thus more effective than one-sided messages (Crowley & Hoyer 1994; Hahn and Lülfs 2014). On the Internet and social media, information (both positive and negative) is only clicks away; thus, transparency and taking responsibility for negative accidents, if any, is likely to help a company establish an honest and trustworthy corporate reputation.

Leveraging third party information sources

CSR communication originating from individual stakeholders, non-profit partners, and other third party sources is likely to have higher perceived credibility relative to that from the corporate sources (Sen et al. 2016; Yoon et al. 2006). Accordingly, managers should find ways to mobilize stakeholders to spread CSR messages. For example, sending press releases to various media outlets, communicating with CSR rating agencies, and recruiting individual stakeholders (e.g., opinion leaders among consumers and employees) to be ambassadors of a company's social cause are effective methods to mobilize different stakeholder groups to communicate the company's CSR initiatives. Such communication, coming from non-corporate, third-party sources, will be perceived as more credible. Social media and mobile platforms, due to their participatory features and focus on user-generated content, are particularly suited for stakeholders-initiated CSR communication.

For certain types of CSR communication, such as standalone CSR reports, companies could boost their credibility by following prominent reporting guidelines (e.g., GRI framework) and obtaining external assurance from auditing firms. In fact, an increasing number of CSR reporting firms adopt the GRI framework and receive external assurance (Junior, Best, and Cotter 2014).

Assessment metrics of digital CSR communications effectiveness

Systematic assessment is critical in ensuring the effectiveness and accountability of digital CSR communication. The familiar adage "you can't manage what you can't measure" certainly applies to digital CSR communication. It is imperative for managers to quantify and calibrate the outcomes of CSR communication endeavors, and leverage the findings to continuously improve and optimize digital CSR communication efforts. Assessment metrics should include both CSR-related outcomes, such as stakeholder awareness and perceptions of a firm's CSR initiatives, and business-related outcomes, such as customer loyalty, employee satisfaction, sales, and overall firm value. Notice that this chapter is about digital CSR *communication* and the effects of such communication on stakeholders and the firm; thus, metrics related to corporate social performance (CSP) are beyond the scope of this chapter, as CSP is mostly determined by a firm's CSR investment and CSR strategy. Further, there already exist various third-party metrics and rankings of CSP, such as those provided by KLD, *Fortune*, *Newsweek*, and others.

We turn to research on institutional legitimacy (Palazzo & Scherer 2006, Suchman 1995) as the theoretical lens through which to identify appropriate assessment metrics. Legitimacy, defined as "a generalized perception or assumption that the actions of an entity are desirable, proper, or appropriate within some socially constructed system of norms, values, beliefs, and definitions" (Suchman, 1995, p. 574), is vital for a company's survival and success because it ensures the continuous flow of resources and the sustained support by stakeholders (Palazzo & Scherer, 2006). Digital CSR communication helps a firm gain legitimacy, because it informs stakeholders of the firm's social initiatives that contribute to the long-term economic, social, and environmental well-being. Through CSR actions, a company enacts and upholds the socio-cultural norms in its institutional environment and attains organizational legitimacy (Handelman & Arnold, 1999; Palazzo & Scherer, 2006). Digital CSR communication, by reducing information asymmetry between the firm and its stakeholders, helps the firm establish legitimacy in the business environment. More specifically, digital CSR communication will (a) shape stakeholders' awareness and knowledge of the firm's CSR engagement, consequently (b) generate positive stakeholder reactions to the firm, and in turn, (c) result in more favorable firm performance. Therefore, we look at three types of assessment metrics, CSR-related, stakeholder-related, and firm performance-related in gauging the effectiveness and accountability of digital CSR communication.

CSR-related metrics

CSR awareness measures the level of general awareness and basic knowledge of a company's CSR initiatives among its stakeholders. In general, stakeholder awareness of firms' CSR activities tends to be low, pointing to the inadequacy of CSR communication or lack of effectiveness of such communication (Bhattacharya et al. 2010; Peloza et al. 2012). Most stakeholders would not actively seek CSR information about a firm, and they do not tend to pay attention to a firm's CSR communication. Thus increasing the effectiveness of digital CSR communication by employing various techniques outlined in the previous section is extremely important. Assessing CSR awareness longitudinally, through a large-scale survey method, enables managers to have a general sense of the effectiveness of the company's digital CSR communication.

Beyond simple awareness, CSR perceptions measure stakeholders' beliefs and evaluations about a firm's CSR, including CSR attributions (i.e., perceived motives of why the firm is supporting a social cause; Sen et al. 2006), CSR fit (i.e., perceived congruence between the firm and its CSR initiative; Zdravkovic, Magnusson, and Stanley 2010), and CSR efficacy (i.e., the extent to which the firm is effective in addressing the focal social issue; Du et al. 2011; Sen et al. 2016), as well as the general evaluations of the firm's CSR reputation. Firms will reap a range of business benefits when stakeholders hold favorable CSR perceptions, such as when stakeholders believe that a firm has intrinsic motives for its CSR initiatives (i.e., genuinely care about societal welfare), is efficacious in improving societal/environmental welfare, and overall has a favorable CSR reputation. Assessing these different facets of stakeholder CSR perceptions using the formats of focus group studies or large-scale surveys would enable the firms to identify potential weaknesses and gaps in their digital CSR communication.

Stakeholder-related metrics

High CSR awareness and favorable CSR perceptions help a firm achieve institutional legitimacy and generate a range of positive stakeholder reactions to the firm. Prior CSR research has documented that, when informed of a firm's socially responsible activities, consumers are likely to form positive product evaluations (Brown and Dacin 1997; Sen and Bhattacharya 2001), have higher purchase intention and customer satisfaction (Luo and Bhattacharya 2006), and be more loyal and more willing to spread positive word of mouth (Sen et al. 2016). Similarly, employees who are aware of their company's CSR initiatives report higher levels of job satisfaction and lower turnover intention, and they are more likely to engage in citizenship behaviors (Du et al. 2015; Greening and Turban 2000). For investors, similar positive effects of CSR communication have been documented (Cone 2015; Dhaliwal et al. 2011; Maignan and Ferrell 2004; Hill et al. 2007).

Accordingly, companies are well advised to monitor metrics on these stakeholder-related business outcomes to ensure that the firms are indeed reaping business benefits as the result of their digital CSR communication. In the consumption domain, managers could assess customer purchase, satisfaction, and loyalty. In the employment domain, they could measure employee job satisfaction, retention rate, and employee citizenship behaviors. In the investment domain, managers could monitor investor intention and turnover (Maignan and Ferrell 2004; Hill et al. 2007), as well as monitoring the breakdown of investor types (e.g., percentage of institutional investors or SRI investors).

Firm performance-related metrics

There has been lots of research examining the relationship between corporate social performance (CSP) and corporate financial performance (CFP; Margolis and Walsh 2003). The CSP-CFP link has been shown to be highly mixed, contingent on a variety of factors. In particular, CSR communication has been shown to be a critical lever that could strengthen the CSP-CFP link (Du et al. 2011; Servaes and Tamayo 2013). Managers need to monitor the effects of digital CSR communication on firm performance, and in particular the CSP-CFP relationship. Relevant firm performance metrics include total sales, market share, financial profitability (e.g., return on assets, return on equity, earnings per share), firm value, and stock returns. Internal and external secondary data sources should also be utilized to acquire information on sales, market share, profitability, and stock prices.

Collecting quantitative data on a variety of metrics outlined in this section would enable the firm to conduct detailed analyses and identify trends, patterns, and performance gaps. These results can be used to understand how variables in our framework (i.e., Figure 4.2.1) relate to each other, and shed light on the effectiveness of digital CSR communication. Tracking the utilization of various digital communication tactics and assessing their effectiveness is important for managers to understand what works and what does not work. Through systematic assessment of metrics, managers will be able to identify the most effective digital communication platforms and techniques that deliver maximal value for the firm.

Conclusions

Given the prominence of Internet and social media technologies, digital CSR communication has gained significant traction and is of increasing importance to firms seeking to reap business benefits from their CSR investment. In contrast to conventional, non-digital CSR communication (e.g., point-of-purchase display, print and TV advertising), communication on digital platforms possesses certain unique features, such as greater media richness and greater level of user participation. We provide an in-depth discussion of the unique characteristics and common types of digital CSR communication, an array of techniques managers could employ to enhance the effectiveness of such communication, and, importantly, metrics for managers to comprehensively and systematically assess the accountability of digital CSR communication.

This chapter highlights the importance of using rich media, encouraging interactivity and active participation by stakeholders in digital CSR communication. Companies should proactively engage stakeholders in the communication process and utilize this opportunity to co-create CSR initiatives (e.g., soliciting stakeholder input and spurring positive word of mouth). Furthermore, we take a contingent view of the effectiveness of digital CSR communication; the effectiveness of such communication in generating coveted business outcomes will depend on a variety of factors, including accessibility of CSR message, media richness, level of stakeholder participation, and importantly, perceived credibility of CSR messages.

The accountability of digital CSR communication is a critical issue in CSR management. This chapter outlines several CSR-related, stakeholder-related, and firm performance-related metrics that managers should monitor to gauge the accountability of digital CSR communication on a continuous basis. By assessing a variety of metrics, managers will be able to empirically establish whether, when, and how digital CSR communication efforts are generating value. This process will enable managers to focus on key communication drivers of business value and leverage factors and techniques that are most effective for their firms in generating coveted business benefits.

References

Bhattacharya, C. B., Sankar Sen, and Daniel Korschun (2010), *Leveraging Corporate Responsibility: The Stakeholder Route to Maximizing Business and Social Value*, Cambridge University Press, Cambridge, UK.
Bhattacharya, C. B., and Sankar Sen (2004), "Doing Better at Doing Good: When, Why, and How Consumers Respond to Corporate Social Initiatives," *California Management Review*, 47(1), 9–24.

Branco, Manuel Castelo, and Lucia Lima Rodrigues (2008), "Factors Influencing Social Responsibility Disclosure by Portuguese Companies," *Journal of Business Ethics*, 83(4), 685–701.

Brown, Tom J., and Peter A. Dacin (1997), "The Company and the Product: Corporate Associations and Consumer Product Responses," *Journal of Marketing*, January, 68–84.

Chakravorti, Bhaskar (2010), "Stakeholder Marketing 2.0," *Journal of Public Policy and Marketing*, 29 (1): 97–102.

Cone (2015), "2015 Cone Communications/Ebiquity Global CSR Study," available at www.conecomm. com/research-from-cone. Accessed March 15, 2016.

Crowley, Ayn. E., and Wayne. D. Hoyer (1994), "An Integrative Framework for Understanding Two-Sided Persuasion," *Journal of Consumer Research*, 20(4), 561–574.

Daft, Richard. L., and Robert. H. Lengel (1986), "Organizational Information Requirements, Media Richness and Structural Design," *Management Science*, 32(5), 554–571.

Dhaliwal, Dan S., Oliver Zhen Li, Albert Tsang, and Yong George Yang (2011), "Voluntary Nonfinancial Disclosure and the Cost of Equity Capital: The Initiation of Corporate Social Responsibility Reporting," *The Accounting Review*, 86(1), 59–100.

Dhaliwal, Dan S., Suresh Radhakrishnan, Albert Tsang, and Yong George Yang (2012), "Nonfinancial Disclosure and Analyst Forecast Accuracy: International Evidence on Corporate Social Responsibility Disclosure," *The Accounting Review*, 87(3), 723–759.

Dawkins, Jenny. (2004), "Corporate Responsibility: The Communication Challenge," *Journal of Communication Management*, 9(2), 108–119.

Deighton, John, Daniel Romer, and Josh McQueen (1989), "Using Drama to Persuade," *Journal of Consumer Research*, 16(3), 335–343.

Du, Shuili, C. B. Bhattacharya, and Sankar Sen (2010), "Maximizing Business Returns to Corporate Social Responsibility (CSR): The Role of CSR Communication," *International Journal of Management Review*, 12(1), 8–19.

Du, Shuili, C. B. Bhattacharya, and Sankar Sen (2011), "Corporate Social Responsibility and Competitive Advantage: Overcoming the Trust Barrier," *Management Science*, 57(9), 1528–1545.

Du, Shuili, C. B. Bhattacharya, and Sankar Sen. (2015), "Corporate Social Responsibility, Multi-faceted Job-Products, and Employee Outcomes," *Journal of Business Ethics, Journal of Business Ethics*, 131(2), 319–335.

Du, Shuili, and Edward. T. Vieira (2012). "Striving for legitimacy through corporate social responsibility: Insights from oil companies, " *Journal of Business Ethics*, *110*(4), 413–427.

Escalas, Jennifer Edson. (2004), "Narrative Processing: Building Consumer Connections to Brands," *Journal of Consumer Psychology*, 14(1/2), 168–180.

Ernst and Young and Boston College (2013), "Value of Sustainability Reporting," available at: www.ey.com/Publication/vwLUAssets/ACM_BC/$FILE/1304-1061668_ACM_BC_Corporate_Center.pdf

Esrock, Stuart L., and Greg B. Leichty (1998), "Social Responsibility and Corporate Web Pages: Self-Presentation or Agenda-Setting?" *Public Relations Review*, 24(3), 305–319.

GlobeScan/SustainAbility (2014), "The 2014 Sustainabilty Leaders: A GlobeScan/SustainAbility Survey," available at www.globescan.com/component/edocman/?view=documentandid=103andItemid=591, accessed April 28, 2015.

Greening, Daniel W., and Daniel B. Turban. (2000), "Corporate Social Performance as a Competitive Advantage in Attracting a Quality Workforce," *Business and Society*, 39(3), 254–280.

Hahn, Rudiger, and Regina Lülfs. (2014), "Legitimizing Negative Aspects in GRI-Oriented Sustainability Reporting: A Qualitative Analysis of Corporate Disclosure Strategies," *Journal of Business Ethics*, 123(3), 401–420.

Handelman, Jay M., and Stephen J. Arnold (1999), "The Role of Marketing Actions with a Social Dimension: Appeals to the Institutional Environment," *Journal of Marketing*, 63(3), 33–48.

Henderson, Lesley, and Jenny Kitzinger (1999), "The Human Drama of Genetics: Hard and Soft Media Representations of Inherited Breast Cancer," *Sociology of Health and Illness*, 21(5), 560–578.

Hill, Ronald Paul, Ainscough Thomas, Shank Todd, and Manullang Daryl (2007), "Corporate Social Responsibility and Socially Responsible Investing: A Global Perspective," *Journal of Business Ethics*, 70(2), 165.

Junior, Renzo Mori, Peter J. Best, and Julie Cotter (2014), "Sustainability Reporting and Assurance: A Historical Analysis on a World-Wide Phenomenon," *Journal of Business Ethics*, 120(1), 1–11.

Kaplan, Andreas. M., and Michael Haenlein (2010), "Users of the World, Unite! The Challenges and Opportunities of Social Media," *Business Horizon*, 53, 59–68.

Kemp, Simon (2015), "Digital, Social and Mobile Worldwide in 2015," available at http://wearesocial.net/blog/2015/01/digital-social-mobile-worldwide-2015/, accessed May 22, 2015.

Klein, Jill, and Niraj Dawar (2004), "Corporate Social Responsibility and Consumers' Attributions and Brand Evaluations in a Product-Harm Crisis," *International Journal of Research in Marketing*, 21(3), 203–217.

Kotler, Philip, and Nancy Lee (2005), *Corporate Social Responsibility: Doing the Most Good for Your Company and Your Cause*, John Wiley and Sons, Inc., Hoboken, NJ.

Korschun, Daniel, and Shuili Du (2013), "How Virtual Corporate Social Responsibility Dialogs Generate Value: A Framework and Propositions," *Journal of Business Research*, 66(9), 1494–1504.

KPMG (2013), "KPMG Survey of Corporate Responsibility Reporting 2013," Available at www.kpmg.com/global/en/issuesandinsights/articlespublications/corporate-responsibility/pages/corporate-responsibility-reporting-survey-2013.aspx, accessed on August 20, 2014

Lee, Min Young, Ann Fairhurst, and Scarlett Wesley (2009), "Corporate Social Responsibility: A Review of the Top 100 US Retailers," *Corporation Reputation Review*, 12(2), 140–158.

Luo, Xueming, and C. B. Bhattacharya (2006), "Corporate Social Responsibility, Customer Satisfaction, and Market Value," *Journal of Marketing*, 70 (October), 1–18.

Maignan, Isabelle, and O. C. Ferrell. (2004), "Corporate Social Responsibility and Marketing: An Integrative Framework," *Journal of the Academy of Marketing Science*, 32(1), 3–19.

Maignan, Isabelle, and David A. Ralston. (2002), "Corporate Social Responsibility in Europe and the US: Insights from Businesses' Self-Presentations," *Journal of International Business Studies*, 33(3), 497–514.

Mangold, W. Glynn, and David J. Faulds (2009), "Social Media: The New Hybrid Element of the Promotion Mix," *Business Horizons*, 52(4), 357–365.

Margolis, Joshua D., and James P. Walsh (2003), "Misery Loves Companies: Rethinking Social Initiatives by Business," *Administrative Science Quarterly*, 48(2), 268–305.

Moreno, Angeles, and Paul Capriotti. (2009), "Communicating CSR, Citizenship and Sustainability on the Web," *Journal of Communication Management*, 13(2), 157–175.

Palazzo, Guido, and Andreas Georg Scherer (2006), "Corporate Legitimacy as Deliberation: A Communicative Framework," *Journal of Business Ethics*, 66, 71–88.

Parguel, Beatrice, Florence Benoît-Moreau, and Fabrice Larceneux. (2011), "How Sustainability Ratings Might Deter 'greenwashing': A Closer Look at Ethical Corporate Communication," *Journal of Business Ethics*, 102(1), 15–28.

Pechmann, Cornelia (1992), "Predicting When Two-Sided Ads Will Be More Effective than One-Sided Ads: The Role of Correlational and Correspondent Inferences," *Journal of Marketing Research*, 29(November), 441–453.

Peloza, John, Moritz Loock, James Cerruti, and Michael Muyot (2012), "Sustainability: How Stakeholder Perceptions Differ From Corporate Reality," *California Management Review*, 55(1), 74.

Perrini, Francesco (2006), "The Practitioner's Perspective on Non-Financial Reporting," *California Management Review*, 48(2), 73–103.

QSR Magazine (2013), "Game Time: Brands' Mobile Games Build Customer Sales, Loyalty." Available at www.qsrmagazine.com/exclusives/game-time, accessed April 6, 2016.

Sen, Sankar, and C. B. Bhattacharya (2001), "Does Doing Good Always Lead to Doing Better? Consumer Reactions to Corporate Social Responsibility," *Journal of Marketing Research*, 38(2), 225–243.

Sen, Sankar, C. B. Bhattacharya, and Daniel Korschun. (2006), "The Role of Corporate Social Responsibility in Strengthening Multiple Stakeholder Relationships: A Field Experiment," *Journal of the Academy of Marketing science*, 34(2), 158–166.

Sen, Sankar, Shuili Du, and C. B. Bhattacharya. (2016), "Corporate Social Responsibility: A Consumer Psychology Perspective," *Current Opinion in Psychology*, 10, 70–75.

Servaes, Henri, and Ane Tamayo (2013), "The Impact of Corporate Social Responsibility on Firm Value: The Role of Customer Awareness," *Management Science*, 59(5), 1045–1061.

Sheehan, Kim, and Lucy Atkinson. (2012). "Special Issue on Green Advertising," *Journal of Advertising, 41* (4), 5–7.

Social Media Examiner (2014), "2014 Social Media Marketing Industry Report," available at www. socialmediaexaminer.com/social-media-marketing-industry-report-2014/, accessed May 22, 2015.

Suchman, Mark C. (1995), "Managing Legitimacy: Strategic and Institutional Approaches," *Academy of Management Review*, 20(3), 571–610.

Tschopp, Daniel, and Ronald Huefner. (2015). "Comparing the Evolution of CSR Reporting to that of Financial Reporting," *Journal of Business Ethics*, 127(3), 565–577.

van Laer, Tom, and Ko De Ruyter (2010), "In Stories We Trust: How Narrative Apologies Provide Cover for Competitive Vulnerability after Integrity-Violating Blog Posts," *International Journal of Research in Marketing*, 27(2), 164–174.

Vickery, Shawnee K., Cornelia Droge, Theodore P. Stank, Thomas J. Goldsby, and Robert E. Markland (2004), "The Performance Implications of Media Richness in a Business-to-Business Service Environment: Direct Versus Indirect Effects," *Management Science*, 50(8), 1106–1119.

Wagner, Tillmann, Richard J. Lutz, and Barton A. Weitz. (2009), "Corporate Hypocrisy: Overcoming the Threat of Inconsistent Corporate Social Responsibility Perceptions," *Journal of Marketing*, 73(6), 77–91.

Wanderley, Lilian Soares Outtes, Rafael Lucian, Francisca Farache, and Jose Milton de Sousa Filho. (2008), "CSR Information Disclosure on the Web: A Context-Based Approach Analyzing the Influence of Country of Origin and Industry Sector," *Journal of Business Ethics*, 82, 369–378.

Yoon, Yeosun, Zeynep Gürhan-Canli, and Norbert Schwarz (2006), "The Effect of Corporate Social Responsibility (CSR) Activities on Companies with Bad Reputations," *Journal of Consumer Psychology*, 16(4), 377–390.

Zdravkovic, Srdan, Peter Magnusson, and Sarah M. Stanley. (2010), "Dimensions of Fit Between a Brand and a Social Cause and Their Influence on Attitudes," *International Journal of Research in Marketing*, 27(2), 151–160.

4.3 The role of social media in communicating CSR within fashion micro-organizations

Claudia E. Henninger and Caroline J. Oates

Introduction

The collapse of the Rana Plaza factory in 2013 – one of the biggest fashion industry accidents in history in which thousands of people died –[1] saw a noticeable increase in corporate social responsibility (CSR) polices introduced by clothing manufacturers seeking to make a difference in current production practices.[2,3] The negative media received by the fashion industry raised public awareness and knowledge of the social and environmental impacts that garments and textiles have on the natural environment and led to consumers demanding changes to be made. This resulted in an increase in CSR activities from the organizations' side, as a direct response to consumers wanting more 'sustainable' actions to be implemented across the supply chain and production process.[4,5] CSR can be defined as "a concept whereby companies integrate social and environmental concerns in their business operations and in their interaction with stakeholders on a voluntary basis"[6] (p. 5). It seeks to "achiev[e] commercial success in ways that honor ethical values and respect people, communities, and the natural environment"[7] (p. 6). CSR provides organizations with the opportunity to legitimize their economic actions, whilst at the same time showing their environmental and social responsibility to a wider audience.[8]

This chapter focuses on three 'sustainable' fashion micro-organizations that are heavily involved in a variety of CSR activities. Micro-organizations employ fewer than ten employees, are dependent on their owner-manager (OM), are vulnerable to increased competition, and have a limited financial budget.[9] Hence, online communication channels become increasingly important as the limited finances of these micro-organizations encourage utilization of new, free digital platforms, such as Twitter and Facebook to broadcast a company's CSR messages to a wider audience.

Past research on CSR has predominantly focused on large organizations and only more recently on small- and medium-sized enterprises (SMEs), which still excludes micro-organizations.[10] Yet within the fashion industry, which contributes £26bn to the UK economy,[11] micro-organizations dominate the business landscape with new designers and brands emerging almost daily. Such organizations contribute 34.9% of private sector turnover and account for over 32% of employment in the UK.[12] The importance of micro-organizations as key economic drivers further justifies this research, which explores three research questions:

RQ1: What does CSR mean in micro-organizations?
RQ2: How do micro-organizations communicate their CSR initiatives to their stakeholders (customers, suppliers, and consumers)?
RQ3: What role does social media play within the process of communicating CSR initiatives?

Literature review

CSR – definitions

Industrial disasters in the fashion industry (e.g., Rana Plaza) have put garment manufacturers in the spotlight and challenged their legitimacy of providing products/services that not only fulfill the needs of the current generation, but also allow for future generations to cater for their needs/wants.[13, 14] In order to counteract poor publicity, more and more fashion organizations emerge that have CSR activities at the core of their business strategy. Toms Shoes, for example, provide a free pair of shoes to a child in need with every consumer purchase from any of their product ranges, whilst H&M utilizes organic materials in their conscious-line collection, thereby promoting worker safety in handling their raw materials and the payment of living wages.[15,16] For micro-organizations, which have a limited budget, and potentially lack business and marketing experience, creating successful CSR activities can be challenging. The extent of their activities will be on a smaller scale compared to that of large or multinational companies, yet it is vital that any organization that wants to be perceived as socially and environmentally responsible matches its stakeholders' expectations.[17] Such expectations can be managed through active communication that supports the organizations' activities and encourages stakeholder engagement.[18,19] It is implied that the magnitude of the CSR activity of an organization is almost irrelevant – as long as the company is actively involved in CSR activities that are clearly communicated to stakeholders and meet their expectations, stakeholders will have a positive image of the brand.[20]

CSR activity is not a new phenomenon, but it has received additional attention after factory incidents in Asia created a bleak backdrop to the fashion industry as a whole. CSR is part of the 'sustainability movement', which has emerged as a 'megatrend'[21] and focuses predominantly on the social aspect of sustainability. CSR has a broad variety of meanings and in this chapter we start from an understanding of CSR as "actions that appear to further some social good, beyond the interest of the firm and that which is required by law"[22] (p. 117). This definition has been used by previous researchers to investigate the motivational drivers underpinning CSR activities can be characterized as moral obligation, sustainability, license to operate, and reputation.[23,24] *Moral obligation* suggests being a 'good corporate citizen',[25] which links to *sustainability*, and establishing and maintaining long-term relationships with the community and other stakeholders. A *license to operate* is concerned with legal requirements introduced by governments and 'forced upon' organizations to act more responsibly. Examples could be labor laws that clearly highlight minimum wage requirements, age restrictions of workers, and/or the use of chemicals in dyes. Last, *reputation* as a motivational driver focuses on creating stakeholder buy-in internally and externally. Community based activities, such as fundraisers or the establishment of leisure and educational facilities are examples of this category. Whilst "no business can solve all of society's problems or bear the cost of doing so . . . each company must select issues that intersect with its particular business"[26] (p. 9). Thus, an organization prioritizes issues of importance, which can be thought of in three different but related ways according to society and the environment[27,28]: 1) issues that are important to society, but do not affect a company's business; 2) a focus on the value chain and thus, issues that impact on the product lifecycle; or 3) issues that affect competitive drivers within a market place.

Although CSR has been criticized as a tool that promotes the agenda of individual organizations, the government, and non-governmental organizations (NGOs), it can also be seen as an important initiative that can attract skilled workers to an organization and improve a company's overall reputation.[29] In today's society, having a favorable reputation is more important than ever, and companies need to continually adapt to consumer demands and expectations.[30] Technological advancements have led to increased fragmentation of communication channels and the emergence of social media platforms, such as Twitter and Facebook.[31, 32] It is no longer enough simply to have a CSR strategy, but rather, it has to be clearly communicated across multiple channels.[33] Stakeholders play an increasingly important role, as they are no longer silent recipients of a message – through social media they have the ability to actively communicate with organizations and be part of their (organizations') CSR conversation. This provides both opportunities and challenges for organizations, which need to be researched further utilizing non-traditional research methods to understand how and what organizations share with and communicate to their audiences.[34]

CSR and social media

The emergence of Web 2.0 has changed the communication landscape for CSR activities by allowing stakeholders to play an active role in the communication process. Web 2.0 is defined as "the philosophy of mutually maximizing collective intelligence and added value for each participant by formalized and dynamic information sharing and creation"[35] (p. 12). Stakeholders now have the opportunity, if they desire, to actively engage in the creation and evaluation of content established by organizations and express their concerns directly. Ideally, this leads to co-creation processes in which both stakeholders and organizations mutually benefit.[36] Research suggests that organizations "need to engage with stakeholders as they have the power . . . to influence the achievement of outcomes"[37] (p. 56). Through interactive communication stakeholders are empowered and gain the opportunity to voice their opinion, whilst organizations can implement changes to create a reputation that is positively perceived by their stakeholders.[38]

Social media has emerged as part of Web 2.0, reshaping the previously existing dynamics in communication between stakeholders and organizations from a one-way process towards dialogic communication.[39, 40] Social media has received attention within the academic literature and is seen as a necessary information channel to distribute brand messages and raise stakeholder awareness of an organization's CSR activities.[41] Real time communication tools (e.g., Twitter, Facebook) allows instant sharing of messages, which can be seen by 'followers' (Twitter) and 'friends' (Facebook), thereby reaching a wide audience in real time.[42] Social media provides a broad range of opportunities for organizations to not only involve stakeholders and the general public in CSR debates, but also to raise awareness about issues within the industry.[43,44] Lee et al[45] insist that it is "imperative for firms to successfully integrate new media into their extant communication strategy" (p. 792). A key challenge associated with social media is the lack of control over any messages that are shared, liked, and re-posted. Stakeholders can search on a multitude of pages and channels and gain access to information organizations were previously able to 'hide'.[46,47]

With social media gaining popularity and providing an opportunity for micro-organizations to broadcast their message to a wider audience at a small or no cost, understanding how and what to communicate becomes a key issue that needs careful consideration. This chapter contributes to knowledge by focusing on an under-researched area (micro-organizations) and filling a gap to utilize innovative sources of research data to explore CSR communication in the twenty-first century.[48]

Methodology

This chapter utilizes an interpretivist research philosophy and is qualitative in nature. The aim of this chapter is to explore in how far micro-organizations communicate their CSR practices through their various digital platforms, specifically social media accounts (e.g., Twitter, Facebook). Due to the nature of this research, which seeks to understand a complex phenomenon within its real life context, a case study approach was deemed appropriate.[49] Case study research allowed for multiple qualitative methodological tools to be utilized, such as in-depth semi-structured interviews, semiotics, and social media analysis.

The three micro-organizations were purposively selected to best answer the research questions. Requirements for their recruitment included: first, they are classified as micro-organizations;[50] second, they operate in the UK fashion industry; third, they have sustainability at their core; and fourth, they self-proclaim 'CSR activities'. Although similar in nature, these micro-organizations differ in size and years of operation (Table 4.3.1).

The exploratory research in each of the micro-organizations was conducted over a three-month period, which resulted in rich data sets. The analysis took several months, in which we iteratively coded data sets up to five times. To guarantee rigor and reliability, the seven step guide of Easterby-Smith *et al*[51] was utilized, which allowed for familiarization with and reflection on the data, conceptualizing and cataloguing of emerging themes, re-coding of the data, linking emerging themes, and re-evaluating the findings. Due to the interpretivist nature of this research, it was seen as vital that themes could emerge naturally, whilst at the same time they could be contrasted and compared. We discussed emerging

Table 4.3.1 Data summary

	Organization 1	*Organization 2*	*Organization 3*
Description	• Est. 2007 • Women's fashion • Upcyling/recycling techniques	• Est. 2002 • Children's wear • Sources in EU	• Est. 2012 • High-end to vintage fashion
Number of interviews (Is)	5	6	7
Interview duration	13:33–57:22 min	10:00–60:00 min	7:51–45:35 min
Interviewee profile	• O/M1, founder • Head of IT, joined in 2008 • Seamstress, joined in 2010 • Apprentice, joined in 2014 • Workshop lead, joined in 2009	• O/M2, founder • Seamstress original member of company • Seamstress, joined in 2006, part-time • Seamstress, joined in 2012 • Production manager, original member of company • Quality manager, joined in 2013	• O/M3, founder • Designer, own business since 2006, joined co-operative in 2012 • Designer, own business since 2001, joined co-operative in 2012 • Designer, own business since 2010, joined co-operative in 2012 • Employee, joined in 2013 • Seamstress/designer, joined 2012
Twitterfeed (TF)		✓	
Semiotics (SE)	Website; blog; newsletter; email; photographs; garment tags		

themes in regular meetings and made sure any discrepancies were re-analyzed. The results were presented to the participants for validation purposes.

It could be argued that the sample and the size of this research act as a limitation, as the context is highly specific: micro-organizations operating in the UK's fashion industry. However, this provides an opportunity to explore an under-researched field, the creative and cultural industries,[52] whilst at the same time purposefully investigating a sector that is of great economic importance.[53] We do not seek to provide any generalizable results but rather bring forward learning points that can be addressed in future research.

Findings

The meaning of CSR in micro-organizations

These micro-organizations believe that their production processes, sourcing, and manufacturing techniques, as well as their end-of-life garment treatment workshops are activities that support their CSR policies and sustainability measures in more general terms. Figure 4.3.1 provides a basic blueprint of these micro-organizations, clearly showcasing the individual steps in the decision-making process of constructing a garment, which starts from the design process, choice of material, sourcing of materials, the production of the collection, the finished product, distribution, purchase by the customer, and the end-of-life treatment of the discarded items. These micro-organizations were established with aspects of sustainability in mind in that they seek to reduce the impact their collections have on the natural and social environment.

The introduction highlighted that research on micro-organizations is limited.[54] When we engaged with these three fashion micro-organizations, we wanted to understand how the owner-managers and their employees interpret CSR activities. OM1 states that she has been actively involved in the community and seeks to incorporate local creative talents into her business. For her, CSR implies providing people with an opportunity to develop their skills further and having a creativity outlet. She insists that

> without me it'd just be a collection of people making things and selling them on market stalls . . . my role really is to take everything away from a village hall craft aesthetic. . . . I feel a bit like it's a massive jigsaw puzzle and I'm in the middle slotting the bits together.
>
> (OM1 Is)

From the interview it becomes apparent that for OM1, creating jobs is an essential part of CSR activities, as providing local people and design and fashion students with work experience and volunteer opportunities are key parts of her definition. An employee supports this view explaining that OM1 "employs everyone that she can, like a little local hat maker and a little lady doing crochet collars . . . she really encourages local makers and doers to keep up and makes use of their skills" (Employee Is). Although the owner-manager's definition fits the McWilliams and Siegel[55] CSR interpretation, the employee's elaboration somewhat contradicts this definition, as CSR is not interpreted as solely doing good within society beyond the interest of the firm and regulations.[56] Even though creating jobs and other opportunities within the local community can be seen as a CSR activity, doing this to gain benefits for the micro-organization in the form of profit does not fit the interpretation of CSR. Thus, their definition of CSR links more closely with the

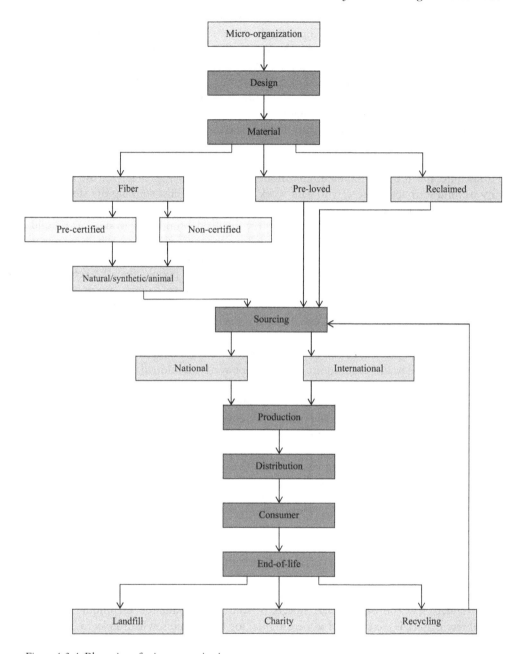

Figure 4.3.1 Blueprint of micro-organizations

interpretation of stakeholder engagement, whereby stakeholders (e.g., employees, community) are seen as a source of opportunity to further the overall business.[57]

OM2 similarly feels that providing employment in the community is an essential part of doing business and showing to be a 'good corporate citizen'.[58] However, OM2 believes that it is her responsibility to go beyond simply providing opportunities locally. In accordance with her product range of children's fashion, she set up a partnership in 2012 with an international agency that supports children in need by donating a certain percentage of her organization's annual profits, which funds educational programs (SE). To ensure that the money reaches the destination, she also undertakes regular trips to the site in Cambodia and supports the agency in their work. OM2's interpretation of CSR activities concurs with various authors,[59, 60] who classify CSR activities as a moral obligation and a license to operate. Employees indicate that they feel proud to be part of the micro-organization and support their owner-manager where they can.

Micro-organization 3 differs slightly from micro-organizations 1 and 2 in that it is a co-operative that is managed by a single individual. OM3 states that for her CSR implies "being part of the community" (Is). OM3 opened her shop with support from the Mary Portas fund and the local council. The money received provides her with the opportunity to fund four apprentices, who gain work experience whilst running the store. OM3 encourages designers to bring forward ideas to raise awareness for the shop. Past activities could be classified as being CSR related, as they involved a fundraiser to support rebuilding parts of the local cathedral (Is; SE). Throughout the research process it became apparent that OM3 believes any activity that involves the local community can be classified as CSR, as "you are making an effort and do social things that people like" (Is). Yet, it seems that these activities are organized as part of an ulterior motive: to raise awareness for the store and get people to shop in their premises, rather than solely to do good. Thus, CSR activities are seen as an opportunity to create a positive buzz for the organization that ideally leads to good publicity.

When discussing aspects of CSR with the owner-managers and the employees, employment opportunities and community involvement were mentioned first, before focusing on the fact that they produce within the UK, source locally – where possible – and organize workshops for the general public to learn about issues of sustainability. For example, all the organizations offer either upcycling and recycling workshops that support people's creativity and educate them on aspects of sustainability (as understood by the owner-manager) (Organizations 1 and 3) or provide apprenticeships that are based on keeping British heritage alive by teaching young adults the craft of sewing (Organization 2).

A commonality between the interpretations is the fact that employment and giving people an opportunity to express their creativity are essential parts of CSR. Only one out of the three companies insists that CSR activities need to go further, by either reinvesting money or donating it to a company related good cause. Underlying all of these CSR activities is the need to increase company awareness and ideally raise profits. This implies that contrary to McWilliams and Siegel's[61] definition that sees CSR as a selfless act to do good, these micro-organizations interpret CSR as a way to advertise their companies and gain recognition in the community, with the aim of promoting their brand and selling products. On the other hand, aspects of sourcing, production techniques, and the actual raw materials are believed to be essential for the business, which links to aspects of sustainability.

CSR communication to stakeholders

Understanding how these micro-organizations interpret CSR is a vital first step in analyzing what channels are used to communicate these activities and in how far these reach the intended audience. All members of these micro-organizations concur that online communication is "the way forward, of course" (OM2 Is). Due to the acknowledged lack of financial resources, social media channels are seen as key tools to stay in touch with stakeholders and bring forward their organizations' messages. An employee (micro-organization 1) states that

> one of the things we do more of . . . is getting people online more involved in us and what we do and how we do it and all the interesting stuff different people that work in the studio are part of . . . cause people like to know things.
>
> (Is)

Thus, digital channels are seen as promotional tools to promote the brand to stakeholders, thereby re-emphasizing their brand's values. Figure 4.3.2 provides an overview of the communication channels identified in these micro-organizations. We focus on social media and online channels only.

Focusing on the 'online' channels first, these micro-organizations utilize both email communication and a company website to broadcast their messages. Both of these 'platforms' only provide an opportunity for one-way communication that is directional in nature. OM2 highlights that "we normally just email people when we've got offers on, it's more for like advertising" (Is). Similar use can be observed in the other two micro-organizations (SE). A reason why the owner-managers neither use emails for promoting their workshops nor their international community engagement is the assumption that consumers seldom read emails and normally delete them straight away (OM3 Is). Thus, OM3 believes that if she needs to communicate something that is important to her and wants people to engage, sending an email is the least favored option (Is).

Organizations 1 and 2's websites provide detailed information on their overall mission, vision, and values and clearly highlights the fact that 'sustainability' is at the core of their business agenda (SE). Micro-organization 1 clearly states that they work together with "local suppliers" and try to build "long-term relationships with the community", whilst working with "upcycling and local fashion systems" (SE). On the other hand, micro-organization 2 emphasizes that they focus on a "green balance" that considers social and

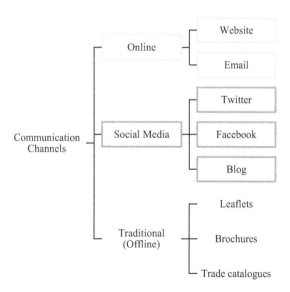

Figure 4.3.2 Communication channels

environmental aspects by producing locally in a "100% sweatshop free environment" (SE). Both websites clearly communicate what their owner-managers believe to be key aspects of CSR: community involvement and fair and safe working conditions. Micro-organization 3's website is very basic and only provides the company's address – neither aspects of CSR nor sustainability are present on this platform. An explanation could be that due to being a co-operative, with designers and makers changing frequently, having a more detailed website would be too time-consuming and hard to maintain.

The role of social media in CSR communication

Social media forms a vital part of the communication strategy of these micro-organizations, as "it's massive! It's a great way to get in touch with people . . . who are interested in your brand and to get people who haven't heard of you to hear about you" (Is). Twitter, Facebook, and the company blogs all allow for dialogic communication, as anyone interested in the tweets and posts has the opportunity to directly respond to the messages sent. All three micro-organizations are extremely vocal on Twitter and Facebook, whilst only micro-organizations 1 and 2 regularly maintain their blogs. The owner-managers insist that they try to update all their social media channels regularly and rather than only posting promotional tweets, they also try to update consumers about their upcoming events (e.g., upcycling workshops), general noteworthy business news, trends in the industry, and responding to queries (SE; TF).

Focusing on the Twitterfeed analysis, it becomes apparent that although all three owner-managers report that they "tweet at least twice a day" (Is) the majority of tweets seem to be in irregular waves. The micro-organizations tweet approximately 20 times a day, if they have an upcoming event, and otherwise only once every two/three days. Looking at the content of these tweets more closely, it can be seen that these micro-organizations associate themselves with various hashtags, such as #sustfash, #ethical, and #local, which fits with the overarching theme of sustainability and CSR. Yet, rather than broadcasting how these companies get involved in the local community and what events they are organizing, these tweets are predominantly promotional in nature:

> Time for [Organization 1]'s back to school & end of summer sale! #sustfash (Tweeted: micro-organization 1)
> Learning from the past with our new Make, Do & Mend feature [. . .] #sustfash #fashion #sustainability (Tweeted: micro-organization 1)
> Made in the UK – (Organization 2) (company name) are delighted to be delivering our Fashion and Textile training here (Tweeted: micro-organization 2)
> Bubble London Homegrown showcases labels that are designed and manufactured in the UK. Come and see us ([Organization 2]) on stand A40. We're completely Homegrown! (Tweeted: micro-organization 2)
> There's still time to buy those last minute gifts! Get down to [Organization 3] lots of lovely, quirky, one-off pieces!! #buylocal #[city's name] (Tweeted: micro-organization 3)
> [Organization 3] is open today. Come in from the rain for some lovely handmade gifts #localshopping (Tweeted: micro-organization 3)

Although these micro-organizations associate themselves with aspects of sustainability, only a minority of tweets communicate CSR activities that are taking place in the individual companies. The engagement rate on Twitter is low or even non-existent. The only dialogues that could be recorded throughout the three month period were of a private nature and lacked further stakeholder engagement. Thus, a key finding that emerges from the data is the fact that Twitter may not be used as effectively as it could be within these micro-organizations. Whilst they are broadcasting messages, whether of a promotional nature or to highlight any CSR activities, these are not received by the audience as an invite to engage. Rather than simply stating facts, it may be beneficial to pose questions and seek feedback from followers, which could lead to higher response rates and more support for their CSR activities.

The Facebook analysis showed similar results. Stakeholder engagement is limited, and the micro-organizations do not utilize this platform to promote their CSR activities. OM1 indicates that

> we want to be a kind of go to brand for not only you know buying clothes, but also for information, ideas and also because we wanna kind of really promote that . . . kind of do-it-yourself kind of grass roots activism . . . but we don't wanna get across too preachy . . . it's a fine balance.
>
> (Is)

Thus, an explanation for why these micro-organizations do not actively promote CSR activities and issues of sustainability through their social media channels may be because they want to be more inclusive and encourage people to explore the brands and their values, rather than emphasizing CSR as their primary concern (Is; SE; TF).

The only social media channel that focuses on CSR activities within these micro-organizations is the blog. OM1 states that she has created her blog so that "you can also learn how to do something to your own clothes, or find out how to . . . and come to our clothes swap and things like that", yet "the blog on the website, which is something we always . . . try to develop . . . unfortunately it's one of those things that always slides and we don't update it as much as we could" (Is). Similar findings could be observed in micro-organization 3. Although OM1 and OM3 feel that the blogs are a good idea and would support them in promoting their community engagement, keeping them updated and maintaining them on a regular basis is too time intensive (Is). Contrarily, OM2 utilizes her blog to post regular updates on the company's relationship with the NGO and indicates what has been achieved with the profits they have made. OM2 further posts pictures and journal entries when she visits the site and specifies how donations have helped children and what happened to those that were previously featured. The blog receives quite a lot of attention, with consumers posting comments of support and sharing the entries on Twitter and Facebook.

These micro-organizations perceive online communication tools as vitally important to share information and broadcast their message to stakeholders.[62] Although stakeholders have an opportunity to engage with these micro-organizations on a variety of platforms, the overall response rate is low. Only micro-organization 2 seems to be able to attract stakeholder engagement through their blog entries, which provide further information on their CSR activities.[63] Various issues emerge from these observations: first, why do stakeholders only engage with the blog rather than with all social media platforms? A possible explanation could be that Twitter only allows for 140 characters to be written for any one post, thus reporting about CSR activities may be challenging, whilst Facebook is predominantly used for personal reasons rather than on a professional level.[64] Second, the lack of control over content that is posted by third parties, as well as the amount of engagement from the side of the stakeholders provide challenges for these micro-organizations.[65,66]

Conclusions

Although social media and digital channels are central to micro-organizations to promote their brand message to a wider audience,[67] a clear line can be drawn between channels that are valuable for promotional purposes and those that can enhance the awareness of CSR activities. Providing links to CSR activities on the company website is essential, as stakeholders usually investigate a company's homepage at least once – either to purchase products or to gain more information about brands. Data indicate that blogs engage stakeholders, as images can be shared, stories told, and detailed information provided about any CSR activities. Due to the nature of Twitter and Facebook, the former with limited characters and the latter with its more personal purpose, neither seem to successfully engage stakeholders nor be utilized by these micro-organizations to promote their CSR activities.

Dialogic communication that enhances stakeholder engagement is vital in today's business world; thus, finding a balance between pushing sales and providing information is key. These three micro-organizations lack a clear strategy to communicate their activities. Information is posted at random and without any clear purpose. Although all three are engaged in CSR activities, none promote them to their full potential, nor provide an opportunity for stakeholders to feedback back on how to enhance individual aspects. This has various practical implications. First, these micro-organizations need to ensure continuous maintenance of their individual channels in order to avoid spamming newsfeeds prior to an event, if they are normally only posting every other day. Digital platforms (e.g., Hootsuite) help to coordinate post by timing news releases and interlinking individual social media accounts. Second, communication experts could help to develop tailored communication strategies that fit the purpose of the individual micro-organization, whilst providing support in using digital channels in a more engaging manner. The lack of a marketing/communication background within all three micro-organizations leaves these owner-managers currently in a trial-and-error state that could be resolved by seeking advice from professionals. Third, within these micro-organizations no social media or digital policy was communicated verbally or was evident in any documentation, which could lead to difficulties in the future, especially if these organizations are to grow into SMEs. Future research should investigate if CSR activities could be promoted better through introducing a digital media policy.

Notes

1 Parveen, S. (2014). *Rana Plaza factory collapse survivors struggle one year on*, BBC [online], retrieved from: www.bbc.co.uk/news/world-asia-27107860, [accessed: 06/08/2014]

2 Colleoni, E. (2013). CSR communication strategies for organizational legitimacy in social media. *Corporate Communication: An International Journal*, 18(2): 228–248.

3 McPherson, S. (2014). *Stylish and sustainable: How brands are getting it right*. Forbes [online], retrieved: www.forbes.com/sites/susanmcpherson/2014/03/18/stylish-and-sustainable-how-brands-are-getting-it-right/#1c68737f2578, [accessed: 17/03/2016]

4 Belz, F.-M., and Peattie, K. (2012). *Sustainability Marketing: A Global Perspective*. 2nd edition, John Wiley and Sons Ltd: Chichester, UK.

5 Mintel (2015). *The Ethical Consumer – UK – July 2015*, Mintel: London, UK.

6 EC (European Commission) (2002). *Corporate Social Responsibility: A Business Contribution to Sustainable Development*. COM (2002) 347 final, Brussels: Commission of the European Communities,

Europa [online], retrieved: http://eur- lex.europa.eu/LexUriServ/LexUriServ.do?uri=COM:2002: 0347:FIN:en:PDF, [accessed: 11/10/2011].

7   White, A.L. (2006). *Business Brief: Intangibles and CSR*. BSR online, retrieved: http://bsr.org/reports/ BSR_AW_Intangibles-CSR.pdf, [accessed: 19/07/2013].

8   Colleoni, op. cit.

9   Chironga, M., Dhal, J., Goland, T. Pinshaw, G., and Sonnekus, M. (2012). *Micro-, Small and Medium-Sized Enterprises in Emerging Markets: How Banks Can Grasp a $350 Billion Opportunity*. McKinsey and Company [online], retrieved from: www.eflglobal.com/sites/default/files/knowledge_center/ MSME-Emerging- Market-Banking-report.pdf, [accessed: 25/01/14].

10   Esposito, A. (2013). Insights about integrated marketing communication in small-and medium-sized Italian enterprises. *Business Systems Review*, 2(1): 80–98.

11   Pozniak, H. (2016). The only way is ethics. *The Guardian, Your Guide to Postgraduate Study* 22 March: 19.

12   Ward, M., and Rhodes, C. 2014. *Small businesses and the UK economy*. UK Parliament [online], retrieved: www.parliament.uk/briefing-papers/sn06078.pdf, [accessed: 14/06/2014].

13   WCED (1987). *Our Common Future (The Brundtland Report), World Commission on Environment and Development*, Oxford University Press: Oxford, UK.

14   Palazzo, G., and Scherer, G. (2006). Corporate legitimacy as deliberation: A communicative framework. *Journal of Business Ethics*, 66(1): 71–88.

15   HandM (2016). *Conscious Fashion*. HandM [online], retrieved: http://about.hm.com/en/About/sustainability/commitments/conscious-fashion.html, [accessed: 17/03/2016].

16   Toms (2016). *One of One*. Toms [online], retrieved: www.toms.co.uk, [accessed: 17/03/2016].

17   Colleoni, op. cit.

18   Morsing, M., Schultz, M., and Nielsen, K.U. (2008). The 'Catch 22' of communicating CSR: Findings from a Danish study. *Journal of Marketing Communications*, 14(2): 97–111.

19   Colleoni, op. cit.

20   Lee, K., Oh, W.-Y., and Kim, N. (2013). Social media for socially responsible firms: analysis of Fortune 500's Twitter profiles and their CSR/CSIR ratings. *Journal of Business Ethics*, 118(4): 791–806.

21   Mittelstaedt, J.D., Schultz II, C.J., Kilbourne, W.E., and Peterson, M. (2014). Sustainability as megatrend: Two schools of macromarketing thought. *Journal of Macromarketing*, 34(3): 253–264.

22   McWilliams, A., and Siegel, D.S. (2001). Corporate social responsibility: A theory of the firm perspective. *Academy of Management Review*, 26(1): 117–127.

23   Crook, C. (2005). *Special Report: Corporate Social Responsibility – The Good Company*. Economist [online], 20 January 2005, retrieved: www.economist.com/node/3555212, [accessed: 11/07/2015].

24   Porter, M.E., and Kramer, M.R. (2006). Strategy and Society: The link between competitive advantage and corporate social responsibility. *Harvard Business Review*, 84(12): 78–92.

25   Sheehan, M. (2013). Corporate citizenship. *Leader to Leader*, 70: 26–31.

26   Porter and Kramer, op. cit.

27   Porter and Kramer, op. cit.

28   Belz and Peattie, op. cit.

29   Franklin, D. (2008). *Just Good Business*. Economist [online], 17 January 2008, retrieved: www.economist.com/node/10491077, [accessed: 11/10/2011].

30   Morsing, M., and Schultz, M. (2006). Corporate social responsibility communication: Stakeholder information, response, and involvement strategies. *Business Ethics*, 15(4): 323–338.

31   Mangold, W.G., and Faulds, D.J. (2009). Social Media: The new hybrid element of the promotional mix. *Business Horizons*, 52(4): 357–365.

32   Kietzmann, J.H., Hermkens, K., McCarthy, I.P., and Silvestre, B.S. (2011). Social media? Get serious! Understanding the functional building blocks of social media. *Business Horizons*, 54: 241–251.

33   De Bakker, F.G.A., and Hellsten, I. (2013). Capturing online presence: Hyperlinks and semantic networks in activist group websites on corporate social responsibility. *Journal of Business Ethics*, 118: 807–823.

34   De Bakker and Hellsten, op. cit.

35   Hoegg, R., Martignoni, R., Meckel, M., and Stanoevska-Slabeva, K. (2006). *Overview of Business Models for Web 2.0 Communities*. GeNeMe, Dreseden, pp. 23–37.

36   Wilson, S.M., and Peterson, L.C. (2002). The anthropology of online communities. *Annual Review of Anthropology*, 31(1): 449–467.

37 Foster, D., and Jonker, J. (2005). Stakeholder relationships: The dialogue of engagement. *Corporate Governance*, 5(5): 51–57.

38 Fieseler, C., and Fleck, M. (2013). The pursuit of empowerment through social media: structural social capital dynamics in CSR-blogging. *Journal of Business Ethics*, 118: 759–775.

39 Dellarocas, C. (2003). The digitization of word of mouth: Promise and challenges of online feedback mechanisms. *Management Science*, 49(10): 1407–1424.

40 Fieseler and Fleck, op. cit.

41 Colleoni, op. cit.

42 Freeman, E., and Moutchnik, A. (2013). *Stakeholder management and CSR: questions and answers.* Uwf UmweltWirtschaftsForum. Berlin: Springer.

43 Kaplan, A.M., and Haenlein, M. (2010). Users of the world, unite! The challenges and opportunities of social media. *Business Horizons*, 53(1): 59–68.

44 Fieseler and Fleck, op. cit.

45 Lee *et al*, op. cit.

46 Kaplan, A.M., and Haenlein, M. (2011). Two hearts in three-quarter time: How to waltz the social media/viral marketing dance. *Business Horizons*, 54(3), 253–263.

47 Kietzmann, J., and Canhoto, A. (2013). Bittersweet! Understanding and managing electronic word of mouth. *Journal of Public Affairs*, 13(2): 146–159.

48 De Bakker and Hellsten, op. cit.

49 Yin, R.K. (2003). *Case Study Research: Design and Method.* 3rd edition, SAGE Publications Ltd: Thousand Oaks, CA.

50 EC, op. cit.

51 Easterby-Smith, M., Thorpe, R., and Jackson, P. (2008). *Management Research.* 3rd edition, SAGE Publications: London, UK.

52 Fassin, Y., Van Rossem, A., and Buelens, M. (2011). Small-business owner – managers perceptions of business ethics and CSR-related concepts. *Journal of Business Ethics*, 98(3): 425–453.

53 BBC Democracy. (2013). *Peers Urge Support for Sustainable Fashion.* 20 March 2013, BBC [online], retrieved: www.bbc.co.uk/democracylive/house-of-lords-21850300, [accessed: 05/07/2013].

54 Esposito, op. cit.

55 McWilliams and Siegel, op. cit.

56 McWilliams and Siegel, op. cit.

57 Sloan, P. (2009). Redefining stakeholder engagement from control to collaboration. *Journal of Corporate Citizenship*, 36: 25–40.

58 Sheehan, op. cit.

59 Crook, op. cit.

60 Porter and Kramer, op. cit.

61 McWilliams and Siegel, op. cit.

62 Hoegg *et al*, op. cit.

63 Fieseler and Fleck, op. cit.

64 Freeman and Moutchnik, op. cit.

65 Kaplan and Haenlein, op. cit.

66 Kietzmann and Canhoto, op. cit.

67 Lee *et al*, op. cit.

4.4 Corporate social responsibility and word of mouth

A systematic review and synthesis of literature

Ezgi Akpinar

Corporate social responsibility in a connected world

There is increasing pressure for companies to be successful in corporate social responsibility (CSR). Part of the pressure is driven by consumers, who expect companies to allocate more efforts to have a societal and environmental impact. The rise of social media enables consumers to be informed about the companies' socially responsible practices in a faster and easier way, and influence companies to act responsibly. Imagine a company is involved in a public harm crisis; it might even take just a couple of hours before the crisis becomes the trending topic in social network websites. Consumers do not only communicate about companies' online, but also through face-to-face (offline) conversations. The informal communication among consumers about product or services, which can occur as face-to-face conversations or online mentions, is called "word of mouth" (WOM), Westbrook (1987). Research has shown that WOM is the one of main drivers of consumers' purchasing decisions, and can be more effective than other forms of paid advertising in creating awareness and persuasion (Godes and Mayzlin 2009; Trusov, Bucklin and Pauwels 2009).

CSR activities can benefit from communication among consumers, which might help raise awareness for the cause and increase recommendation for the products (Vlachos et al. 2015), provide support for the cause or build long-term reputation (Lacey, Kennett-Hensel and Manolis 2015) for being socially responsible. On the other hand, when companies engage in in unsustainable practices or public crises, communication among consumers might make the situation even worse (Xie, Bagozzi and Grønhaug 2015), as news spreads like a wildfire and harms the reputation of the companies. With consumers even more connected, it is clear that WOM and CSR both play an important role, yet less is known about how they act together. For instance, what drives consumers to talk about CSR activities? How could CSR activities lead to positive or negative WOM? How could WOM affect the consequences of corporate social responsibility such as financial returns? Finally, how do WOM components such audience, receiver, content and channel have an impact on propagation of CSR? This chapter addresses these questions, through integrating knowledge from CSR and WOM literatures. First, this chapter provides a background on the importance of interpersonal communication on propagation of both negative and positive CSR. Next, it provides a brief categorization of CSR activities based on distinct outcomes (e.g., focusing on philanthropy, improving operational effectiveness). Next, the chapter presents a systematic review and synthesis of the CSR literature using a conceptual framework adapted from WOM literature (i.e., Berger 2014, King, Racherla and Bush 2014). The systematic review has three main parts. First, the potential drivers of sharing CSR activities are discussed. Second, consequences of CSR activities in terms of WOM are discussed. Third, four components of WOM (sender, receiver, content and channel) that could drive dissemination of CSR activities are discussed. Finally, the chapter ends with concluding remarks including insights on social media metrics for measuring the success of disseminating CSR activities.

This is the first attempt to review the CSR literature using a framework adapted from WOM literature. For each main part of the systematic review, a detailed table is presented, which provides an overview of representative papers categorized based on the relevant phenomena discussed. This chapter will be useful to researchers by showing the most and least explored areas at the intersection of corporate social responsibility and WOM literatures, and provides suggestions for future research. Further, this chapter provides suggestions for marketers to develop efficient communication strategies, which might help them propagate their good deeds and manage crises in a better way.

The role of WOM for corporate social responsibility

Consumers talk about brands. Each day, brands are being mentioned around 3.3 billion times (Keller Fay 2011). Communication among consumers (either offline or online) plays an important role in consumers' decisions. Consumers follow recommendations from friends, colleagues, and other consumer opinions, more than corporate communications such as brand websites and ads (Nielsen 2015). The social talk among consumers about brands can shape which restaurants they go to, movies they watch, and the networking sites they subscribe to (Chevalier and Mayzlin 2006; Godes and Mayzlin 2009; Trusov, Bucklin, and Pauwels 2009). Although the buzz about brands happens mostly offline, more consumers have started to talk about brands online given the rise of social media (Lovett, Peres and Shachar 2013). In social media, consumers can raise their opinions and connect with the rest of consumers in a much more immediate and permanent way. This helps consumers to have more empowerment and democracy over the companies and allows them to collaborate.

One of the important reasons WOM plays an important role in consumers' decision is "trust". Consumers find other consumers' comments and views more trustworthy and sincere, which makes WOM more successful than traditional marketing tools (Cheung and Thadani 2012). Trust is also at the heart of social responsibility. Given the CSR's self-transcendence concept (i.e., protecting the welfare of society and the environment), research suggests that it should convey trust and sincerity among consumers (Torelli, Monga and Kaikati 2012). In fact, it has been shown that trust acts as a mediator role in CSR evaluation frameworks (Vlachos et al. 2009). When stakeholders such as consumers, employees, suppliers or managers perceive that the motivations of the CSR activities are sincere and credible enough, they would be more likely to contribute to the social cause and recommend it to others. Otherwise, perceived hypocrisy (i.e., inconsistency between actions and statements) of the companies might lead to negatively affect beliefs towards CSR activities and therefore reduce support from consumers (Wagner, Lutz and Weitz 2009).

Taken together, "trust" acts as an important facilitator for both information transmission among consumers and perceiving CSR activities positively. When consumers perceive CSR activities positively, they should be more willing to share the information with other consumers. Consumers that receive information about social causes from sources they trust would be more likely to spread the news. Favorable CSR perceptions might also create halo effects, which could make consumers evaluate new products more positively or blame companies less about their product harm crises (Klein and Dawar 2004).

Other than trust, there are several other factors that make consumers share content. WOM literature has presented both micro- and macro-level processes that drive sharing. At a micro-level, research has mostly investigated how psychological processes such as impression management, emotional regulation and social bonding shapes why senders talk and what they say about brands (Berger 2014). In addition, research has explored how communication components such as sender, audience and channel characteristics shapes transmission of information about brands (King, Racherla and Bush, 2014). There is also extensive work on the effect of macro-level processes such as social networks on sharing (Van den Bulte and Wuyts, 2009; Watts, 2004 for review). This chapter focuses on drivers of sharing CSR activities, consequences of CSR activities in relation to word of mouth and the impact of WOM components on propagation of CSR activities.

A systematic review and synthesis of literature

This chapter conducts a systematic review of CSR studies in the past decade and aims to understand: a) key characteristics (drivers and components) that could make information related to CSR spread in the marketplace and b) consequences of CSR in terms of WOM (i.e., publicity of a social cause, propagation of a product crisis, bragging about a charity). Literature in CSR is examined around a conceptual framework adapted from Berger (2014) and King, Racherla and Bush (2014) which both provides a review of WOM literature and have distinct contributions. In addition, based on the current state of knowledge at the intersection these two literatures, new research questions that fill in the gaps are discussed.

Methodology

In order to review the literature, a concept-driven systematic review methodology is applied (Webster and Watson 2002). Using this method, studies in the CSR literature are examined from the perspective of the frameworks adapted from WOM literature (Berger 2014; King, Racherla and Bush 2014). This method enables the creation of a concept matrix that shows what has been done at the cross-section of two literatures and what needs to be done in future research.

For selecting the studies used in the systematic literature review, the highest ranked marketing journals (ranked as 4★ and 4) were picked from the academic journal guide of Association of Business Schools (ABS). The list includes the seven top ranked journals: *Journal of Consumer Research, Journal of Consumer Psychology, Journal of Marketing, Journal of Marketing Research, Marketing Science, International Journal of Research in Marketing*, and *Journal of the Academy of Marketing Science*. In order to search among these journals, databases such as Academic Search Premier, EBSCO, Science Direct, and Emerald Insights were used. To find relevant articles, we have searched for the phrases "corporate social responsibility" and "CSR", which is a common practice in review articles related to CSR literature (i.e., Aguinis and Glavas 2012). Further, to capture various forms of corporate social responsibility including negative behaviors, keywords such as "product harm", "product harm crisis", and "product recall" were also searched. In order to pick the studies for further analysis, two filters were used. First, research articles (not an editorial note or commentary) published between 2006 and 2016 were used. This timeframe has been used since research related to WOM has risen to prominence after 2006 (see for an overview

Lamberton and Stephen 2016).This would allow us to investigate articles at the intersection of CSR and WOM literatures. Second, the studies can apply any method including conceptual frameworks. If the related keywords were only mentioned once or twice or in references, the study was not included in further investigation.We investigated a final list of 71 studies (which are listed in Tables 4.4.1, 4.4.2 and 4.4.3).

To organize the key concepts related to WOM in CSR literature, we adopted the frameworks of both Berger (2014) and King, Racherla and Bush (2014). First, as Berger (2014) suggests, transmitting of WOM can provide five fundamental drivers such as impression management, emotion regulation, information acquisition, social bonding and persuasion. In this work, we investigate studies in CSR literature considering each of these drivers. Second, as King, Racherla and Bush (2015) have outlined,WOM can have diverse set of consequences for the brands as well consumers. We investigated consequences of CSR relevant to propagation. Finally, both Berger (2014) and King, Racherla and Bush (2014) have suggested thatWOM components (receiver, sender, content and channel) can drive what is being shared, therefore the role of these four components in CSR literature are explored. Taking these together, CSR literature is systematically reviewed based on the key WOM dimensions (drivers, consequences and components). Based on the gaps revealed in the systematic review, future research questions are also raised.

Corporate social responsibility: a brief overview

While conducting the systematic review, we have distinguished the studies in CSR literature based on type of activities as discussed in Ragnan, Chase and Karim (2015).The first type focuses on *philanthropy*, which often are not designed to produce profits or directly improve business performance. Some of the examples of *philanthropic* activities include donations of money or equipment to civic organizations, charities, or engagement with community initiatives, and support for employee volunteering.

The second type focuses on *sustainable operations*. Such prosocial initiatives might function within existing business models to deliver social or environmental benefits. They might not necessarily increase revenue, decrease costs, or both. They improve efficiency and effectiveness across the value chain and protect resources that a company depends on, while improving the values the firms stand on. Some examples of responsible activities include reducing resource use, waste or emissions or investing in employee working conditions, health care, or education. Some of these prosocial activities might build and transform the business model. For instance,TOMS is one of these brands that do not just engage in donations, but its business model is also built to be socially responsible.There are also some companies that shift the industry by their sustainable operations. For instance, Tony's Chocolonely, is one of the good examples of transforming the chocolate industry aiming towards slave-free chocolate industry.The company introduced in 2013, is the first "bean to bar" company. The brand produces chocolate brands that are traceable back to the producing farms.

The third type focuses on *cause-related marketing* activities.These activities involve consumers by contributing a specific amount to a non-profit initiative provided by companies. For instance,American Express donated to the Statue of Liberty Restoration Project one penny for each credit card transaction and one dollar for each new credit card issued (Chen and Huang 2016).

Finally, although not ideal, companies also engage in *negative corporate social responsibility*, such as sales of harmful products that result in public crises, unsustainable production facilities that concerns consumers, society and investors, or providing unsustainable working conditions for the employees.

It is important to note that it was not possible to categorize several studies under the three specific categories of positive CSR mentioned above. As the review of Drucker's seminal work noted by Smith (2009) suggests, there is a challenging question about "how much corporate social responsibility is enough?" The limits of social responsibility seem to have wider bounds, and includes issues such as food marketing, obesity, availability of AIDS drugs, labor rights and supply chains. Consistent with this view, several studies explored corporate social activities as a broad construct that captured several dimensions such as community work, corporate governance, diversity, employee relations environment, human rights, and product quality and safety. Similarly, there were also several studies that investigated negative corporate social responsibilities as a general construct. Therefore, we also categorized studies under *general corporate social responsibility*, which did not specifically mention about the type of the activity studied.

Drivers for corporate social responsibility propagation

There are different psychological drivers why individuals talk or share about products or services (Berger 2014). Although, there might be several reasons why individuals share content, four distinct drivers of sharing (impression management, information acquisition, creating support and altruism) overlap the most with current corporate social responsibility literature that has been investigated in this review. We discuss how each of these drivers could drive propagation of socially (ir)responsible actions. Note that each of these drivers have been discussed from different stakeholders' perspective (consumers, organizations, employees, society). Representative studies that are related to the key drivers for sharing each different type of corporate social responsibility are summarized in Table 4.4.1.

Impression management

Individuals share information in order to present themselves and create a good self-impression on others. One way to manage impression is through self-enhancement, which is a basic human need to feel good about oneself (Baumeister 1982). In order to maintain self-enhancement, individuals tend to think positively about themselves and also would like to show their positive features. For this reason, individuals often try to share information that makes them look good, special or ethical, which strengthen one's own self (Richins 1983). Research has shown that individuals also engage in social interactions to receive positive recognition from others (Berger and Schwartz 2011). This basic motivation to self-enhance oneself leads consumers to sharing especially positive experiences about themselves and passing along negative experiences that they heard occurring to others (De Angelis et al. 2012). Consistent with this perspective, consumers might talk about prosocial activities of companies to show that they support such initiatives, which could self-enhancement and provide identity signaling. For instance, imagine a person shares a post online about "Hunger Action Month" campaign, held by Kellogg, that commits to donate two million meals. When others that see this person's post, they may infer about the sender that she/he cares a lot about poverty, hunger and those others in need. Further, talking and spreading about such prosocial initiatives might also make the sender feel good, inferring that they are being altruistic and helpful to the community. For instance, research has shown that when consumers engage in donation behaviors and brag

	CSR (general)	Philanthropy	Sustainable operations	Negative CSR	Cause-related marketing
Impression management	Kang, Germann and Grewal, 2016 Lacey, Kennett-Hensel and Manolis, 2015 Martin, Johnson and French, 2011 Nikolaeva and Bicho, 2011 Torelli, Monga and Kaikati, 2012 Vlachos et al. 2009 Wagner, Lutz and Weitz, 2009 Yoon, Gürhan-Canli and Schwarz, 2006	Berman et al. 2015 Chernev and Blair, 2015 Kull and Heath, 2016 Peloza and Shang, 2011 Sen, Bhattacharya and Korschun, 2006	Luchs et al. 2010 Wagner, Lutz and Weitz, 2009 Peloza and Shang, 2011	Kang, Germann and Grewal, 2016 Peloza and Shang, 2011	Koschate-Fischer, Huber and Hoyer 2016
Identity signaling	Biehal and Sheinin 2007 Martin, Johnson and French, 2011 Korschun, Bhattacharya and Swain, 2014	Chen and Huang 2016 Homburg, Stierl and Bornemann 2013	Ailawadi et al., 2014 Klein and Dawar, 2004 Hensen et al. 2016 Branco and Villas-Boas, 2015	Lei, Dawar, Gürhan-Canli, 2012 Klein and Dawar 2004	
Creating support		Bennett, Kim and Loken, 2013			Kull and Heath 2016 Koschate-Fischer, Stefan and Hoyer, 2012
Information acquisition	Yoon, Gürhan-Canli and Schwarz, 2006 McShane and Cunningham, 2012	Wagner, Lutz and Weitz, 2009	Wagner, Lutz and Weitz, 2009	Zhao, Zhao, and Helsen, 2011 Gijsenberg, Van Heerde and Verhoef, 2015 Kalaignanam, Kushwaha and Eilert 2013	
Altruism	Lacey, Kennett-Hensel and Manolis 2015 Vlachos et al. 2009	Berman et al. 2015	Iyer and Soberman 2016 Ailawadi et al., 2014		Koschate-Fischer, Stefan and Hoyer, 2012

about them, such as by posting it on Facebook, they enhance their self-impression and are perceived as generous (Berman et al. 2015)

Just like individuals, companies also carry out activities to self-enhance themselves. Corporate social responsibilities are perceived as tools that boost companies' reputation and stimulate goodwill among consumers (Chernev and Blair 2015). Our systematic work has revealed that impression management is one of the important functions that corporate social responsibility activities can offer. Consumers evaluate companies based on the impressions they receive from CSR activities such as charities or cause-related campaigns (e.g., Koschate-Fischer, Stefan and Hoyer 2012). Based on the social responsibility activities conducted by the firms, consumers infer positive impression about the companies and become inclined towards talking about the good impression they received from the CSR activities (Vlachos et al. 2009). For instance, Cancer Research UK has conducted "Nomakeupselfie" campaign which asked women to post selfies without make-up with the hashtag #nomakeupselfie. This campaign increased cancer awareness in the society and received around £8m donations (Miranda and Steiner 2014). Imagine this campaign were supported by a cosmetics company, it would give the impression that this company cares about the society and health-consciousness, which could have triggered buzz among consumers that support the campaign.

The impression the companies build through prosocial activities might depend on brand identity, perceived sincerity, fairness and trust mechanisms, which in turn influence whether consumers recommend the products (Vlachos et al. 2009). First, social responsibility is about the self-transcendence concept (i.e., protecting the welfare of all), which therefore contradicts with excessive self-enhancement concept (i.e., dominance over people and resources). Such contradiction arises especially for luxury brands, which might lead to less favorable corporate social responsibility evaluations (Torelli, Monga and Kaikati 2012). Second, trust is an important mechanism for propagation of CSR activities among consumers. There is evidence showing that corporate social responsibilities are evaluated favorably (Yoon, Gürhan-Canli and Schwarz 2006) and lead to higher recommendation intentions (Vlachos et al. 2009) when the motives provide trust to the consumer. Relatedly, the systematic review reveals that "where" and "when" the prosocial activities are communicated matters. Customers might evaluate the campaigns as less sincere if they learn these activities through advertising. It is much more ideal when consumers act as advocates spreading prosocial activities of the firms, rather than ads creating publicity, as consumers are perceived as more trustworthy and sincere. Vlachos et al. (2009) provided support that when consumers trust in corporate social activities, it leads to patronage and recommendation intentions. Further, consumers might perceive the corporate responsible activities hypocritical when companies acknowledge their responsible actions proactively before their irresponsible (contradictory) behavior, rather than reactively. Taking these findings together, companies can get support for their prosocial activities by creating good impression of their activities especially through gaining trust through customers and avoid extreme self-enhancement or publicity.

Finally, although several consumers assume that companies carry out and report their social causes for largely altruistic reasons, one of the main drivers is to manage companies' reputation. In most cases, the firm's institutional environment that are influenced by competitors and media, along with the companies' media visibility publicity efforts create pressure to adopt reporting of the CSR activities (Nikolaeva and Bicho 2011). In fact, supporting this view, research suggests that companies should engage in prosocial activities with strategic reasons based on how their customers demand and place value

(Lacey, Kennett-Hensel and Manolis 2015). As additional evidence suggests, corporate social responsibility activities should be carried out strategically in the present time, as it does not insure against irresponsible behavior that might happen in the future (Kang, Germann and Grewal 2016).

While some studies explored the phenomenon of impression management for corporate social responsibility in general, there were also several studies that specifically focused on certain types of corporate social responsibility such as philanthropy and sustainable activities. Next, these studies are discussed on how they relate to impression management, which could in turn, help these campaigns propagate their socially responsible initiatives among consumers.

More companies produce and promote products that are sustainable with a positive social and environmental impact. The impression of the consumers about the ethics of these products might depend on product characteristics, such as attributes. For instance, Luchs et al. (2010) has shown that products with gentleness-related attributes are valued more ethical than those with strength-related attributes. In the light of these findings, when companies want their sustainability programs to be talked among the public, they would benefit from communicating more of the gentleness-related attributes in their communications, which might also boost preference for the sustainable products.

Further, the effect of corporate responsibility activities on creating a favorable impression and identity are shaped along with firms' other messages and societal norms. Corporate messages often transfer on each other to form judgments, with varying degrees of influence. For instance, a corporate ability (quality) message transferred more to the products than a corporate social responsibility message (Biehal and Sheinin 2007). These findings suggest that in order to give the best impression, companies should balance the communication of CSR messages with other messages of the company. Literature suggests that the organizational and societal environment also influence company identity, which affects the extent to which resources are allocated to ethical and CSR issues (Martin, Johnson and French 2011). Consistent with this view, WOM literature suggests that the buzz around a firm is generated through an echo verse where diverse set of factors (e.g., ads, public releases) influence each other (Hewett et al. 2016), including the environment in which the messages spread (Berger and Heath 2007). Taken together, the consistency of the messages across different activities and fit with the environment is important for creating a good impression about corporate social responsibilities that would spread in the society.

Consumers not only talk about CSR activities but also "unsustainable activities" of companies, such as unethical production standards that pollute the environment, poor standards of labor, and product harm crises. First, research in WOM has shown that sharing negative news might also serve as part of impression management (Schlosser 2005). For example, consumers might talk about companies that fail in corporate social responsibility to show that they are intelligent, competent and in-the-know about such issues. Talking about unsustainable activities that concern the society may provide inferences and status about consumers. Second, the way companies are perceived based on their unsustainable activities or public crises depends on their previous CSR activities, as well as brand characteristics. For less well-known brands, negative publicity might surprisingly help the companies, as they receive more attention (Berger, Sorensen and Rasmussen 2010). Yet, companies should carry out positive activities to amend for the past irresponsible behaviors (i.e., penance mechanism; Kang, Germann and Grewal 2016), as consumers construct attributions based on their prior beliefs (Lei, Dawar, Gürhan-Canli 2012) and, therefore, might blame the companies more if they have involved in negative corporate responsibility before.

Finally, the impact of social responsibility can extend beyond creating goodwill, and spill-over on unrelated consumer judgments. As Chernev and Blair (2015) has suggested, consumers evaluate performance of the products better, even when the charity activities are unrelated to the company's products. Consumers perceive the moral undertone of the companies from their philanthropy actions, and their good will translates to their actions by preferring those companies. These findings have been supported by real word instances of philanthropy, where the effects of such prosocial initiatives extend not only to product evaluations, but also employment, investment domains (Sen, Bhattacharya and Korschun 2006). The spill-over effects of prosocial activities have been also shown to influence the impact of product harm crises on product evaluations (Klein and Dawar 2004). In the light of the findings in literature, companies should not only stimulate consumers to talk about their products but also spread their moral undertones and goodwill, which could in turn extend their good impression or prevent from the adverse effects of product harm crises spreading.

Identity signaling

Individuals share content in order to reveal their self-identity, which is also part of impression management. When consumers talk about certain topics, or consume certain products, they might signal their knowledge or expertise (Packard and Wooten 2013). For instance, consumers talk about food to show that they are foodies or talk about books or movies to show that they are intellectuals. Similarly, using recyclable shopping bags rather than plastic bags reveal that the consumer is environmentally conscious. Just like consumers, companies might also signal their identity through their social causes, and their related communication campaigns. Although literature identity signaling has been studied as one of the factors among impression management, in this review, we have devoted a separate section given the reasonable number of studies that have discussed issues related to it.

Certain types of corporate social responsibility activities might signal more positive identities depending on consumer characteristics. For instance, for consumers with interdependent self-construal, corporate philanthropy leads to better brand images and self–brand connections compared to cause-related marketing, but this is not the case for consumers with independent self-construal (Chen and Huang 2016). Research in WOM literature has revealed that self-construal (independent versus interdependent) also affects what consumers share with others consumers (Akpinar, Verlegh and Smidts 2013). Taken together, targeting specific segments of customers with different type of CSR activities might foster propagation of CSR activities.

Employees, business partners and competitors might also determine the success of CSR activities. First, employees and business partners might construct employee- (or customer-)company identities based on the CSR activities companies carry out. For instance, Korschun, Bhattacharya and Swain (2014) showed that employees identify with firms (i.e., organizational identification) based on the extent to which they perceive that the management supports CSR activities, and this effect is dependent on importance of the CSR to the employee. Relatedly, Homburg, Stierl and Bornemann (2013) showed that philanthropic CSR strengthens customer–company identification. Further, successful implementation of prosocial strategies across a network of employees can create a responsible environment, which might boost sales of environmental products (Hensen et al. 2016). These related works together suggest that the influence about social causes becomes contagious, starting from companies, creating identities on employees and in turn customers. Future work should examine the propagation of identity signaling among companies, employees and customers more in depth.

Finally, the competitive landscape might be also influential for following ethical rules in the market place. The other firms in the competition might create invisible influence, by providing signals for the firms in following responsible behaviors (Branco and Villas-Boas 2015). In the light of these findings, companies should not only maintain good impression of their CSR activities among customers but also employees, business partners and competitors, as research has shown that the impressions about CSR activities can be contagious, affecting various stakeholders simultaneously. Future work could examine to what extent the pressure created by the competitors versus customers affect companies to engage in responsible behaviors.

Creating support

One of the other reasons consumers share content is to generate help or receive support from others. Recent work in WOM literature has shown that sharing content boosts well-being because individuals perceive social support through sharing (Buechel and Berger 2012). Especially for cause-related marketing campaigns, receiving consumers' support is important as they might also influence other consumers and bring in more support for the cause. The more cause-related campaigns spread, the more support can be achieved. Sharing the cause with others might also allow consumers to connect with similar others and reinforce their shared views about the issue (Berger and Heath 2007). For instance, in Expedia's Give Them Wings campaign, which sponsored underprivileged children's holidays, individuals were allowed to contribute to the cause through Facebook activities such as "likes", as well as bookings made through this website. Sharing a campaign to help underprivileged children might connect people who feel similar about certain issues and create social bonding. Spreading responsible activities among communities that have similar interests might reinforce shared views and facilitate more support through social bonding.

Companies can benefit from CSR activities that penetrate through public and, in the meantime, promote its core business values. Kromkommer (a Dutch company) provides a good example. Kromkommer (meaning crooked cucumber) was founded with the mission to save all the fruits and veggies that otherwise would have been wasted because of their looks or overproduction. To be able to make this mission work, they created a totally new business. These social gains have been met by business gains for the company. This initiative is a great example not only for transforming the business but also receiving public support. The company was funded by a crowdsourcing campaign, which received the funds from public.

With the rise of co-creating in marketing, companies involve more consumers in cause-related marketing campaigns where consumers decide which cause to support. Research has shown that the co-created corporate social responsibility programs boost brand related outcomes (Kull and Heath 2016), through giving the consumers the right to choose. The support consumers are willing to provide for corporate social responsibility depends on the nature of the program and the extent to which companies contribute. For instance, when consumers contribute to cause-related marketing programs, they judge the fairness of the prices as sometimes companies increase prices partially to cover the costs of the campaign (Koschate-Fischer, Stefan and Hoyer 2012). Thus, consumers should perceive that their contribution as well as the companies' contribution are balanced. The contribution of corporate sponsorships might even have unintended consequence. Especially in the case of providing support for non-profit organizations. Consumers might be less likely to contribute to non-profit organizations because they might perceive their contribution will be less meaningful comparted to the corporate sponsorship (Bennett, Kim and Loken 2013).

Finally, consumers might share unsustainable activities of companies in order to spread the news to other consumers and, consequently, take vengeance. Especially when consumers become very angry, frustrated or dissatisfied, they might share negative WOM (Bougie, Pieters and Zeelenberg, 2003) and receive support from other consumers. In fact, such cases might even end up being useful for the companies to improve their sustainability. For instance, Nestlé has committed to stop using products that come from rainforest destruction, after the company was attacked by thousands of social media activists on networks such as Facebook and YouTube, initiated by Greenpeace's campaign. This initiative has led Nestlé to transform its business model by committing to sustainable production certified by the Roundtable on Sustainable Palm Oil and also drives changes in the sector. Future work should examine how companies can turn crisis into advantages by exploring the boundaries and conditions of benefiting from negative WOM about companies' public crisis.

Information acquisition

While companies carry out socially responsible activities, they should also care for informing about their activities in the best possible way. Inconsistency between the companies' actual behaviors and stated corporate social responsibility might lead to distrust and uncertainty among consumers, which could be counterproductive for the companies. Perceived sincerity of a company acts as an important informational cue when consumers evaluate CSR activities of the companies (Yoon, Gürhan-Canli and Schwarz 2006). WOM serves as one of the facilitators for providing trust and reducing uncertainty among consumers. Research has shown that when consumers need to seek advice or resolve problems about brands, they communicate with other consumers they trust (Henning-Thurau and Walsh 2004; Zao and Xie 2011). For instance, imagine there is a product harm crisis about a famous chocolate spread brand. Consumers talk among themselves about the potential risks of consuming the product and warn each other. When consumers are uncertain about the product quality, they update their perception about the product over time, acquiring information from others and updating their prior information (Zhao, Zhao and Helsen 2011). Given that consumers spread information at a much faster mode in the era of social media, companies should strategically craft what needs to be communicated to consumers and when to avoid distrust and uncertainty. For instance, research suggests that when there is an inconsistency between the firm's statements and observed behavior, a reactive strategy (i.e., the firm communicates after the observed behavior) might lead to more trust than a proactive strategy (i.e., the firm communicates before the observed behavior; Wagner, Lutz and Weitz 2009). Future work should explore how companies should communicate information about their products especially when they face crisis.

Information provided about the sincerity and authenticity of the prosocial activities are also important from the perspective of the employees. Employees have access to several cues that allow them to assess the authenticity of the activities, such as sustained commitment of the resources, alignment of CSR programs with company's internal activities or emotional engagement of the management and staff (McShane and Cunningham 2012). It might be that a company is carrying out philanthropic activities or activities to improve operational effectiveness, yet the company's employees do not consider those activities as authentic or sincere. Just like consumers, employees that do not find CSR activities authentic might talk about their inferences with other employees but also outside the organization. It is important for organizations to carry out responsible activities that gain both trust of consumers and the employees of companies.

The timing of the information might affect how information propagates among consumers. Although not intended, several companies run into failures such as major delays, and service outrages. Research has shown that such crises affect quality perceptions over time, where losses in performance seem larger than gains in the short run and might even become permanent in the long run (Gijsenberg, Van Heerde and Verhoef, 2015). In case of such crises, companies are concerned that the crisis might spread even further as consumers talk about the bad news. Consistent with this perspective, WOM research has shown that transmission of information among consumers has long carry over effects, which might have both short-term and long-term effects on the performance of the companies (Trusov, Bucklin and Pauwels 2009). Given these findings, companies should especially be cautious about the consequences of negative information spreading in the marketplace.

Finally, companies might learn from their product recall programs and therefore enhance safety. Research has shown that higher numbers of product recall might decrease future recalls and number of injuries (Kalaignanam, Kushwaha and Eilert 2013). Recent work in WOM suggests that social media should not only be used for content generation but also for marketing research (Schweidel and Moe 2014). Given that recent social media listening tools provide possibilities for listening to the voice of customers in a detailed way including sentiment, companies can learn from the consumers' feedback to implement effective product changes.

Altruism

Corporate social responsibilities are supposed to provide unselfish care to the welfare. Yet, it is not clear whether any prosocial behavior is motivated by truly self-less altruistic motivations or by self-serving (i.e., egoistic) altruistic motivations. Research suggests that both drivers could play a role and a truly self-less altruism might help the provider with self-benefit as an unintended consequence such as increase in reputation and or prestige (Ailawadi et al. 2014; Koschate-Fischer, Stefan and Hoyer 2012). A similar argument about the role of self-less and self-serving motivations is also applicable for WOM. Consumers might share content to just help others (e.g., talking about a terrible restaurant experience in order to protect others), but also to show that they care about others. It could be intrinsic altruism that drives people to contribute to prosocial behaviors or communicate their experiences with others, and as a result they might be benefit from their good deeds and WOM.

The clash of two opposing inferences about self-less and self-serving altruistic motivations arise when consumers or companies talk about their social responsibility actions. On the one hand, bragging about the prosocial behavior boosts perceptions of self-less altruism, on the other hand bragging might also signal self-serving altruistic motivations (Berman et al. 2015). The latter motivation might overshadow the self-less motives and, as a result, be counterproductive. Given the two opposing mechanisms that drive social responsibility, one could wonder to what extent these motivations are applied in prac-tice and what would be ideal to use. Research suggests that while managers support the socially responsible actions for largely altruistic reasons, companies should lead these activities with strategic reasons given that customers demand corporate social responsi-bility and value them (Lacey, Kennett-Hensel and Manolis 2015). Regardless of the per-formance of the firms (i.e., in service quality), appropriately motivated corporate social responsibility provides trust to the consumers (Vlachos et al. 2009).

Finally, certain types of corporate social responsibility might be perceived as more altru-istic than some others. For instance, philanthropy is perceived as more altruistic than cause-related marketing campaigns (Chen and Huang 2016). Altruism perceptions might also be affected by consumer characteristics such as self-construal (independent versus interde-pendent). The difference between cause-related marketing campaigns and philanthropy, in terms of altruism perceptions, becomes more salient under interdependent self-construal than independent self-construal. Research on WOM is also consistent with the notion that self-construal affects what consumers share and how they participate in online brand communities (Sinha and Lu 2016). Consumers' intrinsic altruism motivations lead them to engage in online brand communities, and this is especially salient under interdepend-ent self-construal (Lee, Kim, and Kim 2012). Taken together, one could expect that under interdependent self-construal, consumers should be more likely to talk about philanthropy compared to cause-related marketing activities, driven through altruism motives, which could be explored in future research.

The decision of the firms to invest in socially responsible innovations is driven by consumers' altruistic motivations as well as extrinsic motivations. Imagine a consumer purchases a bag that is degradable in nature and toxic free. If these socially responsi-ble features are visible to others in social interactions, consumers would enjoy a social comparison benefit from the product (Iyer and Soberman 2016). Consistent with this perspective, products that are more visible get talked about more and provide social sta-tus cues might become contagious (Berger and Schwartz 2011). The visible features of socially responsible goods could provide consumers more extrinsic benefits (e.g., convey the impression that the person is environment conscious) and therefore get more popular among consumers.

Consequences of corporate social responsibility in terms of WOM

There has been extensive work that has explored the consequences of corporate social responsibility initiatives (see Peloza and Shang 2011; Srinivasan and Hanssens 2009 for a review). The impact of CSR activities on stakeholders and outcomes have been varied and inconsistent. Some studies have focused on comparing different types of CSR activi-ties and measuring the effectiveness of different campaign methods (e.g., Lacey, Kennett-Hensel and Manolis 2015), whereas some others have focused on exploring the effects of CSR activities on certain outcomes (see Table 4.4.2 for a detailed overview). As system-atic review of the studies reveals, the majority of the work done in the area of corporate social responsibility has focused on consequences such as financial performance relation-ships (e.g., Srinivasan and Hanssens 2009); sales (volume)/purchase intentions (Koschate-Fischer, Stefan and Hoyer 2012) and product and brand knowledge (Biehal and Sheinin 2007). While exploring the diverse effects of CSR is important, this review delves more specifically into understanding the contagion of CSR activities. For this reason, in this systematic review, first the studies are categorized based on the outcomes of corporate

Table 4.4.2 Representative articles for consequences of CSR – word of mouth; evaluation of CSR; product/brand evaluation/purchase intention/sales; price/promotion evaluation; trust/credibility/loyalty/reputation/sincerity

	CSR (general)	Philanthropy	Sustainable operations	Negative CSR	Cause-related marketing
Word of Mouth	Lacey, Kennett-Hensel and Manolis 2015 Vlachos et al. 2009		Xie, Bagozzi, and Gronhaug, 2015	Einwiller et al. 2006 Borah and Tellis 2016	Carvalho et al. 2008 Hsu and Lawrence, 2016 Lei, Dawar and Lemmink 2008
Evaluation of CSR	Chabowski, Mena and Gonzales–Padron 2011 Gupta and Sen 2013 Uslay, Morgan and Sheth, 2009 Vlachos et al. 2009 Yoon, Gürhan–Canli and Schwarz 2006	Szócs et al. 2016 Bennett, Kim and Loken 2013 Sen, Bhattacharya and Korschun 2006 Chernev and Blair 2015	Hensen et al. 2016 Newman, Gorlin and Dhar 2014 Sheth, Sethia and Srinivas 2011 Uslay, Morgan and Sheth 2009	Chen, Ganesan and Liu 2009 Einwiller et al. 2006 Gorn, Jiang and Johar 2008 Kalaignanam, Kushwaha and Eilert 2013 Liu, Liu and Luo 2016 Monga and John 2008	Kuo and Rice 2015
Product/brand evaluation/ purchase intention/sales	Biehal and Sheinin 2007 Chabowski, Mena and Gonzales–Padron 2011 Chernev and Blair 2015 Kang, Germann and Grewal, 2016 Torelli, Monga and Kaikati 2012	Chen and Huang 2016 Chernev and Blair 2015 Koschate-Fischer, Stefan and Hoyer, 2012 Kull and Heath 2016 Sen, Bhattacharya and Korschun 2006 Wagner, Lutz and Weitz 2009	Du, Bhattacharya, and Sen 2007 Kashmiri and Mahajan 2010 Klein and Dawar 2004 Luchs et al. 2010 Newman Gorlin and Dhar 2014 Sheth, Sethia and Srinivas 2011 Srinivasan and Hanssens, 2009 Wagner, Lutz and Weitz 2009	Cleeren van Heerde and Dekimpe 2013 Einwiller et al. 2006 Gao et al. 2015 Kang, Germann and Grewal 2016 Klein and Dawar 2004 Lei, Dawar and Lemmink 2008 Pullig, Netemeyer and Biswas 2006 Puzakova, Kwak and Rocereto 2013 Rubel, Naik and Srinivasan 2011 Van Heerde, Helsen and DeKimpe 2007 Zhao, Zhao and Helsen 2011	Koschate-Fischer, Huber and Hoyer 2016 Larson et al. 2008

(Continued)

Table 4.4.2 Continued

	CSR (general)	Philanthropy	Sustainable operations	Negative CSR	Cause-related marketing
Price/promotion evaluation	Winterich and Barone, 2011 Habel et al. 2016	Habel et al. 2016	Iyer and Soberman 2016 Van Heerde, Helsen and DeKimpe 2007	Cleeren van Heerde and Dekimpe 2013	Koschate-Fischer, Huber and Hoyer 2016
Trust/ credibility/ loyalty/ reputation/ sincerity	Gupta and Sen 2013 Luo and Bhattacharya 2009 Vlachos et al. 2009 Yoon, Gürhan-Canli and Schwarz 2006	Habel et al. 2016 Homburg, Stierl, and Bornemann 2013 Szőcs et al. 2016 Torres et al. 2012	Ailawadi et al. 2014 Du, Bhattacharya, and Sen 2007 Habel et al. 2016 Homburg, Stierl and Bornemann 2013 Torres et al. 2012		Gijsenberg, Van Heerde and Verhoef, 2015 Hsu and Lawrence 2016 Lei, Dawar and Gürhan-Canli, 2012 Van Heerde, Helsen and DeKimpe 2007

social responsibilities, and then just the studies that discuss outcomes related to WOM are considered. Note that the effects of corporate social responsibility might have been investigated on a diverse set of outcomes, which is why some studies are listed across a set of consequences, including WOM. Further, WOM or spill-over of socially responsible behaviors might not be only a consequence but also a mediator.

When consumers have positive attitudes towards a company, they are willing to act as advocates and refer the company to other consumers. Lacey, Kennett-Hensel and Manolis (2015) demonstrated that CSR might both act as a catalyst or a hygiene factor for encouraging WOM. On the one hand, corporate social responsibilities of a company might act as a facilitator for consumers in providing positive WOM, when consumers perceive the social responsibility activities favorably. On the other hand, it might prevent consumers from talking about the company favorably when the company's social responsibility efforts are perceived to be not satisfactory or lacking. Further, the influence of CSR on triggering WOM is strengthened by the relationship quality (i.e., trust, commitment) between the customer and the company.

One of the important drivers of getting contagious is being visible (Berger and Schwartz 2011). Consistent with this perspective, the more visible a social good becomes, the more support it might receive from the public. Therefore, companies both invest in the causes as well as publicizing them. For example, Phillip Morris contributed around $75 million to charity and spent around $100 million on a campaign to spread the news (Porter and Kramer 2002). Such practices might lead to distrust among consumers, when they become suspicious about the intrinsic motivations of the firms. Trust is one of the main drivers that makes WOM successful compared to traditional marketing practices. Relatedly, when consumers attribute distrust or hypocrisy to the charity activities of a brand, they are less likely to recommend the brand to other consumers (Vlachos et al. 2009). Therefore, trust acts an important mediator when companies want to publicize their social cause through recommendation of consumers.

Research in WOM shows that emotions influence the likelihood of sharing content. For instance, content that convey high arousal emotions are more likely to be shared than content that convey low arousal emotions (Berger and Milkman 2012). Relatedly, corporate responsible and irresponsible actions might convey emotions that have a mediating role on facilitating positive and negative WOM. For instance, consumers that encounter environmental responsible behavior of a company, might feel gratitude, which could trigger positive WOM for the company. On the other hand, consumers that encounter environmental irresponsible actions, might feel emotions such as contempt, anger and disgust, which could trigger negative WOM for the company (Xie, Bagozzi and Grønhaug 2015). These findings suggest that non-deliberative processes such as emotions can influence how consumers approach social responsibility actions and, as a consequence, provide positive and negative WOM about the companies.

As noted earlier, the likelihood of sharing might depend on consumer psychological characteristics. For instance, research has shown that the extent to which consumers are affected by the negative publicity depend on the consumer–company identification (Einwiller et al. 2006). When consumers that have strong identification with a company and are exposed to moderately negative publicity, it results in less negative associations about the company, compared to consumers that have weak identification. Yet, when the negative publicity is really severe, then the level of identification does not moderate the negative corporate associations. Further, characteristics such as cultural similarity and personal relevance might also affect the extent to which consumers are affected by negative publicity. Research has shown that consumers might be more concerned less about a food contamination that takes place in a close physical or geographical location if there is not much cultural similarity (Carvalho et al. 2008). On the conditions where consumers perceive the crises as personally relevant, then the effect of cultural similarity might be less salient.

Crises such as product recalls can have drastic effects on firms' value. Especially in the digital era, where news spreads relatively quickly over a wide network, the negative effects can be magnified through online WOM. Research has shown that the more negative and faster the growth of online WOM, the worse the effect of product recalls on financial returns (Hsu and Lawrence 2016). Surprisingly, even if companies try to engage in social media by defending against the crises, their attempts get ineffective given the big volume of online chatter. One way to protect the brands from the product crises that becomes magnified in social media environment is to build a strong brand equity. While having a strong brand equity might be useful to protect from product crises, strong associations with other brands in companies' brand portfolio (Lei, Dawar and Lemmink 2008) or other brands in the product category (Borah and Tellis 2016) might create a negative spill-over.

In sum, as the systematic review shows, propagation of corporate social responsibility activities and its public visibility or generation of support from consumers or society at large for social causes, can be influenced by a variety of factors including the relationship quality (i.e., trust and commitment) between the customer and the company, emotions, cultural similarity, personal relevance of the issues or brand equity. The effects of social responsibility and WOM can be directional, where responsible behaviors of the companies can initiate more WOM about the companies and WOM can magnify the effects of social responsibility or product harm crises.

The effects of WOM components on propagation of CSR activities

WOM literature has shown that the characteristics of four components of communication (sender, receiver, message and channel) might have an impact on the likelihood of content being shared. Propagation of a CSR activity can be described using the four components. For instance, the ALS Association – a non-profit organization fighting a progressive neurodegenerative disease – (*sender*) has raised a campaign called the Ice Bucket Challenge (*message*), where it promotes awareness of the ALS disease. In this campaign, the *receiver* of message can also become the sender, if they nominate another person to dump a bucket of ice and water over a person's head and encourage donations to research about this disease (ALS Association, 2017). This message might be broadcast through an online video (*channel*) where the message is sent to a large group of receivers, or might be narrow-casted, where the message is sent only to a person (Barasch and Berger 2014).

So far in our review, the focus has been on *why* the sender shares CSR activities and *consequences* of CSR related to sharing. It is also important to understand how characteristics of the sender, receiver, message or channel may moderate when and how CSR activities are being talked about, interacting with other components of WOM communication. In this section, we will review studies from CSR literature in which the role of sender, receiver, content and channel characteristics will be discussed. Representative studies are summarized in Table 4.4.3.

Table 4.4.3 Representative articles for WOM components on propagation of CSR – sender, receiver, content and channel

	CSR (general)	Philanthropy	Sustainable operations	Negative CSR	Cause-related marketing
Sender	Kashmiri and Mahajan, 2014 Luo and Bhattacharya, 2009	Torres et al. 2012 Homburg, Stierl, and Bornemann 2013	Martin, Johnson and French, 2011 Kashmiri and Mahajan 2010 Luchs et al. 2010 Newman, Gorlin and Dhar, 2014 Hensen et al. 2016	Puzakova, Kwak and Rocereto, 2013 Hsu and Lawrence, 2011 Gao et al., 2015	Koschate-Fischer, Huber and Hoyer, 2016
Receiver	Winterich and Barone, 2011 Gupta and Sen, 2013 Zemack-Roger et al. 2016	Chen and Huang, 2016 Szőcs et al. 2016	Xie, Bagozzi, and Grønhaug, 2015 Klein and Dawar, 2004	Puzakova, Kwak and Rocereto, 2013 Carvalho et al., 2008 Winterich et al., 2015 Monga and John, 2008 Einwiller et al., 2006 Pullig, Netemeyer and Biswas, 2006 Cleeren, Dekimpe and Helsen, 2008	
Content	Robinson, Irmak and Jayachandran 2012 Wagner, Lutz and Weitz 2009	Bennett, Kim, and Loken, 2013 Homburg, Stierl and Bornemann, 2013		Chen, Ganesan and Liu, 2009	Kuo and Rice, 2015
Channel				Hsu and Lawrence, 2016	

Sender

In WOM literature, the impact of the sender has been mostly investigated from the perspective of why the sender shares the content (e.g., self-enhancement, emotion regulation) or consumer psychographics (see King, Racherla and Bush 2014 for a review). In this section, we review characteristics of companies and products that might get CSR activities or negative publicity shared. Note that consumers might act as both receivers (receive the news from the companies, media reports or other consumers) and senders that spread the news about corporate social responsibility activities. In the next section, we discuss the role of consumers as recipients separately.

Research has revealed certain characteristics of companies or products that makes them achieve success in corporate social responsibility. For instance, a company's organizational identity is one of the important features that affects resource allocation to ethical production facilities (Martin, Johnson and French 2011). Some other work has shown that family owned companies provide strong emphasis on corporate social responsibility during recessions which helps to maintain relatively good levels of performance (Kashmiri and Mahajan 2010; 2014). Further, even if a brand is a global one, following local social responsibilities enhances brand equity, which fosters the benefits of corporate social responsibilities (Torres et al. 2012). Although there has been extensive work in WOM that has explored a variety of company/ brand characteristics (e.g., brands that are in the Interbrand [top 100] and more familiar have higher WOM, Lovett, Peres, and Shachar 2013), there is need for research that specifically explores effect of organizational identity, family owned companies, global (versus local) brands on WOM of CSR. For instance, could it be that because family firms are afraid of losing the validity of their own family reputation due to a product crisis (compared to non-family firms), they are more careful about the corporate social responsibilities? Could it be that the impact of global companies bigger than local companies in getting their local social responsibilities contagious? Future research should explore such characteristics of companies that might drive propagation of corporate social responsibilities.

Research has also demonstrated some characteristics of the products/services, employees or supplier of the companies that make CSR activities successful. For instance, product characteristics such as gentleness-related features versus strength-related features (Luchs et al. 2010), intended versus unintended environmental benefits of green products (Newman, Gorlin and Dhar 2014) and humanization of brands (Puzakova, Kwak and Rocereto 2013) have been shown to influence environmental social responsibility activities of the companies. Although, various other features of products or brands (e.g., hedonic versus utilitarian, warm versus competent, being interesting, public visibility, controversy) have been studied in WOM literature (e.g., Berger and Schwarz 2011; Chen and Berger 2013), the features that affect corporate social responsibility suggests new novel ideas for future research. Could it be that consumers are more likely to talk about products with unintended environmental benefits because unintended effects would be more surprising? Would consumers be more likely to talk about socially responsible features that are gentleness-related or strength-related features? Also, one could wonder whether humanized brands that engage in public harm crises receive more empathy and therefore criticized less heavily by public.

Employees also play an important role in creating a socially responsible organizational climate (Hensen et al. 2016). In some cases, the dyad of supplier-company-customer link determines the success of social responsible activities (Homburg, Stierl and Bornemann 2013), whereas in other cases the CEOs' (chief executive officers) financial interests can determine how companies handle product crises (Liu, Liu and Luo 2016). Relatedly, WOM literature has also shown the role of employees in issues such as recruiting and penetrating organizational identity (Keeling, McGoldrick and Sadhu 2013). Combining these perspectives, future work could examine how WOM among employees regarding social responsibilities spread and impact the success of the activities. In addition, CEOs have been heavily criticized due to their high salaries, raising doubts about employment salary and product price fairness. Future work could examine to what extent perceptions about the CEOs trigger more negative buzz when a company becomes involved in product harm crisis.

Finally, research has documented various actions that influence how corporate social responsibility of the companies are perceived. For instance, research has shown that the amount companies donate to company-cause fits for cause-related campaigns affects price fairness and evaluations of the CSR activities (Koschate-Fischer, Huber and Hoyer 2016, Sen and Bhattacharya 2001). Further, corporate social activities along with advertising is more helpful (Luo and Bhattacharya 2009), whereas companies involved in alleviating the potential negative effects of social media during a product recall is not much helpful (Hsu and Lawrence 2011), and ad spending before a product recall about an established product might even make the stock price drop more (Gao et al. 2015). Relatedly, WOM literature has investigated how company initiated activities such as advertising act together with conversations about products (Hewett et al. 2016). Future research could examine how corporate social responsibility or product harm crises might spread counting on the factors such as advertising, sponsored social media activities, type of the brand (new versus established) and fit of the brand with the (ir)responsible corporate issue that might also affect each other.

Receiver

Companies aim to have more customers who talk about them favorably and spread the news to others, who would consequently share positive WOM. Depending on whom the recipient is, senders might have different motivations to share WOM. For instance, a consumer that supports a company's environmental sustainability campaign might share the news with others that would also be interested in such issues to create a common ground and also signal that she/he also cares about the environmental issues (Fast, Heath and Wu, 2009). In CSR literature, various consumer characteristics have been investigated. Below, I provide a review of these characteristics and discuss how they can be influential in propagation of corporate social responsibility.

A diverse set of consumer characteristics have been discussed in literature to have an impact on both responsible and irresponsible actions of the companies, such as self-construal (Chen and Huang 2016; Winterich and Barone, 2011), belief in personality stability (Puzakova, Kwak and Rocereto 2013), geographical residence or cultural similarities (Carvalho et al. 2008; Winterich et al. 2015), thinking styles (Monga and John 2008; Gupta and Sen 2013), justice values (Zemack-Roger et al. 2016; Xie, Bagozzi and Grønhaug 2015), brand attitudes (Klein and Dawar 2004; Einwiller et al. 2006; Pullig, Netemeyer and Biswas 2006), and usage frequency (Szőcs et al. 2016; Cleeren, Dekimpe and Helsen 2008).

Each of the characteristics listed above might raise interesting questions to understand how corporate social responsibility of the companies can propagate among consumers. For instance, research on WOM has shown that word of mouth is more likely when self-construal becomes more interdependent (Lee, Kim, and Kim 2012). Relatedly, research has shown that consumers with interdependent self-construal responded to CRM (customer relationship management) more favorably than philanthropy (Chen and Huang 2016). Combining these two perspectives, future research can investigate whether consumers are more likely to share CRM than philanthropy and whether this tendency can be reversed for causes that are collective identity congruent, which might be salient for interdependent self-construal. Further, research has shown that holistic thinkers are less vulnerable to negative publicity than are analytic thinkers because they consider context-based explanations (Monga and John 2008). Relatedly, research in WOM has shown that consumers would evaluate a product more favorably when some little dose of negative information is enclosed along with a positive information (Ein-Gar, Shiv and Tormala 2012). Further research could examine whether consumers with holistic thinkers would be more likely to share socially responsible news of the companies when some minor negative corporate responsibility are disclosed.

Finally, while some companies try to target broad audiences that seems more likely to spread the news, local and small communities might make the cause spread with a larger volume and speed. For instance, Unilever has been carrying out "Sustainable Tea Agriculture" project in Turkey, which aims to get all the tea from Rainforest Alliance Certified firms. This initiative appeals to a local audience, representing a major milestone towards sustainable tea production in Turkey, but it is also a landmark to boost biodiversity and enrich producers' and consumers' welfare worldwide. Similarly, there might be local negative crises, which might become quickly a global issue. For instance, BP's oil operations in the Gulf of Mexico have become a global concern and been faced with protesters gathering in more than 40 cities worldwide (Bryant 2011). CSR initiatives toward local communities or distant stakeholders might be especially valuable, when such activities get contagious at a global scale, and adds value to the brand's reputation for the close stakeholders.

Content

This systematic review shows that other than the sender and recipient characteristics, there are several dimensions related to the content of responsible and irresponsible activities that have been investigated. For instance, the type of the brand or the product (e.g., luxury brands, humanized brands, hedonic products), specific actions and features (e.g., acknowledging the blame, publicizing the social cause through ads, traits of CEOs), the fit between the relevant stakeholders (e.g., company-cause fit, donor-cause fit) or the timing of campaigns (e.g., proactive versus active CSR campaigns, pre-crisis versus post-crisis advertising) have been studied to explore their effects on the several consequences of CSR that has been outlined in this review.

Some of these dimensions have been also found important in WOM literature. For instance, throughout CSR literature, it has been demonstrated that the fit between the CSR and company or the consumer is important (Robinson, Irmak and Jayachandran 2012; Kuo and Rice 2015; Bennett, Kim and Loken 2013; Homburg, Stierl and Bornemann 2013). The content of CSR campaign should be relevant for the company's mission, identity and core values and consumers to create both value for the companies as well as consumers. Similarly, WOM literature has shown that the fit between the brand and the viral campaigns are also important not only to get viral but also help the brands' bottom line, by making the brand integral part of the viral content (Akpinar and Berger, 2017). Combining the findings from two literature streams, one could suggest that companies should create valuable viral CSR campaigns that benefit both the companies and the society, while getting contagious to spread the cause among consumers to receive more support. One good example of a valuable viral CSR campaign is held by Dove. "Real Beauty Sketches", part of the "The Dove Self-Esteem Project", received more than 100 Million views in just a month, achieving the most viral video of all times. The campaign wanted to boost women's self-esteem by showing that "all women are beautiful." First, this campaign is a successful viral campaign that received high public exposure, which created the awareness about the social cause as intended. Second, it is a valuable CSR campaign that fits Dove's brand mission, identity and core values, which takes "real women" as inspiration and suggests that real beauty is about feeling and looking one's own personal best. To sum, "Real Beauty Sketches" is a valuable viral CSR campaign that benefits both the society and the brand's core values.

The timing of the CSR campaigns might be quite important especially when companies are facing with crisis. Imagine a company recalls their product due to product contamination. Should the company react with a proactive strategy responding to consumer complaints or adopt a passive strategy? How should firms carry out their communication strategy when they conduct conflicting behaviors with their CSR statements? Research suggests that proactive (compared to passive) strategies in recall processes might have a negative effect on firm value, because they might signal substantial financial losses (Chen, Ganesan and Liu 2009). Further, in the case of conflicting CSR behavior with statements, a proactive communication strategy might lead to higher levels of insincerity than a reactive strategy (Wagner, Lutz and Weitz 2009). There is emerging work in WOM literature that investigates the effect of timing on sharing content. When the content being shared reflects positively on the sharer, events that will happen in the future is more likely to be shared (Weingarten and Berger 2017). Combining the findings from CSR and WOM literature, one could wonder whether consumers would be more likely to share CSR actions that will happen in the future or that have happened in the past. Could it be that sharing the future versus past CSR activities moderated whether the consumer is part of the campaign contributing to the cause, which could boost self-enhancement? There is a need for future work that explores the effect of type of content and timing on sharing both positive and negative content related to social responsibility.

Channel

The news about corporate social responsibility actions as well product crises spread from several sources such as newspapers, television, social media, consumer reports, face-to-face conversations among consumers and other communication channels. There is emerging work in WOM literature that has studied how channels affect what people talk about and how. For instance, it has been shown that consumers talk more interesting content online, which is driven by self-enhancement motives (Berger and Iyengar 2013). Building on this knowledge, one could wonder, where do consumers talk about CSR and public crisis? Would it be more helpful for companies when they talk about their good deeds online (which could be more interesting) and communicate about their public crises in other platforms such as public speeches? Relatedly, Hsu and Lawrence (2016) showed that in the case of product recall announcements, companies trying to mitigate the negative effects of social media during a product recall online did not really help the company, as the content provided by the companies becomes almost invisible among the flood of other content. Both in WOM and CSR literature, current knowledge exploring the effect of channels is limited. Future research should explore the effects of channel in combination of other communication components such as sender, receiver and content on the propagation of favorable social responsibility actions and unfavorable ones such as crisis, product recalls.

Regardless of the channel, for CSR activities, achieving two-sided communication between companies and stakeholders is important. First, companies should be proactive in communicating about their efforts or plans in CSR before consumers start a social media backlash due to their unsustainable business practices. Second, companies should communicate interactively with various stakeholders. For example, Unilever's Sustainable Living Lab campaign created an online global dialogue where several stakeholders including businesses, governments, NGOs, scholars and consumers discussed together interactively. This global interactive debate allowed consumers to be active, sharing several aspects on helping to develop solutions to create sustainability at home.

Conclusions

Consumers are heavily influenced by other consumer's opinions, given consumers trust each other more than company generated content. That is why WOM is one of the driving forces that affect consumers' decisions. Companies that are interested in spreading their CSR campaigns in the community should initiate consumers to talk about these campaigns and make them contribute to the social causes. Although, there has been increasing work in the area of WOM and CSR separately, combining these two perspectives is still very recent, thus very little is known how to boost CSR diffusion using WOM.

Due to the extensive knowledge accumulated in the area of CSR, there has been substantial work that provides a good overview of the literature (i.e., Chabowski, Mena and Gonzales-Padron 2011, Crittenden et al. 2011; Hult 2011; Peloza and Shang 2011). Yet, no existing reviews of the CSR literature have explored specifically why content related to CSR is shared by consumers and the consequences related to sharing. This chapter fills that gap with a systematic review and synthesis of the literature by investigating CSR literature through three perspectives of WOM 1) drivers, 2) consequences, and 3) components, raising several future research questions.

Finally, the systematic review showed that the effect CSR and WOM can be directional.

Responsible social behaviors of the companies can make consumers talk favorably about the companies and such positive WOM can make CSR campaigns reach masses of people, which in turn help raise more donation or retrieve more supporters. Consumers might talk favorably about CSR campaigns, influenced by a variety of individual factors such as trust, emotions and commitment to the brand. Given the rise of social media, companies invest considerable amounts of budget and effort in spreading their CSR campaigns in the online world, which can also initiate positive offline WOM. While there is emerging work on the effects of social media on variety of firm performance metrics (e.g., sales, Trusov, Bodapati and Bucklin 2010), future work should understand how social media metrics (e.g., likes, comments) can be used to estimate performance of CSR, which could be measured in a variety of ways (e.g., awareness of the campaign, donation collected, number of supporters, brand equity).

References

Aginis, H. and Glavas, A. (2012). What we know and don't know about corporate social responsibility: A review and research agenda, *Journal of Management*, *38*(4), pp. 932–968.

Ailawadi, K.L., Neslin, S.A., Luan, Y.J. and Taylor, G.A. (2014). Does retailer CSR enhance behavioral loyalty? A case for benefit segmentation. *International Journal of Research in Marketing*, 31(2), pp. 156–167.

Akpinar, E. and Berger, J. (2017). Valuable virality. *Journal of Marketing Research*, *54*(2), pp. 318–330.

Akpinar, E., Verlegh, P. and Smidts, A. (2013). When and why do consumers share product harm information? *Advances in Consumer Research*, *41*, pp. 644–645.

ALS Association. (2017). Your ice bucket dollars at work. [online] Alsa.org. Available at: www.alsa.org/fight-als/challenge.html [Accessed 7 Dec. 2016].

Barasch, A. and Berger, J. (2014). Broadcasting and narrowcasting: How audience size affects what people share. *Journal of Marketing Research, 51*(3), pp. 286–299.

Baumeister, R.F. (1982). A self-presentational view of social phenomena. *Psychological Bulletin, 91*(1), p. 3.

Bennett, C.M., Kim, H. and Loken, B. (2013). Corporate sponsorships may hurt nonprofits: Understanding their effects on charitable giving. *Journal of Consumer Psychology, 23*(3), pp. 288–300.

Berger, J. (2014). Word of mouth and interpersonal communication: A review and directions for future research. *Journal of Consumer Psychology, 24*(4), pp. 586–607.

Berger, J. and Heath, C. (2007). Where consumers diverge from others: Identity-signaling and product domains. *Journal of Consumer Research, 34*(2), 121–134.

Berger, J. and Milkman, K.L. (2012). What makes online content viral? *Journal of Marketing Research, 49*(2), pp. 192–205.

Berger, J. and Iyengar, R. (2013). Communication channels and word of mouth: How the medium shapes the message. *Journal of Consumer Research,* 40 (3), pp. 567–579.

Berger, J. and Schwartz, E.M. (2011). What drives immediate and ongoing word of mouth? *Journal of Marketing Research, 48*(5), pp. 869–880.

Berger, J., Sorenson, A., Rasmussen, S. (2010) Positive effects of negative publicity: When negative reviews increase sales. *Marketing Science, 29*(5), 815–827.

Berman, J.Z., Levine, E.E., Barasch, A. and Small, D.A. (2015). The braggart's dilemma: On the social rewards and penalties of advertising prosocial behavior. *Journal of Marketing Research, 52*(1), pp. 90–104.

Biehal, G.J. and Sheinin, D.A. (2007). The influence of corporate messages on the product portfolio. *Journal of Marketing, 71*(2), pp. 12–25.

Borah, A. and Tellis, G.J. (2016). Halo (spillover) effects in social media: Do product recalls of one brand hurt or help rival brands? *Journal of Marketing Research, 53*(2), pp. 143–160.

Bougie, R., Pieters, R. and Zeelenberg, M. (2003). Angry customers don't come back, they get back: The experience and behavioral implications of anger and dissatisfaction in services. *Journal of the Academy of Marketing Science, 31*(4), pp. 377–393.

Branco, F. and Villas-Boas, J.M. (2015). Competitive vices. *Journal of Marketing Research, 52*(6), pp. 801–816.

Bryant, B. (2011). Deepwater Horizon and the Gulf oil spill – The key questions answered. [online] *The Guardian.* Available at: www.theguardian.com/environment/2011/apr/20/deepwater-horizon-key-questions-answered [Accessed 20 April 2016].

Buechel, E. and Berger, J. (2012). Facebook therapy? Why people share self-relevant content online. In Z. Gürhan-Canli, C. Otnes, and R. (Juliet) Zhu (Eds.), *Advances in consumer research* (Vol. 40, pp. 203–208). Duluth, MN: Association for Consumer Research.

Carvalho, S.W., Block, L.G., Sivaramakrishnan, S., Manchanda, R.V. and Mitakakis, C. (2008). Risk perception and risk avoidance: The role of cultural identity and personal relevance. *International Journal of Research in Marketing, 25*(4), pp. 319–326.

Chabowski, B.R., Mena, J.A. and Gonzalez-Padron, T.L. (2011). The structure of sustainability research in marketing, 1958–2008: A basis for future research opportunities. *Journal of the Academy of Marketing Science, 39*(1), pp. 55–70.

Chen, Y., Ganesan, S. and Liu, Y. (2009). Does a firm's product-recall strategy affect its financial value? An examination of strategic alternatives during product-harm crises. *Journal of Marketing, 73*(6), pp. 214–226.

Chen, Z. and Berger, J. (2013). When, why, and how controversy causes conversation. *Journal of Consumer Research, 40*(3), pp. 580–593.

Chen, Z. and Huang, Y. (2016). Cause-related marketing is not always less favorable than corporate philanthropy: The moderating role of self-construal. *International Journal of Research in Marketing, 33*(4), pp. 868–880.

Chernev, A. and Blair, S. (2015). Doing well by doing good: The benevolent halo of corporate social responsibility. *Journal of Consumer Research, 41*(6), pp. 1412–1425.

Cheung, C.M.K. and Thadani D. R. (2012). The impact of electronic word of mouth communication: A literature analysis and integrative model. *Decision Support Systems, 54*(1), pp. 461–470.

Chevalier, J.A. and Mayzlin, D. (2006). The effect of word of mouth on sales: Online book reviews. *Journal of Marketing Research, 43*(3), pp. 345–354.

Cleeren, K., Dekimpe, M.G. and Helsen, K. (2008). Weathering product-harm crises. *Journal of the Academy of Marketing Science*, *36*(2), pp. 262–270.

Cleeren, K., Van Heerde, H.J. and Dekimpe, M.G. (2013). Rising from the ashes: How brands and categories can overcome product-harm crises. *Journal of Marketing*, *77*(2), pp. 58–77.

Crittenden, V.L., Crittenden, W.F., Ferrell, L.K., Ferrell, O.C. and Pinney, C.C. (2011). Market-oriented sustainability: a conceptual framework and propositions. *Journal of the Academy of Marketing Science*, *39*(1), pp. 71–85.

De Angelis, M.D., Bonezzi, A., Peluso, A.M., Rucker, D.D. and Costabile, M. (2012). On braggarts and gossips: A self-enhancement account of word of mouth generation and transmission. *Journal of Marketing Research*, *49*(4), pp. 551–563.

Du, S., Bhattacharya, C.B. and Sen, S. (2007). Reaping relational rewards from corporate social responsibility: The role of competitive positioning. *International Journal of Research in Marketing*, *24*(3), pp. 224–241.

Ein-Gar, D., Shiv, B. and Tormala, Z.L. (2012). When blemishing leads to blossoming: The positive effect of negative information. *Journal of Consumer Research*, *38*(5), 846–859.

Einwiller, S.A., Fedorikhin, A., Johnson, A.R. and Kamins, M.A. (2006). Enough is enough! When identification no longer prevents negative corporate associations. *Journal of the Academy of Marketing Science*, *34*(2), pp. 185–194.

Fast, N.J., Heath, C. and Wu, G. (2009). Common ground and cultural prominence: How conversation reinforces culture. *Psychological Science*, *20*(7), pp. 904–911.

Gao, H., Xie, J., Wang, Q. and Wilbur, K.C. (2015). Should ad spending increase or decrease before a recall announcement? The marketing–finance interface in product-harm crisis management. *Journal of Marketing*, *79*(5), pp. 80–99.

Gijsenberg, M.J., Van Heerde, H.J. and Verhoef, P.C. (2015). Losses loom longer than gains: Modeling the impact of service crises on perceived service quality over time. *Journal of Marketing Research*, *52*(5), pp. 642–656.

Godes, D. and Mayzlin, D. (2009). Firm-created word of mouth communication: Evidence from a field test. *Marketing Science*, *28*(4), pp. 721–739.

Gorn, G.J., Jiang, Y. and Johar, G.V. (2008). Babyfaces, trait inferences, and company evaluations in a public relations crisis. *Journal of Consumer Research*, *35*(1), pp. 36–49.

Gupta, R. and Sen, S. (2013). The effect of evolving resource synergy beliefs on the intentions – behavior discrepancy in ethical consumption. *Journal of Consumer Psychology*, *23*(1), pp. 114–121.

Habel, J., Schons, L.M., Alavi, S. and Wieseke, J. (2016). Warm glow or extra charge? The ambivalent effect of corporate social responsibility activities on customers' perceived price fairness. *Journal of Marketing*, *80*(1), pp. 84–105.

Hennig-Thurau, T. and Walsh, G. (2003). Electronic word of mouth: Motives for and consequences of reading customer articulations on the Internet. *International Journal of Electronic Commerce*, *8*(2), pp. 51–74.

Hensen, N., Keeling, D.I., Ruyter, K., Wetzels, M. and Jong, A. (2016). Making SENS: Exploring the antecedents and impact of store environmental stewardship climate. *Journal of the Academy of Marketing Science*, *44*(4), pp. 497–515.

Hewett, K., Rand W., Rust, R. R., and van Heerde H. J. (2016). Brand Buzz in the Echoverse. *Journal of Marketing*, *80*(3), pp 1–24.

Homburg, C., Stierl, M. and Bornemann, T. (2013). Corporate social responsibility in business-to-business markets: how organizational customers account for supplier corporate social responsibility engagement. *Journal of Marketing*, *77*(6), pp. 54–72.

Hsu, L. and Lawrence, B. (2016). The role of social media and brand equity during a product recall crisis: A shareholder value perspective. *International Journal of Research in Marketing*, *33*(1), pp. 59–77.

Hult, G.T.M. (2011). Market-focused sustainability: Market orientation plus! *Journal of the Academy of Marketing Science*, *39*(1), pp. 1–6.

Iyer, G. and Soberman, D.A. (2016). Social responsibility and product innovation. *Marketing Science*, *35*(5), pp. 727–742.

Kalaignanam, K., Kushwaha, T. and Eilert, M. (2013). The impact of product recalls on future product reliability and future accidents: Evidence from the automobile industry. *Journal of Marketing*, 77(2), pp. 41–57.

Kang, C., Germann, F. and Grewal, R. (2016). Washing away your sins? Corporate social responsibility, corporate social irresponsibility, and firm performance. *Journal of Marketing*, 80(2), pp. 59–79.

Kashmiri, S. and Mahajan, V. (2010). What's in a name? An analysis of the strategic behavior of family firms. *International Journal of Research in Marketing*, 27(3), pp. 271–280.

Kashmiri, S. and Mahajan, V. (2014). Beating the recession blues: Exploring the link between family ownership, strategic marketing behavior and firm performance during recessions. *International Journal of Research in Marketing*, 31(1), pp. 78–93.

Keeling, K.A., McGoldrick, P.J. and Sadhu, H. (2013). Staff Word-of-Mouth (SWOM) and retail employee recruitment. *Journal of Retailing*, 89(1), pp. 88–104.

Keller Fay (2011). Brands mentioned 3bn times a day in US. [online] kellerfay.com. Available at: www.kellerfay.com/brands-mentioned-3bn-times-a-day-in-us/ [Accessed 20 April 2017].

King, R.A., Racherla, P. and Bush, V.D. (2014). What we know and don't know about online word of mouth: A review and synthesis of the literature. *Journal of Interactive Marketing*, 28(3), pp. 167–183.

Klein, J. and Dawar, N. (2004). Corporate social responsibility and consumers' attributions and brand evaluations in a product – harm crisis. *International Journal of Research in Marketing*, 21(3), pp. 203–217.

Korschun, D., Bhattacharya, C.B. and Swain, S.D. (2014). Corporate social responsibility, customer orientation, and the job performance of frontline employees. *Journal of Marketing*, 78(3), pp. 20–37.

Koschate-Fischer, N., Huber, I.V. and Hoyer, W.D. (2016). When will price increases associated with company donations to charity be perceived as fair? *Journal of the Academy of Marketing Science*, 44(5), pp. 608–626.

Koschate-Fischer, N., Stefan, I.V. and Hoyer, W.D. (2012). Willingness to pay for cause-related marketing: The impact of donation amount and moderating effects. *Journal of Marketing Research*, 49(6), pp. 910–927.

Kull, A.J. and Heath, T.B. (2016). You decide, we donate: Strengthening consumer–brand relationships through digitally co-created social responsibility. *International Journal of Research in Marketing*, 33(1), pp. 78–92.

Kuo, A. and Rice, D.H. (2015). The impact of perceptual congruence on the effectiveness of cause-related marketing campaigns. *Journal of Consumer Psychology*, 25(1), pp. 78–88.

Lacey, R., Kennett-Hensel, P.A. and Manolis, C. (2015). Is corporate social responsibility a motivator or hygiene factor? Insights into its bivalent nature. *Journal of the Academy of Marketing Science*, 43(3), pp. 315–332.

Lamberton, C. and Stephen A.T. (2016). A thematic exploration of digital, social media, and mobile marketing: Research evolution from 2000 to 2015 and an agenda for future inquiry. *Journal of Marketing*, 80(6), pp. 146–172.

Larson, B.V., Flaherty, K.E., Zablah, A.R., Brown, T.J. and Wiener, J.L. (2008). Linking cause-related marketing to sales force responses and performance in a direct selling context. *Journal of the Academy of Marketing Science*, 36(2), pp. 271–277.

Lee, D., Kim, H.S. and Kim, J.K. (2012). The role of self-construal in consumers' electronic word of mouth (eWOM) in social networking sites: A social cognitive approach, *Computers in Human Behavior*, 28(3), 1054–1062.

Lei, J., Dawar, N. and Gürhan-Canli, Z. (2012). Base-rate information in consumer attributions of product-harm crises. *Journal of Marketing Research*, 49(3), pp. 336–348.

Lei, J., Dawar, N. and Lemmink, J. (2008). Negative spillover in brand portfolios: Exploring the antecedents of asymmetric effects. *Journal of Marketing*, 72(3), pp. 111–123.

Liu, A.X., Liu, Y. and Luo, T. (2016). What drives a firm's choice of product recall remedy? The impact of remedy cost, product hazard, and the CEO. *Journal of Marketing*, 80(3), pp. 79–95.

Luchs, M.G., Naylor, R.W., Irwin, J.R. and Raghunathan, R. (2010). The sustainability liability: Potential negative effects of ethicality on product preference. *Journal of Marketing*, 74(5), pp. 18–31.

Luo, X. and Bhattacharya, C.B. (2009). The debate over doing good: Corporate social performance, strategic marketing levers, and firm-idiosyncratic risk. *Journal of Marketing, 73*(6), pp. 198–213.

Lovett, M. J., Peres, R. and Shachar R. (2013). On brands and Word of Mouth. *Journal of Marketing Research, 50*(4), pp. 427–444.

Martin, K.D., Johnson, J.L. and French, J.J. (2011). Institutional pressures and marketing ethics initiatives: the focal role of organizational identity. *Journal of the Academy of Marketing Science, 39*(4), pp. 574–591.

McShane, L. and Cunningham, P. (2012). To thine own self be true? Employees' judgments of the authenticity of their organization's corporate social responsibility program. *Journal of business ethics, 108*(1), pp. 81–100.

Miranda, C. and Steiner A. (2014). No-makeup selfie: Cancer research's lesson on benefits of quick thinking. [online] *The Guardian.* Available at: www.theguardian.com/voluntary-sector-network/2014/dec/03/no-makeup-selfie-cancer-research-fundraising-benefit-quick-thinking [Accessed 20 Dec. 2014).

Monga, A.B. and John, D.R. (2008). When does negative brand publicity hurt? The moderating influence of analytic versus holistic thinking. *Journal of Consumer Psychology, 18*(4), pp. 320–332.

Newman, G.E., Gorlin, M. and Dhar, R. (2014). When going green backfires: How firm intentions shape the evaluation of socially beneficial product enhancements. *Journal of Consumer Research, 41*(3), pp. 823–839.

Nielsen, (2015). Global Trust in Advertising Report. [online] Nielsen. Available at: www.nielsen.com/us/en/insights/reports/2015/global-trust-in-advertising-(2015).html

Nikolaeva, R. and Bicho, M. (2011). The role of institutional and reputational factors in the voluntary adoption of corporate social responsibility reporting standards. *Journal of the Academy of Marketing Science, 39*(1), pp. 136–157.

Packard, G.M. and Wooten, D.B. (2013). Compensatory knowledge signaling in consumer word of mouth. *Journal of Consumer Psychology, 23*(4), pp. 434–50.

Peloza, J. and Shang, J. (2011). How can corporate social responsibility activities create value for stakeholders? A systematic review. *Journal of the Academy of Marketing Science, 39*(1), pp. 117–135.

Porter, M.E., and Kramer, M.R. (2002) The Competitive advantage of corporate philanthropy. *Harvard Business Review,* December.

Pullig, C., Netemeyer, R.G. and Biswas, A. (2006). Attitude basis, certainty, and challenge alignment: A case of negative brand publicity. *Journal of the Academy of Marketing Science, 34*(4), pp. 528–542.

Puzakova, M., Kwak, H. and Rocereto, J.F. (2013). When humanizing brands goes wrong: The detrimental effect of brand anthropomorphization amid product wrongdoings. *Journal of Marketing, 77*(3), pp. 81–100.

Ragnan, K.V., Chase, L. and Sohel, K. (2015). The Truth About CSR. *Harvard Business Review.* January–February, https://hbr.org/2015/01/the-truth-about-csr

Richins, M.L. (1983). Negative word of mouth by dissatisfied consumers: A pilot study. *Journal of Marketing, 47*(1), pp. 68–78.

Rimé, B. (2009). Emotion elicits the social sharing of emotion: Theory and empirical review. *Emotion Review, 1*(1), pp. 60–85.

Robinson, S.R., Irmak, C. and Jayachandran, S. (2012). Choice of cause in cause-related marketing. *Journal of Marketing, 76*(4), pp. 126–139.

Rubel, O., Naik, P.A. and Srinivasan, S. (2011). Optimal advertising when envisioning a product-harm crisis. *Marketing Science, 30*(6), pp. 1048–1065.

Schlosser, A.E. (2005). Posting versus lurking: Communicating in a multiple audience context. *Journal of Consumer Research, 32*(2), pp. 260–265.

Schweidel, D. A. and Moe, W.W. (2014). Listening in on social media: A joint model of sentiment and venue format choice. *Journal of Marketing Research, 51*(4), pp. 387–402.

Sen, S. and Bhattacharya, C.B. (2001). Does doing good always lead to doing better? Consumer reactions to corporate social responsibility. *Journal of Marketing Research, 38*(2), pp. 225–243.

Sen, S., Bhattacharya, C.B. and Korschun, D. (2006). The role of corporate social responsibility in strengthening multiple stakeholder relationships: A field experiment. *Journal of the Academy of Marketing Science, 34*(2), pp. 158–166.

Sheth, J.N., Sethia, N.K. and Srinivas, S. (2011). Mindful consumption: A customer-centric approach to sustainability. *Journal of the Academy of Marketing Science, 39*(1), pp. 21–39.

Sinha, J. and Lu, F. (2016). "I" value justice, but "we" value relationships: Self-construal effects on post-transgression consumer forgiveness. *Journal of Consumer Psychology, 26*(2), pp. 265–274.

Smith, N.C. (2009). Bounded goodness: Marketing implications of Drucker on corporate responsibility. *Journal of the Academy of Marketing Science, 37*(1), pp. 73–84.

Srinivasan, S. and Hanssens, D.M. (2009). Marketing and firm value: Metrics, methods, findings, and future directions. *Journal of Marketing Research, 46*(3), pp. 293–312.

Szőcs, I., Schlegelmilch, B.B., Rusch, T. and Shamma, H.M. (2016). Linking cause assessment, corporate philanthropy, and corporate reputation. *Journal of the Academy of Marketing Science, 44*(3), pp. 376–396.

Torelli, C.J., Monga, A.B. and Kaikati, A.M. (2012). Doing poorly by doing good: Corporate social responsibility and brand concepts. *Journal of Consumer Research, 38*(5), pp. 948–963.

Torres, A., Bijmolt, T.H., Tribó, J.A. and Verhoef, P. (2012). Generating global brand equity through corporate social responsibility to key stakeholders. *International Journal of Research in Marketing, 29*(1), pp. 13–24.

Trusov, M., Bodapati, A.V. and Bucklin, R.E. (2010). Determining influential users in internet social networks. *Journal of Marketing Research, 47*(4), pp. 643–658.

Trusov, M., Bucklin, R.E. and Pauwels, K. (2009). Effects of word of mouth versus traditional marketing: findings from an internet social networking site. *Journal of Marketing, 73*(5), pp. 90–102.

Uslay, C., Morgan, R.E. and Sheth, J.N. (2009). Peter Drucker on marketing: An exploration of five tenets. *Journal of the Academy of Marketing Science, 37*(1), p. 47.

Van den Bulte, C. and Wuyts, S. (2009). Leveraging customer networks. In J.Y. Wind and P. Kleindorfer (Eds.), *The network challenge: Strategy, profit and risk in an interlinked world* (pp. 243–258). Upper Saddle River, NJ: Wharton School Publishing.

Van Heerde, H., Helsen, K. and Dekimpe, M.G. (2007). The impact of a product-harm crisis on marketing effectiveness. *Marketing Science, 26*(2), pp. 230–245.

Vlachos, P.A., Tsamakos, A., Vrechopoulos, A.P. and Avramidis, P.K. (2009). Corporate social responsibility: attributions, loyalty, and the mediating role of trust. *Journal of the Academy of Marketing Science, 37*(2), pp. 170–180.

Wagner, T., Lutz, R.J. and Weitz, B.A. (2009). Corporate hypocrisy: Overcoming the threat of inconsistent corporate social responsibility perceptions. *Journal of Marketing, 73*(6), pp. 77–91.

Watts, D.J. (2004). The "new" science of networks. *Annual Review of Sociology, 30*, pp. 243–270.

Webster, J. and Watson, R.T. (2002). Analyzing the past to prepare to prepare for the future: Writing a literature review. *MIS Quarterly, 26*(2), pp. 13–23.

Weingarten, E. and Berger, J. (2017). Fired up for the future: How time shapes sharing. *Journal of Consumer Research, 44*(2), pp. 432–447.

Westbrook, R.A. (1987). Product/consumption-based affective responses and post-purchase processes. *Journal of Marketing Research, 24*(3), pp. 258–270.

Winterich, K.P. and Barone, M.J. (2011). Warm glow or cold, hard cash? Social identity effects on consumer choice for donation versus discount promotions. *Journal of Marketing Research, 48*(5), pp. 855–868.

Winterich, K.P., Carter, R.E., Barone, M.J., Janakiraman, R. and Bezawada, R. (2015). Tis better to give than receive? How and when gender and residence-based segments predict choice of discount-versus donation-based promotions. *Journal of Consumer Psychology, 25*(4), pp. 622–634.

Xie, C., Bagozzi, R.P. and Grønhaug, K. (2015). The role of moral emotions and individual differences in consumer responses to corporate green and non-green actions. *Journal of the Academy of Marketing Science, 43*(3), pp. 333–356.

Yoon, Y., Gürhan-Canli, Z. and Schwarz, N. (2006). The effect of corporate social responsibility (CSR) activities on companies with bad reputations. *Journal of Consumer Psychology, 16*(4), pp. 377–390.

Zemack-Rugar,Y., Rabino, R., Cavanaugh, L.A. and Fitzsimons, G.J. (2016). When donating is liberating: The role of product and consumer characteristics in the appeal of cause-related products. *Journal of Consumer Psychology, 26*(2), pp. 213–230.

Zhao,Y., Zhao,Y. and Helsen, K. (2011). Consumer learning in a turbulent market environment: Modeling consumer choice dynamics after a product-harm crisis. *Journal of Marketing Research, 48*(2), pp. 255–267.

Part 5

Digital activism and corporate social responsibility

5.1 Digital activism

NGOs leveraging social media to influence/challenge corporate social responsibility (CSR)

Vidhi Chaudhri and Asha Kaul

On October 9, 2014, Greenpeace[1] claimed victory. This time, for getting LEGO to sever its historic marketing partnership with Shell "after coming under sustained pressure from Greenpeace."[2] Dating back to the 1960s, the $110 million marketing partnership involved co-branded LEGO sets, which were sold in retail stores and gas stations across 26 countries.[3]

In a corporate statement issued October 8, 2014, Jørgen Vig Knudstorp, CEO of the LEGO Group confirmed that "as things currently stand we will not renew the co-promotion contract [signed in 2011] with Shell when the present contract ends."[4] However, the statement also expressed disappointment that the LEGO brand was targeted, noting that "Greenpeace ought to have a direct conversation with Shell."[5]

The announcement from LEGO was the culmination of a three-month campaign by Greenpeace, part of an ongoing effort to #SaveTheArctic. A Greenpeace publication explained that LEGO's child and family-friendly values and reputable image was "in bad company" with Shell, and went on to argue that the partnership "makes LEGO complicit with Shell's destructive activities by allowing the oil giant to use this partnership to buy social acceptance."[6]

So how did Greenpeace get LEGO to #SaveTheArctic? With a YouTube video set to the theme song of the LEGO movie "Everything is Awesome." The video of a pristine Arctic constructed with 120 kg of LEGO, slowly submerging in oil, has over 7.5 million views to date and is reportedly the most viral video in Greenpeace history. In addition, millions of supporters signed a petition to end the LEGO–Shell partnership and offline protests were held in many locations around the world.[7]

This is but one case illustrating how non-government organizations (NGOs) and advocacy groups are turning to new and social media to inform, engage, and mobilize. Specifically, this example and others discussed in the chapter highlight how social media afford NGOs new ways to influence and/or challenge large business organizations and their claims of social responsibility (CSR). In the backdrop of growing stakeholder expectations from business to be socially and environmentally responsible and attendant reputation benefits, corporations, more than ever, are working to integrate CSR with corporate strategy. Also, as organizations seek to leverage social media for CSR reputation, new forms of digital activism have profound implications for building and managing reputation.

We start with an overview of the role of NGOs as institutional (CSR) actors, outline the developments in social media adoption by NGOs and their implications for advocacy, explain how new forms of mobilization can undermine corporate claims of social (and environmental) responsibility, present some recent cases, and end with a discussion of managerial and ethical implications.

Setting the context: NGOs as institutional actors

Before we delve into the specifics, we briefly review two key terms central to this chapter, social media and NGOs.

Although we reference both new and social media in the chapter, it is important to highlight their relationship. Social media are variously defined and often used interchangeably with related concepts such as new media, social networks, and others. One definition treats social media as "a group of internet-based applications that build on the ideological and technological foundations of web 2.0, and that allow the creation and exchange of user generated content."[8] Others explain that social media are forms of new media. Both facilitate sharing but social media and their "interactive components has made the ability to comment, respond, share, critique, change and add to information possible on a broad scale."[9] This conceptualization highlights a key dimension that is often the center point of conversations about 'risks and challenges' of social media, and relevant for our purpose, that is, the lack of control. "The increased visibility of interaction, with largely unfiltered peer-to-peer communication" that characterizes social media[10] and cannot be easily controlled makes digital reputation management a daunting task.

Like social media, NGOs defy a singular or unitary classification.[11] For our purpose, we use the following definition of NGOs, "private, not-for-profit organizations that aim to serve particular societal interests by focusing advocacy and/or operational efforts on social, political and economic goals, including equity, health, environmental protection and human rights."[12] NGO is really an umbrella term, and scholars have outlined substantive differences across NGO's goals (self- or other-benefiting NGOs), activities (e.g., advocacy groups, operational NGOs), and identity roles (e.g., partnership and independent NGOs), among others. Here, we focus on advocacy groups that can, broadly speaking, influence business and government practice and decision-making via lobbying, research, agenda-setting, mobilizing public opinion, and organizing boycotts. Advocacy groups are also deemed to represent the marginalized and disempowered in social change efforts, and may do so as *insiders*, working within institutional frameworks, or *outsiders*, by challenging or undermining the system.[13]

It is important to understand the growing influence of NGOs in the international business landscape. In the 1980s, NGOs emerged as important institutional actors in international business, and their influence paralleled the globalization of business, declining state power, and the scrutiny of business practices in developing countries (exploitation of labor, abuse of weak regulatory mechanisms, human rights violations)[14] – developments that have steered civil society engagement with CSR issues. A spate of corporate scandals that created a crisis of leadership and a 'trust-void' further bolstered NGO credibility. Indeed, the *Edelman Trust Barometer* finds that vis-à-vis business, government, and the media, NGOs are the most trusted institution globally.

Accompanying the optimism about NGO influence, however, is a need to be cognizant that the impact of NGOs as CSR drivers is contextual and culturally dependent. In the Western context, NGO pressure is perceived to be a primary driver for CSR. Admittedly, this was not always the case even for NGOs in the Global North. Historically, a firm-centric view and managerial preoccupation with advancing business interests framed activists as working against corporate interests and led to marginalizing legitimate demands and concerns of secondary stakeholders, that is, NGOs. In other institutional contexts such as Singapore or India,[15] NGO impact is still relatively low, attributable to a weak or non-existent role in CSR strategy as well as questions of legitimacy and accountability. For example, a study of the Spanish context found that in spite of their institutional standing and self-perception as CSR change agents, Spanish NGO contribution to CSR is undermined by mutual mistrust among stakeholder groups and concerns about the legitimacy of NGO tactics, demands, and methods.[16]

Institutional variation therefore accounts for differences in NGO relevance, acceptance, and efficacy regarding CSR practice. The role of stakeholders, more generally, and NGOs in particular, is highly situational and depends on a number of variables, including managerial perception of salience. The well-known theory of stakeholder identification posits that stakeholder salience is positively related to the cumulative number of stakeholder attributes – power, legitimacy, and urgency – that managers perceive stakeholders to possess.[17] Instead of being fixed, however, these attributes are variable, socially constructed, and enacted, and collectively determine salience or the "degree to which managers give priority to competing stakeholder claims."[18] That said, institutions and organizations exist in a recursive relationship so just as NGOs reflect existing institutions, they also create and institutionalize new societal norms.

Today, NGOs are key stakeholders and partners in cross-sectoral initiatives for sustainable development, propelled by the institutionalization of CSR and an expansion of business responsibilities from shareholders to stakeholders. A stakeholder approach to CSR assumes a wider scope of responsibility, an appreciation of (diverse) needs and demands, and the ability to create strategic alignment among different stakeholder groups. Going a step further, CSR as 'company stakeholder responsibility' posits that "the very idea of managing for stakeholders is that the process of value creation is a joint process."[19] Therefore, stakeholder involvement in CSR – from incorporating input in CSR design, ongoing dialogue and collaboration in the execution phase, to program monitoring and future changes – has assumed a normative status, underpinning an organization's license to operate.

With this overview, we can claim that institutional actors such as NGOs have a potentially significant role in (re)defining social responsibility and responsible behavior.[20] CSR itself is socially and communicatively constructed which implies that claims about social responsibility are active acts of framing and sense-making that are negotiated with stakeholders.[21] As an 'essentially contested concept' (ECC),[22] CSR meanings and manifestations are fluid and dynamic, and CSR institutionalization is a work-in-progress. NGOs (can) actively participate in the processes of institutional change and the social construction of CSR.

The increasing importance of corporate reputation and corporate social responsibility and new media give advocacy groups a new source of leverage and create opportunities to be heard and noticed by management.[23] To understand what is at stake for corporations, we need to explicate the importance of social responsibility for building corporate reputation and legitimacy.

Building reputation and legitimacy via CSR

Broadly, the CSR concept suggests that business and society are interdependent and that corporate responsibilities extend beyond shareholders to encompass stakeholders such as employees, communities, NGOs, etcetera. The European Commission defines CSR as "the responsibility of enterprises for their impact on society,"[24] signifying CSR as a multistakeholder concept shaped by a confluence of processes and actors (including corporations) that define what is considered appropriate and/or responsible behavior.

Organizations now recognize that being socially responsible yields reputational benefits, an argument firmly entrenched in the business case for CSR.[25] As one of the key drivers for reputation, CSR contributes roughly over 40% toward a firm's reputation.[26] Socially responsible firms generally enjoy stakeholder goodwill and support in the form of purchase, loyalty, recommendation and positive word of mouth, investment, and alignment with organizational goals.[27] If managed carefully, CSR can also shield organizations from reputational damage in times of crisis, although efforts to use CSR as a smokescreen can severely undermine reputation. Having said that, reputations are not static; rather, they are "a continually developing set of evaluative narratives, beliefs, and expectations, built and modified in dialogical communication between the target organization and its publics over time."[28] How stakeholders view an organization vis-à-vis others is an aggregate of several drivers (e.g., CSR, leadership, governance, products, and services), formed over time via direct experience or mediated by information sources. This implies that organizations are not fully in control of their reputation, although they can certainly influence it.

In addition to reputation benefits, organizations accrue social legitimacy from CSR. Legitimacy is "a generalized perception or assumption that the actions of an entity are desirable, proper, or appropriate within some socially constructed system of norms, values, beliefs, and definitions."[29] As an expression of legitimacy or congruence with societal values, CSR lends organizations a license to operate. Like reputation, legitimacy is socially constructed and must be maintained and nurtured over time; discrepancy and misalignment between an organization's actions and (shifting) societal and stakeholder expectations can result in a legitimacy gap potentially threatening the organization's existence.

CSR is a prime example of shifting societal values and expectations, having captured business imagination in the last two decades. In an effort to demonstrate social responsibility and meet the growing demands for transparency, organizations are actively communicating CSR. According to the *2015 KPMG survey of CSR reporting*, 90% of the world's most profitable firms (G250) are now reporting on CSR.[30] *The Global Reporting Initiative* also finds an upward trend in sustainability reporting and predicts that corporate accountability will intensify as technology enables greater stakeholder scrutiny, access, and evaluation of corporate claims. With the attention to CSR and sustainability in the recent past, there has indeed been a profound change in the way we view business–society relations; however, power inequities, wealth concentration, ecological sustainability, climate change, and human rights continue to be pressing social issues that will drive stakeholder assessment of corporate performance.[31]

In the digital age, organizations face new CSR opportunities and risks. Heightened stakeholder interest and scrutiny implies that corporate claims of social responsibility are being closely watched. On the one hand, firms are turning to social-mediated communication to build CSR reputation and engage stakeholders. Higher stakeholder engagement is positively correlated with company–consumer identification and long-term relationships.[32] Ironically, social media's strengths – the potential for connectedness, interactivity, community formation via crowdsourcing and user participation (e.g., MyStarbucksIdea) – are also a source of challenge for organizations.

Now, stakeholders can more easily challenge organizations and demand changes in business practice. For example, when Greenpeace accused Nestle of destroying Indonesian rainforests and endangering orangutan habitats, Nestle was forced to change its palm oil sourcing practices.[33] Nestle instituted the Responsible Sourcing Guidelines as part of corporate efforts to "create shared value and to lead by example."[34] For Nestle, Greenpeace actions amounted to a CSR crisis that threatened the company's reputation, the most valuable corporate intangible asset. Arguably, all crises are associated with some reputational threat, but a CSR crisis (failure to meet stakeholder expectations of societal obligations) can cause far more reputation damage than a product/service crisis.[35]

Paradoxically, just as new media offer opportunities for open and transparent communication between organizations and stakeholder groups, they permit stakeholders to (more easily) challenge corporate claims if they are perceived to be inconsistent with societal norms and value, and/or stakeholder expectations. Indeed, prior CSR efforts may boomerang if they are found to be misleading or just a case of greenwashing (or "green-whitewashing"), that is, representing a product or service as more environmentally friendly than it is, thereby creating a false impression of sustainability.[36] Following the 2010 Gulf Coast oil spill, BP was severely criticized for its inept handling of the crisis and for greenwashing its efforts to go 'Beyond Petroleum' and portray itself as a social and environmentally conscious firm.[37] With stakeholders becoming active participants in setting a CSR agenda and defining social (ir)responsibility, corporate claims can be called out for being hypocritical, as in the case of McDonald's #McDStories campaign. Consumers and former employees weighed in with their worst McDonald's experiences, and the Twitter campaign was pulled within two hours.[38]

So what really is at stake for organizations in a social-mediated environment with vocal stakeholders, specifically NGOs? Existing research considers the impact of NGO challenges on organizational reputation and legitimacy interchangeably without making a conceptual distinction between these related concepts. Deephouse and Carter offer a useful demarcation that permits an appreciation of what is at stake for organizations in the digital realm. They define legitimacy as "the social acceptance resulting from adherence to regulative, normative or cognitive norms and expectations" whereas reputation is "a social comparison among organizations on a variety of attributes, which could include these same regulative, normative or cognitive dimensions."[39] By this understanding, legitimacy is the foundation for all organizations (corporate, non-profit, voluntary, etc.), central to their survival and existence. As long as an organization enjoys social acceptance, a lower reputation (relative to others) does not threaten existence and/or disavowal by stakeholders. Arguably though, recurring (digital) activist campaigns can decisively erode legitimacy by influencing powerful stakeholders via sustained efforts.

As examples in the chapter will show, the ability to leverage social media to challenge corporate claims poses substantive challenge to organizational claims of social responsibility. Next, we delineate key developments in NGO use of social media and elucidate the implications with recent cases of digital activism.

NGO adoption of social media: why, what, and how?

The proliferation of Web 2.0 social networks is regarded by many as a paradigm shift for activism and public engagement.[40] Some have hailed the use of social media as heralding a form of alternative communication that frees activists from the challenges of gaining access to mainstream (mass) media. From this perspective, social media mark a shift in media power whereby activists are much less dependent on television and mainstream newspapers to influence public communication.[41] Already Web 1.0 (websites, email) was seen as a potential equalizer of power between NGOs and corporates via its reach, interactivity and dialogic potential,[42] and it continues to be important for social movements. Social media are a cost-effective tool that allows NGOs to strengthen their outreach efforts, promote engagement by enabling feedback loops, and strengthen collective action through increased speed of communication.[43]

Research among advocacy groups confirms the growing import of social media for both civic engagement (e.g., educating, informing, and platform for expression) and collective action (e.g., mobilization, petition signing).[44] Current trends in social media-based advocacy suggest a hierarchy of sorts where the first stage involves reaching out to people using a host of communication and information dissemination practices (word of mouth, hashtags, use of celebrity); stage two is about building community and strengthening relationships via dialogue and deep engagement; and finally, stage three involves mobilization and call to action.[45] A study of US-based NGOs found widespread use of social networks, primarily Facebook and Twitter, followed by YouTube and blogs. Acknowledging medium-level differences, another study of the top 100 US non-profit organizations found that Twitter is used primarily for providing information (one-way communication), followed by creation of community (e.g., facilitating conversation, response, and dialogue), and call for action (e.g., soliciting volunteers, donations, and lobbying).[46]

Overall, though, most studies thus far find limited evidence of dialogic engagement, confirming that NGOs, like business organizations, are still grappling with the full potential of digitally enabled social change. Much of the current usage falls within a "supersize model" of digital activism which translates to doing more of the same (same processes but bigger scale, speed, and reach); few adopt an alternate "theory 2.0 approach" that fundamentally changes the processes of activism to leverage the full potential of social media.[47] More research is necessary to gain deeper insight into NGO use of social media.

With that said, the adoption of social media present new opportunities for NGOs to strengthen influence. From a stakeholder perspective, social media permit a greater sense of community both within and among stakeholder groups such that members of the same stakeholder group (e.g., NGOs or consumers) can better organize independent of corporate control. Likewise, social media facilitate intergroup relationships for different stakeholder groups to coordinate efforts to influence corporate behavior.[48] Using illustrative cases, the next section elaborates on the specific advantages of social media for advocacy.

NGO strategies of (social-mediated) influence

As said before, NGO pressure has been one of the primary drivers for CSR, and NGO roles and strategies may be varied, including watchdog, consumer and shareholder activism, advocacy, collaboration, and/or a mix of collaborative and confrontational strategies.[49] Many of these tactics are communicative in nature, for instance, NGOs may use a combination of information politics (research and documentation of corporate (mal)practice); symbolic politics (persuasive use of powerful symbols, actions, and stories to frame issues); leverage politics (enlisting support of powerful actors and celebrities "to affect a situation"); and accountability politics (holding corporations accountable to their explicitly stated policies and positions on CSR).[50]

While many of these tactics remain relevant, they are amplified in the digital age. Visibility is the differentiator here – challenges issued by NGOs (and other stakeholders) are more visible, as is the response from the challenged organization. The Integrated Framework for Stakeholder Challenges outlines three elements of a stakeholder-initiated challenge: the challenger, the challenge, and the challenged corporation.[51] In this conceptualization, social media help to promote stakeholder/challenger salience through highly visible and strategic use of public communication; the urgency and legitimacy of the challenge/questionable act is established using rhetorical devices (e.g., research reports, use of emotional appeals) and media action (including traditional and social media); finally, the challenged organization needs to consider how best to respond, given its relative power vis-à-vis the challenger and the organization's prior CSR reputation.[52] This framework provides a multi-perspectival lens from which to consider the dynamics of (NGO-led) CSR challenges and corporate responses and illustrate implications for reputation and legitimacy.

From a legitimacy standpoint, NGO challenges may be viewed as a form of normative delegitimation or "the process by which an organization's normative legitimacy [defined by social norms and values] is diminished through challenges by outside organizations."[53] Because NGOs lack regulatory authority and/or have limited resources, they may employ indirect pressure via critical players – the stakeholders that have some influence over the firm's behavior and economic outcomes – including consumers, shareholders, media, employees, analysts, suppliers, and regulators. The LEGO case is illustrative of normative delegitimation, where Greenpeace used the reputational threat of partnering with Shell as a form of leverage over LEGO. In 2014, the LEGO Group placed sixth for CSR Reputation and ninth among the top 100 global reputable companies in *Reputation Institute*'s annual RepTrak study. When questioned about its tactics to target LEGO, a Greenpeace response highlighted the delicate balance between reputation opportunity and threat: that "Shell gained $116 million in PR from the most recent LEGO co-promotion alone, and Shell achieved a 7.5% worldwide sales uplift during the promotion" necessitated the action because "Shell needs companies like LEGO to help put a friendly face on it's public image – much in the same way the tobacco industry used to partner with famous athletes."[54] The challenge by Greenpeace forced LEGO to evaluate the situation and respond in a manner that had decisive implications for a historic partnership with Shell.

Consider this social media action against Unilever in India.

Unilever: "Kodaikanal Won't"

India-based NGO Jhatkaa.org employed social media to demand Unilever to "make amends now" for a long-standing issue of mercury contamination caused by Hindustan Unilever's (HUL) thermometer factory in Kodaikanal, India. Launched in 2015, the social media movement is an effort to draw attention to an issue that was first spotted the early 2000s when it was reported that HUL was discarding contaminated factory waste. Although the factory was closed in 2001 and glass scrap was sent to the United States for recycling in 2003, activist and corporate accounts differ on important issues of alleged safety and corporate responsibility. In addition to the environmental impacts, the movement claims that factory workers' unprotected handling of mercury led to adverse health problems including death and birth defects.[55]

The social movement is demanding that Unilever 1) clean up all the mercury from Kodaikanal's environment, 2) provide compensation to the workers who have been exposed to mercury in the factory, and 3) provide for long term medical monitoring and health remediation for all the workers and exposed residents of Kodaikanal.

On July 30, 2015, a YouTube video titled "Kodaikanal Won't" challenged Unilever's claims of CSR and reaffirmed the community's stance that "Kodaikanal won't step down until you make amends now." Made with a small budget of Rs. 15,000 (≈US$ 250), the three minute YouTube rap video had close to 1.8 million views in the first week; it documents the health and ecological problems afflicting workers at the mercury factory and calls out Unilever on its claims of safety, compensation, and corrective action.[56] The video has received national and international news coverage as well as celebrity support. Singer Nicki Minaj whose single "Anaconda" provided the inspiration for the viral video, tweeted her support.

The video, online petition, and Twitter action to engage CEO Paul Polman were a response to the apathy of mainstream media and an effort to "put moral pressure" to bring redress to a forgotten issue.[57]

How has Unilever responded: soon after the video was launched, Paul Polman's tweeted, "Working actively solution kodai #UnileverPollutes for several years already Determined to solve. Need others too and facts not false emotions,"[58] prompting an information warfare with both sides publishing their own version of 'facts' and counterclaims in the case.[59] In March 2016, HUL finally signed an agreement to compensate 591 ex-factory workers as a "humanitarian" action: "While extensive studies on the health of our former workers and the Kodaikanal environment have not found any evidence of harm, we take this issue very seriously. In 2016, we reached a settlement with the former workers of Kodaikanal factory on humanitarian grounds."[60]

The fight for environmental clean-up continues on social media using #UnileverPollutes, urging supporters to continue on with the reminder that "it's public outrage, not corporate responsibility, that prompted Unilever to do what it had refused to do for 15 years."[61]

In other instances, the energy sector, in particular, has been the target of what some have called an "online PR war" that "often centers on contested notions of CSR and claims by the oil giants about their environmental impact, which opponents dismiss as 'greenwashing.'"[62] Drawing on the Greenpeace Shell Arctic campaign, a study finds that Greenpeace efforts to stop Shell from drilling in the Arctic relied on the use of humor, irony, and corporate speak.[63] The Arctic Ready campaign launched June 2012, when Greenpeace teamed up with the Yes Men to spoof Shell's Arctic drilling plan with a YouTube video (#ShellFAIL: Private Arctic Launch Party Goes Wrong; published June 7, 2012; 8.5m+ views till date), a fake website (arcticready.com) that mimicked Shell's corporate brand identity, and a Twitter account (@ShellisPrepared) that appeared to be authored by Shell. While the hoax website itself had mixed responses, and critics questioned the ethics of such "brandjacking" (brand hijacking), the social media effort, arguably, undermined the legitimacy of Shell's claims of preparedness, safety, and contingency planning.

In particular, an Ad Generator option on the ArcticReady website allowed users to create parodies of Shell's advertisements and has more than 10,000 ads. Through symbolic visual imagery (e.g., polar bears, melting ice, birds soaked in oil), "mimetic irony" and corporate language (Let's Go, "ocean of possibility") manifested in Greenpeace and user-generated captions (e.g., Some see a frozen wasteland, we see an ocean of possibility. Let's go), Greenpeace Let's Go! Arctic campaign "empowered ordinary citizens by providing them with tools to create and disseminate their own anti-Shell messages." Arguably, the campaign resonated because it challenged corporatism but also because "these messages posed as corporate discourse, then pointed to, exploited, and intensified audiences' distrust of corporate rhetoric and corporate activity, ultimately undermining the legitimacy of corporate action."[64]

The social media action by Greenpeace generated a lot of positive and negative buzz with questions about legality and ethics. User comments on a Greenpeace blog post about the Arctic Ready campaign are illustrative of the mixed sentiment, and a sample (below) encapsulates the ethical concerns surrounding this action:

> This makes me lose faith in Greenpeace as an organisation. Was this approved or is it a solo run? The twitter account and it's messages goes [sic] makes me not believe anything Greenpeace tells me any more. Also there is no indication on the website that Greenpeace is responsible, in other words Greenpeace are lying and in my opinion, even though I am no fan of Shell they should sue you.[65]

Instead of taking legal action, Shell issued a short press release distancing itself from the hoax and highlighting the corporate decision to not press charges:

> Journalists, blog readers and YouTube viewers have recently been targeted with scams launched by organizations opposed to energy exploration in Alaska. A contest on a mock Shell website promotes the creation of fake advertisements. A video purports to show a bungled corporate PR event at the Seattle Space Needle. And a false press release claimed that the company is considering legal action against the scam campaign. The advertising contest is not associated with Shell, and neither is the site it's on. And Shell did not file legal action in this matter. Our focus is on safely executing our operations.[66]

For some, Shell's toned-down response made Greenpeace look like "the real villains"[67] whereas other commentators noted that this was the only plausible option available to Shell, given that legal action would draw more attention to the hoax and likely cause further damage.[68] Although Greenpeace was criticized by some mainstream media for its Arctic Ready hoax, a writer for *Forbes* magazine observed that "Greenpeace has apparently discovered that it's far more effective to ram Shell online than it is to send Greenpeace boats out to protest or to handcuff themselves to drilling equipment in the snow."[69]

What these cases illustrate is the potential of social media to be a power-equalizer. Of course, sustained and large-scale campaigns require a strategic and integrated use of multiple media, offline and online protest actions, petitions, lobbying, and so on. New media do not automatically spell the death of traditional and offline ways of campaigning; rather, they supplement and support conventional campaign strategy while offering new possibilities. Social media have indeed lowered the barriers of access by bypassing traditional media gatekeepers allowing NGOs to directly connect and mobilize their target audiences and enabling these audiences to weigh in on the focal issue (e.g., climate change). The Arctic Ready spoof discussed earlier encouraged users to create their own captions and messages, a form of crowdsourced content that not only reinforced the Greenpeace message but also created a community of supporters and empowered them to participate in a coordinated effort to stop Arctic drilling. This and other social-mediated campaigns permit NGOs and ordinary citizens alike an unprecedented ability "to scrutinize and challenge corporate activity and offer an alternative to business-oriented messages, narratives, and explanatory frameworks."[70] Last but certainly not least, social media allow advocacy groups to issue reputational challenges to powerful and resource-rich corporations with minimum resources (e.g., the case of "Kodaikanal Won't"), forcing them to respond and act appropriately. In sum, new and social media both reinforce traditional mechanisms of influence and present new avenues for digital advocacy.

Implications and discussion

As institutional actors and stakeholders, NGOs are in a position to influence corporate practices and social or environmental responsibilities by engaging in the co-construction and (re)definition of social standards and expectations.[71] Although national differences persist and NGOs continue to be marginalized in some contexts, social media afford them new possibilities to be heard and noticed. Further research should examine contextual differences that shape NGO ability to engage in advocacy to influence business practices.

Cross-cultural and comparative research can yield important insight of institutional differences across and within geographies.[72]

Even then, it would be naïve to gloss over the ethical and pragmatic implications of NGO use of social media. As a case in point, Greenpeace supporters expressed disappointment and a host of other negative emotions after the Arctic Ready and LEGO campaigns challenging the legitimacy of Greenpeace tactics. Admittedly, NGOs, like corporations, face stakeholder scrutiny and need to maintain social legitimacy. As we noted in the beginning, NGOs come in all shapes and sizes with substantive differences in their dealings with business.

Moreover, the efficacy of digital activism, or at least the best way to assess 'success' beyond a few well-documented cases, is yet inconclusive. Malcolm Gladwell critiqued that digital activism is built around weak ties or that increased participation online does not equate to high commitment or motivation. More research is needed but studies are optimistic about the positive spill-over from online participation to offline political engagement.[73] *The 2014 Cone Digital Activism* study also finds that voicing support of social issues on social networks and 'liking' an organization online is a springboard for deeper engagement.[74] As a case in point, on September 28, 2015, Shell announced withdrawal from the Arctic, citing a difficult regulatory environment, disappointing exploration outcome, and high project costs.[75] Whether commercial viability alone explains Shell's decision (after spending USD 7 bn on the project) is beyond the scope of this chapter, but we can argue that Greenpeace ability to influence several touch points – from creating awareness, to information dissemination, mobilizing and sustaining support – played a significant role. Longitudinal studies can deepen our understanding of the specific processes and outcomes of activist campaigns and/or advance new models/ frameworks of influence.

Moving to implications for corporate management, a host of questions emerge: what is at stake for CSR reputation? How should companies respond? Is not responding an option? How should organizations look at their relationship with NGOs (and other stakeholder groups)? There are no easy answers, although there is agreement that corporate reputations are ever more fragile and online reputation management needs to be an ongoing activity. When reputation gaps occur due to inconsistency of corporate claims, or differences in stakeholder expectation and experience with the firm, they need to be addressed before they erupt into full-blown crises.

Of course, there is no one-size-fits-all response. Although a quick and accurate response is 'crisis management 101,' sometimes responding to an online parody, hoax, or rumor may be counterproductive and worsen the situation. No two cases are alike, however, and assessing the potential impact on organizational reputation and business goals can assist the decision about whether (and how best) to respond. In addition, challenged organizations may need to assess their response in accordance with corporate strategy, feasibility and costs of proposed changes.[76]

Finally, can organizations treat digital activism as an opportunity to listen to stakeholders and engage with them? With the exponential growth of social media, the potential for engagement is high. However, studies have found limited organizational effort to engage stakeholders or to have a participant-centered dialogue to find collective solutions to a crisis.[77] Much communication is still one-way, centered on information dissemination, and negative comments are censored or ignored,[78] driven by fear of losing control over corporate messaging.

In sum, the lack of (elusive) control over corporate communication and CSR agendas poses a challenge for communication professionals. Social media engagement requires a change in mind-set from "a logic of control to a logic of communities,"[79] where the corporation is one among many actors. By engaging with online communities, and communicating corporate interest in a transparent and authentic manner, organizations can benefit from the opportunities of the "participatory new media environment."

Notes

1 Considered a front-runner among NGO use of social media, there are several well-documented cases of Greenpeace activism to influence change. Nestle KitKat campaign in 2010 forced the company to change its palm-oil sourcing practices; Zara and other fashion brands were targeted as part of an industry-wide Detox campaign.
2 Vaughan, A. (2014, October 9). Lego ends Shell partnership following Greenpeace campaign. *The Guardian*. Retrieved from www.theguardian.com/environment/2014/oct/09/lego-ends-shell-partnership-following-greenpeace-campaign.
3 Ibid.
4 Comment on Greenpeace campaign and the LEGO® brand. (2014, October 8). Retrieved from www.lego.com/en-gb/aboutus/news-room/2014/october/comment-on-the-greenpeace-cam paign-and-the-lego-brand.
5 Ibid.
6 Greenpeace report. (2014, July 1). Lego is keeping bad company. Retrieved from www.greenpeace. org.uk/media/reports/lego-keeping-bad-company.
7 Duff, I. (2014, Oct 9). How LEGO got awesome to #SaveTheArctic. Blog post. Retrieved from www. greenpeace.org/international/en/news/Blogs/makingwaves/save-the-arctic-lego-dumps-shell/ blog/50917/.
8 Kaplan, A. M. and Haenlein, M. (2010). Users of the world, unite! The challenges and opportunities of social media. *Business Horizons*, 53(1), 59–68. DOI: 10.1016/j.bushor.2009.09.003
9 Pridmore, J., Falk, A., and Sprenke, I. (2013). New media and social media: What's the difference v2.0. Working paper on Academia.edu. [Cited with permission of first author].
10 Ibid.
11 See Yaziji, M., and Doh, J. (2009). *NGOs and corporations: Conflict and collaboration*. Cambridge University Press, Cambridge: UK., for a comprehensive understanding of NGO definitions, classifications, and types.
12 Teegen, H., Doh, J.P., and Vachini, S. (2004). The importance of nongovernmental organizations (NGOs) in global governance and value creation: An international business agenda. *Journal of International Business Studies*, 35(6), 463–483.
13 Ibid.
14 Doh, J. P., and Teegen, H. (2002). Nongovernmental organizations as institutional actors in international business: Theory and implications. *International Business Review*, 11, 665–684.
15 For India, see Chaudhri, V. (March 2015). The promise and challenge of collaboration for CSR: Corporate- NGO engagement. Invited expert article in H. Mäkinen (Ed.) special issue on Corporate Social Responsibility. *Baltic Rim Economies*, 2, 16–17. Published by the Pan-European Institute. For Singapore, see Sriramesh, K., Ng, C. W., and Wanyin, L. (2007). Corporate social responsibility and public relations: Perceptions and practices in Singapore. In S. K. May, G. Cheney, and J. Roper (Eds.), *The debate over corporate social responsibility* (pp. 119–134). New York: Oxford University Press.
16 Arenas, D., Lozano, J. M., and Albareda, L. (2009). The role of NGOs in CSR: Mutual perceptions among stakeholders. *Journal of Business Ethics*, 88, 175–197. DOI 10.1007/s10551-009-0109-x
17 Mitchell, R. K., Agle, B. R., and Wood, D. J. (1997). Toward a theory of stakeholder identification and salience: Defining the principle of who and what really counts. *Academy of Management Review*, 22, 853–886.
18 Ibid.
19 Freeman, R. E., Velamuri, S. R., and Moriarty, B. (2006). Company stakeholder responsibility: A new approach to CSR. Retrieved from www.corporate-ethics.org/pdf/csr.pdf

20 Coombs, W. T. and Holladay, S. J. (2015). How activists shape CSR: Insights from Internet Contagion and Contingency Theories. In A. Adi, G. Grigore, and D. Crowther (Eds.) *Corporate social responsibility in the digital age (Developments in Corporate Governance and Responsibility, Volume 7)*. Emerald Group Publishing Limited, pp. 85–97. DOI: http://dx.doi.org/10.1108/S2043-052320150000007007

21 Schultz, F., and Wehmeier, S. (2010). Institutionalization of corporate social responsibility within corporate communications. Combining institutional, sensemaking and communication perspectives. *Corporate Communications: An International Journal, 15*, 9–29. Also see Christensen, L. T., and Cheney, G. (2011). Interrogating the communicative dimensions of corporate social responsibility. In Ø. Ihlen, S. May, and J. Bartlett (Eds.), *Handbook of communication and corporate social responsibility* (pp. 491–504). Oxford, UK: Wiley Blackwell.

22 Okoye, A. (2009). Theorising corporate social responsibility as an essentially contested concept: Is a definition necessary? *Journal of Business Ethics, 89*, 613–627.

23 Coombs, W. T., and Holladay, S. J. (2012). Fringe public relations: How activism moves critical PR toward the mainstream. *Public Relations Review, 38*, 880–887. DOI: 10.1016/j.pubrev.2012.02.008

24 Corporate social responsibility. Definition retrieved July 29 from https://ec.europa.eu/growth/industry/corporate-social-responsibility_nl.

25 Carroll, A. B., and Shabana, K. M. (2010). The business case for corporate social responsibility: A review of concepts, research and practice. *International Journal of Management Reviews, 12*, 85–105.

26 According to the *Reputation Institute's* RepTrak framework and annual studies. CSR RepTrak scores reflect a firm's performance on three key dimensions: citizenship, governance, and workplace.

27 Ibid.

28 Aula, P. and Mantere, S. (2013). Making and breaking sense: An inquiry into the reputation change. *Journal of Organizational Change Management, 26*, 340–352. DOI: http://dx.doi.org/10.1108/09534811311328380

29 Suchman, M. C. (1995). Managing legitimacy: Strategic and institutional approaches. *The Academy of Management Review, 20*, 571–610. DOI: 10.5465/AMR.1995.9508080331

30 Currents of change: The KPMG Survey of Corporate Responsibility Reporting 2015. Retrieved from www.kpmg.com/CN/en/IssuesAndInsights/ArticlesPublications/Documents/kpmg-survey-of-corporate-responsibility-reporting-2015-O-201511.pdf

31 Sustainability and Reporting Trends in 2025: Preparing for the Future. (2015). A Global Reporting Initiative report. Retrieved from www.globalreporting.org/resourcelibrary/Sustainability-and-Reporting-Trends-in-2025-1.pdf

32 Lee, S.Y. (2015). Can companies gain CSR reputation via social media? In A. Kaul and V. Chaudhri, V. (Eds.), Building reputation through social media. *Vikalpa – A Journal for Decision Makers, 40*, 475–478. DOI: DOI: 10.1177/0256090915618029

33 For more details on the campaign, see www.ft.com/cms/s/0/90dbff8a-3aea-11e2-b3f0-00144feabdc0.html#axzz4FscX5xAb

34 Nestle report. (February 2015). Progress report on responsible sourcing of palm oil. Retrieved July 30, 2016 from www.nestle.com/asset-library/documents/creating-shared-value/responsible-sourcing/progress-report-palm-oil-2014.pdf.

35 Sohn, Y. J., and Lariscy, R. W. (2014) Understanding reputational crisis: Definition, properties, and consequences. *Journal of Public Relations Research, 26*, 23–43. 10.1080/1062726X.2013.795865

36 Greenwashing. (nd). Retrieved from www.sustainablecommunication.org/eco360/what-is-eco360s-causes/greenwashing.

37 Janssen, C., Sen, S., and Bhattacharya, C. B. (2015). Corporate crises in the age of corporate social responsibility. *Business Horizons, 58*, 183–192. http://dx.doi.org/10.1016/j.bushor.2014.11.002

38 Lubin, G. (2012, January 24). McDonald's Twitter campaign goes horribly wrong #McDStories. *Business Insider*. Retrieved from www.businessinsider.com/mcdonalds-twitter-campaign-goes-horribly-wrong-mcdstories-2012-1?IR=T.

39 Deephouse, D. L., and Carter, S. M. (2005). An examination of differences between organizational legitimacy and organizational reputation. *Journal of Management Studies, 42*, 329–360.

40 Lovejoy, K., and Saxton, G. D. (2012). Information, community, and action: How nonprofit organizations use social media. *Journal of Computer-Mediated Communication, 17*, 337–353. doi: 10.1111/j.1083-6101.2012.01576.x

41 Dijck, J., and Poell, T. (2013). Understanding social media logic. *Media and Communication, 1*(1), 2–14. doi: 10.12924/mac2013.01010002

42 Coombs, W. T. (1998). The internet as potential equalizer: New leverage for confronting social irresponsibility. *Public Relations Review, 24*(3), 289–303. Also, Taylor, M., Kent, M. L., and White, W.

J. (2001). How activist organizations are using the Internet to build relationships. *Public Relations Review*, 27, 263–284.

43 Lovejoy and Saxton, 2012

44 Obar, J. A., Zube, P., and Lampe, C. (2012). Advocacy 2.0: An analysis of how advocacy groups in the United States perceive and use social media as tools for facilitating civic engagement and collective action. *Journal of Information Policy*, 2, 1–25. doi: 10.5325/jinfopoli.2.2012.0001

45 Guo, C., and Saxton, G. D. (2014). Tweeting social change: How social media are changing nonprofit advocacy. *Nonprofit and Voluntary Sector Quarterly*, 43(1), 57–79. doi: 10.1177/0899764012471585

46 Lovejoy and Saxton, 2012.

47 Kingston, L. N., and Stam, K. R. (2013). Online advocacy: Analysis of human rights NGO websites. *Journal of Human Rights Practice*, 5, 75–95. doi: 10.1093/jhuman/hus036

48 Capriotti, P. (2011). Communicating corporate social responsibility through the internet and social media. In O. Ihlen, J. L. Bartlett, and S. May (Eds.), *The handbook of communication and corporate social responsibility* (pp. 358–377). Oxford, UK: Wiley Blackwell.

49 Utting, P. (2005). Corporate responsibility and the movement of business. *Development in Practice*, 15, 375–388. doi: 10.1080/09614520500075797

50 Dempsey, S. E. (2011). NGOs as communicative actors within corporate social responsibility efforts. In O. Ihlen, J. Bartlett, and S. May (Eds.), *The handbook of communication and corporate social responsibility* (pp. 445–466). Oxford, UK: Wiley Blackwell.

51 Coombs and Holladay, 2015

52 Ibid.

53 Yaziji and Doh, 2009

54 Greenpeace response to a user comment. Duff, 2014.

55 Factsheet: Response to the claims made by HUL on their website. (2015, August 3). Retrieved from http://kodaimercury.org/factsheet-response-to-the-claims-made-by-hul-on-their-website/

56 Srinivasan, L. (2015, August 6). Meet rapper Sofia Ashraf, the woman behind the 'Kodaikanal Won't' video. Retrieved from www.dnaindia.com/entertainment/report-meet-rapper-sofia-ashraf-the-woman-behind-the-kodaikanal-won-t-video-2111670.

57 Nath, P. J. (2015, August 5). How the Kodaikanal Won't video went viral. *The Hindu*. Retrieved from www.thehindu.com/news/national/tamil-nadu/how-the-kodaikanal-wont-video-went-viral/article7500019.ece

58 Srinivasan, 2015

59 Unilever factsheet here: www.unilever.com/sustainable-living/what-matters-to-you/kodaikanal-india. Petition factsheet here: htmlhttp://kodaimercury.org/factsheet-response-to-the-claims-made-by-hul-on-their-website/

60 Kodaikanal Mercury Factory – Contamination Response, India. Unilever website [Match 9, 2016]. Retrieved from www.hul.co.in/about/our-position-on-kodaikanal-mercury-factory/

61 Victory of Kodaikanal workers against Unilever: Celebrating a brave struggle. (2016, March 9). Retrieved March 31, 2016 from http://www.indiaresists.com/activists-celebrate-unilever-settles-kodaikanal-workers/.

62 McQueen, D. (2015). CSR and new battle lines in online PR war: A case study of the energy sector and its discontents. In A. Adi, G. Grigore, and D. Crowther (Eds.), *Corporate social responsibility in the digital age (Developments in Corporate Governance and Responsibility, Volume 7)*. Emerald Group Publishing Limited, pp. 99–125. doi: 10.1108/S2043-052320150000007008

63 Davis, C. B., Glantz, M., and Novak, D. R. (2016). "You Can't Run Your SUV on Cute. Let's Go!": Internet memes as delegitimizing discourse. *Environmental Communication*, 10, 62–83. doi:10.1080/17524032.2014.991411

64 Ibid., pp. 80–81.

65 User response to a GP blog post. Retrieved from www.greenpeace.org/international/en/news/Blogs/makingwaves/greenpeace-the-yes-men-and-the-inside-story-o/blog/40893/.

66 Hill, K. (2012, July 18). Shell Oil's social media nightmare continues, thanks to skilled pranksters behind @ShellisPrepared. *Forbes*. Retrieved from www.forbes.com/sites/kashmirhill/2012/07/18/shell-oils-social-media-nightmare-continues-thanks-to-skilled-pranksters/#54811e3b651d.
Ironically, Shell's website shows an error message in response to all searches about 'hoax' or 'Greenpeace.'

67 Robbins, M. (2012, July 18). Epic Shell PR fail? No, the real villains here are Greenpeace. *NewStatesman*. Retrieved from www.newstatesman.com/sci-tech/2012/07/epic-shell-pr-fail-no-real-villains-here-are-greenpeace

68 Hill, 2012

69 Hill, 2012

70 McQueen, 2015

71 de Bakker, F. G. A., and Hellsten, I. (2013). Capturing online presence: Hyperlinks and semantic networks in activist group websites on corporate social responsibility. *Journal of Business Ethics, 118,* 807–823. doi: 10.1007/s10551-013-1962-1

72 For example, see Doh, J. P., and Guay, T. R. (2006). Corporate social responsibility, public policy, and NGO activism in Europe and the United States: An institutional-stakeholder perspective. *Journal of Management Studies, 43,* 47–73. doi: 10.1111/j.1467-6486.2006.00582.x

73 Vissers, S., and Stolle, D. (2014). Spill-over effects between Facebook and on/offline political participation? Evidence from a two-wave panel study. *Journal of Information Technology and Politics, 11,* 259–275. doi: 10.1080/19331681.2014.888383

74 2014 Cone Digital Activism Study. Downloaded from www.conecomm.com/2014-digital-activism-study.

75 Shell updates on Alaska exploration. (2015, September 28). Retrieved from www.shell.com/media/news-and-media-releases/2015/shell-updates-on-alaska-exploration.html

76 Coombs and Holladay, 2015

77 Romenti, S., Murtarelli, G., and Valentini, C. (2014). Organisations' conversations in social media: Applying dialogue strategies in times of crises. *Corporate Communications: An International Journal, 19,* 10–33. http://dx.doi.org/10.1108/CCIJ-05-2012-0041

78 Dekay, S. H. (2012). How large companies react to negative Facebook comments. *Corporate Communications: An International Journal, 17*(3), 289–299. http://dx.doi.org/10.1108/13563281211253539

79 Etter, M., and Fieseler, C. (2015). Taking a social stance on social media. *Communication Director, 1.* Retrieved from www.communication-director.com/issues/anticipation-and-disruption/taking-social-stance-social-media#.VwJs4GMVclI.

5.2 Catastrophe, transparency and social responsibility on online platforms

Contesting cold shutdown at the Fukushima nuclear plant

Majia Nadesan

Introduction

The March 2011 Fukushima Daiichi nuclear crisis involved three nuclear meltdowns and one spent fuel pool fire following a major earthquake in Honshu, Japan. Former Prime Minister Naoto Kan described the disaster as "the most severe accident in the history of mankind."[1] Five years later, melted fuel in cracked reactors must be continuously cooled, producing radioactive steam and water that result in ongoing environmental contamination, the scale of which remains unclear.[2] TEPCO claims the Daiichi plant is "under control" but is unable to locate melted fuel from two of the six reactors, even after deploying sophisticated muon scanning.[3] An independent investigation by the Japanese Diet condemned TEPCO's risk and crisis management and criticized government leaders during the early days of the disaster for withholding radiation monitoring data needed by local authorities tasked with evacuations.[4]

Trust between authorities and communities impacted by the disaster was disrupted, especially regarding the perceived risks of nuclear fallout. In response, government and utility authorities promised reform, emphasizing greater transparency and accountability, but skepticism remains high with evacuees resisting re-settlement plans. In this context of distrust, anti-nuclear activists deployed social media to challenge official crisis narratives promoted by TEPCO and the Japanese government and to disseminate dissident accounts produced by a range of individuals and groups. For example, Japanese nuclear physicist Ryugo Hayano attracted many followers for his Twitter posts regarding his "independent" fallout measurements.[5] Citizens set up radiation monitoring to identify "hot spots" of concentrated radionuclides, with the results shared on social media, especially Twitter and Facebook. The Safecast site (http://blog.safecast.org/) illustrates an online "global volunteer-centered citizen science project working to empower people with data about their environment" launched due to perceived failures in official radiation monitoring. In this context of uncertain risks, everyday people within Japan posted videos of high Geiger counter readings at YouTube and shared photos of perceived radiation symptoms (such as bleeding noses, lost nails, and mutated flowers and vegetables).

Social media use in the aftermath of the Fukushima disaster illustrates the rise of Internet-based knowledge production and social activism enabled by interactive platforms.[6] This chapter investigates TEPCO's "webcam" transparency strategy and the online activism surrounding it as company-sourced data were disseminated with the intent of disrupting TEPCO's control narrative. Citizen monitoring of a webcam established at the Fukushima Daiichi site 16 March 2011, and the attendant dissemination of video and screenshots of unusual events on social media, represented a tactical assault against TEP-CO's narrative of control and recovery.

Social media and democracy

Social media is supplementing and, to some degree, replacing traditional mainstream news as the public's primary source of information, but social media content tends to be more overtly editorialized and selectively curated than conventional news reporting. Social media narratives of truth often adopt a populist tone in critiquing corporate and/or government policy[7] and are more open to conspiratorial explanations. The populist flare and capacities for user-generated content are foundational to social media's "democratizing" promises, as social media is thought to facilitate grassroots organizing and influence over governmental and corporate decision-making.

However, research has just begun examining the efficacy of online organizing. Analysis by Schoenmaker and Alexander of an Australian government ban on cattle exports demonstrates that social media can in some instances be a powerful tool for influencing official authorities, particularly when activism is prompted by graphic visual imagery.[8] However, social media's democratizing impact may have limits. In 2006, Li Dollar reported social media activism had not increased governmental responsiveness in China, despite heightened transparency as China moved to create online sites for its government agencies ("e-government").[9] Li Dollar's findings suggest that e-government transparency does not necessarily predict greater democratic responsiveness by authorities, even in a context of heavy social media sharing. The assumption that transparency and activism will automatically lead to more democratic decision-making and corporate social responsibility ignores contextual institutional conditions capable of deflecting populist pressure. In essence, greater democracy does not flow necessarily from increased availability of information, nor from greater social sharing of that information.

Webcams, transparency and democratic participation

Despite uncertain impacts, transparency has been promoted as an important legitimizing construct under neoliberalism and has been actively adopted by governments, in the concept and applications of e-government, and by corporations as a public relations strategy, particularly under crisis conditions.[10] Visual or optic transparency has emerged as a particularly salient transparency regime.

Webcams are perhaps the most iconic deployment of visual transparency, utilized routinely in policing and in the wake of corporate crises, such as the 2010 BP oil spill during which a webcam was installed at the site of the broken well-head. Research on the uses, perceived legitimacy, and social significance of webcam imagery is relatively new. The webcam was invented in 1991 by University of Cambridge computer scientists to monitor the breakroom coffee pot.[11] "Webcam" research tends to address privacy issues involved in remote monitoring and scientific and educational applications. Research on the motivations for webcam watching[12] and webcam blogging[13] have found diverse goals, especially a desire for forming community around shared interests and/or value orientations.

Most research on webcam data investigates the efficacy of webcam pedagogy and the validity of webcam data for scientific research. One study on the scientific use of webcam data concluded that although there are challenges deriving from the typically low-quality images and camera motion, data from camera networks could be usefully deployed "as a means of tracking environmental change in a low cost, highly automated and scalable manner requiring little human involvement."[14] Another study found no statistically significant difference in landscape interpretations by student observers who viewed a landscape by webcam, as compared to those who had viewed the site in person.[15] These studies suggest that webcam data have scientific value, although the limits of which have yet to be determined.

Ultimately, however, webcam and other transparency-regime data (such as documents achieved through Freedom of Information Access requests) have an impact on public dialogue only to the extent that they are officially acknowledged by media gatekeepers, institutional officials, and legal apparatuses. Hence, the admissibility and legitimacy of webcam data ultimately hinge less on absolute measures of validity than on specific social appropriations and acknowledgements by recognized authorities. The analysis offered in this chapter's case study suggests that social responsibility through transparency can be limited by mainstream media gatekeeping and by the perceived illegitimacy of crowd sourced interpretations of ambiguous official data streams.

Method: participatory action research

Having introduced social media activism in Japan and elsewhere following the Fukushima crisis, this study now turns to activists' efforts to challenge the official narrative of "cold shutdown" by documenting atmospheric emissions and other events at Fukushima Daiichi using TEPCO's webcam data. Although the scope of this study is limited, examining the efficacy of webcam data in contesting official risk assessment accounts during two distinct time periods, findings have implications more broadly for the ongoing debates about the role of corporate transparency regimes and efficacy of social media activism.

Case

The Fukushima Daiichi case is particularly interesting because it represents a point of condensation for public debates within Japan about nuclear power.[16] At the time March 2011 earthquake, Japan had 54 operational nuclear power plants. The Fukushima nuclear site consists of Fukushima Daiichi and Daini, located approximately ten kilometers apart. Fukushima Daiichi has six reactors, each with its own spent fuel pool.[17] Cooling failures caused by the earthquakes produced three core reactor meltdowns, four hydrogen explosions, and one reported spent fuel pool fire. On March 17, 2011, European Union Energy Chief Guenther Oettinger described the Daiichi site as "effectively out of control."[18] On 28 March 2011, F. Dalnoki-Veress of the James Martin Center for Nonproliferation Studies at the Monterey Institute of International Studies warned of ongoing, uncontrolled fission activity.[19] Workers, known as the Fukushima 50, voluntarily remained at Daiichi after all others had evacuated to pursue desperate measures to cool melted fuel.

Despite uncertainties in conditions at Fukushima, TEPCO and the government reported that reactor meltdowns were partial and that melted fuel was being cooled throughout the crisis.[20] While mainstream Japanese[21] and US[22] media tended to disseminate the official control frame that minimized risks, social media were deployed by concerned citizens and activists to disseminate alternative and more troubled narratives. These resistance accounts existed tangentially to the official 'control frame' as TEPCO launched an ambitious "roadmap toward restoration" 17 April 2011 that promised to bring reactors and spent fuel pools to a stable cooling condition, mitigate the release of radioactivity, and expedite return of evacuees.[23] In May 2011, TEPCO issued a press release indicating that water injected into the inner containment vessels had cooled melted fuel and that further "large-scale release of radioactive materials" was "unlikely."[24]

Days later, Chief Cabinet Secretary Edano promised the World Economic Forum to promote a more transparent, "risk-resistant society" in response to criticism of Fukushima crisis management: "We will make efforts to improve transparency and more readily share information."[25] TEPCO's earliest efforts at transparency included websites in Japanese and English where decommissioning plans, press releases, and radiation monitoring results were posted. Local municipalities also set up online sites for posting their atmospheric and sewage sludge radiation monitoring data.

Data generated from these transparency regimes were ultimately deployed against TEPCO's control narrative by activists who disseminated webcam screenshots and video clips as evidence of ongoing problems with atmospheric emissions at the plant. This case analysis represents an exploratory study of social media activism using webcam and other data to contest TEPCO's control narrative. The scope of this case analysis is narrowed by focusing on activists' efforts to challenge 1) TEPCO's "road to recovery" in June 2011 after delayed public disclosure that Daiichi had suffered nuclear meltdowns in March, and 2) TEPCO's allegation that "cold shutdown" had been achieved in December 2011 by documenting ongoing atmospheric emissions at Fukushima Daiichi using webcam images and radiation monitoring data.

TEPCO's narrative of control hinged most particularly on its assertion that cold shutdown had been achieved. This assertion made TEPCO's narrative vulnerable because the company had reported that a nuclear reaction, or criticality, potentially occurred on 1 November 2011.[26] If the geometry of melted nuclear fuel meets the right conditions, a fission event can produce a chain reaction of nuclear criticalities resulting in an atomic explosion.[27] In 2012, scientists from the Korea Atomic Energy Research Institute publicly confirmed the theoretical possibility of a criticality occurring in Fukushima's melted fuel.[28] Cold shutdown in December seemed improbable after a criticality in November, especially to webcam watchers.

Webcam watchers deployed screenshots and video to debunk TEPCO's narrative of cold shutdown, arguing that steam eruptions, fires and nuclear criticalities were occurring at the site. Webcam watching and sharing illustrate resistance to the official control narrative as activists followed, analyzed, and shared TEPCO webcam imagery on a variety of social media platforms, including YouTube, Twitter, Enenews, Dropbox, and personal blogs. The nuclear news aggregator site, Enenews was among the most important English-language sites for posting and discussing webcam conditions, as were the blogs Ex-SKF (http://ex-skf.blogspot.com/) and Fukushima Diary (http://fukushima-diary.com/), the latter of which was established by a Japanese citizen who left Tokyo after reporting symptoms of radiation sickness.

Research protocol

The research protocol deployed in this study entailed 5 years of daily ethnographic and textual analyses of Enenews discussion forums and English-language Fukushima social media activism beginning 12 March 2011, grounded in Participatory Action Research (PAR). Ethnographic research guided by PAR acknowledges and validates everyday people's participation in the production of knowledge and social policy.[29] PAR supports social change by documenting alternative epistemologies that challenge dominant regimes of truth. However, PAR's capacity for challenging established truths with alternative epistemologies is contingent ultimately upon institutional acknowledgement of the alternative knowledge and values produced through its research praxis.

Guided by PAR, the research sought to identify and understand how online activists deployed webcam imagery and other data forms to problematize TEPCO's control narrative. The analysis developed here particularly focuses on the "Webcam Discussion Forum" first established in June 2011, followed by a second, focused analysis of the "Webcam Discussion Forum" during November 2011. These time periods were selected because they coincided with webcam watchers' observations of heavy emissions at the plant. Discussion posts were analyzed to identify recurring topics of conversation, discussion themes, and modes of persuasion.

As noted above, Enenews is a news aggregator site that appeared online during the early days of the disaster. Enenews hosted the most frequented English-language discussion of Fukushima cam imagery. As of June 2016, Enenews was ranked 153,579 in Japan and 69,699 in the United States by Alexa. Enenews' first post was dated 23 March 2011.[30] On 22 May 2011, the "general discussion" forum was established, with the second post on this forum alerting readers to a video from the online TEPCO webcam that had been saved and uploaded to YouTube.[31] Enenews established a dedicated webcam discussion forum 26 June 2011 to facilitate conversation about the cams.[32]

The name "webcam watchers" came to designate those individuals who participated in the Enenews forum, as well as posting screenshots, video clips, and analyses at other sites. Some webcam watchers triangulated data streams by integrating their analyses of webcam imagery with TEPCO's official radiation monitoring data, Japanese municipal radiation monitoring data, US Environmental Protection Agency Radnet data, and meteorological information concerning the jet stream location. The availability of these additional data streams illustrates e-government transparency.

Findings

The Japanese government and nuclear industry, supported by the same US entities, promoted a narrative of expert control that was problematized in social media by activists who challenged the cold shutdown and promoted alternative narratives of plant conditions. Enenews was an important platform for anti-nuclear online activism and helped frame discussion agendas through its curated, daily-updated assortment of headlines drawn from scientific studies, government reports, and corporate press releases and news coverage. For example, Enenews' post from 7 June 2011, "More serious than a meltdown – Japan Gov't now raising possibility that fuel had a 'melt through,'"[33] illustrate how the site fed challenges to TEPCO's narrative of a cold shutdown through its selective curation of news.[34] Webcam watchers drew upon curated headlines to support their interpretations of atmospheric "emissions" believed to be caused by ongoing nuclear activity in melted fuel, especially beginning in June 2011 and continuing through December 2011.[35]

The popularity of Fukushima webcam watching grew with the establishment of the first dedicated "Webcam Forum" 26 June 2011,[36] spurred by apparent fires at the site recorded and uploaded to YouTube, as illustrated by the first comments on the forum reporting possible flames visible on the webcam.[37] Debate about observations and interpretations encouraged webcam watchers to save and share video clips and screenshots, especially at YouTube and Dropbox.[38] Fukushima webcam watchers who saw smoke and steam, rather than ordinary fog, routinely had to defend interpretations, despite their efforts to triangulate data, as some commentators questioned the poor quality of the cams and the ability of the watchers to differentiate between normal fog and radioactive emissions.[39]

Webcam watchers often sought to validate their interpretations of "criticality" events at Daiichi with meteorological patterns and atmospheric radiation data. Webcam watchers were tutored in atmospheric circulations by the Austrian Central Institute for Meteorology and Geodynamics (ZAMG) and Norwegian Institute for Air Research (NILU). Both organizations had posted online visual representations (using FLEXPART) of the atmospheric dispersion of Fukushima fallout using source terms provided by TEPCO.[40] NILU's graphic was uploaded to YouTube as early as 29 March 2011.[41] In November 2011, ZAMG and NILU released a joint press release documenting the institutes' measurements of radioactive xenon and cesium released between 11 March 2011 and mid-April 2011, offering higher source terms than provided by TEPCO.[42]

In November 2011, TEPCO and the Japanese government jointly declared that cold shutdown was achieved at Fukushima Daiichi and that nuclear power would remain vital to economic and political security. The announcement was surprising because conditions at Daiichi failed to meet ordinary criteria for cold shutdown, which require that the reactor core temperature is stabilized below 95 degrees Celsius. The Japanese newspaper, *The Mainichi* described TEPCO's use of the phrase in a December 2011 article, "What is a 'Cold Shutdown' at the Fukushima Nuclear Plant?"[43] The article compared the typical technical use of "cold shutdown" with the Japanese government's deployment, the latter of which did not preclude spontaneous fission events and atmospheric emissions.

The November 2011 announcement of a "cold shutdown" by the Japanese government coincided with sightings by webcam watchers of unusual events at Daiichi, as illustrated by comments and links to YouTube video clips posted on the Fukushima webcam discussion forum 6 November 2011.[44] Commentators suggested that fires were visible in units 3 and 4 based on the extent of "emissions" visible on the cams, which were allegedly documented in screenshots and video clips.

Webcam watchers and others seeking to fracture the control narrative during this period drew upon 'diverse forms of evidence.' In particular, activists widely shared and discussed a 11 November 2011 TEPCO press release reporting radioactive xenon gas (Xe133 and Xe135) was detected in the unit 2 containment vessel. The detection suggested a nuclear criticality occurred, an interpretation promoted by webcam watchers who reported fires.[45] Additional evidence for criticalities was derived from municipal sewage sludge monitoring data routinely shared by Japanese bloggers[46] and by independent radiation monitoring results, also shared through social media.[47] Expert testimonials were also widely shared as evidence of anomalous events at that time.[48] For example, Fukushima Diary posted a video clip of remarks made by Uehara Haruo, the former president of Saga University, who warned the Free Press Association (17 November 2011) of a potential "hydrovolcanic explosion" should melted fuel reach the river running under the Daiichi site.[49] Webcam watchers seized upon the idea of an extended "hydrovolcanic explosion" to explain their interpretation of plant conditions. Accordingly, activists deployed diverse data, including data generated from government and scientific sources, to fracture the official control narrative, legitimize alternative interpretations of plant conditions, and to agitate for more transparency.

However, webcam watchers were not successful in their efforts to get mainstream media to examine screenshots as evidence of anomalous events. None of the webcam images or video clips from this period were ever discussed in mainstream media. A Google search found few "mainstream" media references to the webcams: 1) a reference in *Forbes* magazine 31 March 2011 telling readers the webcam was black because it was night;[50] 2) references to a worker who appeared directly before the Fukushima webcam and pointed insistently at the camera in 2011;[51] 3) an image of "mystery steam" rising over reactor 3 published by *The Ecologist* 31 December 2013;[52] 4) a report by *RT* published in January 2014 alleging that "plumes of mysterious steam" had been detected rising from unit 3 by "surveillance cameras";[53] 5) followed in February 2014 by an unremarkable image of the Fukushima plant from the webcam published at *The Ecologist*;[54] with the last found reference; 6) an announcement of, and links to, the Fukushima webcams published by *Euronews* in October 2014.[55] *The Japan Times* published an article dated 18 July 2013 alleging steam had been seen rising over reactor 3,[56] although the source of the information was not reported. In 2016, Reuters posted a webcam clip from TEPCO webcam 1 of a sizeable earthquake near the plant on 22 November. The earthquake triggered a small tsunami that temporarily halted cooling at Daini.[57] Although the power disruption was reported at Daiini, the webcam clip of the earthquake was taken from TEPCO webcam 1, trained on Daiichi units 1 and 2.

Discussion

Japan's government is encouraging citizens to return to the former restricted 20-kilometer exclusion zone, while support is being withdrawn for Fukushima's radiation refugees.[58] TEPCO continues to struggle to find and contain nuclear fuel at Daiichi and has been criticized for poor social responsibility for exploiting works and for withholding information,[59] especially about water contamination levels and leaks.[60] Despite these problems, the narrative of expert control and cold shutdown prevailed.

Alternative narratives of plant conditions did not migrate into mainstream media often, even when sourced by high-profile figures, such as Mitsuhei Murata, Japan's former ambassador to Switzerland, who in 2014 declared that Fukushima remained "out of control," posing an unprecedented "global security issue."[61] Nonetheless, social media activists persist in their efforts to contest TEPCO's control paradigm using online platforms, including Enenews, to promote their alternative narratives.

Webcam watching had no discernable impact on mainstream news or political discussion of conditions at the plant beyond the few references cited above, as of 2016. Webcam watchers' sustained failure to problematize the cold shutdown outside of online platforms eroded participation in webcam watching and sharing. In 2015, it became impossible to post new comments sequentially on the webcam forum because of technological glitches, effectively ending four years of protracted discussion at Enenews. Webcam watching participation and discussion dropped off significantly as a result, although a few watchers continue to record observations on personal blogs and at a new, less-trafficked platform (http://caferadlab.com/forum-5.html). Interest in webcam screenshots rises after periodic reports of earthquakes centered near the plant.

Social media's Fukushima epistemologies appear to exist in an "alternative" e-public sphere. The nature of this emerging e-public sphere remains unmapped, but this case study demonstrates that online activism can adopt norms of argumentation and evidence to articulate and propagate divergent narratives, particularly in crises situations marked by high levels of uncertainty and ongoing risks. Divergent Fukushima narratives failed to effect desired change within the time period studied but will potentially be re-vitalized in adapted form in the wake of future crises.

Conclusions and managerial implications

This chapter has demonstrated that the Fukushima nuclear crisis engendered grassroots opposition to nuclear power.[62] Social media played an important role in shaping and sharing alternative narratives of the disaster that contested official pronouncements of cold shutdown. This chapter has demonstrated how the public relations imperatives of transparency, when coupled with new technologies of visualization (such as webcams), fueled resistance to the official control narrative.

TEPCO and the Japanese government responded to criticism of their crisis management by promising greater transparency. Webcams were established and radiation monitoring data were posted online. Concerned citizens in Japan and elsewhere drew upon these data streams to belie official pronouncements of the cold shutdown. The deployment of webcam imagery as part of a campaign to problematize the official narrative illustrates the complexities of evaluating the democratizing potential of social media activism.

Webcams are new technologies, and the validity of their data streams remains untested, even when the webcams are owned and operated by official authorities. In the case analyzed here, TEPCO and government officials simply failed to acknowledge activists' challenges, even when such challenges relied upon official data. Mainstream media followed suit, marginalizing social media activism in online platforms whose highly editorialized content problematizes legitimacy in the broader court of public opinion. This study's findings support previous conclusions that Fukushima social media content lacked perceived legitimacy.[63] Consequently, neither transparency nor social media activism were sufficient to challenge the official control narrative regarding plant conditions outside of online platforms.

Honma Ryu's 2012 bestselling Japanese-language book, *Dentsu and Nuclear Coverage*, argues that the Japanese advertising and public relations conglomerate Dentsu actively contained mainstream media coverage of the Fukushima disaster on behalf of TEPCO, one of the company's leading clients.[64] Dentsu is the fifth largest media communication group globally and controls a significant share of Japan's corporate advertising budgets. Ryu's book raises unanswered questions about mainstream media gatekeeping that should be explored further in future research.

Limitations and recommendations for further research

This project concludes that social media activism apparently failed to shape Japan's mainstream media coverage and nuclear policy, as the country remains committed to re-starting reactors and re-settling evacuated populations.[65] In their account of challenges facing PAR research, Whitman, Pain and Milledge observed frequent failures by formal authority structures, systems, and policies to acknowledge and incorporate alternative accounts of contested issues and terrains. This study concludes that democratic responsiveness to social media activism is selective, with some issues engendering less responsivity, particularly when tied to highly politicized energy and natural security issues.

However, this research study is limited in several ways. First and foremost, it is very difficult to know whether webcam data have influenced public discourse from "behind the scenes." The popularity of circulating images of Fukushima emissions, mutated vegetables, and bloody noses on social media may have encouraged mainstream news outlets to run their own Fukushima news stories. Although mainstream news has promoted a "recovery" narrative, many stories have also included very critical reports on the problems of ongoing radioactive water production at the site and the missing corium mysteries. The role of social media in fueling this coverage remains unclear.

In June 2016, TEPCO's president apologized publicly for a "cover-up" of the Daiichi meltdowns.[66] China called for full transparency on plant conditions. Hence, the control narrative remains fragile and subject to revision. In this context of ongoing uncertainty, Japanese citizens still monitor radiation in hotspots and food and share their results in community lectures and on social media.[67] Fukushima evacuees have not been persuaded by the government to return to their localities, fearing exposure to radioactive contamination.[68] Social media activism continues with unclear effects, suggesting more research is needed to understand the dissemination and efficaciousness of persistent alternative narratives in the wake of catastrophic accidents.

Notes

1 Kan, N. (2013, October 28). Encountering the Fukushima Daiichi accident. *The Huffington Post*. Available from, www.huffingtonpost.com/naoto-kan/japan-nuclear-energy_b_4171073.html, accessed October 29, 2013.

2 Mukerjee, M. (2016, March 8). Crippled Fukushima reactors are still a danger, 5 years after the accident. *Scientific American*. Available from, www.scientificamerican.com/article/crippled-fukushima-reactors-are-still-a-danger-5-years-after-the-accident1/?WT.mc_id=SA_ENGYSUS_20160310, accessed March 10, 2016.

3 Nagano, T. (2015, March 20). TEPCO believes nearly all nuclear fuel melted in Fukushima reactor, *The Asahi Shimbun*. Available from, http://ajw.asahi.com/article/0311disaster/fukushima/AJ201503200050, accessed March 21, 2015

4 The Fukushima Nuclear Accident Independent Investigation Commission, Japan National Diet (2012). The Official Report of the Fukushima Nuclear Accident (Executive Summary). Available from, http://naiic.go.jp/wp-content/uploads/2012/07/NAIIC_report_hi_res2.pdf, accessed December 29, 2012.

5 Glionna, J. (2011, December 18). Japan less likely to trust officials, main media, since disaster. *The Los Angeles Times*. Available from, www.latimes.com/news/nationworld/world/la-fg-japan-distrust-20111218,0,7635674.story, accessed December 19, 2011.

6 Riedlinger, M. and Rea, J. (2015). Discourse ecology and knowledge niches: Negotiating the risks of radiation in online Canadian forums, post-Fukushima. *Science, Technology, and Human Values*, 40(4), 588–614. DOI: 10.1177/0162243915571166

7 Harris, L. (2011). When your communication gets in a spin – the battle of policy versus populism. Proceedings of the *PRIA National Conference PR Directions*, 25 October 2011, Sydney.

8 Schoenmaker, S., and Alexander, D. (2012). Live cattle trade: The case of an online crisis. *Social Alternatives*, 31(2), 17–21.

9 Li Lollar, X. (2006). Assessing China's E-Government: Information, service, transparency and citizen outreach of government websites. *Journal of Contemporary China*, 15(46) 31–41.

10 Nadesan, M. (2011). Transparency and neoliberal logics of corporate social responsibility, in O. Ihlen, J. Bartlett, S. May (eds.) *The Handbook of Communication and Corporate Social Responsibility*, Malden, MA: Wiley-Blackwell, 252–275.

11 Did you know? (2015, March). *Discover*, 36(2), 2.

12 Koskela, H. (2011, August). Hijackers and humble servants: Individuals as camwitnesses in contemporary controlwork. *Theoretical Criminology*, 15(3), 269–282.

13 Kitzmann, A. (2015). Re-visiting the web cam and the promises and perils of the fully networked age. *Biography*, 38(2), 273–278.

14 Morris, D., Boyd, D., Crowe, J., Johnson, C., and Smith, K. (2013, May). Exploring the potential for automatic extraction of vegetation phenological metrics from traffic webcams. *Remote Sensing*, 5(5), 2200–2218.

15 Kolivras, K., Luebbering, C., and Resler, L. (2012). Evaluating differences in landscape interpretation between webcam and field-based experiences. *Journal of Geography in Higher Education*, 36(2), 277–291. doi:10.1080/03098265.2011.621165

16 Aldrich, D., Platte J., and Sklarew, J. (2015, July 20). Despite meltdowns, a tsunami and public opposition, Japan may soon restart a nuclear power plant – or several. *The Washington Post*. Available from, www.washingtonpost.com/blogs/monkey-cage/wp/2015/07/20/despite-meltdowns-a-tsunami-and-public-opposition-japan-may-soon-restart-a-nuclear-power-plant-or-several/, accessed July 21, 2015.

17 *Integrity Inspection of Dry Storage Casks and Spent Fuels at Fukushima Daiichi Nuclear Power Station* (16 November 2010). Available from, www.nirs.org/reactorwatch/accidents/6-1_powerpoint.pdf, accessed April 30, 2011.

18 Shirouzu, N., and Smith, R. (2011, March 17). U.S. sounds alarm on radiation, *The Wall Street Journal*, A1, A12.

19 Dalnoki-Veress, F. (2011, 28 March). What was the cause of the high C1-38 Radioactivity in the Fukushima Daiichi Reactor #1. *Lewis Arms Control Wonk*. Available from, http://lewis.arm scontrolwonk.com/files/2011/03/Cause_of_the_high_Cl38_Radioactivity.pdf, accessed April 3, 2011.

20 See Nadesan, M. (2013). *Fukushima and the Privatization of Risk*. Houndmills: Palgrave Macmillan, 43–47.

21 Imtihania, N., and Marikoa, Y. (2013). Media coverage of Fukushima nuclear power station accident 2011. *Procedia Environmental Sciences*, 17, 938–946.

22 See for example Pascale, C. (2016). Vernacular epistemologies of risk: The crisis in Fukushima. *Current Sociology*, 65, 3–20, DOI: 10.1177/0011392115627284

23 Lochbaum, D., Lyman, E., Stranahan, S., and Union of Concerned Scientists. (2014). *Fukushima: The Story of a Nuclear Disaster*, London: The New Press. p. 163

24 Nakayama, M., and Okada, Y. (2011, May 16). Tepco says fuel in 2 reactors may have melted. *Bloomberg*. Available from, www.bloomberg.com/news/2011-05-16/tepco-says-fuel-in-2-reactors-may-have-melted.html, accessed May 17, 2011.

25 Tonkin, S. (2011, May 18). Japan government draws lessons from March quake, pledges greater transparency. *World Economic Forum*. Available from, www.weforum.org/news/japan-government-draws-lessons-march-quake-pledges-greater-transparency, accessed May 19, 2011.

26 Inajima, T., and Okada, Y. (2011, November 2). Tepco detects nuclear fission at damaged Fukushima power station. *Business Week*. Available from, www.businessweek.com/news/2011-11-01/tepco-detects-possible-nuclear-fission-at-fukushima-reactor.html, accessed November 3, 2011.

27 See Zoellner, T. (2010). *Uranium: War, Energy, and the Rock that Shaped the World*. New York: Penguin Books, pp. iv–vi. And Wikipedia (2016, February 10). *Nuclear chain reaction*. Available from, https://en.wikipedia.org/wiki/Nuclear_chain_reaction, accessed February 11, 2016.

28 Jeong, H., Ryu, E., Song, J., Ha, K., and Song, Y. (2012). Evaluation of possibility for reactor corium re-criticality in Fukushima NPP accident, *Transactions of the Korean Nuclear Society Spring Meeting Jeju, Korea*, May 17–18, 2012.

29 Whitman, G., Pain, R., and Milledge, D. (2015). Going with the flow? Using participatory action research in physical geography. *Progress in Physical Geography*, 39(5), 622–639. doi:10.1177/03091333 15589707. p. 622–623.

30 Smoke/steam rising from all 4 reactor units – Workers evacuated (VIDEO). (2011, March 23). *Enenews*. Available from, http://enenews.com/nhk-at-7pm-et-smokesteam-rising-from-all-4-reactor-units-workers-evacuated-video.

31 FORUM: Discussion Thread for May 26–June 1, 2011 (2011, May 26). *Enenews*. Available from, http://enenews.com/energynews-energetic-thoughts/comment-page-1#comments. The specific comment link is http://enenews.com/energynews-energetic-thoughts/comment-page-1#comment-71092.

32 Fukushima webcam discussion thread June 26, 2011–December 14, 2011. (2011, June 26). *Enenews*. Available from, http://enenews.com/fukushima-webcam-discussion-thread/comment-page-1#comments, accessed June 27, 2011.

33 More serious than a meltdown – Japan Gov't now raising possibility that fuel had a "melt through". (2011, June 7). *Enenews*. Available from, http://enenews.com/breaking-more-serious-than-a-melt-down-japan-govt-now-raising-possibility-that-fuel-had-a-melt-through-at-all-3-reactors, accessed June 8, 2011.

34 'Melt-through' at Fukushima? / Govt report to IAEA suggests situation worse than meltdown. (2011, June 8). *The Daily Yomiuri Online*. Available from, www.yomiuri.co.jp/dy/national/T110607005367.htm, accessed June 8, 2011.

35 Samples: www.dropbox.com/s/6c1j0jnp061w7uc/Scary%20Fukushima%20Webcam%20Imagery%202.pdf

36 Fukushima webcam discussion thread. (2011, June 26). *Enenews*. Available from, http://enenews.com/fukushima-webcam-discussion-thread/comment-page-1#comments, accessed June 27, 2011.

37 Ibid.

38 Ibid.

39 Webcam discussion thread (2011, June 27). *Enenews*. Available from, http://enenews.com/fukushima-webcam-discussion-thread/comment-page-2#comment-100741, accessed March 7, 2016.

40 Norsk Institutt for Luftforskning, Fukushima. (last modified 2011–05–13 10:26). Available from, http://transport.nilu.no/products/fukushima, accessed March 25, 2016.

41 NILU's graphic was uploaded to YouTube as early as March 29, 2011. Available from, www.youtube.com/watch?v=UKdsjyUB_dI, accessed March 30, 2011.

42 Austrian Central Institute for Meteorology and Geodynamics (ZAMG) and Norwegian Institute for Air Research (NILU) (2011). Press release reactor accident Fukushima – new international study on emissions of radioactive substances into the atmosphere. Available from, www.zamg.at/docs/aktuell/20111021_fukushima_review.pdf, accessed June 5, 2012.

43 What is a "cold shutdown" at the Fukushima nuclear plant? (2011, 17 December). *The Mainichi Daily News*. Available from, http://mdn.mainichi.jp/perspectives/news/20111217p2a00m0na015000c.html, date accessed December 17, 2011.

44 Webcam discussion thread. (2011, November 6). *Enenews*. Available from, http://enenews.com/fukushima-webcam-discussion-thread/comment-page-17#comment-152184, accessed March 7, 2016.

45 Krypton-85 up over 14,000% in one day at Reactor No. 2 (2011, November 2). *Enenews*. Available from, http://enenews.com/just-in-krypton-85-up-over-14000-in-a-day-at-reactor-no-2-kr-85-used-to-detect-plutonium-separations, accessed November 3, 2011.

46 Ex-SKF (2011, September 7). Radioactive iodine in sewer sludge in Oshu City, Iwate. Available from, http://ex-skf.blogspot.com/2011/09/radioactive-iodine-in-sewer-sludge-in.html, accessed September 8, 2011.

47 Mochizuki (2012, January 20). Iodine-131 measured from snow in Hachioji Tokyo. *Fukushima Diary*. Available from, http://fukushima-diary.com/2012/01/iodine-131-measured-from-snow-in-hachioji-tokyo/, accessed January 21, 2012.

48 Xu, S., Freeman, S., Hou, X., Watanabe, A., Yamaguchi, K., and Zhang, L. (2013). Iodine isotopes in precipitation: Temporal responses to 129I emissions from the Fukushima nuclear accident. *Environmental Science and Technology*, 47, 10851–1085.

49 Mochizuki (2011, November 19). Architect of Reactor 3 warns of massive hydrovolcanic explosion. *Fukushima Diary*. Available from, http://fukushima-diary.com/2011/11/architect-of-reactor-3-warns-massive-hydrovolcanic-explosion/, accessed March 25, 2016.

50 Davidson, O. (2011, March 31). Don't panic: Why the Fukushima webcam is black. *Forbes*. Available from, www.forbes.com/sites/oshadavidson/2011/03/31/dont-panic-why-the-fukushima-webcam-is-black/#3ef334fb1e12, accessed March 21, 2016.

51 Koh, Y. (2011, August 31). Worker's eerie show on Fukushima Daiichi webcam. *The Wall Street Journal*. Available from, http://blogs.wsj.com/japanrealtime/2011/08/31/workers-eerie-show-on-fukushima-daiichi-webcam/, accessed August 31, 2011.

52 Tickell, O. (2013, December 31). Fukushima meltdown? Mystery steam rising over Reactor 3. *The Ecologist*. Available from, www.theecologist.org/News/news_round_up/2217953/fukushima_meltdown_mystery_steam_rising_over_reactor_3.html, accessed March 17, 2016.

53 Plumes of mysterious steam rise from crippled nuclear reactor at Fukushima. (2014, January 1). *RT*. Available from, www.rt.com/news/fukushima-steam-nuclear-reactor-064/, accessed March 15, 2015.

54 Fukushima leaks 23 TBq of radioactive water. (2014, February 20). *The Ecologist*. Available from, www.theecologist.org/News/news_round_up/2291438/fukushima_leaks_23_tbq_of_radioactive_water.html, accessed March 21, 2016.

55 Live webcams on the damaged Fukushima nuclear power plant. (2014, October 1). *Euronews*. Available from, www.euronews.com/2014/01/10/live-webcams-on-the-damaged-fukushima-nuclear-power-plant/, accessed October 30, 2014.

56 Steam seen in Fukushima reactor 3 building: Unit still subcritical, Tepco assures. (2013, July 18). *The Japan Times*. Available from, www.japantimes.co.jp/news/2013/07/18/national/steam-seen-in-fukushima-reactor-building/#.VtCbHeaYI2Y, accessed July 19, 2013.

57 Obayashi, Y. and Lies, E. (2016, November 22). Tsunami hits Japan after strong quake near Fukushima disaster site. *Reuters*. Available from, www.reuters.com/article/us-japan-quake-idUSKBN13G2DC, accessed December 5, 2014.

58 Takahashi, N., Negishi, T. and Semba, S. (2015, September 1). Fukushima evacuees prepare for eventual return, but most are choosing not to. *The Asahi Shimbun*. Available from, http://ajw.asahi.com/article/0311disaster/fukushima/AJ201509010062, accessed September 2, 2015.

59 Kumai, H. (2015, August 25). Panel blames TEPCO's negligence for delay in information disclosure. *The Asahi Shimbun*. Available from, http://ajw.asahi.com/article/0311disaster/fukushima/AJ201508250044, accessed September 4, 2015.

60 TEPCO withheld Fukushima radioactive water measurements for 6 months. (2014, January 9). *The Asahi Shimbun*. Available from, http://ajw.asahi.com/article/0311disaster/fukushima/AJ201401090060, accessed January 10, 2014.

61 Murata, M. (2014, August 26). To prevent Fukushima from causing the ultimate global catastrophe, Solartopia.org. Available from, http://solartopia.org/mitsuhei-murata-to-prevent-fukushima-from-causing-the-ultimate-global-catastrophe/ima, accessed August 26, 2014.

62 Miller, D. (February 20, 2014). Japan's anti-nuclear movement, post 3–11. *Japan Subculture*. Available from, www.japansubculture.com/japans-post-311-antinuclear-movement/, accessed February 27, 2016.

63 Utz, S., Schultz, F., and Glocka, S. (2013). Crisis communication online: How medium, crisis type and emotions affected public reactions in the Fukushima Daiichi nuclear disaster. *Public Relations Review*, 39, 40–46.

64 Gaulène, M. (2016). Does the advertising giant Dentsu pull the strings of the Japanese media? *Asia Pacific Journal: Japan Focus*, 14(11.5), http://apjjf.org/2016/11/Gaulene.html, accessed June 13, 2016.

65 Takahashi, et al. Fukushima evacuees prepare for eventual return (above).

66 AP. (2016, June 21). TEPCO: Delay in declaring "meltdown" was a cover-up. *The Asahi Shimbun*. Available from, www.asahi.com/ajw/articles/AJ201606210075.html, accessed June 21, 2016.

67 Takahashi, Y. (2015, February 24). Hot on the trail of radioactivity, despite dwindling public interest in the issue. *The Asahi Shimbun*. Available from, http://ajw.asahi.com/article/0311disaster/fukushima/AJ201502240004, accessed March 22, 2016.

68 Fukushima cleanup fails to convince as just 10 to 20% of evacuees seek return. (2015, February 25). *The Asahi Shimbun*. Available from, http://ajw.asahi.com/article/0311disaster/fukushima/AJ201502250050, accessed March 22, 2015.

5.3 Plotting CSR narratives

CSR stories by global fashion brands after the collapse of Rana Plaza in Bangladesh

Angela Mak and Suwichit Chaidaroon

Introduction

The practices of corporate social responsibility (CSR) among multinational corporations (MNCs) in developing countries have gained attention among scholars and practitioners in various fields as the interactions among MNCs and various stakeholders in such international contexts can be complicated, multi-faceted, and dialectical.[1] Stakeholders of MNCs including policy makers in host countries, local beneficiaries and communities, and organizations themselves affect and are affected by one another. These social actors exercise their influence on one another through CSR communication with different levels of power and most likely through different modes of communication.[2] Hence, CSR communication in this context can be seen as an act of negotiation among these parties.

The emergence of digital media has allowed us to communicate texts, images, and sounds in a more vivid and interactive manner. Unlike the traditional analogue media, audiences of digital media can receive and appreciate their digitally encoded messages mostly on the computer screens or mobile devices.[3] These messages could be sent in such forms as digital videos, digital games, and digital imageries. In addition, the rapid rise of social network sites, or social media, has enabled us to share digital messages through our networks on social media much more easily.[4] These new media platforms have immense implications for corporate communication and CSR practices as corporations nowadays not only upload their printed sustainability reports online but also share video clips about their CSR projects on their corporate sites and via social media such as Facebook and YouTube.[5] The interactivity between digital media and social media has, therefore, impacted CSR communication.

While digital and social media could serve as effective CSR communication tools, they also provide the opportunities for local stakeholders to voice their opinions, needs, and concerns. The tremendous growth of academic literature on social media from public relations discipline has identified the issues of transparency, authenticity, influence, engagement, and dialogue when corporations use social media to communicate with their stakeholders.[6,7] Considering the multidimensional nature of digital media presented on social network sites, it is important to understand how texts, sounds, and images tell CSR stories and engage various stakeholders in CSR dialogues.[8,9]

This paper aims to analyze CSR communication through video on the social media platform. In particular, the study will explore how CSR stories are constructed and in what ways digital media enriches CSR narratives. The study will focus on a case of global fashion brands' social responsibility after the collapse of Rana Plaza in Bangladesh in 2013. These fashion brands outsourced Bangladeshi garment factories and demonstrated their social responsibility in videos through various social media channels. More descriptions of the case will be provided in subsequent sections. A close reading of these multimodal texts will reveal not only the power of CSR stories in shaping the audience's perception but also uncover the negotiation of values and/or morals that stakeholders represent in the constructed narratives as these stories were crafted as a response to the disaster, attempting to positively frame organizations in the garment industry and to suppress the accused abusive workplace conditions. The analysis will highlight how corporate communication practitioners resolve these competing and/or conflicting values among the stakeholders represented in the stories.

Narrative approach to CSR communication

Even though CSR initiatives could be communicated rationally through sustainability reports and data to verify the outcomes (i.e., business and social impacts) of corporate CSR efforts, one common way to illustrate CSR effectiveness is through stories.[10] This narrative approach to CSR claims that "social reality can be regarded as being mainly negotiated and organized through the interplay of different actors' stories, which communicatively construct norms and morality through 'sensegiving' and 'sensemaking' processes and in which they mainly build on such societal narratives." By analyzing CSR stories we could see the diverse expressions of stakeholders presented explicitly or implicitly. CSR stories are usually crafted as a response to preceding situations, and the organizations as well as stakeholders are presented as characters in the stories. As this chapter will illustrate in the subsequent section, how the organizations directly and indirectly involved in the past tragedy or crisis will influence the process of crafting CSR stories.

The communicative use of narratives has been extensively linked to the psychological processes of sensemaking and sensegiving in the academic literature. Fisher (1984) posits that human beings are *homo narrans* as we tend to assign meanings to our experiences in a story format that we could share to others.[11] Scholars in the business discipline in particular demonstrated that organizational members tend to make sense (Weick, 1995) or construct meanings to the challenges they face in their organizational experiences such as when their companies encounter downsizing through stories.[12] Therefore, the manager's primary role is to give a sense of comfort and certainty to organizational members most likely through stories in such situations (Gioia & Chittipeddi, 1991).[13] In other words, setting up organizational strategies is a process of narrative sensegiving (Barry & Elmes, 1997).[14]

CSR stories, in many instances, are dialectical as they become "competing, counter statements, or corrective to the stories of another group."[15] It is very common for corporations to develop their CSR initiatives and tell their CSR stories as a response to previous crises, boycotts, or newly launched policies.[16] The case of Rana Plaza collapse in 2013 is an illustration of the call for CSR practices among global fashion brands that outsourced from garment manufacturers in Bangladesh. This eight-story commercial garments factory in Bangladesh totally collapsed, killing over 1,100 workers. Bangladesh, the world's second largest garment exporting country, faced acute criticism in this regard for not ensuring social and environmental responsibilities in the workplace.[17] Global brands that outsourced products from Bangladesh also faced severe criticism for not exercising their CSRs properly that ultimately could lead to similar tragic occurrences in the future.[18] It is timely to study how global fashion brands communicate their CSR effort in Bangladesh after the collapse across digital platforms. The case is a perfect illustration on how CSR stories are constructed and serve as portrayals of stakeholders in various competing roles.[19]

Multimodal discourses of CSR videos

New technology has allowed us to present and receive information synchronously and asynchronously as well as through features beyond simple text-based presentation. Using digital videos on social media has become a popular tool for corporate communication practitioners to interact with various stakeholders and presenting CSR stories is what most modern corporations do to report their social performance to publics in an accessible manner. This new communication tool enables us to enrich our messages through sounds, images, lights, camera angles, and vivid actions, features called semiotic resources.[20] As the variability of communication elements become available, narratives on social media videos appear to represent a more complex structures of significations of meanings and ideas. Values in corporate CSR videos are, therefore, subtly presented through these multimodal resources.

As this case captures CSR stories of global fashion brands and their various stakeholders told in their social media videos, this paper aims to analyze their narratives and pose the following research questions:

RQ1: How are the global fashion companies that outsourced from manufacturers in Bangladesh and their stakeholders portrayed and integrated in CSR video narratives?

RQ2: How do multimodal features of digital media facilitate these CSR narratives in meaning construction?

Method

To address the above research questions, this study employed two interrelated qualitative textual analysis approaches. First, the authors have compiled CSR videos of global fashion brands across different digital platforms (i.e., YouTube, Vimeo, Facebook, Google Plus, Instagram and Twitter) that outsourced Bangladeshi factories and conduct a preliminary narrative analysis to identify the emerging narrative genres of CSR in this context.[21] Knowing the narrative genres, or the recurring type of text in this CSR context, allows us to see the pattern of archetypal CSR stories.[22] Then, based on the interpretivist reading, structural analysis of those CSR stories were performed to analyze how the stories were told, what characters in the stories represented, how the concept or act of CSR was constructed by each corporate story, and finally what morals/values the stories portray through the digital media platform. Specifically, we paid attention to who were portrayed as the protagonists and victims in the clip, what dilemmas or social problems caused CSR initiatives, and what heroic actions were highlighted.

Second, a multimodal discourse analysis was performed to uncover the underlying informational values represented in CSR videos on social media. While this research approach is new, it has proved useful in revealing the negotiated ideologies through various modes of texts. For example, a study by Wang (2016) analyzed "Singapore Girl" TV advertisements by Singapore Airlines and found that gendered representations were manipulated to build the brand based on a well-rounded narrative structure.[23] Dash, Patnaik, and Suar

(2016) based on their analysis of Indian TV food and beverage commercials, discovered the construction of global identities of consumers based on how consumption was represented in the ads.[24]

To identify the discursive construction of CSR narratives among garment brands involved in Rana Plaza catastrophe, we first paid attention to basic element of multimodal discourse.[25] We identified the *foreground*, or what was made important, and *background* of each video. These foregrounding and backgrounding elements may include settings, light, narration, music and sound. *Modal density*, the degree to which social actors or characters in the video display their level of attention/awareness to certain things was also investigated to discover what was made salient and why.

After these basic elements were identified, the researchers followed Kress and Van Leeuwen's (2006) framework for multimodal discourse analysis by paying attention to how framing, salience, and informational value construct the meanings of the entire video clip.[26] We paid attention to scenes and shots of the video as we analyzed the frames of each clip. Then we focused on how certain issues were made salient as the videos highlighted the aural and visual intensity for that particular section. Finally, we interpreted the informational value by asking ourselves what information was made explicit and what was made implicit as we watched each clip and code our texts.

To enhance the credibility of our analysis, the two researchers first conducted a close observation of each video and paid attention to the characters, and forms of the narratives as well as framing, salience, and informational value of multimodal CSR video discourses independently before making a consensus on their interpretations.[27] In addition, since the research team was assisted by a Bangladeshi native and the non-Bangladeshi nationals, the insider's and outsider's views on interpreting CSR stories were both acknowledged. The information provided by the Bangladeshi research assistant allowed us to understand the cultural contexts as we interpreted the stories. Therefore, the analysis incorporated both emic and etic perspectives.[28]

Findings

To analyze CSR communication of this case study, our research team identified three groups of companies based on their degree of direct responsibility to the collapse of the plaza. We referred to the document prepared by the Clean Clothes Campaign, an independent non-profit organization that aims to improve working conditions and empower workers in garment industries in developing countries.[29] As a third party organization, the Clean Clothes Campaign developed a report to identify garment companies that outsourced Bangladesh for their production during the collapse and determined whether those companies had direct involvement with the collapse of the Plaza. After we identified the global garment brands based on the Clean Clothes Campaign's data, we then traced the companies that posted CSR videos on social media. The first group could be named the so-called *wrongdoers* as they employed the garment factories in Rana Plaza during the catastrophe and hence needed to conduct CSR activities as a response to the situation. This group included such companies as Benetton, Primark, and Walmart. Walmart was included in this category as the company has its line of clothing and ex-fashion designer of Walmart was interviewed in the news documentary "Made in Bangladesh – the fifth estate" to unveil the fast fashion industry's manufacturing issues in Bangladesh.[30] The second group included such companies as Matalan who used the Plaza before the collapse. These *malefactors* conducted their CSR initiatives to repent their guilt, even though they were not directly responsible for the disaster given that their involvement with the plaza was prior to the disaster but during the crisis they did not outsource workers from Rana Plaza. Two other organizations including the ACCORD and Alliance for Bangladesh Worker Safety were included in this category, as they were formed by brands that joined together for their CSR efforts in Bangladesh even though they were not the wrongdoers directly. The final group included the heroes or the garment brands who were not involved in the situation at all but seized the moment to be CSR leaders in the industry by stepping in to help Bangladesh's garment workers. This category included such companies as H&M and VF.

Altogether, eight video clips reporting CSR efforts by eight organizations representing the three groups were collected for multimodal discourse analysis in this project. The research team analyzed videos from companies that employed the direct approach in posting the videos of their CSR activities by themselves as well as those who partnered with NGOs and posted their videos in collaborations with others. The following section presents findings of our analysis as we discuss the portrayals of characters/stakeholders in the clips as well as the effects of multimodal features on the construction of meanings among the *wrongdoers*, *malefactors*, and *heroes* in this case. Three distinct narrative patterns were discovered by these three groups of global fashion brands in response to our research questions that aimed to explore how the brands and stakeholders were presented as well as how meanings were constructed in the digital videos.

Wrongdoers: impressionist tales of benevolent heroes to save the world

The lack of workplace safety, which was the main cause of the catastrophe, was mentioned but it was not made the sole CSR issue in Bangladesh among these companies.[31] CSR initiatives of this group addressed a wide range of issues that may or may not directly respond to the collapse of Rana Plaza. Benetton, Primark, and Walmart constructed such social issues as poverty, poor children lacking education, and women's inequality in Bangladesh as dilemmas that induce their heroic CSR activities. While these efforts may be seen as their genuine intention, it could also be interpreted as an attempt to sway the attention from the actual cause of Rana Plaza collapse.

All three *wrongdoers* employed multimodal resources to enhance their narratives and sensationalize their CSR efforts in various degrees. Benetton's entire clip, for example, portrayed the life of Shiuly, a female factory worker survivor from Rana Plaza collapse and how she was assisted by BRAC, an NGO partner of Benetton to return to her normal life. In the clip, Shiuly said, "After I returned home, I felt totally hopeless. . . . What good is being alive if I can't do anything and feed my three children?" The clip showed how Shiuly's miserable life was turned positive through various scenes of Shuily attending mental therapy sessions with other factory workers, doing daily activities by herself and working in her own grocery store.

Primark and Walmart, on the other hand, included some elements of narratives with some direct interviews of their administrators. Primark, in particular, focused their CSR activities on helping female workers to have better quality of lives. They made this issue salient through different frames of eliciting the female victims' stories and interviewing third party to endorse the benefits of garment factories in the country. For example, a woman in a slum said during the clip, "It upsets me to think I could earn some money. If I had the opportunity to work, it would help me to run my family better. If I was properly educated with adequate savings from a job, I could plan a better life, live in an improved environment and take better care of my children. I wouldn't have to live in this slum area."

It was a smart move of Primark as the company did not respond to this poverty problem by praising themselves but the video then presented a discussion with Ms. Sayeeda Roxana Khan, a social development specialist from an NGO who explained:

> Entering the garment industry, women started to earn for themselves and they started to get their voices. They started articulating their thoughts and their needs. They can choose whom they want to marry and when they want to marry, and they started cherishing a new dream. In a garment factory, all workers do not need too many skills. She learned the job on the job. It's hard work. A senior operator can earn up to 10,000–12,000 Taka per month with the overtime. So that kind of life meets all their living expenses and they can take care of the education … health of their family.

Walmart's CSR video also illustrated that the company initiated several projects such as workplace safety, empowering women, and teaching critical life skills to workers but the ultimate aim of their CSR activities was to reduce poverty in Bangladesh. It seems that these stories help legitimize the benefits of garment industry to Bangladesh. CSR videos in this wrongdoers category made it explicit that without the existing garment industry, social problems in Bangladesh would not have been improved this much. Therefore, rather than being blamed as the cause of the catastrophe, positive societal contributions by companies in garment industry should be acknowledged. Sensational narratives based on effective uses of lights, sounds, and tones to arouse emotions and sympathy seem to play an important role in CSR communication in the video clips of companies in this category. Table 5.3.1 summarizes our analysis of the *wrongdoers'* CSR videos.

Malefactors: symbolic tales of professional heroes to improve workplace safety

Organizations in this category demonstrated a distinct approach to construct their CSR narratives on the videos. The Alliance for Bangladesh Worker Safety and ACCORD are organizations formed by garment brands who did *not* outsource to Rana Plaza directly during the crisis but they have been using labor in the plaza somehow for their production, hence, the *malefactors*. Both the Alliance and the ACCORD focused their CSR efforts on workplace safety issue and they made it salient in their video clips through the portrayals of serious safety inspection processes. Various frames of interviews with inspection specialists also highlighted their commitments to the high standard workplace safety and stories the specialists told were used to illustrate the serious and professional safety inspection practices in both video clips.

To illustrate, the Alliance's clip explained the inspection processes in three areas: 1) structural design of buildings, 2) fire safety, and 3) electrical aspects. Mr. Niladri Shekhar Saha, one of the inspectors in charge of fire safety assessment said during the interview,

> On today's audit, we found a few faults, and found a few things were right. There were smoke detectors in many places but one or two places they got unexpectedly blocked. We would ask them to fix those. We also saw the hose reel system, extinguishing system. They have put those in accordance with the Alliance standards.

This clip not only showed Mr. Saha during in the interview but also himself in action during the inspection. The fact that any issue not up to the safety standard found would

Table 5.3.1 Summary of CSR videos of "wrongdoers" global fashion brands in response to the collapse of Rana Plaza

Company	CSR initiatives in the clip	Summary of narratives & characters	Multimodal features highlighted
Benetton	Partnering with BRAC to help victims from Rana Plaza collapse	Shiuly, a female worker survivor went to the BRAC training center (with the funding support from Benetton) and received the start-up funds to run her grocery store to regain her strength and support her family with three children. She said, "One day I got a call and was asked to visit a BRAC office. There I was given motivation to be strong and not losing my will power." She ended the video by saying, "I hope I can grow as an entrepreneur and expand my business and now, I am doing well."	*Scenes/setting*: 1) therapy group session at BRAC; 2) living place of Shiuly with her children; and 3) grocery shop that Shiuly is running her own business. *Images & symbols*: 1) Shiuly meditating on bed and recounting how hopeless she was from losing her leg to raise 3 children; 2) Shiuly walking in the neighbourhood after the training workshop; and 3) Shiuly running her grocery store using a calculator
Primark	Activities to alleviate poverty and improve women's lives	The clip interviewed a few female workers to highlight financial benefits the garment industry brought to Bangladesh and to sensationalize the hardship these women encountered. For example, one female in a slum said, "I wanted to continue my education, but my parents said I had to get married. My parents arranged my wedding, there was no other way. I don't work, I stay at home and cook for my family."	*Scenes/settings*: 1) slum area; and 2) females in Bangladesh get to work in a factory to change their life *Images & symbols*: using documentary style with contrasting backgrounds to show Primark provided job opportunities for women and transformed their lives.
Walmart	Activities to alleviate poverty, improve workplace safety and improve women's lives	This clip highlighted various CSR efforts of Walmart. At the beginning, it sensationalized the hardship as the narrator said people lived with just less than $2 per day and implied then that garment industry helped improve this poverty problem in the country. Then the clip presented Walmart's CSR that addressed such issues as improving lives of female workers and workplace safety both through interviews with the administration team and by showing some employee training sessions.	*Scenes/settings*: 1) poverty areas in Bangladesh; 2) training classroom; 3) safe workplace environment; and 4) workers doing work together to increase the safety standards. *Images & symbols*: 1) urban poverty in Bangladesh; 2) various safety activities undertaken by the Alliance; 3) "collective effort" with group of workers standing together; and 4) a curious face of a young girl as if she is looking into the future full of hopes and promises.

be reported and must be corrected demonstrated the seriousness and professionalism of this practice.

One important aspect of CSR video narrative found in the Alliance's and ACCORD's clips was the use of symbols to represent certain values. As discussed earlier, these two organizations were formed by brands indirectly responsible for Rana Plaza collapse. These fashion brands may have previously hired workers in the plaza and caused fires in other factories before the tragedy that got the international attention. In their CSR narratives, three values were made salient in many scenes through relevant symbols. First, since the Alliance and ACCORD are collaborative efforts, they used pictures of meetings, events, and activities participated by various stakeholders from different ethnicities. The meetings before and after inspections, in particular, illustrated a collaboration between Bangladeshi workers at different levels as well as the non-Bangladeshi. Second, the use of advanced technology for inspection also symbolized professionalism and accountability as this process was taken seriously and records were taken. Finally, most inspectors wore or used protection gears such as helmet, mask, gloves, fire extinguisher, which were symbols for safety, security, and better future for both factories and garment industries in Bangladesh. Therefore, the symbolic construction of meanings in these CSR narratives was quite compelling.

While the pattern of narratives by the Alliance for Bangladesh Worker Safety and ACCORD was compatible in terms of the safety issue they address, Matalan which was also in this *malefactors* category addressed their CSR effort to a different issue. As an individual fashion company, Matalan developed a project to help poor children in Bangladesh called "School of Hope." The stories of this project were presented in the clip together with interviews with Matalan management and its NGO partner Hope Worldwide Bangladesh. Cinematographic elements were used to induce compassion among viewers for children in Bangladesh and symbols were again used to show that Matalan was a part of happiness it brought to children in Bangladesh. For example, there was one scene showing the technical and sourcing director playing football with Bangladeshi kids in school. Even though Matalan's video was very different from those of ACCORD & the Alliance because the former is a fashion company, the latter are organizations formed by different brands for a specific purpose, one thing in common for these organizations is the fact that symbols plays an important role in their narratives.

Heroes: pledging tales of corporations' resolution to uplift workers' lives

In previous categories of wrongdoers and malefactors, the fashion brands we investigated involved in Rana Plaza either directly or indirectly. This last category included the brands that seized the opportunities to help Bangladesh through their CSR efforts and included such companies as H&M and VF. These brands were not involved in Rana Plaza collapse and had never been related to other fire accidents in Bangladeshi garment factories before. Both companies' CSR video clips we analyzed were presented their management teams to discuss their CSR initiatives with different approaches. VF employed a "dry" method, as they had their three top management people to explain their main CSR issue which was workplace safety. There were no other cinematic elements to enhance what these three people's interviews and the stories were narrated through their talks only. H&M, on the other hand, incorporated both interviews and other scenes including workers in action in the factories, training sessions for workers to enhance their narratives of CSR.

Table 5.3.2 Summary of CSR videos of "malefactors" global fashion brands in response to the collapse of Rana Plaza

Company	CSR initiatives in the clip	Summary of narratives & characters	Multimodal features highlighted
Matalan	Helping poor children through the "School of Hope" project with Hope Worldwide Bangladesh	The ray of hope at the beginning signifies the future of hope in the next generation through this education program. A HOPE representative said, "65% of children in Bangladesh are not able to go to school but playing on the streets and working in a factory for a while." The ethics director of Matalan said, "HOPE has a track record to do the right thing" so they chose HOPE to partner to provide proper education and guaranteed careers. The children of the factory workers go to school are also provided with "chicken, fish and vegetables" and "some children never ate chicken in life and they have to teach them to eat chicken."	*Scenes/settings:* 1) inside classroom of daily situation of the children; and 2) outside classroom like playground and school kitchen, with interactions with the key project members. *Images & symbols:* 1) schoolchildren (aged 3–7) vs. kids wandering in villages/cities; 2) key project members' happy faces spending time with the kids at school; and 3) ray of light (hope) at the beginning of the video.
The Alliance for Bangladesh Worker Safety	Workplace safety	The video provided an introduction to the Alliance. It depicted three areas of workplace inspection, i.e., building, fire, and electrical safety through interviews and demonstration of inspection process. A lot of symbols were used to show the professionalism and commitment to a high quality standard. The lead assessor, for example, said while investigating the building of factory, "We tested the strength of the concrete by using the rebound hammer. The Alliance standards allow a maximum life load of 42PSF," as he was using that "rebound hammer" in his hands.	*Scenes/settings:* 1) meeting room with top management from different brands; 2) training workshops with workers and supervisors; 3) factory environment for inspection process; and 4) nurse bed for health check-up. *Images & symbols:* 1) people from different ethnicities and work positions joining the Alliance; 2) technical equipment for inspection; and 3) upbeat music during the inspection process.
ACCORD	Workplace safety	Anecdotes from workers in Bangladesh proclaiming that "a safe workplace is our right." A lot of shots about inspections with emphasis on "checks," "visits," "fire safety," "monitor," and "report". A Bangladeshi government inspector said, "in these three years we expect to work intensively with ACCORD to complete the assessment and follow-up activities."	*Scenes/settings:* 1) interviews done in the offices; 2) factory scenes of making clothes; and 3) lots of shots focusing on inspections and equipment. *Images and symbols:* 1) protection gear (e.g., helmet, mask, gloves, and fire extinguisher); 2) equipment for inspection; 3) smiles from workers; and 4) corporate faces of key parties.

However, though the presentation approaches differed, it appeared that their key messages of CSR videos had something in common. While the *wrongdoers* and *malefactors* seemed to construct the dilemma and address their CSR activities to such basic needs such as health, safety, poverty, and education, H&M and VF addressed their CSR activities to the higher levels of human needs. This issue was made salient in their clips in many scenes. Wickie Carroll, supply chain from VF, for example, said in the clip,

> There is no conflict of interest between making a profit and treating people right. . . . We are totally committed to workers, safety, whether it is a plant we own or a contract factory, we don't see any difference. . . . VF is committed to Bangladesh for a long term . . . to stay there and make it a better country.

This quote highlighted a strong commitment of the company towards safety regardless of the ownership of the factories, a different angle than just focusing on the inspection process in the previously mentioned CSR videos from the *malefactors* category.

To illustrate more vividly how the narratives of this *heroes* group appealed to the higher level of human needs, H&M put their CSR effort to improve workers' motivation to succeed and address such issues as workers' awareness of their right and their bargaining power for higher wage.[32] For example, one female worker in the clip said,

> I was very poor when I came here from the countryside, I started as a helper. After a while, I was promoted to operator and was paid more. My life has improved and I can now support my son and my husband. I can afford to send my son to a good school. He wants to become a doctor.

This quote suggested the consequence of H&M's CSR effort in bringing the best out of individuals. The most highlighted part of this H&M's CSR video was the scene when the company's CEO, Karl-Johan Persson, negotiated with the prime minister of Bangladesh to raise the minimum wages as the narrator said, "H&M is the first fashion company to have developed the pioneering global strategy for a fair living wage." It is obvious that his efforts seem to construct a strong heroic position of H&M as the company does not only assist the workers at the basic needs level but also the higher level, the awareness of their right in the overall economic system. Table 5.3.3 summarizes our analysis of the *heroes*' CSR videos in this case.

To conclude, the three emerging tales from these global fashion brands in the case answered the two research questions in this study. As our first research question asked how the companies and the stakeholders were portrayed in CSR videos, the three tales depicted the brands in each category as benevolent, professional, or heroic. Bangladeshi workers were also illustrated differently, ranging from victims of the disaster, professional workers, and active volunteers for other workers in the community. The three tales were also responses to the second research question that asked how multimodal features facilitate the construction of meaning process. The benevolence of the *wrongdoers*' tales was constructed through sounds, sight, and imagery of poor living condition of the workers to arouse sympathy. The professionalism of the *malefactors*' tale was, on the other hand, constructed through symbols of safety equipment and process of inspection to name a few.

Table 5.3.3 Summary of CSR videos of "hero" global fashion brands in response to the collapse of Rana Plaza

Company	CSR initiatives in the clip	Summary of narratives & characters	Multimodal features highlighted
VF	The VF We Care project focuses on workplace safety not only through inspection and technical assistance but also financial support for fire protection equipment	CSR video of VF was pretty dry, as cinematic effects seemed to be deliberately omitted. The clip merely showed three administrators of VF talking about their CSR efforts in improving workplace safety and poverty in Bangladesh. Stories were merely told orally from the three administrators, and the clip was much less sensationalized when compared to others.	*Scenes/settings*: 1) interview format only with three administrators talking about three focus areas (i.e., workplace safety, workers training & financial assistance to garments suppliers & traders); and 2) VF logo appeared several times. *Images & symbols*: 1) three administrators; and 2) logos of VF & the Alliance.
H&M	Improve workers' skills and increase awareness of worker's right through the fair living wage program and H&M training center in Bangladesh since 1999	IFC, The World Bank official said, "Textile is one of the key economic sectors for us in Bangladesh. . . . and H&M has been a great partner for us in our initiatives towards sustainability and growth." A female H&M worker said, "my life has improved and I can now support my son and my husband." The CEO met and discussed with the prime minister in Bangladesh to "put forward our [H&M] demands for higher minimum wages." The H&M training center was set up back in 1999 to make sure that workers got the skills and work as operators in the factory. It is also "the first fashion company to have developed the pioneering global strategy for a fair living wage."	*Scenes/settings*: 1) thriving city with young workers going to work in factories; 2) H&M working complex with modern high-rise buildings; 3) pleasant working environment for workers with mask-protection; and 4) training from managers to workers. *Images & symbols*: 1) women workers (i.e., gender empowerment); 2) CEO and Sustainability Manager of H&M as industry CSR leader; 3) CEO meeting with Prime Minister for CSR advocacy and fair living wage; and 4) H&M training center.

Discussion and conclusion

The emerging distinct patterns of CSR narratives in the analyzed videos reflected the effective uses of lights, sounds, camera angles and movements, or semiotic resources in persuading the audience to accept the good deeds these corporations intended to portray in their CSR initiatives. While it could be argued that these narrative styles also exist in the text-based communication, our analyses indicated the more deliberate usages of these semiotic resources on digital media platform. The impressionist tales by the *wrongdoers*, for instance, swayed the audience from the actual cause of the collapse of the building due to the lack of safety measure by arousing emotions of the audience through the victims of poverty or other social issues. The symbolic tales of the *malefactors* highlighted professionalism in the safety auditing process. It would have been much harder for readers of a textual report to visualize how the process had been conducted even with some still images as illustrations. With the digital videos, the audience could see the process with their own

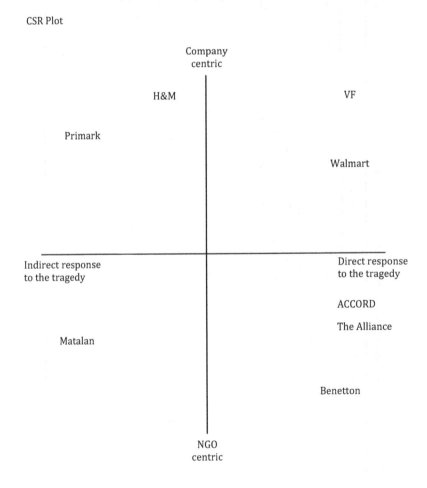

Figure 5.3.1 CSR narrative

eyes. Therefore, it is argued that these new technologies have made CSR narratives more vivid and convincing to the audience.

In addition, the narratives constructed by the three groups of organizations demonstrated different patterns or structures by two factors. First, the issue that each fashion brand addressed in their CSR efforts could be a direct or indirect response to Rana Plaza tragedy. The organizations that aim to improve workplace safety certainly address their CSR activities to the collapse while those who focus on education, women's right, or poverty do so indirectly. At the same time, CSR stories could present the companies as heroes or depict a third party such as experts or NGOs as protagonists who help solve social problems. These two factors form a diagram that allows us to plot the stance of these global fashion brands and how they constructed meanings through their narratives. The X axis of the diagram represents the degree to which the organization's' CSR respond to the collapse directly while the Y axis represents the degree to which their CSR stories are company centric or NGO centric.

The rhetoric of CSR narratives relies heavily on the construction of heroes and the framing of dilemmas that victims in Bangladesh faced in their lives. Figure 5.3.1 allows us to diagnose the stance of each organization through their CSR narrative. H&M as well as VF, specifically, are confident enough to present themselves as the protagonists who emerge to resolve social problems in Bangladesh confidently as they were not involved in the disaster, while other brands had to rely on a third party or NGOs to establish more trusts with stakeholders. Interestingly, the direct or indirect response to the tragedy does not depict a clear pattern of organizational stance as all *heroes, malefactors,* and *wrongdoers* focus their CSR efforts in different ways. Yet, most of them included the issue of workplace safety, which was lacking prior to the collapse of Rana Plaza. This fact is consistent with the previous argument by Wehmeier and Schultz (2011) that CSR narratives are inherently dialectic, as the storyline is developed as a response or correction to the previous problems or counter statements.[33] While the digital videos alone may represent diverse

Table 5.3.4 List of URLs to the CSR video clips by organizations analyzed in this chapter. All these links were available as of July 2017.

Categories	Organization	Video Title and URL
Wrongdoers	Benetton	Story of a Rana Plaza tragedy survivor – Shiuly: www.youtube.com/watch?v=J0r-mEdfsfs
	Primark	Primark HERproject: www.youtube.com/watch?v=O587xl3LiKI
	Walmart	Walmart in Bangladesh: https://vimeo.com/103183709
Malefactors	Matalan	Matalan HOPE School: www.youtube.com/watch?v=6YuVBl1Bk1c
	The Alliance for Bangladesh Worker Safety	Alliance Assessment Process : www.youtube.com/watch?v=2uBk5dKAqCE
	The ACCORD	ACCORD 2nd Anniversary 2015: https://vimeo.com/134818206
Heroes	VF	VF We Care – Bangladesh: https://vimeo.com/95857203
	H&M	H&M in Bangladesh: www.youtube.com/watch?v=WY4FeUYMFzM

perspectives, the fact that these digital CSR videos were posted on social media allow for dialectical interactions form various stakeholders online.

The construction of hardship and difficulty encountered by the Bangladeshi workers was primed and made salient through the multimodal features, enhancing the heroic quality of the organizations either directly or indirectly. Showing scenes of how female victims from the collapse struggle, how Bangladeshi kids live their poor lives, how unsafe their workplaces are highlights the fact that organizations that help Bangladesh to resolve these issues really do good deeds and hence deserve the legitimate status to still employ laborers in this country. The texts (scripts), sights, and sounds in the videos work together to create such emotional effects to its fullest. These multimodal CSR stories, arguably, aim not only to inform but to draw the audience to accept the stance of the organization emotionally.

The use of digital video allowed the companies to engage the audience through their CSR stories as it goes beyond summarizing the CSR project in a linear manner by merely describing the purpose, stakeholders, and outcomes. Digital media serves as a communication platform that allows narratives to reach their maximum dramatic effects as the audience is drawn by appreciating the frames stories aim to highlight, identifying with the main characters/heroes, and accepting the values conveyed in the narratives. This usage of CSR videos could be an effective approach for CSR communication in this digital age, where mere text-based narratives could limit potential. Moreover, with the power of social media where these digital videos of corporate CSR initiatives can be accessed and shared by any stakeholders,[34] it is imperative that corporations that aim to use video as a platform to tell their CSR activities create genuine, authentic, and transparent narratives as stakeholders also have the power to support, questions or challenge them.

Notes

1 Mak, A.K.Y., Chaidaroon, S.S. and Pang, A. (2016) 'MNCs and CSR engagement in Asia: A dialectical model', *Asia Pacific Public Relations Journal*, 16(1), pp. 37–60.

2 Curtin, P.A., Gaither, K.T. and Gaither, T.K. (2007) *International public relations: Negotiating culture, identity, and power*. Thousand Oaks, CA: Sage Publications.

3 Feldman, T. (1996) *An introduction to digital media*. London: Routledge.

4 boyd, danah m. and Ellison, N.B. (2007) 'Social network sites: Definition, history, and scholarship', *Journal of Computer-Mediated Communication*, 13(1), pp. 210–230. doi: 10.1111/j.1083–6101.2007.00393.x.

5 Berg, K.T. and Sheehan, K.B. (2014) 'Social media as a CSR communication channel: The current state of practice', in DiStaso, M.W. and Bortree, D.S. (eds.) *Ethical practice of social media in public relations*. New York: Routledge, pp. 99–110.

6 McCorkindale, T. and DiStaso, M.W. (2014). The state of social media research: Where are we now, where we were and what it means for public relations. *Research Journal of the Institute for Public Relations*, 1(1). Available from www.instituteforpr.org/wp-content/uploads/TinaMarciaWES.pdf [Accessed 19th November 2016]

7 Khang, H., Ki, E. and Ye, L. (2012) 'Social media research in advertising, communication, marketing, and public relations, 1997–2010', *Journalism and Mass Communication Quarterly*, 89(2), pp. 279–298. doi: 10.1177/1077699012439853.

8 Colleoni, E. (2013) 'CSR communication strategies for organizational legitimacy in social media', *Corporate Communications: An International Journal*, 18(2), pp. 228–248. doi: 10.1108/13563281311319508.

9 O'Riordan, L. and Fairbrass, J. (2008) 'Corporate social responsibility (CSR): Models and theories in Stakeholder dialogue', *Journal of Business Ethics*, 83(4), pp. 745–758. doi: 10.1007/s10551–008–9662-y.

10 Wehmeier, S. and Schultz, F. (2011) 'Communication and corporate social responsibility: A storytelling perspective', in Ihlen, Ø., Bartlett, J., and May, S. (eds.) *The handbook of communication and corporate social responsibility*. Malden, MA: Wiley-Blackwell (an imprint of John Wiley and Sons Ltd), pp. 467–488.

11 Fisher, W.R. (1984) 'Narration as a human communication paradigm: The case of public moral argument', *Communication Monographs*, 51(1), pp. 1–22. doi: 10.1080/03637758409390180.

12 Weick, K.E. (1995) *Sensemaking in organizations*. Thousand Oaks: Sage Publications.

13 Gioia, D.A. and Chittipeddi, K. (1991) 'Sensemaking and sensegiving in strategic change initiation', *Strategic Management Journal*, 12(6), pp. 433–448. doi: 10.1002/smj.4250120604.

14 Barry, D. and Elmes, M. (1997) 'Strategy retold: Toward a narrative view of strategic discourse', *Academy of Management Review*, 22(2), pp. 429–452. doi: 10.2307/259329.

15 Wehmeier, op. cit.

16 Heath, R.L. (2004) 'Telling a story: A narrative approach to communication during crisis', in Millar, D.P. and Heath, R.L. (eds.) *Responding to crisis: A rhetorical approach to crisis communication*. Mahwah, NJ: Lawrence Erlbaum Associates, pp. 167–188.

17 Taplin, I. (2014) 'Who is to blame? A re-examination of fast fashion after the 2013 factory disaster in Bangladesh?', *Critical perspectives on international business*, 10(1/2), pp. 72–83. doi: 10.1108/cpoib-09-2013-0035.

18 Bearnot, E. (2013) 'Bangladesh: A labor paradox', *World Policy Journal*, 30(3), pp. 88–97. doi: 10.1177/0740277513506386.

19 Tarek, K.M. and Mak, A.K.Y. (2017) 'Fashion CSR by global brands vs. social enterprises: A closer look after the Rana Plaza collapse in Bangladesh', *Media Asia*. doi: 10.1080/01296612.2017.1374631

20 Kress, G.R. and Van Leeuwen, T. (2006) *Reading images: The grammar of visual design*. 2nd edn. London: Taylor and Francis.

21 Czarniawska, B. (2004) *Narratives in social science research*. London: Sage Publications.

22 Campbell, K.K. and Jamieson, K.H. (1978) *Form and genre: Shaping rhetorical action*. Falls Church: Speech Communication Association.

23 Wang, J. (2015) 'Multimodal narratives in SIA's "Singapore Girl" TV advertisements – from branding with femininity to branding with provenance and authenticity?', *Social Semiotics*, 26(2), pp. 208–225. doi: 10.1080/10350330.2015.1092277.

24 Dash, A.K., Patnaik, P. and Suar, D. (2016) 'A multimodal discourse analysis of glocalization and cultural identity in three Indian TV commercials', *Discourse and Communication*, 10(3), pp. 209–234. doi: 10.1177/1750481315623892.

25 Norris, S. (2004) 'Multimodal discourse analysis: A conceptual framework', in LeVine, P. and Scollon, R. (eds.) *Discourse and technology: Multimodal discourse analysis*. Washington, DC: Georgetown University Press, pp. 101–115.

26 Kress, op. cit.

27 Brummett, B. (2009) *Techniques of close reading*. Thousand Oaks, CA: Sage Publications.

28 Brislin, R.W. (1983) 'Cross-cultural research in psychology', *Annual Review of Psychology*, 34(1), pp. 363–400. doi: 10.1146/annurev.ps.34.020183.002051.

29 Clean Clothes Campaign (2015) *Rana Plaza actual and potential donors, listed by G7 country*. Available at: www.cleanclothes.org/safety/ranaplaza/rana-plaza-actual-and-potential-donors-listed-by-g7-country/view (Accessed: 30 March 2016).

30 *Made in Bangladesh – the fifth estate* (2014) Directed by CBC News.

31 Barua, U. and Ansary, M.A. (2016) 'Workplace safety in Bangladesh ready-made garment sector: 3 years after the Rana Plaza collapse', *International Journal of Occupational Safety and Ergonomics*, pp. 1–6. doi: 10.1080/10803548.2016.1251150.

32 Maslow, A.H. (1943) 'A theory of human motivation', *Psychological Review*, 50(4), pp. 370–396. doi: 10.1037/h0054346.

33 Wehmeier, op. cit.

34 Kaplan, A.M. and Haenlein, M. (2010) 'Users of the world, unite! The challenges and opportunities of social media', *Business Horizons*, 53(1), pp. 59–68. doi: 10.1016/j.bushor.2009.09.003.

Part 6

Digital methodologies and corporate social responsibility

6.1 A new content analysis methodology appropriate for CSR communication

Edward T. Vieira, Jr. and Susan Grantham

Introduction

This study proposes a content analysis (CA) component to standard CA methods by distilling content in a manner that potentially reduces labor and the time required to run the analysis. This technique further identifies the structure of the text by providing the most influential words, word clusters, and the connections among the clusters.

Corporate social responsibility (CSR) reporting and content analyzing can easily involve thousands of pages involving many hours of unitizing and coding content. The goal of this chapter is to suggest a complementary technique in conjunction with standard CA methodologies. We describe and explain this method, which is based on network principles, then we apply it to ExxonMobil CSR content.

First, deploying text network analysis (TNA), the discovery of influential words and larger themes comprised of word clusters are determined by way of an inductive computational model that initially includes all text words. The analysis identifies the message structure by detecting the most influential words, the relationships among text words, and the overall structure of the message using network analysis principles. Once the manifest structure of the text is discovered, the researcher is free to analyze the text employing any number of strategies whether qualitative and/or quantitative.

Second, informed by the Landscape Model of Reading Comprehension (LMRC), the computation involves the contextual placement of words as networks of potential "meaning" starting from individual influential words to interpretable latent thematic communities which together form an overall central message.[1,2,3] Words, word cluster assignments, and the connection among clusters are based on network-based algorithms. We suggest that this method mimics how the reader processes and understands text.

With the growth of the web and the availability of large quantities of user generated content, which changes constantly,[4] TNA provides an opportunity to expeditiously and systematically reduce content to manageable levels identifying the most influential and connected words from which a researcher can distill themes and messages including some that are not always evident. This can be advantageous for CSR CA where time-sensitive communications and reactions to those communications can be tabulated consistently and interpreted in as little time as a day. Additionally, large amounts of CSR-related content can be easily examined for trends or changes over time taking into consideration the influence of passing events. TNA can also be applied to speeches, Twitter, Facebook, blogs, books, discussion forums, and reports, as well as observational and interaction analysis. Theme opinion leaders in a network can be identified based on the number and nature of themes and individuals connected to them. Last, TNA CA can aid in pretesting CSR communications in order to optimize message effectiveness.

We begin with a description of the LMRC followed by a review of the TNA methodology.[5,6,7] Next we survey other computational approaches. Last, we apply TNA to introductory letters from ExxonMobil's 2002 and 2012 Corporate Citizen Reports (CCR).[8,9] The letters provide an easily understandable comparison of text content. We conclude with a brief description of some strategies for interpreting and presenting TNA results into meaningful themes and content for discussion.

Conceptualization

LMRC

We propose the LMRC Model (the receiver perspective) as the conceptualization for applying network analysis techniques to CA.[10,11] The Landscape Model is predicated on memory and concept construction during the reading process.[12] The reader identifies and activates or associates semantic connections between and among each word, phrase, or concept in the text of existing knowledge structures. Yeari and van den Broek describe the reader's information processing as following these steps.[13] First, there is the act of reading. Second, text elements from immediately preceding reading cycles retain some of their activation. Third, elements from prior read text during the reading activity are (re)activated through an automatic associative process. Finally, readers engage in intentional, constructive processes, by which they strategically (re)activate concepts from prior reading cycles. Therefore, the number and kinds of relationships among units of observation and the strengths of these relationships are critical to text comprehension.

The Landscape Model can be operationalized using mathematical tabulations. The message is more than the word count. It is context and created meaning from context. Because of the complexities involved in designing a computational content analysis system that comprehensively captures the factors involved with processing, understanding, and interpreting text, our focus is limited to a strict, computational definition of reading the words and their comprehension resulting in derived meaning.

We do not address context and exogenous variables, such as reader personal and environmental characteristics or exigencies, but we do acknowledge their role in this process.[14] That is to say, the utility of TNA rests in the automatic identification of linguistic networks manifestly operating in the analyzed texts. Beyond that, the researchers attach meaning to word relationships either through qualitative or mixed (such as incorporating intercoder reliability) methodologies that reveal meaning at a paradigmatic level involving the cultural contexts of meanings (e.g., real-world exigencies, codes, metaphors, narratives) that shape meaning for the people who produced the CSR messages, the targeted audiences, and the researchers themselves.

TNA

Informed by the LMRC, TNA is an inductive and algorithmic unsupervised method based on network principles. Like other competing computational techniques, it is time-saving and cost-effective. Various computational methods offer approaches that claim to accurately analyze text. For instance, the computational Syntagmatic Paradigmatic model informed by

String Edit Theory uses an algorithm to extract propositional information from text into manageable sectors.[15] Durbin, Earwood, and Golden developed a Hidden Markov Models algorithm to compare with human coding decision-making on test data.[16] Landauer and colleagues developed the Latent Semantic Analysis procedure.[17] McNamara makes an argument for multi-level modeling in a review of various computational latent semantic models.[18] Shaoul and Westbury have studied computational lexical semantic models.[19] Many models were able to replicate the human coding of words into complex themes.

However, other than Paranyushkin's research, we found no extant literature applying computational network-based principles to CA that integrate levels of meaning in the analysis.[20,21] Such an analysis would include word counts, contiguous co-occurrences of words, word clusters, the connection between and among clusters, and an overall text structure.

How does TNA differ from other high dimensional unsupervised methods such as HAL, LSA, and HiDEx?[22] These computational approaches calculate words, their co-occurrences, and groups of co-occurrences in relation to the unit of measurement only. On the other hand, TNA computes influential words, the number of connections of these influential word, and the nature of these connections within and between word clusters based on between centrality (*BC*) and degree (*D*) network principles. *BC* and *D*, which will be discussed in detail later, are measures that analyze the importance of words in relation to other words because it is the combination of words that allow us to formulate meaning from what we read.

People read, perceive, and interpret text based on word and text characteristics. The process starts with single words building relationships and later meaning through their association with other words, thus constructing higher orders of networks and understanding as more and more content is integrated. For instance, in the sentence, "ABC Company's CSR focuses on worker safety, worker benefits, and community development," "ABC Company" alone provides little meaning per se other than the company name. Yet, in the context of worker and community-focused CSR, we have a better understanding about ABC Company and its CSR efforts.

TNA informs our methodology in a manner consistent with the Landscape Model. TNA is manifest text analysis based on networks.[23,24,25,26] Two of the basic measures in network analysis are degree (*D*) and betweenness centrality (*BC*).[27,28] *D*s are the number of connections a word possesses (direct connections to other words). They are co-occurrences. A word with a high *D* serves as a hub within a word cluster. Words and their connections to other words provide what is called in Landscape Theory anaphoric clarity. It results from cohort activation, which is the association of read words to previously read words in the text.[29] This is an automatic process with no conscious cognitive effort. The process identifies referents for objects and other direct word associations (connections).

Word influence is not assessed simply by frequency or co-occurrences of words, but by relative placement in the text in relation to other words or cohorts where context provides a measure of influence and meaning at potentially more than one level. As in the "ABC Company" example, if the word CSR often appears among such words as worker safety, worker benefits, and community development, we might conclude that the company's CSR focuses on its workers and local communities where it operates. *BC* expands the analysis because it captures the important relationships in this process as a measure of how often a word appears on the shortest paths between two other words in the network.[30,31]

A word with a high *BC* thus connects and potentially provides meaning in conjunction with the other two words as well as within a larger context or among word clusters. *BC* connections allow for the interpretation of meaning at a higher level involving perceived themes as well as the overall text structure to become apparent to the reader. Because *BC* circulates meaning, the reader can connect the dots and can see the bigger picture as the message unfolds.

TNA measures provide us with summary measures including Ds and *BCs*; a modularity index, which refers to the presence of prominent word clusters in the text; and a count of strongly linked clusters. Together these measures provide the text structure. In the following section, we apply this method. In a study by Vieira and Grantham, TNA demonstrated a high correlation with other measures of LMRC suggesting concurrent validity.[32] Correlations ran from 0.94 to 0.97.

In summary, TNA facilitates analogical and metaphoric meaning and interpretation by reducing the amount of (read) text to a manageable level based on *BC* and *D* network principles informed by the LMRC theoretical framework. The influential words are identified as a result of their centrality in connection to other words, as well as their number of direct connections to other words. This approach reduces the text to the most influential content and provides the manifest structure needed so that the researcher can consider analogical and metaphoric meaning as well as individual characteristics, contextual considerations, and sociological factors as part of the interpretation process.

From influential words, word clusters, and text structure to themes and message structure

After TNA uncovers the influential words, world clusters and the overall text structure, what is next? As depicted in Figure 6.1.1, the complete process offering a number of paths for ascribing meaning to TNA results and the options are by no means exhaustive and mutually exclusive. As we can see, TNA is a two-stage process.

Stage one is TNA. It provides the text structure and manifest content influential words, word clusters, and the connections among those clusters. The text structure provides key words and how those key words are connected to other words and word clusters. A word that serves as a bridge to many other words, thus, circulating meaning throughout the text, will have a high betweenness centrality score. A word that is heavily connected within its word cluster will have a high degree score and thus operates as a hub within the cluster. The most influential words will score high on both measures and thus play a key role in the overall message.

Stage two involves examining words and word clusters and assigning meaning to them, thus, uncovering themes, message structure, and the overall message. Stage two can be conducted in different ways, often blending approaches, and is guided by the researcher's approach and conceptual framework. The researcher introduces expertise, context, reader-based factors or attributes and may include variables exogenous to the text, which all provide greater meaning and understanding of the text corpus. Therefore, this method allows for the discovery of latent constructs not evident in the manifest content. Moreover, more quantitative techniques can be implemented along with researcher expertise through a process of reification where intercoder reliability measures are introduced. This is an attempt to quantify words and word clusters in preparation for additional statistical analysis aimed at accurately ascribing meaning to the text as well as possibly introducing exogenous variables into the analysis.

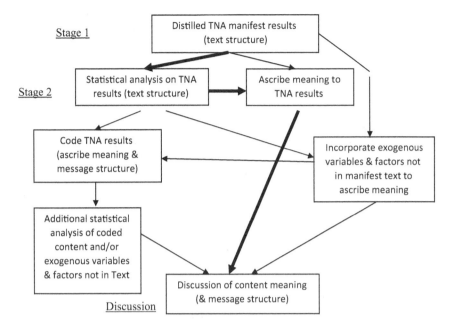

Figure 6.1.1 Strategies for deploying TNA

Note: The message structure refers to the meaning of words and relationships between and among words to form themes as calculated by word influence, word clusters, and the overall message using TNA betweenness centrality and degree measures.

In this study, we followed the path indicated by the bold arrows in Figure 6.1.1. First, the TNA was run. Next, we ran a number of statistical analyses in order to determine manifest and structural differences among the words and word clusters. Last, we used face validity to suggest and discuss the message structure, key constructs, and themes in the context of ExxonMobil's CSR.

Methodology

The text source is ExxonMobil's CEO welcome letters, located in the company's CCR for 2002 and 2012.[33,34] The relatively small amount of content makes it easy to run a comparative assessment. Notwithstanding contrasting views on the usage of inferential statistics to analyze network data, we will employ statistics because of the following reasons.[35] We assume that the letters introduce CCR content, serve as samples, and are thus representative of the CCRs' content. Our unit of analysis consists of the 100 most influential nodes, which are the most salient and representative data in the two letters. They are based on the highest betweenness centrality scores. Because of these data characteristics, the usage of inferential statistics is appropriate.

The TNA methodology is informed by the LMRC, which is a computational approach to text comprehension and analysis.[36,37,38] Rather than simply counting word frequencies, this method tabulates the strength and relationships among words suggesting how individuals read and comprehend text.[39,40] We posit that during and after reading the text, the reader will form a mental model of Exxon's CCR efforts based on the CEO letters.

Data preparation

We employed the following TNA methodological steps starting with preparing the text for analysis.[41,42] First, prepositions and other words that bind the text together but do not specifically contribute to the content are removed: such words as "the," "to," "at," and so forth. Second, the remaining words are replaced with their appropriate stem words using the Krovets Stemmer algorithm.[43] This stemmer essentially transforms the plurals or tenses of a word to its singular and present tense. For instance, "continuing" is replaced with "continue" or "issues" is replaced with "issue." It can be modified to include plural or other forms depending on the research goal. Next, all words are changed to lower case in order to avoid counting the same word as two different items. Modifications can be made to include similar upper and lower case words. Last, unnecessary spaces, symbols, and punctuation, and numbers were removed.

The next step involved converting the normalized text data into an Extensible Markup Language (XML) format, which is used to graph data. We ran the data in Gephi, an open source application that produces graphical visualizations and offers optional analytic procedures.[44] The data were encoded using the two-pass approach developed by Paranyushkin.[45,46] First, the normalized text was scanned using a two consecutive word scan. For each word that first appears in the scan, it is recorded as a new word and a value of one was assigned to the word connection. If the pair already exists, the weight of the corresponding connection is incrementally increased by one. Each paragraph is scanned and tabulated separately, with each paragraph representing a reading cycle. The second pass uses a five consecutive word scan and follows a similar procedure as the initial two-word scan. The five-word pass starts at the first word of a paragraph and terminates once it reaches the last word of the paragraph. It then jumps to the next paragraph and starts again from the first word. The two-word pass approach permits the discovery of the general text structure as well as word clusters, which serve as the basis of themes within the entire text. Paranyushkin found that the five-word scan further differentiates clusters into more fine-tuned groups by weighing the closest contiguous connections and then extending the connections to five words.[47,48]

TNA was run on the 2002 and 2012 CEO letters to ascertain the most influential words and the nature of their relationship with other words. Once the distillation was complete, we qualitatively assessed the results for latent content and themes. Along these lines, we endeavored to discover similarities and differences in the central themes between ExxonMobil's 2002 and 2012 CCR, as sampled in the CCR's CEO welcome letters for the two years under study.

Results

Study 1 – 2002 CEO letter structural properties

Table 6.1.1 depicts the structural properties of the 2002 CEO letter. Some of these measures are relative. Considering the limited size of the text, the analyzed words are restricted to the 100 most influential words per letter. A larger text might very well include more words. In this case, there are 329 direct connections on the two and five consecutive word scans. The average *BC* was 411.56 (*SD* = 614.96). The *BC* measure represents how often a word appears on the shortest paths between two other words in the text.[49,50] The higher the *BC* score, the more influential the word because it links other words and circulates potential meaning associated with those other words as well as potentially connecting word clusters. *D*s are the number of direct connections a specific word has to other words. The *D* was 6.66 (*SD* = 2.58), which is in the low medium range count of 5–10 direct connections per word.[51,52] Eight themes were detected. Modularity was 0.00, indicating less dense word clusters. Any modularity measure > 0.40 suggests the presence of strongly connected clusters.[53,54]

Key words

BC is the basis for determining word influence. The key words were *business* (*BC* = 3933.18, *D* = 18), *exxonmobil* (*BC* = 3230.34, *D* = 21), *economic* (*BC* = 1903.99, *D* = 11), and *respect* (*BC* = 1714.26, *D* = 10). Although all four had above average *D* scores, *business* and *exxonmobil* had the highest *D*s, which followed a pattern similar to their *BC*s, suggesting that these key words serve to connect themes and contribute to the overall text structure. There was less of a hub (strong theme intra-connected) role because none of the themes were dense. Also, *economic* and *respect* provided a similar role but were not as influential. See Table 6.1.2.

Themes

Of the eight detected potential themes, five comprised 82% of the words. Within each of the five clusters, the four most influential words were responsible for 57–83% of betweenness centrality within their respective theme. Because they comprised most of the words, the analysis of the 2002 letter focuses on the dominant five themes. Note that this is an arbitrary decision based on the reported percentages above. The top four words per cluster's *BC*s ranged from 220.04 to 3933.18 (M=431.19, Md=204.56, SD=657.10, and the coefficient of variation (CV) is 152.39%). The top four words per cluster's *D*s ranged from 4 to 21 (M=6.78, Md=6.00, SD=2.76, and CV=40.67%). The *BC* descriptives suggest that a few words were driving betweenness centrality. No significant differences in average *BC*s or *D*s were found among the five themes ($F[4,77] = 0.719, p = 0.58$ and $F[4,77] = 0.80, p = 0.53$, respectively).

Table 6.1.1 2002 CEO Letter Structural Properties

Property	Measures
Word count	100
Direct connections count	329
Average betweenness centrality	411.56 (*SD* = 614.96)
Average degree	6.66 (*SD* = 2.58)
Theme count	8.00
Modularity	0.00
Strongly connected themes	0.00

Note: Initial word count was 395.

Table 6.1.2 2002 CEO letter descriptive measures

Themes & within theme words	Percentage of text	Mean BC	Mean D
1 ExxonMobil is a good global corporate citizen	0.49	389.90	6.64
Citizenship (hub)		1697.26	9.00
Standard		931.54	11.00
Good		809.96	12.00
High		772.70	11.00
2 Success requires understanding and respect for people	0.18	429.00	6.33
Respect (hub)		1714.26	10.00
People		1651.88	5.00
Operation		885.80	9.00
Understanding		466.72	4.00
3 ExxonMobil devotes all of its resources to meet challenges	0.15	410.38	7.40
ExxonMobil (hub)		3230.34	21.00
Challenge		1434.09	12.00
Director		220.04	6.00
Dedication		197.93	6.00
4 Economic Prosperity is necessary for societal welfare	0.14	278.44	6.14
Economic (hub)		1903.99	11.00
Society		377.34	6.00
Developing		355.34	6.00
Environment		202.00	6.00
5 ExxonMobil's longevity and long-term competiveness	0.13	692.62	7.62
Business (hub)		3933.18	18.00
Require		1382.24	10.00
Policy		1006.60	6.00
Aspect		756.88	7.00

Note: Measures are relative to the entire text for the given year.

Word Cluster 1: ExxonMobil is a good global corporate citizen

Here, citizenship ($BC = 1697.26$, $D = 9$), standard ($BC = 931.54$, $D = 11$), good ($BC = 809.96$, $D = 12$), and high ($BC = 772.70$, $D = 11$) were the most influential words within this theme comprising 49% of BC. There was a section entitled "Our Long-Term Responsibility." The word citizenship drove this word cluster and consisted of 22% of the letter's words. Its average BC was 389.90 ($SD = 382.02$) and D was 6.64 ($SD = 2.74$). The citizenship word served as a hub and was linked to other themes throughout the letter. The following quotations capture this finding (Italicized words are community nodes):

> This *report* describes how we *translate* our *commitment* to *good corporate citizenship* into *action*. . . . We pledge to be a *good corporate citizen* in all the *places* we *operate worldwide*. . . . We will maintain the *highest ethical standards* . . . proud of its *high standards* of *safety*.

In short, the company's good global corporate citizenship was demonstrated by its high safety and ethical standards.

Word Cluster 2: success requires understanding and respect for people, safety, laws,
and the environment

Here, *respect* (BC = 1714.26, D = 10), *people* (BC = 1651.88, D = 5), *operation* (BC = 885.80, D = 9), and *understanding* (BC = 466.72, D = 4) were the most influential words within this cluster, comprising 61% of BC. This theme comprised 18% of the words. The average BC and D scores were 429.00 (SD = 492.23) and 6.33 (SD = 1.37), respectively. The following text represents this theme:

> And to do business successfully for this long and on this scale also requires a deep *respect* for and *understanding* of different *people* and *cultures*, and a keen appreciation of what our role in society should be . . . comply with all *applicable laws* and *regulations*, and *respect local* and *national cultures*. We are *dedicated* to *running safe* and *environmentally responsible operations*.

Here, *respect* functions as a hub within this cluster and *respect for people* is linked to other themes.

Word Cluster 3: ExxonMobil devotes all of its resources to meet challenges

Here, *exxonmobil* (BC = 3230.34, D = 21), *challenge* (BC =1434.09, D = 12), *director* (BC = 220.04, D = 6), and *dedication* (BC = 197.93, D = 6) were the most influential words within this cluster, comprising 83% of BC. This theme comprised 15% of all words. The average BC and D scores were 410.38 (SD = 852.39) and 7.40 (SD = 4.07) respectively. *exxonmobil* in the context of *challenge* operated as the hub of this cluster. Thus, *exxonmobil* followed by *challenge* drove this theme. This theme was circulated throughout the letter as well. The following text represents this theme: "*ExxonMobil is called* upon to *address* an ever-*broadening range* of *issues* and *challenges*. The *resourcefulness, professionalism*, and *dedication* of the *directors, officers*, and *employees* of *ExxonMobil make* it possible for us to meet these *challenges.*" The idea of challenge was linked to other themes.

Word Cluster 4: economic prosperity is necessary for societal welfare and a quality environment,
and energy use is necessary for economic growth

Here, *economic* (BC = 1903.99, D = 11), *society* (BC =377.34, D = 6), *developing* (BC = 355.34, D = 6), and *environment* (BC = 202.00, D = 6) were the most influential words within this theme comprising 73% of BC. This theme comprised 14% of all words and was driven by the word *economic*. The following text represents this theme: "Energy use grows as *economic prosperity* increases. And there is a *proven* link between *economic development* and *advances* in *societal welfare* and *environmental improvement* – particularly in the *developing areas* of the *world*." The average BC and D scores were 278.44 (SD = 480.54) and 6.14 (SD = 1.51), respectively. The word *economic* was the hub of this theme and linked to other themes in the letter.

Word Cluster 5: ExxonMobil's longevity and long-term competiveness attests
to its core competencies

Here, *business* (BC =3933.18, D = 18), *require* (BC = 1382.24, D = 10), *policy* (BC = 1006.61, D = 6), and *aspect* (BC = 756.88, D = 7) were the most influential words within this theme, comprising 79% of *BC*. This theme comprised 13% of the total words. The average *BC* and *D* scores were 692.62 (*SD* = 1055.05) and 7.62 (*SD* = 3.43), respectively. The following text represents this theme:

> To do *business successfully* for this long and on this *scale requires* that we be on the *leading* edge of competition in every *aspect* of our business. This *requires* that ExxonMobil's substantial resources financial, operational, technological and human – be employed wisely and evaluated regularly.

This theme was about *the business of business* and was linked to other themes in the letter. Clearly, *business* is the hub and a concept that circulates throughout the letter.

Study 1 discussion

In the 2002 letter, we found four influential words and five theme clusters accounting for 82% of the text. Compared to the overall letter measures, the modularity was 0.00, indicating no prominent or dense themes. However, the words *business, exxonmobil, economy, respect*, and *citizenship* (close to respect) were a common thread in all of the themes. *exxonmobil* and *business* especially served as hubs within their primary word clusters. The "*exxonmobil* is a good global corporate citizen" theme did not include one of the four most influential words, but it supported this message. Essentially, the letter suggested that economic prosperity is necessary for the welfare of society, including a safe environment and the availability of energy: *exxonmobil* is a good corporate citizen because it *understands* and *respects* people, safety, laws, and the environment by devoting its resources to meet the world's energy *challenges* (in support of economic prosperity).

In short, the connected message in the text is primarily that ExxonMobil's business of energy provides economic/energy benefits to society, followed by its concern for society, together making it a good corporate citizen. Figure 6.1.2 provides a graphical depiction of the influential words and their relationships to other words forming themes that represent ExxonMobil's CSR message.

Study 2–2012 CEO letter structural properties

Table 6.1.3 represents the structural properties of the 2012 letter. Again, the analysis was limited to the 100 most influential words; 495 direct connections comprise the letter text. The average *BC* was 247.58 (*SD* = 266.54). The average *D* was 9.18 (*SD* = 4.52). Seven clusters were detected. The modularity was 0.50, which suggests the presence of prominent themes.

Key words

The most influential words were *exxonmobil* (*BC* = 1697.26, *D* = 22), *risk* (*BC* = 1153.92, *D* = 24), *respond* (*BC* = 1059.80, *D* = 8), and *performance* (*BC* = 832.74, *D* = 23), which is based on their high betweenness centrality scores. They accounted for 51–97% of their respective theme's *BC*. Then, *exxonmobil, risk*, and *performance* had similarly high degree scores, revealing that these key words were not only prominent in the entire text, but also played an important role as hubs within their primary word clusters. On the other hand, *respond* had fewer direct connections (lower *D*), yet, it was connected to most of the clusters as suggested by its high *BC* reinforcing its message that ExxonMobil is responsive. See Table 6.1.4.

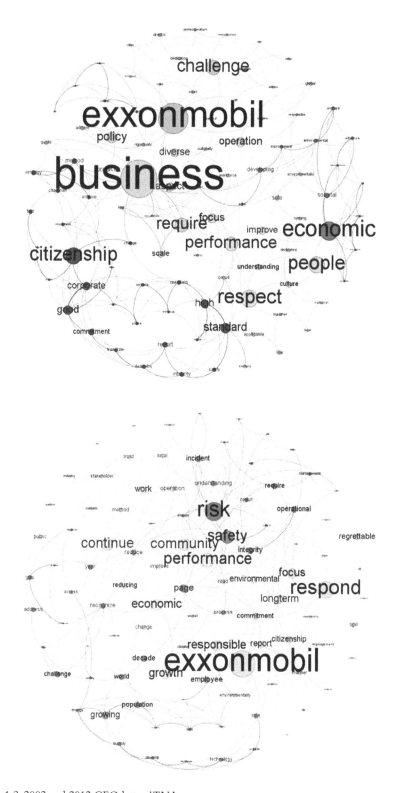

Figure 6.1.2 2002 and 2012 CEO letters' TNA

Note: Larger words represent greater text network influence based on *BC*.

Table 6.1.3 2012 CEO letter structural properties

Property	Measures
Word count	100
Direct connection count	459
Average betweenness centrality	247.58 (SD = 266.54)
Average degree	9.18 (SD = 4.52)
Theme count	7.00
Modularity	0.50
Strongly connected themes	3.00

Note: Initial word count was 846.

Table 6.1.4 2012 CEO letter descriptive measures

Themes & within theme words	Percentage of text	Mean BC	Mean D
1 ExxonMobil has a long-term commitment for the ...	0.24	255.93	8.54
ExxonMobil (hub)		1697.26	22.00
Responsibility		607.98	14.00
Long-term		496.84	16.00
Growing		415.15	9.00
2 Managing risk	0.22	288.37	11.18
Risk (hub)		1153.92	24.00
Safety		787.09	22.00
Community		718.53	18.00
Focus		588.00	18.00
3 ExxonMobil's economic and environmental performance	0.18	256.23	10.17
Performance		832.74	23.00
Economic		627.93	16.00
Growth		607.77	14.00
Environment		389.23	15.00
4 ExxonMobil continuously address stakeholders' concerns	0.16	190.65	8.75
Continue		727.01	18.00
Work		398.66	14.00
Address		238.25	7.00
Trust		223.80	10.00
5 ExxonMobil is responsive	0.06	303.30	4.83
Respond		1060.01	8.00
Regrettable		378.00	4.00
Spill		222.83	5.00
Oil		96.50	4.00

Note: Measures are relative to the entire text for the given year.

Themes

The Strongly Connected Components measure indicated three prominent theme clusters. In fact, seven clusters were identified of which three comprised 64% of the words. However, we only analyzed the top four word clusters because they accounted for 80% of the words. Additionally, because of its unique relationship to the text, we included a minor word cluster, which included one influential word. Respond or responsiveness to oil spills touched on all of the themes, yet it was rarely addressed directly.

The themes' *BCs* ranged from 0 to 1697.26 (M = 255.45, Md = 179.29, SD = 282.21, and CV = 110.48%). The *Ds* ranged from 3 to 24 (M = 9.34, Md = 8.00, SD = 4.65 and CV = 49.79%). Like the 2002 letter, the *BCs* suggest that some words are present throughout the themes.

Word Cluster 1: ExxonMobil has a long-term commitment to the betterment of society

Here, *exxonmobil* (BC = 1697.26, D = 22), *responsibility* (BC = 607.98, D = 14), *long-term* (BC = 496.84, D = 16), and *growing* (BC = 415.15, D = 9) were the most influential words within this theme, consisting of 52% of the cluster's *BC*, and within this theme, there is a section entitled "Our Long-Term Responsibility." The cluster's average *BC* was 255.93 (SD = 342.89) and D was 8.54 (SD = 4.10). The *exxonmobil* word drove this theme and consisted of 24% of the text words. It served as the hub of this dense cluster and was present throughout the letter. The following quotation captures this theme: "*ExxonMobil* is focused on the *long term*. Our projects- and their impacts -span generations, not business or political cycles. Our *long-term* perspective helps us focus on our *responsibilities* for *environmental* protection, social *development* and economic *growth*." The theme communicates that ExxonMobil is seriously committed to its long-term responsibility for the environment while contributing to society and the economy suggesting that the company provides jobs, economic growth, and other related societal benefits.

Word Cluster 2: managing risk through safe operations that protect communities and the environment

Here, *risk* (BC = 1153.92, D = 24), *safety* (BC = 787.09, D = 22), *community* (BC = 718.53, D = 18), and *focus* (BC = 588.00, D = 18) comprises 51% of the theme's *BCs*, and this cluster contains 22% of the text words. The average betweenness centrality was 288.37 (SD = 297.30) and average D was 11.18 (SD = 5.62). This cluster is densely connected through the *risk* and *safety* hubs. Although *risk* is a hub, the word is present throughout the letter. The following captures this cluster.

> We responded *immediately* with a *focus* on *community safety*, restoring the environment and understanding the cause of the *incident*. When working to *ensure operational integrity*, our *goal* is to *manage risk* and to *avoid incidents* such as these. . . . Strong results require effective *risk management*.

The emphasis is to maintain the safety of the community and to avoid *incidents* by focusing on managing risk and ensuring operational integrity. The implicit message was that risk is minimized in order to assure *community* safety. Controlling risk is linked to other themes such as *community, safety,* and *economic* growth.

Word Cluster 3: ExxonMobil's economic and environmental performance

Here, *performance* (BC = 832.74, D = 23), *economic* (BC = 627.93, D = 16), *growth* (BC = 607.77, D = 14), and *environment* (BC =389.23, D = 15) accounted for 53% of this theme and comprised 18% of the letter's words. The BC mean is 256.23 (SD = 227.60) and the D mean is 10.17 (SD = 4.64), indicating a tightly woven cluster in which economic *performance* is the hub while accounting for environmental concerns. It includes a section entitled "Commitment to Performance." The following are sample excerpts: "We have established systematic *policies* and *processes* to measure, monitor and *improve* our *economic*, social and *environmental performance*. . . . We look forward to continually *improving* our performance and *contributing* to innovation and *growth* in the decades to come."

Word Cluster 4: ExxonMobil continuously addresses stakeholders' concerns

Here, *continue* (BC = 727.01, D = 18), *work* (BC = 398.66, D = 14), *address* (BC = 238.25, D = 7), and *trust* (BC = 223.80, D = 10) were the most influential words within this theme, comprising 52% of BC. This word cluster has 16% of the total words. The BC and D scores were 190.65 (SD = 172.99) and 8.75 (SD = 3.45), respectively. The following text represents this theme:

> Industry must *work* to *build stakeholder trust*. With every new technological advance comes a renewed obligation to *address public* questions and *concerns*. That is why we must *continue* to engage with *communities* about how we systematically mitigate *risk* in our *operations*. . . . It is important that we *continue* listening to those who have a *shared stake (stakeholders)* in this and other *issues* so that we can *continue* to *build* their *trust*. We look forward to *continually* improving our performance and contributing to innovation and growth in the decades to come.

This theme concentrates on continued effort and the need to continuously address stakeholders' concerns and build trust.

Word Cluster 5: ExxonMobil is responsive

Here, *respond* (BC = 1060.01, D = 8), *regrettable* (BC = 378.00, D = 4), *spill* (BC = 222.83, D = 5), and *oil* (BC = 96.50, D = 4) are the most influential words within this cluster, comprising 97% of BC. This theme consisted of 6% of the total analyzed text. The BC and D scores were 303.30 (SD = 393.71) and 4.83 (SD = 1.60), respectively. Then, *responsiveness* is the cluster hub, yet, it also was connected throughout the letter. The cluster focuses on the Mayflower oil spill. The following text represents this theme:

> In early 2013, ExxonMobil Pipeline Company *responded* to a crude *oil spill* in *Mayflower, Arkansas* – a *regrettable* event for which we are deeply sorry. We *responded* immediately with a focus on community safety, restoring the environment and understanding the cause of the incident.

No significant differences in BC means were found among the five themes (F[4,81] = 0.318, p = 0.87). However, there was a difference in D means by word cluster (F[4,81] = 2.89, p = 0.03). The ExxonMobil *responsiveness* cluster's mean D was significantly less that the other themes. Since the test of homogeneity of variance was significant ($p = .04$), we used the Games–Howell post hoc test. Clusters 1–3 were densely connected indicating strong themes. The clear proactive messages are that ExxonMobil has a long-term commitment to the betterment of society by managing risk through safe operations that protect communities and the environment, while also maintaining its economic performance.

Study 2 Discussion

In the 2012 letter, we found four influential words and four themes accounting for 80% of the text. Modularity was 0.50, suggesting prominent themes. Since the themes' mean *BC*s were unremarkable, the drivers throughout the letter were the influential words *exxonmobil*, *risk*, and *responsiveness*. In the case of *exxonmobil, risk*, and *performance*'s high *D*s, they served as the hubs for their clusters, and *responsiveness* was not a hub, but it was influential because of its high *BC*, indicating that it was present throughout the letter along with the other influential words.

It is worth noting that one theme did not include an influential word but comprised 16% of the words, including *continue* and *work*, which were cluster hubs. The message is that ExxonMobil is focused on addressing stakeholder concerns and building trust through continued work in these areas. The word *continue* was a reinforcer throughout the text, communicating that ExxonMobil's CSR efforts are continuous.

These measures suggest that the overall 2012 letter's message centers on ExxonMobil's performance based on the company's continuous management of risk and its responsiveness to all stakeholders' concerns and situations. Figure 6.1.2 provides a graphical depiction of the influential words, their relationships to other words, and the identified word clusters.

Comparing 2002 and 2012

The 2002 and 2012 CCR CEO letters' word counts were 395 and 846, respectively. The 2002 letter is one page and the 2012 letter is two pages. Lee R. Raymond was CEO and chairperson in 2002. The same position was held by Rex W. Tillerson during 2012. Table 6.1.5 depicts the *BC*s and *D*s for the top 4 influential words in the letters. ExxonMobil was a central word in both letters. The chi-square test revealed a significant difference between 2002 and 2012 *BC* scores per influential word ($X^2[6] = 7631.65$, $p < .001$). The chi-square test for the *D* scores was also significant ($X^2[6] = 63.16$, $p < .001$).

Since the *F*-tests for difference between the 2002 and 2012 letters' variances for *BC* and *D* were significant ($p < 0.001$), a separate variance two–sample t-test was conducted comparing each letter's mean *BC* and *D* for the dominant themes. The *BC* means were significantly different ($M_{2002} = 431.19$, $SD_{2002} = 657.10$, $M_{2012} = 255.45$, $SD_{2012} = 282.21$, $t[108] = 2.23$, $p = 0.03$). The *D* means were also significantly different ($M_{2002} = 6.78$, $SD_{2002} = 2.76$, $M_{2012} = 9.34$, $SD_{2012} = 4.65$, $t[140] = -4.35$, $p < 0.001$). Overall, the 2002 letter demonstrated greater *BC* and the 2012 letter indicated greater *D*. Generally, the influential words in the 2002 letter were more central throughout the letter. In other words, the key words were present throughout the letter and connecting the themes through a central message. On the other hand, the 2012 letter focus was on the presentation of discrete themes.

Table 6.1.5 Chi-square-test for differences of betweenness centrality and degree scores for top four most influential words by each letter

Most influential words	BC		D	
	2002	*2012*	*2002*	*2012*
Business	3933.18	0	18	3
ExxonMobil[1]	3230.34	1697.86	21	22
Economic	1903.99	627.93	11	16
Respect	1714.26	0	10	0
Risk	0	1153.92	0	24
Respond	0	1060.01	0	8
Performance	1374.45	832.74	9	23

Note: [1]Appeared in the top four words for *BC* in 2002 and 2012 letters.

General discussion

This study offers a complement to CA, which identifies manifest content as part of the CA process informed by the Landscape Model of Reading.[55] TNA focuses on reader information processing and comprehension and network analysis principles and methods. It comprises three levels of analysis. Individual words, the relationships of individual words to other words forming word clusters, which can be interpreted as themes, and the over-arching text message. The analysis offers a number of options throughout the process. The steps are systematic and straightforward.[56,57]

As demonstrated in the 2002 and 2012 ExxonMobil CEO CSR letters, the properties of these words and word clusters are primarily based on betweenness centrality and degree network principles and measures. Using an algorithmic method, word clusters are extracted, which then can be interpreted as is or subjected to additional statistical analyses.

There were content similarities and differences between the decade-apart corporate communication report letters. Understandably, ExxonMobil was the primary word in both letters. Figure 6.1.2 illustrates the words and themes of the two letters. In the 2002 letter, the use of the words *business, exxonmobil, economy, respect,* and *citizenship* (close to *respect*) was the common thread throughout the letter, as suggested by their high betweenness centrality scores. The message structure involved linking ExxonMobil's business as good for the economy and emphasized the company's understanding of respect and citizenship in its societal role. On the other hand, the 2012 letter's word structure was essentially based on discrete themes, as indicated their high degree scores. The only exception was the word "ExxonMobil," which was the common thread in the letter. The 2012 letter emphasizes five themes that were not interwoven into a unified message.

Table 6.1.6 contrasts the letter's themes. The tone of the 2002 themes suggests concerns that must be considered for ExxonMobil to be a good citizen. They take into account stakeholder interests and indicate the importance of their remaining competitive. On the other hand, the 2012, suggests a more specific and proactive role to simply being a "good" citizen. The letter communicates ExxonMobil's commitment to the betterment of society as evidenced in different discrete themes such as reducing risk in order to protect the environment and communities, and being responsive to all stakeholder needs as well. The 2012 message structure suggests proactive CSR efforts presented as salient points; whereas,

Table 6.1.6 Themes in the 2002 and 2012 ExxonMobil CEO CCR letters

2002

Theme 1: ExxonMobil is a good global corporate citizen.
Theme 2: Success requires understanding and respect for people, safety, laws, and the environment.
Theme 3: ExxonMobil devotes all of its resources to meet challenges.
Theme 4: Economic prosperity is necessary for societal welfare, a quality environment, and energy use is necessary for economic growth.
Theme 5: ExxonMobil's longevity and long-term competiveness attests to its core competencies.

2012

Theme 1: ExxonMobil has a long-term commitment to the betterment of society.
Theme 2: Managing risk through safe operations protects communities and the environment.
Theme 3: ExxonMobil's economic and environmental performance.
Theme 4: ExxonMobil continuously address stakeholders' concerns.
Theme 5: ExxonMobil is responsive.

Note: The word clusters comprising the themes were based on the 100 most influential words based on betweenness centrality.

the 2002 is more of a general message covering ExxonMobil's understanding of the good global corporate citizenship role relative to the communicated motifs.

Although a potentially useful tool for CA researchers, TNA utilizes algorithms that cannot identify meaning at the paradigmatic level or provide the cultural contexts of meanings (e.g., real-world exigencies, codes, metaphors, narratives) that shape understanding not only for the people who produced the CSR messages but for targeted audiences as well.

Incorporating a TNA component in CA has many applications involving many strategies some of which are suggested in Figure 6.1.2. The application lends itself to larger text CA reducing the amount of text to a manageable level and thus allowing for exogenous variables to be incorporated. TNA can be used to examine CSR reports over time in order to discover whether issues change and perhaps change in response to external events such as financial crises or oil spills. Factors unique to specific (and strategic) industries can be studied in terms of messaging and reported performance standards. For instance, in the case of the oil industry, inherent environment and employee safety risks reporting and messaging can be compared to official records. Last, from a public relations standpoint, this methodology can be used to evaluate content before dissemination in order to manage message effectiveness.

Conclusions

If the research goal is to include the entire text in CA through discovering influential words and their meaning, as well as higher levels of meaning through word clusters, then TNA is an option that can reduce a large text corpus into a smaller manageable amount of words for analysis.

TNA has the potential for extensive usage throughout CSR research including big data applications. It can be applied to speeches, social media such as Twitter and Facebook, blogs, books, discussion forums, reports, and as well as observational and interaction analysis. Results can be expeditiously and easily generated. In addition to post publication CA, this method can be utilized in prepublication testing to assure that the intended message is clear.[58]

Notes

1 D.N. Rapp and P. van den Broek, "Dynamic Text Comprehension: An Integrative View of Reading," *Current Directions in Psychological Science*, 14 (2005): 276–279.

2 P. van den Broek, D.N. Rapp, and P. Kendeou, "Integrating Memory-Based and Constructionist Approaches in Accounts of Reading Comprehension," *Discourse Processes*, 39 (2005): 299–316.

3 P. van den Broek, K. Risden, C.R., Fletcher, and R. Thurlow, "A 'Landscape' View of Reading: Fluctuating Patterns of Activations and the Construction of a Stable Memory Representation," in B.K. Britton and A.C. Graesser (Eds.), *Models of Understanding Text* (1996) Mahwah, NJ: Erlbaum, 165–187.

4 S. Du and E.T. Vieira, Jr., "Striving for Legitimacy Through Corporate Social Responsibility: Insights From Oil Companies," *Journal of Business Ethics*, 110/4 (2012): 413–427.

5 M. Yeari and P. van den Broek, "A Cognitive Account of Discourse Understanding and Discourse Interpretation: The Landscape Model of Reading," *Discourse Studies*, 13/5 (2011): 635–643.

6 D. Paranyushkin, "Visualization of Text's Polysingularity Using Network Analysis," *Nodus Labs*, Berlin, Germany. (2012): http://noduslabs.com/.

7 D. Paranyushkin, "Identifying the Pathways for Meaning Circulation Using Text Network Analysis," *Nodus Labs*, Berlin, Germany. (2011): http://noduslabs.com/.

8 *ExxonMobil*, "2012 Corporate Citizenship Report" (2012): www.exxonmobil.com/Corporate/community_ccr.aspx.

9 *ExxonMobil*, "2002 Corporate Citizenship Report" (2002): www.exxonmobil.com/Corporate/community_ccr_archive.aspx.

10 Paranyushkin, 2011, op. cit.

11 Paranyushkin, 2012, op. cit.

12 Van den Broek, Risden, Fletcher, and Thurlow, op. cit.

13 Yeari and van den Broek, op. cit.

14 W.J. Potter and D. Levine-Donnerstein, "Rethinking Validity and Reliability in Content Analysis," *Journal of Applied Communication Research*, 27 (1999): 258–284.

15 S. Dennis, "An Unsupervised Method for the Extraction of Propositional Information from Text," *Proceedings of the National Academy of Sciences*, 101 (2004): 5206–5213.

16 M.A. Durbin, J. Earwood, and R.M. Golden, "Hidden Markov Models for Coding Story Recall Data," in *Proceedings of the 22nd Annual Cognitive Science Society Conference* (2000) Mahwah, NJ: Erlbaum: 113–118.

17 T.K. Landauer, P.W. Foltz, and D. Laham, "An Introduction to Latent Semantic Analysis," *Discourse Processes*, 25 (1998): 259–284.

18 D.S. McNamara, "Computational Methods to Extract Meaning from Text and Advance Theories of Human Cognition," *Topics in Cognitive Science*, 3 (2011): 3–17.

19 C. Shaoul and C. Westbury, "Exploring Lexical Co-Occurrence Space Using HiDEx," *Behavior Research Methods*, 42/2 (2010): 393–413.

20 Paranyushkin, 2011, op. cit.

21 Paranyushkin, 2012, op. cit.

22 Shaoul and Westbury, op. cit.

23 L.C. Freeman, "Centrality in Social Networks Conceptual Clarification," *Social Networks*, 1 (1979): 215–239.

24 M.E.J. Newman, "The Structure and Function of Complex Networks," *Society for Industrial and Applied Mathematics Review*, 45 (2003): 167–256. Permalink: http://dx.doi.org/10.1137/S003614450342480.

25 Paranyushkin, 2011, op. cit.

26 Paranyushkin, 2012, op. cit.

27 Freeman, 1979, op. cit.

28 L.R. Izquierdo and R.A. Hanneman, "Introduction to the Formal Analysis of Social Networks Using Mathematica" (2006) Retrieved from http://luis.izquierdo.name.

29 Yeari and van den Broek, op. cit.

30 Freeman, 1979, op. cit.

31 Izquierdo and Hanneman, op. cit.
32 E.T. Vieira, Jr. and S. Grantham, "Text Network Analysis and the Computational Landscape Model: A Study of Concurrent Validity," *American Communication Journal*, 18/1 (2016): 1–16.
33 ExxonMobil, 2002, op. cit.
34 ExxonMobil, 2012, op. cit.
35 R.A. Hanneman and M. Riddle, "Introduction to Social Network Methods," University of California, Riverside, C.A. (2005) Retrieved from http://faculty.ucr.edu/~hanneman/.
36 Rapp and van den Broek, op. cit.
37 P. van den Broek, "Using Texts in Science Education: Cognitive Processes and Knowledge Representation," *Science*, 328 (2010): 453–456.
38 Van den Broek, Risden, Fletcher, and Thurlow, op. cit.
39 T. Linderholm, S. Virtue, Y. Tzeng, and P. van den Broek, "Fluctuations in the Availability of Information During Reading: Capturing Cognitive Processes Using the Landscape Model," *Discourse Processes*, 37 (2004): 165–186.
40 Y. Tzeng, P. van den Broek, P. Kendeou, and C. Lee, "The Computational Implementation of the Landscape Model: Modeling Inferential Processes and Memory Representation of Text Comprehension," *Behavioral Research Methods, Instruments and Computers*, 37 (2005): 277–286.
41 Paranyushkin, 2011, op. cit.
42 Paranyushkin, 2012, op. cit.
43 R. Krovetz, "Viewing Morphology as an Inference Process," *SIGIR 1993 Proceedings of the 16th Annual International ACM SIGIR Conference on Research and Development in Information Retrieval.* (1993).
44 M. Bastian, S. Heymann, and M. Jacomy, "Gephi: An Open Source Software for Exploring and Manipulating Networks," *Association for the Advancement of Artificial Intelligence.* (2009) https://gephi.org/.
45 Paranyushkin, 2011, op. cit.
46 Paranyushkin, 2012, op. cit.
47 Paranyushkin, 2011, op. cit.
48 Paranyushkin, 2012, op. cit.
49 Freeman, 1979, op. cit.
50 Izquierdo and Hanneman, op. cit.
51 Paranyushkin, 2011, op. cit.
52 Paranyushkin, 2012, op. cit.
53 V.D. Blondel, J.L. Guillaume, R. Lambiotte, and E. Lefebvre, "Fast Unfolding of Communities in Large Networks," *Journal of Statistical Mechanics: Theory and Experiment*, P10008. (2008) DOI: 10.1088/1742-5468/2008/10/P10008.
54 L.C. Freeman, "Visualizing Social Networks," *Journal of Social Structure*, 1/1 (2000). Retrieved from www.cmu.edu/joss/content/articles/volume1/Freeman.html.
55 Van den Broek, Risden, Fletcher, and Thurlow, op. cit.
56 Paranyushkin, 2011, op. cit.
57 Paranyushkin, 2012, op. cit.
58 M.D. Slater, "Content Analysis as a Foundation for Programmatic Research in Communication," *Communication Methods and Measures*, 7/2 (2013): 85–93.

6.2 #CSR on Twitter

A hashtag oversimplifying a complex practice

Ana Adi

Introduction

This chapter focuses on the emerging discourses and themes associated with the CSR hashtag on Twitter as a way of discovering concerns, issues and key conceptual associations for the field. By identifying the accounts that influence and drive these conversations online, this chapter aims to invite a wider discussion about how CSR is portrayed on Twitter by a savvy public as well as how these messages shape understanding of what CSR is and its role and mechanisms.

The chapter will first examine Twitter's relevance as a study environment and the academic fascination and attention it currently enjoys, elaborating on the differences between the public, unorganised discourses and other forms of online dialogue and discussion it enables, including private conversation and hashtag chats. It will then proceed with a brief overview of the multitude of perspectives and definitions of CSR, a necessary reference point for the data analysis later included in this chapter. The current state of research into digital CSR will then be explored, where I argue that this is heavily focused on how CSR is communicated, implemented or undertaken by organisations rather than examine how various groups perceive it and understand it. As academic literature, consultancy groups and organisations promote a wide variety of definitions of what CSR is or should be, an exploration of the general, open discourses about CSR in an open forum such as Twitter will help understand what are the most frequently associated perspectives with the practice. For CSR to be widely embraced by organisations of any kind, it is not sufficient that it is known by professionals and specialists only. Twitter acts as an open forum, whose users' postings are by default visible and accessible even to those not registered with the platform. Moreover, its bite-size messages when containing links become gateways to further, more in-depth information and thus become a source of reference and information. The identification of the CSR perspectives promoted on Twitter will thus help understand perceptions, or potentially misconceptions of CSR, an essential step in furthering dialogue about the profession but also in increasing the uptake of the practice.

The methodology proposed therefore is exploratory and qualitative, even if the dataset used would also enable quantitative analysis. The results indicate that CSR messages on Twitter shared under the hashtag are first and foremost associated with those about sustainability. Driven by a select few, the association of CSR with sustainability on Twitter indicates the prevalence of a very narrow perspective of the field. This, I argue, is prone to misrepresent CSR and diminish its importance for organisations. As I warn against the danger of considering the most frequent associations and depictions of CSR to be representative for the profession and against considering that the loudest voices are also the most suited to lead the discussion, I conclude by suggesting that, for CSR at least, the meaningful conversation is more individual and thus hidden away from this general view.

The fascinating Twitter

According to Statista.com, Twitter is the ninth most popular social network[1] in the world, with 320 million active users registered at the beginning of 2016[2] or 23% of the all the adult internet users.[3] Twitter's points of differentiation from its competitors remain its real-time 140-character-long updates, the easiness to join the platform and its "public by default" approach to its users' status updates. In terms of usage the platform is very popular with celebrities and entertainers, its top ten most followed users are from this field. A few exceptions are made by @BarackObama, ranking fourth, and @YouTube and @Twitter, ranking fifth and ninth, respectively.[4]

It is often suggested that news breaks on Twitter nowadays,[5] with the London Riots[6] or Osama Bin Laden's death[7] in 2011 being among the popular examples mentioned. Equally, the real-time character limit of its updates make Twitter an appealing second screen[8] platform which enables, among others, the monitoring of sentiment and reaction of people watching[9] or attending[10] an event. Twitter thus emerges as a popular platform and tool with journalists, communicators, politicians and activists, its brevity of updates and ease of use promising not only message control but also access to a wide audience.

It is thus no surprise that Twitter has also received increased attention from researchers in recent years and it is for this open forum character and its potential to coagulate elite or grassroots networks that Twitter makes the focus of this chapter as well.

Holcomb, Gross and Mitchell,[11] for instance, examined how large groups of "elite" journalists are using the medium while Cozma and Chen[12] studied more closely the practices of foreign correspondents. In either case, instead of being a reporting environment, Twitter's use emerges to be promotional, with the journalists pushing their own content and linking to the website of the organisation they are affiliated with. The same promotional, unidirectional use is also noticed by Vergeer, Hermans and Sams,[13] whose analysis of Twitter use by candidates running for the European Parliament in 2009 indicates that politicians reluctantly engage with the medium and when they do, they do it predominantly for electoral campaigning. This is also supported by Lilleker, Tenscher and Stetka's[14] findings according to which political parties are also using the medium as a campaign tool, aimed at increasing visibility of the party policies and positions and obtaining support for their campaigns. Corporations are facing the same challenge. Adi and Grigore's[15] analysis of Pfizer's use of social media including Twitter across their European accounts shows clearly how the channel, although brand consistent and integrated with the company's other digital accounts, is not more than an un-engaging, self-centred mouthpiece for the organization.

Activist groups are no different either. The research carried by Adi into various Occupy groups – from the small scale[16] to the iconic[17] – also point out that activists and protesters too use the medium to promote their own causes. While it can be argued that Twitter provides them with a voice and an opportunity to formulate and share their own perspectives, Adi's research also points out that Occupiers are reaching out to audiences similar to them, preaching thus to the already converted.

This raises numerous questions about the success of the platform, the imagined audiences addressed and their potential of forming a public sphere, its potential to predict user choices and about its true potential for dialogic exchanges, whether between organisations and users or between peers. The research undertaken in these circumstances needs to be audience-focused rather than source/messenger-focused. Additionally, research should focus more on the rules, etiquette and patterns of interaction among users and their effects rather than the strategies to communicate to them.

Colleoni, Royya and Arvidsson[18] suggest that if defined as a social medium, communication among users on Twitter displays an "echo chamber-like structure of communication" which is indicative of a higher level of homophily, "higher homogeneity in interpersonal networks as well as common sense expectations".[19] It is perhaps this higher level of homogeneity that also gives Twitter a predictive potential (after all users follow other users based on their shared interests which in time reveals the formation of issue or interest networks). The analysis of Tumasjan et al.[20] of more than 100,000 tweets "published in the weeks leading up to the federal election of the national parliament in Germany which took place on September 27th, 2009",[21] for instance, reveals that Twitter is not only used extensively for political deliberation but that "the mere number of messages mentioning a party reflects the election result"[22] with the political sentiment reflecting the offline political landscape by displaying a strong correspondence between the messages and the political positions of the parties analysed. If this is the case, one might assume that the frequency of conversations on any topic would help identify public, or depending on the nature of the group, expert opinions and perceptions. It is, therefore, this feature of Twitter that is of interest to the chapter but rather than aiming to identify the potential outcome of a political debate, the aim here is to identify the general discourses about corporate social responsibility (CSR), a topic that has increased in visibility and importance in the past years.

In fact, if one considers the Reputation Institute's[23] seven dimensions of reputation (performance, product/service, innovation, workspace, governance, citizenship and leadership) proposed to calculate an organisation's reputation score, CSR is playing a major role in influencing business success as the dimensions of workspace, governance and citizenship are all featured in CSR definitions. And if CSR is and should be playing such an important role in shaping an organisation's reputation, the questions that thus emerge are "what are Twitter users saying about CSR?" and "who are the CSR promoters, supporters and influencers?". This chapter addresses these questions.

CSR on Twitter and beyond

Communication and reflections of CSR online, especially the use of websites, make the subject of the biggest part of CSR research (see Chaudhri and Wang's[24] analysis of 100 Indian IT companies on how they convey their CSR information via their websites; Basil and Erlandson's[25] analysis of 159 Canadian websites and their declared internal and external CSR activities; and Bravo, Matute, and Pina's[26] banking websites assessment of CSR use as a corporate identity expression vehicle, among others). Some studies however also investigate Twitter. Adi and Grigore's[27] analysis of Pfizer's Twitter use across their European accounts paints a brand consistent presence where the messages shared reflect the company's values. However, overall, the channel is company-focused, un-engaging and push-like; it is a true mouthpiece for the organisation. Low levels of interactivity are also identified by the analysis of Etter, Plotkowiak and Stanoevska-Slabeva[28] of 30 central corporate Twitter accounts, which indicates that organizations use different strategies to communicate that differ in intensity and interactivity of CSR communication. This is

later expanded by Etter[29] to show that low levels of interactivity of online CSR communication are due to a reactive interaction approach and lack of specialization.

> When companies communicate about CSR in Twitter, it is predominantly about the
> topics environment, climate change, and philanthropy, rather than employee relations,
> human rights, or governance. This trend can be explained by the CSR initiatives of
> the companies and the configurations of interest stemming from different institu-
> tional affiliations (Nielsen and Thomsen, 2007). Furthermore, the analysis shows that
> a particular strategy does not favor certain CSR topics. Rather, it is the choice of
> communicated topic rooted in the strategic choice of particular CSR initiatives.[30]

Lee, Oh and Kim's[31] analysis of Fortune 500 companies in the Twitter sphere "reveals that
a higher CSR rating is a strong indicator of an earlier adoption, a faster establishment
of online presence (followers), a higher responsiveness to the firm's identity (replies and
mentions), and a stronger virality of the messages (retweets)". This also shows, they argue,
that socially responsible firms can take advantage of proactive stakeholders' participation
without having to invest further resources into their communication than those already
in place. While this is in line with the findings of Saffer, Sommerfeldt and Taylor[32] (they
suggest that Twitter interactivity influences the quality of organization – public relationships), this also shows that early adoption and inclusion of CSR communication within
the general social media strategy of an organization is necessary. Finally, Colleoni's[33] work
featuring a network analysis of the CSR community investigating the level of reciprocity
and communication dynamics, indicates "that neither the engaging nor the information
strategies lead to alignment" between the communication strategy of the organization
and their CSR agenda. On the contrary, she argues that "the assumption of the more the
dialog, the more the communality seems to fail to portray the complexity of the communicational dynamics".

Current CSR communication research looking at Twitter therefore focuses mainly on
the uses and implications of using the platform by organizations and the strategies (communication or otherwise) that they employ. While valuable and insightful, there is a need
to identify and understand the general depictions and perceptions of CSR and to consider
the dynamics of Twitter as a network shaping them. While looking at the organisation-
specific interests and their broadcasting, reacting and engaging strategies provide researchers with numerous case studies, what is currently under-researched is the prevalent and
publicly accessible association or definition of CSR.

Especially in the case of CSR, Twitter is both an open forum and an elite network. It is
an elite network because practitioners and people aware of the topic would be more likely
to follow it and contribute to it. Equally, it is an open forum because anyone within the
extended networks of the Twitter users sharing messages about CSR could follow or join
these conversations. This can also be done by anyone interested in the acronym. Twitter
thus has the potential to inform practitioners and elites but also influence the perceptions
of the "passers-by". Identifying these perceptions and identifying their source is extremely
important.

Speaking about perceptions and portrayals of CSR, Bhattacharya, Rao and Glynn[34]
suggest that consumers could be willing to support socially responsible companies while
Sen and Bhattacharya[35] and others[36] indicate that CSR can affect consumers' purchase
intentions. This has led businesses, managers and even CEOs to instrumentalise CSR

and undertake the activities that yield higher stakeholder support.[37] The lexical analysis of De Wolf, Mejri and Lamouchi[38] of CEO letters also supports these findings, showing that executives' discourse is not spontaneous but rather stake-driven and generally found to refer to wide subject areas such as economy, environment, ethics and human rights. Benefits to the bottom line are seen among these stakes, as well as links with sustainability. A similar pragmatic approach to CSR is also shared by small business owner-managers.[39] Internally, "employee trust partially mediates the relationship between CSR and employee attitudinal and behavioral outcomes".[40] The two qualitative studies of Hansen et al. show for instance that "employees who perceived their employer to be more socially responsible were less likely to consider leaving the company . . . and more likely to engage in OCB [organizational citizenship behavior]".[41]

While certainly understanding that various groups (from consumers to employees and customers) are important, there is nothing yet in the literature assessing general discourses on CSR in a public and open arena such as Twitter, yet content about CSR is shared daily on Twitter. This chapter aims to address this void. In order to do so, considering the definitions associated with CSR is important as they can provide guidance into the understandings promoted online. The following section provides a brief overview of these definitions.

CSR: definitions and perspectives

"Derided as a joke, an oxymoron and a contradiction in terms by the investment and business community",[42] CSR has become after the 1990s a highly coveted topic, with institutions like the World Bank and the United Nations praising the practice and even promoting their own guidelines. This also resulted in a renewed scholarly interest, with multiple theoretical frameworks interpreting and measuring it emerging; whether stake-holder, leadership, management or resource-based focused,[43] all the definitions and paradigms on CSR being informed by the area of specialism of the investigating scholars.

Corporate social performance (CSP), for instance, provides such a management perspective on CSR, considering economic and public responsibilities as well as the social responsiveness of an organisation. The proposed model of global citizenship (concerned with the way culture influences how an organisation's responsibilities are defined and distributed[44]) also encompasses management views. So does the concept of ecological citizenship proposed by Crane, Matten and Moon, which focuses mostly on the collective responsibilities resulting from the relationship between globalization, environmental issues and the new cosmopolitanism.[45] Corporate citizenship (CC),[46] on the other hand, is seen both in management and political sciences approach literature; two limited views of CC equate it wither with strategic philanthropy or with CSR. Matten and Crane,[47] however, proposed an extended perspective on CC which "exposes the element of 'citizenship' and conceptualizes CC as the administration of a bundle of individual citizenship rights – social, civil and political – conventionally granted and protected by governments".

The environmental perspective on CSR is strongly represented by the concept of corporate sustainability. Managers and businesses seeking to apply the concept are recommended to satisfy six criteria: eco- and socio-efficiency, eco- and socio-effectiveness, sufficiency and ecological equity.[48] Linked to it is the concept of the triple bottom line, an accounting framework also referred to as "people, planet and profits" which incorporates social, environmental and financial dimensions of performance.[49]

More recently, a marketing perspective is brought forward with the 3C-SR model proposed by Meehan, Meehan & Richards.[50] The 3Cs: commitments (ethical and social), connections (with partners in the value network) and consistency (of behaviour over time) are explained by the authors to be essential in building successful CSR programmes.

Regardless of the perspective however, CSR is outlined in broad terms as integral to the relationship between business and society. The definitions thus proposed focus on the impact of CSR on business: whether

> social (reflecting the relationship between businesses and society), environmental (focusing on the impact and/or contribution of businesses on the natural environment), economic (referring to the socio-economic or financial aspects of a business including the description of CSR in terms of a business operation), stakeholder and voluntariness (reflecting and voluntarily abiding to ethical principles which span beyond the legal obligations).[51]

Yet, with so many definitions proposed by scholars and practitioners, the question of how CSR is portrayed on Twitter, an open forum and elite network at the same time, is fundamental. This would help potentially understand the public perceptions or misconceptions about CSR and thus provide both scholars and practitioners with a benchmark and a point of reference for their future discussions and analyses about the practice, its communication or impact.

Methodology

This chapter aims to answer two questions: "what are Twitter users saying about CSR" and "who are the CSR promoters, supporters and influencers".

In order to capture these narratives, Socioviz,[52] an online platform enabling the collection and visualisation of up to 5,000 tweets based on given search criteria, was used to collect the data.

The search criteria input into Socioviz's search engine was "#CSR". Chang defined hashtags as a "bottom-up user proposed tagging convention" that "embodies user participation in the process of hashtag innovation, especially as it pertains to information organization tasks".[53] They are one of Twitter's communication norms, helping capture the boundary between individual and collective discourses as well as between formal and informal ones.[54] Moreover, the use of hashtags enables users to incorporate their posts into an ongoing global discussion which can either be perceived as self-promotion[55] or as a demonstration of solidarity.[56] Hashtags also enable users to join topic-focused and sometimes live conversations[57] which Highfield[58] classifies as "issue publics" and Cook et al. describe as "more passionate users producing seemingly higher quality tweets".[59]

The collection of tweets with the hashtag narrowed the search and ensured that the messages thus captured were meant to the associated with the topic.

The data was collected in three different periods: 23–29 August 2015, 14–21 December 2015 and 23–29 January 2016 aiming thus to capture a wider time span of messages linked to the topic. The 15,000 tweets[60] thus collected were analysed using first Socioviz's automatically reported hashtag frequencies, the most active and most influential accounts as well as user network visualisation and hashtag network visualisation. These were used as entry points into the data as a means to identify conceptual associations with the CSR hashtag as well as identify those driving and shaping the Twitter discussion about CSR. These hashtag frequencies will help answer the first research question. This is also what Adi[61] did in her analysis of "#publicrelations" tweets as a means to identify general perceptions about public relations on Twitter, thus establishing a precedent for the method.

In order to confirm the emerging themes suggested by the hashtag frequency and its exploration, a combination of Wordle's[62] most frequent words summary and an in-depth keyword search within each dataset was then performed, similar to what Grigore, Adi and Theofilou[63] used in their analysis of online digital reflections of pharmaceutical companies.

To answer the second research question, an analysis of the most active and the most influential accounts repeatedly featuring in the top ten of the three weeks analysed was conducted. This included Foller.me's[64] last 100 tweets activity summary reports which were collected on 22 February 2016. Foller.me, a free analytics platform, has previously been used identify specific Twitter accounts activity, interests and level of interaction (whether promotional and self-referential or engaging and dialogical) by Adi and Moloney[65] and more recently Adi[66] in their analyses of Occupy.

Results

#CSR emerging narratives: sustainability (RQ1)

From the 15,000 tweets collected on #csr, more than a quarter are retweets (1383 in August, 1259 in December and 1262 in January) meaning that the dataset contains multiple duplicated data points. While the value of retweets is generally still being debated, whether they show interest, support, agreement or endorsement, the fact that one in four tweets is being repeated shows to a degree interaction and engagement with the content.

Table 6.2.1 shows the top ten most used hashtags associated with the data collected. The presence of #csr as the top most used hashtag is not surprising, as it is this hashtag that has been used as a search term to collect the data. This is also confirmed by a word frequency analysis of the entire dataset, with Table 6.2.2 capturing the most frequent words (not only hashtags) as identified by Wordle and thus showing that not only is the hashtag often used but that also the content of the tweets makes direct reference to CSR. Based on these frequencies, it can be assumed that the content shared is directly related to sustainability, environmental/green conversations or job search and/or promotion. Associations with

Table 6.2.1 Top ten most used hashtags associated with #CSR on Twitter

	23–29 August 2015	14–21 December 2015	23–29 January 2016
1	csr (5021)	csr (5013)	csr (5028)
2	sustainability (913)	medical (623)	sustainability (676)
3	green (413)	sustainability (580)	green (206)
4	jobs (210)	customer (345)	tweetmyjobs (199)
5	susty (130)	green (267)	rse (110)
6	seasonal (102)	jobsinuk (137)	earthtweet (107)
7	socialresponsibility (91)	imhiring (135)	esg (89)
8	esg (86)	jobs (126)	sustainable (80)
9	job (76)	socent (83)	earth (76)
10	business (76)	sales (82)	charity (69)

Table 6.2.2 Most frequent words within the #CSR dataset

	23–29 August 2015	14–21 December 2015	23–29 January 2016
1	csr (4966)	csr (5042)	csr (4950)
2	RT (3553)	RT (3106)	RT (3130)
3	sustainability (1012)	apply (733)	sustainability (799)
4	green (410)	customer (705)	corporate (367)
5	social (359)	sustainability (654)	business (326)
6	corporate (239)	medical (652)	social (296)
7	jobs (216)	service (620)	responsibility (256)
8	business (193)	green (341)	apply (221)
9	help (184)	getajobusa (292)	green (218)
10	@caelusgreenroom (177)	hiring (258)	tweetmyjobs (199)

charity and business also emerge, however, these are considerably less frequent within the dataset. These frequencies thus suggest that messages shared are most often depicting notions of corporate sustainability and only in a very small number refer to the limited concept of strategic philanthropy (the narrow and insufficient depiction of CC according to Matten and Crane).

A deeper exploration of the data shows that when used on its own, #CSR is generally associated either with self-promotional content or with shared articles including advice and guidelines. This, to a degree, reflects what Xifra and Grau[67] found out in their analysis of 653 tweets about public relations that Twitter is "a good tool for disseminating information about experiences, case studies, ideas and theoretical approaches".[68]

> #CSR Skills: What you need and why. Not your traditional list! https://t.co/dSGDph CeBP https://t.co/B14nG6jac1 (@ZINGmore, 29.01.2016)
>
> This will impact #CSR reporting no doubt. . . . Obama Moves to Expand Rules Aimed at Closing Gender Pay Gap https://t.co/upC2W3MLdP (@matthewtgard ner, 29.01.2016)
>
> How Smart Companies Build Relationships with Millennial Audiences in 2016 (hint: #CSR): https://t.co/ZcfVnCm05S (@Garrett_H, 21.12. 2015)
>
> #CSR Webinar: Building Better Movements to Create Greater Impact | Jan 14 11am PST | https://t.co/N2BxkZ7mV8 (@ManausCSR, 19.12.2015)
>
> Focused on five priorities, our #CSR report outlines our moves for positive global impact: https://t.co/tZu1DN2jbP (@CiscoCSR, 19.12.2015)
>
> Meeting in Nicaragua with Community Relations group of large Guatemalan Holding company to design Community involvement strategy #CSR (@Celinapt, 28.08.2015)

However, most of the time, the hashtag is used concomitantly with others showing variety in how users approach and classify the content they share.

Considering portrayals and perceptions of CSR, hashtags such as #sustainability, #susty (sustainability), #green, #socialresponsibility, #charity, and #esg (environment, social and governance) all reflect elements associated with definitions of CSR. While charity is generally associated with philanthropy and is usually linked with the first understandings of CSR[69] and later reworked into the narrow and incomplete understanding of CC, sustainability, governance and environmentally conscious initiatives (green) are more recent additions. Unlike philanthropy, these last concepts are resonating with the principles promoted by the European Union's definitions of CSR[70] as well those promoted by the UN Global Compact initiative.[71] Additionally, sustainability and green associated hashtags, besides being testimony to a user base that is knowledgeable about the subject, show a preference for the triple bottom line framework. This confirms the earlier assumption that Twitter users are aware of and give preference to the concepts of corporate sustainability and environmental citizenship. However, comparing the references to people, planet, profits and other conceptualisations within the tweets recorded with the full proposals of both the EU and the UN Global Compact (includes financial markets, supply chain and governance, sustainable development, the environment, value chain and customer and local communities) the approach included here is much narrower and thus very limiting.

Around a fifth of the messages shared every month are linked with sustainability hashtags, whether #sustainability, #esg, #susty or others. When used only in relation with #CSR, the tweets are sharing information about new reports releases, tips on measurement and strategy improvement, industry news, positions on CSR approaches such as CC or triple bottom line. Moreover, many of the tweets using both #sustainability and #csr are shared by @greeneconpost, the account of *Green Economy Post*, "a blog portal that provides (. . .) green business and career information, news and commentary" based in the Greater Seattle area[72]:

> 2015 Review: Europe – Driving change https://t.co/Yku8txWtPZ #CSR #sustainability (@Ethical_Corp, 21.12.2015)
> Automakers Beat Emissions Standards for Third Straight Year https://t.co/VSZHxhGpkD #sustainability #csr (@greeneconpost, 21.12.2015)
> 3p Weekend: The Foodie's Travel Guide to the World's Most Sustainable Restaurants http://t.co/T5CjIOV4wu #sustainability #csr (@greeneconpost, 28.08.2015)
> Oregon Occupation Update: Multiple Arrests, One Fatality https://t.co/wL3CRgr2jQ #sustainability #csr (@greeneconpost, 27.01.2016)

#susty and #esg are also used together and they too have a user that promotes them more often: @iioannoulbs, a professor of strategy at the London Business School who explores "whether, how, and the extent to which the modern business organization contributes towards building a #sustainable future".[73]

#green is also at times associated with #sustainability and #csr. In the December and January datasets, for instance, the tweets containing all three hashtags are often originating from @CaelusGreenRoom and include a link to the caelusgreenroom website which aims to share "#green, #sustainability and #csr news, videos and discussion".[74]

> Easy Ways to Be Eco-Friendly at Work – #green #sustainability #csr https://t.co/5QM4NABIhj (@CaelusGreenRoom, 19.12.2015)
> Aligned Data Centers Introduces the First Pay-for-Use Data Center – #green #sustainability #csr http://t.co/mXmSqQQH74 (@CaelusGreenRoom, 28.08.2015)
> Analysts' recommendations much less negative for firms with high #CSR scores https://t.co/4uRvV7nX5G #susty #esg #sri @LBS (@iioannoulbs, 20.12.2015)
> In countries with a credit-based financial model, firms score lower on social performance https://t.co/Oi9NQ8kzkJ #csr #susty @LBS (@iioannoulbs, 27.01.2016)

This indicates that certain hashtags are user specific (whether these users are influential will be discussed later in this chapter). Each user prefers a combination of hashtags for their tweets. These combinations of keywords not only become synonymous with a user but they capture their view and definition of CSR. I would argue that @greenpost and @caelusgreenroom's approach to CSR is closer to that of corporate sustainability while @iioannoulbs's is closer to the conceptualizations of CC.

The charity hashtag is present in the top ten most frequent hashtags only in January, although it is present in the other datasets too, but is less frequently used. In all cases, the hashtag is associated with other hashtags such as volunteering, employee engagement or team building which take its meaning beyond its basic philanthropy meaning and bring it closer to the conceptualisations of global citizenship and creating shared value:

> Great article on Employee Volunteering and Giving Programs! – https://t.co/ K0PkV95w3f #EmployeeEngagement, #charity, #CSR (@we2o_, 28.01.2016)
>
> #teambuilding2016 #eventprofs Innovative ways to engage and motivate teams AND support #CSR goals #charitybikebuild https://t.co/zq4p9QuOCH (@O3engage, 27.01.2016)

Tweets using the charity hashtag also include shared materials praising the value and impact of CSR or, at times, recognising partnerships and collaborations.

> @Cowgills @BLGCofficial 2016 patrons certificate has arrived! Proud to support you again #CSR #charity #Bolton https://t.co/wEAxLHUiIB (@Cowgills, 29.01.2016)
>
> Running a #CSR, #charity or #philanthropy project? Manage your #socialvalue with myGVE! https://t.co/XtKQned5Rg https://t.co/HBQyYM8LPQ (@Global ValEx, 28.01.2016)
>
> How involvement with a #charity can make you better at your job! Raising morale and providing a new perspective #CSR https://t.co/qPAQyFpPTF (@alicelamb84, 28.01.2016)
>
> We thank Mr. Yuji Nakata & @konicaminolta for their encouragement & support to us.
>
> #EducationMatters #charity #CSR https://t.co/Hd8m0hukmW (@smilefounda tion, 27.01.2016)

Overall, #CSR on Twitter is a hashtag using a specialised vocabulary seemingly addressing a professional, specialist audience. The messages are informational and at times promotional. This combination is typical for Twitter. The portrayals of CSR indicate a preference for the concept of corporate sustainability followed by that of CC. In fact, views of citizenship (whether corporate, environmental or global) are mostly portrayed in these tweets, other models and definitions (such as creating shared value, 3C-SR described in an earlier section) being almost inexistent from these online narratives. Such approaches portray CSR in the service of businesses and their interest, rather than consider the contribution and responsibility of corporations towards communities in particular and society as a whole. To this deficient image of CSR contributes a small group of users who consistently use the same hashtag associations (green, sustainability, esg) as if aiming to be identified with them or aiming to establish these associations within their networks.

#CSR emerging narratives: job search and the confusing acronym (RQ1)

The dataset also reveals a high concentration of job-related messages, around 5–10% in each 5,000-tweet batch. Although not as high as in Adi's[75] findings about #publicrelations shared content on Twitter, where 15% of the tweets were job related, this confirms that Twitter is used by professionals as a recruitment platform. The hashtags recorded vary from month to month (from #jobs and #job in August to #jobsinuk, #tweetmyjobs or #imhiring in December and January):

> #Seasonal #CSR [Part-Time] needed in #Nashville at David's Bridal. Apply now! #jobs http://t.co/POWqJm7u3Z http://t.co/y9EmKZM8PK (@NeuvooPTPit, 29.08.2015)
>
> New #job: Manager, Code of Conduct, London https://t.co/IBbgbzv873 #jobs #greenjobs #csr (@acre, 29.01.2016)

The job postings however also reveal a confusing use of #csr, where the acronym stands for "customer service representative" rather than "corporate social responsibility". Most of these tweets originate from the United States and have as a source recruitment agencies. This also explains the presence of #medical and #customer hashtags in the December dataset; all messages including these hashtags were recruitment focused:

> #Customer Service Representative – Bilingual Dallas – ##CSR #Medical Apply: https://t.co/yqX9Npu8Tw (@GetAJobUSA, 21.12.2015)
>
> #Customer Support Lead San Francisco – ##CSR #Medical #SanFrancisco Apply: https://t.co/iK4erz53BB (@GetAJobUSA, 21.12.2015)

While this clearly shows the disadvantage acronym-based hashtags present – the same letters can be a codification for multiple phrases – it can also indicate a lack of awareness on the recruiters' part for what CSR stands.

> #Immediate #Job Opening in #Austin TX! #Customer Service Representative for #SouthAustin Office #ApplyNow http://t.co/Ld5r55G2Hf #CSR #Jobs (@Int HumanCapital, 29.08.2015)
>
> Apply to this job: Customer Service Representative in Ann Arbor, MI https://t.co/DfJX1cJ83q #job #csr (@variantpartners, 27.01.2016)
>
> #Customer Service Representative #CSR – #CSR #CSRJobss #MO #TweetMy Jobs Apply: https://t.co/sF0Z57NS6m (@ChaiberiaJobs, 28.01.2016)

This however cannot be assumed about @GetAJobUSA, as their messages, although containing #CSR, also include the type of job recruited for: teller, dispatcher, appointment manager.

CSR influencers: between academia and CSR portals (RQ2)

According to Socioviz, an active account is one that shares information very frequently, whereas an influential account is one that receives a higher number of retweets and mentions.

Table 6.2.3 provides an overview of what the most active and most influential accounts are within the three datasets, the usernames in bold letters being those that repeatedly make it in the top. While the presence of other accounts shows that conversation and attention on Twitter vary at different times and thus confirms the dynamism of the platform, the presence of common accounts reveals the existence of users who not only identify with the hashtag but consistently and strategically use it in their tweets. These are: @csr_rt, @csrwire, @caelusgreenroom, @redmond_ted and @triplepundit. Out of these five, four are associated with online publications (so specialist media) or news aggregators dedicated to CSR, and only one is a personal account. @redmond_ted's account, "husband (PartNerd), father, architect, amateur photographer, social entrepreneur, weight lifting enthusiastic, proud geek, dreamer tweeting @bluedotregister"[76] is also the youngest Twitter account with the smallest network (see Table 6.2.3).

Interestingly, out of the four media outlets, @csr_rt is the only one based in Germany and linked with a public relations' practitioner account; @csrwire, @caelusgreenroom and @triplepundit are all US-based but declare a "global" location. This could potentially suggest a difference in both awareness and perception: CSR is better known and more spoken of in the United States, yet associated with sustainability and environmental protection, whereas CSR in Europe is associated with the strategic practice of public relations. Equally, this can also show that the US-based publications are also aiming to reach a global audience, hence the listing of their location in this way. Of course, language differences should also be considered. This chapter relies on an English language dataset, so other languages referring to corporate social responsibility might not be included.

With regards to frequency of posting, @csr_rt is undeniably the most active account, occupying the first position in all three datasets, with 1637 tweets in August, 1526 tweets in December and 1579 tweets in January or around 30% of the entire dataset. However, the account's entire activity is based on retweeting messages containing the #csr hashtag, making it highly active but also unidirectional and non-interactive. Even in these circumstances, the account still makes it among the most influential list, a small percentage of its content being itself retweeted by its followers.

@csr_rt, @caelusgreenroom and @triplepundit are recorded as both most active and influential accounts by Socioviz. Observing their activity captured in Table 6.2.4, it can be concluded that high frequency of activity leads to high visibility and in turn to higher influence. After all, both @csr_rt and @triplepundit have relatively low follower numbers compared to the amount of information they share.

Influence however does not necessarily have to be linked with an account's ability to reach out and connect to other users, whether by mentioning them or replying to them. As seen in Table 6.2.4, all media accounts display very high numbers of mentions in their tweets (anywhere from 99/100 in the case of @redmond_ted to 56/100 in the case of @csrwire; @csr_rt has no mention at all in its messages). Similarly, all accounts display very low conversation rates, from no replies at all in @csr_rt's tweets to 13/100 from @caelusgreenroom. This lack of conversation and interactivity and high level of sharing of information mirrors Adi's[77] findings about #publicrelations. While the content shared about #csr is less self-serving than that about public relations, the influential users' activity is still generally one-way and non-conversational. Twitter's brevity of its messages could render the platform less prone to fruitful conversation and dialogue and more suited for information pushing: the unidirectional sharing of content without the expectation of a response. This could, in part, explain the influential users' observed communication

Table 6.2.3 Top ten most active and most influential users #CSR on Twitter (data obtained from Socioviz)

	23–29 August 2015		14–21 December 2015		23–29 January 2016	
	Most active	Most influential	Most active	Most influential	Most active	Most influential
1	**@csr_rt**	@westjet	**@csr_rt**	**@triplepundit**	**@csr_rt**	**@csr_rt**
2	**@csrwire**	@flyclopedia	@getajobusa	**@csr_rt**	@tribesovereign3	**@triplepundit**
3	@paneendrabellur	@elainecohen	@lilmsmatchmaker	@theofficialsbi	@chaiberiajobs	**@caelusgreenroom**
4	@stapietrend	@amansinghcsr	**@csrwire**	**@caelusgreenroom**	@csrgood	@forbes
5	**@caelusgreenroom**	@leokaye	**@redmond_ted**	**@csrwire**	@iristandards	**@csrwire**
6	**@redmond_ted**	@csrtist	**@caelusgreenroom**	@wrdiamonds	**@caelusgreenroom**	@svenmul
7	@remarkablemag	@davestangis	**@triplepundit**	@ahambhumika	@nancylevine	@tiffanyandco
8	@csrpictures	@drmeyer1	@ughtechjobs	@leokaye	**@triplepundit**	@sust_train
9	@srasia2015	@walidmichael	@csrpictures	@lbs	**@redmond_ted**	@justmeans
10	@togovern		@atah442	@ioannoulbs	@greeneconpost	@ethical_corp

Note: Recurrent accounts appear in bold.

Table 6.2.4 Top influentials and most active using #csr. Data captured with Foller.me on 22 February 2015.

Account	Year created	Tweets	Followers	Following	Replies	Tweets with @ mentions	Tweets with #	RTs by the account	Tweets with links	Tweets with media
@CSR_RT	2011	401,289	5,141	50	0/100	0/100	97/100	100/100	73/100	28/100
@CSRWire	2008	86,709	44,167	4,704	8/100	56/100	77/100	5/100	79/100	4/100
@Caelusgreenroom	2011	19,627	55,316	31,807	13/100	66/100	100/100	21/100	100/100	0/100
@Triplepundit	2008	92,878	40,469	896	1/100	98/100	86/100	35/100	99/100	0/100
@Redmond_Ted	2014	15,900	525	387	0/100	99/100	96/100	96/100	99/100	0/100

patterns. However, as the status provided to influentials goes beyond that of "pushing relevant information" and more towards inspirational people and role models, there is an unspoken expectation that these accounts should engage with others in a dialogical manner and through engaging exchanges.

Speaking of influence, Socioviz's recorded top ten influencers in every dataset presents a mixture of consultants (@amansinghcsr), NGOs (@ahambhumika), media (@forbes) and academics (@lbs, @iioannou). However, the recurrence of only a small number of accounts within this list brings questions both about maintaining visibility on Twitter as well as about achieving the influential status. For instance, @iioannou needed only 19 retweets and mentions to qualify on this list yet each dataset records around 1,000 tweets being shared daily using the hashtag.

Conclusions: diminishing CSR

As previous studies show, Twitter is a platform suitable for information dissemination as both Xifra and Grau and Adi indicate in their conclusions. #CSR tweets include information relevant to the profession and the field, oftentimes reiterated, repeated and repackaged showing that there is interest in the topic but perhaps not as much initiative. Twitter's setup is in part responsible for this outcome: in its ultra-fast-paced information refresh rate, retweeting content is much easier and faster than generating original material.

This chapter reveals that the CSR hashtag is mostly associated with #sustainability, #green and #jobs. This also shows that wider approaches to CSR such as shared value or global citizenship (which posit CSR at the service of society and as a wider responsibility of organisations of any kind towards multiple stakeholders, including their employees) receive far less attention and support than the triple bottom line approach: people, planet, profit. It is, of course, valuable that Twitter users have access to information that shares, debates and discusses sustainability, but this limits the scope and application of CSR. Moreover, this misleads users into associating CSR with a profit enhancing and environment-saving (or maybe just greenwashing) practices. If considering these frequent portrayals as the most visible narratives and associations of CSR, then businesses and consultants on Twitter either are unaware of the wider concepts of CSR proposed by academia, the EU or the UN Global Compact, have difficulty in grasping them or have no interest in doing so. This therefore points to a need for these promoters to be more active on Twitter and to moderate more often and more frequently discussions about CSR, where the concepts of social responsibility (as in what is responsibility, towards whom, who and what is social, can businesses perhaps be designed considering social, environmental responsibilities first and then profits) are clarified and where measurable and applicable measures of CSR practice, impact and communication are identified.

From a research perspective, further studies could use quantitative content analysis and link the content of CSR tweets with existing CSR definitions, helping thus confirm whether indeed the Twittersphere favours truly one approach over the others.

In comparison with Adi's study, the job-related posts are not related to corporate social responsibility but rather with customer service representatives. This highlights once more Twitter's embedded challenge for its users: the brevity of its message size forces users into using acronyms, some of which will stand for more than one combination of words.

This dataset also included company generated messages but compared to Adi's #publicrelations's research these are less self-serving. Research into CSR communication undertaken by organisations reviewed in this chapter indicates that there are low levels of interactivity, lack of specialisation and high levels of reactivity rather than proactivity. This is certainly indirectly confirmed by this dataset: the fact that corporations do not consistently use the #CSR hashtag means they fail to label their messages referring to these activities. As such, not only are they missing an opportunity to be visible, but they are also failing to inscribe their messages into the wider discourse of socially responsible practices. Further research could also revisit this dataset to identify whether and, if so which corporations and consultancies are using the #CSR hashtag and then further analyse their Twitter activity. This would bring together the research of general narratives on Twitter carried out here with that of organisation-specific communication.

Finally, this chapter also shows that some of the most active accounts are also among the most influential ones. This suggests that frequency could be a strong predictor of influence; however, further studies and different methodologies should be used to explore this potential. The chapter also shows that there are some differences between the most influential accounts (those referred to the most) and the most active accounts (those sharing the most information), beyond their activity type. The top three most influential accounts are generally affiliated with individuals acting as consultants or representing their consultancies; they are conversational and equally discuss and share matters related to CSR or sustainability. The top most active accounts, however, are generally automated and run by agencies or consultants and only retweet information. This confirms Adi's findings that messages on Twitter are non-conversational; however. unlike her findings, the CSR hashtag messages do seem to contribute to the advancement of the profession, its standards or its associated research. Further analysis into this or related datasets could help confirm this.

Notes

1 Facebook, WhatsApp and Facebook Messenger occupy the first, second and fourth position in this ranking.
2 Statista.com. (2016). *Leading Social Networks Worldwide as of January 2016, Ranked by Number of Active Users (in Millions)*. Available from: www.statista.com/statistics/272014/global-social-networks-ranked-by-number-of-users/ [Accessed 15 March 2016]
3 Duggan, M., Ellison, N. B., Lampe, C., Lenhart, A. and Madden, M. (2014) Demographics of Key Social Networking Platforms. *Pew Internet*. Available from: www.pewinternet.org/2015/01/09/demographics-of-key-social-networking-platforms-2/. [Accessed 3 July 2015].
4 Twittercounter.com (2016). *Twitter Top 100 Most Followers*. Available from: http://twittercounter.com/pages/100?utm_expid=102679131-70.Cf2Z6uGtR42NAFBYKQT74A.0andutm_referrer=https%3A%2F%2Fwww.google.de%2F [Accessed 16 March 2016].
5 Sakaki, T., Okazaki, M., and Matsuo, Y. (2010, April). Earthquake shakes Twitter users: real-time event detection by social sensors. In *Proceedings of the 19th International Conference on World Wide Web* (pp. 851–860). New York: ACM. Available from: http://www.ra.ethz.ch/CDStore/www2010/www/p851.pdf
6 Vis, F. (2013). Twitter as a reporting tool for breaking news: Journalists tweeting the 2011 UK riots. *Digital Journalism*, 1(1), 27–47.
7 Shedden, D. (2015). Today in Media History: In 2011, Twitter Broke the News of Osama Bin Laden's death. *Poynter.com*. Available from: www.poynter.org/2015/today-in-media-history-in-2011-twitter-broke-the-news-of-osama-bin-ladens-death/340913/ [Accessed 16 March 2016].
8 Giglietto, F., and Selva, D. (2014). Second screen and participation: A content analysis on a full season dataset of tweets. *Journal of Communication*, 64(2), 260–277.
9 Highfield, T., Harrington, S., and Bruns, A. (2013). Twitter as a technology for audiencing and fandom: The #Eurovision phenomenon. *Information, Communication and Society*, 16(3), 315–339.
10 Zhao, S., Zhong, L., Wickramasuriya, J. and Vasudevan, V. (2011). Analyzing twitter for social tv: Sentiment extraction for sports. In *Proceedings of the 2nd International Workshop on Future of Television*

(Vol. 2, pp. 11–18). Available from: https://pdfs.semanticscholar.org/d99c/21adb61a5d080e4de3b5 2a4d1c01fc4719e0.pdf

11 Holcomb, J., Gross, K., and Mitchell, A. (2011). *How Mainstream Media Outlets Use Twitter: Content Analysis Shows Evolving Relationship.* The Project for Excellence in Journalism, Pew Research Center. www.journalism.org/node/27311.

12 Cozma, R., and Chen, Kuan-Ju. (2012). "What's in a Tweet? Foreign Correspondents' Use of Social Media." *Journalism Practice*, 7(1), 33–46. doi:10.1080/17512786.2012.683340.

13 Vergeer, M., Hermans, L., and Sams, S. (2013). Online social networks and micro-blogging in political campaigning: The exploration of a new campaign tool and a new campaign style. *Party Politics*, 19(3), 477–501.

14 Lilleker, D. G., Tenscher, J., and Stetka, V. (2015). Towards hypermedia campaigning? Perceptions of new media's importance for campaigning by party strategists in comparative perspective. *Information, Communication and Society*, 18(7), 747–765.

15 Adi, A., and Grigore, G. (2015). Communicating CSR on social media – the case of Pfizer's social media communications in Europe. In A. Adi, G. Grigore, and D. Crowther (Eds.), *Corporate social responsibility in the digital age.* Emerald Group Publishing Limited.

16 Adi, A. and Moloney, K. (2012). The importance of scale in Occupy movement protests: A case study of a local Occupy protest as a tool of communication through Public Relations and Social Media. *Revista Internacional de Relaciones Publicas*, 4(II), 97–12.

17 Adi, A. (2015). Occupy PR: An analysis of online media communications of Occupy Wall Street and Occupy London. *Public Relations Review*, 41(4), 508–514.

18 Colleoni, E., Rozza, A., and Arvidsson, A. (2014). Echo chamber or public sphere? Predicting political orientation and measuring political homophily in Twitter using big data. *Journal of Communication*, 64(2), 317–332. Available from: http://tecjor.net/images/4/49/Echo_Chamber_or_Public_Sphere_Predicting_Political_Orientation_and_Measuring_Political.pdf [Accessed 20 March 2016].

19 Colleoni et al, op. cit., p. 328.

20 Tumasjan, A., Sprenger, T. O., Sandner, P. G., and Welpe, I. M. (2010). Predicting elections with Twitter: What 140 characters reveal about political sentiment. *ICWSM*, 10, 178–185. Available from: www.aaai.org/ocs/index.php/ICWSM/ICWSM10/paper/viewFile/1441/1852Predicting [Accessed 20 March 2016].

21 Tumasjan et al., op. cit., p. 178.

22 *Ibid.*

23 Reputation Institute (2016). *The Global RepTrak® 100: The World's Most Reputable Companies.* Available at: www.reputationinstitute.com/research/Global-RepTrak-100. Retrieved April 5, 2016.

24 Chaudhri, V., and Wang, J. (2007). Communicating corporate social responsibility on the internet: A case study of the top 100 information technology companies in India. *Management Communications Quarterly*, 21, 232–247.

25 Basil, D. Z., and Erlandson, J. (2008). Corporate social responsibility website representations: A longitudinal study of internal and external self-presentations. *Journal of Marketing Communications*, 14(2), 125–137.

26 Bravo, R., Matute, J., and Pina, J. M. (2011). Corporate social responsibility as a vehicle to reveal the corporate identity: A study focused on the websites of Spanish financial entities. *Journal of Business Ethics*, 107, 129–146.

27 Adi and Grigore, op. cit.

28 Etter, M., Plotkowiak, T., and Stanoevska-Slabeva, K. (2011). CSR communication strategies for Twitter: Microblogging as a tool for public relations. In *61st Annual Conference of the International Communication Association (ICA) 2011. Boston, MA.* Retrieved April 3, 2012.

29 Etter, M. (2014). Broadcasting, reacting, engaging – three strategies for CSR communication in Twitter, *Journal of Communication Management*, 18(4), 322–342.

30 Etter, op. cit.

31 Lee, K., Oh, W.Y., and Kim, N. (2013). Social media for socially responsible firms: Analysis of fortune 500's Twitter profiles and their CSR/CSIR ratings. *Journal of Business Ethics*, 118(4), 791–806.

32 Saffer, A. J., Sommerfeldt, E. J., and Taylor, M. (2013). The effects of organizational Twitter interactivity on organization – public relationships. *Public Relations Review*, 39(3), 213–215.

33 Colleoni, E. (2013). CSR communication strategies for organizational legitimacy in social media. *Corporate Communications: An International Journal*, 18(2), 228–248.

34 Bhattacharya, C. B., Hayagreeva, R., and Ann, G. M. (1995). Understanding the bond of identification: An investigation of its correlates among art museum members. *Journal of Marketing, 59*(October), 46–57.

35 Sankar, S., and Bhattacharya C. B. (2001). Does doing good always lead to doing better? Consumer reactions to corporate social responsibility. *Journal of Marketing Research, 38*, 225–243.

36 Swaen, V. (2003). Consumers' perceptions, evaluations and reactions to CSR activities. *Online Posting, 7.*

37 Sankar and Bhattacharya, op. cit., pp. 225–243.

38 De Wolf, D., Mejri, M., and Lamouchi, R. (2012). How do multi-national corporations CEOs perceive and communicate about social responsibility. *Journal of Finance and Accounting, 3*(1), 18–34.

39 Fassin, Y., Van Rossem, A., and Buelens, M. (2011). Small-business owner-managers' perceptions of business ethics and CSR-related concepts. *Journal of Business ethics, 98*(3), 425–453.

40 Pa Hansen, S. D., Dunford, B. B., Boss, A. D., Boss, R. W., and Angermeier, I. (2011). Corporate social responsibility and the benefits of employee trust: A cross-disciplinary perspective. *Journal of Business Ethics, 102*(1), 29–45.

41 Ibid, p. 41.

42 Paul Lee, M.-D. (2008). A review of the theories of corporate social responsibility: Its evolutionary path and the road ahead. *International Journal of Management Reviews, 10*(1), 53–73.

43 McWilliams, A., Siegel, D. S., and Wright, P. M. (2006). Guest editors' introduction: Corporate social responsibility: Strategic implications. *Journal of Management Studies, 43*(1), 1–18.

44 Crisan, C., and Adi, A. (2016). A new paradigm: How social movements shape corporate social responsibility after the financial crisis. In T. Theofilou, G. Grigore, and A. Stancu (Eds.), *Corporate social responsibility in the post-financial crisis era. CSR conceptualisations and international practices in times of uncertainty*. London, UK: Palgrave Macmillan.

45 Crane, A., Matten, D., and Moon, J. (2008). Ecological citizenship and the corporation: Politicizing the new corporate environmentalism. *Organization and Environment.*

46 Crane, A., Dirk, M. and Moon, J. (2008). *Corporations and citizenship*. Cambridge: Cambridge University Press.

47 Matten, D., and Crane, A. (2005). Corporate citizenship: Toward an extended theoretical conceptualization. *Academy of Management Review, 30*(1), 166–179, p. 1.

48 Dyllick, T., and Hockerts, K. (2002). Beyond the business case for corporate sustainability. *Business Strategy and the Environment, 11*(2), 130–141.

49 Slapper, T. H., and Hall, T. J. (2011). The triple bottom line: What is it and how does it work? *Indiana Business Review, 4*–8, Available from: www.ibrc.indiana.edu/ibr/2011/spring/pdfs/article2.pdf. [Accessed 22 August 2016].

50 Meehan, J., Meehan, K., and Richards, A. (2006). Corporate social responsibility: The 3C-SR model. *International Journal of Social Economics, 33*(5/6), 386–398.

51 Dahlsrud, A. (2008) cited in Adi, A., Crowther, D., and Grigore, G. (2015). Introduction to corporate social responsibility in the digital age. In A. Adi, G. Grigore and D. Crowther (Eds.), *Corporate social responsibility in the digital age* (p. 2). Emerald Group Publishing Limited.

52 Socioviz is available at http://socioviz.net/SNA/eu/sna/login.jsp

53 Chang, H-C. (2010). A new perspective on Twitter Hashtag use: Diffusion of innovation theory. *ASIST 2010*, October 22–27, Pittsburgh, PA, p. 1.

54 Gibbs, M., Meese, J., Arnold, M., Nansen, B., and Carter, M. (2015). #Funeral and Instagram: death, social media, and platform vernacular. *Information, Communication and Society, 18*, 1468–4462.

55 Halpern, D., Valenzuela, S., and Katz, J. E. (2016). "Selfie-ists" or "Narci-selfiers"? A cross-lagged panel analysis of selfie taking and narcissism. *Personality and Individual Differences, 97*, 98–101.

56 Zappavigna, M. (2015). Searchable talk: The linguistic functions of hashtags. *Social Semiotics, 25*, 274–291.

57 This is the case of Twitter chats or event hashtags.

58 Highfield, T. (2012). Talking of many things: Using topical networks to study discussions in social media. *Journal of Technology in Human Services, 30*(3–4), 204–218.

59 Cook, J., Kenthapadi, K., and Mishra, N. (2013). Group Chats on Twitter. Paper presented at the International World Wide Web Conference (IW3C2). WWW 2013, May 13–17, Rio de Janeiro, Brazil, p. 10.

60 5,000 tweets × 3 search periods = 15,000

61 Adi, A. (2015). # publicrelations on Twitter: Pushers, talkers, influencers on spamming PR and job hunting. *Revista Română de Comunicare Și Relații Publice*, *17*(3), 41–57.

62 *Wordle, a free Java-based application visualising input text. The word* clouds created "give greater prominence to words that appear more frequently in the source text". www.wordle.net/

63 Grigore, G., Adi, A., and Theofilou, A. (2015). Digital reflections of pharmaceutical companies and their CSR communication strategies. In *Corporate Social Responsibility in the Digital Age* (pp. 221–239). Emerald Group Publishing Limited.

64 *Foller.me,* "a Twitter analytics application that gives you rich insights about any public Twitter profile". https://foller.me/

65 Adi and Moloney, op.cit.

66 Adi, op.cit.

67 Xifra, J., and Grau, F. (2010). Nanoblogging PR: The discourse on public relations in Twitter. *Public Relations Review*, *36*(2), 171–174.

68 Ibid, p. 173

69 Carroll, A. B. (1999). Corporate social responsibility evolution of a definitional construct. *Business & Society*, *38*(3), 268–295.

70 "Corporate social responsibility (CSR) refers to companies taking responsibility for their impact on society. The European Commission believes that CSR is important for the sustainability, competitiveness, and innovation of EU enterprises and the EU economy. It brings benefits for risk management, cost savings, access to capital, customer relationships, and human resource management". Available from: http://ec.europa.eu/growth/industry/corporate-social-responsibility/index_en.htm. [Accessed 27 April 2016].

71 *UN Global Compact is* "a call to companies to align strategies and operations with universal principles on human rights, labour, environment and anti-corruption, and take actions that advance societal goals". Available from: www.unglobalcompact.org/what–is–gc. [Accessed 24 April 2016].

72 Greenconpost bio on Twitter: https://twitter.com/greeneconpost?lang=de

73 Iioannoulbs bio on Twitter: https://twitter.com/iioannoulbs

74 Caelusgreenroom bio on Twitter: https://twitter.com/caelusgreenroom

75 Adi, op.cit.

76 Redmond_ted bio on Twitter: https://twitter.com/redmond_ted

77 Adi, op. cit.

Index

Note: Page numbers in *italic* indicate a figure, and page numbers in **bold** indicate a table on the corresponding page.